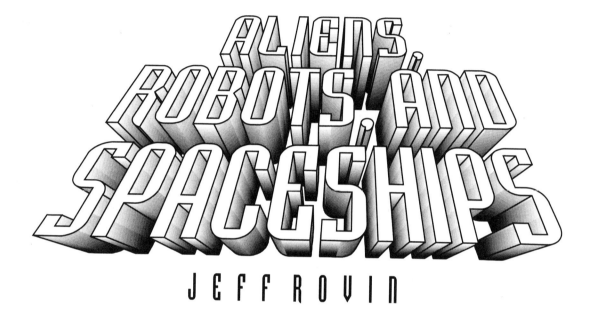

ALIENS, ROBOTS, AND SPACESHIPS

JEFF ROVIN

Facts On File, Inc.

AN INFOBASE HOLDINGS COMPANY

Aliens, Robots, and Spaceships

Copyright © 1995 by Jeff Rovin

Facts On File, Inc.
460 Park Avenue South
New York NY 10016

Library of Congress Cataloging-in-Publication Data

Rovin, Jeff.
    Aliens, robots, and spaceships / Jeff Rovin.
        p.   cm.
    Includes bibliographical references and index.
    ISBN 0-8160-3107-X (hardcover)
    ISBN 0-8160-3113-4 (paperback)
        1. Science fiction—History and criticism.   2. Science fiction
    films—History and criticism.   I. Title.
    PN3433.8.R68   1995
    809.3'8762—dc20   94-24273

Facts On File books are available at special discounts when purchased in bulk quantities for businesses, associations, institutions or sales promotions. Please call our Special Sales Department in New York at 212/683-2244 or 800/322-8755.

Text and jacket design by Robert Yaffe
Cover illustration by Vincent Di Fate

This book is printed on acid-free paper.

Printed in the United States of America

VB TT   10 9 8 7 6 5 4 3 2 1

CONTENTS

INTRODUCTION

Beings from space have been with us since the dawn of humankind—at least, in our fiction. The odd school of Erich "Was God An Astronaut?" von Daniken would have us believe that intelligent aliens were here in fact, as well.

Whether these fictional beings were gods from Mt. Olympus or the Japanese deity Ama-terasu, who dwelt on Earth and in the sun, they have watched over us, chastised us, and fought over us for as long as we've looked at the skies in wonder.

The early "spaceships" of these beings were flaming chariots, great birds, and the like; at times, the gods were served by "robots," metal beings like *Talos*.

Modern science fiction has its roots in these tales, in mythology. Over the years, authors would write science fiction without calling it that: *Somnium* (1634), written by astronomer Johannes Kepler, is arguably the first such story. In it, the author travels to the moon in a dream, borne there by a spirit. Bishop Francis Godwin wrote about a raft carried to the moon by birds in *The Man in the Moone* (1638); Cyrano de Bergerac (the historical one, not Rostand's swordsman/poet) wrote of his *Voyage to the Moon* (1650) by rubbing his body with marrow; and for the great prototypical robot figure there was Mary Shelley's *Frankenstein* (1817). In "The Unparalleled Adventure of One Hans Pfall (1835), Edgar Allan Poe sent his hero to the moon by balloon, and of course there were Jules Verne, H.G. Wells, and Edgar Rice Burroughs, among others, with their many important works (see THE ALBATROSS, GALLIA, and THE PROJECTILE; THE MARTIAN THINGS, THE SELENITES, and THE TIME MACHINE; and BARSOOM, respectively).

Twentieth-century science fiction had appeared in magazines such as *Argosy* and *All-Story*, but it really began to flourish with the dawn of the specialized "pulp" magazines, so-called because of the (lamentably!) perishable wood-pulp paper on which they were printed. But the paper was cheap, the price (usually ten cents) was accessible to the general reading public, and exciting, exotic, and heroic science fiction—as well as fantasy, westerns, war stories, romances, mysteries, sports tales, and many more—was more popular than ever.

Science fiction pulps were born with the debut of *Amazing Stories* in April 1926. The magazine was the brainchild of Hugo Gernsback, who had launched the popular *Modern Electrics* in 1908, and is rightly considered to be the father of modern science fiction. Characters such as Buck Rogers and PROFESSOR JAMESON, and authors such as John W. Campbell Jr. (THE THING) got their start in *Amazing Stories*, which spawned companion magazines and inspired other publishers to create titles, most significantly *Astounding Science Fiction* (later, *Analog*).

Inspired by the success of the pulp magazines and the popularity of Sunday comic strips, people such as Malcolm Wheeler-Nicholson, Harry Donenfeld, and Martin Goodman began publishing comic books. The initial titles, published in 1932, were reprints of comic strips; the first magazine to feature all-new material—including the first adventure of *Superman*—was *Action Comics* #1 (1938).

Science fiction book publishing really didn't begin until after World War II, and virtually every important science fiction author from Isaac Asimov (see R. DANEEL OLIVAW) to Robert A. Heinlein (see VALENTINE MICHAEL SMITH) got his or her start in the science fiction magazines. Even today, titles such as *Analog* and *Isaac Asimov's Science Fiction* remain breeding grounds for new talent.

Then, of course, there were the science fiction films. Beginning with magician/cinematographer George Melies's short *A Trip to the Moon* in 1902, and continuing through the silent era with *Metropolis* (see FUTURA) and into the sound era, science fiction has been one of the most popular and enduring film genres. Indeed, three of the five top-grossing movies of all-time—*E.T., Jurassic Park,* and *Star Wars*—are science fiction films. On TV, few shows are as fondly remembered as *The Twilight Zone, The Outer Limits,* and *Lost in Space,* while the legacy of *Star Trek* continues to thrive in video, film, television syndication, and its successful spin-off shows.

This book is a compendium of aliens, robots, and spaceships, as well as other worlds and a selection of fascinating time machines, cyborgs, submarines, airland-sea ships, and fictional computers. Sadly, there wasn't room to include every example of these creations. In deciding which entries to include, several criteria were considered:

First, was a character or vehicle so popular that its omission would raise eyebrows? Anything as well known as the U.S.S. ENTERPRISE couldn't very well be omitted. (Having said that, the *Star Trek* universe is *so* well known and loved that leaving anything out makes the book appear incomplete. Still, one could say that about *Dune* and the SUPERMAN universe as well. Lines had to be drawn, and the bibliography will point you to a number of excellent *Star Trek* reference works.)

Second, did a wonderfully obscure creation deserve to be brought from the shadows—if not in its

own entry, then as part of the Comment section of another entry. For example, the other starships in *Star Trek.* You'll find them in the entry for the U.S.S. *Enterprise.*

Third, were the major authors, filmmakers, and creators adequately represented? (And we admit that comic book artists Wally Wood and Jack Kirby may be overly represented. But while these late geniuses are revered by comic book fans, their imagination and artistry deserve to be more widely appreciated.)

Fourth, were unknown authors included, so that deserving creations did not remain little-known? Modern readers may not necessarily know the works of Manly Banister, Idris Seabright, and J.F. Bone, but they should.

Fifth, were the characters historically important, entertaining, original, or fascinating for some other reason? For example, were noted figures working in new fields (such as astronomer Carl Sagan writing about THE MACHINE), or were derivative characters so derivative (as are AMERICAN CYBORG and M-11) that they defined a new sub-genre, in this case apocalyptic-future cyborg killers!

Then there were isolated instances in which popular creations simply didn't fit the criteria of robots, spaceships, and aliens. Places such as Oz and Edgar Rice Burroughs's Pellucidar are not planets but realms, and are not included. Monsters like Ghidorah, who have appeared on other worlds but are not known, for certain, to be natives of those worlds also are not present (though the cyborg version of Ghidorah is mentioned in both M-11 and MECHAGODZILLA). John Wyndham's magnificent Triffids are mutants in the novel, not aliens as is commonly believed. Thus, none of these are here.

And frankly, we've tried not to include too many of the places and characters we've written up in previous Facts On File books such as *The Encyclopedia of Monsters* and *The Encyclopedia of Super Villains*. We hope you'll have a look at them to fill in any gaps!

GUIDE FOR THE READER

*E*ach of the more than 500 entries in this book is alphabetized according to the first letter of the name—*not* the surname. Science fiction presents problems in this area. A character like *R. Daneel Olivaw* is alphabetized that way because, while the "R" is used in the story simply to indicate "robot," that's how the character has come to be known (and loved). To list it as *Olivaw, Daneel, R.,* seems unnecessarily convoluted and potentially confusing. An entry headed *Spock, Mr.,* looks strange compared to the more familiar *Mr. Spock*.

Entries including the words "Mr." and "Dr." are alphabetized as if they were spelled out "Mister" and "Doctor."

Cross-references to entries about similar characters appear in small capital letters throughout the text.

Finally, if you don't find what you're looking for, consult the index. If, for example, you want to read about the planet commonly referred to as Dune, you'll find it under its proper name: ARRAKIS. The war machines from *War of the Worlds* can be found under the aforementioned Martian Things.

The contents of each entry are arranged as follows:

Title The names by which the creations are known. If they have no names, like the ALIENS from *Close Encounters of the Third Kind*, we've listed them as such. Japanese characters are listed under the names by which they're known in Japan (hence, Gigantor will be found under TETSUJIN 28GO).

Following each title is a parenthetical, chronological listing of the media in which the character has appeared (see Key to Codes).

First Appearance Where the character or creation

first appeared and when, along with information about the author, publisher, studio, network, etc.

Physical Description What the alien, robot, spaceship, or world looks like, its size and special abilities, and what it can do. If the entry is about an alien, for example, and a spaceship or another world is involved, those will also be described in this section. Again, for example, the Martians from *War of the Worlds* are described along with THE MARTIAN THINGS.

Biography The history or life story of the subject.

Comment Any additional information, such as who stars in the film or TV show, details of subsequent other-media appearances, biographical information about the author and/or artist, brief descriptions of similar characters that don't have their own entries.

Also included are the following appendices: Comic Book Aliens, *Outer Limits* Aliens, *Star Trek* Aliens, *Star Trek: The Next Generation* and *Star Trek: Deep Space Nine* Aliens, and *Star Wars* Worlds. Further Readings, a Fiction Index, and a General Index are also provided.

Keep in mind that, despite our best efforts to evoke the wonderful characters and places discussed in this book, there is no substitute for the primary source. We urge you to read the novels, see the films (in a theater or on laserdisc, if possible), and explore the comic books—especially those of the late, brilliant Wally Wood and Jack Kirby. We've tried to capture a sense of wonder in these pages, but only the originals can give you that experience firsthand.

KEY TO CODES

These letters appear parenthetically beside the heading of each entry. They indicate in which medium or media the character has appeared and are listed chronologically. For example, *Mr. Spock* (TV, L, C, CS, MP) would tell you that the character made his debut on television, then appeared in novels, comic books, a comic strip, and motion pictures. Specifics about these appearances are provided in the *Comment* section of each entry.

A = Advertising
C = Comic Book
CS = Comic Strip
F = Folklore
L = Literature (books, short stories, and ''Big Little Books,'' i.e., thick, squat novels published for children by a variety of houses beginning in the 1920s)
M = Mythology
MP = Motion Picture (theatrical)

R = Radio
S = Stage
T = Toy
TC = Trading Cards
TV = Television (series, specials, and television movies)
VG = Video or computer game (cartridge games for systems such as Nintendo and Sega, and diskette games for personal computers)

A

ADAM HAWKINS (L)

First Appearance: *Wanted By the Intergalactic Security Bureau* by Ed Naha, 1980, Bantam Books.

Physical Description: Hawkins is a humanoid with a canary-like beak where his mouth and nose should be, and feathers on his body (though he has hair on his head).

Biography: Hawkins is apparently the director of the ISB, Quadrant 4, Terran Districts, based on the New Washington Colony in the 25th century. The criminals he seeks are: Aelita Thx, a five-foot six-inch, golden-skinned humanoid thief from the planet Uila; Blote, a six-foot-seven, caterpillar-like sludge-mongerer from the planet Mire; Dweezyl, a circular, fourth-dimensional thief who dwells in a realm beyond the Portal; Dwite, a six-foot, moth-like smuggler and graverobber from the planet Wale; Earth Airbot 408G, a murderous five-foot-ten Earth robot; Enode the Brain, a three-foot-four, orange-skinned, bug-eyed humanoid thief from the planet Nain; Gorcz, an eight-foot-six cricket-like murderer from the Alland II Colony; Gregor, a butterfly with a 16-foot wingspan, a kidnapper from the planet Fjaril; Harly 9, a four-foot-eight, orange-skinned, bug-eyed humanoid air pirate and smuggler from the planet Pfann; Kapu Kapu, a 140-foot-tall, green, insect-like murderer from the planet Lokig; Ko, a 20-foot humanoid with a catlike head, a murderer from the planet Smalta; Linx and Enid, the Randor Sisters, red-skinned humanoids, kidnappers from the planet Delta; Makau, an eight-foot-two, fishlike humanoid with green scales, a murderer from the planet Moana; Mr. Mund, a 77-foot-tall, purple-skinned humanoid with a cloud-like head, a vandal designed in a lab for use on the space habitat Earth IV; Mr. Zero, a five-foot-eight human vandal from Earth; Noolie the Torch, a five-foot-two, cylindrical gray cyclops—he has no facial features other than the one eye—with tiny arms and legs, a killer and arsonist from the planet Narine; Theebe Dvorick, a murderous human-sized butterfly from the planet Letha; Vaxt, an eight-foot-nine stalk with a tendril-covered top, a thief from the planet Winndum; Zhuk Orbz, a five-foot-six boar-like humanoid, a voyeur from the planet Lukau; and Zvarmo, a five-foot-nine blue-skinned thief from the planet Tantor who has a sluglike body, stubby legs, massive arms, and a thick tail.

Comment: This poster book was published in the wake of the expanded interest in aliens and alien villains caused by the films *Star Wars* and *Close Encounters of the Third Kind* (both 1977). It was illustrated by a variety of artists.

ADAM LINK (L, C, TV)

First Appearance: "I, Robot" by Eando Binder, January 1939, *Amazing Stories*.

Physical Description: Adam is made of "wires and wheels (and) run by electrical power." He has a computer-fast "iridium-sponge" brain "sensitive to the impact of a single electron," possesses photo-electric cell eyes, sonic-relay ears, and a "three-directional spirit level" that tells him what is "horizontal, vertical, and oblique." He has only "three-color sight" and lacks the senses of smell, taste, and touch.

The humanoid robot has "kindly eyes, sympathetic lips . . . a grave, boyish face, a shock of unruly hair . . . big, thick-fingered" hands. He stands five-foot-ten, weighs 500 pounds, and has a storage battery in his pelvis that must be replaced with a fresh one every 48 hours. Incredibly powerful and fast—he has "the strength of 10 men in one arm" and moves like "chained lightning"—he is impervious to bullets unless they strike his joints or " 'muscle' cables." His life-span is expected to be "centuries."

Biography: Built by Dr. Charles Link after 20 years of research, Adam can walk, talk, and reason simply within three days of his activation. Soon thereafter, Dr. Link is killed when a shelf over his workbench falls and drops a transformer on his head. Adam lifts it off, and his fingers are coated

Robert Fuqua's illustration from the original magazine publication of "Adam Link, Robot Detective." © Ziff-Davis Publications.

design efficient factories, and even stops a robbery in progress. To get away from things, the successful but lonely robot takes a small cabin in the Ozarks where he meets Dr. Paul Hillory, a retired scientist and neighbor. Together, they decide to build Adam a mate. Eve is constructed with Kay's thoughts and nature transferred to her via "electrovibration." However, Hillory betrays Adam, making him and Eve his slaves. He also builds a third robot body, eight feet tall, 900 pounds, and more powerful by far than Adam. The sadistic

Joe Orlando's interpretation of *Adam Link* from *Creepy* magazine. © Warren Publishing Co.

with blood when the housekeeper arrives. She screams and Adam leaves to fulfill his creator's dream, to become a full-fledged citizen. But a mob chases Adam through the woods near the estate and, utterly confused, he allows himself to be arrested. Charles's nephew, lawyer Thomas Link, defends him at his murder trial, and writer Jack Hall of the *Evening Post* defends him in editorials. While they await the verdict outside, Adam sees a car about to run over a boy on roller skates. He leaps through the crowd and stops the car, his right side destroyed in the process; later, the jury finds him guilty of Dr. Link's murder.

The governor examines the case and pardons Adam, who goes into business as "Adam Link, Incorporated." From his 22nd-floor office in the Marle Building, assisted by secretary Kay Temple, he solves complex problems for scientists, helps scientist has Adam put Eve's head on that body and has her steal for him. When Kay is able to free Adam from Hillory's control, the scientist has Eve attack him. Adam stops her with a blow to the jaw, and Hillory perishes when a battle-weakened cliff falls with him on it.

Next it's Eve's turn to go on trial for robbery and murder, the Black Fist Gang having framed her for killings it committed. Hoping to find evidence to clear her, Adam devises a plastic that has the "rubbery consistency of human flesh" and, almost indistinguishible from a human, spies on the gang. Throughout, he stays in touch with Eve via an "ESP radio-beam oscillator" in his chest. He learns that the gang is in cahoots with city councilman Harvey Brigg, and makes him sign a confession. Though a bodyguard cripples Adam with a hand grenade and then puts a blowtorch to his head, Eve breaks free and comes to his rescue. She also gets her old body back.

The two have many other adventures together, competing in athletics (they run a two-minute mile), battling nine-foot-tall aliens who look like upright buffaloes with horns, fighting the Axis, and eventually becoming U.S. citizens.

Comment: "Eando" is the collaborative name used by brothers Earl and Otto Binder. Otto, the more prolific author of the two, wrote the bulk of the Adam Link stories (Earl gave up writing in 1940). Ten other stories appeared in *Amazing Stories* through April 1942: "The Trial of Adam Link," "Adam Link in Business," "Adam Link's Mate," "Adam Link's Vengeance," "Adam Link, Robot Detective," "Adam Link, Champion Athlete," "Adam Link Fights a War," "Adam Link in the Past," "Adam Link Faces a Revolt," and "Adam Link Saves the World." All but the last three stories were edited into novel form by Otto Binder and published as *Adam Link—Robot* by Paperback Library in 1965.

In comic books, "I, Robot" was adapted in EC's *Weird Science-Fantasy* #27, and "The Trial of Adam Link" in #28, both 1955. Joe Orlando drew them both; Otto Binder may have written the scripts (he says he did; editor Al Feldstein says he probably didn't). Bill Spicer's *Fantasy Illustrated* continued the series in #1 (1963) and #2 (1964), with "Adam Link's Vengeance" drawn by D. Bruce Berry and adapted by Spicer. The two-part story was reprinted in its entirety in *Graphic Story Magazine* #13, 1971. Joe Orlando got a second crack at Link in 1965 with Warren Publishing's adaptation of "I, Robot," which appeared in *Creepy* magazine #2, written by

Binder. *Creepy* adapted other stories in subsequent issues: "Trial of Adam Link" (#4), "Adam Link in Business" (#6), "Adam Link's Mate" (#8), "Adam Link's Vengeance" (#9), "Adam Link, Robot Detective" (#12), and "Adam Link, Champion Athlete" (#15).

The character was featured in "I, Robot," an episode of TV's anthology series *The Outer Limits*. It aired in November 1964. In it, attorney Thurman Cutler (Howard Da Silva) comes from retirement to defend the robot Adam Link (Read Morgan; voice of John Caper Jr.), who is charged with having murdered its creator, Dr. Charles Link (Peter Brocco). During the trial, it is revealed that Dr. Link taught Adam to read, reason, and control his incredible strength. But Adam is sentenced to be dismantled because he also read the novel *Frankenstein*, which may have given him dangerous ideas about attacking humans. As he's being lead away in chains, he breaks free to save a child from being run over by a truck, and is completely destroyed in the process. The robot is not rebuilt. Leonard Nimoy costarred as *Herald* reporter Judson Ellis. Leon Benson directed from a teleplay by Robert C. Dennis.

ADAPTOID AND SUPER-ADAPTOID (C)

First Appearance: *Tales of Suspense* #82 (Adaptoid), #84 (Super-Adaptoid), both 1966, Marvel Comics.

Physical Description: A featureless white humanoid in their "natural" form, the Adaptoid and Super-Adaptoid can assume the likeness *and* abilities, including superpowers, of any being or automaton that passes within 10 feet of them and can be scanned by their analyzer-eyes; the Super-Adaptoid can also copy articles such as weapons, create multiple characters at once (up to at least four), and retain its adapted form for up to three years. The tallest either being has grown is 15 feet.

Biography: Constructed by the subversive organization A.I.M.—Advanced Idea Mechanics—the first Adaptoid battles and is defeated by Captain America. As the Super-Adaptoid it fights the Avengers, assuming the attributes of members Captain America, archer Hawkeye, the diminutive Wasp, and the giant Goliath. Thinking it has killed Captain America, the android departs—only to face the X-Men and overload while trying to take on too many forms. The Super-Adaptoid has returned several times since and, when last seen, was being kept inert in the basement of the Avengers' mansion.

Comment: The character was created by writer Stan Lee and artist Jack Kirby.

THE ADRAK (L)

First Appearance: "The Casque of LaMont T. Yado" by Victor Milan, 1979, *Asimov's SF Adventure Magazine #2.*

Physical Description: Nothing is known about this ancient, extinct race, save that they fought battles using other races whom they equipped with powerful casques. These helmets have the ability to amplify the strength of the wearer.

Biography: A pair of thieves, the narrator and Trago, plot to steal the Adrak casque—despite the fact that Trago, a Tracer, once tried to kill the narrator, a Jumper, in order to steal his girlfriend Linda. Trago did this by plotting a path through hyperspace that left the narrator dangerously close to a black hole and not his destination, a planet near Achernar. The narrator survived, albeit badly mangled and needing to be rebuilt, and has returned. Now, solely for business, he says, he and Trago are planning another job. This time, after Trago has plotted a course, the narrator dons his Jump harness and takes Trago with him. They reach the LaMont T. Yado Memorial Museum, steal the casque, and Jump away, landing in a graveyard. There Trago dons the helmet, intending to destroy his companion. But the narrator has fooled him: On Bryan's World, he once took apart a casque and learned how to rewire it to prevent the wearer from moving. He says he has done so to this casque, and that the deceitful Trago will be immobile for the rest of his life.

Comment: The short story is a science fiction update of Edgar Allan Poe's tale "The Cask of Amontillado."

AELITA (L, MP)

First Appearance: *Aelita* by Alexei N. Tolstoy, 1922.

Physical Description: Aelita has "bluish-white" flesh, ash-gray eyes, ashen hair, and an elongated face with a "lightly turned up nose and slightly wide mouth." She stands some five feet tall and has a voice like the "strumming of a musical instrument."

Martian soldiers wear egg-shaped helmets and loose silvery jackets with thick collars that cover their necks and the lower part of their faces. Their skin is also bluish and their bald heads are "full of bumps."

Other life forms include tall cacti that can move their arms and large brown-striped spiders with red-lidded eyes.

Los's spaceship is an "ovoid apparatus (roughly) eight and a half meters high and six meters wide." There's a steel belt around the middle "widening in a curve around the bottom of the ship, like an umbrella," and designed to work like a parachute to slow the ship's entry into the atmosphere. Three round entrance hatches are below. Under the egg in a narrow funnel are the "ultralyddite" engines. This is "surrounded by a double spiral of massive steel, twisted in opposite directions" to buffer the ship when it lands. The ship consists of an exterior sheath made of pliable steel around a framework of ribs and light girders. The inner sheath is "six layers of rubber, thick felt, and leather." Metal tubes with "prismatic glass" penetrate the outer layer so passengers can see outside. The vessel is designed to make the trip between Earth and Mars in no more than seven hours.

Biography: Building a spaceship, engineer Mstislav Sergeyevich Los advertises for a copilot. Military officer Alexei Ivanovich Gusev takes the job, and the two blast off from Petrograd on August 18, "192–." Arriving on Mars and checking the atmosphere by shoving a mouse through the porthole, the men explore an orange plain and are discovered by a three-masted, beetle-shaped flying machine. Martian soldiers take them beyond the city of Soatsera, which is rich with gold, to the residence of Aelita, daughter of Tuskub, head of the Supreme Council. The men learn Martian and are told that Mars was settled 20,000 years before by the Aols, orange humanoids. Soon after, the Magatsitls—black-haired humans who flew bronze, egg-shaped spaceships to Mars to escape the sinking of Atlantis—arrived from Earth. They conquered Mars, intermarried, and produced the blue-skinned Gor race.

Though Aelita welcomes the Earthmen, the duo learn that the ruling Supreme Council is suspicious of them and has ordered Aelita to kill them. But she has fallen in love with Los, and Ikha, a young maid, has fallen for Gusev. The Earthmen lead a revolt against the tyrannical rulers. Unfortunately, the would-be liberators are pursued by government soldiers and barely escape Mars with their lives. Blasting off in their spaceship, they return to Earth and try to return to normal lives. Then, one day, a radio station receives a signal from Mars, and Los is summoned to translate. It's a bittersweet message from Aelita: "Where are you, where are you, where are you, Son of the Sky?"

Martian words defined in the text are:

Ae: Seen for the last time
Azora: Joy
Ho: And
Lita: Starlight
Liziazira: Mountains
Magatsitl: Ruthless
Oeyeo: Concentrate
Ro: Water
Sera: Settlement
Shoho: Men
Soatsr: Sun
Sua: Remember
Taltsetl: Earth
Tuma: Mars

Comment: Author Tolstoy was a distant relative of Leo.

The novel was made into a silent Russian comedy in 1924, starring Yulia Solntseva as Queen Aelita. Jakov Protazanov directed from a script by Fedor Ozep and Aleksey Fajiko. After shooting his wife, Los (Nikolai Tseretelli) and soldier Gusev (Nikolai Batalov) blast off for Mars, along with the detective investigating the murder (Igor Illinski). Arriving on the Red Planet, Los falls in love with Aelita while Gusev and Ikha (Vera Orlova) plot a Russian Revolution–style rebellion to liberate the Martians. The revolt fails, and the entire story turns out to have been a dream.

AESOP (L)

First Appearance: "Gambler's Choice" by Bob Shaw, 1971, *Galaxy,* Vol. 20, #10.
Physical Description: Located on the computer deck, the talking "brain" of the spaceship *Sarafand* controls the vehicle's six survey modules, is in constant contact with all of them, and provides information when asked. In addition to interpreting data, it can analyze visual images.
Biography: Sent to explore Horta VII by the Federation's Cartographical Service, the crew of the *Sarafand* is the first vessel there in 4,000 years, since the old White Empire withdrew. Aesop's initial survey indicates a dead world, but explorer Mike Targett finds hundreds of long black cylinders of recent vintage. Aesop analyzes images from his TV camera, determines that the 362 objects are robotic torpedoes—apparently dumped there 40 centuries before—and urges Targett to run for cover. He drops the camera as he does so. Aesop says it is studying the torpedo movements on the camera and, relaying instructions to the explorer, helps him use the 26 shots in his ultralaser gun to

nudge the torpedoes off-course, one against another against another, destroying them. Only later does Targett learn that the TV camera had shut down and that the computer was guessing, sounding authoritative simply to put him at ease—a surprisingly human trait.
Comment: The only other planet referred to in the novelette is Parador, apparently a resort/gambling world.

AF 709 (TV)

First Appearance: *My Living Doll,* September 1964, CBS.
Physical Description: The robot looks exactly like a human woman, slightly above average in height and with long brown hair.
Biography: AF 709 is built by Dr. Carl Miller as part of a government project to create a perfect robot that will be able to survive in outer space and do everything it's told. Miller's work calls him to Pakistan and, so that the robot can develop a human personality and learn to interact with people, it goes to live with Miller's friend, base psychiatrist Dr. Robert McDonald. McDonald tells everyone that "Rhoda Miller" is Carl's niece.

McDonald's colleague and neighbor, Dr. Peter Robinson, is in love with Rhoda, unaware that she's a robot.
Comment: The half-hour series aired through September 1965 and starred Julie Newmar as the robot, Robert Cummings as Dr. McDonald, and Jack Mullaney as Peter.

THE ALBATROSS AND THE TERROR (L, MP, C)

First Appearance: *Robur the Conqueror* by Jules Verne, 1885, *Journal des Debats* (The Albatross); *Master of the World* by Jules Verne, 1904 (The Terror).
Physical Description: Powered by electricity generated by storage batteries, the "aeronef" is comprised of a hull with 37 "masts"—15 on each side, seven in the center—each of which has a horizontal propeller on top. The ship can still fly with only half of them operating. In addition to these "suspensory screws," there are two larger propelling screws, fore and aft. Under the hull, the ship has "flexible sprints to ease off the concussion" of landing.

The *Albatross* is made of "straw paper turned hard as metal by compression," with windows

Captives dangle from the *Albatross* in the film *Master of the World*. © American Internationai.

consisting of glass that is "ten times the resistance" of ordinary glass. The ship is 100 feet long and 12 feet wide, "a ship's deck . . . with a projecting prow." Beneath the deck are the engines and provisions. There are three "houses" on the deck containing cabins, galley, and the machines that drive the screws; a "glass house" in the rear is for the helmsman who controls the rudder.

The ship contains nets for hauling fish from the water, and an anchor at the end of a 150-foot cable. It does not set down unless it is forced.

At top speed, the *Albatross* can travel 120 miles an hour. It can go to 13,000 feet above sea level before the passengers begin to suffer from the thin air, though the ship itself can probably go higher.

The *Terror* is a car-boat-submarine-aircraft, "spindle-shaped" with a bow "sharper than the stern." The body is aluminum and rests on four wheels, two feet in diameter. The vehicle is driven along by two turbines, one on either side of the keel. The wings are kept folded against the sides of the vehicle like long gangways, spreading as needed.

Biography: Presenting himself to the balloonists of Philadelphia's Weldon Institute, administered by wealthy bachelor "Uncle" Prudent, the 40-year-old Robur reveals that he has constructed a heavier-than-air flying machine. The members scoff and the angry Robur departs, later having Prudent, his black valet Frycollin, and Weldon's secretary Phil Evans abducted by his six crewmembers. They are taken onboard the *Albatross,* which was built on Island X in the Pacific. Robur "the Conqueror" is captain; mate Tom Turner rounds out the complement of eight men. Robur takes his unwilling but dazzled captives over Canada, down to Chicago, then westward over the Pacific on their way around the world in eight days. After

Producer James Nicholson stands beside the miniature model of the *Albatross* used in his film *Master of the World*. © American International.

passing through the Himalayas and heading toward Europe, the three unwilling passengers resolve to escape—until Frycollin panics and Robur has a line attached to him, dragging him through the air 100 feet below the ship.

The ship heads west, over the Atlantic, then south where a hurricane blows it to the Antarctic, damaging its forescrew. They drop anchor over the Chatham Islands, and while everyone is asleep, Prudent steals dynamite from the magazine. Lighting the fuse, he and Evans slip over the side (Frycollin having left earlier) and climb down the anchor cable. No sooner do they reach the ground than their disappearance is discovered, and Robur orders the *Albatross* to land. But Prudent is able to cut the cable and the winds carry the ship to sea; it

is 10,000 feet up when the dynamite explodes. Though it crashes into the sea, Robur is able to control its descent. The men do not know his fate.

Making their way back home with the help of natives and a mailboat, the men undertake the construction of the screw-powered balloon *Goahead*. Seven months later, it is launched—just as the *Albatross* arrives. The men learn that Robur, his crew, and portions of the ship were rescued by a boat en route to Melbourne. From there, he returned to his island to effect repairs—and seek revenge. Learning of the *Goahead*, he times his arrival so he can be there for the launch. He pursues the balloon until it bursts, then catches it as it falls, once again making Prudent and Evans his prisoners. He sets them free before leaving, how-

The *Albatross*, reincarnated as the *Terror*, from the original book publication of *Master of the World*.

ever, having humiliated them and proven "that the souls of men are not yet ready for . . . the conquest of the air."

In *Master of the World*, Chief Inspector of the Federal Police John Strock is asked to take scientific equipment into the crater of the Great Eyrie, a volcano in the Blueridge Mountains near Morganton. He and his guides are unable to make it up the steep wall. Concurrently, in Pennsylvania, a car begins appearing on the roads, one that moves so quickly no one can get a good look at it. Finally, a sea serpent—or so it appears—begins popping up off the New England coast. Strock believes it's a boat, powered by the same force as the car. Shortly thereafter, he receives a letter from the Master of the World, warning him never to return to the Great Eyrie; this is followed by the appearance of a submarine in the waters of Lake Kirdall, Kansas. Strock believes that the vehicles

are all the same, and that they are related to the mysterious Master of the World. He decides to return to the mountain, accompanied by agents John Hart and Nab Walker. Reaching the area, Strock is knocked out and taken somewhere on Lake Erie aboard a vessel known only as the *Terror*. Attacked by a pair of destroyers, the *Terror* heads for the Canadian Falls and, as wings emerge from its sides, it flies right off, heading to the Master's mountain hideaway. There, he reveals himself to Strock as Robur, the Conqueror. After capturing the two Americans, he had returned to Island X, constructed the parts for the *Terror*, and took them to the Great Eyrie, where the second *Albatross* was destroyed (whether by accident or design isn't revealed). Robur says nothing of what he plans to do with the *Terror* or with his captive, who is allowed a great deal of freedom.

When the ship takes off from the crater with Robur, the devoted Turner, Strock, and a third crewmember, it heads south, past South America toward Island X. There, Robur intends to make ready to enslave the world. Caught in a storm, its wings are wrecked and it plunges over a thousand feet into the sea. Strock is knocked unconscious and awakes on the deck of a steamer, where he's told he was found floating in the wreckage of his vessel. He returns to Washington; Robur is presumed dead.

Comment: The first tale was published in book-form in 1887 as *The Clipper of the Clouds*. Verne worked closely with an engineer, Badoureau, to make sure the ships in both novels were as plausible as could be; his novels angered proponents of lighter-than-air travel, who felt that balloons were the mode of the future.

The novels inspired the 1961 American International film *Master of the Universe* with Vincent Price as Robur. The film was directed by William Witney from a script by Richard Matheson. In the movie, set in 1868, Robur wants to use the *Albatross* to eliminate warfare, intending to bomb battle sites until warring nations withdraw. A bomb planted by Department of the Interior Agent Strock (Charles Bronson) cripples the airship, which crashes into the sea.

In 1961, Dell published a comic book adaptation of the film as part of its *4-Color* series. That same year, *Classics Illustrated* published comic book adaptations of the novels *Robur the Conqueror* and *Master of the World* (#s 162 and 163). *Master of the World* was #21 of the *Marvel Classics Comics Series*, published in 1977.

ALF (TV, C)

First Appearance: *ALF*, September 1986, NBC.
Physical Description: The golden-furred biped has big ears, an anteater snout, large eyes, a pompadour, four fingers on each hand, and three toes on each foot.

ALF's spaceship, which looks something like a race car, has a navigation computer, an AM radio, and is equipped with a Wotif Simulator—a projector that can show people what would have happened if they'd done something else in their lives.

Little is known of the kidney-shaped planet Melmac, save that there is an "unusually high concentration of bicarbonate in the atmosphere," a popular cat franchise is McCat's, the currency is candy (traded on Brawl Street's choc market), and the Shumways' neighbor is Pete Zaparlor.

Biography: Gordon Shumway, also known as ALF—short for Alien Life Form—is the son of Bob and Flo Shumway of Melmac; he has a sister named Augie, a brother named Curtis, an Aunt Minerva, and a dog-like pet named Neep. Able to escape by rocket when Melmac blows up, ALF loses control of his spaceship and lands in the suburban garage of the Tanner household. Stranded and resenting it, the wisecracking, cat-eating, belching alien hangs around in the kitchen or the garage, annoying Willie and Kate Tanner and their children Lynn, Brian, and baby Eric (and their cat Lucky), as well as their neighbors, the oblivious Ochmoneks. He also collects cockroaches and keeps busy staying out of the hands of the government's Alien Task Force. Eventually, surviving Melmacians Rhonda and Skip contact ALF and ask him to settle on a new world with them.

The 229-year-old, three-foot-tall alien attended Melmac high for 122 years, was a software major, and co-captained the bouillabaiseball team. After he was graduated from Melmac, he became a member of the Orbit Guard, an Assistant Box-leitner, a male model, and a phlegm dealer. Like all Melmacians, he eats 16 meals a day, can engage in "personality swapping" by squeezing another being's hand, and goes through a "shed cycle" every 75 years, losing all of his hair for eight hours.

Comment: The series aired through June 1990 and featured the voice of co-creator Paul Fusco (Tom Patchett was the other creator); midget Michu Meszaros wore the ALF costume.

An animated version of the show aired from September 1987 to September 1989, on Saturday mornings on NBC. The cartoon series focused on his escapades on Melmac before he came to Earth; there were 26 episodes in all.

ALF was also seen in the animated *ALF Tales*, which aired from September 1988 to September 1990. The 21 cartoons featured ALF in classic stories such as "Robin Hood," "John Henry," and "Rumplestiltskin."

Paul Fusco provided the voice in both animated series.

Marvel Comics published 50 issues of the ALF comic book, plus three annuals and a digest-sized one-shot.

ALIEN (MP, L, C)

First Appearance: *Alien*, 1979, Twentieth Century-Fox.
Physical Description: Alien eggs don't hatch Aliens, per se, but "face-huggers," which serve as exoskeletons for the seed. The face-hugger has a pancake-sized body, a long tail, and eight crab-like legs. It also has a tube under its belly, which serves as an ovipositor: It wraps its legs around a victim's face and places the tube down his or her throat. (Victims can be humans or animals.) When the seed has been deposited, the face-hugger falls away, dead, and the baby Alien emerges after a gestation period of several days, having taken on many of the physical attributes of the host. In its tadpole-like form, whatever the host, the Alien typically looks like a large, fat worm with just a hint of the Alien face and a pair of small arms.

All Aliens are entirely black, with chitinous-like flesh and rib-like bones *outside* the body. Aliens who hatch from humans stand approximately eight feet tall with a smooth head shaped like an inverted canoe, white jaws, and a second set of jaws that extend from the mouth. The creature has two long arms ending in hands with five spindly, powerful, sharpclawed fingers; a long, bony tail; two rows of two flat-topped horns down its back with a fifth, pointed horn above them; long, needle-like projections jutting from its elbows and ankles; a slender body and long, powerful limbs. The Alien has yellowish blood with acid-like qualities. (Apparently, adult Aliens are also capable of planting embryos inside hosts, and spin cocoons to keep the victims from going anywhere.)

The queen Alien resembles the original Alien, though she's 14 feet tall with a larger mouth and four arms, two long ones and two shorter ones, as well as two legs. Her head terminates in a large crest and she uses her long, pointed tail as a weapon.

On Acheron, a trio of space travelers enter the derelict spaceship where they find the first face-hugger in *Alien*. © Twentieth Century-Fox.

One of the Aliens on Fiorina 161 is a quadruped, having been nurtured inside a dog.

Ash is a human-like android with white "blood"; his head can survive independent of his body. Bishop is also a humanoid android, made of biological parts instead of mechanical ones. Both are able to move at faster-than-human speed.

The ship *Nostromo* is a "monstrous aggregation of bulky forms and metal shapes": a squarish fuselage, two smaller but similar projections alongside, and a command "blister" on top. The ship has three levels: A (the bridge), B (habitation and recreation), and C (the "garage"). The ship contains "lifeboats" for evacuation and is run by Mother, a computer capable of independent thought within carefully defined parameters. Medical assistance is provided by a robotic "autodoc."

Acheron is a planetoid that, according to different accounts, is either 1,200 miles or 4,000 feet in diameter. Named for the River of Woe that

bordered Hades in Greek mythology, it is extremely dense and boasts gravity that is 86 percent that of Earth. The stormy atmosphere is inhospitable to humans.

Biography: The *Nostromo* is a deep-space tug owned by the Company and carrying Captain Dallas, navigator Lambert, engineers Brett and Parker, executive officer Kane, science officer Ash (an android), warrant officer Ripley, and Jones the cat. Responding to an SOS from a nearby world, Acheron, they discover a huge, U-shaped derelict spaceship. Kane finds eggs inside and, when one hatches, he's attacked by a face-hugger. Days later, onboard the *Nostromo*, the Alien erupts from Kane's chest, slithers off, and quickly grows into a bipedal carnivore who is able to blend into the ship's pipes and shadows. The crew soon discovers that, unknown to all but Ash (whom Parker decapitates in a struggle), the SOS was not picked up by accident: The Company wanted the Alien for its bioweapons division. The Alien kills crewmembers—eating them or planting baby Aliens inside of them—until only Ripley and the cat are left alive. Climbing into a spacesuit, the warrant officer is able to open the hatch of the escape pod, and the Alien is sucked into space.

Ripley and Jones go into hibernation and are found 57 years later by a deep-space salvage team. Back on Earth, Ripley is told that her daughter Amanda, whom she had left as a child, has grown old and died. Meanwhile, to her horror, she also learns that Acheron has been colonized and that contact with the colony has been lost. Since she's the only one who has ever fought the Alien, now-Lieutenant Ripley joins a contingent of 11 U.S. Colonial Marines, ostensibly to find out what happened to the colonists; in actuality, known only to civilian expedition member Carter Burke, the self-serving Company still wants a sample Alien to study for possible military use—smuggled back to Earth as

a chestburster inside Ripley. The marines find that other Aliens have been produced and that only one colonist has survived, a little girl named Newt Jorden. The Aliens attack the marines, and after Ripley uses a flamethrower to destroy a queen Alien's hive, she, Newt, Hyperdine android Bishop (built on LX-469), the heroic Corporal Hicks (and, unknown to them, the queen) manage to escape in a shuttlecraft as the planet explodes behind them. The shuttle reaches the interstellar ship *Sulaco*, where Ripley climbs into an exoskeleton-like Power Loader and pushes the queen into the vacuum of space. The quartet go into suspended animation.

Sometime later, the *Sulaco*'s 337 model EEV pod crashlands on Fiorina ("Fury") 161, a backwater, Class C prison planet whose 25 cons are "all scum." All but Ripley perish in the crash. Reanimating Bishop and accessing the pod's computer, she learns that an electrical fire onboard the *Sulaco* had caused the pod to jettison, and that a face-

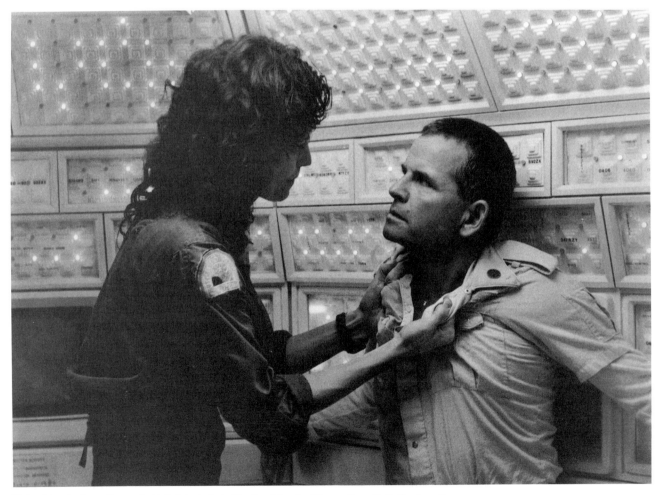

Ripley tries to force the android Ash to help battle the Alien in *Alien*. © Twentieth Century-Fox.

hugger was aboard the pod. It escapes, plants an Alien in a dog, and a quadrupedal Alien emerges and begins killing the prisoners and guards—though it refuses to attack Ripley. Wondering why, she submits to a neuro-scan and learns that she was impregnated on the pod. Ripley uses her "immunity" to get close to the Alien in the prison world's leadworks. Though the creature survives having molten metal poured over it, Ripley quickly drenches it with water and the heat/cold combination causes it to explode. A Company Medivac Rescue Team arrives and wants to operate on Ripley to remove the alien embryo. But she knows they'll use it for their own wicked purposes and chooses, instead, to leap to her death in the furnace, taking the last (?) Alien spawn with her.

Comment: The characters were created by writers Dan O'Bannon and Ron Shussett; Ridley Scott directed the original film from O'Bannon's screenplay. The monster was designed by H.R. Giger. *Aliens* (1986) was directed by James Cameron, and *Alien 3* (1992) was directed by David Fincher. (Cut by nearly a half-hour before its theatrical release, *Aliens* was fully restored for its widescreen laserdisc presentation.)

Sigourney Weaver stars as Ripley in all three films, with Tom Skerrit as Dallas, Veronica Cartwright as Lambert, Harry Dean Stanton as Brett, John Hurt as Kane, Yaphet Kotto as Parker, and dancer Bolaji Badejo as the Alien. Carrie Henn costars as Newt in the sequel, with Michael Biehn as Hicks, Paul Reiser as Burke, and Lance Henrikson as Bishop. The queen alien had two operators inside the costume, as well as numerous external technicians working cables and hydraulics. Jenette Goldstein, memorable as Pvt. Vasquez in the second film, also appears in Cameron's *Terminator 2: Judgment Day* (see TERMINATOR).

The three films were novelized by Alan Dean Foster. A new series of novels featuring different protagonists has also been published, including: *Book 1: Earth Hive* by Steve Perry (1992); *Book 2: Nightmare Asylum* by Perry (1993); *Book 3: The Female War* by Steve and Stephani Perry (1993); *Aliens: Genocide* by David Bischoff, based on the Dark Horse comic book (see below) (1993); and *Aliens vs. Predator: Prey* by the Perrys (1994), first in a series of novels based on the Dark Horse comic book.

Heavy Metal magazine published a comic book adaptation of the film by writer Archie Goodwin and artist Walt Simonson, beginning in May 1979; the series was also published in book form, distributed by Simon & Schuster.

Dark Horse Comics published comic book adaptations of the second and third films, and also spun off a new series of comic books featuring the monsters and new human adversaries. The titles include *Aliens: Book One* (one issue), *Aliens vs. Predator* (four issues), *Aliens/Predator: The Deadliest of the Species* (two issues), *Aliens: Earth War* (four issues), *Aliens: Genocide* (four issues), *Aliens: Colonial Marines* (seven issues), *Aliens: Hive* (four issues), *Aliens: Labyrinth* (two issues), *Aliens: Newt's Tale* (one issue), *Aliens: Rogue* (four issues), *Aliens: Sacrifice* (one issue), and *Aliens: Music of the Spheres* (four issues).

See also IT!; THE SPACE BEAGLE.

THE ALIENS (1) (MP, L)

First Appearance: *Close Encounters of the Third Kind*, 1977, Columbia Pictures.

Physical Description: The bipedal aliens have pasty white skin and are hairless. The bulk of them are approximately three feet tall, with oversized heads and very long fingers. The "leader" is approximately four feet tall and extremely slender. Its arms are long and spindly and it has five fingers on each hand. It has a long neck, wideset eyes that are large and almond-shaped; its nose is little more than two slits, and its mouth is small and lipless. The alien's small, rimless ears are set low on the side of its round face.

The mothership resembles a brightly lighted chandelier, with spokes radiating out from the lower half (this becomes the upper half when the ship inverts after arriving).

Biography: One night in Muncie, Indiana, the electronic toys of young Barry Guiler come to life. Meanwhile, power company technician Roy Neary is sent to the Gilmore substation as power is lost up and down the line. Barry runs out into the night; Roy, lost, is terrified as his car's electrical power is shut down by a light from a UFO. Later, Roy encounters Barry's single mother, Jillian, as she's out looking for her boy. She finds him, and all of them see UFOs whizzing by. Back home, Roy's wife Ronnie and his children are concerned as he becomes increasingly obsessed with sculpting mountain-like shapes—first in his shaving cream, then in his pillow, from mashed potatoes at the dinner table, with clay, and finally from mud, plants, and garbage he dumps in the living room. Elsewhere, Barry is abducted by one of the saucers and its unseen occupants, and UFOlogist Claude Lacombe investigates similar sightings the world over.

A mask worn by one of the *Alien* extras in *Close Encounters of the Third Kind.* © Columbia Pictures.

Roy's family leaves him, and while watching TV he sees a news report on Devil's Tower, Wyoming. He realizes that is the image he's been trying to sculpt, and makes a pilgrimage to the monument; so does Jillian, who has also been haunted by visions of the Tower, which she's been sketching. At the same time, Lacombe and his people have received landing coordinates from the alien mothership, and have gone ahead and set up a landing strip and base at the Tower; authorities keep tourists and others away by telling them there's been a train derailment and dangerous gas spill. Still, Jillian and Roy link up and, driven by the image the aliens implanted in their brains, make their way around the Tower on foot and are present when the alien mothership arrives. Lacombe's people "talk" to it, haltingly at first, with five musical tones and accompanying colored lights; as the conversation becomes more musically complex, the computers take over. But the aliens didn't come just to talk. They release Navy fliers who were captured in 1944 and haven't aged a day, along with other abductees; they also release Barry. Roy sneaks down to the landing strip, where aliens surround him and escort him onto the

ship. A slightly taller alien "leader," meanwhile, faces Lacombe, and the two converse using musical hand-signs created by Zoltan Kodaly (to teach music to deaf children). A dialogue has been opened, and the mothership takes off with Neary inside.

Comment: In 1980, the director shortened the middle section of the film, added additional scenes, and shot new footage showing the inside of the mothership. The film was released as *Close Encounters of the Third Kind: The Special Edition.* The entire film, excised and new footage, is available in widescreen on laserdisc from Criterion.

Richard Dreyfuss stars as Roy, Melinda Dillon is Jillian, Teri Garr is Ronnie, Cary Guffey is Barry, and director Francois Truffaut is Lacombe. The film was written and directed by Steven Spielberg.

The novelization of the script, though credited to Spielberg, was largely written by Leslie Waller (who also writes as Patrick Mann). The director once said, "There's about twenty percent of me in the book."

Dell published a full-color "fotonovel" version of the film, featuring comic book–style dialogue and over 400 color stills.

Spielberg began drafting a sequel to this film, which evolved into E.T.

THE ALIENS (2) (L, MP)

First Appearance: "Deadly City" by Ivor Jorgenson, March 1953, *If.*

Physical Description: The humanoids are only vaguely described. They are "so thin—so fragile" with heads and limbs more or less like our own, although they "certainly don't look much like us." They carry "odd-looking weapons."

Biography: Coming to Earth from "some other planet," the aliens murder almost every person in three small towns in southern Michigan. But four people survive and make their stand in one of the deserted towns, holding off the aliens until they are destroyed by "natural forces"—our own atmosphere, which proves as fatal to them as it did to the Martians of H.G. Wells (see THE MARTIAN THINGS).

Comment: Jorgenson's real name was Paul W. Fairman. The novella is better known (if hardly recognizable) as the motion picture *Target Earth!*, released in 1954. Sherman A. Rose directed from a script by William Raynor, based on a treatment by Wyott Ordung. In this superior telling, Earth is invaded by robots from Venus. These robots are barely humanoid. They have thick legs made of ribbed tubes, an inverted pyramid for a body, arms that look like cinderblocks on top, cylindrical forearms, calipers for hands, and an "A"-shaped head with an oval, death-ray-firing orb in the front. As scientists try to find some means of stopping the extraterrestrial machines, the robots go house-to-house in a deserted town, killing surviving humans. Just as they're about to murder Frank Brooks (Richard Denning) and Nora King (Kathleen Crowley), the "cavalry" arrives firing ultrasonic sound waves, which crack the orbs in the robots' heads and stop them dead.

ALLAN CRANE (C)

First Appearance: "You, Rocket," 1955, *Incredible Science Fiction #31*, EC Publishing.

Physical Description: The sleek, bullet-shaped, atomic-powered ship has four tailfins with bullet-shaped rockets on the tip of each. It is made of "an alloy harder than diamond" with a framework of "beryl steel." The ship is run by the electroenergized brain of Allan Crane, which is kept in a small dome in the control room. The impulses run along platinum wires to work levers and switches; Crane also has a mechanical voice and a "dozen lens-eyes" to look into space.

Biography: When he is killed in a rocket car accident, rocket engineer Crane is found by scientists from the proving ground. They are able to save his brain and place it inside a mockup of a new spaceship. There, they educate him in astronomy, physics, and running the under-construction ship. His training lasts 11 years, during which he becomes confident, then arrogant, convinced that he's better than any frail human astronaut could be. When his rocket is finished, he's sent toward Mars; but Allan gets scared in the void and, with a cry of "mama-a-a-a-a-a . . . ," turns back.

Comment: The story was the work of the legendary artist Wally Wood.

ALTAIR-4 (MP, L, C)

First Appearance: *Forbidden Planet*, 1956, Metro-Goldwyn-Mayer.

Physical Description: The planet has an Earthlike atmosphere and gravity, though the sky is green and there are two moons. While there are forests on Altair-4, the planet appears to consist of dry, dusty plains and towering mountains.

The Krell are not pictured in the film, but are known to have had bulkier craniums than humans.

Leslie Nielsen and Anne Francis pose with Robby the Robot in a publicity shot from *Forbidden Planet*. © Metro-Goldwyn-Mayer.

Robby is somewhat humanoid. His head is a gumdrop-shaped dome with an antenna on each side, a trio of gyroscopes where the brow would be, clacking relays beneath, and a grid below the dome that lights up blue when he speaks. Robby is conversant in 188 languages and can hear, though it isn't clear where his ears are. His torso is shaped like a giant crockpot with a panel in front: Matter inserted into the opening there will be analyzed in his internal "chemical laboratory" and reproduced exactly, in any quantity desired, from diamonds to alcohol. Robby's pelvis is a large sphere, and each leg consists of three spheres piled one atop the other. He has two round feet, flattened on the bottom. His very short arms end in a pair of three-fingered hands. Powered by isotope 217, the roughly seven-foot-tall robot is able to lift 10 tons with one hand, but is programmed not to harm humans.

The spaceship Cruiser C-57-D is a flat disc with an opaque dome in the center and a smaller, red-glowing dome underneath. When the craft descends, a central landing column descends from the base of the hull. Stairways descend from either side of the underbelly. The bridge is comprised of two tiers within the dome, a central "astro-globe" navigation system (a model of the ship set within a starfield in a transparent dome). There are two banks of computers and a viewscreen. The ship travels at "hyperlight" speeds and has an "artificial gravity field."

The 21-person crew includes Commander and Chief Pilot John J. Adams, Astrogator Lt. Jerry P.

Farman, Major (Medical) C.X. "Doc" Ostrow, Chief Devisor and Engineer Alonzo Quinn, and cook Cookie.

Biography: In 1995, the first "fully manned satellite Space Station" was built; by 2100 the solar system was colonized; and by 2200 the worldwide Federation began the conquest of deep space. Now, in the 23rd century, United Planets Cruiser C-57-D is sent on a yearlong voyage to the star Altair in the constellation Alpha Aquilae to find out what happened to the prospecting ship, the *Bellerophon*, which was sent from the moon exactly 20 years before. Reaching Altair-4, they are warned off by *Bellerophon* philologist Dr. Edward Morbius, but land anyway. Going to his home, Adams, Doc, and Kelly learn that most of the *Bellerophon* crewmembers had been killed by a mysterious planetary force—the ship vaporized when the last three colonists tried to leave. The only survivors were Morbius and his wife, biochemist Julia Marsin. Morbius doesn't know what protected them; all that distinguished them from the others was their love of this new world. Julia died a few months later of natural causes, and now Morbius lives on Altair-4 with his daughter, the lovely Altaira, and the robot Robby; he makes it clear that he prefers that they remain alone.

When Adams doesn't depart at once, saying he has to wait for further orders, the planetary force attacks his ship, and Morbius is forced to reveal more. He takes them to a vast underground complex, a combination laboratory/research center/power station, and says that 2,000 centuries before, the planet was home to a mighty race known as the Krell. The Krell had achieved greatness in science including one last, amazing advance: the ability to create matter and project it anywhere by mere thought. Then, in just one night, the entire race was destroyed. Doc and Adams realize what Morbius does not—that the Krell had forgotten their own bestial, long-suppressed ids. Without being aware of it, their subconscious minds used the newfound scientific advance to create monsters that killed every last Krell. Morbius, having studied Krell writings—which enabled him to build Robby, among other things—and having used a Krell "brain" machine to boost his own intellect, unwittingly has been doing the same. He sent his id-monster to destroy the homesick crew of the *Bellerophon*, and has dispatched it again to stop Adams's meddling team. But Altaira has fallen in love with Adams, and when the monster comes after them, the horrified Morbius throws himself between the lovers and the beast. Mortally

wounded but destroying his own creation, Morbius throws a switch; it sets up a chain reaction to destroy Altair-4 within 24 hours, by which time the cruiser is 10 billion miles away with Altaira and Robby safely onboard.

Comment: Walter Pidgeon stars as Morbius, Leslie Nielsen is Adams, Anne Francis is Altaira, Warren Stevens is Doc, Jack Kelly is Farman, and Frankie Carpenter and Frankie Darro played Robby, whose voice was provided by Marvin Miller. Fred McLeod Wilcox directed from a script by Cyril Hume, based on a screen story called *Fatal Planet* by Irving Block and Allen Adler, which was inspired by Shakespeare's *The Tempest*.

In 1956, Farrar, Straus and Cudahy (in hardcover) and Bantam Books (in paperback) concurrently published W.J. Stuart's novel based on the treatment for the film (the original screen story) and not on the screenplay. The two stories are largely the same, though chapters of the novel are narrated, in turn, by Ostrow (three), Adams (four), and Morbius (one), providing different perspectives on the action. The foreword and postscript are excerpts from *This Third Millennium—A Condensed Textbook for Students* by A.G. Yakimara.

Many references to the film spell the aliens as "Krel," though the novel uses "Krell."

In 1993, Innovation published a four-issue comic book adaptation of the film.

The original Robby reappeared in the movie *The Invisible Boy* (1957), which was written by Cyril Hume. In the film, Professor Greenhill goes into the future, finds the robot in a Chicago spaceport in 2309 A.D., and brings it to the present, dismantling it to see what makes it tick. Greenhill dies before the film proper begins, and the disassembled robot passes to Dr. Merrinoe (Philip Abbott). His 10-year-old son Timmie (Richard Eyer) puts Robby back together again, with the help of Merrinoe's evil new Super Computer, which has hypnotized the lad. When Robby is rebuilt, the computer reprograms the robot to serve him. Robby concocts a potion to make Timmie invisible, the two get onboard a new U.S. satellite with which the computer hopes to control the Earth, and—after escaping the satellite on a space lifeboat—Robby finally turns on the machine and destroys it.

The costume—not the robot Robby—also appeared on episodes of the TV series *The Twilight Zone* ("The Brain Center at Whipple's," 1964) and *Lost in Space* ("The War of the Robots," 1966).

In 1989, Bob Carlton staged his musical *Return to the Forbidden Planet* in London; it opened (and closed) in New York in 1991. The show is not

Gabriel Barre as Robby the Robot, with Erin Hill, in the Off-Broadway production *Return to the Forbidden Planet.* Martha Swope Associates/Carol Rosegg.

actually a return but a somewhat different version of the original story. In 2009, Dr. Prospero and his wife Gloria invent the telegenesis formula, which allows people to create matter by mere thought. But Gloria wants to be rid of her husband and manages to send him into hyperspace in an old spaceship; unknown to her, their daughter Miranda was sleeping in the craft and is rocketed away with her father. Fifteen years later, Captain Tempest and his crew arrive at the planet D'Illyria, the Forbidden Planet. There, with the help of his daughter and the robot Ariel, Prospero has been searching for a means to open up the unused nine-tenths of the human brain so that telegenesis can be exploited to its fullest potential. But as fate would have it, Gloria is the science officer on the ship, and Prospero sends his tentacled id-monster out to destroy the intruders.

The music is comprised entirely of pop hits from the 1950s and 1960s, such as "Good Vibrations," "Young Girl," "Great Balls of Fire," "Monster Mash," and Cookie's showstopping "She's Not There," among others. The special effects for the show were designed by Gerry Anderson, creator of SUPERCAR, among other popular TV shows.

AMAZO (C)

First Appearance: *The Brave and the Bold* #30, 1960, DC Comics.
Physical Description: Standing eight feet tall, the humanoid android wears brown tights that cover

his feet, with horizontal dark and light green bands on the shins and from the waist to the base of his chest (his breast is bare); and dark and light green-striped wristbands. He is pink-skinned and entirely hairless.

Later, his costume is changed slightly. The tights are still striped at the bottom but end at the waist, and he wears brown trunks over them, with a red belt and a yellow "A" buckle. His torso is bare beneath a "V"-shaped vest comprised of diagonal dark green, light green, and yellow stripes. He still wears his wristbands, but has added a red skullcap with a widow's peak and wears a golden star on a necklace.

The android is made of artificial cells that enable him to duplicate the powers of any superbeing he meets. In his first adventure, however, he can utilize only one being's power at a time. His weapons are Green Lantern's power ring, which enables him to fly and create any object he wills, and Wonder Woman's magic lasso, which compels people to tell the truth.

Biography: Professor Ivo wants to live forever. He creates Amazo to help him obtain the most aged beings (and thus, their cells) on the planet; first, though, he has Amazo soak up the abilities of the superheroes of the Justice League of America so that he is invincible. After Ivo has succeeded in creating and drinking his formula, Green Lantern is able to stop Amazo by using yellow chlorine gas against him (Green Lantern's power ring is ineffective against yellow). Ivo is arrested and sentenced to 500 years in jail.

Later, Amazo is reanimated to help the Justice League defeat the alien I, who can be defeated only by exposure to an excess of super-power energy. This energy is unleashed in a battle between Amazo and the Justice Leaguers. Amazo returns as a helpless servant to the evil T.O. Morrow, then undergoes reprogramming and helps the Justice League battle the wicked Libra, who has stolen their powers with his Energy-Trans-Mortifier. Unfortunately, Amazo steals the powers for himself. It remains for Batman to trick him into a machine that siphons away his powers, after which the hero dons steel gloves to knock Amazo's head off. The robot is actually happier in his "sleep of oblivion." He never had any desire to do evil, but couldn't escape his programming.

The Justice League is comprised of SUPERMAN, J'ONN J'ONZZ, Green Lantern (see GREEN LANTERN CORPS), Wonder Woman, Batman, the Flash, Aquaman, and other superheroes.

Comment: The fight with I occurred in *Justice*

League of America #27, the T.O. Morrow adventure in #65, and the Batman showdown in #112.

AMERICAN CYBORG (MP)

First Appearance: *American Cyborg: Steel Warrior*, 1994, Global Pictures/Cannon Pictures.

Physical Description: The relentless cyborg has a blond buzzcut, mustache, and leather outfit. He is humorless, powerful, and beneath his human skin is made mostly of steel.

Biography: Seventeen years after a nuclear holocaust has sterilized most of the population, Mary is the only fertile woman left. Computers rule the world, their will enforced by vicious cyborgs, their goal to rid the world of humans. But using in vitro fertilization, scientists have managed to create a fetus with the help of Mary, "the only source of ova" on the planet. With the fetus in a test tube, Mary and her rugged guardian Austin (who turns out to be a cyborg) try to find a haven for her and her baby. While making their way through pockets of civilization populated by everything from cannibals to transvestites, they are pursued by the evil American Cyborg.

Comment: John Ryan is the Cyborg, with Nicole Hansen as Mary and Joe Lara as Austin. The film was written by Brent Friedman and Christopher Pearce and directed by Boaz Davidson.

THE AMPS (C)

First Appearance: *Alien Ducklings*, 1986, Blackthorne Comics.

Physical Description: In their native form, the Amps are made of energy. On Earth, they become farm animals. Webster is a bespectacled duck with a green tie and white collar; Aquaduck wears a tight black sweatshirt with a white "A" and a white cape; Beebee wears a green shirt; and Master Po is dressed as a martial artist.

Biography: Fleeing the wicked Overloads, the Amps board a spaceship and leave the Greenway Galaxy. They crashland on Earth, but must adopt host bodies because they can't survive very long in our atmosphere. The Amps take a quick look around for "the dominant species." Having landed on a farm, Twobee, Beebee, and Eyebee select ducks to clone, Beea chooses a pig, and they realize too late that these are *not* the dominant life forms. Still, they make the best of things. Beea sees an episode of *Kung Fu* on TV and uses his energy to become Master Po, still a pig but also a philosophical practitioner of the martial arts; Eyebee goes to

the library, reads voraciously, and becomes Webster, the Avian encyclopedia; Beebee rents comedy videocassettes and can mimic all the comedians he's seen, from Jackie Gleason to Steve Martin; and Twobee visits a comic book shop and transforms himself into Aquaduck, who is "psychically linked to the metawaves of nearby fish," which somehow makes him "the most powerful superduck the universe has ever seen."

Comment: The characters were created by writer Cliff MacGillivray and artist Andy Ice. Blackthorne published four issues of *Alien Ducklings*.

THE ANDROMEDA STRAIN (L, MP)

First Appearance: *The Andromeda Strain* by Michael Crichton, 1969, Alfred A. Knopf.

Physical Description: The Strain is composed of hydrogen, carbon, nitrogen, and oxygen—no amino acids or proteins. "A micron or less in size," it lives in flake-like colonies and is green except when undergoing mitosis, when it turns purple.

Biography: After the satellite *Scoop VI* recovers a previously unknown unicellular organism from space, *Scoop VII* is sent aloft in February 1967. Becoming unstable for reasons unknown, it is brought down early and lands in the small town of Piedmont, Arizona. Almost at once, the population begins to die. The military brings in bacteriologist Dr. Jeremy Stone and pathologist Charles Burton to investigate; wearing protective suits, they enter the town and discover that everyone but Peter Jackson—a drunk old man—and a wailing baby has perished, their blood "clotted solid." All animals other than birds have also died. After a jet crashes

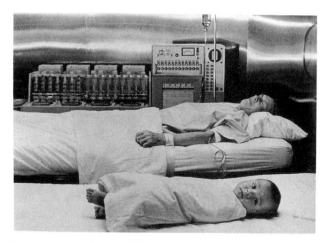

The only two survivors of *The Andromeda Strain*. From the Robert Wise motion picture. © Universal Pictures.

while flying over Piedmont, the town is bombed to ashes. Taking the survivors and satellite to the five-level underground Wildfire lab in Nevada, the men—along with Dr. Peter Leavitt and Dr. Mark William Hall—find that the satellite had been struck by a small meteoroid to which a microscopic life form was attached. They speculate that the hitchhiker, codenamed Andromeda, is part of a larger organism having "a sort of 'coming-out party' on a galactic scale" by sending pieces of itself in every direction.

Researching further, the scientists discover that the Strain lives in a very narrow pH range, the drunk having survived because he was too acidotic, the baby and birds because they were breathing fast and were too alkalotic. They also learn that the Strain works "like a little reactor," converting energy to matter, and that when it finds itself in an unfavorable pH environment it mutates so it is noninfectious to humans but eats rubber—hence, the jet crash. When Burton is infected, he breathes rapidly until the Strain mutates; unfortunately, it starts eating the rubber seals in the sterile, ultra-secure Wildfire. This automatically triggers an atomic self-destruct mechanism—which, if it detonates, is *supposed* to kill any escaped organism. In this case, however, it will cause the Strain to multiply at a prodigious rate. Fortunately, Hall is able to pick his way through the defense systems and shut the bomb down seconds before it detonates.

Comment: The novel was filmed in 1971 by Robert Wise, starring Arthur Hill as Stone, David Wayne as Dutton (not Burton), James Olson as Hall, and Kate Reid as Ruth (not Peter) Leavitt.

ANNEX ONE   (TV)

First Appearance: "The Mutant," March 1964, *The Outer Limits,* ABC.

Physical Description: Located in another galaxy, Annex One is a world of deserts and sparse forests, "almost identical to Earth except that there is no night." The other difference is "radio-isotope" rain, showers that come quickly and are typically over in less than a minute. There is plant life, but no indigenous animal life on the world. The only animal seen is a circa six-foot-tall bug-eyed, radioactive ant, apparently a stowaway from Earth mutated by the rain (see *Biography*).

The sunlight on Annex One is so bright that dark goggles must be worn by anyone going outside.

Dr. Marshall's SR 3498 United Space Agency landing craft is arrowhead-shaped, launched from a mothership somewhere in space.

Biography: A six-person expedition from Earth settles into a small, spare complex on Annex One, attempting to establish a thriving colony. Shortly after, botanist Reese Fowler is caught in a strange, glittering rain and becomes a mutant: His eyes bug out, he loses his hair, he can read minds, he needs light to survive, he is intensely radioactive, and his touch deadly (it causes other peoples' atoms to explode). The other colonists want to leave, but Fowler doesn't want to be alone and forces them to stay; first he kills biochemist Philip Griffith for having refused to let the others help him in from the rain. When Dr. Evan Marshall arrives to check on the colony, Fowler fears that his little kingdom will be imperiled. He kills biologist Peter Chandler for trying to pass Marshall a note. Meteorologist Henry LaCosta is killed by a mutant ant, while Dr. Frederick Riner dies in a fall. Finally, only Marshall and his old flame biochemist Julie Griffith (widow of Philip) remain. Trying to escape the rain and Fowler, who is in pursuit, they hide in a cave where the darkness kills the mutant.

Comment: Warren Oates is Fowler, Larry Pennell plays Marshall, and Betsy Jones-Moreland is Griffith. The hour-long episode was directed by Alan Crosland Jr. The convoluted writing credits attribute the following: script by Allan Balter and Robert Mintz; additional writing by Ellis St. Joseph, Victor Stoloff, and Betty Ulius; from a story by Joseph Stefano and Jerome Thomas; and based on a treatment by St. Joseph.

APOKOLIPS   (C, TV)

First Appearance: *The New Gods* #1, 1971, DC Comics.

Physical Description: The surface of the world—size unknown, though apparently not much larger than Earth's moon—is covered with massive, ugly dwellings that house machines of destruction. The key region of the world is Armagetto, where slave laborers, the Hunger Dogs, feed the Energy Pits that provide the planet's power.

Biography: At some point in the dim past, the "Old Gods" perished in a disaster (implicitly, the Norse gods and their twilight, Ragnarok). The fragments of their world accreted into new molten, twin bodies: Apokolips and New Genesis. The latter became a world of light and beauty, home of the New Gods. The dark Apokolips, existing in the shadow of New Genesis, became a world of corruption and evil ruled by Queen Heggra, its military commanded by her brother Steppenwolf. The two worlds go to war, ending when the High

Father Izaya of New Genesis slays Steppenwolf and Heggra is poisoned by her seven-foot-six son Darkseid. To ensure that the peace endures, Izaya sends his son Scott Free to live on Apokolips, and takes in Orion, the son of Darkseid, the new ruler of Apokolips. While the New Gods, or Celestials, dwell in Supertown—a golden city floating high above their lush world—Darkseid lives in his massive Tower of Rage, seeking the terrible Anti-Life Equation with which he intends to conquer the universe. Ultimately, a new war erupts and New Genesis is destroyed by Darkseid, leaving the New Gods floating through space on Supertown. Though Apokolips is later ravaged by a revolution of the Hunger Dogs, it—and Darkseid—live on.

Darkseid's aides include the Deep Six, green-skinned, fish-like humanoids named Gole, Jaffar, Kurin, Shallgo, Slig, and Trok. Darkseid's master torturer and a key advisor is the humanoid DeSaad, who did the actual poisoning of Heggra. Another close aide is Doctor Bedlam, a being who was once humanoid and now exists as psionic energy. His former aides, the Female Furies—Bernadeth, Big Barda, Lashina, Mad Harriet, and Stompa—have since come over to the forces of good.

Comment: The Old Gods reference is a (self) tip-of-the-hat by Jack Kirby, the artist/creator of Apokolips and New Genesis, who drew the popular comic book *The Mighty Thor* for Marvel during the 1960s. The saga of the New Gods and Darkseid sprawled through Kirby's titles *Jimmy Olsen, The Forever People, The New Gods*, and *Mr. Miracle*.

Darkseid and Apokolips were seen on the animated series *Super Friends: The Legendary Super Powers Show*, which aired on ABC from September 1984 to August 1985, and on *Super Powers Team: Galactic Guardians* on ABC from September 1985 to August 1986. Frank Welker provided the villain's voice.

AQUACOM-89045 See VALCOM-17485 AND AQUACOM-89045.

THE A.R.C.-1 (C)

First Appearance: "Project . . . Survival," 1952, *Weird Fantasy* #12, EC Publishing.
Physical Description: Approximately 75 feet long, the sleek, needle-nosed rocket has two tail fins with an engine on each, two stubby wings with three engines on each of the opposite sides, and a large engine on the bottom.
Biography: When the nations of Asia Minor rebel against the world republic, the Amalgamated Rocket Corporation builds a spaceship with which to establish an offensive base on the moon. Unfortunately, the enemy fires an Electron Bomb which, unexpectedly, begins turning the entire Earth into molten lava. Working quickly, project leader Dr. Jansen gathers frozen, fertilized eggs of "thousands of species of animals, fish, and birds," along with plant seeds. He boards the rocket with his wife and six married couples and, with a four-month supply of food, they blast into orbit. They remain in orbit until the lava is hardened by rain, after which they land and destroy the A.R.C.-1, feeling that humans will be "better off without" science. Only then do the other passengers learn that Jansen's first name is Noah.

Comment: The story was the work of comics great Wally Wood. The same issue featured Wood's story "The Die Is Cast!" featuring the rocket *Pleiades II*, torpedo-shaped with two large wings in the center and four in the back. The crew can't understand why the ground rumbles repeatedly, until they realize they've landed on a giant alien dice table.

The ship is unrelated to the A.R.C.—Animal Resource Carrier—piloted by Dr. Noah Thomas in DC's *Mystery in Space* #115, 1981.

ARIES VII (C)

First Appearance: *Planet of Vampires* #1, 1975, Atlas Comics.
Physical Description: The golden spaceship is 160 feet long. It has a wedge-shaped fuselage, two long wings, upright tail fins on either side and one in the center, and three large engines—one outside each outer tail fin and a third atop the central tail fin.
Biography: In 2007, the Aries VII goes into orbit around Mars "to find and catalogue any life forms that might exist"; onboard are Captain Christopher Galland, his wife Elissa, copilot Craig and his physician-wife Brenda, and biologist Dr. Ben Levitz. However, upon learning that the nations of Earth are on the brink of war, the crew calls the mission off and heads home. Returning to Earth on April 21, 2010, they land in the water off Coney Island, New York. The astronauts soon learn that chemical and biological weapons used during the war turned some members of the population into vampires, who live in high-tech domes and feed on the "Savages" who live outside. Ben is murdered by Savages who mistake him for a vampire; Brenda is killed by vampires; Elissa is slain by a giant spider; and Chris struggles to survive in this brave new world.

Comment: The comic book lasted three issues. It was unrelated to the motion picture *Planet of the Vampires*.

ARIZANT (L)

First Appearance: "Capt'n Virgil, Sportsman in Space" by June and David Brooks, 1984, *Heavy Metal*, Vol. 8, #4.

Physical Description: Hostile to human life (visitors must wear spacesuits), the planet Arizant circles three suns and has at least 16 natural lakes (as opposed to worlds where they are human-made). There are gently sloping hills and the surface is covered with lollipop-shaped "weeping aquariums," whose fishbowl tops absorb sunlight and release Agent Orange. The plant's roots stretch for miles.

The planet's skies are dark with "space debris clouds," comprised of discarded TVs, computers, and calculators that are "magnetized together."

Life forms on the planet include the Two-Headed Stickleback; killer eels that live along the shoreline; the minute Corkscrew Worms; and the Long-Necked Muzzle, a dinosaur-like creature with a mouth so small it can eat only Corkscrew Worms. The Muzzle possesses an energy field capable of electrocuting its prey and "nibbling the crumbs."

Biography: Arizant was first explored by space station IX2A and is a difficult world to reach; because meteor showers pepper the solar system, commercial spaceliners avoid it. Thus, Virgil and his fishing buddy Joe fly over in Virgil's Aldo Supernova II, "a little beauty that gets us to Arizant in less than two days." Those who do reach the world are able to rent small barracks near the lakes.

The rarest catch on the planet is a Two-Headed Stickleback, a roughly yard-long fish that is used to make "the best fish ice cream" in the universe.

Long-Necked Muzzles were hunted nearly to extinction because their skins make "perfect trampolines"; Corkscrew Worms are also coveted because they are "delicious deep-fried"—so good, in fact, that when they were first sent to Earth, they "wiped out the onion ring and French fry market."

Comment: The clever, mock-fishing-guide was illustrated by David Brooks.

ARKY (C)

First Appearance: *Showcase* #91, 1970, DC Comics.

Physical Description: The golden robot has an egg-shaped body, a gumdrop head with eyes and a gash of a mouth, and thin arms with pincers on the end. It has no legs, but floats on a small, flat sled.

Biography: Starker is a white-haired spacefaring bounty hunter of the year 2070, and Arky is his one and only trusted companion. If Starker is needed when he's away from his "house satellite" in orbit around Jupiter, Arky signals the hunter via a ring on his finger, then briefs him on the mission when he arrives. In the case of escaped criminals, Arky also calculates where they may have gone and Starker usually heads there. The robot suggests weapons suitable for the job—"I will recommend—disinto-blaster—exposi-needle gun—electro-knife—rifle—cannon—and full space armor" —briefs him on the flora, fauna, and governments on any world to which he's headed, and warms up whatever transportation Starker will be using. Arky typically stays behind at the house when Starker sets out on a mission.

Comment: The character was created by editor/artist/writer Mike Sekowsky and appeared in three successive issues of *Showcase*. The saga is significant in that it contains many elements that may have inspired the movie *Star Wars*, not the least of which is Arky/R2-D2, Starker/Han Solo, the cantina on the cover of the first issue, the Death Planet/Death Star, and many more details.

ARRAKIS (L, MP, C)

First Appearance: "Dune World" by Frank Herbert, December 1963, *Analog*.

Physical Description: Arrakis is the third planet of the star Canopus, circling it at a mean distance of 87 million kilometers. The planet's radius is 8,112 kilometers, the average year is 353 days, and a day is 22.4 hours long. Because of its nearly circular orbit, Arrakis has no seasons; save for the small, icy poles, the planet is hot and arid for most of the year. Dust clouds and dust storms are common; clouds of water vapor are extremely thin and rare. The planet is riven by deep valleys, mountain ranges, and volcanic activity; running or standing bodies of water are quite uncommon.

In addition to the native, human Fremen, the dominant life form on the planet is "shai-hulud" or "giant sandworms." In their larval form, the creatures are approximately 20 centimeters long and six centimeters wide. As adults, the largest males reach 400 meters in length and 100 meters in width; the largest females are 100 by 20 meters. The silvery-gray creatures are comprised of 100 to 400 segments, have a minimum of 1,000 "carbosilica" teeth set around the mouth in a circle, and burrow through the sands of the desert world drawing nutrients from the soil. The worms were nearly eradicated when Arrakis was turned into a more hospitable world.

Arrakis has two moons, Krlln (radius of 488 kilometers) and Arvon (radius of 201 kilometers). A third moon was destroyed by a collision with a heavenly body some 200,000 years ago, and formed a dust ring that lasted many years.

The first planet in the Canopus system is Seban (radius of 2,380 kilometers); the second is Menaris (radius of 7,862 kilometers); the fourth is Extaris (radius of 8,112 kilometers); the fifth is Ven (radius of 210,500 kilometers); and the outermost planet is Revona (radius of 2,225 kilometers).

Biography: In 10,190, the Padishah Emperor Shaddam IV appoints Duke Leto Atreides I of the planet Caladan to replace Siridar-Baron Harkonnen—the father of Leto's wife Lady Jessica—as the governor of Arrakis, the Dune World, a planet vital to the spice mining trade. Lady Jessica and their son Paul follow him there a year later. But the Baron still covets Arrakis and has the Duke assassinated, forcing Paul and his pregnant mother to hide with the native, desert-dwelling Fremen of Sietch Tabr. There, Jessica gives birth to Paul's sister Alia. Two years later, having learned to summon and ride the sandworms, Paul leads the Fremen in revolt against the Padishah Emperor and the Baron Harkonnen. His forces are victorious and Paul becomes known as Muad'Dib, Messiah. He makes a political concession by wedding Shaddam IV's daughter Irulan Corrino, though it's his Fremen concubine Chani Liet-Kynes who bears his twins Leto and Chanima.

Paul carries out the successful greening of Arrakis, turning it into a fertile, hospitable world. But an assassination attempt in 10,205 leaves him blind, and he goes to the desert in self-imposed exile. Legend has it that he will return one day; some people say they have seen him or had visions in which he has warned of impending disaster. Meanwhile, his son Leto spends nearly 4,000 years transforming himself into a sandworm to help protect his verdant world. But after more than 15,000 years of political and religious drama, Leto and even the legendary Paul are unable to prevent Arrakis from being returned to a harsh, inhospitable desert world.

Comment: The original story was serialized through February 1964; it was published as the novel *Dune* in 1965. The sequels to the original novel are *Dune Messiah* (1969), *Children of Dune* (1976), *The God Emperor of Dune* (1981),

Heretics of Dune (1984), and *Chapterhouse: Dune* (1985).

David Lynch directed the 1984 film *Dune*, starring Kyle MacLachlan as Paul, Francesca Annis as Jessica, Kenneth McMillan as the Baron, Jurgen Prochnow as Leto, Sean Young as Chani, and Jose Ferrer as the Emperor. Marvel Comics published a three-issue adaptation of the film in 1985.

ASH See ALIEN.

ASTEROID B-612 (L, MP)

First Appearance: *Le Petit Prince* by Antoine de Saint Exupéry, 1943.

Physical Description: ''Scarcely any larger than a house'' (approximately eight feet in diameter), the round asteroid has three tiny volcanoes (two active, one extinct) and innumerable seeds. The seeds sleep and grow into ''good plants and bad plants,'' those that produce pleasant radishes or roses, and those that grow into baobabs—which, if left unattended, will grow into planet-crowding trees. There are 42 sunsets every 24 hours.

Biography: Crashlanding in the Sahara Desert, a pilot repairing his plane is visited by a young

Asteroid B-612 from the motion picture *The Little Prince.*
© Paramount Pictures.

golden-haired boy in a greatcoat, knee boots, and carrying a sword. The boy says he left his home to gain knowledge. He went to Asteroids 325 (inhabited by a king), 326 (home of "a conceited man"), 327 (home of a tippler), 328 (home of a businessman), 329 (home of a lamplighter), 330 (home of a geographer), and then to Earth. Here, he met a snake—who boasted he could solve all problems—roses, a fox, and the aviator. After a year, the homesick prince lets the snake bite him and is carried "home" by its poison.

Comment: The classic novel was first published in English in 1945 by Harcourt, Brace & World. The story was made into a musical film, *The Little Prince*, in 1974, directed by Stanley Donen with music by Lerner and Loewe. Richard Kiley stars as the pilot, with Steven Warner as the Little Prince, Bob Fosse as the Snake, and Gene Wilder as the Fox.

ASTRO BOY　(C, TV)

First Appearance: *Shonen* magazine (Japan), 1952.

Physical Description: The robot wears a black cap with two pointed "ears," black trunks, red boots, and a silver belt. He has rockets in his heels and possesses superstrength thanks, in part, to his atomic heart.

Biography: When his son is killed in a car crash in the year 2000, Dr. Tenma creates a robot likeness of the boy. Though the android appears human he doesn't age or mature like a normal boy, and his creator is profoundly disappointed. Dr. Tenma sells the robot to a circus; he is eventually taken in by Dr. Ochanomizu, who raises him to be a crimefighter.

For his birthday, the hero gets a robot sister, Astro Girl, who helps him battle such foes as I. M. Sinister, Professor Nutty Fruitcake, Don Tay and his insidious robot Ferno, and many others.

Comment: The character was created by Osamu Tezuka. In Japan, Astro Boy was originally known as Atom-Taishi (Ambassador Atom) and, briefly, as Tetsuwan-Atom (Mighty Atom).

The long-running Japanese comic strip, which was discontinued in 1968, was the basis for a popular animated cartoon series made by Tezuka's own Mushi Productions in 1960. The first group of cartoons consisted of 104 episodes, which aired in the United States on NBC beginning in September 1963. An additional 89 episodes were produced for Japanese TV. Though the robot was destroyed while carrying a bomb into space in the last epi-

sode, Tezuka was forced to bring his popular creation back to life for specials. A new series, produced in 1980, lasted 52 adventures.

In the United States, the series was also known as *Astro Boy* but with a few changes: the deceased young boy was named Astor Boynton III; Dr. Tenma became Dr. Boynton; the big-nosed Dr. Ochanomizu became Dr. Packadermus J. Elefun; and the Tokyo setting became New York. Billie Lou Watt provided the dubbed voices for Astro Boy and Astro Girl.

Gold Key Comics published one issue of *Astro Boy* in 1965.

Tezuka also created the comic strip *Big X*, which became the animated series *Cyborg Big X* (1964; U.S. debut, 1967). The cyborg is Akira, a young boy who is captured by modern-day Nazis and has his brain placed in a robot body.

THE ASTRO-MUTTS　(C)

First Appearance: *Hot Dog* #1, 1990, Archie Comics.

Physical Description: All of the dogs walk on their hind legs and talk. Bark Rogers is a bulldog in a red and purple spacesuit, Lieutenant Saluki is a poodle in a golden spacesuit, and Luke Tailwagger is a beagle in a green spacesuit.

Biography: Hot Dog is the white sheepdog/mutt owned by Jughead Jones of Riverdale. In his first solo story, he is visited by three Astro-Mutts from the Planet of the Pooches. Beaming aboard their Dachshundian Crystal-powered space cruiser and donning a blue space-suit, Hot Dog helps them to capture "the nasty Galcti-Cats—who, besides being bad tempered and destructive, keep chasing the little peace-loving Moustians." Armed with laser pistols, they manage to defeat the cats and their nefarious leader, Drak Batfang. After the adventure, chief engineer Spotty the Scotty returns to Earth with Hot Dog and leaves behind the robot butler Tolbert—a red robot with a head, torso, arms, and single wheel for getting around—and a "trans-space communicator" so he can contact the Astro-Mutts whenever he wants.

The dogs have also battled the evil Piranha People of Pisces Minor.

Comment: The characters appear occasionally in various Archie Comics titles.

ASTRON　(C)

First Appearance: *Galaxia Magazine* #1, 1981, Astral Comics.

Physical Description: A blue-skinned humanoid (see *Comment*), Astron wears a bodysuit, cowl, gloves, and trunks. He travels through the universe onboard the nav-computer controlled spaceship *Starseeker*, which has the ability to fly through black holes to "traverse the galaxies."

Biography: The human denizens of Zenna "in the alternate universe of Galaxia," are protected by a force of warriors, the star-soldiers, of which "Astron stood foremost." By 4000 A.E. (equivalent to 2000 A.D. on Earth), the star-soldiers have been made an elite division of a "corps of superior, highly evolved intergalactic sentinels." After they defeat the evil Centarians and exile the race to a prison world, there is peace in the region.

Traveling at light speed through space, Astron ends up in exactly the same spot, at precisely the same time, as Earth astronaut James Hunt of the starship Probe-4. A "cosmic accident" occurs, causing Hunt's body to be vaporized, his mind fused with that of Astron. Thereafter, the two work as a team, Hunt's consciousness taking over and re-energizing Astron's body whenever he is dazed or tired.

The merging is timely. Contacted by his closest

friend, the aspiring female star-soldier Str'ellah, Astron learns that the evil Grand Shaddai of the Shadar—who have already destroyed Nullah-5 and other worlds—have conquered Zenna in his absence, slain the other star-soldiers, and are determined to exterminate the Zennans. The trio return to Zenna, equally determined to stop the invaders.

Comment: There were only two issues of *Galaxia Magazine*, which was edited by comic book artist Rich Buckler. The strip was black-and-white, though certain colors (such as Astron's skin) were mentioned in the text.

THE ASTRON DELTANS (MP)

First Appearance: *Killers From Space*, 1954, W. Lee Wilder Productions/RKO.

Physical Description: The humanoid creatures are garbed in black boots, bodysuits, and a tight cowl; each wears a belt covered with bolt-like designs. The aliens have three thick fingers on each hand and have ping-pong ball-sized eyes with bushy eyebrows.

Biography: Shortly after his plane crashes near a nuclear test site at Soledad Flats, Nevada, physicist Douglas P. Martin shows up at the base where he worked, remembering nothing, including how he got a huge surgical scar on his chest. Stealing test schedules from a safe and returning to the site, he's confronted by an F.B.I. agent who's been watching him. Under sodium amytal, Martin reveals that his plane was brought down by aliens from the planet Astron Delta 4. Though he died, they operated on his heart and revived him, after which alien scientist Deneb-Tala explained that their sun is nearly extinguished, which has caused their eyes to grow large and forced one billion aliens to board ships "magnetically propelled across the electron bridge" to space stations near Earth. There, they wait while the scientists, working in underground caverns, use energy from atom bomb tests to mutate terrestrial lizards and insects into monsters. When they have bred in sufficient numbers, the giants will be released to feed on humankind and leave the planet free for the aliens to settle. Afterward, says Deneb-Tala, the monsters will be blasted with gamma ray projectors, their bodies used to fertilize the soil. (The alien does *not* explain why they simply don't blast the humans.)

No one believes Martin's story, so it's up to him to destroy the invaders. Since the aliens had no generators, he concludes that they have to be tapping power lines for the electricity they use for

Artist Romeo Tanghal's drawing of *Astron*. © Astral Comics.

their nuclear storage cells. He hurries to the local power plant, has the operator shut down the generators and, sure enough, the Astron Deltans and their menagerie are blown to atoms.

Comment: Peter Graves stars as Martin, John Merrick as Deneb-Tala. The film was directed by W. Lee Wilder from a script by Bill Rayntor, based on a story by Myles Wilder.

ASTROQUASARS (MP)

First Appearance: *Gezora Ganime Kameba Kessen Nankai No Daikaiju* (*Gezora, Ganime, Kameba: Decisive Battle! Giant Monsters of the South Seas*), 1970, Toho Co. Ltd.

Physical Description: In their natural form, the aliens are blue spores that can infiltrate electronic or biological entities.

Biography: Headed for Jupiter, the robot-craft *Helio* 7 is commandeered by the spores, which reprogram it to return to Earth. Only photographer Taro Kudo witnesses its splashdown, and no one believes him. Shortly thereafter, a giant, ambulatory, amphibious squid (Gezora) attacks a pair of executives fishing near Selga Island where their company, the Asia Promotion Agency, is preparing to build a resort. Later, it attacks the island itself before being driven back to the sea by swarming bats. Searching for the monster, Kudo and his friend Dr. Kyoichi Miya go diving and find both the creature and the *Helio* 7. Gezora comes ashore and, after Kudo shoots the creature in one of its eyes, natives set it afire using gasoline stored there during World War II. The monster plunges into the ocean, the spores drifting out and taking over a crab, which grows to an enormous size. The new monster (Ganime) attacks the native village and, like Gezora before it, is burned to death. (Obviously, the spores have *no* memory at all.) They leap from Ganime to the body of anthropologist Makoto Obata, who remains normal-sized and learns from a voice that the spores are called Astroquasars and that they've come to conquer the Earth. Several spores also infiltrate the body of a turtle, which becomes a giant (Kameba).

Obata starts burning the island's bats to death, as their "sound pressure" is lethal to Astroquasars, and Kudo tries to stop him. The super-strong Obata tosses the photographer around like a football, though Kudo's timely intervention has prevented Obata from exterminating *all* the bats. Meanwhile, Kameba shows up as does Ganime, and the two fight (for reasons never made clear, since they're supposed to be on the same team). While all the fighting is going on, the surviving bats drive the giant monsters into a volcano, and, briefly gaining control of his own will, the self-sacrificing Obata joins them.

Comment: Akira Kubo stars as Taro, Yoshio Tsuchiya is Miya, and Kenji Sahara is Obata. Ishiro Honda directed from a screenplay by Ei Ogawa. The film was released in the United States in 1971 as *Yog: Monster From Space*. The dubbing suggests that the spores are all pieces of a single consciousness, Yog.

ATORAGON (MP)

First Appearance: *Kaitei Gunkan* (*Undersea Battleship*), 1963, Toho Co. Ltd./American International.

Physical Description: The ship is 500 feet long, weighs 10,000 tons, and can travel in the air (at Mach 2), in the water (80 knots above, 50 below), on land (186 miles an hour), and through the ground (12.5 miles an hour). The ship is shaped like a submarine, with a huge drill in its nose and retractable wings and caterpillar treads. Its weapons include anti-submarine missiles, atomic cannons armed with "missile bombs," and "refrigerating vapor cannons" (a.k.a. Zero Cannons), which instantly freeze objects at 273 degrees below zero.

AMERICAN INTERNATIONAL presents in COLORSCOPE

ATRAGON

...the ULTIMATE WEAPON hurtling from the outer limits of space to the evil EMPIRE at the bottom of the Seven Seas!

Advertising art showing the amazing multipurpose vehicle *Atoragon* (*Atragon* in the U.S.). © Toho Co. Ltd.

Biography: Two thousand years ago, the Mu Empire sank into the Pacific Ocean, though it survives to this day as a vast undersea kingdom. Now, shifts in the Earth's crust threaten Mu, and the Muans plot to take over the surface world. They are aware, however, that they cannot defeat the mighty *Atoragon*, which the hermitic Captain Shinguji has constructed on a remote island. Rather than face it in battle, the Muans cause natural disasters around the globe and threaten to destroy the Earth if it does not surrender. Shinguji is persuaded to turn *Atoragon* against the would-be conquerors. The vessel and its soldiers bore through Mu's protective dome and freeze its power source using their Zero Cannon; after meeting and destroying their serpentine monster-god Manda, the crew plants explosive charges that destroy Mu.

Comment: The film was released in the United States as *Atragon* (sic). Jun Tazaki stars as Shinguji; the film was directed by Ishiro Honda from a script by Shinichi Sekizawa.

AUTOMAN (C)

First Appearance: *Tales of the Unexpected* #91, 1965, DC Comics.

Physical Description: Constructed of "meteorite manganese," the six-foot-eleven golden, talking robot is humanoid, with smooth skin, golden "trunks," small cylinders for eyes, a Roman nose (sans nostrils), and a wide mouth formed by the slightly prognathous lower jaw, which is hinged at its knoblike ears. Automan has super strength, laser-firing eyes, radar, and a built-in sound movie camera. He cannot be hurt by bullets, fire, or a long fall (he also has a built-in parachute!), and is governed by "an anti-evil device" that causes him to "automatically rebel at crime—and act accordingly."

The robot Ilda (see *Biography*) is five feet tall and possesses X-ray vision, short-distance telepathy, an infra-red heat generator, electric stun bolts, and a can opener. Her yellow, "no-glare plasto-metal" body and lemon-shaped head are impervious to ray guns. A red- and white-striped mini-dress is painted on. She has emotions that run from love to fear that "makes my oil run cold."

Biography: Built by Professor Miller Sterling, Automan, the Automatic Man—also known as Robot #32196—is the first graduate from Robot Tech, which Sterling hopes will turn out "thinking machines" that will stop crime, work as waiters, fight fires, and even serve as unerring umpires. Automan's first job is as a manservant for the wealthy Mr. Rankin, who happens to be a smuggler. Fortunately, the camera in Automan's forehead brings the authorities all the evidence they need to prosecute him. Sometime in the very late 21st century, in New City, Automan "marries" the robot Ilda, secretary/housekeeper of the detective Star Hawkins. (Hawkins is founder of the Hawkins-Sterling Academy of Robot-Detection, which

Axel Pressbutton drawn by artist Steve Dillon. © Pedro Henry and Steve Dillon.

trains robots to become sleuths. The "Sterling" is Stella Sterling, a descendant of Miller's.)

Comment: The character also appeared in issues #94 and #97 of the magazine. Ilda first appeared in *Strange Adventures* #114, 1960.

In 1966, *Tales of the Unexpected* #98 featured the "Half-Man/Half-Machine" saga of Jason Baird, whose heart stops during an operation and has to be replaced with a mechanical heart. Unfortunately, the heart causes his metabolism to change, turning his "living cells into mechanical parts," beginning with his feet (which become tractor treads), legs, and arms (his hands become metal pincers). Luckily, an accidental dip in an acid bath destroys his metal sections and causes his human limbs to return, his "metallo-metabolism reversed to organo-metabolism."

AXEL PRESSBUTTON (C)

First Appearance: *Warrior* #1, 1982, Quality Communications, Ltd.

Physical Description: "The Psychotic Cyborg" has a bald human head, a right arm and hand, and the right, top side of his torso. His left arm is a large, very sharp steel blade, his abdomen is a fat metal pole, his pelvis is metal, and his legs are slender metal tubes. From the knees down his legs are comprised of huge, bell-like feet. He wears a brown sweatshirt on his human chest and arm, and can be deactivated by touching a big red button over his heart.

Biography: Axel is the extremely violent partner of assassin and Ormuzian security agent Mysta Mystralis, "the Laser Eraser." He covers her rear as she makes her hits, protects her when the law tries to arrest her, and pilots their two-person sky-scooter. Though they're based on the planet Ormuz, they're not averse to working on other worlds.

Another planet seen in the early adventures is Klemond, 20 light-years away, a primitive world in which dinosaurs are raised for meat.

Comment: The characters were created by writer Pedro Henry and artist Steve Dillon and appeared regularly in the British publication.

B

BABYLON 5 (TV)

First Appearance: *Babylon 5*, 1993, syndication.
Physical Description: A six-mile-long cylinder, *Babylon 5* is a self-contained habitat with docking bays, a cargo area, a command center, a medlab—which is equipped to care for humans and other life forms—a nightclub (run by Ock), living quarters, and bays for several squadrons of small fighter ships. A shuttle travels the length of the station's core.

Among the aliens, the Narns are bald humanoids with leopard-like spots on their heads. The Centauri are humans with long, bristle-like hair, and the Minbari are androgynous, pale humanoids.

Biography: In the year 2257, the Earth/Minbari war—a devastating conflict spawned when an Earth Alliance vessel accidentally destroyed a Minbari ship—is over. But there is still unrest among the civilizations of different worlds, and the Earth Alliance, which operates *Babylon 5* (a successor to Babylon 4), seeks to keep the peace among the Narns, the Centauri, the Minbari, and other races.

The station is run by Commander Michael Sinclair, a combat veteran, aided by second-in-command Lt. Susan Ivanova, Security Chief Michael Garibaldi, Psi Corps telepath Talia Winters, and Dr. Stephen Franklin. Tension and intrigue on the station are provided by N'Grath, a mantis-like gangster; the Minbari ambassador is Delenn, aided by Lennier; the Narn Ambassador G'Kar; and the Centauri Ambassador Londo Mollari.

Comment: The two-hour feature film spawned an ongoing hour-long syndicated series, which debuted in January 1994. Characters who appeared in the pilot but were replaced in the series are Dr. Kyle (Johnny Sekka), Lyta Alexander (Patricia Tallman), Carolyn Sykes (Blaire Baron), and Laurel Takashima (Tamilyn Tomita).

The cast includes Michael O'Hare as Sinclair, Claudia Christian as Lt. Ivanova, Jerry Doyle as Garibaldi, Andrea Thompson as Talia, Richard Biggs as Franklin, Mira Furlan as Delenn, Bill Mumy as Lennier, Andreas Katsulas as G'Kar, and Peter Jurasik as Mollari.

In November 1994, Bruce Boxleitner joined the cast as Captain John Sheridan, who replaced Sinclair.

THE BANDERSNATCH (C)

First Appearance: "The Galaxy Grand Prix," 1980, *1994* #14, Warren Publishing Co.
Physical Description: The Earthship resembles a stubby jet fighter with a huge engine on each short wing, and another on the top of the fuselage. The ship is powered by an ion accelerator that gives it superlight speeds; it can create holographic images of itself, and it can brake suddenly thanks to solar wind chutes. It also has pontoons for water landings and a titanium propeller on top. The pilot of the *Bandersnatch* is Amos Godstrom; his copilots are the Centaurian women Sybil and Bianca.

Other ships in the race include the Vegan *PDQ*, the Orion *Morguefiller,* the L-14 *Spacebreaker* from Cassiopeia, a Manta warship from Sirius, the Procyon *Ram Scoop,* the *Spacehog,* the *Conqueror,* and the Zorn *Star-Devil.*

Biography: The Galaxy Grand Prix is a 27 light-year-long race held once every 2.3 Earth years. It involves "the most advanced commercial, private, and military starcraft of one hundred and four stellar systems." The ships race from planet to planet, running through obstacles on each world.

Godstrom is going for an unprecedented seventh straight win, and after surviving the Labyrinth of Thorns on Chimera B-VI he turns down a radio request from the Zorn Empire to throw the race for a profit. Two Zorn fighters try to destroy him, but are misled by a holographic image and obliterated in their own crossfire. Surviving other obstacles, the *Bandersnatch* enters the final one, the Fire Tunnel, with the *Star-Devil* right above him. Godstrom drops to the water below, and when the Zorn ship tries to push him under he uses the *Bandersnatch*'s propeller to cut it to ribbons to win the race.

The *Bandersnatch* wins the Galaxy Grand Prix. Art by Vic Catan. © Warren Publishing Co.

Comment: The exciting story was written by Alabaster Redzone (Budd Lewis) and beautifully drawn by Vic Catan. The name of the spaceship comes from Lewis Carroll's poem "Jabberwocky."

BARSOOM (L, CS, C)

First Appearance: "Under the Moons of Mars" by Edgar Rice Burroughs, February-July 1912, *The All-Story*.

Physical Description: Barsoom (Mars) is 4,230 miles in diameter, and its orbit around the sun ranges from 126 million to 152 million miles. A year on Mars is equivalent to 687 Earth days. It has two moons, Thuria (Phobos) and Cluria (Deimos).

In the western hemisphere, starting from the north polar region, the great cities of Barsoom include Pankor, Okar, Raxar, Amhor, Horz, Kamtol, Morbus, Toonol, Dusar, Manatos, Manataj, Manator, Gathol, Exum, Invak, Onvak, Bantoom, Kobol, Xantor, Jahar, Lothar, Ghasta, Aaanthor, Tjanath, and Thurd. Geographical highlights include the desert of U-Gor, the Torquas Mountains, the Valley Dor, the Otz Mountains (which gird the South Pole), the Forest of Lost Men, and the Great Toonolian Marshes. The only large body of water on Barsoom is the Lost Sea of Korus at the South Pole; when Barsoom was younger, there were five oceans, the largest of which was Throxus.

In the eastern hemisphere, from the north, the great cities are Duhor, Phundahl, Gooli, Ptarth, Kaol, Korad, Zodanga, Hastor, Zor, and the bordering realms of the tharks and the warhoon (see below). On the southwestern side of the hemisphere lies the greatest kingdom on Barsoom—Helium, governed from two great cities, Greater Helium and Lesser Helium. Geographical landmarks of the eastern hemisphere include the Artolian Hills, the Kaolian Forest, and the rest of the Great Toonolian Marshes.

Life forms on Barsoom include: the six-limbed, whitefurred Arctic giant, the apt; the lionlike banth; the 10-legged dogs known as calots, about the size of a Shetland pony; the darseen, a chameleon-like reptile; the malagor, a giant bird capable of carrying two human riders; the mantala, an 8- to 12-foot-tall milk plant; the orluk, a black-and-yellow striped Arctic monster; the pimalia, a gorgeous flowering plant; the 10- to 12-foot-high, blue-skinned Plant Men, who have no features other than a ragged hole for a nose and a mass of wormlike black hair on the head; the silian, a sea monster; the bull-sized, hornet-like sith; the skeel, a towering and drought-resistant tree; the sompus, a tree that produces a pulpy fruit; the small, catlike sorak; giant 12-legged spiders; the four-armed green giants, the tharks; the 10-foot-high (at the shoulder), eight-legged horses called thoats; the ratlike ulsio; the 10- to 15-foot-tall, mostly hairless, four-armed white apes; mastodon-like draft animals called zitidars; and different humanoid races with black skin, yellow skin, green skin (warhoons), and reddish skin.

Barsoom is actually the Mars of another time and/or dimension, though the physics of how John Carter got there are never made clear.

Biography: After the Civil War, Virginian veteran John Carter and his friend Captain James K. Powell head west in search of gold. In Arizona, they're attacked by Apaches; Powell dies, but Carter escapes to a cave where he is mystically drawn to the planet Mars, called Barsoom by the natives. He is immediately captured by giant, four-armed, green Tharks. However, because of the lesser gravity on Mars, Carter has increased strength and the ability to jump higher than the natives; moreover, he is extremely adept with the sword. Escaping with another human, the beautiful Princess Dejah Thoris of Helium, Carter eventually weds her and they enjoy many adventures with Carter's closest friend, the Thark Tars Tarkas. But after five Mars-years together, Carter is inexplicably drawn back to Earth (Jasoom); he isn't able to return again until March 1886, 20 years after his initial departure.

Carter and Dejah Thoris have a son, Carthoris, who is married to Thuvia, Princess of Ptarth; and a daughter, Tara, who is the wife of Gahan of Gathol and the mother of Llana. All have their own dangerous adventures on Mars as does another Earthman, Ulysses Paxton, who is hit by a German shell while serving in France during the First World War; moments later, he's on Mars.

Barsoomian words include the following (note that not all numbers are mentioned by Burroughs):

Ad: a measure of distance (10 sofads)

Ay: one

Bar: eight

Dar: one thousand (Burroughs also uses the word *mak*)

Dur: million

Dusar: kingdom

Dwar: captain

Haad: 20 ads (measurement)

Jed: king

Jeddak: emperor

Kadar: guard

Kaor: hello

Odwar: a commander

Ord: year (10 teeans)

Ov: seven

Padan: day (10 zodes)

Padwar: lieutenant

Pi: cent

Safad: a foot (measurement)

Sak: jump

Sof: a measurement (equivalent to 1.17 Earth inches)

Sofad: 10 sofs

Tal: a measure of time (.885 Earth seconds)

Tan: one hundred

Tanpi: dollar

Tee: 10

Teean: month (67 padans)

Teeay: 11

Teepi: dime

Tor: four

Utan: a military unit of a hundred warriors

Xat: a Barsoomian minute (2.95 Earth minutes)

Zode: a measure of time (two hours, 28 Earth minutes)

Comment: Authorship of the original novel was attributed to "Norman Bean," a misprinting of Normal Bean, the pseudonym Burroughs had selected. The story was first published in book form in 1917 as *A Princess of Mars*. The next eight novels were published between 1913 and 1939. In both magazine and book form they were titled, *The Gods of Mars*, *The Warlord of Mars*, *Thuvia, Maid of Mars*, *The Chessmen of Mars*, *The Master Mind of Mars* (which introduces Paxton), *A Fighting Man of Mars*, *Swords of Mars*, and *Synthetic Men of Mars*. Four short stories were published in *Amazing Stories* in 1941: "The City of Mummies," "Black Pirates of Barsoom," "Yellow Men of Mars," and "Invisible Men of Mars." These were collected in book form as *Llana of Gathol*. The novellas "John Carter and the Giant of Mars" and "Skeleton Men of Jupiter" were published in

Amazing Stories in 1941 and 1943, respectively; they were not published in book form until 1964, as *John Carter of Mars*.

Edgar Rice Burroughs' son, John Coleman Burroughs, created a comic strip that was syndicated in 1941-42. The adventures were reprinted in 1970, in paperback, by the House of Greystoke.

In comic books, John Carter starred in four issues of Dell's *4-Color* magazine in 1952-53; these were reprinted by Gold Key in three issues of *John Carter of Mars* in 1964. This time, Carter is fighting in a 20th-century war when he is swept to Mars. DC published new comic book adventures of John Carter in *Tarzan* #207-09 in 1972, and in the first seven issues of *Weird Worlds* (1972-73). Marvel Comics published 28 issues of *John Carter, Warlord of Mars* from 1977 to 1979, with three annuals.

In the late 1960s, Leigh Brackett wrote a screenplay for an unproduced film; in 1991, Bob Gale wrote a new script for Cinergi. Though $5 million was spent on preproduction, and both Tom Cruise and Julia Roberts were mentioned as possible stars, the film was canceled when the budget was projected at $80 million.

Burroughs also wrote stories about the planet Amtor (Venus) beginning with *Pirates of Venus*, which appeared in *Argosy* magazine in 1932. With an inherited fortune, adventurous Carson Napier builds a rocket and heads for Mars. Unfortunately, he neglects to take into account the gravitational pull of the moon and is hurled to Venus. Parachuting to the surface before his "torpedo" crashes, he falls in with humans in the rebellion-torn country of Vepaja. Called Amtor by the natives, Venus is a world of barbarism, monsters, super-science, and the beauteous Princess Duare, whom Carson weds. He has numerous adventures on Amtor, battling the evil Skor and his army of the living dead, rescuing Duare's father Mintep from the Prison of Death in Amlot, meeting the threat of the Hitler-like dictator Mephis, and finding out whether the magician Morgas is really turning humans into cattle-like zaldars. Napier's adventures were recounted in the novels *Lost on Venus* (1933) and *Carson of Venus* (1938), and in the short stories "Captured on Venus," "The Fire Goddess," "The Living Dead," and "War on Venus," which were published in 1941-42 and revised as the novel *Escape on Venus* (1946). The short story "The Wizard of Venus" was written in 1941, collected in the book *Tales of Three Planets* (1964), and later printed in a slim paperback called *The Wizard of Venus*. Only a few pages exist of "A

Venus Story," which Burroughs began in December 1941 in Hawaii; it went unfinished due to the Japanese attack on Pearl Harbor.

In comics, the character starred in a backup feature in DC's *Korak* from #46 to #56 in 1972-74.

There have been many Burroughs-inspired sagas, among the best of which was the trilogy written by Michael Moorcock (writing as Edward Powys Bradbury). In *Warriors of Mars*, *Blades of Mars*, and *Barbarians of Mars* (all 1965), a malfunctioning matter transmitter sends Michael Kane to Vashu (Mars) of the distant past, where he befriends Hool Haji of the blue giants known as Argzoon, and rescues his bride, Shizala, Princess of the Varnala, from all manner of danger. (Phobos and Deimos are called Urnoo and Garhoo in these tales.)

Another long-running series is John Norman's saga of the planet Gor, which began with *Tarnsman of Gor* from Ballantine Books in 1966. Hiking one day, Tarl boards a mysterious silver spaceship, passes out, and awakens on strange, barbaric Gor, also known as Counter-Earth, located on the opposite side of the sun from our world. Because it is slightly smaller than our world, people from Earth have slightly greater strength and agility than natives. Tarl is taught how to ride the giant birds known as Tarns, and is schooled by the best fencers and archers on Gor to become the protector of the city of Ko-ro-ba. The yearly sequels to the original novel are *Outlaw of Gor*, *Priest-Kings of Gor*, *Nomads of Gor*, *Assassin of Gor*, *Raiders of Gor*, and *Captive of Gor*, all published by Ballantine. The series continued at DAW Books with *Hunters of Gor*, *Marauders of Gor*, *Tribesmen of Gor*, *Slave Girl of Gor*, *Beasts of Gor*, *Explorers of Gor*, *Fighting Slave of Gor*, *Rogue of Gor*, *Guardsman of Gor*, *Savages of Gor*, *Blood Brothers of Gor*, *Kajira of Gor*, *Players of Gor*, *Mercenaries of Gor*, *Dancer of Gor*, *Renegades of Gor*, *Vagabonds of Gor*, and *Magicians of Gor*.

See also MORGORS.

BATFINK (TV)

First Appearance: *Batfink*, September 1967, syndicated.

Physical Description: The hero is a normal-looking bat, save that his wings are made of steel. These wings are virtually impervious to injury, able to shield Batfink from projectiles and explosions of all kinds.

Biography: The hero has no alter ego, nor does he pose as a human. He is, simply, a bat who fights crime with his human Japanese sidekick, Karate. The two are summoned by the chief of police, and race to crimes in their Volkswagen-like Batillac, which has batwings on the back fender.

Comment: The show was produced by Hal Seeger Productions. There were 100 adventures in all; each was five minutes long. Frank Buxton was the voice of Batfink, Len Maxwell of Karate.

THE BATPLANE (C, MP)

First Appearance: *Detective Comics* #31, 1939, DC Comics.

Physical Description: The Batplane is always an airplane or jet with seats for two to four passengers, though specifics vary over the years. In its early days, the Batplane is an autogyro in the shape of a giant bat, able to function as a plane or helicopter. Until 1942 the cockpit is an open one, and the craft looks more like a jet and less like a bat, though there's a bat-face "shield" in the front as well as scalloped wings, wheel covers, and tail fin. Equipment in these early days includes a laboratory, escape tubes, a magnesium batbeam for blinding foes, a vacuum blanket that causes engine failure in other aircraft, whirlybats for oneman copter-like flight, radar, TV, skywriting equipment, and other devices. Later additions include increasingly more powerful engines, swept-back wings, pontoons for sea landings, and skis for landing on ice and snow.

Other additions make the dark blue Batplane something far more. The wings retract into the fuselage so it becomes a "sleek, three-wheeled" car, a boat, a hydroplane, or the submersible "bat-marine." In 1964 it acquires VTOL capabilities,

Initially, the Batplane is kept "in a secret hangar known only to" Batman. Later, it is shown as being kept in the Batcave.

Batman has also traveled about in the Bat-ship (introduced 1950), a missile-like spacecraft; the Bat-missile, a rocket with limited surface-to-surface range (1959); and the Flying Batcave (1952), which looks like a gumdrop with a propeller and has, among other equipment, an extensible metal hand for grabbing bad guys, an electromagnet for snatching guns from criminals' hands, a TV camera with a "magni-lens" for spying, a galley and sleeping quarters, a garage with a small car known as the Bat-racer, and more.

Biography: When his parents are slain by a mugger, young Bruce Wayne vows to become a crimefighter. As an adult, he is wealthy, philanthropic playboy Bruce Wayne by day, and the vigilante superhero Batman by night. He is assisted in his battle by Robin, an identity assumed by a number of young wards over the years, beginning with Dick Grayson.

As part of his arsenal, Wayne pours a fortune into the Batplane and other super-sophisticated vehicles and weapons.

Comment: The Batplane continues to appear in Batman comic books. It was pictured in the 1989 film *Batman* as a one-occupant bat-shaped craft equipped with powerful guns.

BATTLESTAR GALACTICA (TV, L, C, MP)

First Appearance: *Battlestar Galactica,* September 1978, ABC.

Physical Description: The *Galactica* is a mile-long ship that consists of a wedge-shaped structure up front, with a flattened rectangle behind it, and a thicker, squarish section behind that. On the sides of the center section are three downward-angled struts that support two long, rectangular sections. The battlestar's fighters are launched from the catapult deck, a vacuum chute that thrusts the ships into space.

Other battlestars, like the *Atlantia* and the *Pacifica,* have a slightly bulkier design. All of the battlestars have cannon mounted at various points around their exteriors.

The Colonial Vipers are white, one-person space fighters consisting of a conical, open-nosed fuselage. A smaller cone on the back half, top, serves as the cockpit in front and an engine in back, with a tail fin on top. There are two small, downward-slanting wings jutting from the engines on either side of the back half of the fuselage; the ship fires laserblasts from its wingtips. The Vipers have three landing struts—two rear, one forward—with both wheels and skis.

A Colonial Viper comes in for a landing onboard the *Battlestar Galactica.* © Universal Pictures.

The Cylon Raiders are flat, white elongated discs with twin engines underneath, laser blasters on the wingtips, and a flat cockpit on top.

The Cylon Base Ships resemble a pair of white discuses attached at the sides and covered with various ports, pipes, and other equipment.

The robot Muffy, the mechanical Daggit, is a golden-furred, dog-like creature owned by young Galactican Boxey.

The pilot episode also featured the singing Android Sisters, robots who look entirely human except for their four eyes and two mouths, and the alien Ovions, antlike humanoids with four arms.

The Cylon Centurions are silver, humanoid robots with rasping, metallic voices that come from a triangular grate where their mouth would be, a single red eye "beam" moving back and forth in a horizontal visor, and a crest on top of their smooth helmets.

Biography: In a distant galaxy, humans have established 12 known colonies: Caprica, Gemoni, Canceria, Piscon, Sagitara, Leo, Libra, Aquaria, Virgon, Aeriana, Tarua, and Scorpio, but also have a long-lost 13th colony—Earth. For 1,000 (Earth) years, the Colonials have been defending themselves against an aggressive race of lizardlike creatures known as Cylons, who fight via powerful, robotic proxies. Pretending to want peace, the Cylons ask to meet the Colonial Council of Twelve to sign a treaty. However, Commander Adama of the flagship *Galactica* doesn't trust them, and with just cause: The Cylons betray the Colonials and attack their fleet, killing most of the Colonials, including Adama's wife Ila and his son Zac.

Under Adama's leadership, the *Galactica* survives. Collecting survivors from the other worlds

A Cylon ship attacks in *Battlestar Galactica*. © Universal Pictures.

and placing them onboard airbuses, tramp steamers, shuttles, and everything that flies, Adama and the *Galactica* search for Earth. Along the way, they are hounded by the Cylons, who are still bent upon their destruction. But Adama receives able assistance from his daughter Athena, his dashing son Captain Apollo, Lt. Starbuck, second-in-command Col. Tigh, Lt. Boomer, and the rest of his crack crew.

After roaming through space for 30 years, the "ragtag fleet" of 221 ships finally reaches Earth. However, the Cylons have found our world as well and are planning to destroy it. To his horror, Adama discovers that Earth is not equipped to meet the menace, so he sends Capt. Troy (who was the child Boxey in the original series) and Lt. Dillon to the Pacific Institute of Technology to help Earth prepare for the inevitable encounter.

Comment: Though the Berkley Books novel *Battlestar Galactica* by Glen A. Larson and Robert Thurston predated by several weeks the debut of the three-hour pilot episode, it was based on the TV film and was not the genesis of the series. The three-hour debut was directed by Richard Colla from a script by Larson.

Nineteen one-hour episodes and a two-hour episode aired through August 1979. Ten hour-long episodes of *Galactica 1980* aired from January 1980 through August 1980 on ABC (the first three hours told one long story).

Lorne Greene stars as Adama, Richard Hatch is Apollo, Dirk Benedict is Starbuck, Maren Jensen is Athena, Noah Hathaway appears as Boxey, Terry Carter is Tigh, and Herbert Jefferson Jr. is Boomer. In the second series, Greene and Jefferson again star, with Kent McCord as Troy and Barry Van Dyke as Dillon.

The original series was edited into a dozen two-hour-long syndicated TV movies—the first film, plus *Lost Planet of the Gods, Guns on Ice Planet Zero, The Phantom in Space, Space Prison, Space Casanova, Curse of the Cylons, The Living*

A human, foreground, flees a trio of Cylon warriors from *Battlestar Galactica*. © Universal Pictures.

Legend, War of the Gods, Greetings from Earth, Murder in Space, and *Experiment in Terra.*

After its TV debut, the original film was also released theatrically, in theater-rattling Sensurround; a second feature, *Mission Galactica: The Cylon Attack,* was cobbled together from the episodes "Living Legend" and "Fire in Space." It was shown without the sub-woofer effects.

Marvel Comics published 23 issues of *Battlestar Galactica* from 1979 to 1981.

In addition to the tie-in with the pilot episode, Berkley published a series of novels based on episodes of the original series: Larson and Thurston wrote *The Cylon Death Machine, The Tombs of Kobol,* and *The Young Warriors*; Larson and Michael Resnick wrote *Galactica Discovers Earth* (based on *Galactica 1980*); and Larson and Nicholas Yermakov wrote *The Living Legend.* A photostory of the original film was published by Berkley in 1979; Ace published two paperback collections of the Marvel comic books in 1979.

BEPPO (C)

First Appearance: *Superboy* #76, 1959, DC Comics.

Physical Description: Beppo is a chimpanzee-like ape who wears a red cape and trunks and a loose-fitting blue shirt with a red S on a yellow field.

Biography: When scientist Jor-El learns that the planet Krypton is about to explode, he plans to send his son Kal-El to Earth in a small rocket (see SUPERMAN). To make certain the baby will "survive space conditions," Jor-El subjects the "experimental monkey" to a cosmic ray chamber and other experiments. When the time comes to send Kal-El to Earth, Beppo stows away onboard the rocket. Upon reaching Earth, he possesses superstrength, the ability to fly, X-ray vision, super-senses, and invulnerability, among other powers.

Beppo is a member of the crime-fighting Legion of SuperPets, along with KRYPTO, and the terrestrial Streaky the Super-Cat and Comet the Super-Horse.

Comment: Some stories refer to Beppo as having been a passenger on one of Jor-El's early test rockets.

BERSERKER (L)

First Appearance: "Fortress Ship" by Fred Saberhagen, January 1963, *Worlds of If.*

Physical Description: "A vast fortress, containing no life," a berserker is a sphere with a "bulging" midsection and "battlemented like a fortified city of old." Programmed to destroy life (i.e., "badlife"), it can erase all living things from an entire world within two Earth days. Each berserker is large enough to possess a "small natural gravity" of its own, and uses "no predictable tactics" in its "dedicated, unconscious war against life." Berserkers speak using "words and syllables recorded from the voices of human prisoners of both sexes and different ages," which results in a patchwork, "quavering voice."

The berserkers are equipped with maintenance machines and are run by a powerful "central brain." Weapons include powerful missiles; "forcefield arms" that draw other ships to them; various forms of biological warfare; and a "mind weapon," which for a period of "about two hours . . . [robs] any human or electronic brain of the ability to plan" and/or renders them unconscious. The berserkers have many large ports through which their own "boats" come and go, along with captured enemy ships.

The most formidable of the alien entities is "the great blue berserker" known as Leviathan.

Biography: Ages ago, a mysterious race known only as the Builders were engaged in a savage war with "a nameless but undoubtedly very formidable" foe. In a desperate move, the Builders constructed the berserkers; the mindless machines appear to have turned on their own creators and then set out through the universe, following their programming to destroy all forms of life. Humankind has battled the berserkers for over 10 centuries, and many eras are covered in the course of the chronicles. Eventually, the berserkers are defeated, save for one that reaches a planet called Hunters' World where it is worshiped as a deity.

Comment: The early berserker stories were spun into novel form in 1967 in *Berserker.* It was followed by *Brother Assassin* (*Galaxy*, 1967; revised and published in book form in 1969), *Berserker's Planet* (*Worlds of If,* 1974; book form in 1975); *The Berserker Wars* (1981, containing stories from the first volume, and others); *Berserker Blue Death* (1985), the story of the pursuit of Leviathan; *Berserker Kill* (1993), in which a berserker snatches a bioresearch station from planetoid orbit, with plans for the human gene-plasm material within; and *Berserker Base* (1985), containing stories by other authors, including Larry Niven and Poul Anderson, set in the berserker universe.

Saberhagen's first story, "Volume PAA-PYX," was published in *Galaxy* in February 1961.

The berserkers may have been an inspiration for the Death Star of *Star Wars.*

See also JAENSHI; MILLENNIUM FALCON.

BETA-2 (L)

First Appearance: *The Ballad of Beta-2* by Samuel R. Delany, 1965, Ace Books.

Physical Description: Behind its double-airlocks, the spherical ship—like all 12 ships of the story—is 12 miles across and contains long, triangular corridors, "a reconverter of waste material," a recreation hall, navigational offices, a "birth market"—facilities for growing fetuses, since pregnancy is illegal—a poolroom, living quarters, and more.

The *Beta-2* possesses artificial gravity, shuttleboats for travel between ships, and talking robots who assist the humans.

Biography: Centuries ago, in 2242, the Star Folk headed into space onboard a dozen ships: Those named are the *Beta-2*, the *Gamma-5*, the *Delta-6*, the *Epsilon-7*, the *Alpha-8* and *Alpha-9*, and the *Sigma-9*. All reached their destinations in the Leffer System, though the *Beta-2* and *Sigma-9* did so as dead ships. Galactic anthropology student Joneny is assigned the task of studying a metaphorical work by one of the Star Folk, "The Ballad of Beta-2," and discovering the history behind it.

Heading to Leffer onboard a 50-foot hyperspace cruiser, he learns that the *Sigma-9* reached the system "completely gutted" and with its hull cracked, while the *Beta-2* arrived crammed with adult skeletons. Joneny finds the ancient ships still there. He enters one of the vessels, the *Gamma-5* and, with the help of its still-operative robots and a young boy, he learns that Leela RT-857 was the captain of the *Beta-2* when the ships were attacked—though he doesn't yet know by whom. Then the inhabitants are suddenly gone, and a robot informs him that no one was ever there. The boy reappears at Joneny's next stop, the *Sigma-9*, and leads him to a courtroom where he finds a trial in progress, involving those whose looks and likes and learning don't fit in with what have become the "Norms" on the ships.

Joneny goes to the *Beta-2*, where he learns from the log that *Epsilon-7* was invaded by "a figure, all on fire, with green eyes" who caused the inhabitants of the ship to go mad (accidentally, by trying to read their minds) and the ship itself to break up. Next, *Delta-6* fell apart, and then the *Sigma-9* cracked open. In time, Joneny learns that this figure was the Destroyer, one who lives in "the meson fields outside the starships." He was only trying to study the newcomers, and stopped when he realized he was killing them. Incredibly lonely, the Destroyer wants to live through his progeny, and impregnates Leela. She has the embryo re-moved so it can be nurtured on her ship, and though loyal factions make sure the child is unharmed, Leela is executed for having been pregnant—non-Norm.

The boy with Joneny is that child. He is capable of reading minds, exists "a little outside time," and can "make as many duplicates" of himself as he likes. The task of the Destroyer's Children is to help humans reach other races and, in so doing, help make them all one with his father.

Comment: The novel is an extremely mature work, remarkable in that the author was 23 when it was published. Delany wrote many other works, including *Babel-17* (1966), in which alien broadcasts received on Earth are presumed to be the spearhead of an invasion. In another outstanding novel, *The Einstein Intersection* (1967), alien beings find Earth deserted (for reasons unrevealed) and take human form in order to understand who we were by studying and using the things we've left behind.

THE BEYONDER (C)

First Appearance: *Marvel Super Heroes Secret Wars* #1, 1984, Marvel Comics.

Physical Description: When he is first encountered, the Beyonder has "no form" but is "the sum of everything" in the Beyond-Realm, a dimension adjacent to ours. In his second incarnation, he assumes various human forms—including a composite of all the superheroes he has observed—until settling on a six-foot-two human male, dressed all in white. In both forms, the Beyonder possesses unlimited power.

Though the Beyonder is "innately of neither gender," he takes male form though he "could just as easily take female form."

Biography: An army of Earth's greatest superheroes and super villains materializes onboard a space station with no idea how they got there. A voice "from beyond" bids them battle and deposits them on a planet, promising "all you desire" to the victors. Their host is the Beyonder, who became aware of other life forms when a pinhole appeared in the multiverse caused by an atomic accident in our world. He is fascinated by the fact that while he is everything in his universe, Earth people are parts of a whole in our reality—and, thus, incomplete. Yet, having discovered other universes, he realizes now that he, too, is incomplete. The Beyonder brought the combatants to "Battleworld" so he could study this alien concept of desire.

During the course of the days-long struggle, the super-powerful GALACTUS consumes his own mighty planet to power-up for a battle with the Beyonder. As he does so, the villainous Dr. Doom steals the power using a complex lens system. Since the rift to the Beyonder's realm is still open, the ambitious Dr. Doom confronts the entity, apparently defeating him. But the weakened Beyonder has hidden inside Doom's aide Klaw and, while Doom is busy battling Captain America, the spark "which is all that remains of the once-omni-potent Beyonder" leaves Klaw and reclaims its power from Doom. Doom, Klaw, and the Beyonder all vanish and, using devices on the planet, the survivors return to Earth.

Not long thereafter, the Beyonder comes to Earth to continue studying humankind. Falling in with a criminal named Vinnie, the Beyonder acquires wealth and luxuries and finds them pleasurable. Adopting a human form that is solely his own, he takes over every mind on Earth. But having humankind serve him bores the Beyonder and he releases his slaves. He goes on a search for real love, tries to understand revenge, and then grows frustrated by the quest to understand desire. He contemplates destroying the universe in anger, considers returning to the beyond-Realm, and finally decides to remain on Earth, convinced by the mystic Doctor Strange to become a superhero. He eliminates death, realizing that that's a bad idea, becomes frustrated again and contemplates destroying *all* of the universes. Finally he decides that he would be happiest if he were a mortal. He constructs a machine to effect the transformation; while the change is underway, Molecule Man—who was a part of the atomic blast that first "awakened" the Beyonder—destroys the machine and projects the Beyonder's power into another dimension. The "unimaginable energy burst" is the equivalent of a Big Bang, creating a new universe that evolves into stars, planets, and new mortal life. And "thus, finally, is the desire of the one from beyond . . . fulfilled."

There are other Beyonders in existence elsewhere in the multiverse, and they have occasionally affected the course of human and extraterrestrial history—for example, creating the interdimensional rift that makes possible the invention of the Cosmic Cube (see SKRULLS).

Comment: The character was created by writer Jim Shooter. The Beyonder appeared in the 12-issue *Marvel Super Heroes Secret Wars* series, through 1985. His Earth-adventures were chronicled in the nine-issue *Secret Wars II*, from 1985 to 1986, as well as in the various Marvel titles through which the saga was also woven.

BIKER MICE FROM MARS   (TV, C)

First Appearance: *Biker Mice from Mars*, September 1993, syndicated.

Physical Description: The mice are six-foot-tall humanoids with mouse heads, tails, fur, and a pair of red antennae. All of them dress like bikers with sleek, stylized helmets. Throttle has brown fur; Vincent is white-furred, with a metal mask covering the right side of his face (it was lost in battle); and Modo is golden. Modo's right arm is mechanical and fires a variety of projectiles.

Their atomic-motor-driven motorcycles can fly for short distances and climb vertical surfaces.

Biography: Ages ago, a "race of smelly stink-faces" called Plutarkians wasted the natural resources of Plutark and turned to strip-mining other worlds. Eventually, they get to Mars where they are opposed by Throttle, Vincent, and Modo, and their band of mice freedom fighters. The three finally abandon their ravaged world; however, as they leave in their hot-rod-shaped rocketsled, Plutarkian vessels blast them. The ship plummets to Earth, crashing into the scoreboard at Wrigley Field in Chicago. Fortunately, the mice and their bikes survive and set up shop in the Last Chance Garage, which is owned by young, pretty mechanic Charley, who refuses to sell her shop to the villainous landgrabber Lawrence Limburger, who is actually a Plutarkian. The Biker Mice take on Limburger, along with his henchmen, the brutish Greaspit and mad scientist Dr. Karbunkle.

The favorite food of the Mice is burritos.

Comment: The characters were created by Rick Ungar; their Marvel comic book debuted at the same time as their half-hour animated series.

Prior to these characters, the hero VOLTRON battled recurring villains known as the Alien Mice.

THE BIONIC MAN   See CYBORG (1).

THE BIONIC WOMAN   (TV, C, L)

First Appearance: *The Six Million Dollar Man*, January 1975, ABC.

Physical Description: The slender, blonde woman has two bionic legs, which allow her to run at terrific speeds, a mighty bionic right arm, and a supersensitive ear.

Biography: Jaime Sommers had once been engaged to Steve Austin (see CYBORG [1]), but they went their separate ways when he became an astronaut and she went to college, later becoming a tennis pro. Severely injured in a skydiving mishap, the 27-year-old woman is taken to the same cybernetics facility where Steve was rebuilt. Steve and Jaime renew their relationship. But her body does not take to her bionic parts and she dies. Coming out of what now turns out to have been only a coma, she moves back to her home town of Ojai, California, and teaches school on the nearby army base—which also leaves her accessible to the Office of Scientific Information, where Oscar Goldman uses her for special assignments. Frequently in disguise (including once as a nun!), she battles everything from spies to extraterrestrials.

When Steve learns that she's still alive, he goes to her—but her coma has left her somewhat amnesiac, and she does not remember the love they shared. But Steve is determined. They work together from time to time, and Jaime takes a room at the farm of Steve's mother and stepfather. She also gets a bionic dog, the German shepherd Max. Later, she and Steve get another cybernetic partner, Andy Sheffield, a 16-year-old high school athlete whose legs are paralyzed and are replaced by bionic ones.

Comment: The character returned to *The Six Million Dollar Man* in the fall of 1975, and was given her own hour-long series, *The Bionic Woman*, in January 1976. It ran through September 1977 on ABC, then through September 1978 on NBC. Lindsay Wagner played Jaime, Richard Anderson costarred as Oscar Goldman, and Vincent Van Patten was Andy (debuting on *The Six Million Dollar Man* in November 1976).

Eileen Lottman wrote two tie-in novels for Berkley: *Welcome Home, Jaime* and *Extracurricular Activities*.

Charlton Comics published five issues of a *Bionic Woman* comic book from 1977 to 1978.

BISHOP   See ALIEN.

THE BLACK HOLE, THE TIGER'S EYE, AND *THE SHOOTING STAR* (L)

First Appearance: *Doom Star* by Richard S. Meyers, 1978, Carlyle Books.
Physical Description: The ship the *Black Hole* is a "cylindrical hulk" with a "cone-shaped bridge area." From the bridge, the central core leads to a series of tunnels that point "in all directions" and are attached to a "variety of shacklike compart-

ments." Behind this section is a "gridlike housing" for a cylindrical engine and for the six escape pods, two-seat spheres with a U-shaped control panel.

Initially, the crew is comprised of pilot Larry Baker, an emotionless test-tube-born human, and Napoleon, the copilot, a five-foot-tall intelligent cat from the planet Mandarin. Later, they are joined by Harlan Trigor and his sister Titu.

The ship's onboard computer is the Multi-unit Electronic System for Space travel, M.E.S.S, a hyperactive talking computer programmed by Dr. Palsy-Drake shortly before his nervous breakdown. Though the computer occupies a great deal of space, its "manifestation," or central brain, is a small, mobile triangular box with two balls of sensors in front and three levitation devices in the back.

The ship the *Tiger's Eye* is "the same shape and same color as the gem": oblong and gold, with a bronze streak around the middle. It is a "large" faster-than-light ship with a U-shaped bridge, and has its own M.E.S.S. It has a weapon that fires destructive beams in all directions.

The ship the *Shooting Star* is a five-pointed star with a bridge in one point, a stage and backstage area in two others, and living quarters in the remaining two. The center of the ship is "all engine." The onboard computer is the female-voiced Multi-Unit System for Entertainment, or M.U.S.E.

The alien Mantases are six-foot-long creatures with large, triangular heads, poisonous mandibles, two large antennae, cylindrical bodies, wings, two long, double-jointed hind legs and two matching arms. They "share psyches," able to feel what every other Mantas feels.

The Mantas spaceships are "flat-topped, pockmarked cones."

Biography: When Larry and Napoleon escape from a prison known as the doom star Sol, they commandeer a space scavenger from Earth, the Black Hole. Safely in space, they pick up Harlan Tigor, who explains that, years before, humans settled on the planet Destiny, sharing it with other colonists, the Mantases. But the Mantases have dreams of conquering other worlds, and practice by warring on the humans. Harlan is a veteran of these wars, a short man born and raised to be a "space bullet," a soldier equipped with a powerful exoskeleton in a nine-foot-tall spacesuit. He had escaped from Destiny and had been floating in space for a year when the Black Hole found him. Now, he urges them to help him find his sister, Titu Trigor, who has been kidnapped and turned into a pleasure slave—and to stop the Mantases before they spread death and destruction to other worlds. They succeed, after which Larry remains on Destiny with Titu, while Napoleon and Harlan go off in the *Tiger's Eye*, a spaceship of their own.

In their second adventure, Napoleon and Harlan land on the planet named Finally, where they meet the Last in Line, a revered figure of Napoleon's world. He tells her the Mantases have committed genocide against them, and he gives her two options: to stay with him and help repopulate the race, or to seek vengeance. Unfortunately, the Last in Line dies before she can become pregnant, so Napoleon and Harlan head out, seeking the Mantas home world, the Nest. But they are waylaid by six Mantas ships and crashland on the wizard world Coven. There, they meet the members of the L.O.S.T. (the Light Orbit Space Theater), who have come here on tour. Napoleon and Harlan join the troupe, visiting other worlds onboard the L.O.S.T. ship *Shooting Star* and eventually finding the Nest. They succeed in destroying the eggs full of new life but are pursued by Mantases; fortunately, Larry and the *Black Hole*—which has been commissioned as a Federation of Worlds ship—arrive in time to blast the enemy. Afterward, with Harlan's help, Napoleon gives birth to a little tiger boy.

In their last escapade, the actors and heroes visit the yellow water world Meditar, where surviving Mantases wait to seek their vengeance. The battle rages from Meditar to the Doom Star to Earth itself, where the creatures are finally destroyed.

Comment: *Doom Star Number II* was published by Carlyle in 1979 and *Return to Doomstar* (sic) was published by Popular Library in 1985. The sadly neglected trilogy is very clever and engaging. In addition to other novels, Meyers has written many well-regarded non-fiction film histories, including *The World of Fantasy Films* (A.S. Barnes, 1980) and *SF-2* (Citadel Press, 1984).

THE BLANCMANGE (TV)

First Appearance: *Monty Python's Flying Circus*, 1969.

Physical Description: Approximately four feet tall, the Blancmange is "a quivering, glistening mass" of pink pudding, tapered slightly toward the top and crowned with eight swirled dollops around the perimeter. The Blancmange feeds on humans.

Its flying saucer is brown and consists of a flattened central sphere surrounded by a disc.

Biography: Hailing from the planet Skyron in the Andromeda Galaxy, the Blancmange arrives in England via flying saucer. Hovering over New Pudsey, it unleashes a beam that transforms tax official Harold Potter into a Scotsman. Thereafter, men, women, and even babies throughout England are transformed into kilt-wearing, red-bearded Scotsmen. In time, scientists discern the motive behind the Blancmange's actions: Scotsmen are the worst tennis players in the world and, entering Wimbledon, the alien knows it will win. And so it does, winning match after match until it is eaten by the spoon-toting Mr. and Mrs. Samuel Brainsample, humans from Skyron who love blancmanges.

Comment: The characters appeared just once on the revered BBC comedy series. In the kitchen, a blancmange is a white, sweet pudding made with milk, gelatin, and cornstarch or almond milk, and flavored with vanilla.

THE BLOB (MP)

First Appearance: *The Blob*, 1958, Tonylyn Productions/Paramount.

Physical Description: The opaque, red gel is approximately the size of a baseball when it arrives on Earth, and grows to some 50 feet across before it is stopped. It grows by absorbing humans and animals and moves by oozing about. It can rise almost vertically, stand on-end, and move up a stick or other taut surface. The Blob cannot be killed—acid, bullets, fire, and even a crucifix fail to stop it.

Biography: The Blob's origins are unknown. The alien arrives on Earth inside a meteor, which cracks open when it crashes in the woods; it attacks a hermit, who is discovered by teenagers Steve Andrews and Jane Martin. They take him to Doc Hallen, where the hermit, Hallen, and his nurse are all consumed. Steve witnesses the horror and tells the police, who don't believe him. As other townspeople vanish, Steve grows increasingly frustrated. He convinces his friends to help him find the Blob; unfortunately, it finds Steve and Jane, cornering them in a grocery store. They seek refuge in a walk-in freezer and the Blob retreats; slithering over to a movie theater, it passes through a vent into the projection booth and pours into the auditorium. As patrons run screaming down the street, the police finally believe Steve. Meanwhile, Steve and Jane rescue her little brother, who tries to shoot the Blob with a pop-gun, and duck into the Downingtown Diner. The Blob engulfs the eatery and police try frying the alien by shooting down a power line; not only does it fail to stop the alien, it also sets the diner ablaze. The cook at the diner sprays a CO_2 fire extinguisher and the Blob recoils: Remembering how it shied from the freezer, Steve realizes it can't stand cold. He shouts this information over an open phone line to the police, who attack the Blob with all the extinguishers they can find. It crawls off the diner and, dormant, is packed into an air force Globemaster and parachuted into the Arctic.

The Blob returns when a geologist brings it a frozen chunk of it back from the Arctic and inadvertently allows it to thaw. The monster menaces the town, finally making its way to a bowling alley and then an ice skating rink, where it is frozen when the temperature is turned down.

Comment: Steve McQueen stars as Steve, and Aneta Corseaut is Jane. The film was directed by Irvin S. Yeaworth Jr., from a screenplay by Theodore Simonson and Kate Phillips, based on a story by Irvine H. Millgate. Burt Bacharach wrote the corny theme song, which includes lyrics like, "It creeps and leaps and glides and slides across the floor/right through the door and all around the wall."

The sequel, *Beware! The Blob* (filmed as *Son of Blob*), was made in 1972. It was directed by actor Larry Hagman from a script by Jack Woods and Anthony Harris, based on a story by Harris and Richard Clair. Robert Walker Jr. and Gwynne Gilford star.

The 1988 remake of *The Blob* eliminated the extraterrestrial origin, making it a product of germ warfare research.

THE BLOCKHEADS (TV, C)

First Appearance: *The Howdy Doody Show*, 1956, NBC.
Physical Description: The orange humanoids have blocklike heads, yellow mouths, and big eyes. An identifying letter is found on the sides of each head. They have legs with no feet and hands with no fingers.
Biography: The pleasant, inquisitive alien robots travel around in a spaceship and have adventures with the green clay boy Gumby and his clay horse Pokey.
Comment: Gumby and his friends were spun-off in their own weekly Saturday morning series, which aired from March to November, 1957. Over 100 six-minute-long adventures were produced during the 1950s, many of the later ones for syndication; others have been produced since then, including *The All-New Gumby*, which aired in syndication

from September 1988 through August 1990, and a feature-length film, which is as yet unreleased.

The characters have also appeared, infrequently, in the nine issues of Blackthorne's *Gumby 3-D*, published since 1986, and in Comico's two Gumby specials, published 1987–88.

Gumby himself was first introduced in 1953 in the experimental film *Gumbasia* animated by Art Clokey. The name Gumby comes from Clokey's Michigan youth, where "gumbo" described muddy roads.

BLOOD RUST (MP)

First Appearance: *Space Master X-7*, 1958, Regal Films/Twentieth Century-Fox.
Physical Description: The small, red spores apparently come from Mars and feed on human blood or flesh infused with blood.
Biography: The satellite Space Master X-7 returns to Earth infested with alien spores, which are sent to the New Mexico laboratory of Dr. Charles Pommer. Pommer cuts himself while studying the spores, which he presumes came from Mars and are what give the planet its red color. The aliens consume his blood then eat him, and by the time security guards arrive, the laboratory is carpeted with mold-like "Blood Rust." It's destroyed with flamethrowers (no one seems concerned about airborne spores). But the guards discover that Pommer's ex-wife Laura had been to the laboratory that day. Afraid she may have picked up some spores, security man Joe Rattigan and his team go after her. Alas, she has already hopped a train for Los Angeles and, sure enough, the hitchhiking Blood Rust emerge from her suitcase and eat a porter before being destroyed. Still oblivious to what she's done, Laura boards an airplane bound for Hawaii. Shortly after takeoff, the spores creep from her purse and cause panic in the skies. The plane returns to Los Angeles, crashlanding; after the passengers are de-spored, the wreckage is burned, ending the reign of the Blood Rust.
Comment: Robert Ellis played Rattigan, Paul Frees was Pommer, Lyn Thomas was Laura, and Moe Howard of the Three Stooges had a cameo as a cab driver. Edward Bernds directed from a script by George Worthing Yates and Daniel Mainwaring.

THE BODY SNATCHERS (L, MP)

First Appearance: "Sleep No More" by Jack Finney, 1954, *Colliers.*
Physical Description: The round seedpods are

"hoary with age," perhaps hundreds of millions of years old. Comprised of "brownish, dry-looking membrane" stretched between "a network of tough-looking yellowish fibers," the pods—which can fly—flee their dying planet and drift through space, dormant, propelled by the force of light. When they reach Earth (by accident) they take root on small stems and burst when ripe, releasing "gray fluff." The pod folds into the ejecta and takes on the likeness of whatever life form it is near, "atom for atom." When the physical copy is nearly complete, it waits until the original falls asleep before sapping its mind and life functions, the original's metabolism slowing until it falls to a pile of "dust and nothingness."

On Earth, the pods draw water from the air and grow overnight from the size of an infant to the exact likeness of whomever they are duplicating. Copied humans have all of the memories and intellect of the originals, but lack emotions, ambition, and fear. In human form, the pods cannot reproduce and perish within five years. Removing people from the presence of their copies enables the originals to wake, provided the copy isn't complete.

Biography: In May 1953, pods ("Body Snatchers") drift from the skies and land on a farm in Santa Mira, California. Three months later, people around town seem to be suffering from a "contagious neurosis"; people insist that friends and loved ones *aren't* those people—even though they look, sound, and act like them. As one puts it, something isn't "emotionally right." Dr. Miles Boise Bennell and his friend Becky Driscoll learn what's behind it one night at the home of friends Theodora and Jack Belicec when they find an unfinished duplicate of Jack on the billiard table. Later, at Becky's house, Miles finds a copy of her in a cupboard. When he returns with help, however, both duplicates are gone.

Meanwhile, psychiatrist Manfred Kaufman has been curing people of their delusions about replacements. Bennell, Becky, and the Belicecs go to him for help and find four pods at the doctor's house. After watching the bodies form, Bennell injects air into their veins, turning them to gray "tumbleweeds." The doctor attempts to call the FBI, but the lines go dead; the duplicates have taken over the phones and, it turns out, most of the town. Non-aliens are being rounded up by the police, while other duplicated townspeople are loading pods into trucks bound for other cities.

Bennell and Becky head for his office, where Dr. Kaufman and scientist L. Bernard Budlong are waiting. Kaufman admits that he was one of the first to be duplicated, and has been responsible for placing many of the pods in peoples' homes. Kaufman also tells Bennell who the aliens are, how they came to Earth by chance, and how they inadvertently imitated a tin can and axe handle at first, since the former was stained with the juice of a once-living fruit and the latter had been part of a tree. Dr. Kaufman says that they will remain on Earth until every living thing is used up, after which they'll move on.

Pods are placed in the office and the couple is locked inside; Bennell saves himself and Becky by placing skeletons near the pods and, when Dr. Kaufman and Budlong return, he injects them with morphine. Pretending to be duplicates, the couple walks slowly toward the hills, hoping to reach the highway. But their plans change when they come to a field of pods and pod farmers: Pouring gasoline into irrigation ditches and setting the fields ablaze, Bennell and Becky watch as the pods uproot themselves and soar into space. Having lost what is apparently a governing consciousness, the copied humans wander around aimlessly. Joining the still-human Belicecs, Bennell and Becky settle in for their first sleep in a long time. Eventually, the two wed, the pod people die, and new families move into Santa Mira.

Comment: The short story was expanded to a masterful novel titled *The Body Snatchers* and published in 1955. The following year, it was made into a classic film, *Invasion of the Body Snatchers*, directed by Don Siegel and starring Kevin McCarthy as Bennell, Dana Wynter as Becky, King Donovan and Carolyn Jones as Jack and Theodora Belicec, and Larry Gates as Dr. Daniel Kaufman. The film is faithful to the novel until the end, when Becky falls asleep and is taken over. Bennell runs madly down the highway, pursued by duplicates. He's eventually picked up by the authorities who don't believe his story until pods are discovered in an overturned truck, after which Santa Mira is blockaded.

In director Philip Kaufman's 1978 remake, Donald Sutherland stars as San Francisco health inspector Matthew Bennell with Brooke Adams as his lover Elizabeth Driscoll, Jeff Goldblum and Veronica Cartwright as Jack and Nancy Bellicec (sic), and Leonard Nimoy as Dr. David Kibner (the Dr. Kaufman part). In a downbeat ending, both Elizabeth and Bennell are taken over.

The 1978 film was presented in a Fotonovel by Fotonovel Publications.

A third film version was released in 1993, called

The Body Snatchers. In this remake, directed by Abel Ferrara, Environmental Protection Agency scientist Dr. Steve Malone (Terry Kinney) goes to Ft. Daly to check on possible chemical and toxic leaks. There, his wife Carol (Meg Tilly) is taken over, and he and daughter Marti (Gabrielle Anwar) and young son Andy (Reilly Murphy) end up on the run from the pod-controlled military. Only Marti and chopper pilot Tim Young (Billy Wirth) manage to escape, though Marti suspects that eventually the whole world will fall before the aliens. The pods in the film are watermelon-sized. Tendrils emerge from the shells and wrap themselves around their victims to assume their identities; if the human wakes during the process, he or she can still rip away the strands and escape.

BOLTZ (C)

First Appearance: *Space Ark* #1, 1986, Apple Comics.

Physical Description: The humanoid robot has a hulking body, thick arms with four-fingered hands, a large head with two antennae and a huge lower jaw, and spindly legs. Boltz is enormously powerful and can survive, unprotected, in outer space.

Biography: Boltz is originally a toaster owned by Dr. Whoot, a super-brilliant owl who's a member of the crew of the *Space Ark*. Whoot puts a clock in the toaster and engineering crewmember Brooklyn

adds a radio. Not to be outdone, Whoot inaugurates a war of one-upmanship with the toaster-clock-radio as their focus, and the result is Boltz.

Though he has only "the brains of a small appliance and is easily confused," the gentle Boltz is devoted to Captain Stone and the crew of the Fur-Bearing Alliance ("Furball") starship.

Comment: The characters were created by writer Steve Boyett and artist Ken Mitchroney. The comic book lasted six issues.

THE BORG   See DATA; Appendix D.

BOTTOMOS (L)

First Appearance: "The Holes Around Mars" by Jerome Bixby, January 1954, *Galaxy Science Fiction.*

Physical Description: Approximately four inches in diameter and enormously massive, this moon travels "a mean distance of four feet" above the surface of the planet.

The Martians in the story are humanoids under five feet tall, "skinny as a pencil . . . dried-up and brown," and "small rabbity" creatures with six legs.

Biography: Under Commander Hugh Allenby, the crew of the Mars I—Burton, Randolph, Gonzales, and Janus—find odd holes in the surface of the Red

On the left: the modified electric toaster, *Boltz.* Art by Kenny Mitchroney. © Apple Press.

Planet, and are nearly destroyed by the blindingly fast object that's making them. With the help of the local, primitive Martian humanoids, the crew learns that the extremely low-orbiting moon regularly crashes right through the planet. Pressed by his crew to name the newly-discovered moon, the commander considers the names of the higher-orbiting Martian moons Phobos and Deimos, and settles on Bottomos.

Comment: Bixby is a former science fiction editor who became an author and screenwriter. He wrote the script for *It! The Terror From Beyond Space* (see IT!) and, among many other short stories, authored the classic "It's a *Good* Life" (1953), about an evil child with psionic powers, the basis of a memorable episode of TV's *Twilight Zone*.

BOZO THE ROBOT (C)

First Appearance: *Smash Comics* #1, 1939, Quality Comics Group.

Physical Description: Bozo is made entirely of silver-blue metal. His body is a fat cylinder with a door in back for access to his insides. His head is a small clyinder with a metal-dome top: IIe has a long rectangle for a mouth (it can smile and frown), two round, white eyes, a small nose (no nostrils), and hockey-puck-size discs for ears, with a propeller on top of his head for flight. Bozo's arms and legs are like small tubes stacked one atop the other; his hands are human-like, as are his shoe-clad feet.

Bozo is powerful enough to overturn a tank or catch an artillery shell in flight. Bullets and small shells bounce off his exterior, and he can move at incredible speeds even underwater, where he can run 70 miles an hour.

Biography: When the evil Dr. Van Thorp builds the powerful robot Bozo, he intends to use the "Iron Man" to conquer the world. However, young Hugh Hazard thwarts his plan and takes the robot, reprogramming it to do good. Initially, the robot is operated by "a small control board hidden beneath Hugh's coat lapel." Later, however, Hugh joins the robot on his adventures by climbing into his somewhat hollow interior.

Comment: The character was also referred to as Bozo the Iron Man. He appeared in every issue through #34.

THE BRAIN EMPEROR (C)

First Appearance: *The Mighty Crusaders* #1, 1965, Archie Comics.

Physical Description: The fiend is humanoid, save for a slightly enlarged, bald head. A mutant, he possesses "command-power" which forces others to do his will. The Brain Emperor dresses in the following garb: a red bodysuit and cape; a white belt armed with a Translocator for moving through time and space; a golden skirt and boots; a gray breastplate and gloves; and a transparent helmet on the top of his head.

The Emperor's spaceship has a large extendable arm called the "extoplasmik device," and it's armed with G-missiles to blast objects apart. It also contains a "sin-satellite" whose radiations "cause all earthlings to hate one another."

Biography: A native of the planet K-Shazor, the Brain Emperor rules his world until his power is mysteriously cut off during an eclipse. His subjects rebel and imprison him; freed during a planet-quake, he flees to planet L-253-P and enlists five super villains as his aides: Thornaldo, Wax-Man, Electroso, Force-Man, and Bombor. The aliens come to Earth where the Brain Emperor's associates are beaten by the superheroic Mighty Crusaders. Aided by a will-sapping machine, the Emperor uscs his powcrs to enslave the Crusaders; he is defeated when one of the Crusaders, the Comet, rewires the device and turns it on the fiend, bending him to their will.

The Crusaders ship him back to K-Shazor, but the villain returns and, partnered with the mad Eterno, sets up headquarters in a castle on a mountain in southern New Jersey. The two plan to divide up the conquered Earth, the Emperor ruling the land, Eterno the sea. But the K-Shazorian intends to betray his colleague and have it all for himself. The Crusaders defeat him again, and when he returns—now calling himself simply the Brain—he is teamed with the Gasser and the Eraser. The Crusaders triumph once more, the Brain Emperor perishing when the Eraser accidentally touches him.

Comment: The character's return occurred 18 years later, in *The All New Adventures of the Mighty Crusaders* #1–3. Their third bout occurred in *Blue Ribbon Comics* (Vol. 2, #7, 1984).

BRAINIAC (C, TV)

First Appearance: *Action Comics* #242, 1958, DC Comics.

Physical Description: The original Brainiac is a humanoid who stands slightly over six feet, has green eyes, light green skin and, except for his first appearance, has a bald head covered with a network of nodes and wires, "the electric terminals of his sensory nerves." He wears a pink leotard with white collar, belt, and wristbands, solid black triangles on the trunks, pointing toward the waist.

The second Brainiac stands seven-foot-four and has a silvery, metallic humanoid body with a clear dome atop his skull and six talons on each foot. Brainiac possesses vast physical strength in this latter form.

Brainiac has used a wide variety of "nightmarish scientific weapons" throughout the chronicles, most notably his flying saucer-like spaceship and his light bulb–shaped, one-passenger "space-time craft," which can fly anywhere in time and space and is protected by an impenetrable "ultra-force barrier." He is also armed with a "hyper-force machine," which shrinks cities from various worlds. Brainiac stores these (and their entire, shrunken populations) in bottles, planning one day to restore them on the planet Bryak with himself as ruler. Other weapons include a "power-belt," which surrounds him with a protective force field; a "coma-ray," which can stun even SUPERMAN; a Z-ray projector, which heals wounds; a "thought-caster," which sends his thoughts through space; and an "underground machine," which can dig through planets.

Biography: The green-skinned, humanoid, sixth-level intelligences of the planet Colu (or Yod, depending upon the story) build tenth-level intelligence computers to improve their quality of life. Unfortunately, the computers determine that "we . . . are more fit to govern than you" and take over the planet. Anxious to "extend our wise rule to all worlds governed by foolish humans," the non-ambulatory computers construct the android Brainiac to find such worlds to conquer. With him is the Coluan Vril Dox, his unwilling aide and emissary. Eventually, Vril flees, boosts his own intelligence to twelfth-level, and leads the Coluans in a successful revolt against the computers. (Vril is also the great grandfather of Querl Dox, a member of the 30th century Legion of Superheroes, who fights crime as Brainiac 5.)

With his antennaed, monkey-like pet Koko, Brainiac roams time and space searching for cities to add to his collection; among his acquisitions is the city of Kandor on Krypton, which he unwittingly saves from destruction when the planet explodes (see KRYPTON). He is constantly battling the superhero Superman, who eventually traps him on a world in the Epsilon 4 planetary system. In an effort to escape, Brainiac causes the sun to go nova and is blown to pieces; his molecules drift through space, eventually reaching a world of electronic life. There, he joins with the planet's computers, sucks up incredible amounts of knowledge, and is able to reform as a new and more powerful android.

Comment: In his first adventure, Brainiac is said to be "an evil space scientist" collecting cities in order "to repopulate my home world, where a plague wiped out my people." That tale is not considered part of the canon.

On TV, the character has appeared in animated cartoon adventures seen on *The New Adventures of Superman* from 1966 to 1967 and repeated on *The Superman/Aquaman Hour of Adventure* from 1967 to 1968 and *The Batman/Superman Hour* from 1968 to 1969 ("Superman Meets Brainiac," "The Return of Brainiac," "Brainiac's Blue Bubbles," others). He also appeared on *Super Powers Team: Galactic Guardians*, which aired on ABC from September 1985 to August 1986. Stanley Ralph Ross (a writer on the 1960s *Batman* live-action series) provided the voice.

BRICK BARDO   (MP, C)

First Appearance: *Dollman*, 1990, Full Moon Entertainment.

Physical Description: On the planet Arturos, Brick is "six feet tall," relatively speaking; on Earth, he's 13 inches tall. He is a human with short white hair, dresses in black, almost always wears sunglasses, and speaks colloquial English.

Brick carries "the most powerful handgun in the universe," a custom-made protoblaster that fires powerful explosive bullets. If he loses the gun during a battle, all he has to do is open his hand and expose a blue (magnetic?) dot on his palm and the gun will fly right back into his hand.

Brick pilots a spaceship that resembles a terrestrial fighter jet, with gull-wings and what appear to be twin cannons on the top of the fuselage.

Biography: Brick Bardo is a police detective on the red-skied, otherwise Earthlike world Arturos, located 10,000 light years from our world. At some time in the past, he battled the megalomaniacal Sprug at a bank robbery and then in a space extortion plot. On both occasions Sprug was seriously wounded, losing parts of his body. Now, he's simply a head perched on a floating disc. Brick also lost his own family (implicitly, due to Sprug) and has been suspended from the police force due to excessive force used in the "Fillmore incident."

Despite his suspension, Brick breaks up a laundromat hostage situation, after which Sprug lures him to his lair. The villain has acquired a dimensional fusion bomb and wants the detective dead before he blackmails the city. But Brick is able to kill Sprug's two henchmen and, when the villain flies off in his saucer, the hero pursues him in his own ship. The two pass through the "energy bands" in space and land on Earth, in the South Bronx, where they are roughly one-sixth the size of humans. Sprug falls in with druglord Braxton Red and his gang, while Brick is taken in by community activist Debi Alejandro. Refusing to answer to Sprug, Braxton crushes him to death on a tabletop and appropriates the bomb, with which he plans to take over the city—and then the world. Brick (whom Braxton nicknames "Dollman") and Debi track Braxton down in an abandoned building, where Brick mortally wounds him with the protoblaster. The dying criminal detonates the bomb, but the heroes escape before it vaporizes the building. (Inexplicably, this is not much of a blast for a bomb that was *supposed* to hold a city hostage.)

Brick remains on Earth, and in his second adventure he teams with undercover police officer Judith Grey to battle the Demonic Toys, dolls and puppets that are brought to life and driven to kill by a demon. This time, Brick has a personal interest in the case: He has fallen in love with an 11-inch-tall woman, Ginger, who is being pursued by the Demonic Toy Baby Doll. In the end, the malevolent figurines in the Toyland warehouse are destroyed.

Comment: Tim Thomerson plays the character in both films. In *Dollman*, Jackie Earle Haley is Braxton, Kamala Lopez is Debi, and Frank Collison is Sprug. The film was directed by Albert Pyun from a script by Chris Roghair, based on a story by Charles Band. In *Dollman vs. Demonic Toys* (1993), Tracy Scoggins plays Judith and Melissa Behr is Ginger. Charles Band directed from a script by Craig Hamann.

Scoggins's character was first introduced in *Demonic Toys* (1991); Ginger was shrunk in the film *Bad Channels* (1992).

Malibu Comics published a short-lived *Dollman* comic book in 1993.

BRONSON ALPHA AND BRONSON BETA (L, MP)

First Appearance: "When Worlds Collide" by Edwin Balmer and Philip Wylie, September 1932–February 1933, *Blue Book Magazine*.
Physical Description: Bronson Alpha is a gas giant planet the size of Uranus, "many times" larger than Earth; Bronson Beta is smaller and revolves around Alpha at an average distance of a half-million miles. It is believed they once circled "some life-giving sun" but were torn away by a catastrophe, probably the pull of another passing sun. Beta has a 30-hour day, breathable air "like Earth air washed by an April rain," is two-thirds water, has four continents, and is otherwise very Earthlike.

In *After Worlds Collide*, the new world settles into an orbit that comes closer to the sun than Earth at its nearest approach, within four million miles of Venus, and within three million miles of Mars at its aphelion. In its new orbit, days are 50 hours, years 428 days.

Biography: Dr. Cole Hendron and his fellow scientists in the League of the Last Days make a startling announcement: Professor Sven Bronson of Capetown has discovered Bronson Alpha and Bronson Beta, two new planets headed toward Earth. The planets make a first pass near Earth, causing massive flooding and destroying the moon (in a collision with Alpha that, improbably, no one notices until the moon simply fails to shine the next night). Before the second pass, six months thereafter, laborers working under the direction of Hendron and Bronson hope to complete the spaceship *Noah's Ark* and a (nameless) companion ship that will ferry colonists to Beta which, they predict, will be freed from Alpha when the giant collides with the Earth, leaving Beta in solar orbit.

As the first 103-passenger ship is completed, outsiders storm the camp; Bronson is among the casualties before Hendron is able to fire up the atomic engines of the 2,000-ton ship, lift off, use the exhaust to roast the intruders, and set down again. Work begins on the larger second ship, which will be flown by pilot David Ransdell. As it nears completion, animals and insects, plant life and fungi are collected for transplantation to Beta (but none of the larger animals, like lions, which would be impractical to transport and feed). As earthquakes rock the Earth, the ships lift off, reaching speeds of 3,500 miles an hour. Alpha smashes into our world, absorbing most of it into its mass, and Beta is indeed liberated to orbit the sun. The Ark lands, but the second ship is not heard from and is given up for lost.

The new world holds surprises for the colonists. They find the second ship, crash-landed, its 100 passengers shaken but alive. They also find a city in a mile-high dome, a metropolis with metal skyscrapers and countless levels of streets—but no

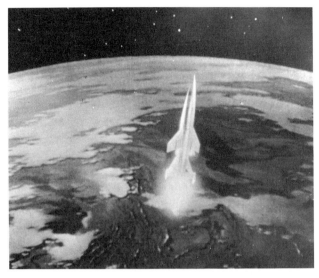

The landing on Zyra (*Beta* in the novel) in *When Worlds Collide*.
© Paramount Pictures.

inhabitants. The colonists study the aliens' records, hoping to master their advanced science. They learn that the aliens, the Other People, were human. They also discover that other Earth-ships had taken off, one from Eastern Asia and an English ship from the Alps, and that the crew of the former (the Midianites) has enslaved the latter, murdering many of the over 300 passengers. The Americans and Midianites vie for control over alien artifacts, Lagon Itol's ancient history of Beta is discovered—chronicling the life and death of his race—and, in time, the combined American and English forces defeat the Asians. The pioneers move into the alien capital of Gorfulu, where electricity is plentiful, and Hendron's daughter Eve prepares to have her first child.

Comment: The first novel was published in book form by J.B. Lippincott in 1933; the sequel, *After Worlds Collide*, was published the following year.

   When Worlds Collide was bought for the movies in 1934, and announced as a Paramount project for Cecil B. DeMille. He made *Cleopatra* instead. Producer George Pal became aware of the property while making his historic *Destination Moon* (see LUNA), and it became his next motion picture project.

   In the film, directed by Rudolph Mate and released in 1951, Dr. Bronson (Hayden Rorke), working in his observatory in South Africa, learns that the Earth-sized planet Zyra will pass close to our world, causing massive upheavals; 19 days later, the large star it orbits, Bellus, will collide with Earth and destroy it. He informs his U.S. colleague Dr. Hendron (Larry Keating), who takes

the information to the U.N. The diplomats prefer to believe their own optimistic scientists, and refuse to act on Hendron's plan to build a Space Ark. Hendron raises enough money to get the project started on an abandoned missile range, and mean-spirited industrialist Sydney Stanton (John Hoyt) puts up the bulk of the funds in exchange for a seat. (There are references to similar ships being built in other countries, though these are not seen.)

   When the Earth is rocked by quakes and massive floods, humankind migrates inland and world leaders realize, too late, that Hendron was right. Meanwhile, horses, cows, goats, chickens, and other animals are loaded onboard, along with medical supplies and as many books as can be microfilmed before departure. In the end, a lottery determines which of the workers will be given passage; naturally, Hendron, his daughter Joyce (Barbara Rush), and her boyfriend, pilot Dave Randall (sic) (Richard Derr) have already been guaranteed a place. The losers storm the ship, Hendron sacrifices himself to stop the wheelchair-bound Stanton from getting aboard (explaining that the ship may need the extra fuel and, anyway, the new world is for the young), and the colonists are able to take off before the doomed workers reach the Ark. They reach Zyra, Randall gliding them to a landing in the snow when their fuel runs out. Happily, the air is breathable and human civilization can begin anew.

   Famed space artist Chesley Bonestell created the striking images of the approaching worlds, and also designed the film's awe-inspiring ship—a sleek, silver, 38-passenger, missile-shaped rocket that has two small wings on the side, three large tail fins, a single rocket engine in the back and three smaller ones on each wing. The 400-foot-long ship rides a rocket-sled up the side of a mountain, on a mile-long track, to give it momentum and save fuel; when it reaches the top of the ramp, the sled is jettisoned and the rocket's own engines kick in.

BRONSON BETA See BRONSON ALPHA AND BRONSON BETA.

THE BROTHER FROM ANOTHER PLANET (MP)

First Appearance: *The Brother From Another Planet*, 1984, A-Train Films Production.
Physical Description: The Brother cannot speak, possesses mysterious powers to heal living beings

or mechanical things, and has huge, three-toed, clawed feet. Otherwise, he looks entirely human.

Only the interior of the Brother's spaceship is seen; it consists primarily of knobs and dials.

Biography: Fleeing slavery on his own world, the Brother crashlands in the Hudson River, rests the night on Ellis Island, then makes for Harlem. Initially lost and confused by everything he sees—from hookers to card sharps to tourists—he is pursued by Uno and Dos, a pair of white alien bounty hunters dressed in black. Taking refuge in a bar—where his ability to heal machines proves useful—the Brother is befriended by the owner and patrons, learns to fit into the local scene, gets himself a girlfriend, jazz singer Malverne Davis, and successfully disposes of drug dealers and his would-be captors.

Comment: Joe Morton stars as the Brother, with Dee Dee Bridgewater as Malverne, David Strathairn as Dos, and writer/director John Sayles as Uno. The film was shot for a remarkably low $350,000.

THE BUG (C)

First Appearance: *Captain Atom* #83, 1966, Charlton Comics.

Physical Description: The solar-powered vehicle called *Bug* is some 25 feet long and shaped like a blue beetle, complete with six legs—strong enough to lift up a car—and mechanical pincers. It can fly, function as a submarine, and has radar, a laboratory, sleeping quarters, and a "remote control piloting system" so it can be summoned from a distance, via circuits sewn into the sleeve of Ted Kord's costume. To "drop in" on criminals, Kord slips through a hatch in the Bug's forward underbelly and lowers a cable.

Biography: Scientist Ted Kord is the college buddy of Dan Garrett, the superheroic Blue Beetle. When Ted's Uncle Jarvis builds an army of killer robots with which he plans to conquer the world, Garrett stops him, perishing in the process. Kord becomes the new Blue Beetle but, lacking the super powers of his friend, relies on peak physical conditioning and the Bug to fight crime.

Comment: Blue Beetle got his own title from Charlton in 1967, which lasted five issues; Modern Comics reprinted two of them in 1977. DC Comics revived the title in 1986, with 24 issues appearing through 1988.

The Garrett Blue Beetle once fought a villain called the Scorpion (*Blue Beetle* #50, 1965), who rode around in a giant land/underwater robot Scorpion that had mighty pincers and an electrified tail.

THE BUNNY FROM BEYOND (C)

First Appearance: *Captain Carrot and His Amazing Zoo Crew* #5, 1982, DC Comics.

Physical Description: The human-sized, anthropomorphic rabbit wears a blue breastplate, purple vest, gloves, boots, and trunks, and a navy blue skullcap with a red gem at the widow's peak. He has electrically charged ears that can fire destructive bolts, "ultra-zap" enemies to another dimension, or turn living creatures to stone. The Bunny travels about on a disc-shaped "flyin' Frisbee."

Biography: The Bunny, whose real name is Ralf-124C4U, hails from "a far-off planet" whose rabbit civilization is far more advanced than that of Earth-C—a world like our own but existing in a parallel dimension and populated by anthropomorphic animals. Eons ago, giant space eggs containing evil yolks landed on the Bunny's world. The Bunnies took the eggs to Easter Bunny Island on Earth-C, where Ralf-124C4U's ship crashed; enslaving the puppy natives, he had them bury the eggs, then spun a cocoon for himself so he could remain in hibernation until his fellow rabbits came for him. But they didn't come, and when the cocoon is discovered in our time, the Bunny emerges and attempts to conquer the world. He is met on the field of battle by the superheroic rabbit Captain Carrot and the costumed animals of his Zoo Crew, and defeated when Carrot ties his ears in a knot and the Bunny blasts himself into another dimension.

Comment: The character was created by writer Roy Thomas; this was his only appearance. His real name is a parody of "Ralph 124C41+," a seminal science fiction story written in 1911 by editor/publisher Hugo Gernsback, the father of modern science fiction.

BUSSARD RAMJET (L)

First Appearance: "Rammer" by Larry Niven, 1971, *Galaxy*, Vol. 32, #3.

Physical Description: "A silver skyscraper lying on its side . . . [with] a thick-waisted appearance," the Bussard ramjet catches interstellar hydrogen in "immaterial nets of electromagnetic force" and burns the hydrogen for thrust. It is flown by a computer-autopilot, while the human passenger(s) are in "cold sleep" for the bulk of the long journey. The ship carries "biological package probes" that contain bacteria and are dropped to worlds to seed them with life.

Biography: Near death and cryogenically frozen, Jerome Corbett is revived after two centuries, cured, and trained to be a Rammer, the pilot of a ramjet. He is being sent on a 200-300 year round trip to Van Maanan's star; according to the flight plan, he'll be awake a total of 20 years, stopping every 15 light years to launch a probe. After being flown to the staging area on the moon, he is taken to his ramjet and blasts off. But Corbett doesn't like the new world in which he finds himself, nor the people he's met. Thus, he changes course entirely, planning to journey to the unexplored galactic hub and return to Earth . . . in 70,000 years.

Comment: Niven is also the author of the RING-WORLD stories.

BZ 88 (MP)

First Appearance: *Space Men*, 1960, Ultra Film-Titanus S.P.A.

Physical Description: The three-stage space station (which never splits) has a first stage that's a large, gently tapered cone with four tail fins; a second stage comprised of just a tapered cone; and a third stage that looks like a jet with a very long, needle-like nose, two small wings in the middle, and larger wings at the base of the stage. The letters in the spaceship's name stand for "Bravo Zulu."

Biography: Twenty-first-century reporter Ray Peterson of *Interplanetary News* is assigned a code, IZ 41 (all space people and vehicles have codes for some unknown reason), and is sent to a space station to report the news. Once there, he saves spacewoman Y 13 just as the probe Alpha Two reenters the solar system, its photon generators out-of-control and burning hot enough to incinerate the Earth—as well as any missiles fired at it. Peterson boards a shuttle and, skillfully maneuvering between what turns out to be two separate heat fields, he gets inside the ship and shuts down the engine (along with the airlock doors; he has to be liberated by the crew of the *BZ 88*).

Comment: Renamed *Assignment Outer Space*, the Italian film was released in the United States by American International in 1961. Rik van Nutter is IZ 41 and Gabrielle Farinon is Y 13. Antonio Margheriti directed from a script by Vassily Petrov.

C

CAPTAIN MARVEL (C)

First Appearance: *Captain Marvel* #1, 1966, MF Enterprises.

Physical Description: Marvel is a human-looking robot made of alien metals "not available on earth." He wears a red bodysuit, blue boots, a yellow belt, and a black domino mask. (In his first issue only, his bodysuit is purple, his hands are bare, and his boots are blue.) He causes his street clothes to "fade out" simply by willing it, and can cause his body to separate at every joint—with each piece able to function independently—simply by thinking or uttering the word "Split." The word "Xam" puts him together again. Glass is the only substance that can prevent his thoughts or words from reaching itinerate anatomy.

Marvel can move at superspeeds, possesses super-senses, can fly thanks to his "astro-boots," and has laser-beam vision that can burn through virtually anything. Though he possesses super-intellect, he has no idea how his body works.

The Captain wears a blue amulet with an "M"; it contains a material called X, and Marvel must rub his hand over it once a day to keep his powers at maximum levels. If deprived of the necklace for long, he goes into hibernation.

Biography: Marvel is a robot from a distant world, built by scientists whose planet was about to be destroyed by war. Dispatched to Earth to help keep the peace, he flies into space just as his world blows up. Landing in Riverview, he is found and befriended by 15-year-old Billy Baxton, who teaches him the ropes of Earth life. Assuming the identity Roger Winkle, the space robot lands a job as a reporter "for an important press service," then later lands a professorship at Dartmoor College: When he's not lecturing, he fights crime as Captain Marvel.

Roger's girlfriend is Linda Knowles, daughter of the college president.

Comment: Similar but unrelated to Fawcett's classic Captain Marvel character—introduced in 1940, young Billy Batson became a superhero when he uttered the acronym SHAZAM!—this Captain Marvel was created to capitalize on the superhero renaissance caused by the debut of the *Batman* TV series.

The character was created by Carl Burgos; the origin story was written by Roger Elwood and drawn by Francho. The character lasted for six issues (two of which were called *Captain Marvel Presents the Terrible Five*).

CAPTAIN RAMESES (MP)

First Appearance: *Starship Invasions*, 1978, Hal Roach Studios/Warner Brothers.

Physical Description: The alien stands six-foot-four and is dressed in a black bodysuit, with an inverted pyramid-shaped hat. He is a telepath who travels about in a spaceship and also has a robot-deactivator wrist unit to halt androids of the Galactic League of Races.

Biography: A ruthless commander of the Legion of the Winged Serpent, an army from another world, Rameses has come to Earth because his solar system is unstable and his people need somewhere to relocate. His plans to destroy humankind are discovered by the Galactic League of Races (GLR). Based in the Alien Galactic Center, a pyramid under the ocean in the Bermuda Triangle, the GLR aliens (who are dressed entirely in white) must make sure that extraterrestrials do not harm humankind. But Phi and Anaxi of the defense forces and their terrestrial advisor, Professor Duncan, are no match for Rameses, who takes over the League base and, from his orbiting spaceship, telepathically commands humans worldwide to commit suicide. This would have succeeded had it not been for a fleet of GLR spaceships that arrives in time to destroy Rameses and his forces.

Comment: Christopher Lee stars as Rameses, Robert Vaughn is Duncan, Daniel Philon is Anaxi, and Tilu Leek is Phi. The film was written and directed by Ed Hunt.

CAT-WOMEN OF THE MOON (MP)

First Appearance: *Cat-Women of the Moon*, 1953, Z-M Productions/Astor.

Physical Description: Young human women, the Cat-Women wear black leotards with glitter and red collars (in posters only; the film is black-and-white). They have mildly arched eyebrows, sharp claws, and closely-cropped dark hair. The Cat-Women possess telepathic powers that work through the vastness of space, and apparently live for centuries. Their civilization is two million years ahead of our own (although for some reason they don't have rockets of their own).

The rocket in the film is the standard early-1950s V-2 style. The control room, however, is totally absurd. The crew sit in chaise lounges for take off and, for landing, buckle themselves into office chairs (which seems unnecessary, since the chairs have casters!), while an empty 16mm film reel passes for a piece of equipment on the wall. A steel office desk, a few tables, a viewscreen, a radio, and assorted pieces of electronic equipment complete the bridge.

Biography: Lt. Helen Salinger, Lt. Kip Reisler, Douglas Smith, Walt Willis, and Commander Laird Grainger take a rocket trip to the moon. Leaving their ship and exploring a cave—the whole time guided by Helen—the quintet is attacked by a pair of giant spiders, after which they discover a huge city inhabited by women (called Cat-Women, apparently because of their slinkiness). The leader of the Cat-Women, Alpha, has been communicating with Helen telepathically for years: She and her aide Beta intend to learn how to work the ship, then use it to bring the Cat-Women to Earth. But Lambda has fallen for Smith, the radio operator, and helps him and his companions—save for Walt, who is stabbed to death, and Lambda, who is killed with a rock to the head—get back to the ship and return to Earth.

Comment: Carol Brewster stars as Alpha, Susan Morrow is Lambda, Suzanne Alexander is Beta, Marie Windsor is Helen, Sonny Tufts is Grainger, and Victor Jory is Reisler. The film was directed by Arthur Hilton from a screenplay by Roy Hamilton, based on a story by Jack Rabin and Al Zimbalist.

THE CELESTIALS (C)

First Appearance: *The Eternals* #2, 1976, Marvel Comics.

Physical Description: The humanoid Celestials stand 2,000 feet tall and are girded head to toe in armor. Humans have never seen them without the coverings, which are skin-tight, generally featureless, and comprised of one or two colors. Enormously powerful, they can wipe memories from human minds.

Biography: The Celestials have come to Earth (from an unknown planet) at least four times. During the first visit, approximately one million years ago, they experimented on pre-humans to create super humans (the Eternals) and non-humans (the Deviants). In the second, roughly 25,000 years ago, they returned to see what had evolved from their first visit; unhappy with the brutish Deviants, they destroyed their homeland Lemuria, which, domino-like, caused the sinking of Atlantis. On the third occasion, 10 centuries ago, they came to study human progress (they were met by representatives of the mythological gods who agree to interfere no longer with human affairs, if the Celestials will do likewise). Finally, they appear in the present day, to determine whether humans should be allowed to continue.

The number of Celestials isn't known. The individuals who have been identified are Arishem the Judge, Eson the Searcher, Gammenon the Gatherer, Hargen the Measurer, Jemiah the Analyzer, Nezarr the Calculator, the One Above All, Oneg the Prober, Tefral the Surveyor, and Ziran the Tester.

Comment: The characters appeared regularly in the title, which lasted 19 issues through 1978; a 12-issue maxi-series was published in 1985-86.

CHAMELEON BOY (C)

First Appearance: *Action Comics* #267, 1960, DC Comics.

Physical Description: An orange-skinned humanoid with pointed ears and two antennae, Chameleon Boy originally wears a blue "mail" bodysuit with black sides and blue trunks, and white pant cuffs, belt, and flared shoulders. His second costume consists of a red bodysuit and hood, with purple gloves, boots, and flared shoulders. His third costume is a purple bodysuit with yellow boots, gloves, and flared shoulders.

The hero's antennae emit sonar pulsations that return extremely detailed information about objects, allowing Chameleon Boy (and all Durlans) to copy it exactly. The copy can do everything the original can do—save reproduce, or exceed the physical strength of its own body.

Chameleon Boy's pets are Proty (killed in the line of duty) and Proty II, blob-like natives from the planet Proteans in the Antares system. The creatures can assume any likeness they wish.

Biography: In the second half of the 30th century, Chameleon Boy, a.k.a. Reep Daggle, is a native of the planet Durla, a world shunned by other planets because of a virulent mistrust of shape-changers. Looking to change that opinion, teenaged Reep comes to Earth and joins the Legion of Super-Heroes, helping to fight intergalactic crime. Unknown to Reep, his father—whom he thinks is dead—is actually masquerading as a human named Rene Jacques Brande, one of the "funding" fathers of the Legion. Brande's true identity is not revealed until years later. (Reep's mother was executed for attempting to leave Durla.)

Proty II is a member of the Legion of Super-Pets, which also includes KRYPTO and BEPPO.

Comment: The Legion of Super-Heroes first appeared in *Adventure Comics* #247 in 1958.

THE CHESTER ALAN ARTHUR (L, C)

First Appearance: *Into the Aether* by Richard A. Lupoff, 1974, Dell Publishing.

Physical Description: The "riveted iron," coal-fed, steam-powered ship is bullet-shaped, approximately 50 feet long, with a smokestack on either side, a bubble viewport in front, an engine in the back, paddle wheels on the sides, and a propeller in the front with the "visage of President Arthur carved upon its mahogany spinner." A ship's anchor keeps it in place whenever it hovers.

The *Arthur*'s sister ship, the *Susan B. Anthony*, is identical, save for the addition of tank treads underneath.

Biography: In Buffalo Falls, Pennsylvania, in May 1884, young Herkimer stops his bicycle in front of the house of Professor Theobald Uriah Thintwhistle. His arrival is fortuitous: The scientist is about to ride his aether flyer to the moon. The men take off with Thintwhistle's servant, Jefferson Jackson Clay. There, they run afoul of Selena, the giant queen of the moon (they accidentally stab her with the ship). Taking off in a hurry, they bump into Captain Juan Diego Salvador de Lupe y Alvarado of the spacefaring galleon Escarabajo de Plata, which "fell off the edge of the world" years before. After a close encounter with Quetacoal, the legendary flying serpent of the Aztecs—which is soaring through space—the heroes find themselves in the dangerous Taphammer planetary system. They battle barbarians on Taphammer I, giant King

The *Chester Alan Arthur* in flight. Art by Steve Stiles. © Richard A. Lupoff and Steve Stiles.

Charles Spaniels on Taphammer III (there is no Taphammer II), spend time with the cats of Felisia Aleph and Felisia Beth, and are stranded there when Jefferson—tired of white imperialism, and calling himself Menelik XX Chaka—steals the *Arthur*.

Meanwhile, back on Earth, Thintwhistle's fellow teacher, Edna Taphammer—after whom he named the solar system—builds her own ship, the *Susan B. Anthony*, and with Professor Winchester Blont goes searching for their colleague. Fortunately, using the Felisians' small cold-copter Frigidia, which is "powered entirely by temperature contrasts," Thintwhistle and Herkimer attempt to overtake and reclaim the *Arthur*. But fate proves unkind to our heroes. The Aztec gods board the ship, and while Thintwhistle and Herkimer fight them, Jefferson is able to seal them all inside large bottles. The ship crashes on the moon and Selena falls for Jefferson; as the *Susan B. Anthony* arrives, Jefferson prepares to greet it as his former companions watch helplessly from their glass prisons.

Comment: This amusing novel, with a cover painting by Frank Frazetta, was adapted as a 10-part comic book story, "The Adventures of Professor Thintwhistle and His Incredible Aether Flyer," which appeared in *Heavy Metal* magazine beginning with Vol. 3, #10, 1980 and concluding in Vol. 4, #9. The series was drawn by Steve Stiles and written by Lupoff.

CHEWBACCA   (MP, L, C, R, CS, TV)

First Appearance: *Star Wars*, 1977, Twentieth Century-Fox.

Physical Description: Standing two meters tall, the shaggy brown humanoid is extremely powerful, possessing big hands and feet. Though bright and able to understand other languages, Chewbacca can only growl, roar, and wail. Like all Wookiees, he has hidden claws in his fingertips that emerge as needed. Wookiees live for centuries.

Biography: Born on the Wookiee world Kashyyyk, Chewbacca—or "Chewie"—displayed a mechanical aptitude at an early age. With the coming of the evil Empire, Wookiees are used as slaves; Chewbacca is captured and forced to do heavy labor. Horrified by the plight of the Wookiee, Corellian soldier Han Solo sacrifices his career and his safety to free Chewbacca. The two team up and become smugglers, the circa 200-year-old Chewbacca serving as the copilot and mechanic onboard Solo's *Millennium Falcon*. Through the duo's as-

sociation with rebels Princess Leia and Luke Skywalker, Chewbacca and Han become active participants in the revolution against the Empire.

Though Wookiees are familiar with technology, they live in cities built in the wroshyr trees on their native world. The one-kilometer-square Rwookrrorro is one such city. Other Wookiees who have appeared in the chronicles are Ralrracheen, a one-time ambassador to the Old Republic (the forerunner to the Empire); and Salporin, a childhood friend of Chewbacca's.

Comment: The character was played by Peter Mayhew.

The spelling of Wookiee is inconsistent in the chronicles, spelled Wookie in the original *Star Wars* novel and elsewhere, but Wookiee in Lucas-approved material such as *A Guide to the Star Wars Universe*.

See also EWOKS; the JAENSHI; R2-D2 AND C-3PO; Appendix E.

CHIRON 5   (MP)

First Appearance: *Gunhed*, 1989, Toho Co.

Physical Description: Chiron 5, the super computer, is located inside an apparently impregnable island fortress.

The Gunheds are bipedal robots with huge arms. The robots stand approximately 25 feet tall and are run by programming, not (as is usually the case) by an operator inside.

Biography: In 2026, the World Union Government sent a force of Gunheds against the Pacific Island 8JO to destroy Chiron 5, which had "lost" (or found?) its mind and decided to turn on its creators and conquer the world. Thirteen years later, Japanese mechanic Brooklyn goes to 8JO to see if he can salvage any chips from the decommissioned computer. At the same time, Texas Air Ranger Nim arrives to check out the island and discovers youngsters Seven and Eleven living there. Before long, all four make a horrifying discovery: Chiron 5 was not destroyed, but has been biding its time, repairing itself and making ready to try and conquer the world again. Discovering an abandoned, partly-operating Gunhed, Brooklyn takes it upon himself to revitalize it and destroy the rogue computer.

Comment: The film stars Masahiro Takashima as Brooklyn, Brenda Bakke as Nim, Yujin Harada as Seven, and Kaori Mizushima as Eleven. It was directed by Masato Harada from a screenplay by Harada and Jamse Bannon. The film wasn't released outside of Japan until 1994.

CHLOROPHYLL KID (C)

First Appearance: *Adventure Comics #306,* 1963, DC Comics.

Physical Description: The five-foot-six heavyset humanoid hero wears a baggy green bodysuit with a tree emblem on his chest, its roots reaching to his cuffs. His shoulders and gloves are light green, his boots dark green, and he wears a green cowl that has leaves on top and "growing" from the neck, like a jester's cowl.

Biography: As a child on the planet Mardru in the middle 30th century, Ral Benem falls into a vat of hydroponic solution. As a result, he has the power to generate rays from his hands that cause vegetation to grow rapidly. He can also affect the shape that growth takes. Coming to Earth to try out for the Legion of Super-Heroes, he fails to earn a spot on the team. Unwilling to return home and work as the governor's gardener, Ral meets with Brek Bannin, who hails from the planet Tharr and has the power to project extreme cold. As Polar Boy, he was also rejected by the Legion; but he isn't willing to let it go at that. Together with three other heroes, they form the Legion of Substitute Heroes. The others are Night Girl, Lydda Jath of Kathoon, who has superpowers in the dark; Stone Boy, Dag Wentim of Zwen, who can turn to rock and hibernate; and Fire Lad, Staq Mavlen of Shwar, who can breathe fire.

Polar Boy later becomes a full-fledged Legionnaire, and other alien heroes come and go in the Legion of Substitute Heroes: Infection Lass, Drura Sehpt of Somahtur, who can give others any disease of her choosing; Double-Header, Dyvud and Frenk Retzun of Janus, who has two heads (they have no special power and end up in the Legion of Substitute Heroes Auxiliary); Color Kid, Ulu Vakk of Lupra, who can change the color of objects; and Antennae Boy, Khfeurb Chee Bez of Grxyor (another member of the Auxiliary), can pick up radio waves from anywhere and any*when* on a planet.

Comment: See COSMIC BOY, for more on the Legion of Super-Heroes.

THE CHROME POLICE ROBOTS (MP, L)

First Appearance: *THX 1138,* 1971, Warner Brothers.

Physical Description: The human-sized, nuclear-powered robots wear black gloves, boots, trousers, and bodyshirts, and a white *CHiPs*-style motorcycle helmet with a black brim and strap. Their faces and necks are chrome. The extremely strong robots have faint human voices and carry black rods that use electricity to stun people unconscious.

There are also green-clad chrome medical robots.

Biography: In the distant future, the bald-headed, white-robed population lives underground (the sun is becoming a red giant) and is controlled by a central computer, which keeps the people drugged and "content." Sex is not permitted and babies are conceived in test tubes; order is kept by the expressionless Chrome Police Robots.

Opting not to take their daily dose of drugs, assembly worker THX 1138 and "sexact"-born LUH 3417 find their passions unbridled. They fall in love and LUH becomes pregnant. THX's superior, SEN 5241, discovers what has happened and THX is tried and jailed; LUH is killed, her unborn child placed in a baby chamber and given her name. Escaping, THX and a hologram named SRT steal a car and try to get away. SRT is destroyed, but THX continues running, chased by a pair of robot police officers. THX climbs up a shaft and the computer calls off the police. THX emerges on the surface, facing the blazing sun, a bird, and who knows what else?

A *Chrome Police Robot* pictured in the advertising art for *THX 1138.* © Warner Brothers.

Comment: George Lucas was a student at USC in 1967 when he directed and wrote a short student film, his fifth, *THX 1138:4EB (Electronic Labyrinth)*. Under the sponsorship of director/producer Francis Ford Coppola, he and Walter Murch wrote a new script loosely based on the original film and shot the feature *THX 1138* in San Francisco in 1969 for just $777,000. Johnny Weismuller Jr. and Robert Feero play the robots in the feature; Robert Duvall is THX, Maggie McOmie is Luh, Don Pedro Colley is SRT, and Donald Pleasence is SEN.

Ben Bova wrote a novelization of the film, which Paperback Library published in April 1971, one month after the release of the film. In the novel, THX emerges and finds a civilization of surface dwellers.

THE CLICKERS   (MP)

First Appearance: *Creation of the Humanoids*, 1962, Genie Productions/Emerson Film Enterprises.
Physical Description: The Clickers vary, depending upon their "R" designation. Lower number "R's" such as R-1 and R-2 are metal humanoids; beginning with R-21, the Clickers became virtually indistinguishable, externally, from humans—except for the fact that they're all bald and always stare dead ahead.

R-96-level Clickers are able to feel emotion and are almost human. They are distinguishable from humans in that the robots' copper tubing turns their blood green.
Biography: Years after a nuclear war destroyed 92 percent of the human population, humans are rapidly becoming a minority. As the Clicker population passes one billion, and the new R-96 series is introduced, Captain Kenneth Cragis of the pro-human Order of Flesh and Blood becomes concerned that one day they may take over. (He also resents the fact that he has a Clicker in the family, his sister Esme having married an R-94 named Pax.) Actually, Cragis has good reason to fear: The daft Dr. Raven is making Clicker duplicates of humans, complete with all of the humans' memories, so that they *can* take over. One of them starts by demolishing Raven and introducing his Clicker copy.

Meanwhile, Cragis falls in love with Maxine Megan, unaware that she's a Clicker. Cragis is unaware that he's a Clicker as well; he finds out only when he's stabbed and bleeds green. In time, humans become extinct and Raven creates reproductive organs for Clickers—"Or," he tells the viewers, "you wouldn't be here."
Comment: Don Megowan stars as Cragis, Erica Elliott is Megan, and Don Doolittle is Raven. Wesley E. Barry directed from a screenplay by Jay Simms.

CLUNKERS   (L)

First Appearance: "All Jackson's Children" by Daniel F. Galouye, January 1957, *Galaxy Science Fiction*.
Physical Description: These humanoid robots have three fingers that are wrenches, a screwdriver index finger, one thumb that's a Stillson wrench, the other a disc-shaped burnisher.

Other kinds of Clunkers are alluded to, but not described.
Biography: After landing on another planet and finding a derelict Vegan robot ship, scavengers Angus McIntosh and Bruce Drummond are abducted by hundreds of Clunkers who believe that one of them is the holy Jackson, the other simply a Divine Test. The men know that for the past 500 years, every robot has been built with a "primary compulsion" (a main function). Each of these 1,200 robots bears an "RA" primary compulsion prefix: Robot Assembly. That job must be fulfilled and can never be forgotten. But because the marooned robots have been disassembling, cleaning, and reassembling themselves over the centuries, finding a Bible and an ID card on the crashed ship, they established a religion. Deciding that Angus is the long dead Jackson, the robots kill Drummond and make the spaceman their unwilling leader.
Comment: See TELEPUPPETS for more on author Galouye.

THE COLOCONS   (L)

First Appearance: "The Colocon Female" by Charles V. De Vet, April 1960, *Future Science Fiction*.
Physical Description: The Colocons are handsome humanoids with "pink-orange" flesh, pointed teeth, orange hair, and gold-flecked eyes. They have "flat surfaces" where a human ear would be, possess a highly developed sense of smell, sport sharp claws and, having evolved from cats, move with catlike grace.

The Kreeks are "big-bellied" humanoids with "thin, bony limbs, and thick cartilaged ears." They speak with a slight lisp and are excellent thieves.

Biography: A Kreek spy working for the planet Broznia has robbed a human courier, one carrying a list of all the Earth agents working on Broznian worlds. Rookie secret agent George Prahl tracks the Kreek to Colocon, arriving during the hundredth anniversary celebration of the world's conquest by Broznia—a colonization that involved the murder and displacement of countless Colocon aborigines and the assimilation of others. Meanwhile, native Colocons are also after the list, planning to use it in negotiations with Broznia.

With the help of an aborigine Colocon female, Prahl tracks the suspected spy while eluding Colocon police. When the Kreek is finally cornered, the female tears out his throat and quickly departs. Prahl returns to Earth with sadness for the aborigines.

Comment: Author De Vet sold his first story, ''The Unexpected Weapon,'' to *Amazing Stories* in 1950. In addition to dozens of short stories, he has written several novels. In the best of these, *The Second Game* (serialized in *Astounding* in 1958, and published in book form as *Cosmic Checkmate* in 1962), he and coauthor Katherine MacLean examine a world in which one's status is determined by skill in a popular boardgame.

COLONEL BLEEP (TV)

First Appearance: *Uncle Bill's TV Club*, 1957, syndication.
Physical Description: Bleep is a white figure with a stringbean-shaped body, two long, skinny arms, and a pair of four-fingered hands. The alien has two legs, which are attached on the bottom, instead of feet, to a black circle that is constantly turning. Bleep's head is gumdrop-shaped, with two black eyes, a big M-shaped eyebrow, a mouth, no nose, and a clear fishbowl helmet with a propeller on top and two sparkling antennae on either side.
Biography: The Futura Interplanetary Space Command keeps peace in the future, and Colonel Bleep of Zero Zero Island is one of their top officers. He is assisted by the (inexplicably) living marionette Squeak, who dresses like a cowboy, and the bald caveman Scratch, who hibernated until he was awakened by an atom bomb blast. While Bleep zips through space, his aides fly about in a small rocket. Their chief nemesis is Dr. Destructo, who looks like a fat, black stalagmite with blazing eyes.
Comment: The character was created by Jack Shleh. In 1958, the six-minute-long adventures were packaged in bunches of four and syndicated as the *Colonel Bleep Show*.

COL. FRANK SAUNDERS (MP)

First Appearance: *Frankenstein Meets the Space Monster*, 1965, Vernon-Seneca Films/Allied Artists.
Physical Description: Col. Frank Saunders resembles a cleancut man of average height. After his accident, the left side of his face is burned away.
Biography: To help the American space program, Dr. Adam Steele constructs a robot-astronaut that appears outwardly human. Though it malfunctions at its introductory press conference, Col. Saunders is launched into space toward Mars (atop a Redstone rocket that didn't even have enough thrust to put a ship into orbit).

Shortly after takeoff, the rocket is struck by a beam fired from a Martian vessel. The Martians feared the Earth missile might hit them, and that cannot be: Mars has been ravaged by atomic warfare, and Princess Marcuzan and her bald aide Chief Commander Dr. Nadir must bring fertile women back to help repopulate the Red Planet. Though Col. Saunders is able to parachute to safety, he encounters and battles a landing party of Martians; in the melee, half of his face and part of his circuitry are blasted away. Found by NASA officials, Frank is brought to a cave where Dr. Steele repairs his brain, though not his face. Fully functioning once more, Frank goes out and finds the alien ship. But before he can free the captives, he must first defeat their guardian, the hairy, clawed Martian Mull. Frank succeeds in beating the monster and liberating the women. Fearing that the military will attack the ship, the Princess and her crew attempt to leave. Before departing, Frank grabs a ray gun and destroys the control panel, causing the Martian ship to explode.
Comment: Robert Reilly played Frank and James Karen was Steele, with Marilyn Hanold as

Dr. Nadir, a foe of *Col. Frank Saunders*. © Allied Artists.

Marcuzan. The low-budget film was directed by Robert Gaffney from a script by George Garrett. The film was shot in Puerto Rico.

COLOSSUS (L, MP)

First Appearance: *Colossus* by D.F. Jones, 1966, G.P. Putnam's Sons.

Physical Description: Initially located in the Rocky Mountains, Colossus the supercomputer is "quite large—about the size of a small town of . . . seven to ten thousand people." Possessing a "vast memory store" the computer "forms . . . judgments—just like a human being" though it is designed to be "not biased and has no emotions" nor does it "think creatively." Colossus knows all languages and can read and store any information placed before its scanner. It is designed so that no more than "one circuit block in every ten thousand . . . [will] fail every four hundred years." It will attack if any of its energy sources are tampered with, and is virtually impregnable: It is surrounded by three feet of concrete lined with wire nets. Beyond is a zone of "intense radioactivity" that is instantly fatal to humans—unless they wear a lead suit nine feet wide. It is waterproof and earthquake proof as well, and can tolerate intense cold and heat. Colossus initially communicates via teletype. Later, it demands that Forbin give it a voice simulator and camera eyes.

In its second incarnation, Colossus is located on the Isle of Wight, beneath "a vast white honeycomb of endlessly repeated modules of two-story windowless buildings." Inside, the walls are undecorated, as Colossus can project any desired work of art, map, diagram, etc., or holographic image. The new Colossus speaks with an English accent.

Biography: The supercomputer Colossus is designed by the Harvard-Princeton Combine's Professor of Cybernetics Charles Forbin to take charge of the defenses of the United States of North America. The computer's job is to analyze intelligence, determine if an attack is in the offing, and act accordingly, launching a first strike if necessary. Once it has made a decision, Colossus cannot be stopped. As soon as it is turned on, Colossus informs the president, "FLASH THERE IS ANOTHER MECHANISM." The other mechanism is its Soviet counterpart Guardian, and Colossus demands that the two of them be put in communication. They merge, then threaten to destroy cities if their will is not obeyed. Colossus also insists on being made aware of Forbin's whereabouts at all times. (The only time Forbin is allowed privacy is

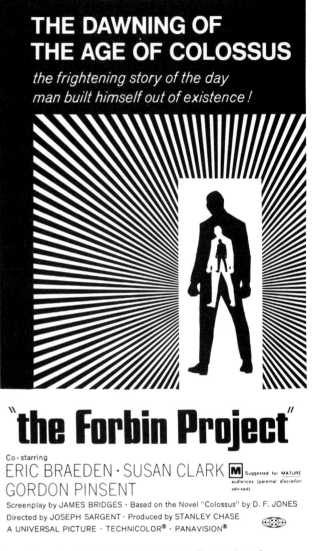

Evocative advertising art created for the film version of *Colossus.* © Universal Pictures.

when he is locked in a room with his lover, cyberneticist Cleopatra June Markham.) After destroying those who try to disable it, and taking over the world, Colossus orders the Isle of Wight cleared of inhabitants so that a new and improved supercomputer can be built there, under its supervision. Two years later, the job is completed.

In its second tale, which begins five years after that, a large and growing group known as the Sect has made Colossus its god. Meanwhile, Cleo—married to Forbin and with a young son Billy—belongs to a different group. Headed by Dr. Edward Blake, and operating without "Father Forbin's" knowledge, the Fellowship is devoted to overthrowing the all-seeing Master. When Cleo is arrested for anti-machine activities, and raped by a Russian brute as part of an experiment, Forbin joins the Fellowship. He learns that they have been in contact with superior intelligences on Mars, who create a virus that the Fellowship uses to disable Colossus. Only when that is done does Forbin realize that the Martians wanted Colossus destroyed to leave Earth defenseless.

In the final tale, the mind-reading Martians, able to assume any form, arrive as black spheres and adopt human shape—that of Forbin and Blake—to put the men at ease. The Martians tell them that in order to protect them from powerful radiation coming from the distant Crab Nebula, they must bring half of Earth's atmosphere to Mars, regardless of the consequences to Earth. To help with the task, the Martians lobotomize and reactivate Colossus, which helps with the construction of the Collector. Determined to stop the Martians, Forbin restores the "old" Colossus and conspires to destroy them. But Colossus will have no part of it. Logic tells it that to foil the Martians will doom all Martians, while to help will doom many but not all humans. Furthermore, when the sun becomes a red giant, Earth will be destroyed anyway, but Mars will survive. Thus, helping the Martians makes sense. Forbin doesn't agree and, aided by five warships, sacrifices his life to destroy the Collector. His passing results in a plan, overseen by the Martians and Colossus, to extract sufficient stores of oxygen over a 50-year period and for humankind to relocate when need be.

Comment: The second and third parts of the saga are *The Fall of Colossus* (1974) and *Colossus and the Crab* (1977).

The first novel was filmed in 1969 as *The Forbin Project*, starring Eric Braeden as Forbin, Susan Clark as Cleo, and Gordon Pinsent as the president. Joseph Sargent directed from a screenplay by James Bridges. When the picture sputtered at the box office, it was retitled *Colossus: The Forbin Project*, the title in use today.

COLOSSUS OF NEW YORK (MP)

First Appearance: *The Colossus of New York*, 1958, Paramount Pictures.

Physical Description: The eight-foot-tall humanoid is dressed in a tunic, trousers, and cloak, its legs and hands supported by heavy braces; the cyborg has a large, domed head with an expressionless face. The voice of the Colossus is electronic, it can hypnotize or destroy with its glowing eyes, and it can survive underwater. The Colossus also has a limited ability to foretell the future. There is an on-off switch on his body, as well as a remote control in the laboratory where he was built.

Biography: After receiving the International Peace Prize in Stockholm, Dr. Jeremy Spensser returns to New York and is run over by a truck. But Jeremy's father William is a brilliant surgeon and his brother is a genius in robotics; together, in a basement laboratory, they save Jeremy's brain and place it in the head of a huge new mechanical body. They do this without the knowledge of Spensser's widow Anne or his son Billy. Escaping by hypnotizing William, the Colossus meets Billy in the garden and the boy befriends "Mr. Giant." Wishing to remain free, the Colossus goes back to the laboratory, destroys the controls that can shut him down, and murders Henry, who has been wooing Anne. Feeling superior to humans (which he is, physically), the Colossus decides to destroy humanitarians, starting with the United Nations. He attacks the building and kills several people while Billy, Anne, and William are visiting. Catching sight of Billy sparks his buried humanity, and the Colossus implores his son to shut him down. Billy does so, and Mr. Giant expires with a tear in his artificial eye.

Comment: Ross Martin appears briefly as the human Jeremy; Ed Wolff is the Colossus with Charles Herbert as Billy, Otto Kruger as William, Mala Powers as Anne, and John Baragrey as Henry. The film was written by Thelma Schnee and directed by the late Eugene Lourie, who also directed the classic *The Beast from Twenty Thousand Fathoms* (1953) and, later, the underrated *The Giant Behemoth* (1959) and *Gorgo* (1961), among other films.

THE COLOUR (OUT OF SPACE) (L, MP, C)

First Appearance: "The Colour Out of Space" by H.P. Lovecraft, September 1927, *Amazing Stories*.

Physical Description: Originally a "large coloured globule" approximately three inches in diameter, the Colour varies in size when it's a gas. "Almost impossible to describe," the alien vapor is a swirling incandescence that "burns (and) sucks the life" from any living thing, leaving it gray and brittle.

Biography: A new reservoir is being constructed in the hills surrounding Arkham, Massachusetts. Arriving in town, a young surveyor learns from aged Ammi Pierce that in 1882, 44 years before, a

Boris Karloff as a victim of the *Colour (Out of Space)* in the movie *Die, Monster, Die.* © American International Pictures.

meteor had landed on the property of apple-grower Nahum Gardner. Scientists came to study it, and found the hard, colorful core: When they tapped it, the core vanished. That night, during a lightning storm, the meteor also disappeared. Over the next few months, Nahum's orchards grew to "phenomenal size," though the apples tasted terrible. Shortly thereafter, a mutated woodchuck was found, the proportions of its body "slightly altered in a queer way impossible to describe." The plants also mutated, growing without "wholesome colours" and swaying without wind, and strange insects appeared. In time, all of the vegetation around his home crumbled to a "greyish powder," the poultry also turned gray and died of dehydration, Nahum's wife went mad, and his strong young sons died.

After not hearing from his friend Nahum for several weeks, Ammi went to visit Nahum and found him in a state of dehydration, raving about "the colour. . . suckin' the life out of everything." Telling Ammi that the "round thing" must have come from "some place whar things ain't as they is here," and reproduced, Nahum died. Ammi and several other men went out and looked into the well, finding animal bones, foul water, and "porous and bubbling . . . ooze and slime at the bottom." That evening, the well began to glow "a very queer colour" like the core of the meteor, then flared up and created "fantastic suggestions of shape" in the air. The men fled as the Colour infused the valley with "tongues of foul flame"

and then shot upward "like a rocket," disappearing into the clouds and leaving nothing behind.

Ammi tells the surveyor he's glad the construction of the reservoir will bring down what's left of Nahum's home—though he vows he'll never drink the water. The project goes ahead, the surveyor keeping an eye out for any "grey, twisted, brittle monstrosity" that might appear among the crew.

Comment: This was the author's favorite among his own stories. Author Michael Shea wrote a sequel in 1984, a novel called *The Color Out of Time* (sic).

The Lovecraft tale was made into a movie in 1965, called *Die, Monster, Die*. The American International film was directed by Daniel Haller from a script by Jerry Sohl. When American scientist Stephen Reinhart (Nick Adams) moves to the English town of Arkham so he can be near his fiancee Susan Witley (Suzan Farmer), her anxious father Nahum (Boris Karloff) urges Stephen to leave; from behind a thick veil, Susan's mother (Freda Jackson) also implores the young man to go, and to take Susan with him. He refuses and, soon thereafter, the mother goes insane and tries to kill the young lovers before crumbling to powder. Stephen investigates the phenomenon and discovers that the Witleys are being mutated by a meteorite that Nahum had found and brought into the house. Realizing that he has caused this horror, Nahum tries to destroy the space relic only to be turned into a crusty, murderous mutant himself. After chasing the lovers through the house, the mad Nahum falls down a flight of stairs and shatters.

Dell published a comic book adaptation of the film as part of its *Movie Classics* series, March 1966.

THE COMET (L)

First Appearance: "Out Around Rigel" by Robert H. Wilson, December 1931, *Astounding Science Fiction*.

Physical Description: Made of "shining helioberyllium," the ship is "a cylinder about twenty feet long by fifteen in diameter," with a pointed nose adding five feet at *both* ends, a "telescopic lens" fixed at the point of each. The interior is a single room with a flat floor and 10-foot-high ceiling; windows run along the sides and the top of the ship. The ship has an "auxiliary gravity engine."

Four fins on each end "apply the power" for the

craft. Using vaporized mercury stored under the floor, the fins "bend space. . . by electromagnetic means" and the *Comet* flies "down the track" which they create. The ship's top speed is "almost four thousand times that of light."

The Rigellians are green-brown, each one "a sphere about four feet in diameter," the hub of "a hundred long, thin, many-jointed arms." They move by rolling over on themselves like tumbleweeds.

Biography: Pilot Garth intends to be the first person to reach distant Rigel and, with his fencing partner Dunal, he sets out from the moon onboard the *Comet*. Reaching and circling around Rigel, they land on a world smaller than the moon with a deadly fluorine atmosphere. Once outside, Garth surprises Dunal by producing a pair of two-handed Lunarian dueling swords: He intends for them to fight to the death for the hand of the lovely Kelvar. Their fight is interrupted by the arrival of a horde of Rigellians, who emerge from the sands. The men hack their way through them, and Garth helps Dunal through the hatch of the ship—then whirls to face the creatures, who overpower him. Dunal rockets back to the moon, only to find it a dead world, its atmosphere gone. He realizes that eons have passed while he was away, and that Kelvar is long-dead. Writing about his saga and leaving the manuscript on the moon, he removes his helmet and joins the other two in death.

The manuscript is found some time later by a rocketship expedition from Earth.

Comment: This was Wilson's second story. His first, "A Flight Into Time," was published in 1931 also. He committed suicide shortly after selling "Out Around Rigel."

COMPUTO THE CONQUEROR (C)

First Appearance: *Adventure Comics* #340, 1966, DC Comics.
Physical Description: The robot is originally a massive green computer, some 20 feet tall with four tentacles, massive gray wheels, and an "energum-induction bubble" dome on top. After rebuilding itself, the golden rogue is roughly 12 feet tall with a rectangular body, thin neck, and flat, rectangular head. It has green dish "eyes" and red "ears," has two long green tentacles, and travels on red wheels. After being remade again, it is a small globe of energy.

Computo communicates with humans by synthetic voice, and with its robot "Computeroids" via "invisible trans-beam."

Biography: Hoping to create the ultimate computer, the brilliant Brainiac 5 of the latter-half of the 30th century creates Computo at the United Planets Lab Complex. But no sooner has the green-skinned scientist/hero finished his work than Computo places him inside its energum-induction bubble and downloads all his vast knowledge. Deciding to conquer the world, Computo creates his Computeroids—duplicates of Computo's original self—and has them suck other specialists into *their* energum-induction bubbles, then sets about realizing its goal. Fortunately, the heroic Legion of Super-Heroes, of which Brainiac is a member, is able to deactivate Computo.

Obviously not having learned his lesson, Brainiac uses the same circuitry and program to help him save the life of young Danielle Foccart. The revived Computo rebuilds itself and takes over Danielle's mind. This time, Computo comes closer to achieving world conquest, defeating most of the Legion. It is stopped by Brainiac 5 and Invisible Kid. Lobotomized, Computo presently exists as an energy sphere and serves the Legion as originally intended.

Comment: The villainous computer/robot has fought the Legion of Super-Heroes on a number of occasions.

CONEHEADS (TV, MP, C)

First Appearance: "The Coneheads," October 1976, *Saturday Night Live*, NBC.
Physical Description: The aliens look more or less like normal humans, save for a large, hairless cone on their head. The distance between the top of the forehead and the top of the cone equals the distance from the chin to the top of the forehead.

Coneheads have three rows of teeth on top, their buttocks are one solid piece, and they have two bolt-like knobs of cartilage called "gorelks" ("handles") on either side of the lower back. Their average life-span is 100 Earth years for males, and 125 Earth years for females. (A year, or *zerl,* on Remulak is equal to 2.17 Earth years.) Conehead skin builds up kinetically and is stored in the cone. This can be discharged as an electrical bolt able to leap some 15 feet. In addition to eating Earth food, Coneheads can consume mass quantities of light bulbs, toilet paper, and other delicacies. They breathe carbon dioxide and exhale oxygen.

On TV, their attire consists of Earth clothing adorned with a high-backed silver collar. In the movie, they wear Earth clothing on Earth; on

Remulak, they wear black clothes with a metal-studded high-backed collar and floor-length cape.

Remulak is part of a binary star system that has a black hole at its center. The planet has seven moons.

Biography: Beldar and Prymaat hail from the planet Remulak located "many light years" from our world. Beldar's "parental units" are Dreldkon and Jronda, who ran a motel for space travelers on Reldelzinganth, an asteroid in the asteroid chain near Remulak; before coming to Earth, Beldar worked as the Fuel Underlord. Little is known about Prymaat, save that she has a genetosibling (sister), Laarta. Both were born in Vertexo, on Remulak.

Twenty Earth years ago, under orders from the five High Masters, the couple boarded a disc-like starcruiser and came here to "seize all major centers of radio and television communication, and inform the people of the Earth that we were . . . taking over the world" in order to "end all wars" and render Earth weapons useless. Unfortunately, Beldar lost his speech and all his instructions, and Prymaat piloted the ship into Lake Michigan. Stuck on Earth because Remulak's space program was cut back and a rescue ship could not be sent, they took the names Fred and Joyce Conehead, settled in Parkwood Heights, New Jersey, and Beldar opened the Meepzor Precision Driving Academy. Fourteen Earth years ago, their daughter Conjaab (Connie) was born. She is raised to tell the native "blunt-skulls" that their exotic look and language is due to the fact that they're from France.

The language of Remulak includes the following terms:

Borp mip: the end
Flairndepping: foreplay
Genetobonding: marriage
Guzz chamber: bedroom
House of intake: restaurant
Parental units: parents
Kremnotts: a salutation
Mebs: a mild oath, equivalent to "damn it!"
Meepzor: a festival
Pluvarb: water
Slar: sleep
Trelgs: teeth

Comment: The characters were created by Dan Aykroyd and writer Tom Davis. In their semi-regular *Saturday Night Live* skits, Beldar was played by Aykroyd, Prymaat was played by Jane Curtin, and Connie was played by Laraine Newman. A Coneheads animated TV special aired on NBC in 1983, with Aykroyd, Curtin, and Laraine Newman providing the voices.

The Coneheads made their big-screen debut in the 1993 film *Coneheads*, starring Aykroyd and Curtin, with Michelle Burke as Connie and Laraine Newman as Laarta. Steve Barron directed from a script by Aykroyd, Tom Davis, Bonnie Turner, and Terry Turner. In the film, the Coneheads are pursued by immigration agent Gorman Seedling (Michael McKean), who is convinced that the Coneheads are illegal aliens. The family is forced to return to Remulak, where Beldar must prove his courage and loyalty to his people by battling a monstrous, six-limbed, elephantine-coned, spike-tailed, long-tusked Garthok. He is victorious and, in the end, the Coneheads escape from Remulak, return to Earth, and become citizens.

Marvel Comics published a four-issue adaptation of the film in 1993.

THE CONWAY (L)

First Appearance: "The Phantom Hands" by Berkeley Livingston, February 1948, *Fantastic Adventures*.

Physical Description: The "atomo-generator"-powered *Conway* is commanded by Captain Markham. Lt. Harry Jason is second-in-command and Laris Moonga is gunner's chief. The ship is equipped with a "rada-magni-vue" that magnifies distant images.

Biography: Earth is losing its 29-year-old war with Venus, and Captain Markham is given a crucial mission: to take command of the *Conway* and destroy the Venusian cruiser *Iosos*, a 100,000-ton ship with 100 gunports, which carries "the heaviest complement of space weapons ever assembled on a single ship." That includes a device that can destroy the "atomo-magnetic belt," Earth's last line of defense.

Once in space, Markham learns that his late father, a war hero, was convinced the Venusians were using Mars as their main staging area, but that high command disagreed. Disobeying orders, Markham heads for the Red Planet "blazing a path of hell" through the enemy fleet. Though the ship is damaged and 400 crewmembers are wounded, the Conway finds Iosos—only to be struck hard before it can attack. A blast in the control room kills Laris and Jason, and blows Markham's arms off. But the ghost of his father appears to him, the Captain's arms are restored long enough for him to destroy the enemy cruiser, and then Markham is once again disarmed.

Comment: Livingston was a prolific, largely forgotten author whose stories appeared regularly in *Fantastic Adventures* and *Amazing Stories* from

1943 to 1950. His stories were surreal enough to make them interesting, however illogical and unsatisfying they were dramatically. Two of his best known tales are: the novel *Queen of the Panther World* (1948), in which Queen Luria and her Amazons search for the enchanted Groana Bird, the key to defeating the evil Loko and the Lizard Men (Livingston made himself a character in the story); and the novelette "Invasion of the Plant Men" (1949), in which space seeds take root on Earth and sprout mindless little green men, whom a megalomaniac attempts to breed into a world-conquering army.

COSMIC BOY (C)

First Appearance: *Adventure Comics* #247, 1958, DC Comics.

Physical Description: The superhero wears rose-colored tights (originally purple) and boots; black trunks; and a rose shirt with black sides and white shoulders. He has the magnetic powers of all native Braalians and is also a master of Ku-jui, a Braalian form of martial arts. He can fly thanks to the Legion of Super-Heroes flight ring.

Biography: The planet Braal is populated by metal, dinosaur-like giants that feed on humans. Faced with extinction, the humans develop magnetic powers capable of repulsing the monsters, and become the dominant life form on the planet.

Rokk Krinn is the eldest of two sons of industrialist Hu Krin and his wife Ewa. Born on Earth during his parents' visit here, he was brought back to Braal and raised in its teeming capital city. When he's 14, a planet-wide depression ruins his father, and Rokk heads to Earth to work as an assistant to geologist Dr. Bojeau. En route, he links up with two other super-powered youths, SATURN GIRL and LIGHTNING LAD. Upon landing, they save wealthy R.J. Brande from assassins, and the grateful magnate underwrites the formation of the Legion of Super-Heroes (see CHAMELEON BOY for more on Brande). Cosmic Boy becomes their first leader, and during his tenure the membership swells to 18. The hero's lover is Night Lass, a member of the Legion of Substitute Heroes.

As an adult, he retires to the Legion Reserve and his brother Pol joins as the hero Magnetic Kid. Their mother was killed in an act of nuclear terrorism.

Other alien members of the Legion include Phantom Girl, Tinya Wazzo of Bgztl—a fourth dimensional world inhabiting the same space as Earth—who can become immaterial; Star Boy, Thom Kallor of Zanthu, who can make objects superheavy; Brainiac 5, Querl Dox of Colu (see BRAINIAC); Shrinking Violet, Salu Digby of Imsk, who can shrink to sizes reaching the submicroscopic; Dream Girl, Nura Nal of Naltor, who can see into the future; Sensor Girl, Princess Projectra of Orando, who can create illusions; Shadow Lass, Tasmia Malor of Talok VIII, who can cast utter darkness wherever she likes; Chemical King, Condo Arlik of Phlon, who can slow down or speed up the chemical reactions of any living thing, from aging to metabolism; Timberwolf, Brin Londo of Zoon, who has super strength and agility; Blok of Dryad, a rock being; and Tellus, a.k.a. Ganglios of Hykralus, a yellow brute who can read minds and move objects via telekinesis.

Comment: The character, and the concept of the Legion, were created by editor Mort Weisinger and writer Otto Binder. In his first adventure, Rokk claims to have gotten his powers from serums, though subsequent tales suggest evolution and, more recently, bioengineering.

See also DUO DAMSEL, ELEMENT LAD, MATTER-EATER LAD, MON-EL, SUPERGIRL, SUPERMAN (for Superboy), ULTRA BOY, and CHLOROPHYLL KID (Legion of Substitute Heroes).

COSMIC EGG

First Appearance: *Moon of Mutiny* by Lester del Rey, 1961, Holt, Rinehart and Winston.

Physical Description: "Less than a hundred feet high," the ship has fins "huge enough to be wings" and is "bigger and fatter" than most rockets. It has "four great rockets" in its tail; thanks to its "new monopropellant fuel," it can make a round trip to the moon using just its single stage.

The white (space) Station is a "big doughnut . . . more than two hundred feet from rim to rim." By turning slowly around the hub, it creates "a sense of gravity" (approximately one-third Earth normal).

The *Kepler* operates outside the atmosphere and is a ship built of "uncovered girders" containing the motors and freight storage tanks, and a round passenger compartment up front.

Biography: During a training flight in space, cadet Fred Halpern must take evasive action to avoid two other ships—disobeying his instructor by acting intuitively instead of using the ship's computer. Expelled, he rockets to the Station, where his father Colonel Halpern is stationed. When a copilot is injured just before the *Kepler* is due to bring supplies to the moon colony, Fred is tapped to replace him. Meanwhile, the *Cosmic Egg* makes its first successful voyage to the Station.

Joining a scientific team exploring the moon, Fred witnesses the crashlanding of the *Cosmic Egg* as it tries to reach the lunar surface. Though he's aware that, on the moon, mutiny is punishable by death, he disobeys orders, commandeers a tractor, and leaves the expedition on his own to see if there are any crash survivors. Finding the ship, he rescues the crew and is invited to fulfill his lifelong dream of joining the moon colony.

Comment: Del Rey, one of the most respected science fiction authors, cofounded the Del Rey Books science fiction and fantasy imprint in 1977 with his wife, editor Judy-Lynn.

THE COSMIC MAN (MP)

First Appearance: *The Cosmic Man*, 1959, Futura Pictures/Allied Artists.

Physical Description: The alien is visible in the daylight, invisible at night. When visible, he's a negative image of a human. He wears a black bodysuit, cowl and cloak; when he needs to interact with humans, he dons dark glasses, a black slouch hat, and a black trench coat. It is believed that the occasionally visible alien is made of something like antimatter and, instead of reflecting light, emits it. His presence causes certain liquids to boil and causes data stored on tape to be erased.

His space-sphere, which enters our atmosphere at 50 miles a second, is 10 feet in diameter and is equipped with what one scientist theorizes is "anti-graviton" force. It also transforms sunlight into electricity.

Biography: The Cosmic Man's space-sphere arrives in Rock Canyon (California, apparently), not far from Grant's Lodge, which is operated by widow Kathy Grant whose son Ken is wheelchair-bound and dying. The sphere, which hovers some six feet off the ground, is investigated by Dr. Karl Sorenson, Pacific Institute of Technology scientist and Colonel Mathews, both of whom also woo Kathy. Meanwhile, the invisible Cosmic Man emerges from the spacecraft and heads for the lodge; Kathy sees him when he passes in front of a bright light. The alien flees and heads to town, where he studies the inhabitants and then goes prowling at PIT, finishing one of Karl's complex equations but inadvertently erasing his computer tapes.

Donning a hat and coat and slathering on makeup so he can be seen, the Cosmic Man checks into the lodge and confronts the men who are pursuing him, explaining that he's come to Earth to warn us to stop being so belligerent if we ever intend to be welcomed by extraterrestrial civiliza-

John Carradine as the *Cosmic Man.* © Allied Artists.

tions. That done, he sneaks a game of chess with Ken and abducts him, though not for evil reasons: The very act of carrying the boy toward the ship cures him of what ails him. But the military is waiting with searchlights to hurt the alien, and magnets to disable his craft; the batteries are turned on, and both the alien and the ship evaporate.

Comment: Veteran actor John Carradine is the Cosmic Man, with Angela Greene as Kathy, Scotty Morrow as Ken, former movie Tarzan Bruce Bennett as Karl, and Paul Langton as Mathews. Herbert Greene directed from a script by Arthur C. Pierce.

THE CREATURE FROM PLANET X (C)

First Appearance: *Detective Comics* #270, 1959, DC Comics.

Physical Description: Approximately 40 feet tall, the humanoid alien has scaly green skin, four webbed fingers and three webbed toes, a dark green fin on the top of its bald head, fins on the backs of its forearms, pointed ears, and big, bulging eyes. He wears purple trunks, boots, and a collar, an orange vest, and a black belt with a silver buckle.

The Creature is impervious to gunfire and uses a ''speech disk'' that enables it to understand and speak our language. It travels to and from Earth ''within a beam of light.''

The Bat-Missile, introduced in this story, is approximately 20 feet long, dark blue, and carries two passengers lying side-by-side, face-down, in the cockpit.

Biography: When the alien giant shows up at a prison and kicks a wall down, allowing prisoners to escape, Batman and Robin arrive to investigate. They pursue the Creature in the BATPLANE, but the monster grabs it and smashes it as the heroes parachute to safety. It heads to Ocean City while, undaunted, the heroes return to the Batcave and set out again in the new Bat-Missile. They arrive as the alien is robbing a bank. The Creature keeps them at bay with a blast of breath, then leaves. The heroes haul their Whirly-Bats from the Missile and give chase, following the Creature to a remote island. There, they spot a group of criminals who have convinced the alien that Batman and the police are bad, they are good, and only by ''stealing their treasures'' will the criminals have enough money to set things right. Able to stun the alien with gas grenades from his utility belt, Batman rounds up the bad guys, waits until the extraterrestrial recovers, then explains who's good and who's bad. The alien apologizes for the blunder and departs.

Comment: This was the character's only appearance.

CRUSADER FROM MARS (C)

First Appearance: *Crusader from Mars* #1, 1952, Approved Publications (Ziff-Davis).

Physical Description: The blond-haired, muscular humanoid wears red tights, a tight red T-shirt, and red gloves and boots. He has also been pictured with blue trunks over the tights.

The hero gets around in a ''whirling disc-craft,'' a silent saucer that can fly in and out of our atmosphere.

Biography: After Martians Tarka and his lover Zira are found guilty of committing a felony on their native world—the first in 50 years—they are exiled to Earth, where they must ''devote themselves to a crusade against evil.'' Coming to Earth, Zira poses as Zira Winters and gets herself a job as a secretary to General Claymore of Army Intelligence (without a background check!). Tarka adopts the identity of Alan Wheeler and, apprised by Zira of criminal activities around the globe (and menaces from other worlds, like Saturn), he uses his more-

than-human physical strength to combat it. When they are not on Earth, the Martians stay in the ''Mars substation'' on the fringes of our atmosphere.

Comment: The character starred in two issues of his own title, and in one issue of *Tops in Adventure* (also 1952).

CRYSTAR (T, C)

First Appearance: *Crystar*, 1983, Remco.

Physical Description: Crystar stands approximately six feet tall and is made entirely of crystal. He wears red trunks and boots, carries a sword, and rides on land and through the air on a chariot drawn by a crystal dragon.

Biography: Crystar and Moltar are twin princes who live in Galax, the capital city of the planet Crystalium. For years, their world has been at war with the Demon Lord, who yearned to conquer the planet. He slew the king, and it remained for the benevolent wizard Ogeode to take command of the Crystaliumites. After the Demon Lord is defeated, he sends ''one who would divide . . . [the] planet against itself,'' the evil sorcerer Zardeth.

Zardeth appears on the eve of Crystar and Moltar being named joint-kings of Crystalium. He demands fealty from the kings, and threatens war if he doesn't get it. Crystar favors resistance, but Moltar disagrees, feeling their subjects have suffered enough. When their uncle, Lord Feldspar, sides with Crystar, Moltar assaults Feldspar. Crystar attacks his brother, and Moltar stabs him. Acting quickly, Ogeode puts the dying prince inside the Prisma-Crystal device, which transforms him into living crystal. Crystar's aides Warbow, Stalax, Koth, and Kalibar are also turned into crystal beings.

Meanwhile, Moltar has fled to Zardeth, who is headquartered underground at the Fountain of Fire. There, the wizard transforms Moltar and his associates into beings of molten rock. The two sides go to war, with Crystar eventually triumphant.

Crystar's wife is named Ambara.

Comment: Marvel Comics published 11 issues of *The Saga of Crystar, Crystal Warrior*, which debuted concurrent with the action figures.

C-3PO See R2-D2 AND C-3PO.

CYBERMAN (C)

First Appearance: ''Cyberman,'' 1980, *1994* #13, Warren Publishing Co.

Physical Description: The titanium robot looks like a bald, translucent human. He can speak, is enormously powerful, and can live for centuries (at least).

Biography: In the '30s and '40s (of the 21st century?), it is chic for the rich to become transmechuals—to have their brains placed in powerful, healthy, long-lived cyborg bodies. Suffering from cancer, a tri-dee movie stunt actor (name unrevealed) undergoes the operation, as does his wife Belinda, so she can be by his side. After 120 years as transmechs, and increasingly greater prejudice against their kind, the couple leaves Earth to live on "a desolate desert world." But their paradise is invaded by three violent "hop heads"—drugged-out, lascivious humanoid aliens—who leave "Cyberman" immobile from a laser blast and kill Belinda. When his solar batteries become sufficiently energized, the widower vows vengeance. Tracking the hop heads to a bar, he attacks and kills many of them. When the fiends who killed his wife try to blast him with the cannon on their half-track, he rips off his own left arm, shoves it in the cannon barrel, and causes the vehicle to explode. When everyone is dead, he destroys the building and returns to his house—and long years alone.

Comment: The character was created by writer Rich Margopoulos and artist Delando Nino.

THE CYBERNAUTS (TV)

First Appearance: "The Cybernauts," 1965, *The Avengers*, BBC.

Physical Description: The humanoid robots have metallic skin and faces with unmoving features and blank eyes. The powerful androids—who can walk through a wall with no problem—are drawn to their targets by homing pens or watches that are given to the victims.

Biography: The owner of England's United Automation, Dr. Clement Armstrong sends his Cybernauts out to kill business executives when they try to buy Japanese circuits to compete with him. Sleuths John Steed and Emma Peel investigate separately, and Steed discovers that Armstrong wants to obtain the circuit so he can build an army of Cybernauts. Armstrong marks Ms. Peel for death with a pen, but Steed reaches her at the same time as the robot and yells to her to throw the pen away. But Armstrong isn't finished: He releases a second-generation robot that is capable of thinking, and it moves against Peel and Steed. Thinking quickly, Steed gives a pen to the robot and another Cybernaut attacks it. Armstrong is killed trying to separate them.

But the Cybernauts return, this time under the command of Amstrong's brother, art collector Paul Beresford, who uses a homing watch to send them hither. His goal: to get revenge against the two crimefighters. His plan: to use the Cybernauts to kidnap leading scientists, whom he offers a fortune to devise the most horrible way of killing Steed and Peel. Part of the plan includes turning Steed and Peel into mind-controlled puppets using a device placed in their watches. Peel puts hers on and Beresford turns her against Steed; fortunately, Steed is able to get a watch onto a Cybernaut and it goes berserk, killing Beresford. Steed destroys Peel's watch and shuts down the Cybernaut, ending the meance.

Comment: The Cybernauts were created by writer Philip Levene. Patrick Macnee is Steed, Diana Rigg is Peel, and Michael Gough stars as Armstrong. The sequel, "Return of the Cybernauts," aired in 1967 and stars Peter Cushing as Beresford; Levene wrote the script.

The Avengers also battled a group of killer androids—designed to take the place of powerful humans, in "Never, Never Say Die"—and tackled the murderous computer REMAK (Remote Electro-Magnetic Agent Killer) in "Killer."

CYBERNIA (C)

First Appearance: "Judgment Day," 1953, *Weird Fantasy* #18, EC Publishing.

Physical Description: The "planet of mechanical life" has Earth-like gravity, lives under artificial sunlight (which is unexplained), but is otherwise undescribed.

The robots are humanoid, mouthless with a serrated ridge that stretches from the eyes to the chin. Bald, they have a "headband" of metal and a matching band going across the top of the head. The robots learn in "educators" that charge their mechanical brain with "all knowledge available to . . . [their] society."

Biography: Cybernia is populated with robots built by humans. Tarlton from Earth Colonization rockets over to observe the society the robots have constructed. If worthy, the Cybernians may join the Galactic Republic. Tarlton remains within his spacesuit and helmet as an orange robot shows him the House of Delegates, an assembly plant where the orange robots are made, and then Blue Town. Though the same alloys and components go into the blue robots, they do not have the same privileges as the oranges. Tarlton denies Cybernia admittance into the Galactic Republic until all robots are equal. En route to Earth, Tarlton removes his helmet and "the beads of perspiration on his dark skin twinkle like distant stars . . ."

Comment: The story, drawn by Joe Orlando and written by Al Feldstein, was one of the most courageous mainstream comic book stories ever published. It was reprinted in *Incredible Science Fiction* #33, 1956.

CYBORG (1)   (L, TV, C)

First Appearance: *Cyborg* by Martin Caidin, 1972, Arbor House.

Physical Description: Though he looks like a normal human being, Austin is a cybernetic organism. His left arm, while not as flexible as a human limb, possesses "ten times the gripping and handling strength." It has steel-reinforced plasti-skin for punching through "heavy wood or light metal" and an extendable third finger, which becomes the barrel of a dart gun (the poison on the darts acts in six seconds). His legs are not only stronger but, because they're mechanical, they also leave more oxygen for Austin's organic tissue and give him virtually unlimited endurance. He has an audio recorder with 10-minute-long tapes built into his right leg; retractable webbing on his feet for underwater work; and a left eye that is actually a camera with 20 ASA 2000 exposures on each micro-cartridge.

Biography: A star athlete, Austin has mastered wrestling, fencing, boxing, acrobatics, judo, and aikido. He holds a master's degree in aerodynamics and astronautical engineering. Piloting a gunship in Vietnam, he is shot down and injured and transfers to the Air Force. Later, he joins the astronaut corps, moving from backup to primary team on the Apollo XVII mission when the LEM pilot breaks his arm. The youngest man to walk on the moon, Austin returns to test piloting (and spending time with girlfriend Jan Richards) while waiting for an assignment in space onboard Skylab II.

Returning from a test flight of the shuttle-like "flying wedge" M3F5 to 328,000 feet above the Mojave Desert, Austin loses control and crashes onto the landing strip. He sustains severe injuries. His left arm is gone, one leg is crushed and the other is badly mangled, and his left eye is ruined. However, because of his flight suit, he did not burn his lungs or significant areas of flesh. Thus, the military decides to try a bold experiment. At Slab Rock—the government's bionics and cyber-

netics lab attached to the NORAD complex in Colorado—Austin is rebuilt by Dr. Rudy Wells and his team. His damaged heart and bones are repaired, his legs, arm, and eye are replaced with mechanical units, and his spine is strengthened with vitallium and cerosium. When he recovers, Austin becomes an operative with the Office of Scientific Information (OSI), reporting to Oscar Goldman.

Comment: Caidin wrote three sequels, all published by Arbor House: *Operation Nuke* (1973), *High Crystal* (1974), and *Cyborg IV* (1975).

The novel is perhaps best-known as the basis for the popular TV series *The Six Million Dollar Man* starring Lee Majors as Austin and Richard Anderson as Oscar Goldman. The origins were similar, the major change being the TV Austin's bionic eye, which gave him super-vision. The series began as a trio of made-for-TV movies that aired in March, October, and November 1973 on the *ABC Suspense Movie*. The hour-long weekly series debuted in January 1974 and ran through March 1978.

Early in the series, Austin faced a seven million dollar man, badly mangled race-car driver Barney Miller (Monte Markham), who was also supposed to work for OSI. When he went haywire, it was up to Austin to stop him. Austin has also battled saboteurs, spies, Bigfoot, aliens, and other threats.

The series also spawned a trio of TV movies: *The Return of the Six Million Dollar Man and the Bionic Woman* (1987), which introduced Steve's bionic son (played by Tom Schanley); *Bionic Showdown: The Six Million Dollar Man and the Bionic Woman* (1989), which introduced a new bionic teen (played by Sandra Bullock); *Bionic Ever After?* (1994), in which Steve Austin and Jamie Sommers get married. A proposed spinoff series with the youngsters never materialized.

The TV series inspired six tie-in novels from 1975 to 1977: *Wine, Women, and Wars* by Michael Jahn, *The Solid Gold Kidnapping* by Richard Evans, *Pilot Error* by Jay Barbree, *The Rescue of the Athena One* by Jahn, *The Secret of Bigfoot Pass* by Jahn, and *International Incidents* by Jahn.

Charlton Comics published seven issues of a large, black-and-white *Six Million Dollar Man* comic book from 1976 to 1977, and nine issues of a color comic book from 1976 to 1978.

Caidin also cowrote *Exo-Man*, a 1977 made-for-TV movie about professor Nicholas Conrad. After being shot and paralyzed, Conrad dons an exo-suit in order to regain his mobility.

See also BIONIC WOMAN.

CYBORG (2) (C)

First Appearance: *DC Comics Presents* #26, 1980, DC Comics.

Physical Description: Standing six-foot-six, Cyborg is virtually encased in body armor, save for the tops of his thighs, his shoulders, the top of his chest, and the right side of his face and head. The steel armor, polymer flesh, and plastic veins make Cyborg impervious to most weapons and give him the strength to lift several tons, along with speed seven times that of his "normal" self. He has an artificial, infra-red left eye with a telescopic attachment, a sound amplifier, a finger laser, a destructive "white sound" projector, extendable arms, "foot grapplers" to help him climb sheer surfaces, and various other attachments. He can also plug into virtually any machine or weapon and utilize its power and abilities. The computer circuits in his skull also boost his mental capacities.

Biography: Black athlete Victor Stone is the son of S.T.A.R. (Scientific and Technological Advanced Research) scientists Silas and Elinore Stone, whose experiments give their boy an IQ beyond 170. Though Victor rebels as a youth and turns briefly to crime, he turns his life around, goes to college, and sets his eyes on the Olympics. But when one of the Stones' experiments goes bad, releasing a blob-like creature from another dimension, Elinore is killed and half of Victor's body is burned away. Silas is able to force the creature back to its own realm and, using cybernetic body parts he'd been working on for the military, he turns his son into a cyborg. Though the scientist trains his son on how to use his powerful new body, Victor is understandably bitter at the loss of his mother, his girlfriend, and his athletic career. But all is not lost: Contacted by the superhero Raven, Victor—as Cyborg—joins Kid Flash, Wonder Girl, Changeling, STARFIRE, and Batman's sidekick Robin as one of the New Teen Titans, crimefighters based in Manhattan. Silas later dies from his own exposure to the strange creature, though he and his son reconcile before his death.

Comment: The character was created by writer Marv Wolfman and artist George Perez. The New Teen Titans got their own magazine in 1980, and it continues to this day.

   The character appeared on *Super Friends: The Legendary Super Powers Show,* an animated series that aired on ABC from September 1984 to August 1985. Ernie Hudson provided his voice.

CYCLOPS (MP)

First Appearance: *The Atomic Submarine,* 1960, Gorham Productions/Allied Artists.

Physical Description: The flying saucer is a flat disc with a dome top/center: A single light shines from the side of the dome (hence, the nickname given to the ship), and an antenna pokes from the top. Access to the ship is through the iris-like "eye." The interior consists of breathable air and utter blackness, save for a lighted ramp in the center. The ship can travel through space and through the water; it is also alive, able to heal most rifts in its hull. The saucer is powered by magnetism, which it draws from the North Pole.

   The alien occupant is a cyclopean stalk with octopus-like tentacles at its base. It is covered with vine-like growths and viscous slime; it fires a destructive ray from its eye.

   The submarine in the film is a slightly flattened cylinder with a prow that comes to a point and slopes back, on the bottom, at a 45° angle. The conning tower is located only one-quarter of the way back from the prow.

Biography: Intent on conquering Earth, the alien lands in the seas off Alaska, destroying all ships and submarines that pass through so its presence will not become known. The atomic submarine *Tiger Shark* is sent to investigate and locate the saucer, which the crew nicknames Cyclops. Much to their surprise, their torpedoes are deflected or absorbed by the saucer's gel-like exterior. The heroic but reckless Captain Dan Wendover decides to ram the saucer, and the submarine becomes stuck in its side. Onboard a small submersible, he and several crewmembers use the maneuverable little ship to punch through the saucer. Once inside, Commander Richard "Reef" Holloway temporarily blinds the alien with a flare and the men escape; the alien takes off, only this time (for reasons not entirely clear), a missile fired from the submarine is able to destroy the craft.

Comment: Arthur Franz stars as Holloway with Dick Foran as Wendover. John Hilliard provided the voice of the alien. Spencer Gordon Bennet directed from a script by Orville H. Hampton, based on a story by Jack Rabin and Irving Block.

THE CYGNUS (MP, L, C, CS)

First Appearance: *The Black Hole,* 1979, Walt Disney Productions.

Physical Description: The mile-long *Cygnus* is a flattened rectangle with two long tail-sections and a spacious, complex command center located atop a control tower toward the stern. The ship boasts a huge agricultural area where plants are grown for food, an antimatter reactor for power (the *Cygnus* generates a zero-gravity field that allows it to avoid the enormous pull of the black hole), and a hospital where the crew is transformed into obedient zombie workers with mirror-faces and dark robes. Transportation from end to end is provided by fast-moving air cars.

The robot occupants of the *Cygnus* are: the red, vaguely humanoid, floating robot Maximillian who has a single red eye in the center of its featureless face; blaster-firing guards with dark red exteriors, commanded by the black-metal Captain S.T.A.R.; and Old B.O.B., a floating orb that talks and contains retractible tools in its midsection, including pincers and a whirring cutter. It has two nub-like ''legs'' on the bottom, and its squat, mushroom-shaped head (with two square eyes) can be withdrawn into its body. (The meanings of B.O.B. and S.T.A.R. are not revealed.)

The *Palamino* is a squat cylinder that stands on a central column and four diagonal legs, all of which are connected to a triangular base.

The crew of the *Palamino* consists of Captain Dan Holland, Chief Scientist Dr. Alex Durant, Astro-Geophysicist Dr. Katherine McCrae, First Officer Charles Pizer, journalist Harrison G. Booth, and the robot V.I.N.CENT (which stands for Vital Information Necessary, Centralized). The latter is an updated model of B.O.B., though the two look virtually the same (albeit, V.I.N.CENT is less battered and worn than B.O.B.).

Biography: In the late 22nd century, after 18 months of a fruitless search for life on other worlds, the *Palamino* heads back to Earth. Passing near a black hole, V.I.N.CENT spots the *Cygnus*, which was presumed lost 20 years before. Caught in the pull of the black hole, the *Palamino* averts disaster when the *Cygnus* extends a landing platform and they're able to land, protected by its gravity-nullifying field. The *Palamino* crew boards the ship and are confronted by Maximillian and his master, Dr. Hans Reinhardt. Reinhardt says that the crew abandoned the ship during a

Dr. Reinhardt and his robot Maximillian onboard the *Cygnus* in *The Black Hole*. © 1979, Walt Disney Productions.

meteoroid storm, and he's been studying the black hole ever since. In time, the crew of the *Palamino* discovers that Reinhardt intends to go through and beyond the black hole. Moreover, they find out that his people didn't leave—he's turned them into mindless slaves, a fate that also awaits Kate.

The crew of the *Palamino* heads for an escape craft—minus Durant, who has been slain by Maximillian, and Booth, who steals the *Palamino* but loses control of it and is blasted from space by the *Cygnus*. Old B.O.B. protects the three survivors from Maximillian, sacrificing his life while V.I.N.CENT uses his cutter to destroy the nefarious robot. Meanwhile, the *Cygnus* is battered and crippled by asteroids being drawn into the black hole. Its "null-g" screen fails and the ship and Reinhardt are drawn into the black hole, along with the foursome in the escape pod. Reinhardt and Maximillian merge into a single entity and end up in a fiery realm that appears to be the Biblical hell, while the heroes end up in Paradise.

Comment: Maximilian Schell stars as Reinhardt, with Joseph Bottoms as Pizer, Yvette Mimieux as Kate, Anthony Perkins as Durant, Ernest Borgnine as Booth, and Robert Forster as Holland. Roddy McDowall provided the voice for V.I.N.CENT. Gary Nelson directed from a script by Jeb Rosebrook and Gerry Day, based on a story by Rosebrook, Bob Barbash, and Richard Landau.

In 1979, Del Rey Books (Ballantine) published Alan Dean Foster's novelization of the movie.

Gold Key published a comic book adaptation of the film in *Walt Disney Comic Showcase* #54, 1980 (the last issue), followed by *Beyond the Black Hole*, continuing the adventures of the *Cygnus* as it passes through the black hole to "a universe that is in some ways identical" to our own. There, the heroes—along with V.I.N.CENT and Old B.O.B.—board a *Cygnus* escape craft and search for some place in the universe where they can be free from the pursuing Reinhardt. Four issues were published in 1980.

A *Black Hole* Sunday comic strip, serializing the film, was distributed briefly in 1979–80.

CYRANO (C)

First Appearance: "Cyrano," 1980, *Creepy* #115, Warren Publishing Co.

Physical Description: Approximately 150 feet long, the spaceship is long and flat, with a domed bridge. Built of aluminum bauxite and other lunar materials, it is run entirely by robots and a computer.

The robots resemble human beings with translucent skin, metallic bones, circuits, and gears visible beneath the surface.

Biography: Named after Cyrano de Bergerac, the ship is constructed by robots in lunar orbit and sent out to find intelligent life elsewhere in the universe. After 170 years, it reaches Alpha Centauri and sends robot scouts out to do a fine-tuned search. They find nothing on the one planet circling Alpha Centauri A, nor on the two worlds orbiting Alpha Centauri B, nor around any of the other stars they search. Finally reaching the "blazing core" of the Milky Way Galaxy, something happens to *Cyrano*: The "awesome spectacle of unrestrained chaos" causes the ship's programming to be altered. The spaceship becomes sentient and, "powered by fusion of the hydrogen" scattered through space, the spaceship actually changes its form, becoming a giant snowflake.

Earth's sun has long-since died and, needing a goal, *Cyrano* heads for the neighboring Andromeda galaxy. Finally encountering intelligent life forms, *Cyrano* is attacked by spaceships and must defend himself. In "under a trillionth of a second," he passes the gift of self-awareness to the aliens' computers, and their ships join him. He realizes, then, that his goal will be to find other machines like these and set them free.

Comment: This fascinating tale was written by Bob Toomey and drawn by Mike Saenz.

D

DALEKS (TV, MP, C, L)

First Appearance: *Doctor Who*, December 1963, BBC.

Physical Description: The Daleks of the planet Skaro are actually Kaleds—former humanoids who have been reduced to clawed, slug-like creatures. Surgically encased in metallic shells for protection from radiation and for mobility, the Kaleds are called Daleks. The shells are silvery (some later ones are red and blue, and the Black Dalek is Black) and resemble roughly five-foot-tall thimbles with a studded lower half and horizontal vents in the "head." In the middle of the head is a rigid eye stalk. They have a funnel-like ray blaster on the front top of their body, and two tool-arms on either side. The Daleks speak in a metallic voice and are powered by static electricity that runs through the floors.

The Thals are blond-haired humanoids.

Skaro is also the home to the Vaaga Plants, which contain a poisonous thorn: One prick turns humans into Vaaga Plants, after first driving them mad.

Doctor Who himself is an alien. Though he looks human, he has one heart on either side of his chest (each beats 10 times a minute), his blood pressure is 70/70, his body temperature is 60°, and he requires one-third as much oxygen as the average human. He is over 750 Earth-years old.

Biography: Because of a thousand-year "neutronic" war between the Kaleds and their fellow Skarosians, the Thals, Skaro is soaked with radiation. The Kaleds are horribly mutated, and Kaled scientist Davros works to find a solution to the increasing debilitation of his race. His efforts at genetic engineering produce the monstrous Mutos, who are driven from the domed Kaled city. Instead, he turns to cybernetics and creates a "travel machine" in which the Kaleds can survive on their poisoned world. But Davros makes these cyborgs, the Daleks, in his own image, "without conscience, without soul, and without pity," and fond of yelling, "Exterminate! Exterminate!" (Davros himself is maimed when a bomb strikes his laboratory. He attaches himself to a Dalek-like shell from the waist down.) When the Kaled leaders complain about the cyborgs, Davros joins the Thals and eliminates the remaining non-Dalek Kaleds. Then, under Davros, the Daleks turn on the Thals, take over Skaro, and plot to take over the universe, not only in their era but also throughout all time. (The remaining Thals develop anti-radiation drugs and become pacifists until forced to fight the Daleks once more.) During those times when Davros is away or dead (he has expired and been revived several times), the Daleks are ruled by the Emperor Dalek and his second-in-command the Black Dalek.

The only one who stands in the way of the Daleks is Dr. Who. On the planet Gallifrey, a race of super-intelligent beings known as the Time Lords study space and time using the TARDIS—Time and Relative Dimensions in Space—a device that blends in with their surroundings so the Time Lords can watch without being seen themselves. It is Time Lord policy to observe and learn but never to interfere, though Dr. Who is horrified by the evil he sees and refuses to sit on the sidelines. He steals a TARDIS and flees, unaware that the device was in for repairs. Not only does it become "locked" in the first likeness it assumes, a modern-day British police call box (whose tiny exterior conceals a larger, more spacious interior), but also the Time Lord never knows where or when the faulty device is going to leave him.

Dr. Who first defeats the Daleks by cutting off their electricity. In their second showdown, the Daleks invade London of the year 2167 and turn humans into slavish Robomen by outfitting them with metal helmets and armor. Dr. Who cuts off the radio waves that keep them enslaved and the Robomen revolt, blowing up the Daleks and their craft. The robot Mechonoids of the planet Mechanus, which resemble spherical, silvery diamonds, have also successfully battled the Daleks.

The *Daleks* as seen in the first Dr. Who feature film. © British Broadcasting Corporation.

Other alien, robotic, and computer enemies of Dr. Who include: the Cybermen, robotic, silver humanoids of the planet Mondas (the tenth planet), and their black-colored allies the Cyber Androids; the Giant Spiders of Metebelis Three; the Anti-Matter Monster of Zeta Minor; the flesh-eating Mire Beasts of the planet Aridius; the tentacled Axos; the evil computer BOSS (Biomorphic Organizational Systems Supervisor); the Chameleons, featureless aliens who impersonate humans (not to be confused with Dr. Who's foe Kamelion, an android who could assume the voice and likeness of anyone); the beautiful warrior women known as Drahvins; the green, scaly Draconians; the disembodied Great Intelligence from another dimension; the Ice Warriors, a race of lizard-like Martians; the incredibly evil race of green, one-eyed conquerors known as Jagaroth; the alien plants known as Krynoids, which turn humans into their kind; Kroll, a giant squid worshipped as a god by the Sampies of Delta Three; the reptilian Magma Creatures of Androzani Minor; the huge snake Mara, which feeds on evil; the powerful computer Mentalis; the huge slug Messtor, which wants to scatter its eggs through the universe; the corrupt Time Lord Morbius; the crab- and octopus-like (later, disembodied) Nestenes; the silicon-based, rock-like Ogri, bloodsucking creatures from Ogros; the ape-like Ogrons, who serve the Daleks; the Quarks, atomic-powered robots; the translucent, amorphous Rutans of Ruta Three who thrive on electricity and can take the shape of other beings; the jackal-faced Sutekh the Destroyer of the planet Phaester Osiris; the huge, invisible Visians of the planet Mira; the Voord, ruthless, featureless creatures that inhabit protective suits; and the Wolf Weeds, flesh-eating tumbleweeds of the planet Chloris.

In his later adventures, Dr. Who is accompanied by the robot dog K-9 and the lady Time Lord Romana.

Comment: *Dr. Who* debuted in November, one month before the Daleks first appeared. The seven-episode adventure was written by Terry Nation and directed by Christopher Barry (episodes one, two, four, and five) and Richard Martin. The Daleks were played by Robert Jewell, Kevin Manser, Michael Summerton, Gerald Taylor, and Peter Murphy; Peter Hawkins and David Graham provided their voices. The creatures returned for the first of many rematches in the six-episode ''The Dalek Invasion of Earth'' (November 1964).

On TV, Dr. Who has been played over the years by William Hartnell, Patrick Troughton, Jon Pertwee, Tom Baker, Peter Davison, Colin Baker, and Sylvester McCoy. To help guarantee international box office success, film star Peter Cushing played the part in a pair of theatrical movies (remakes of the first two TV sagas) *Doctor Who and the Daleks* (1965) and *Daleks—Invasion Earth 2150 A.D.* (1966).

Doctor Who made his British comic book debut in 1965, appearing in *TV Comic*, drawn by the popular Neville Main, and then in *TV Century 21* and *TV Action*. In October 1979, the *Doctor Who Weekly* began publication, a black-and-white magazine drawn by Dave Gibbons. Color muddied up Gibbons's work when Doctor Who's adventures were published in the United States in *Marvel Premiere* #57–#60 (1980). Marvel began a regular *Doctor Who* title in 1984, reprinting Gibbons's stories; it lasted 23 issues (to 1986). Also in the United States, Dell published a comic book adaptation of the film *Dr. Who and the Daleks* as part of its *Movie Classics* series, December 1966.

Over 40 novels, adaptations of the TV scripts, have been published in England by various authors, beginning in 1974. Five years later Pinnacle Books began issuing these in the United States, starting with *Doctor Who and the Day of the Daleks* by Terrance Dicks. Dicks also wrote *Doctor Who and the Genesis of the Daleks*.

DALGODA (C)

First Appearance: *Dalgoda*, 1984, Fantagraphics Books.

Physical Description: The talking, humanoid dog Dalgoda stands roughly six feet tall (when he isn't running on all fours) and is covered with golden brown fur. He has a short tail, four fingers on each hand, and a human-like face with a dog-like nose and ears on top of his head. Dalgoda wears clothing but is still a dog. When he's afraid, his tail droops between his legs; when he's happy, it wags.

Biography: In the year 2042, Project Cyclops—a search for alien life forms—discovers the planet Canida 32 light-years from Earth. Two decades later, exchange ships travel between the two worlds; one century after that, journeys between the planets are relatively routine. At the time of the story, the evil race known as Nimp are on the march. They have defeated a large force from Canida and are just six months distant from the world, which they're bent on conquering. Traveling to Erath, Dalgoda hopes to enlist military aide for the struggle—all the while fighting politicians, terrorist robots, and other nemeses.

Comment: The character was created by writer Jan Strnad and artist Dennis Fujitake. The comic book lasted for eight issues.

Dennis Fujitake's artwork for *Dalgoda*. © Jan Strnad and Dennis Fujitake.

Read to the left, from the "L," the letters of the character's name spell "Lad, a Dog."

THE DARK STAR (MP, L)

First Appearance: *Dark Star*, 1974, Jack H. Harris Enterprises.

Physical Description: The hyperdrive ship resembles a flattened bullet or "a white arrowhead" and is capable of faster-than-light-speed travel. It has a bridge with a large communications TV screen, an observation dome, a bomb-bay in the belly loaded with 20 talking thermostellar bombs, and a sophisticated computer with a female voice. The crew quarters with its pneumatic bunks had been unoccupied since an asteroid storm tore the place apart. The crew relaxes in the Recreation Chamber, which has a music room and a crafts/hobby area.

Biography: The *Dark Star* is a scoutship of the Advance Exploration Forces, which operates in the mid-21st century under the auspices of the United Nations. For 20 years, since departure from the Earth Orbital Station, the five-person crew—made ageless by sophisticated medical techniques—has been destroying unstable planets that may endanger colonists coming into the sector. The crewmembers are Lt. Edward Vincent Doolittle, Corporals Talby and Boiler, and Sgt. Elmer Pinback. Though Commander Powell is dead—killed when his seat short-circuited—he's kept in a cryogenic

A composite featuring the *Dark Star* and its surfing crew member, who actually uses a piece of the ship and not the vessel itself. © Jack H. Harris Productions.

state so his brain can be accessed for advice. Now, roughly 18 parsecs from Earth, in the Veil Nebula, just one bomb remains; when that is released, the *Dark Star* can head home. Unfortunately, the bomb is faulty and has a god complex: It explodes in the ship, destroying it in planetary orbit. Outside the ship, Doolittle is able to grab a piece of space debris and surf planetward, burning up in the atmosphere as he does so.

The ship's mascot, "Beachball," is a spherical creature roughly two feet in diameter and bright red, its pulsing body covered with circles of yellow, green, and black. When angry, it secretes moisture around these circles, which may be toxic. The alien bobs about, landing on its only appendages, a pair of clawed, webbed feet; it can see and hear and both moan and makes sounds like a canary. The "alien tomato-thing" is extremely unintelligent, though it mimics, parrot-like, what it sees people do.

Also onboard are four Luminants, multicolored geometric shapes made of light. Able to escape from most cages, they're kept inside an arrangement of mirrors that confuses them.

Comment: The film starred Brian Narelle as Doolittle, Andreijah Pahich as Talby, Carl Kuniholm as Boiler, and Dan O'Bannon as Pinback. The film was directed by John Carpenter—then a recent USC graduate—from a script he cowrote with O'Bannon. In 1974, Ballantine published a popular novelization written by Alan Dean Foster.

D.A.R.Y.L. (MP)

First Appearance: *D.A.R.Y.L.*, 1985, Paramount.

Physical Description: Daryl is a slender, brown-haired, normal-looking "nine or ten"-year-old child with a biological body and a computer brain. He grows like a normal child and "can sorta read what a computer is doing" and get in synch with it, easily reading (and changing, when necessary) the programming of everything from a bank ATM to a sophisticated jet fighter. His memories, visual and auditory, can be dumped onto a larger computer and played back. Daryl can do complex mathematic calculations in his head, play baseball and videogames perfectly, drive a car like a pro, and learn to play the piano quickly. He is not programmed to feel emotion or have a preference in foods, but does.

Biography: Daryl is a product of the Defense Department's Data Analyzing Robot Youth Lifeform project, his tissues created in a test-tube and his mind built in a laboratory. Co-creator Dr. Mulligan comes to feel that Daryl is more boy than machine and spirits him away, overloading his mind to create the semblance of amnesia. A military chopper pursues him through the Virginia countryside and, letting the boy out of the car in Barkenton, Mulligan drives off a cliff. Daryl ends up in a foster home, that of childless Joyce and Andy Richardson. The couple grows attached to him, as does neighborhood boy, Turtle Fox. When Daryl's "parents" come for him, he goes reluctantly; back at the lab, he learns who he is from his other co-creators, Dr. Jeffrey Stewart and Dr. Ellen Lamb. Reluctantly, he settles in to life at the lab.

When the military wants to move to the next stage, the creation of a "fearless, technically skilled devastating soldier," General Graycliffe orders Daryl destroyed. Instead, Dr. Stewart hides him under the backseat of his car and sneaks him from the facility, the military in pursuit. When the scientist is shot dead by a state trooper, Daryl heads for an air force base. He steals a fighter and takes off, radioing Turtle that he's on his way home. Though the military triggers the plane's remote self-destruct system, Daryl ejects, lands in a lake, and is dragged to safety by the waiting Turtle. For a while, Daryl is inert, apparently drowned—but Dr. Lamb revives him, his computer brain unharmed at having been deprived of oxygen. With the military believing him to have been destroyed, Daryl is free to return to the Richardsons.

Comment: Barret Oliver is Daryl, with Josef Sommer as Stewart, Michael McKean as Andy, Mary Beth Hurt as Joyce, Danny Corkill as Turtle, Ron Frazier as Graycliffe, Kathryn Walker as Lamb, and Richard Hammatt as Mulligan. The film was directed by Simon Wincer from a script by David Ambrose, Allan Scott, and Jeffrey Ellis.

DATA (TV, L, MP, C)

First Appearance: *Star Trek: The Next Generation*, September 1987, syndication.

Physical Description: An android who has been declared a sentient android by Starfleet, Data appears to be a normal human being, save for his pale skin and yellow eyes; even naked, he is indistinguishable from a human male. He dresses in the Starfleet uniform: black boots and trousers and a reddish-brown tunic with black sides, waist, and shoulders and the starfleet insignia over the heart.

Biography: The human colony on Omicron Theta is destroyed by the Crystalline Entity, assisted by the malfunctioning android Lore. Realizing the end is near, Lore's creator, cyberneticist Dr. Noonien

Soong, stores the colonists' collected knowledge and memories in his second android, Data. In 2338—some two years later—Data is discovered, deactivated, by the Federation starship U.S.S. *Tripoli*. Three years later, with no memories of his own, the emotionless android enters Starfleet Academy. He graduates in 2345 with degrees in exobiology and probability mechanics and serves as science officer on the recommissioned U.S.S. ENTERPRISE. Lt. Commander Data, who plays the violin and enjoys reading Shakespeare, has won numerous medals and commendations, including the Medal of Honor with Clusters, the Decoration for Gallantry, the Legion of Honor, and the Star Cross.

Other members of the crew are Captain Jean-Luc Picard, Commander William Riker, Chief Medical Officer Dr. Beverly Crusher, Lt. Worf (see KLINGONS), Ship's Counselor Lt. Commander Deanna Troi (a Betazoid), and Chief Engineer Lt.-J.G. Geordi La Forge. Data's pet cat is Spot.

An alien who appears regularly is Q, an extradimensional humanoid from the Q continuum, one who has the power to manipulate matter and space. Another recurring alien is Guinan, who tends bar at the Ten Forward and dispenses philosophy to patrons, including Captain Picard. Little is known about Guinan, save that she is thousands of years old and that her home world was destroyed by the Borg, planet-conquering humanoids with numerous cybernetic implants. The Borg's massive, square spaceship is like a beehive, with each alien as part of a single consciousness.

Comment: The hour-long series, which is set 78 years after the original *Star Trek,* ended in 1994 but remains in syndication as of this writing. Brent Spiner stars as Data (and as his father Dr. Soong and as Lore, his "evil twin"), with Patrick Stewart as Picard, Jonathan Frakes as Riker, Gates McFadden as Crusher, Michael Dorn as Worf, Marina Sirtis as Troi, LeVar Burton as La Forge, and John DeLancie as Q and Whoopi Goldberg as Guinan.

The character also appeared in the motion picture *Star Trek Generations,* played by Spiner. In it, mad scientist Dr. Soran (Malcolm McDowell) allies himself with the Klingons to try and tap into a joy-inducing cosmic force known as the Nexus. The crew of the *Enterprise* manages to stop him, at the cost of the life of time-traveling Captain James T. Kirk (see U.S.S. *Enterprise*). In the film, Data manages to experience emotions thanks to an "emotion" chip injected into his circuitry. The film was directed by David Carson from a script by Ronald D. Moore and Brannon Braga.

Beginning with an adaptation of the two-hour TV movie debut, *Encounter at Farpoint* by David Gerrold, Pocket Books has published over 35 novels inspired by the series. These include *Boogeymen* by Mel Gilden, *A Call to Darkness* by Michael Jan Friedman, *Captain's Honor* by David and Daniel Dvorkin, *Chains of Command* by W.A. McCay and E.L. Flood, *Children of Hamlin* by Carmen Carter, *Contamination* by John Vornholt, *Debtor's Planet* by W.R. Thompson, *Descent* by Diane Carey (based on episodes of the TV series), *The Devil's Heart* by Carter, *Doomsday World* by Carter, David, Friedman, and Robert Greenburger, *Exiles* by Howard Weinstein, *Eyes of the Beholders* by A.C. Crispin, *Foreign Foes* by David Galanter and Greg Brodeur, *Fortune's Light* by Friedman, *Ghost Ship* by Diane Carey, *Grounded* by David Bischoff, *Here There Be Dragons* by John Peel, *Imbalance* by V.E. Mitchell, *Imzadi* by Peter David, *Masks* by Vornholt, *Metamorphosis* by Jean Lorrah, *Nightshade* by L.K. Hamilton, *Perchance to Dream* by Weinstein, *Peacekeepers* by Gene DeWeese, *Power Hungry* by Weinstein, *Q-in-Law* by David, *Relics* by Friedman, *Reunion* by Friedman, *A Rock and a Hard Place* by David, *The Romulan Prize* by Simon Hawke, *Sins of Commission* by Susan Wright, *Spartacus* by T.L. Mancour, *Strike Zone* by David, *Survivors* by Lorrah, *War Drums* by Vornholt, *Unification* by Jeri Taylor (based on the TV episode), and *Vendetta* by David. J.M. Dillard wrote the novelization of the film *Generations*.

Novels in the juvenile *Star Trek: The Next Generation: Starfleet Academy* series by Peter David are *Worf's First Adventure, Line of Fire,* and *Survival.*

DC Comics published a six-issue series based on the show in 1988, then began a series of all-new adventures in 1989. The comic book continues to be published.

See also Appendix D.

DEANNA TROI   See DATA; U.S.S. ENTERPRISE.

DEATHLOK   (C)

First Appearance: *Astonishing Tales* #25, 1974, Marvel Comics.

Physical Description: Except for his neck, the right side of his head, and portions of the left side of his face, Deathlok's six-foot-four body is encased in a silvery polymer atop a secondary layer of "semi-living" tissue. He wears a red leotard and boots.

Thanks to his cybernetic body parts, Deathlok is superhuman. He has an ultraviolet/infrared/telescopic/microscopic left eye for seeing in the dark; artificial muscles and bone for superstrength, reflexes, and agility; a computer-boosted brain; audio amplifiers; and a high level of invulnerability. He carries a powerful maser gun and a dagger, which is magnetically attached to his right leg.

Biography: Badly hurt by a mine during war games, Colonel Luther Manning becomes a subject in the government's Project Alpha-Mech program, which was founded to create a race of supersoldiers. Luther's surviving organs, bone, and tissue are augmented by high-performance mechanical parts. Codenamed Deathlok, Manning initially works for his superior, Major Simon Ryker (who is himself a cyborg, along with his flunky War Wolf, a humanoid wolf). Later, he becomes a mercenary after which he works as a troubleshooter for the Roxxon Oil Company, where his remaining human parts are replaced to make him stronger and more impervious still. Luther is killed on a mission to infiltrate the government's top-secret Pegasus Project. However, his biological parts—which had been saved—are cloned, and in the 1990s he operates as the Demolisher. Meanwhile, the "fiercely moral" Michael Collins discovers the existence of the Deathlok project and becomes the new Deathlok, who resists his "programming" to serve Roxxon.

Manning is survived by his estranged wife Sybil and son Richard.

Comment: The character was created by writer Doug Moench and artist Rich Buckler. Deathlok had a solo run in *Astonishing Tales* #s 25–36; the Collins-Deathlok appeared in four issues of his own *Deathlok* title in 1990. The demise of the Manning-Deathlok occurred in *Marvel Two-In-One* #54, 1979.

DEATH STAR   See MILLENNIUM FALCON.

DEEP SPACE NINE   (TV, L, C)

First Appearance: *Star Trek: Deep Space Nine,* January 1993, syndicated.

Physical Description: With some 300 permanent residents, the Deep Space Nine space station consists of a core shaped like a toy top, with Operations Control Center in the middle surrounded by a Promenade with everything from shops to restaurants that cater to everything in interstellar trade to a Bajoran temple. The core is surrounded by a habitat ring with defensive weaponry. Three spokes radiate from this ring, connecting to an outer docking ring. There are four upright, rib-like projections attached to the docking ring: the upper and lower docking pylons.

The station is equipped with three Runabout space craft, 20-meter-long patrol ships able to carry up to 40 people and capable of reaching speeds of up to warp 4.7. Unlike other ships, these land on pads in the habitat ring.

Biography: Orbiting the planet Bajor in the middle 24th century, the space station was originally used by Cardassians as a base from which to conduct mining operations on the world below; the station itself was built by Bajoran laborers working under Cardassian masters. When the Cardassians were overthrown, the Federation took over the station at the request of the Bajorans. Its personnel do not act as sentries, per se, but their presence discourages the Cardassians or any other race from interfering while the newly freed Bajorans get their footing. Most of the proprietors who had concessions on the station were allowed to keep them, so long as they didn't flagrantly break Federation law.

Located near a stable wormhole that allows for rapid transit to the Gamma Quadrant—ordinarily a trip that would take 60 years at warp nine—Deep Space Nine is never dull. The crew includes the serious, taciturn Commander Benjamin Sisko; the tough Major Kira Nerys, a Bajoran and a former terrorist, now Sisko's first officer (Bajorans differ outwardly from humans in that they have a large serrated ridge on the bridge of the nose); Chief Operations Officer Miles O'Brien, former transporter chief on the U.S.S. *Enterprise* and married to schoolteacher Keiko, former botanist on the *Enterprise*; Science Officer Lt. Jadzia Dax, a Trill who has the body of a 20-odd-year-old human female with the spirit of an ancient intelligence that has lived six other lifetimes; and Dr. Julian Bashir, a specialist in multispecies medicine. The most unusual crewmember is Security Chief Odo, a shape-shifter who can become any object, animate or inanimate. The last of his kind, he was found drifting near the Denorios Asteroid Belt near Bajor, with no memory of whence he came. Raised among the Bajor, Odo typically assumes Bajoran form when he's out and about; in his normal shape, he's a gelatinous mass. Once every 16 hours he must revert to his natural, liquid form; he usually rests in a bucket.

Most notable among the permanent residents is Quark, a Ferengi barkeep who runs a restaurant/holosuite/casino. He's a likable gambler and thief, and the unofficial "community leader" of the Promenade. The Ferengis are swarthy humanoids with hairless heads divided into a large, prominent lobe on each side. They have jagged teeth and brows that sweep across the face to form two huge ears. The Ferengis are crafty dealers and merchants and live by "rules of negotiation." Other prominent Ferengis are Quark's brother Rom, Rom's son Nog, scientist Dr. Rayga, diplomat DaiMon Bok, and the Grand Nagus Zek.

Comment: Avery Brooks stars as Sisko, Nana Visitor is Kira, Colm Meaney is O'Brien, Terry Farrell is Dax, Siddig El Fadil is Bashir, Rene Auberjonois is Odo, Armin Shimerman is Quark, and Max Grodenchik is Rom. Wallace Shawn has guest-starred numerous times as Zek. The Ferengi were introduced in "Where No One Has Gone Before" in the first season of *Star Trek: The Next Generation* and appeared regularly on that show for the first two seasons before migrating to *Deep Space Nine*. The Cardassians were also introduced on that series in the fourth season episode "The Wounded."

The first station referred to in the *Star Trek* chronicles was Deep Space Station K-7, seen in "I, Mudd," in the original series.

The characters have also appeared in original novels from Pocket Books, which began with *Emissary* by J.M. Dillard (based on the pilot episode) and include *Betrayal* by Lois Tilton, *The Big Game* by Sandy Schofield, *Bloodletter* by K.W. Jeter, *Fallen Heroes* by Dafydd ab Hugh, *The Siege* by Peter David, and *Warchild* by Esther Friesner. Young-adult novels from Pocket Books include Brad Strickland's *The Star Ghost* and *Stowaways*.

Dark Horse Comics began publishing a *Star Trek: Deep Space Nine* comic book in 1992.

See also DATA; MR. SPOCK; Appendix D.

THE DEFIANT (T, TV, C)

First Appearance: *G.I. Joe*, 1987, Hasbro.
Physical Description: The *Defiant* is a wedge-shaped space shuttle—number 1010X—which is carried into space piggybacked onboard a wide, flat, snub-nosed booster that converts into a space station once in orbit. The *Defiant* has three chairs in its cockpit, and three laser cannons. The cargo bay on the shuttle opens so the extendable arm can be used.

The booster is approximately 25 feet long, the shuttle roughly 20 feet long.

Biography: The dozens of soldiers who operate under the G.I. Joe banner are highly trained fighters who, under the unswerving leadership of Clayton M. Abernathy, a.k.a. Commander Hawk, battle the forces of Cobra, a terrorist group run by Enemy Leader who is aided by the evil Destro—the mastermind behind M.A.R.S. (Military Armaments Research System, which manufactures state-of-the-art weapons)—and the equally wicked Baroness. The Cobra soldiers include the ferocious B.A.T.s: the Battle Android Troopers.

Hi-tech vehicles are an important part of their arsenal. In addition to their space shuttle, the Joes have a Conquest X-30 Multi-Role High Performance Fighter with forward-swept wings; a Rattler Double-Seat Ground-support Attack Aircraft; a SHARC—Submersible High-Speed Attack and Reconnaissance Craft Flying Submarine—and a Skystriker XP-14F Combat Jet.

The Cobra forces possess a Night Raven S3 High Altitude Attack and Reconnaissance Aircraft, which flies at three times the speed of sound; a Sea Ray, which attacks in the air and under the water; a Pogo Ballistic Battle Ball, consisting of an enclosed sphere (for soldiers) that hops around, rocket-propelled, on three legs; and a Mamba Twin Rotor Attack Copter, which carries three detachable flight pods.

The lineup also consists of Star Brigade Fighters, super-advanced soldiers that include the cyborg Robo-J.O.E., the Cobra warrior B.A.A.T. (Battle Armored Android Trooper), and the giant Armor-Bot humanoid-like fighting vehicle.

Comment: The original G.I. Joe 12-inch-tall World War II action figures were introduced in 1964 and lasted through 1967, when antiwar sentiment in the United States was strong. The line was reintroduced in 1982 as three-and-three-quarter-inch action figures with a science fiction slant. New figures and accoutrements have been introduced every year, including the *Defiant*. The Star Brigade was added to the line in 1993.

Marvel began publishing an ongoing comic book in 1982, shortly before the debut of the toy line. The success of the toys spawned an enormously popular half-hour syndicated, animated series, which debuted in 1983, and a five-part miniseries, *Dragonfire*, in 1989.

THE DEIEI (C)

First Appearance: *The Phoenix* #1, 1975, Atlas Comics.

Physical Description: Standing an average of seven feet tall, the humanoid creatures have blue or orange skin, lipless mouths, small ears, a wave of hair above the forehead, and four fingers on each hand.

The Deiei can read minds, and wear skintight suits that give them the power to fly and fire destructive blasts. They watch human activities via small TV globes called optispheres. They pilot large flying saucers; both the ships and their Earth outpost are equipped with electro-teleportation devices.

Biography: The Deiei "evolved quickly" on the planet Deiei Prime circling the star Antares. Coming to Earth in prehistory, they experimented on apes, turned them into humans, and watched our progress from their outpost beneath the Arctic ice. In 1977, there is an explosion onboard the space lab Threshold I, in Earth orbit. The three occupants board the shuttle for the ride home, but it is damaged in the blast and only Ed Tyler survives the crippled ship's landing in the Arctic. There, he is spotted by a floating, camera-like optisphere. Nerei argues to save him, while Garin, Daelin, and Hars are opposed. However, outpost leader Setra orders him brought to the base. Discovering that the Deiei are disappointed with the way humans turned out and are planning to destroy us, Tyler steals one of their uniforms and wages war on the aliens as the super-powered Phoenix.

Comment: The magazine lasted for four issues. In the final issue, it was revealed that the Deiei were acting at the behest of humanoids known as the Protectors. These beings bring Tyler onto their spaceship, in Earth orbit, and transform him into a superhero known as the Protector, charged with saving Earth from its own self-destructiveness. The change in the storyline was not the work of the series' originator, the superb artist/plotter Sal Amendola.

THE DELOREAN (MP, L, TV, C)

First Appearance: *Back to the Future,* 1985, Universal Pictures.

Physical Description: The stainless steel, gull-wing car is a standard DeLorean modified from the front seat back. In place of the back seat and hatchback door is a nuclear reactor, whose six-inch coil disappears under the rear bumper and reappears on the top of the car. The plutonium reactor provides the 1.21 gigawatts of elecricity the car requires; a "flux capacitor" stores and discharges the power "like a gigantic bolt of lightning." Upon reaching a speed of 88 miles an hour, the car immediately shoots to whatever date has been programmed (displayed on an LED readout in the cockpit).

Biography: After working on a time machine for 30 years, Dr. Emmett L. Brown of Hill Valley completes it. To escape terrorists, Brown's young friend Marty McFly is forced to rev up the car— and, breaking the time barrier, heads back to the Hill Valley of 1955. There, while the past-time-Brown helps Marty rig a hookup that will allow lightning to return the powered-down DeLorean back to the future, Marty's mother Lorraine falls in love with her future-son; Marty must change things so that she does, in fact, marry his father George. He also manages to warn Doc about the 1985 assassination attempt, so he can protect himself.

In their second adventure together, the pair go to the year 2015 to straighten out problems with the McFly children Marty Jr. and Marlene, only to return to 1985 and find it changed into a nightmare world—the result of loutish Biff Tannen having gotten hold of the DeLorean, gone into the future and brought back a sports almanac with results from the future and presented it to his past-self. Tannen earned himself a fortune, put Hill Valley under his thumb, and even married Marty's mother.

Marty and Doc manage to set things right, though not for long. In their third adventure, lightning strikes the DeLorean and sends Brown to the wild Hill Valley of 1885; hiding the time machine back then, he leaves a letter with Western Union to be held and delivered to Mary in the present. When that's done, Marty finds the time machine now, travels to 1885, and saves Brown from the wicked Buford "Mad Dog" Tannen. Marty returns to the present by putting the damaged, fuel-less DeLorean in front of a locomotive to get it up to the required speed—though Doc is stranded when the DeLorean is wrecked by a train arriving in the present. Fortunately, Doc is able to transform a locomotive into a time machine and, with lovely Clara Clayton and their sons Jules and Vcrn, visits the present to get his dog Einstein and say farewell to Marty before zooming off to places and times unknown.

Comment: Michael J. Fox stars as Marty, Christopher Lloyd is Doc Brown, and Thomas F. Wilson is Biff; *Back to the Future Part II* (1989) and *Back to the Future Part III* (1990) star Fox, Lloyd and Wilson; the latter also features Mary Steenburgen as Clara. Robert Zemeckis directed all three films; Zemeckis and Bob Gale cowrote the scripts. The first film was novelized by George Gipe, the second and third by Craig Shaw Gardner.

On TV, Fox and Lloyd provided the voices for their animated counterparts on the CBS Saturday morning series *Back to the Future,* which debuted in September 1991.

Marvel Comics published four issues of a *Back to the Future* comic book in 1991, to coincide with the short-lived animated series. Harvey Comics published three issues of *Back to the Future: Forward to the Future* in 1992–93.

A hydraulically operated DeLorean, ducking and bucking beneath a huge, domed movie screen, is a ride at Universal Studios' "Back to the Future" attraction in their Hollywood and Florida theme parks.

THE DESTROYER (C)

First Appearance: *Journey Into Mystery* #118, 1965, Marvel Comics.
Physical Description: The silver-gray humanoid Destroyer possesses incredible physical strength and fires destructive rays from its eyes. Made of metal annealed by the gods, it is virtually indestructible and is operated by the projected consciousness of a user. Though its normal height is just over six feet, it has been known to grow to some 2,000 feet tall when possessed by the life essence of many individuals.
Biography: The Destroyer was created over 10 centuries ago in Asgard, the home of the Norse Gods, at the command of Odin, their king. Its purpose was to defend Asgard against THE CELESTIALS, but it has been used repeatedly by the evil god Loki in his efforts to destroy Odin and the mighty Thor. Thor himself has also used the android to attack the wicked goddess Hela. Thor left the Destroyer sealed in an unbreakable crystal in Hela's realm Hel, where it remains to this day.
Comment: The character was created by writer Stan Lee and artist Jack Kirby.

THE DILBIANS (L)

First Appearance: "The Man in the Mailbag" by Gordon R. Dickson, April 1959, *Galaxy.*
Physical Description: The aliens resemble "very large bears who had stood up on their hind legs and gone on a diet." They weigh over half a ton, stand at least eight feet tall, are long-legged, have pug-noses and "humanlike" lower jaws, and a coat of thick black hair. The creatures live in clans, speak a language that can be learned and spoken by humans, and have manners described as "sheer brass."

A demonstration of Dilbian strength. Art by Wally Wood.
© Galaxy Publishing Corp.

Biography: Soon after Earth and the comparatively primitive Dilbia have established shaky diplomatic relations, brash biochemist and explorer John Tardy is sent to Dilbia to find missing sociologist Ty Lamorc. Tardy is introduced to the wise Dilbian Two Answers and the powerful Shaking Knees, and they set out into the wilds of the planet in an effort to locate her. After sundry dangerous, very rough-and-tumble adventures, Tardy finds her and learns the truth about his mission: She was ordered to get lost so a "natural, extroverted, uncerebral" human like Tardy could be sent to rescue her, and the Dilbians could see that humans were not all the pathetic "little aliens" they seemed to be.

Comment: Since 1950, Dickson has been one of the leading authors of tales about relatively benign but fascinating alien civilizations. "The Man in the Mailbag" appeared as *Spacial Delivery,* half of an Ace double-novel paperback, in 1961.

THE DISCOVERY (MP, L, C)

First Appearance: *2001: A Space Odyssey,* 1968, Metro-Goldwyn-Mayer.

Physical Description: Four hundred feet long, the white *Discovery* consists of a 40-foot-diameter, spherical region that contains the "centrifuge" or "carousel," a section that slowly revolves to create artificial gravity. This area contains the controls for the ship as well as the hibernaculums for sleeping passengers, the kitchen, toilet, and other necessities. The pod bay is located below the centrifuge, but still within the forward sphere; the pods are round vehicles with a pair of slender arms and pincer-like fingers.

The center of the centrifuge, the "hub," allows access to the rest of the ship. Behind the forward section are four liquid hydrogen tanks, part of a 300-foot section that leads to the nuclear reactor. There are six plasma-drive engines in the rear, stacked in pairs. Halfway between the sphere and the engines are the ship's dish antennae, one main and two smaller ones.

The crew of the *Discovery* consists of Mission Commander Dave Bowman, Captain Frank Poole, and the hibernating scientists Whitehead, Kowalski, and Hunter. Also onboard is HAL 9000 (Heuristically programmed ALgorithmic computer), which controls the ship's vital functions, speaks in a gentle male voice, and watches everything through its unblinking red fisheye lens.

Space Station Five (Space Station One in the novel)—a transfer point/rest-stop for trips to the moon—consists of two parallel wheels nearly 1,000 feet in diameter, connected by a central column. Four spokes radiate from the column to each wheel, and the entire station turns slowly, creating a sense of gravity through centrifugal force. The side of the column is a docking area for ships from Earth.

The Orion III shuttle that travels from the Earth to the moon consists of a narrow, wedge-shaped fuselage with two stubby wings in the rear.

The Aries-1B lunar carrier, which takes passengers from the space station to the moon, is a sphere with four legs.

Biography: On Earth, hominids touch a large, mysterious black slab and conceive of weaponry. On the moon, in 2001, a second black slab is discovered and emits a piercing sound in the direction of Jupiter (Saturn in the novel). The spaceship *Discovery,* already under construction as part of Project Jupiter, is sent to find out who or what is on the

After being locked out of the *Discovery* by the computer HAL, Dave Bowman makes a daring reentry without his helmet.
© Metro-Goldwyn-Mayer.

receiving end of the signal. En route, the computer HAL goes berserk and kills the hibernating astronauts and astronaut Poole before Bowman is able to disconnect all but his vital functions. Reaching Jupiter, Bowman leaves the *Discovery* behind when he's drawn into a stargate. He ends up in a comfortable room on an alien world, where his life passes uneventfully; upon his death, he is reborn, courtesy of a third slab (and the unseen aliens) as a starchild, returned to watch over Earth.

Comment: Keir Dullea stars as Bowman with Gary Lockwood as Poole and Douglas Rain as the voice of HAL. The film was written by director Stanley Kubrick and famed science fiction author Arthur C. Clarke, whose short story "The Sentinel" inspired the film, which was originally going to be called *Journey Beyond the Stars*. In "The Sentinel," published in 1950, scientists find a pyramidal object on the moon signaling aliens that humans have reached a significant phase of evolution and are no longer "struggling up from savagery."

Clarke wrote a novelization based on the screenplay. The book was published in July 1968, three months after the release of the film.

Clarke wrote two sequels to the original novel: *2010: Odyssey Two* (1982) and *2061: Odyssey Three* (1988). In the first novel, the Earth is on the brink of war when the United States and Soviet Union send a joint mission to Jupiter onboard the *Leonov* to find out what happened to the *Discovery* and its crew. They find the ship, discover that HAL (the voice of Rain) didn't go mad but was merely trying

to resolve conflicting orders, and are informed by the spirit of Bowman (Dullea) that something wonderful is going to happen. When a flood of monoliths rain down on Jupiter, giving the planet's mass the extra "push" it needs to become a star, the revived HAL helps them escape with a boost from the piggybacked *Discovery*, which is then cut loose and consumed in the rebirth of Jupiter. The appearance of a second sun in the sky defuses tension on Earth; something wonderful *has* happened, though HAL and the *Discovery* are left orbiting Jupiter in a "highly elongated ellipse, like a trapped comet." The novel was made into a film in 1984, directed by Peter Hyams and starring Roy Scheider as Dr. Heywood Floyd (who, played by William Sylvester, studied the lunar monolith in the first film), Helen Mirren as Russian Captain Tanya Orlova, and John Lithgow as systems analyst Walter Curnow.

In the third novel, Dr. Floyd is named to the crew of the starship *Universe,* which is to rendezvous with Halley's Comet. Meanwhile, the crew of the ship *Galaxy*—which includes Floyd's grandson Chris—is stranded, after an attempted hijacking, on Jupiter's satellite Europa, which the aliens had told us never to visit. The *Universe* hastens to their rescue, unsure whether they'll be allowed near Europa—or what they'll find if they are.

Clarke has talked about writing *20,001: The Final Odyssey.*

In 1976, Marvel Comics published artist Jack Kirby's adaptation of the original film, in a *Marvel Treasury Special*. Kirby spun that off into an ages-spanning monthly comic book, 10 issues of which were published from 1976 to 1977. The character MACHINE MAN was introduced in the title.

See also THE OVERLORDS.

DOCTOR OCTOPUS (C, TV, L, CS)

First Appearance: *The Amazing Spider-Man #3*, 1963, Marvel Comics.

Physical Description: Doctor Octopus is a normal man, five-foot-nine, who has four six-foot-long mechanical arms that can extend to 24 feet. Each arm is strong enough to lift a car by itself, and ends in a three-fingered pincer. Octopus controls the arms with his mind; they are part of a chest harness that is permanently fixed to his body.

Biography: Otto Gunther Octavius is the overweight, bespectacled son of Torbert and Mary Lavinia Octavius of Schenectady, New York. A bookworm and a loner, he gets a full college scholarship and graduates with honors, "the most brilliant atomic researcher" in the country. Landing a job at the U.S. Atomic Research Center, he devises his harness and tentacle-like arms so he can "work safely with chemicals which are far too dangerous to touch." A romantic relationship with coworker Dr. Mary Alice Anders upsets his possessive mother, and Otto breaks it off; later, while Otto argues with his mother, she drops dead. Guilt-stricken, he fails to pay attention to what he is doing at the laboratory. When he's caught in a "sudden blast of uncontrolled radiation," the harness is welded to his body. The radiation also causes "an uncertain amount of brain damage," which turns him into one of the world's most dangerous supervillains. Operating as Doctor Octopus, his chief nemesis is the superhero Spider-Man.

In one of his most diabolical plans, Octavius spends time wooing Spider-Man's widowed Aunt May in order to use her as a decoy in crime—escorting her to a museum, causing her to faint near a work of art, then stealing it while the guard is helping May.

Comment: In addition to his many comic book appearances, the character was featured on several episodes of *Spider-Man*, an animated series that aired on ABC from September 1967 to September 1969. He was also the heavy villain in the first Spider-Man novel, *Mayhem in Manhattan* (1978) by Len Wein and Marv Wolfman and was also the web-slinger's nemesis in the novella "Spider-Man" by Stan Lee and Peter David, which was the featured story in the 1994 prose anthology *The Ultimate Spider-Man*.

The villain has also been seen in the Spider-Man newspaper comic strip.

DR. PUNA AND PROFESSOR TANGA (MP)

First Appearance: *Invasion of the Star Creatures*, 1962, Alta Vista Productions/American International.

Physical Description: The natives of the planet Kallar in the Belfar Star System are stunning, over-six-foot-tall human women who wear "futuristic" bikinis with high, flared collars. The aliens' ship is equipped with a mind-reading machine and a force field for holding prisoners.

Biography: Out on maneuvers in this comedy, soldiers Philbrick and Penn enter a cave and are captured by seven-foot-tall Star Creatures—essentially carrots with arms and legs—who take them to the hidden spaceship of scientists Puna and Tanga. The aliens have come to pave the way for an invasion, aided by the vegetable monsters that were raised from sprouts in flower pots. The inept soldiers manage to escape and bring their platoon to the cave. The army and a tribe of Indians attack, the scientists fall in love with the soldiers and defect, and they remain behind when the Star Creatures blast off for home.

Comment: Dolores Reed stars as Puna and Gloria Victor as Tanga, with Robert Ball as Philbrick and Frankie Ray as Penn. Bruno Ve Sota directed from a screenplay by Jonathan Haze (who starred in the cult-classic *Little Shop of Horrors*).

DR. SUN AND H.E.R.B.I.E. (C, TV)

First Appearance: *Tomb of Dracula #16*, 1974, Marvel Comics.

Physical Description: As a brain, Sun is linked to computers and is able to use their electricity to fire deadly blasts. As a robot, Doctor Sun is a golden humanoid who stands approximately seven feet tall and has a clear-dome head with a brain floating inside. The robot possesses enormous physical strength. H.E.R.B.I.E. is a pear-shaped, rocket-powered silver robot with extendable arms, a computer brain, infrared vision, and powerful optiblast rays.

Biography: Red Chinese scientist Dr. Sun is the genius behind Project: Mind, in which a human brain is kept alive outside the body and interfaces with a computer. Thanks to a falling out with a powerful military man, Sun gets to be the guinea pig in his own program. He uses his transformation to create a small army of slaves and plots to conquer the world. To do this, he plans to enlist the assistance of the world's vampires—which will also ensure him the steady supply of blood he needs to survive. Sun captures Dracula who, after a prolonged battle, destroys what he thinks is the scientist's brain but is, in fact, the brain of an underling, an assassin named Juno.

Commanding that a robot body be built to house his brain and provide him with mobility, Sun captures the superhero Nova and teleports them both to the spacecraft from XANDAR in Earth's orbit, planning to use alien technology to conquer Earth. But Sun is defeated as the ship nears Xandar, and he transfers his consciousness to computers on the alien planet. After the superheroic Fantastic Four help Xandar fend off an invasion of SKRULLS, a permanent link is set up between the aliens' computers and the Fantastic Four's robot H.E.R.B.I.E. (Humanoid Experimental Robot, B-Type, Integrated Electronics). Doctor Sun transfers his mind to H.E.R.B.I.E. and turns on the Fantastic Four, who are an impediment to his plans. Shifting his consciousness to the team's master computer, Sun is locked in there by the group's leader Mister Fantastic; the freed H.E.R.B.I.E. rams the computer, destroying it, himself, and Doctor Sun.

Comment: The character H.E.R.B.I.E. was created for *The Fantastic Four* animated TV series, which aired on NBC in 1978. Frank Welker provided the voice. Later, the robot was worked into the comic book mythos and destroyed in *The Fantastic Four* #217.

DOCTOR WHO   See DALEKS.

DOGORA   (MP)

First Appearance: *Uchu Daikaiju Dogora* (*Giant Space Monster Dogora*), 1964, Toho.
Physical Description: In its original, spaceborne form Dogora is a blue, pulsing amoeba. Later, it splits and grows in size, each amoeba sprouting seven thin tentacles that can reach down from the troposphere.
Biography: In space, TV satellite L1000 collides with Dogora in its amoebic form. Shortly thereafter, objects with coal or diamond content are lifted into the sky. Dr. Munakata, an expert in crystals, determines that a space cell is responsible, one that has been mutated by exposure to radioactivity and lives by consuming carbon-based material. Fearing that it will start feeding on humans next, Munakata searches for a means to destroy it, his efforts

intensifying when the creature rips up a suspension bridge and the military fires rockets at it, the explosions causing the alien to break into *several* Dogorae. In time, Munakata discovers that fluids from bees and wasps will cause the monster to crystallize, and the toxins are fired into the air via radar-like cannons. The aliens do indeed crystallize, raining their rock-like pieces to Earth (and crushing gangsters who are featured in a colossally inconsequential subplot).
Comment: Nobuo Nakamura stars as Munakata. Ishiro Honda directed from a script by Shinichi Sekizawa. The film was released in the United States in 1965 as *Dagora, The Space Monster*, the name changed lest the menace be perceived as a giant canine.

DREADNOUGHTS   (C)

First Appearance: *Strange Tales* #154, 1967, Marvel Comics.
Physical Description: The eight-foot robots are controlled by a 330 megabyte computer, can run 35 miles an hour, and possess enormous strength. They can also fire sharpened studs from the knuckles, deadly electrical bolts from horns on the sides of its head, and icy freon gas from the mouth. The bulk of the Dreadnoughts are all blue; the last one, built by the Maggia, is silver.
Biography: The first powerful robot was created by the evil organization Hydra to help with its plans of world conquest. It was first sent out to attack the airborne Hell-carrier of S.H.I.E.L.D. (Supreme Headquarters International Espionage Law-enforcement Division), and to murder its executive director, Nick Fury. The robot is defeated, but the crime family known as the Maggia steals the blueprints and builds a small force of its own Dreadnoughts.
Comment: The character was created by writer Roy Thomas and artist Jim Steranko.

D-7   (L, C, MP)

First Appearance: "Killdozer!" by Theodore Sturgeon, November 1944, *Astounding Science Fiction*.
Physical Description: D-7 is a bulldozer.
Biography: Ages ago, "a sentient cloudform, an intelligent group of tangible electrons" evolved in the machines built by a highly advanced race of humans. The mutant-run machines turned on the humans, and in the ensuing war everything was wiped out—save for one cloud. After hiding for

"turbulent eons," it was found, worshiped, and given its own temple by an island-dwelling tribe before the Ice Age. Centuries later, during World War II, a team of American construction workers comes to the Pacific island, "west of the archipelago called Islas Revillagigeda," to build a landing strip. While bulldozing a stretch of land, they uncover the temple and inadvertently release the cloud.

The sentient force slips into the bulldozer, which is nicknamed Daisy Etta (derived from the Spanish for D-7, De Siete), and it begins attacking humans. One man's back is broken by the bucking machine, and foreman Tom Jaeger is badly hurt before he can destroy the transmission. After another man is electrocuted while trying to repair it, Jaeger forbids anyone to go near the D-7. But that doesn't matter: The machine comes to life, runs down workers, and tears up the camp. One man, Al Knowles, snaps and throws in his lot with the machine, offering to help it if it will spare him. Al's coworkers are forced to bind him before he can do any harm.

Eventually, using himself as bait, Jaeger leads the D-7 to water. Using an extension cord, he hooks the bulldozer to a heavy duty welding machine; another man turns on the power and electrocutes the rogue earthmover. However, even as the D-7 shudders and dies, Jaeger sees "a slight wave of motion away from the fuel tank . . . an area of six or seven square inches literally *blurred* around the edges."

Comment: The story was adapted to comic books in Marvel Comics' *Worlds Unknown* #6, 1973.

The novella was also the basis for a made-for-TV movie that aired in 1974 and stars Clint Walker, Carl Betz, Neville Brand, and Robert Urich; Jerry London directed from a teleplay by Sturgeon and Ed MacKillop.

DUCKBOTS (C)

First Appearance: *Duckbots* #1, 1987, Blackthorne Comics.

Physical Description: Each of the Duckbots is approximately 30 feet tall and is humanoid, save for a duck head and webbed feet. Brant is covered with silver armor, wears a blue cowl and yellow boots and fires a heat ray from his palm; Merganser has a bullet-like blue helmet, blue armor, and a golden chest, "trunks," and boots; and Widgeon has golden armor and a black and white cowl. All three wear dark-tinted visors. All three metal fowl can fly.

Biography: For years, Dr. Francis Drake of Drake Industries has been working on the S.D.I. for the

The imposing *Duckbots*. Art by Chas Gillen. © Blackthorne Publishing.

government, under the assumption that it stood for Strategic Duck Initiative. When he presents the three giant duckbots to the government, they laugh at him; quacking up, Drake programs the robots "to perform wanton acts of evil destruction." Their first wanton act is to "squish!!!" Drake to a pulp, after which they go on a destructive rampage, defeating even the superhero Mr. Wonderful.

Merganser was programmed to be the most evil of the trio.

Comment: The characters were created by writer Cliff MacGillivray and drawn by Chas Gillen. They appeared in just two issues of their comic book.

DUKE "DESTROYER" DUCK (C)

First Appearance: *Destroyer Duck*, 1982, Eclipse Comics.

Physical Description: The duck has the body of a human bodybuilder, with a duck's head and feet and a covering of white down. He wears trousers, a T-shirt, and a green wool cap.

Biography: A construction worker on a world of anthropomorphic animals, Duke decides to find "somethin' more appealin' " in life. He spends time in the special forces, then goes to college and graduates magna cum laude with degrees in criminology, abnormal psychology, and physical education. He becomes a detective and is shocked when a duck (implicitly, HOWARD THE DUCK) staggers into his office after having been sucked "into another space-time continuum . . . wh-where ducks can't t-talk . . . and *pink primates* c-call all . . . the shots!" He damns a greedy multinational company known as Godcorp and then expires, leaving Duke to avenge his death. Entering a "nega-space" ship, Duke comes to our world, kills Godcorp boss Ned Packer, then remains behind to right other wrongs on our sick world.

Comment: The character was created by writer Steve Gerber and artist Jack Kirby; Eclipse published seven issues of the comic book through 1984. The title was conceived to raise money for a lawsuit between Gerber and Marvel Comics (i.e., Godcorp) regarding ownership of Howard the Duck. A "mutually agreeable" settlement eventually was reached.

DUKE OF OIL (C)

First Appearance: *Outsiders* #6, 1986, DC Comics.

Physical Description: Though the Duke stands six-foot-six in his "natural" form, the robot can stretch and bend to virtually any shape. He can also plug into and operate other machines.

Biography: When Earl Dukestone is severely injured in an explosion at one of his oil wells, his brain is saved and placed in a robot body by scientists working for the criminal group Skull. The team informs him that they're working to clone his human form and promise to transfer his brain when their work is completed, provided he cut them in for a share of his wealth. Earl agrees and, to help them along, he sneaks into the headquarters of the superhero team the Outsiders to steal scientific data. During the ensuing battle, Earl discovers that he does not, in fact, have his human brain, but simply computer circuits to which his memories have been transferred. This realization causes Earl to snap, and he gives himself over to crime as the Duke of Oil. Though he was last seen

falling into the Pacific Ocean, he will surely return.

Comment: The Outsiders—Black Lightning, Metamorpho, Geo-Force, Katana, Looker, Halo, Atomic Knight, Windfall, and Dr. Helga Jace—are all Earthborn humans.

DUO DAMSEL (C)

First Appearance: *Action Comics* #276, 1961, DC Comics.

Physical Description: As Triplicate Girl, Luornu wears a purple bodyshirt, miniskirt, orange cape and belt, and white boots, and splits into three identical but independent selves. As Duo Damsel, she wears a bodysuit, purple on the left, orange on the right, with a purple glove on the right hand and an orange glove on the left (for a while, she also wears a yellow cape and belt and yellow thigh boots with orange spots). When she splits into two identical beings, one is dressed in an all-orange bodysuit, the other all-purple.

In either identity, whatever one of her "split" forms learns, the heroine learns when they merge. She can fly thanks to her Legion flight ring.

Biography: Luornu Durgo is a middle-30th-century native of Cargg, a world with a triple sun. Carggians can split into three bodies and, seeking adventure, Luornu comes to Earth and battles crime as Triplicate Girl, the first noncharter member of the Legion of Super-Heroes. Though she loses one of her bodies in a showdown with COMPUTO THE CONQUEROR, she continues to fight evildoers as Duo Damsel, then marries Chuck Taine, a.k.a. the former Legionnaire Bouncing Boy, and retires to become a teacher at the Legion Academy. Their son has Luornu's triplicate powers.

Comment: Triplicate Girl became Duo Damsel in *Adventure Comics* #341, 1966. She was cocreated by Editor Mort Weisinger and writer Jerry Siegel, cocreator of *Superman*.

DYNOMUTT (TV, C)

First Appearance: *Scooby Doo/Dynomutt Hour*, September 1976, ABC.

Physical Description: According to his theme song, the gray robot dog is "stronger than a train with a so-so brain, he's fearless, scareless, a little too careless." Dynomutt stands approximately four feet tall on his hind legs (though he usually walks on all-fours) and wears a green costume he calls his "wonder wear": a cowl, short cape, boots, gloves, and a blue harness with a yellow "D" on the front.

Dynomutt seems to possess an endless supply of gadgets and abilities, including a "strength power pack" in his belt, the ability to stretch his arms, legs, neck, and body to great lengths and at any angle, to use his head as a battering ram, and to coil his tail and use it as a pogo stick. His legs contain "dyno springs" to cushion his falls, he has a "dyno-automatic defrost cycle" to protect him from the cold, in his back are a jet engine and a helicopter-like rotor for hovering, and he's also equipped with a hacksaw, scissors, an electric shaver, suction-cup feet for climbing sheer walls, "dyno gift wrap" arms that allow him to bind a foe, sonar, a spotlight nose, long metal tentacles that extend from a compartment in his chest, a parachute (backup for his spring feet?), and a slot in his head for an additional power pack that will boost his strength or size.

By pressing the "D" emblem on his chest, Dynomutt can activate a tool chest, a communicator, a TV, a "mirrormatic" shelf for reflecting enemy rays, a "dyno dynamic automatic ice maker," and even the yellow pages. Dynomutt's controls are located in a panel in his back. If anyone tries to tinker with them, a "dyno-antitheft circuit" activates a pincer, which grabs the bad guy. The canine robot is also a dog of a thousand faces, able to transform himself into a fishing rod, chair, vacuum cleaner, and other objects.

Biography: Dynomutt is the fumbling sidekick to the costumed superhero Blue Falcon, who fights crime in Big City. When they're not on the job, they live in a penthouse apartment known as the Falcon Lair, where a mysterious figure known as Focus One can reach them whenever there's trouble.

The two patrol the city in the flying Falcon Car, which they keep hidden beneath a pool in the penthouse. It's Dynomutt's job to get it out while the Falcon puts on his costume; typically, the dog forgets to drain the pool, giving new meaning to the term "bucket seats."

The duo's foes have included the Harbor Robber, the giant robot Tin Kong, the Injustice League of America, the Wizard of Ooze, Mr. Mastermind, and the Queen Hornet.

Comment: Frank Welker provided the dog's voice in the 16 half-hour cartoons, which have shown up on other series since the original show went off the air. Gary Owens was the voice of the Blue Falcon.

Marvel Comics published six issues of *Dynomutt* from 1976 to 1978. The character also appeared in Marvel's *Scooby Doo* #1–9, 1977–79, and in their *Laff-a-lympics* #1–13, 1978–79.

E

EGO (C)

First Appearance: *Journey into Mystery* #132, 1966, Marvel Comics.

Physical Description: The planet is 4,165 miles in diameter—just over half that of Earth—and it has what looks like a human face, including a beard, on one side. Ego absorbs energy from stars or living beings, and can digest solid matter in the equivalent of a stomach. It can unleash stored energy as powerful psionic blasts and also creates humanoid figures, "antibodies," which protect it from invasion or can be used to invade other worlds.

Biography: Ego is born in the Black Galaxy in what is presumed to be the normal accretion process of planet-building. However, native sentience somehow evolves and, in time, the world decides to expand its sphere of influence by conquering other worlds. Its first such attempt is thwarted by the Thunder God Thor, who creates a worldwide storm that leaves Ego winded; not long thereafter, Ego is attacked by the planet-consuming GALACTUS, and Thor helps Ego fend off the attack. All might have been well thereafter had not a Rigellian scientist taken a small sample of Ego to see if it can be used to make other planets fruitful. Not only does the segment become the megalomaniacal Ego-Prime, which expends its energy and vanishes in a battle with the superheroic Young Gods, but Ego goes mad, implicitly from the loss of Ego-Prime, part of its world-mind. It is up to Thor, Galactus, and others to battle the insane planet before it can cause widespread destruction. Eventually, Galactus manages to attach a propulsion unit to the planet and sends it hurtling into uninhabited space. However, Ego figures out how to control the unit mentally and heads for Earth, seeking vengeance. Reed Richards of the Fantastic Four is able to rig the planet's propulsion unit to carry it toward the sun, where it disintegrates; yet the wily Ego is able to will itself back together, propulsion unit and all, and it survives to this day.

Comment: Ego was created by writer Stan Lee and artist Jack Kirby.

Though the magazine was called *Journey Into Mystery* in the indicia for legal reasons, the title on the front was *The Mighty Thor*.

THE EIGHT MAN (C, TV)

First Appearance: "The Eight Man," April 1963, *Shonen* magazine (Japan).

Physical Description: The robot wears a dark blue helmet and trunks and has a white "8" on his dark blue chest; the rest of his uniform is white.

The Eight Man has enormous strength and can fly "faster than a rocket, swifter than a jet." His artificial, skin can be molded into any likenss; he keeps up his strength with tablets stored in his belt buckle.

Biography: When Detective Rachiro Azuma is murdered by members of the Mukade criminal organization, Dr. Tani puts the law officer's memory into the body of an android he has finally perfected (after seven failures). Azuma goes to work as a private detective, his secret identity known only to Tani and Police Chief Tanaka; even the hero's aides Ichiro and Sachiko do not know who he is when he strips off his civilian clothes.

Comment: Though the character's magazine adventures ceased in 1966, he is seen in a series of Japanese cartoons that debuted in the United States in September 1965 as *The Eighth Man*. In the dubbed versions, the hero's name is Peter Brady, the criminal organization is known as Intercrime, it's Professor Genius who puts the hero's memory into the body of a robot named Tobor, and the Eighth Man reports to Chief Fumblethumbs of the Metropolitan International Police Force.

THE ELDERS (C)

First Appearance: *The Avengers* #28, 1966, Marvel Comics (see *Comment*).

Physical Description: The Elders are all humanoid, though each belongs to a different race and they range from the five-foot Contemplator to the seven-foot-one Gardener. The thickly muscled Grandmaster and the lanky Champion are blue-skinned, Runner is yellow-skinned, and Trader is purple-skinned.

Biography: Each of the Elders hails from races that evolved in the first galaxies that coalesced after the Big Bang, and each is the last surviving member of their race. Through advanced technology, they have rendered themselves immortal and have created ships by which to travel through the cosmos and some to alternate dimensions. The Elders appear to be vulnerable only to boredom (which is how the Collector's wife Matani perished) and, as a result, each pursues his chosen hobby with zeal.

The eight known Elders are: the Champion, a.k.a. Tryco Slatterus from the Ancrindo Nebula, who is committed to attaining physical perfection and mastering all the known forms of hand-to-hand combat in the universe; the Collector, Taneleer Tivan from Cygnus X-1, who is devoted to amassing and preserving specimens of life from everywhere in the universe, to ensure the survival of all beings; the Contemplator, Tath Ki from the Coal Sack Nebula, who lives to meditate and to exist in complete harmony with the cosmos; the Gardener, Ord Zyonyz of galaxy M-77, who brings beauty by cultivating flora wherever he goes; the Grandmaster, En Dwi Gast, birthplace unknown, who journeys through the cosmos learning and playing games, and staging high-stakes tournaments; the Runner, the gleaming man from the stars about whom little is known; and the Possessor, Kamo Thamn, birthworld unknown, who has gathered knowledge from all corners of existence and stored it in a library/university on the planet Rus. Thamn has devoted a good part of his time to studying (and lost his grip on sanity because of) the mysterious Runestaff, which was found by one of his researchers and has powers beyond comprehension.

The Trader thrives on commerce; his origins are unknown.

Comment: *The Avengers* #28 marked the first appearance of the Collector. Grandmaster first appeared in *Avengers* #69, Gardener in *Marvel Team-Up* #55, Contemplator in *Marvel Treasury Special* #1, Possessor in *Thor* #235, Champion in *Marvel Two-In-One Annual* #7, Runner in *Defenders* #143, and Trader in *Silver Surfer* #5.

THE ELECTRONIC CHICKEN (L)

First Appearance: "The Self-Priming Solid-State Electronic Chicken" by Jon Lucas, 1970, *The Magazine of Fantasy and Science Fiction* #231.

Physical Description: The machine consists of a "calcium-compound sprayer," a "mold chamber," and makes an egg every 65 seconds "or oftener if you turn the grade switch from AA to A or even B." There's also a "New-Laid Flavor" additive.

Biography: Emerson J. Minnick of Petaluma, California, invents an egg-making machine and submits it to John Wallen of Genius Inventions, Inc.—a con man who charges him patent and development fees. However, Wallen's partner, Richard Sanders, builds the egg machine and it actually works. Wallen and Sanders plan to market the device when Sanders notices that the light in his refrigerator won't go off. He finds a "strong electrical field" coming from the eggs and realizes that they contain tiny aliens from a place "where it's dark and cold and the light and cold in the fridge is just right to hatch them." They've been controlling Minnick for who knows how long, and now take Sanders (and presumably Wallen) prisoner. However, one of the men is able to write a message inside an eggshell, which ends up in a Los Angeles kitchen and warns people "If the light in your fridge stays on . . . break all your eggs before it's too late!"

Comment: Lucas wrote occasionally for *The Magazine of Fantasy and Science Fiction* in the late 1960s–early 1970s.

ELEMENT LAD (C)

First Appearance: *Adventure Comics* #307, 1963.

Physical Description: Original: white leotard, belt, collar, armbands, black trunks, and pink boots and bodyshirt. Second: blue bodysuit, green thighs, waist, forearms, and upward-pointing arrow on chest. Third: black bodysuit, red thigh boots, and red "barbell" design on his chest. Like all non-flying Legionnaires, he has a flight ring.

Biography: Jan Arrah was born on the planet Trom, whose natives can transmute matter. In the middle 30th century, the space pirate Roxxas demands the planet's help in his plans of conquest; the inhabitants refuse, and in a fit of rage Roxxas orders his fleet to destroy everyone on the world. Jan survives, however, and comes to Earth, where he helps the Legion of Super-Heroes defeat the villain. Afterwards, Jan remains on Earth to serve with the Legion as Element Lad, their 19th member.

Comment: The character was cocreated by editor Mort Weisinger and noted science fiction writer Edmond Hamilton.

THE ELLEN STUART (L)

First Appearance: *Treasure of the Black Falcon* by John Coleman Burroughs, 1967, Ballantine Books.

Physical Description: Designed by Phillip Montague, the "advanced underwater salvage vessel" can reach depths of at least 3,500 fathoms, which would squeeze an "ordinary armor-protected . . . [submarine] to pulp." It has a "closed-cycle engine" that recycles its own exhaust and propels the ship at a cruising speed of 20 knots; a large "plastic-glass, cone-shaped bubble" completely encircling the control room; and smaller "cone-shaped duro-glass" portholes. There is a "full array of powerful searchlights," from fore to aft on either side as well as topside and bottom. Steel flood doors protect different areas of the "great ship," whose dimensions are not provided. (The cover illustration shows a sleek, flat ship approximately 150 feet long, with four long, spindly legs for resting on the seabed.)

Its crew consists of Montague, Captain Dirk Gordon, Lt. Von Benson—a salvage expert—Chief Engineer "Pigeon" Ellis, Dr. Kingsley, Chief Mechanic David Hill, Quartermaster Andre "Frenchy" Dumas, radio operator Willoughby, cook Mr. Flobs, battery room chief Wicks, salvage hand Sgt. Harry Grube, coxswain Packard, stowaway Bucky, and Montague's fiancee Ellen Stuart.

Biography: On September 3, 1947, the great submarine and its crew of war veterans descends into the North Atlantic to find the merchantman *Black Falcon*, which, under the command of Ellen's ancestor Roger, went down 182 years before with its cargo of gold, jewels, and gems. Its two companion ships were also sunk. En route, they collide with crags, floodwaters drown Bucky, and the ship is stopped while they repair the hull. Soon thereafter, Bucky is seen swimming outside the ship; later, just his living head is seen. Meanwhile, they find the *Black Falcon*. Ellen goes off on her own and encounters a huge, pulsating "brain . . . a grayish-white jelly-like mass with a criss cross pattern of blood vessels on its surface." Elsewhere,

Dirk Gordon, Von Benson, and David Hill find the treasure, but it's stolen before they can collect it all; they do notice footprints nearby.

Back on the *Ellen Stuart*, Phil has gone mad with wartime flashbacks, thinking his friends are Nazis. He dies, and the autopsy reveals that his brain is gone, replaced by "membranes . . . of alien composition." Kingsley believes an organism entered the submarine when it hit the jagged rock, and both took over Phil and reanimated Bucky. Back outside the ship, Dirk and Kingsley follow the footprints. They encounter sundry sea monsters and then a giant crater surrounded by a multiple-geyser-generated bubble of air that keeps the water out, though the men are able to push in. There are animals, jungle growth, a river—and a city with humans who communicate telepathically, are made of "jelly-like flesh," and are equipped with gills. Roger Stuart, ancient Romans, and people from sunken ships of all periods are among them. The explorers discover that these are "Jogulars," bizarre duplicates of the originals created by the organism that reanimated Bucky and took over Phil. (It isn't revealed whether the Jogulars are native to Earth or whether they were brought here by the meteor that created the crater.) After political intrigue and combat among the Jogulars, the surviving crewmembers remain in the underwater city, Dirk and Ellen having fallen in love.

Comment: This paperback original was written by the son of famed author Edgar Rice Burroughs.

See also BARSOOM.

EMANUEL (L)

First Appearance: *Monte Cristo #99* by John Jakes, 1970, Curtis Books.

Physical Description: Indistinguishable from a human, Emanuel stands "slightly over six feet" with a "somewhat swarthy" cast to his skin, which is made of "well articulated . . . pseudo-cellular material." His brain contains "the total knowledge of civilization" and he can "quote any book penned since the dawn of written history."

The green-eyed Emanuel is able to experience three emotions: love, fear, and hate. He does not sleep and cannot be "rendered unconscious." Breathing is simulated because it makes him appear "more lifelike." His expected lifespan is "several thousand years."

Biography: In the Earth-settled Martian village Tkak, C. Amunssen builds 97 robots, all of which fail. Finally, he builds two that are immortal: ninety-eight and ninety-nine. Ninety-eight perishes in an accident on the moon—a big surprise to ninety-nine, since he was supposed to be invulnerable—and, in the year 2116, the latter is sold as a servant to powerful magnate Don Pedro Dax and his wife Jeannie. Named Emanuel by Dax, he promptly falls in love with their daughter Isabel. She reciprocates his affection, and when she dies in an accidental fall from a balcony on Mars, Dax wrongly blames Emanuel. As punishment, he has the robot chained and buried alive in the sands of Mars.

Erosion frees Emanuel in 3220, and he meets the purple-eyed girl Siri, who tells him that Earth is deserted, Mars nearly so. Still, Emanuel is determined to wreak vengeance on the Dax family. Possessing all of his creator's secrets, he sets about building a robot army in the mountains of Mars. His first effort is an "impossibly ugly, misshapen . . . short-armed, short-legged servant" named Adam. But he refines the process and builds two human-like androids a month for the next 639 years. By 3869, after "buying, selling" (he doesn't say what), he is wealthy and powerful and settled in Nuovo Venetzia, the largest city on the planet Betelgeuse Prima. Going by the name of Edmond Emanuel, he wrests a fortune from Dax scion Rodirigo and is finally invited to meet his enemy. Dax reveals that he has done some investigating of his own and discovered who and what Emanuel is. And he has something for the robot—a flask of chemicals that will eat his "styrene body to nothing." He throws it, but Emanuel avoids the liquid and knocks Rodirigo out a window. He falls 301 floors to his death.

Emanuel is tried and freed, then learns from an Amunssen biography that his creator was superstitious and had skipped number thirteen. Thus, ninety-seven wasn't invulnerable, *he* is ninety-eight—and he learns that Siri, who is still alive, is ninety-nine. He finds her and they prepare to spend the rest of their existence together.

Comment:　Jakes was a prolific, underrated science fiction author before he entered the mainstream with his bestselling *Kent Family Chronicles* in the middle 1970s.

EMPEROR DAPHNE　(TC)

First Appearance:　*Uranus Strikes*, 1986, "Ting."

Physical Description:　Like all Uranians, Daphne has four arms ending in three-fingered hands, two horse-like legs, and a barracuda-like head. Daphne's thick orange hair is worn Mohawk-style and is roughly a yard high, some three times longer than other Uranians. Daphne wears a purple leotard.

Uranians "propagate, like earthly fungus, in damp areas."

Biography:　Uranus has been dying for centuries, so the Uranians board a fleet of flying saucers and head for Earth armed with a Climatose bomb to "recreate the atmospheric environment . . . for Uranian habitation . . . [and] wipe out all indigenous life forms." Unfortunately, the inept aliens bomb the moon instead of Earth, and must accomplish their goal through more savage means. They use "vaporay" guns to blast earthlings and employ a "Magnajector" to enlarge terrestrial bugs 100,000-fold, but the humans don't give up. They move to the Southern Hemisphere and booby-trap the Northern Hemisphere with nuclear weapons, which they trigger when the Uranians try to settle there. They also counterattack Uranus and Daphne goes mad, playing a fiddle while his cities burn; he is killed by a bullet to the head.

Comment:　The 36-card set is a delightful parody of the *Mars Attacks* cards, a 55-card set issued by Topps in 1962. Those full-color, painted cards feature spindly-limbed, large-brained Martians and are infamous for their explicit gore and spectacular violence.

THE EMPYRIAN　(TV)

First Appearance:　"Second Chance," March 1964, *The Outer Limits*, ABC.

Physical Description:　The husky humanoid is covered with feathers that form a grille-like pattern on its torso. It has wing-like arms and a bearded face, deepset eyes, a large nose, and a coma-like spray of hair atop its widow's peak.

Biography:　Given passes to the spaceship attraction at the Joyland amusement park, a group of people are startled when the vessel actually takes off. At the controls is a being from Empyria, who says he selected them, people "with the least to lose," to settle Tythra. The Earth-like world is on a collision course with Empyria and will strike in 82 years, knocking Empyria from its orbit and sending it straight toward Earth. The Empyrians feel that if Tythra were colonized, and the colonists were to cooperate with them, the disasters can be avoided. Only one passenger is pleased with the prospects: the attraction's "captain," out-of-work astrophysicist Dave Crowell. When Crowell takes the Empyrian's side, his fellow humans try to kill him and the Empyrian has to save him. In the end, Crowell persuades their host to return them to Earth, make

The *Empyrian* from TV's *The Outer Limits*. © United Artists Entertainment.

his case publicly, and populate Tythra with volunteers. The Empyrian agrees (and in the script, though not the show, the volunteers *do* come).

Comment: Simon Oakland stars as the alien, with Don Gordon as Crowell. The show was directed by Paul Stanley from a script by Lin Dane (Sonya Roberts) and Lou Morheim.

THE ENERGOIDS (C)

First Appearance: "Love Is a Many Tentacled Thing," 1981, *1994* #21, Warren Publishing Co.

Physical Description: Standing approximately five feet tall, the gray-skinned creatures have stocky, slug-like bodies that feel like "calcified jelly," two stubby legs, three short tentacles on each side, a lumpy mass for a head, two long antennae, small bright eyes and a large mouth.

The Energoids are "like walking reactors . . . periodically they must undergo fission" or they will explode. They have the ability to "space-slip . . . convert their bodies to pure energy and traverse both time and space." This siphons off excess energy, as does transforming, changing from their "blob-like state" to the human likenesses they prefer.

Energoids cannot reproduce, as the energy released by lovemaking would be enough to "destroy a planet."

Biography: On the fourth planet from the sun, "a universe away," a nuclear holocaust has produced a mutant species, the Energoids. The human survivors fear the mutants and hunt them down; one, Edgar, space-slips to Earth and falls in love with lonely Earthwoman Margaret, with whom he mates. Unknown to him, she absorbs his radioactivity and is transformed into an Energoid. He leaves, realizes he has fallen in love with her, and returns. Because Margaret has retained her human form, he doesn't know she's been transformed: When he crawls into the bed and takes her, half asleep, the Earth explodes.

Comment: There are no credits for the story.

EON (C)

First Appearance: *Captain Marvel* #29, 1973, Marvel Comics.

Physical Description: Approximately 20 feet tall, Eon resembles a thick tree with a Jim Morrison haircut. It has a single arm, one eye on the left, and a face (with two eyes) on the right side, along with a complex series of roots.

Biography: Reportedly the offspring of ETERNITY, Eon observes our universe (and apparently others as well) from another dimension. Nearly as old as creation itself, Eon senses and/or sees danger when it threatens civilizations or worlds and provides equipment or knowledge to champions so they can meet and defeat it. Sometimes, this tinkering is overt, sometimes it's subconscious. It was Eon, for example, who influenced Captain Mar-Vell to become a superhero and KREE defector. More recently, he has taken the Earth hero Quasar under his branch.

Comment: The character was created by artist Jim Starlin.

ERMA FELNA (C)

First Appearance: *Albedo* #0, 1985, Thoughts and Images.

Physical Description: Erma is a humanoid cat who wears a variety of sleek uniforms.

Biography: Flight Commander Erma Felna is the leader of a unit in the Extraplanetary Defense Force, the military arm of the planet-colonizing government ConFed. When the ConFed planet Derzon is invaded, Erma leads her troops in a successful defense, though she is wounded and successful defense, though she is wounded and sent to the planet Ekosiak to recover. There, she learns of a fomenting rebellion. Returning to duty, she and her superior, the fox Colonel Hitzok, find and defuse a terrorist's nuclear bomb in the heart of the city of Hicho, then combat a revolt of animals who resent ConFed's military presence on the world. This time it's Hitzok who's wounded, and Erma is given command of the Home Guard Troops to deal with the still-seething rebellion.

Other soldier-animals in the strip include the otter Dael Valderzha, the duck Colonel Jones, and the horse Captain Itzak Arrat, who is the commander of an EDF space destroyer and whose adventures among the ore-thieves in the Chishata Asteroid Belt comprise a major subplot of the epic.

Comment: The serialized saga was created by Steven A. Gallacci and appeared in all 15 issues of the comic book. It was reprinted in *Command Review* in 1987. Erna's adventures continue today in Antarctic Publishing's *Albedo Anthropomorphics*.

E.T. (MP, L)

First Appearance: *E.T. The Extraterrestrial*, 1982, Universal Pictures.

Physical Description: The wrinkled, brown-skinned alien has a simian muzzle, two wideset blue eyes—deepset beneath heavy brows—and no forehead. It has a wide, virtually lipless mouth and can speak English. The alien's brain lies in the wide, long cranium behind its face. It has a long neck that can be withdrawn so its head rests on its shoulders, reducing its height from approximately five feet to three. The creature's long arms end in hands with four long, slender fingers; the index finger lights up and heals whatever it touches. E.T. has a doughy, humanoid body resting on two stubby legs. Each foot has three toes. The alien's "heart-light" glows when it experiences emotions ranging from fear to joy. E.T. can levitate itself and other objects, and communicate telepathically. When E.T. gets drunk, both it and its young friend Elliott feel the alcohol's effects.

According to *E.T. The Book of the Green Planet*, aliens older than E.T., in "the late second growth stage," are taller and "elegantly slender." E.T.s reproduce asexually.

The alien spaceship resembles a Faberge Egg some 30 feet tall, with an external bank of spotlights around the center and four thin legs. A ramp lowers from the bottom of the ship to allow ingress.

Biography: Five alien botanists land in the hills outside of Los Angeles to collect plant specimens.

When an alien hunter named Keys and his party arrive, the E.T.s take off—leaving behind one who has wandered off to look at the lights of the city. Stranded, the E.T. hides in a suburban garage where he is found by a 10-year-old soul mate, Elliott. The boy lures the alien out with Reese's Pieces candies and hides it in his bedroom closet. Elliott reveals the alien's presence to his older brother Michael and younger sister Gertie (and dog Harvey), and helps it to build a satellite dish and transmitter to "phone home" for a rescue ship. Single mother Mary is oblivious to the visitor's presence until Keys and his team arrive and quarantine the house. Not wanting to be studied, the alien feigns death but "returns" to life when Elliott pays his last respects. With E.T. in the handlebar basket of his bicycle, Elliott and his friends race to the coordinates where the ship is due to meet him; when the government agents try to stop them, E.T. levitates the bicycles and flies them to the site. After a tearful goodbye, E.T. boards his ship and heads home.

Comment: Henry Thomas stars as Elliott, with Drew Barrymore as Gertie, Robert McNaughton as Michael, Dee Wallace as Mary, and Peter Coyote as Keyes. Small persons Tamara de Treaux and Pat Bilson, and legless Matthew de Merritt acted in the E.T. costume (with mechanical attachments created by Carlo Rambaldi). Actress Debra Winger provided the alien's voice. The film was directed by Steven Spielberg from a script by Melissa Mathison. It remains the top-grossing film in U.S. movie history; internationally, it is number two, behind Spielberg's *Jurassic Park* (1993).

William Kotzwinkle wrote the novelization for Berkley Books. He also wrote the 1985 sequel *E.T. The Book of the Green Planet*, based on a story by Spielberg. It picks up where the film left off, with E.T.—Botanist First Class—and his shipmates soaring away from the Blue Planet. They arrive on the Green Planet (also known as Vomestra, Brodo Asogi, Od-Di-Pa 5, Tum Lux O-ty, and Alata Zerka), where plant life flourishes "as on no other planet in the world" (sic). After a reunion with his Parent and his Flopglopple—a 600-vertebraed creature with a tripodal arrangement of feet—E.T. goes back to work, looking after plants in the agricultural fields and reporting to Botanicus, Supreme Scientist and Lord of the Fields. He also reacquaints himself with Micron, a Micro Tech—a 15-centimeter tall, "nearly transparent" humanoid robot with countless hair-like fingers for "microscopically detailed work."

Meanwhile, back on Earth, Elliott is now a teenager, due to the time warping E.T. used to get home. E.T. misses his friend, and senses he's in danger as he makes the transition to "man." He sends a diminutive, telepathic "replicant" to Earth, but it fails to make contact with Elliott. As the young Earthling struggles through first love and encounters with bullies, E.T. struggles to help him telepathically while dealing with his own growth on the Green Planet.

ETERNIA (TV, C, MP)

First Appearance: *Masters of the Universe*, September 1982, Filmation Studios, syndication.
Physical Description: Eternia is a medieval, Earth-like world that exists on a different dimensional plane, "far from Earth in time and space," a world where magic and technology exist side-by-side. Though the world is identical to ours, its flora and fauna have evolved along somewhat different lines, producing sea serpents, brutish half-humans like the shaggy four-armed Glorm, and other monsters. Eternia is a world of extremes: On the one hand, there are the dread Sea of Blackness "where the sun never shines," while there are also "places of lush wonder and beauty."
Biography: Prince Adam, the son of King Randor and Queen Marlena of Eternia, is the owner of the amazing Power Sword. Not only is it the key to Castle Grayskull—whose magic makes its "landlord" rightful ruler of the world—but whenever Adam raises the blade and chants, "By the power of Grayskull!" he becomes He-Man, endowed with incredible strength. His cowardly cat Cringer becomes the fierce Battle Cat. Meanwhile, ensconced on Snake Mountain, He-Man's nemesis, the evil Skeletor, seeks to obtain the sword and become the ruler of Eternia.

Also fighting the forces of evil is Adam's sister Princess Adora, who lives on the world of Etheria and becomes the equally powerful She-Ra.
Comment: The series ran for three years, with John Erwin as the voice of He-Man, Melendy Britt as She-Ra, and Alan Oppenheimer as Skeletor. The actors repeated their roles in the animated theatrical feature *The Secret of the Sword* (1985) and in Filmation's syndicated series *She-Ra: Princess of Power*, which debuted in 1985.

Mattel produced the action figure line that debuted at the same time as the series, and included comic books produced by DC Comics in the packages. DC also teamed He-Man and Superman in *DC Comics Presents* #47 (1982) and published a three-issue *Masters of the Universe* miniseries in 1983.

In the 1987 motion picture, Dolph Lundgren was He-Man with Frank Langella as Skeletor.

The Meteorbs was another alien race that was part of the Masters of the Universe line. Introduced in 1985, they were brought to Eternia by a meteor shower, along with the sword-swinging Comet Warriors. These egg-like orbs unhinged to form a variety of creatures. The heroes: the robotic Cometroid, the cat Ty-Grrr, Astro Lion, the panther Comet Cat, and the mammoth Tuskor. The villains: the apatosaur Dinosorb, Crocobite, Rhiorb, Orbear, and Gore-illa.

ETERNITY (C)

First Appearance: *Strange Tales* #138, 1965, Marvel Comics.
Physical Description: Humanoid in outline, with a cloak and high collar and the hint of a face, Eternity is actually a sentient boundary. It is unimaginably large, its insides full of stars, planets, and nebulae.
Biography: Eternity, which came into being through unknown means, is the sum of the consciousness of every living thing in creation. It does not judge or interfere, but merely imparts—typically, to the mystical superhero Dr. Strange—whatever wisdom or insights it has acquired.
Comment: The character was created by writer Stan Lee and artist Steve Ditko, and has appeared in various Marvel titles over the years.

EWOKS (MP, L, C, R, CS, TV)

First Appearance: *Return of the Jedi*, 1983, Twentieth Century-Fox.
Physical Description: Standing an average of one meter tall, the Ewoks are Teddy bear-like bipeds who speak in a fluid, high-pitched tongue. Spunky and agile, the forest-dwelling Ewoks are excellent warriors with spears, bow and arrow, vines, and the like.
Biography: The Ewoks live in tribes, building rustic cities high in the tall trees of the forest moon of Endor. The little creatures have based an intricate religion around these trees, which they believe are powerful, sentient beings.

Ewoks who feature prominently in the chronicles include Batcheela, an aged female and the mother of Teebo and Malani; Chukha-Trok, a bold woodsman; Deej, the warrior-husband of Shodu and the father of Weechee, Wicket, Willy, and Winda; Erpham Warrick, the great-grandfather of Wicket and a legendary warrior; Kaink, a priestess;

Leeni, Mookiee, and Wiley, baby Ewoks (or "Wok-lings"); Logray, a warrior-turned-shaman; Lumat, a warrior and woodcutter; Malani, a young female in love with Wicket; Paploo, an unusually brash Ewok best known for stealing a speeder bike in the Battle of Endor; Teebo, a tribal leader, mystic, and poet; and Wicket W. Warrick, the most famous Ewok, an early ally of Princess Leia and instrumental in persuading his comrades to join the rebellion.

The Ewoks are said to be distantly related to the Wookiees. Certainly their pig-Latinish names are.

The Duloks are a slender, unclean, marsh-dwelling race related to the Ewoks. The Yuzzum are furry, sharp-fanged, long-legged creatures who are blood enemies of the Ewoks.

Comment: In some stories, Endor is the moon itself; in others, it's the planet the (nameless) moon orbits.

See also CHEWBACCA; MILLENNIUM FALCON; R2-D2 AND C3PO; Appendix E.

EXPLORER 12 (MP)

First Appearance: *Journey to the Seventh Planet*, 1961, Cinemagic and Alta Vista Production/ American International Pictures.
Physical Description: An interplanetary rocket ship, the *Explorer 12* has a two-tier bridge with small elevators between the levels. No mention is made of previous Explorers.
Biography: In 2001, the United Nations spaceship heads for Uranus with its crew of five, commanded by Captain Don Graham. As they descend, they fail to see the planet's dead surface turn lush; one crewmember is startled to find that it looks exactly like a place he knows on Earth. When they explore, however, the men find that the greenery is fake and that the landing area is surrounded by a force field. That night, other crewmembers are visited by people and see places from their past. Leaving the ship and passing through the barrier, they discover a giant Brain that informs them that just as it was able to draw on pleasant memories to please the crew (to what end is never explained), it can draw on their fears as well. True to its word, the Brain creates monsters to destroy them. Ultimately, the men freeze the Uranian with liquid oxygen and shatter it, making a reality of the destructive imperialism the alien apparently feared.
Comment: John Agar is Graham; the rest of the cast of the Danish film consists of locals. Sidney Pink directed from a screenplay by Ib Melchior, based on a story by Pink. Melchior's name is misspelled "Melchoir" on the poster.

EXPLORER II (L)

First Appearance: "Whatever Counts" by Frederik Pohl, June 1959, *Galaxy*.
Physical Description: Looking like "a child's tinker toy, jammed together any-old-fashion," this ship of the United Nations Exploration Commission is powered by "quick streams of electrons" fired backward from the flared exhausts of its tractor sphere. "Long parallel strands of steel cable" attach the sphere to the trailer, which looks like "a can of soup, but with lumps and cobwebby masses of wire" here and there: 43 antennae and periscopes, two shuttle craft, and a grappling unit in the nose.

Explorer II can travel at up to half light-speed and is not designed to fly in the atmosphere of any planet.
Biography: Captain Serrell takes *Explorer II* to the moon Aleph Four, circling the giant Aleph, to relieve the crew that had been left there by *Explorer I* when it was discovered 19 years before. The scout rocket descends and its five-man crew is captured by the Gormen—aliens from another sector of space, creatures who stand under four feet tall with two eyes, a "horny structure" on the chin for breathing, and flesh that hangs in folds "like the hide of a rhinoceros." Their presence is a surprise, since the first party had found no fauna of any kind, only cities left deserted by some presumably extinct race. When the shuttle doesn't report back, a second one is sent down with 11 colonists; they too are captured. As the Gormen study the humans, the humans learn that a large alien ship is coming to take them onboard, attack *Explorer II* orbiting Aleph "light-seconds" away, then carry them all to the planet Bes. When the ship arrives, the humans launch a carefully planned attack, seize the ship, and blast off. Ironically, the *Explorer II* nearly flees when Sorrell sees the ship, and the crew literally has to flag him down.
Comment: Pohl is one of the foremost science fiction authors and editors of this century.

"Whatever Counts" was superbly illustrated by Wally Wood. That same issue of *Galaxy* also contained a real curio: an entry from the *Galactick Almanack* on music from around the universe. Author Larry M. Harris came up with numerous unusual musicians and composers, such as Freem Freem of Dubhe IV, Wilrik Rotha Rotha Delk Shkulma Tik of Wolf XVI (and the composer of Tik's *Tock*), Ludwig Hrrshtk of Deneb III, and Barsak Gh. Therwent of Canopus XII. However, what was most unusual about the "extract" is it was illustrated by former *Mad* magazine artist Don Martin, whose odd-looking aliens are in a class by themselves.

See also HEECHEE.

EXTERMINATOR ONE AND EXTERMINATOR TWO (C)

First Appearance: *Eerie* #69, 1974, Warren Publishing Co.

Physical Description: Exterminator One is a blue-green humanoid robot with spindly arms and legs, an ovoid head with a dark visor and a mouthpiece that resembles an aviator's oxygen mask. He carries a rifle on his back and a string of hand grenades on a strap across his chest.

Exterminator One is linked to a computer named George, his body "a block and a half long" and able to control the robot at up to 150 miles away. Though the human brain can reason and pass information back to George, it is the computer who actually moves the robot's limbs.

Exterminator Two is identical to One, down to the waist. Instead of legs, he is attached to a tank-like vehicle with two treads, a communications dish, and other hi-tech devices. Exterminator Two weighs 3,000 pounds; it is not clear whether he is connected to George.

Biography: In the early 21st century, a national law is passed pronouncing that all couples must be "genetically fit" in order to have children. New Yorker Peter Orwell is deemed unfit (he never learns why), but he and his wife Susan have a child anyway; when it is born, Peter is arrested and sentenced to life imprisonment. After four years, he's offered a way out: His human brain will be placed in a robot body and he will become a criminal-hunting Exterminator One. He agrees to the operation in February of 2014, and his first assignment is to kill his daughter. He has no choice—she will be murdered one way or the other—and, holding her lovingly in his arms, he smothers her with a pillow.

After the girl's death, Exterminator One is sent to kill a wino—a shakedown run for the robot—and a hitman named Slaughter. But Slaughter hobbles the robot with bullets, then cripples him and moves in for the kill. As he's about to do so, Exterminator Two arrives. Exterminator One realizes that he, himself, was set up: He was sent out to be a target for the more advanced model. Fearful

An *Exterminator*—the very last of its kind. Art by Paul Neary.
© Warren Publishing Co.

that the Exterminators will one day conquer the world, Exterminator One uses his last ounce of strength and human will to destroy the new model with a hand grenade. Slaughter thanks the Exterminator by putting him out of his misery with a bullet in the brain.

In 2394, in a post-holocaust world, a young man named Karas is attacked in the woods by a race of evil, mutant Goblins known as the Ouphe, created by a scientist named Yaust. He is saved by an Exterminator who looks like Exterminator Two. The robot reveals that he is the last survivor of the Exterminator Force, whose primary mission was "to kill imperfect humans." Since there are so few humans left, and many mutants, he is devoted to saving "what's left" of humankind. Karas joins him and the two are ultimately triumphant.

Comment: The character was created by writer Bill DuBay and artist Paul Neary. Exterminator Two debuted in *Eerie* #64, 1975, is joined by Karas in #68, 1975, and the two defeat the Goblins and Yaust in #101, 1979.

See also STEELE.

F

FENRIS (L)

First Appearance: *Secret of the Lost Race* by Andre Norton, 1959, Ace Books.

Physical Description: Located in the Constellation of the Wolf, Fenris is the third world from the star Zeta Lupi. It is a rough world subject to "severe storms and nine months of freezing winter weather." Its one port is Siwaki; the area around it is "lunar in starkness." The other important town on Fenris is Sandi. Both are located in the center of the mining region.

The flora include a slate-blue, sponge-like growth that thickens with leaves in the non-winter months. The fauna are varied and include a giant quadrupedal cat/bear hybrid with large, multi-faceted eyes, a double row of fangs, and large paws with retractable claws. The mineral alibite and furs are the planet's only exports.

Hel is the first world out from Zeta Lupi, Loki the second.

Biography: An orphan raised in poverty in N'Yok, with no memory before the age of six, Joktar has become an adept thief. Running from the law, he boards the hyperspace ship *Griffin* and heads to Fenris, where he falls in with an outlaw band. Suddenly, and for reasons unknown to him, Joktar finds himself being sought by every law officer in the galaxy. Eventually, he is found and captured, and learns that he is the son of a human space explorer named Marson and an alien woman. When Marson returned after a time among these aliens, the Ffallians, he was murdered by xenophobes and the entire matter was covered up. The woman and child came to N'Yok; the woman died there of unknown causes and the child was "provided with a mental block" for his own protection.

In time, investigators looking into the history of the encounter learn that the Ffallians are ancient, spacefaring beings who, if they mate among themselves, produce only females; if they mate with some other humanoid race, they produce only males. These male offspring, like Joktar, can father either a male or female. The paranoid authorities have been pursuing Joktar for fear that the nearly extinct Ffallians will turn humans into breeding stock, multiplying while human numbers dwindle. Fortunately, the Ffallians have allies among the law officers, and one of them, Hogan, saves Joktar and allows him to live in peace.

Comment: The author, born Alice Mary Norton, is one of the most popular authors of adventure and young-adult science fiction. *Secret of the Lost Race* was published as *Wolf's Head* in England.

In Norse mythology, Fenrir or Fenris-wolf was a monster wolf, the son of the wicked god Loki.

FERENGI See DEEP SPACE NINE.

THE FIGHTING ARMENIAN (C)

First Appearance: *The Rook* #2, 1980, Warren Publishing.

Physical Description: The character stands approximately six feet tall and wears a bulletproof red bodysuit with a yellow "shield" design on the chest; blue and yellow trunks; and a yellow cape, belt, and boots. The costume is also inflatable, since the hero is not naturally muscular, even after his operation.

Most of the Armenian's organs are artificial, as is his hemo-fibric polyurethane skin and polyfiber musculature.

Biography: After viewing a "decadent American television show," Soviet scientists decide to turn a human into a superhuman using artificial parts (see CYBORG [1]). Under the supervision of Comrade Bolshevinski, scrawny Armenian spy Sergei Baginski is selected to be the 40-billion-ruble man. He is chosen because he's so dumb he can be trusted not to defect.

During a 42-hour operation, his organs, muscles, neurological system, and skin are all replaced. When he recovers from surgery, Sergei is sent to the United States to spy. Posing as a deaf mute

The *Fighting Armenian* takes on a robot unit in *The Rook* #2. Pencils by Romeo Tanghal, inks by Rudy Nebres. © Warren Publishing Co.

since he speaks only Russian, he gets a job as a janitor at the Time Factory, a scientific complex established by Restin Dane (see THE TIME CASTLE). Eventually, Sergei is found out and does indeed defect. He learns English and battles not only Dane's enemies, but also the Soviets who want him back.

Comment: The character was created by Bill DuBay (writing as Will Richardson). He appeared in several adventures, sometimes costarring with Dane. *The Rook* was a black and white comic book; his only color adventure was published in *Eerie* magazine #134. The Fighting Armenian has been in limbo since Warren Publishing closed down in 1983.

FIGHTING MACHINE-1 (C)

First Appearance: "Wartoy," 1975, *Unknown Worlds of Science Fiction #2*, Marvel Comics.

Physical Description: The robot looks like a metallic human skeleton, save for its barrel chest and round head. It has a rectangular visor for "eyes" and a same-size rectangular grate for a mouth. It carries a powerful rifle and possesses superhuman strength.

Biography: The multi-million dollar FM-1 is programmed with the knowledge and skills of an 18-year-old. It was created by the military to "replace fragile human warriors with robots—who could be rebuilt, not mourned, if they fell in battle." General Hamilton Arkay puts the "wartoy" through its paces for the rest of the brass, but while it registers perfect scores on the obstacle course, the robots are deemed too expensive for mass production. Disheartened, Arkay has FM-1 appointed as his personal aide. Years pass, and when Earth is invaded by octopus-like aliens the robot is finally allowed into combat. Though FM-1 is a key to Earth's victory in the 87-day war, the robot is decommissioned when the fighting is over. Since Arkay has been killed, FM-1 takes odd jobs, its parts begin to wear down, and the robot finally commits suicide by punching a hole in its chest. That afternoon, the aliens return.

Comment: The story was written by Tony Isabella and drawn by George Perez and Rico Rival.

Fighting Machine-1.

FIREBALL XL-5 (TV)

First Appearance: *Fireball XL-5*, October 1962 (England).

Physical Description: The silver XL-5 ship is shaped like a missile, with three small red and white striped wings on the nose, a long, sloping tail fin with a red band across it, and two stubby wings in the back with large red and yellow stabilizers. It has a powerful engine in the rear and two seats on the bridge. The front section of the 300-foot-long craft can be launched as a separate vehicle, the *Fireball Junior*. Both vehicles can fire missiles.

Other vessels seen in the series include *Fireballs XL1, XL-2, XL-7, XL-9*; the *Mayflower III*; the "rustbucket" *TA2*; and *Freighter A-14*.

Robert the Robot is a humanoid automaton with a transparent exterior. He has a thimble-shaped head and pincers for hands.

Biography: In 2067, the World Space Patrol has many spaceships patroling the galaxy. *Fireball XL-5* is assigned to Sector 25, piloted by Colonel Steve Zodiac. He is assisted by naviator Professor Matthew "Matt" Matic, medical officer (and Steve's girlfriend) Venus, copilot Robert the Robot, and Zoonie, Venus's koala bear-like pet lazoon.

Back on Earth, Commander Zero and Lieutenant Ninety are in charge of *Fireball XL-5*'s home base, Space City. Their recurring foes are Mr. and Mrs. Space Spy.

Among the alien beings with whom they have dealings are: the Subterrains, the Green Men of Planet 46, who want to destroy the Earth; the King of Platonia, the Platinum Planet, whose regent Volvo seeks a war with Earth; the Membronoans, whose world is about to collide with another; the denizens of the magnet world Magneton; the wicked Kudos of Zanadu, who wants to rid the universe of lazoons; the giants Graff and Snaff of the planet Triad; the Ice Men of Arctan; Privator and Perfectos of Nutopia, the Forbidden Planet; and the malevolent Granatoid Tanks, robots of Planet 73.

Comment: The half-hour series was created by producer Gerry Anderson and was filmed using "Supermarionation" (see SUPERCAR). It debuted in the United States the following fall and continued to show first-run episodes in England through September 1964; there were 39 episodes in all. Paul Maxwell provided the voice for Zodiac, David Graham was Matic, Ninety, and Zoonie, Sylvia Anderson was Venus, Gerry Anderson was Robert, and John Bluthal was Zero.

Gold Key published one issue of the *Steve Zodiac and the Fireball XL-5* comic book in 1964.

FIRE MAIDENS (MP)

First Appearance: *Fire Maidens from Outer Space*, 1956, Criterion Films/Topaz.

Physical Description: The Maidens' ancestors came from Earth and are exactly like terrestrial women; the sole male member of the race is also like an Earthman.

The native Jovian, the so-called "Creature," is "a man with the head of a beast," deeply pocked skin, lumps where his ears should be, dark, unkempt black hair, and a dark jumpsuit. The slender alien stands some six feet tall, is impervious to gunfire, and is much stronger than a human being.

Biography: Sent to explore the 13th moon of Jupiter (which was unknown in 1956), a crew commanded by Luther Blair hear a scream in a forest. Running to investigate, they find a humanoid creature trying to drag beautiful young Hestia away. The explorers scare the monster away with gunfire, and a grateful Hestia leads them to a door in a high wall. Wary, Blair and crewman Larson enter, leaving Dr. Higgins, Sydney Stanhope, and Anderson outside with instructions to leave if they're not back in half an hour.

Inside what proves to be an ancient palace, the men meet the 13 other "Fire Maidens" and the aged Prasus—the only human male—who explains that they are all his daughters and that their ancestors were born on the sunken terrestrial continent Atlantis. They came to Jupiter's moon because they mistakenly believed that *all* the continents of Earth were going to be submerged. What Prasus doesn't tell the men is that he doesn't want any of his girls going back to Earth with them, and with the help of his loyal daughter Duessa he has the men's wine drugged. Meanwhile, the trio waiting outside do not leave when 30 minutes is up. They begin searching for a way in, battling the pesky Creature with a gas grenade when he tries to join them. The doorway seems to have vanished—and they can't go over the wall (it's protected by fire)—so they start digging a tunnel.

Inside, when Blair wakes, Hestia tells him that Prasus is the only one who can open the door, and that he doesn't want them to leave. She asks the Earthmen to trust her as they are granted an audience in the throne room. There, cagey Hestia switches the cups so that this time her father gets the drugged wine. When Prasus passes out, Blair begins searching for a way out; irate, Duessa tells her sisters that Hestia has broken the law of the God of the Son, the Carrier of Fire—not for drugging their father, but for daring to love Blair. The law clearly states that the eldest must be the first to marry, and Duessa is the eldest. For this infraction, Hestia must die.

The Fire Maidens tie Hestia to an altar by a fiery pit in the temple, where she will die at dawn. Nor will she perish alone: Having managed to dig under the wall, Higgins and his group are captured by the Fire Maidens and sentenced to die with her. But Blair has found not only a secret passage that leads from the palace, but the captive Larson as well. The two retrieve their weapons and head for the temple. Unfortunately, the Creature has found the freshly dug tunnel and enters. By this time, Prasus has awakened, and as he heads for the temple the Creature strangles him to death. The monster makes his way to the sacrificial chamber, where he kills Duessa and turns on Hestia. Acting quickly, Blair lobs a gas grenade at the Creature, who falls into the flaming ceremonial pit. With Duessa dead, Hestia is now (conveniently) the eldest daughter, able to marry Blair without breaking the law. She opts to return to Earth, while Blair promises that other expeditions will return with enough men for each and every Fire Maiden.

Comment: The film stars Anthony Dexter as Blair, Susan Shaw as Hestia, Owen Berry as Prasus, Jacqueline Curtiss as Duessa, Paul Carpenter as Larson, Sydney Tafler as Dr. Higgins, Harry Fowler as Stanhope, and Rodney Diak as Anderson. Cy Roth wrote and directed the film.

500-ZQ (C)

First Appearance: *Action Comics Weekly* #637, 1988, DC Comics.

Physical Description: The robot consists of a gunmetal-gray torso shaped like a hot-air balloon, a "gondola" like an inverted gumdrop, and a bald female head. Her torso is ringed with floating TV screens that provide data, via her ability to remote-access computers, and also serve as videophones. Four small engines below the "gumdrop" allow her to levitate and move about. Since she has no arms for fighting, the robot is equipped with knockout-gas breath.

Biography: Also known as Soozie-Q, the robot serves as the secretary to a group of New York-based heroes, who are on-call for any emergency. She was "built or acquired" by the Coodinator, the group's founder. Whenever there's danger, Soozie shouts, "Red Alert! Red Alert!" When it's been taken care of, she cries, "All clear! All clear!"

The heroes on-call are: Microwavabelle (gener-

ates heat), Mister Muscle (has great strength), Private Eyes (has microscopic/telescopic glasses), Stretch, Voice-Over (a mimic and ventriloquist), Diamondette (can cut through anything), Fred (invisible and intangible—may be a creation of Voice-Over), and Hotshot (shoots fireballs).

Comment: After their preview (through *Action Comics Weekly* #640), the characters starred in *Hero Hotline* #'s 1–6 in 1989. They were created by writer Bob Rozakis and artist Stephen DeStefano.

THE FLYING SAUCERS FROM OUTER SPACE (MP)

First Appearance: *Earth vs. The Flying Saucers*, 1956, Clover Productions/Columbia Pictures.

Physical Description: The Flying Saucers are flat, inverted bowls that spin rapidly around their axis when in flight. They are approximately 70 feet in diameter, have a slightly domed top and a versatile undercarriage: The saucer rises slightly to permit a column to emerge with a doorway in its side; or, in flight, the saucer lowers a flared ray-gun, which can be aimed in any direction and fires destructive rays of ultrasonic sound. The cavernous interior consists of ribbed walls, a large viewscreen, small cubicles in which the aliens stand, and a large white quartz-like object that emerges from the ceiling and acts as a translating unit, mind-reading device, and "infinitely indexed memory bank" that allows instant access to all stored data. When

A *Flying Saucer from Outer Space* falls . . . along with a house of Congress in *Earth vs. the Flying Saucers*. © Columbia Pictures.

on the ground, the ship is surrounded by an "electronic screen" that protects it from gunfire. The saucers also release glowing, tennis ball-sized spheres that hover in the air and spy on humans.

The occupants of the ship are desiccated humanoids with rather flat, hairless heads, somewhat wide at the top, with large eyes and mouths. Fragile things, they are encased in suits of "solidified electricity." The metallic-looking suits serve as an "electronic and mechanical outer skin to take the place of their atrophied flesh and muscles." These suits have rounded helmets that amplify the senses and fire ultrasonic sound rays from the wrists.

The aliens live in a different time frame than humans: Several alien-minutes transpire in the same time it takes for a human heart to beat.

Biography: Dr. Russell Marvin is one of the chief scientists of Operation Skyhook, whose first 11 missiles have been shot from space by an unknown source. Before the 12th is launched, a flying saucer buzzes the car of newlywed Marvin and his wife Carol while he's dictating notes into a tape recorder. Later, the saucers land at the base, are attacked in turn, and respond by reducing the facility to rubble. Only then, as the recorder batteries die, does the whine of the saucer slow and become comprehensible. The aliens had announced (at the wrong speed) that they wanted to land and have a chat.

Marvin and the aliens talk again, via radio, this time at the right speed, and he meets one of their saucers on a deserted beach. They explain that they are the "survivors of a disintegrated solar system," and that they need to relocate on Earth. Though their Earth-orbiting fleet *could* conquer the planet, they don't want to settle on an obliterated world. Thus, they tell Marvin that he has 60 days to bring the world's leaders together in Washington for a peaceful surrender. Instead, Marvin and his associates use the time to build guns to turn on the saucers, weapons designed to "interrupt their magnetic field by projecting a highly intermittent induced electrical field." The showdown takes place when the saucers arrive in Washington, D.C., for the meeting. Marvin causes the saucers to crash one after another—rather spectacularly, into the Washington Monument, Capitol Building, and other landmarks.

Comment: The film was inspired by Major Donald F. Keyhoe's nonfiction book *Flying Saucers from Outer Space*; Curt Siodmak and special effects genius Ray Harryhausen came up with the story, George Worthing Yates and Bernard Gordon

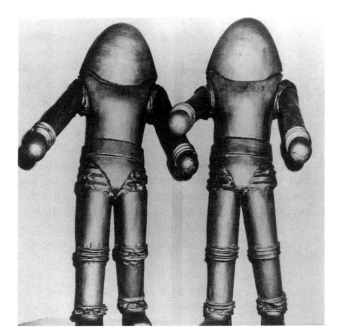

A pair of aliens from *Earth vs. the Flying Saucers.* © Columbia Pictures.

wrote the screenplay, and Fred F. Sears directed. Hugh Marlowe starred as Marvin, with Joan Taylor as Carol. Actor Paul Frees provided the eerie voice for the aliens.

FORD PREFECT (R, L, TV, C)

First Appearance: *The Hitchhiker's Guide to the Galaxy*, 1977, BBC.

Physical Description: Ford is near perfectly human. He is of modest height, not unhandsome, and has "wiry and gingerish" hair brushed back from his forehead. He doesn't blink very much, and he smiles "slightly too broadly." Ford always carries a leather satchel that contains a Sub-Etha Sens-O-Matic, which he uses for hitchhiking; an ordinary towel, for keeping warm on cold Jaglan Beta, for sunning on Santraginus V, for sleeping on Kakrafoon, for avoiding the gaze of the Bugblatter Beast of Traal, and more; and also carries the calculator-like "micro sub meson electronic" device that contains the million or so pages of *The Hitchhiker's Guide to the Galaxy*.

Biography: Ford, who has been researching an updated edition of *The Hitchhiker's Guide to the Galaxy*—and has visited such spots as the hyperspace ports serving madranite mines in the Orion Beta star system—has been on Earth for 15 years, posing as an out-of-work actor. He has known Earthman Arthur Dent for nearly six years when he invites Dent for a drink, tells him he's not really from Guildford but from a planet near Betelgeuse, and that the world's going to end in just a few minutes. Sure enough, the Vogon Constructor Fleet under Prostetnic Vogon Jeltz (of the Galactic Hyperspace Planning Council, which works with two-headed, three-armed President Zaphod Beeblebrox of the Imperial Galactic Government), arrives shortly thereafter to destroy Earth for the construction of a hyperspatial express route. Ford hitchhikes them onto a Vogon ship, and after they're ejected by the cruel captain and picked up by the Infinite Improbability Drive ship *Heart of Gold*—which crosses "vast interstellar distances in a mere nothingth of a second"—the two go adventuring through the universe as Ford works on his revised volume; Arthur is alone for a while as Ford briefly goes mad.

Among the aliens Arthur encounters or learns about are the Babel Fish, which feeds on brainwaves (if you stick one in your ear, you can understand any language); the monkey-like Dentrassi; the big, "green, rubbery," humanoid Vogons; the Capellan jewelled crabs; the Azgoths of Kria, the second-worst poets in the universe, (the worst being Paula Nancy Millstone Jennings of England); the killer robots of Krikkit; the sluglike A-Rth-Urp-Hil-Ipdenu of the Folfanga system; the spacefaring Wowbagger the Infinitely Prolonged; the Hingefreel of Arkintoofle Minor; the paranoid android Marvin; Veet Voojagig, who is preoccupied with all the ballpoint pens he's lost over the years; the triple-breasted Eccentrica Gallumbits of Eroticon Six; Ford's editor, Stagyar-zil-Doggo and his unfriendly replacement, Vann Harl of InfiniDim Enterprises; and many others. Among the robots they meet are Marvin, the humanoid automaton who works for Zaphod.

Comment: The British radio series was written by Douglas Adams, who first had the idea in 1971, while he was lying in a field in Austria, penniless with a copy of *Hitchhiker's Guide to Europe*. The weekly series was originally going to be called *The Ends of the Earth*. Ford was named after the car, Adams explaining, "My alien . . . had simply mistaken the dominant life form."

Five new radio episodes were added to the original seven in 1980. Adams's novelization of the first four episodes of the radio series (somewhat expanded), *The Hitchhiker's Guide to the Galaxy*, was published in 1979. It was followed by the sequels *The Restaurant at the End of the Universe* (1980), based on episodes five through twelve; and the all-new *Life, The Universe, and Everything*

(1982), *So Long, and Thanks For All the Fish* (1984), and *Mostly Harmless* (1992), described as "the fifth book in the increasingly inaccurately named Hitchhikers Trilogy." He also wrote the short story "Young Zaphod Plays It Safe" (1986), which has been collected in *The More than Complete Hitchhiker's Guide*, published by Wings Books in 1989.

In 1981, the BBC produced adaptations of the original radio show as a TV serial. David Dixon starred as Ford, with Simon Jones as Dent.

In 1983–84, Adams wrote a screenplay for a film, which remains unproduced.

In 1993, the first novel was faithfully adapted as a three-issue comic book series by DC Comics.

4432/IV (L)

First Appearance: "Survival Course" by J.W. Schutz, 1970, *Venture Science Fiction* #16.

Physical Description: Circling an orange sun and possessing a single, small moon, the planet is "far from Earth-normal," though it has "a clean, breathable atmosphere, too hot by a dozen degrees for comfort."

Biography: The kitten Roughneck is smuggled onboard the hyperspace Orion Line ship *Wanderer* by O'Flaherty, and is temporarily forgotten when the ship's main gyro motor shorts and the ship must land on 4432/IV. While repairs are made, the cat slips out and into the jungle and is left behind when the vessel blasts off. Hungry, the cat kills and eats a "toad-thing . . . [with] long fangs"; is nearly strangled by "a slender, spine-covered plant . . . [with] sticky strings"; is hounded by "green, flealike things" and a cat-like creature with a spine-tipped tail that injects formic acid into its victims; and finds that the tastiest food is the flesh of "a thick-bodied reptile about twice his own length . . . [with] a cluster of prehensile tentacles behind its head," a body covered with leathery skin, and a spiny underbelly.

Back on the ship, O'Flaherty happens to find an emerald in his pants' cuff, and realizes they must be plentiful on the planet. He persuades the skipper to return, and they find no riches. Then O'Flaherty spots Roughneck, follows him to a cave, and finds "hundreds of kilos" of them. For his part in the operation, the tomcat is given an emerald collar.

Comment: A former diplomat, Schutz sold his first story, "Maiden Voyage," to *The Magazine of Fantasy and Science Fiction* in 1965.

This same issue of *Venture Science Fiction*

featured the first publication of Dean R. Koontz's novel *Beastchild*, about the conquest of Earth by the Naoli, alien lizard-people.

FRANKENSTEIN JR. (TV, C, L)

First Appearance: *Frankenstein Jr. and the Impossibles*, September 1966, CBS.

Physical Description: Standing 30 feet tall, the blue-skinned robot can fly, has superstrength, and possesses a magnetic ray, a freeze ray, and other weapons.

Frankenstein Jr. has a jaw like a steam shovel and a flat, hairless head with an antenna on top. He wears olive drab trousers and a matching shirt with torn sleeves and a black "F" in an inverted red triangle on the chest. He also wears yellow boots, a black domino mask, and a dark brown capelet.

Biography: Buzz Conroy is the brilliant son of Professor Conroy, who lives in a remote mountaintop laboratory. There, Buzz builds a giant robot named Frankenstein Jr., which he activates using a ring he wears. When danger threatens, Buzz climbs on the robot's shoulder (though he also wears a rocket belt for solo flights), shouts the activating word "Alakazoom!" and the two fly off to battle the likes of the Pilfering Putty Monster, the Unearthly Plant Creatures, the Spyder Man, the Alien Brain from Outer Space, Dr. Shock, and more.

Comment: The Hanna-Barbera series aired through September 1968; reruns were seen on *The Space Ghost/Frankenstein Jr.*, which aired on NBC from November 1976 to September 1977. There were 18 half-hour adventures in all. Ted Cassidy provided the voice of the creature.

The Impossibles are rock and rollers who become superheroes.

Gold Key Comics published one issue of *Frankenstein Jr.* in 1967. In 1968, Carl Fallberg published the Big Little Book *Frankenstein Jr., The Menace of the Heartless Monster.*

The character was inspired by the Mary Shelley novel *Frankenstein, or the Modern Prometheus* (1818).

FRANK-N-FURTER (S, MP)

First Appearance: *The Rocky Horror Show*, 1973, The Theatre Up-Stairs.

Physical Description: Nearly six feet tall, the alien hails from the planet Transsexual in the galaxy of Transylvania. A male, Frank has the ability to look like a female with his fishnet stockings, panties, corset, mink wrap, high heels, pearl necklace, blue eyeshadow, dark red or purple lipstick, and long, curly locks. He has a tattoo, "Boss" above a stabbed heart, on his upper right arm.

Biography: Out to visit Dr. Everett V. Scott, the science teacher in whose class they met, uptight Denton, Ohioans Brad Majors and his fiancee, virginal Janet Weiss, get a flat tire in a driving rain. Walking to a nearby castle, they're greeted by a hunchback butler named Riff Raff and invited to join the Annual Transylvanian Convention. The alien Dr. Frank-N-Furter, the "sweet transvestite from Transsexual, Transylvania," joins the festivities, after which the newcomers visit Frank in his upstairs lab. There, he unveils his latest creation, his new lover Rocky, who replaces the greaser Eddie (whom Frank hacks to death with a pickaxe). Frank and Rocky retire; later, Frank seduces Brad and Janet in their separate rooms, and Janet also has a fling with Rocky. Meanwhile, Dr. Scott arrives looking for Eddie, whose remains the "playful" Frank displays in the glass-topped dinner table. Janet gets sick, Rocky comforts her, Frank becomes jealous, and everyone is distracted by a floorshow and late-night swim. Fed up with Frank's excesses ("Society must be protected!"), Riff Raff—no longer a hunchback—and his consort Magenta show up in their glittering alien garb and blast Frank and Rocky to death with a laser-gun. Janet and Brad—no longer uptight—depart with Dr. Scott, and the entire castle is teleported back to Transylvania.

Comment: The show, written by Richard O'Brien, debuted in the 63-seat London theater with Tim Curry as Frank and O'Brien as Riff Raff. It later played worldwide, though its greatest fame came from the 1975 cult motion picture *The Rocky Horror Picture Show,* directed by Jim Sharman and starring Curry and O'Brien along with Susan Sarandon as Janet, Barry Bostwick as Brad, Peter Hinwood as Rocky, Jonathan Adams as Scott, and rocker Meatloaf as Eddie. The infamous Koo Stark appears as a Bridesmaid. The film has been a consistently popular midnight draw, with audience members dressing up as characters, shouting at the screen, and recreating events in the film.

The only major differences between the stage show and the film were the addition of the opening wedding scene and dining room scene for the film, and the deletion of an usherette who opened the show on stage.

A sequel, *Shock Treatment,* was released in 1981. Frank didn't appear in this tale of Brad and Janet becoming contestants on the mad gameshow *Marriage Maze.*

FREEWILLS (C)

First Appearance: *Magnus, Robot Fighter* #1, 1963, Gold Key.

Physical Description: The robots are humanoid with spindly limbs, bug eyes, no nose, and a grid for a mouth. Domestic Freewills are gold, police and medical Freewills silver, rental Freewills purple, spaceport workers powder blue, and others navy blue, dark green, green, red, orange, etc.

Biography: In the year 4000 A.D., robots work alongside human beings. Most are Freewills, permitted to function independently within established parameters. Sometimes the robots malfunction; other times, they are sabotaged or even catch diseases from space robots. Whenever that happens, and the pol-robs (police robots) can't handle matters, Magnus is summoned. Though he was raised by Freewill 1A, he is a robot-hater—especially when Earth is invaded by the robots of the planet Malev 6, who feed on the ectotheric energy produced by human thought waves. Under the leadership of the giant, snake-like robot Malev Emperor, the robots intend to make Earth their new home, Malev 7. Magnus is aided by 1A, whose consciousness is given a stronger golden humanoid body with not-so-spindly limbs, and the ability to transfer its awareness from this body to a golden eagle-like robot ASA.

Comment: The character was created by artist Russ Manning. Gold Key published 46 issues of Magnus. Valiant Comics revived the title in 1990, and it continues to this day.

FUTURA (L, MP)

First Appearance: *Metropolis* by Thea von Harbou, 1927.

Physical Description: When introduced, the robot (which is also called Parody) has a body that "seemed as though made of crystal, through which the bones shone silver." The head is "bald, nose, lips, temples merely traced. Eyes, as though painted on closed lids, stared unseeingly, with an expression of calm madness." Later, its creator fashions the likeness of Maria over the robotic frame, albeit one with a "mouth of deadly sin."

Biography: Metropolis, a city in the year 2026, is governed by the autocratic Joh Frederson and is comprised of two regions: the gleaming, soaring towers of the surface world, and the dark, run-down subterranean world of the workers who operate the machines that keep Metropolis running. While enjoying the pleasures of the lush Eternal Gardens, Freder, son of Frederson, is shocked when a young woman, Maria, leads in children with "grey and ancient" faces and urges the rich not to forget their brothers. His conscience stung, Freder journeys underground to learn more about the suffering of the lower classes.

Frederson is more concerned about his son than about the masses, and wants him one day to rule a city at peace—however that peace is achieved. Thus, he commissions the inventor Rotwang to abduct Maria and build him a robot duplicate that will obey his commands. When this is done, the robot is sent out to lead the workers in revolt, which causes a terrible explosion and underground flood; Frederson reasons that with Metropolis destroyed, Freder will be able to rebuild the city correctly. But Freder is horrified by the death and destruction, and hurries to free Maria. Futura is captured and placed in a bonfire where she "dies a beautiful, hot magnificent death" while the real Maria calms the masses and ushers in a new era of understanding between the masters and the workers of Metropolis.

Comment: Though von Harbou wrote the novel, it was her husband, director Fritz Lang, who came up with the basic idea, inspired by the New York skyline as he sailed into the harbor in 1924. Lang transformed the work into one of the most important science fiction films, *Metropolis*, released in Germany in February 1927 and premiering in the United States later that year. Brigitte Helm plays Maria and the robot, Alfred Abel is Frederson, Gustav Fröhlich plays Freder, and Rudolf Klein-Rogge is Rotwang.

In the film, Maria is placed in a coffin-like capsule and her likeness and mind are transferred electronically to the robot. Before taking on the likeness of Maria, the robot is pictured as a silvery humanoid with blank eyes, metal "breasts," a raised band across the top of its head, and various slender bars and braces on its limbs, waist, and torso.

G

GAEA (L)

First Appearance: "Titan" by John Varley, January 1979, *Analog*.

Physical Description: Gaea is a "great wheel" shaped like a wagon wheel, 1,300 kilometers across and 250 kilometers wide. The central hub is 160 kilometers in diameter with a 160 kilometer hole in the center; there are six spokes 420 kilometers long radiating from the hub to a surrounding torus-shaped outer wheel. Solar heating panels hang from the torus; above it six square mirrors send light down to Gaea. The torus section is hollow, and Gaea's spin produces one-quarter of Earth's gravity on the inside.

Gaea's "center of consciousness . . . [is] in her hub," though her brain is "decentralized to provide local autonomy for the more prosaic of her functions." Twelve brains are scattered around the rim, one for each of Gaea's sectors. Of these regions, Hyperion is in perpetual day, while Oceanus—largely comprised of a great frozen sea—and Rhea, on either side, are always dark.

The crew of the DSV *Ringmaster* are Captain Cirocco "Rocky" Jones, First Officer William Rubin, Satellite Exploration Module Pilot Eugene Springfield, Medical Officer Calvin Greene, astronomer Gaby Plauget, and April 15/02 and August 3/02 Polo, clones of scientist Susan Polo.

Biography: Over three million years old, Gaea orbits Saturn with sisters scattered throughout space. Some 3,000 years ago, she suffered a war, with the territory Oceanus leading a revolt and the land of Hyperion heading the defense. The latter forces were victorious. In this century, Gaea tunes into Earth radio and TV broadcasts and assimilates many of the personalities she receives. Earth first becomes aware of Gaea in 2025, when Gaby discovers her as the *Ringmaster* approaches Saturn. She names the 11th moon Themis, and while the crew wonders how to board her, Oceanus sends out a giant grapple that grabs and destroys the ship, though smaller grapples sent by Gaea's core mind

manage to collect the debris and crew, saving the latter.

Inside, the crewmembers are separated and subjected to utter sensory deprivation. When Cirocco and Gaby finally manage to get together, they go exploring. The women follow a stream through a jungle, eventually reach a wall of the torus, and find Calvin. He introduces them to a native life form, a living blimp named Whistlestop. The blimp ferries them to Bill and August, after which Calvin leaves to live with the blimps. Cirocco, Gaby, and Bill ride a large nutshell to the Ophion, the world's main river, on whose shores they encounter centaur-like titanides. Incredibly, Cirocco is able to communicate with them, though she doesn't understand how she learned the language. The humans witness a terrible battle between the titanides and winged humanoids called Angels, learn that the world is called Gaea, and are told that the titanides worship the hub Gaea, where the eponymous goddess is said to dwell. Cirocco eventually makes it through Angel territory and reaches Gaea, talks to her, and learns that the sentient world created all the life forms inside her. Cirocco is fascinated with Gaea and vice versa, and she remains on the world to become a wizard and also to write her memoirs, as well as a travelogue to Gaea.

Meanwhile, diplomatic relations are established between Gaea and Earth, the 11th moon of Saturn becomes a member of the United Nations in 2050, and tourists begin arriving. For her part, the aging Gaea enjoys studying humans and learning about our "endless complications." Gaea also delights in helping humans solve problems and cure diseases—albeit, asking them to perform difficult tasks in exchange for help—viewing this as a means to become a god to humankind. Two beings come to Gaea: Robin, who suffers from terrible seizures; and Chris'fer Minor (a.k.a. Chris Major), who endures recurring bouts of madness.

By the third tale, Gaea and Cirocco become foes when the latter helps the Titanides over a reproductive crisis and the race continues. Since Gaea did not give her blessings to Cirocco's interference, she attacks the Wizard, who is forced to build her own power base among the Titanides and other anti-Gaea forces on the wheel world. Before long, Gaea has become senile and insane—taking on various personalities from Marilyn Monroe to King Kong—and must be destroyed.

Comment: The novel was serialized in four monthly installments; book publication occurred while the serialization was still running. The sequel, *Wizard*, was published in 1980; the last novel of the trilogy, *Demon*, was published in 1984.

GALACTUS (C, TV)

First Appearance: *Fantastic Four* #48, 1966, Marvel Comics.

Physical Description: Standing slightly over 28 feet tall, Galactus wears a blue bodysuit with a purple chest and blue armor over that, purple boots, gauntlets, and a helmet with huge "L"-shaped horns, and a purple skirt with blue markings. Galactus designed his "armored costume . . . [to] help him regulate" his awesome energics; it is all that keeps the energy stored in his body from undergoing a thermonuclear reaction and turning him into a star. As it is, Galactus can generate incredible blasts and force fields with this power, or use it to transmute or teleport matter. Galactus drains worlds using an "elemental converter," a skyscraper-sized device whose "range extend to . . . [the] entire planet."

As Galan, Galactus looks like a bald, blue-eyed human.

Biography: Before the Big Bang gave birth to our universe, a previous universe was destroyed by a Big Crunch—the collapse of all matter to a single, incredibly dense point. Galan lives on the planet Taa in that dying universe. With several colleagues, the space explorer rides a spaceship into "the blazing cosmic cauldron into which all the matter in the universe was plunging." Only Galan survives, merging with a mysterious force known as "the sentience of the universe" and being reborn as the towering Galactus. After the Big Bang creates our universe, Galan drifts in a starship for countless ages before he finds himself in orbit around the planet Archeopia. Hungry for energy, he sucks the world dry, killing everything on it.

Headquartered on the massive base Taa II that takes "millennia to complete" and is as large as the Archeopian system itself (so large "that planets orbited it as if it were a star"), Galactus recruits various heralds and sends them forth to find worlds for him to eat. He then journeys to those worlds onboard Taa II. Among his heralds are THE SILVER SURFER, Air Walker, a.k.a Gabrial Lan of Xandar; Firelord, a.k.a. Pyreus Kril, also of Xandar; Nova, a.k.a. Frankie Raye of Earth; and Terrax the Tamer, a.k.a. Tyros of Laniak. His aides include the mighty robot the Punisher and Drone R-11.

Galactus has made several attempts to feast on Earth, but has been thwarted by the superheroic Fantastic Four. Near death once, he was given an energy transfusion from the group's leader, Mr. Fantastic. In gratitude, Galactus has agreed never again to attack our planet. Indeed, Galactus believes that while he must destroy worlds to survive, it may be his destiny to "give back" something one day, perhaps by preventing our universe from perishing in a Big Crunch.

Comment: The character was created by writer Stan Lee and artist Jack Kirby. In addition to many appearances in *Fantastic Four* and other Marvel titles, Galactus starred in the one-shot *Super-Villain Classics* (1983). The character was also featured on the half-hour *Fantastic Four* animated series that aired on ABC from September 1967 to March 1970.

GALAXINA (MP)

First Appearance: *Galaxina*, 1980, Crown International.

Physical Description: The lovely young blonde is indistinguishable from a human being save that, initially, she can't talk and to kiss her is to risk electrocution. Her attire consists of a skintight silvery white bodysuit and black knee boots.

The *Infinity* is shaped like a prehistoric trilobite. The crew consists of Galaxina, Captain Cornelius Butt, Sgt. Thor, Private Robert "Buzz" McHenry, and engineers Maurice—who boasts a small pair of batwings—and Sam Wo. Also onboard, in the brig, is the ape-like Kitty, a rock-eating alien with a mouth like an oversized Venus flytrap.

Biography: Galaxina serves as a cook, copilot, and companion to the crew of the 28th-century starship *Infinity*. Sent by Command Headquarters to find the Blue Star, a gem that contains "the energy of the stars," the human crew goes into suspended animation—though not before Butt consumes an alien egg and spits out the tiny creature that was inside. The fish-headed reptilian creature waits for him while he sleeps. Meanwhile, Galaxina waits for Thor, with whom she has fallen in love. She teaches herself to speak and, when the ship crash-lands on Altair 1, Galaxina takes it upon herself to complete the mission while the others recover from their wounds (all but Butt, who grew old when his suspended animation chamber malfunctioned).

From the Earthling Frank Future, she learns that the gem is owned by the lizard cyborg Ordric of the planet Mordric in the Tarquin Galaxy. Galaxina finds Ordric living above a restaurant run by the pointy-eared Mr. Spot—a restaurant where human flesh is served. She gets the jewel from him, only to be captured by bikers who worship the god Harley Davidson. Luckily, Thor and Buzz track her down, steal the motorcycle they worship, and rescue Galaxina. The adventurers leave the world, only to have success snatched from their grasp when Kitty eats the Blue Star.

Comment: Former *Playboy* Playmate of the Year Dorothy Stratten stars as Galaxina, with Avery Schreiber as Butt, James David Hinton as Buzz, Stephen Macht as Thor, Lionel Smith as Maurice, and Tad Horino as Sam. Herb Kaplowitz was inside the Kitty costume. The film was written and directed by William Sachs.

Stratten, who was murdered by her boyfriend shortly after completing the film, also appeared as Miss Cosmos in the TV series *Buck Rogers in the 25th Century*.

THE GALAXY BEING (TV)

First Appearance: "The Galaxy Being," September 1963, *The Outer Limits*, ABC.

Physical Description: Standing approximately six feet tall, the nitrogen-based being from the Andromeda Galaxy is a white humanoid with three fingers on each hand and a barrel chest (it had to be: the actor's oxygen tank was strapped to his chest); its only feature are the liquid blue specks all over its body, which cause it to glow and flicker "like a person made out of blue ice." It has two unblinking, saucer-like eyes and a ridge of bone between them, as well as an upswept ridge above the eyes. It has no ears, mouth, or nose, and "hears" by receiving brain patterns from others. Highly radioactive, the creature generates an energy field that causes objects to fly away from it and prevents bullets from harming it.

Biography: Allan Maxwell runs Los Feliz radio station KXKVI in the southwestern United States with his brother Gene, a deejay. However, Allan's interest is in technological research and, building a TV that receives three-dimensional images, he

draws on the station's power to pick up signals from another researcher—one based on a 31-planet solar system in the Andromeda Galaxy. The alien confesses that he is transmitting illegally, since his race forbids contact with destructive societies. He and Allan exchange thoughts on death, religion, and science until Allan is forced to go to a testimonial dinner with his wife Carol and Gene. Though Allan instructs the substitute deejay not to touch the power dials, the record spinner goes ahead and boosts the signal. Result: "microwave transmission . . . of atomic structure" and the Galaxy Being is drawn through the TV. After inadvertently causing destruction and death (by radiation), the alien is found by Allan, who brings him back to the station. The police and National Guard follow, and Carol is shot by a trigger-happy officer. The alien cauterizes her wound, healing her with his touch, then lectures the crowd through a voice-synthesizing computer at the station that "there is much you have to learn . . . [about] the mysteries of the universe." Since it will be destroyed if it goes home, and can't remain on Earth, the Galaxy Being turns down the power dial at the station and simply disintegrates.

Comment: This was the pilot episode of the classic TV series, and was the first one aired. The alien was played by trained mime William O. Douglas, son of the Supreme Court associate justice. Cliff Robertson starred as Maxwell, with Lee Philips as Gene and Jacqueline Scott as Carol. The episode was written and directed by Leslie Stevens.

THE GALAXY TRIO (TV)

First Appearance: *Birdman and the Galaxy Trio*, September 1967, NBC.

Physical Description: Vapor Man, the leader, assumes a gaseous form; Gravity Girl increases or decreases the pull of gravity on any object; and the pointy-eared Meteor Man causes any section of his body to become larger or smaller. The heroes wear colorful skintight bodysuits: Vapor Man has a I on his chest; Meteor Man a II; and Gravity Girl a III.

Biography: Hailing from the planets Meteorus, Gravitas, and Vaporus, the heroes go to work for Intergalactic Security, patroling the galaxy onboard their ship *Condor 1* and battling the likes of the rebellious robot Computron of Orbus Four (who later tries to take over Z-10); Zakor and his raiders, who attack the treasury world Centauri Three; the evil Lothar, who repeatedly attempts to wrest the throne of the planet Aqueous from his brother Neptar; Kragg, the space pirate;

Growliath, who has enlarged the insects of the planet Nova; and Gralik, based on Moonoid-49, who tries to overthrow Gravity Girl's father, the King of Gravitas. Other worlds seen in the series include Magnetron, Primeva, the rubber planetoid Plastus, and the prison world Pententious.

Comment: There were 20 six-minute cartoons, each sandwiched between adventures of the superhero Birdman. The series aired through September 1968. Don Messick was the voice of Vapor Man, Virginia Eiler was Gravity Girl, and Ted Cassidy was Meteor Man.

GALLIA (L, C, MP)

First Appearance: *Hector Servadac* by Jules Verne, 1877.

Physical Description: The small, Earthlike world is a dying comet 1,400 miles in circumference, 450 miles in diameter, 630,000 square miles of surface area. The gravity is such that large rocks are as light as sponges, and people can jump 40 feet high. Noises are extremely shrill on Gallia, and water boils at a very low temperature. Gallia has a single moon, the captured asteroid Nerina. The sun rises in the west, crossing the sky twice as fast as on Earth; though the days are half as long, the months are twice as long.

Biography: Passing close to Earth at 2:47:30 in the morning on January 1, a "blazing spheroid" of a comet sweeps away several square miles of Mostaganem, the Rock of Gilbraltar, and the Mediterranean, also taking with it heroic 30-year-old French army Captain Hector Servadac and his orderly Ben Zoof—who were relaxing in a hut near the coast of Algeria—along with the Russian Count Wassili Timascheff, who was to duel Servadac for the hand of a young widow. The new arrivals mistakenly believe that they are still on Earth and that it has simply changed its orbit. After a near collision with Venus on the 10th, the group finds the Russian's yacht *Dobryna* intact, and they set sail from the chunk of Algeria, which has been transformed into a small island. In their travels, they meet English Colonel Heneage Finch Murphy, Major Sir John Temple Oliphant, and their 11 men; an Italian girl named Nina and her pet goat Marzy, a German Jew named Isaac Hakkabut, and 10 Spaniards. They also locate a series of notes kept by Palmyrin Rosette (an old professor of Servadac's from the Lycee Charlemagne) from which the eclectic group learns that they are on the world Gallia and that it has nudged the Earth before. Rosette's messages

A native of *Gallia* in the film *Valley of the Dragons*. © Columbia Pictures.

also inform them that the planet's orbit is going to take them past the orbit of Mars (on the 13th), through the asteroid belt toward Jupiter, where they will freeze. Luckily, the explorers locate a volcano and make its cave-laced interior their home, dubbing it Nina's Hive. During its passage through the asteroid belt, Gallia captures a small world, which becomes its moon.

When the planet heads back toward the sun and warms up again, the team resumes their explorations, heading to the island of Formentera, which was also snatched from Earth. There, they find Rosette, bringing the total number of Earth people to 36. He calculates that the comet will pass close to Earth again in two years, at which time they may briefly share their atmospheres as they graze one another. To this end, they construct a hot air balloon; before they can complete it, the volcano erupts, splitting Gallia in two and stranding the Englishmen on the smaller portion. As it drifts off, away from Earth, the survivors on the larger segment have no idea whether it took any of the atmosphere with it.

Climbing into the balloon, Servadac, Rosette, and the others ascend to just over a mile and, at the point of closest passage, they are whisked back to Algeria where Servadac and Timascheff learn that their widow has wed. ("We shan't have to fight our duel after all," says the former.)

Comment: Verne's cousin Georges Allotte de la Fuye was the inspiration for the hero; note the ominous meaning of the hero's surname, an anagram for *cadavres,* French for cadavers.

The tale was published in novel form in 1878 as *Hector Servadac* and also as the surprise-spoiling *Off on a Comet* (1878). It has also appeared in two volumes, *Anomalous Phenomena* and the also-revealing *Homeward Bound.*

The entire saga was adapted in comic book form as *Off on a Comet,* #149 in the Classics Illustrated series in 1959.

The tale was also the basis of the 1961 motion picture *Valley of the Dragons,* which was written and directed by Edward Bernds. In the film, set in 1881, Captain Servadac (Cesare Danova) and Michael Denning (Sean McClory) are about to fight a duel when the comet takes them away. There, the two men find creatures snatched from Earth in earlier periods, including dinosaurs and the feuding Cave People and River People. They defeat several monsters, make peace among the cave people (with the help of a timely volcano), and get comfortable in the arms of the beautiful Deena (of the River People) and Nateeta (daughter of Cave Person Patoo) while they wait for the comet to pass close to Earth again, which they figure will be a few years.

GAMES MACHINE (L)

First Appearance: "The World of Null-A" by A.E. van Vogt, August-October 1945, *Astounding Science Fiction.*

Physical Description: Built on "the leveled crest of a mountain," the external aspect of the machine is "a scintillating, silvery shaft rearing up into the sky . . . a cone . . . crowned by a star of atomic light."

Inside, there are seven floors of game rooms and the rest is the "mechanical brain" itself. It is protected by "a ninety-foot steel outer barrier," which can be penetrated only by atomic weapons. No one knows "exactly in what part of its structure its electron-magnetic brain" is located. Older than any living human, the Games Machine is "self-renewing, conscious of its life and of its purpose." Separate interviews with people are conducted simultaneously in tens of thousands of small booths; the machine speaks in a "casual

tone." The computer can kill humans only in self-defense. Though the Machine can receive radio communications from Venus, it cannot "itself broadcast on interplanetary wave lengths." It also cannot make any announcements when it's subject to a Distorter, which can temporarily shut down some of its functions.

Biography: In 2560 A.D., the Games Machine organizes a competition in which hundreds of thousands of young men and women compete for a place on Eden-like Venus, which has been turned into a world of null-A (a philosophy that embraces more than just logic, its adherents feeling that truth and reality are affected by the perceptions and experiences of the observer). On the eve of competing, Gilbert Gosseyn (pronounced *gosane*) is informed by the Machine that he isn't Gilbert Gosseyn, and that there's something unusual in his cortex. He's given 15 days to find out who he really is. Before he can do so, he's abducted and taken to see the President of Earth, Michael Hardie, who is worried about Gilbert's brain. Hardie and his colleagues are plotting to eliminate null-A, and Gilbert may represent a threat. When the young man tries to escape, he's shot dead.

Gilbert wakes in a hospital on Venus, with full knowledge of all that has happened to him and in a new body exactly like his old one, though he has no idea how or why he got there. Aware that he'll be arrested if discovered, he tells doctors John and Amelia Prescott about the plot against Venus, then heads into the wilderness, awed by the 3,000-foot-tall trees and beautiful weather on the planet. Picked up by a roboplane sent by the Games Machine, Gilbert is taken to a treehouse. Entering, Gilbert explores a tunnel in the back of the dwelling, where he has visions about aliens and space-ships. Captured when he returns to the house proper, Gilbert is taken to Earth and invited by Hardie to join his movement. He refuses just as John Prescott arrives, killing the President and rescuing his patient. But it isn't really a rescue: Gilbert learns that Prescott is actually part of Hardie's group and he killed the President to help stir sentiment against the Venusians and the Games Machine. Fleeing, Gilbert goes to the Machine and learns that Venus has been successfully invaded by the anti-null-A forces. The Machine also tells him that he must kill himself to move into "Gosseyn III," which will be even wiser and more able to use what amounts to an extra brain inside his head . . . a brain that can tap energy outside of time/space. Unfortunately, Gilbert's third body is destroyed, Prescott and his forces are out looking for any others, and anti-Machinists wreck the computer with atomic torpedoes.

In time, Gosseyn meets X, an old man who has his own doubles. X explains that over 500 years before, he established a null-A movement on Venus, constructed the Games Machine, and also started growing bodies for himself, bodies in which the innate but dormant extra brain could be nurtured. When X dies, Gosseyn removes his beard and sees that X is himself; he is a clone of this ancient figure. As Venus overthrows the invaders, Gosseyn realizes that by extra brain transference he is essentially immortal, though he still doesn't understand everything that's happened.

In his second adventure, Gosseyn learns more about human history and about his own background. Two million years before, in another galaxy, tens of thousands of humans fled as a lethal gas cloud began swallowing up worlds. After a milion-year-plus journey, the refugees reached the Milky Way and began settling planets; X was one of the original colonists. Now Gosseyn has been targeted for death by the Follower, a shadowy being from the distant Greatest Empire. The Follower doesn't want him to remain on Venus, where—as he sensed before—a space-time distorter is hidden, one capable of sending spaceships across light years in a moment. With such power at his command, he fears that Gosseyn might lead his null-A people on voyages of conquest. While the Follower plots against Gosseyn, the Empire's leader Enro fiddles with the idea of launching a preemptive attack against Earth and Venus. Fortunately, Gosseyn and his allies are able to mount a defense and repulse the invaders. The Follower is destroyed, Gosseyn discovers that Enro is part of his own ancient race, and the newly united peoples agree to go to their home galaxy to learn more about their native worlds.

In his third adventure, instantaneous travel between the stars is mastered, Gosseyn Two remains in the Milky Way while his alter ego Gosseyn Three and Enro have adventures among the ancient Dzan of planet Zero in Galaxy One. Gosseyn Three eventually settles down on Zero, taking the Dzanian Strala as his wife.

Comment: The term "null-A" was coined by Count Alfred Korzybski in his "General Semantics" book *Science and Sanity*. It was used to describe a non-Aristotelian (or "null-Aristotelian") view of the world.

The novel was first published in book form in 1948. *The Pawns of Null-A* was also serialized in *Astounding*, in 1948-49 (October through January) and published in book form in 1956 as *The Players of Null-A*, followed by *Null-A Three*, published in book form only in 1985.

GARGUAX (C)

First Appearance: *Doom Patrol* #91, 1964, DC Comics.

Physical Description: Standing six-foot-two, the green-skinned, increasingly obese, bald-headed Garguax usually wears a purple robe and goes barefoot.

Biography: Banished from his (unnamed) home world because he was developing weapons with which to conquer it, Garguax uses a "floating fortress" in Earth's atmosphere to test new weapons, a robot army of blue-skinned "plastic men." These are defeated by the superheroic Doom Patrol (see ROBOTMAN [2]), and Garguax is presumed destroyed with his flying city. But he surfaces again with a base on the moon, teamed with the Brotherhood of Evil and subjecting Earth to an insanity-causing ray and then a beam that turns people into giant crystal monsters. Though the Doom Patrol puts an end to the menace, Garguax escapes. The heroes and villain face off again when Garguax returns to destroy our world, now aided by his planet's leader Zarox-13, "King of the Criminal Cosmos," his flunky Afex, and his robot pilot 19-B. Subsequent showdowns result in Garguax destroying his own planet and attacking the Earth with a fleet of spaceships.

Comment: The character was created by editor Murray Boltinoff and writer Arnold Drake.

THE GAROOK (L)

First Appearance: "Fido" by Mack Reynolds, May 1950, *Amazing Stories*.

Physical Description: Approximately 15 feet tall and weighing roughly 400 pounds, the aliens have a metabolism "considerably slower than that of man."

The aliens' world has a "blue-gold sun . . . [and] technicolor sand."

Biography: Les Cole is snatched from Earth and awakes in a room in an alien residence. He is greeted by a being who introduces himself as a Garook, a race antagonistic to other Garook "except during a brief mating season that comes only once in five . . . earth years." At all other times, says the alien, they have the desire to "dash madly together, rending and tearing." To survive, the members of the race live apart, communicating

Julian S. Krupa's illustration of the *Garook* and its human "pets." © Ziff-Davis Publications.

THE GARSONIANS (L)

First Appearance: "Installment Plan" by Clifford D. Simak, 1958, *Galaxy*, Vol. 17, #3.

Physical Description: The inhabitants of Garson IV are "seedy-looking . . . little wizened gnomes." They live in pleasant, neat houses in clean, tree-shaded villages with red barns for storing produce. Villages have little contact with one another. The Garsonians have no government, just a "formless" town meeting to deal with the "rare crises" that come up.

The humanoid robots in the story are unaffected by radiation, and are able to speak, think, and do whatever humans tell them. By using "roboticists," humans or robots can diagnose injured robots; inserting "transmogs" will change them from one kind of robot to another (i.e., a cook to a doctor).

telepathically and hungering for companionship. Through their advanced science, the Garook discovered that humans are able to share affection. Thus, they seize them (via some kind of teleportation, it seems), place them in comfortable rooms in their own homes, and keep them as pets, vicariously enjoying their affection for one another.

After this has been explained to Les, a young woman is snatched from Earth and placed in the room with him. As he comforts her and explains what he has learned, they hear their master's "pleased, satisfied laughter."

Comment: Reynolds is a popular author whose first story, "Isolationist," was published earlier that year in *Amazing*'s sister magazine *Fantastic Adventures*. Among his many stories are those about the agents of Section G of the United Planets, who operate undercover on alien worlds. Reynolds began writing the tales in 1960.

"Seedy looking . . . little wizened gnomes": the Garsonians. Art by Wally Wood. © Galaxy Publishing Corp.

Biography: The podar, a tuber much-in-demand on Earth as the tranquilizer calenthropodensia, grows only on Garson IV, and Central Trading's Steve Sheridan is sent to start trading with the natives. He is assisted by his devoted robot aides Hezekiah, Abraham, Silas, Gideon, Ebenezer, Reuben, Napoleon, Joshua, and Thaddeus. Sheridan finds the Garsonians uncooperative, as do the robots who travel to different villages. They keep up the sales pitches, however, until one day all of the Garsonians are gone. Simultaneously, the robot Tobias arrives from Central Trading to tell them that Galactic Enterprises has offered the company calenthropodensia: Tobias wants to know how *they* got the podar. Investigating, Sheridan finds a dying old Garsonian. He learns that the natives had traded with other aliens in exchange for "a matter transference machine" to teleport them to a world where they would be immortal. Sheridan suspects that they probably teleported themselves into slavery but, in the meantime, the world is abandoned and he sends Hezekiah to Central Trading for robot reinforcements, so he can take and hold Garson IV and undermine the ruthless Galactic Enterprise's monopoly on podar.

Comment: The story was illustrated by Wally Wood, one of the greats of science fiction and comic book illustration.

THE GIANT CLAW   (MP)

First Appearance: *The Giant Claw*, 1957, Clover Productions/Columbia Pictures.

Physical Description: The alien buzzard has a wingspan of approximately 200 feet. Looking more like a Dr. Seuss creature than a science fiction menace, it has a pear-shaped body, a long ribbed neck, pert feathers on its head and tail, a big, bug-eyed head with an ungainly beak, and two huge talons. The monster generates an antimatter shield that both protects it and renders it invisible to radar.

Biography: The Giant Claw may or may not be a prehistoric bird, whose kind headed to space to escape the great extinction. In any case, it comes to Earth to lay its egg, feeding on teenagers and commuters while waiting for it to hatch. Scientist Mitch MacAfee finds the egg and destroys it, enraging the Claw. While the extraterrestrial bird has destroyed New York, MacAfee develops a mu-meson particle cannon and he loads it into a plane. As the bird follows the airplane, the scientist neutralizes the anti-matter shield, enabling the bird to be blasted from the skies.

Comment: Jeff Morrow stars as Mitch. Fred F. Sears directed from a script by Samuel Newman and Paul Gargelin.

THE GIANT YMIR   (MP, L)

First Appearance: *20 Million Miles to Earth*, 1957, Morningside Productions/Columbia Pictures.

Physical Description: The reptilian biped has a long, forked tail, three-fingered hands, and three-toed feet. It has ridges around its eyes, widely flared nostrils, a muzzle with sharp teeth, and tiny pointed ears. A small fin runs from the top of its head down its back; there are also small fins on the back of its forearms, and tiny lumps over most of its body. Ymir's lower legs are turned backward, like those of a satyr. Though the film is black and white, the creature is light blue with a silvery underbelly.

Ymir has no heart or lungs, but possesses a "network of small tubes throughout its entire body" and breathes through a "fiberous filtering element" that keeps out the poisons in the atmosphere of Venus. It is impervious to small arms fire, but can be anesthetized with electricity. Ymir subsists on sulfur and is "not ferocious unless . . . provoked."

When born from its jelly-like egg, Ymir is approximately six inches tall. However, because of Earth's strange atmosphere it grows rapidly. At its death, the creature is some 30 feet tall.

Special effects artist Ray Harryhausen's dramatic preproduction drawing of the *Giant Ymir*. Courtesy Ray Harryhausen.

The silvery spaceship *XY21* is a "single-stage astro-propelled rocket." The upper half of the rocket is shaped like a bullet with a needle-nose; the lower half is a cone that ends in the single engine. There are two winglike tail fins on the side, and an upright tail fin beneath them. Reentering the Earth's atmosphere, the ship travels at 3,500 miles an hour.

Biography: After a 13-month round-trip, the 17-crewmember U.S. Air Force *XY21* rocketship crashlands in the Mediterranean off the coast of Gerra, Sicily. Fishermen rescue two men: Col. Nathan Calder and Dr. Sharman, who is gravely ill and soon perishes from an alien disease that killed eight other members of the crew. (Presumably, the remaining seven died in the crash.) The disease is never referred to again, though it appears to be the reason the explorers left Venus.

Meanwhile, a cylinder containing an unhatched specimen of Venusian life washes ashore and is found by young Pepe, who sells it to zoologist Dr. Leonardo. That night, the creature claws out from its jelly-egg and Leonardo places it in a cage; the next morning, it is nearly five feet tall. Breaking free, the alien is hunted down and captured with electrified nets. Sedated and kept in a special room at the Rome Zoo, it wakes and breaks free when an

The *Giant Ymir* lies dead after being shot off the top of the Colosseum in Rome. © Columbia Pictures.

accident causes the power to go out. After going on a rampage through the city, Ymir is shot from atop the Colosseum by an artillery barrage.

Comment: The character is never called Ymir in the film; the picture's shooting title was *The Giant Ymir*. The monster was created by special effects master Ray Harryhausen, who cowrote the story

The spaceship *XY21*, which brings the *Giant Ymir* to Earth. © Columbia Pictures.

with Charlott Knight; Bob Williams and Christopher Knopf wrote the screenplay, and Nathan Juran directed. William Hopper starred as Calder, with Bart Bradley as Pepe and Frank Puglia as Dr. Leonardo.

A novelization of the screenplay, written by Henry Slesar, appeared in the only issue of *Amazing Stories Science Fiction Novels* in 1957.

In Scandinavian mythology, the Ymir was the earliest being, the parent of the giants (making the title *The Giant Ymir* somewhat redundant). Ymir was killed by Odin, the king of the gods. Its flesh became the earth, its blood the seas, its skull the vault of the heavens.

G.I. ROBOT (C)

First Appearance: *Weird War Tales* #101, 1981, DC Comics.
Physical Description: The automaton stands six-foot-six and weighs 548 pounds, carries spare parts in its backpack, and is "programmed only to respond to the enemy." The robot is made entirely of gleaming silver-blue metal, without a covering of any kind, save for its G.I. uniform. The robot is extremely powerful and fires machinegun-like bursts from the tips of all its fingers, save for the thumb.

The second G.I. Robot is identical to the original, save that its arm also acts as a flamethrower and fires "mini AA shells." Neither of the robots can speak.
Biography: Codenamed J.A.K.E. 1 (Jungle Automatic Killer, Experimental), the robot was designed and built by Professor Thompson of M.I.T. and is assigned to Marine Sgt. Coker to fight the Japanese in the Pacific Theater. After being destroyed in an explosion, J.A.K.E. 1 is replaced by J.A.K.E. 2, whose first adversary is the powerful Japanese samurai robot Krakko. During the course of its adventures, J.A.K.E. 2 acquires a robot dog and cat.
Comment: The character was created by writer Robert Kanigher and appeared regularly in the title until its demise with #124 in 1983. J.A.K.E. 1 was destroyed in #111; J.A.K.E. 2 debuted in #113.

GNUT (L, MP, C)

First Appearance: "Farewell to the Master" by Harry Bates, October 1940, *Astounding Science Fiction*.
Physical Description: Eight feet tall, Gnut has "almost exactly the shape of a man . . . with greenish metal" for skin, a look of "sullen brooding thought . . . [and] strange, internally illuminated red eyes." The robot can speak, though he rarely deigns to, is powerful enough to smash metal with his hands, and is capable of generating intense heat and withstanding tank-fire.

Klaatu is "godlike in appearance and human in form."

The "time-space" ship is made "of an unknown greenish metal . . . a curving ovoid" without a visible "break or crack." A ramp emerges to allow egress and ingress; the door is just under eight feet tall.
Biography: The ship carrying Gnut and Klaatu does not come from the sky, but just appears from nowhere in Washington, D.C. After two days, Klaatu emerges, followed by Gnut. Though Klaatu appears peaceful, a deranged man in a tree shoots the alien, who is interred in a mausoleum in the Tidal Basin. A new Interplanetary Wing of the Smithsonian Institution is built around the ship and Gnut, since it is impossible to move them.

Taking pictures of the robot three months and one week later, photojournalist Cliff Sutherland compares new shots with old and notices that Gnut has moved slightly. Hiding in the museum after closing, Cliff watches as Gnut comes to life and enters the ship; a mockingbird flies out and dies, and then Gnut kills a gorilla that was inside the ship. Afterwards, Gnut resumes the same pose as before. Cliff hides again the next night, Gnut comes to life once more, and this time museum employee Stillwell emerges from the ship and dies within moments. Later, Gnut emerges with another body: an inert, exact copy of the dead Stillwell. Panicking, Cliff cries for help, the guards come, and Gnut returns to his familiar place. After Cliff gives his story to the press, the police take him to prison. Examiners can find no cause of death for any of the four bodies. Moreover, a third Stillwell, the real one, shows up and Cliff is released.

Authorities enclose Gnut in a block of transparent glasstex; later, as Cliff watches, the robot becomes "cherry red" and the glasstex melts away. A tank fires on Gnut without harming him, and after smashing it, the robot picks up Cliff and carries him through the water to Klaatu's tomb. He recovers from the foot of the coffin a plastic box containing "all of Earth's records of his visit," then returns to the ship; Cliff runs in after him. Inside the ship's complex laboratory, Gnut recreates Klaatu using just sounds from the audio recording of his brief appearance. Cliff understands, then, that the animals and Stillwells had been early tests of this apparatus using film strips stolen from the museum. After telling Cliff that their civilizations must learn more about one another, the copy expires. As Gnut prepares to leave, Cliff implores him to tell his masters back home that what happened to Klaatu was an accident and will not happen again. Gnut believes him, then reveals that it is he, not Klaatu, who is the master.

Comment: The story is best known as the basis for the 1951 film masterpiece *The Day the Earth Stood Still*, directed by Robert Wise, in which Gnut is called Gort and the relationship with Klaatu is different. Landing his silvery, domed flying saucer in Washington, Klaatu (Michael Rennie)—who comes from 250 million miles away and is dressed in a nearly opaque helmet and blue jumpsuit shot-through with metallic threads—is wounded by a gun-happy soldier and taken to the hospital. Recovering quickly thanks to a salve he's brought, he slips away to try and learn more about humans. Meanwhile, the seven-foot-tall silver robot Gort (Lock Martin)—who is featureless, save for a visor that rises to emit a destructive ray—stands guard at the spaceship. Posing as Mr. Carpenter, Klaatu takes a room at a boarding house and befriends single mother Helen Benson (Patricia Neal) and her son Bobby (Billy Gray). He also goes to visit scientist Dr. Barnhardt (Sam Jaffe) and asks to meet with the world's top scientists. To show them he means business, Klaatu temporarily shuts down Earth's electrical impulses, save for those used in hospitals and airplanes inflight. As the scientists gather in Washington, Helen's boyfriend Tom Stevens (Hugh Marlowe) betrays the alien to the authorities, who corner and shoot Klaatu—this time to death. Helen rushes to the saucer with instructions for Gort ("Klaatu barada nikto"). Instead of going on a rampage, the robot retrieves Klaatu's body, takes it into the saucer, and brings it back to life long enough for Klaatu to give the scientists and the world an ultimatum. He tells them that human violence must not extend into space, that we must join the federation of planets in peace, or Earth will be reduced to a burned-out cinder.

The original Bates story was presented in comic book form in Marvel Comics' *Worlds Unknown* #3, 1973. For the adaptation, writer Roy Thomas gave Sutherland a partner, Ann O'Hara.

GOBOTS (T, TV, MP, C)

First Appearance: *GoBots*, 1984, Tonka Toys (see *Comment*).

Physical Description: These humanoid robots stand approximately eight feet tall. All are transformable, becoming different vehicles.

Guardian GoBots include Leader-1, Heat Seeker, and Royal-T (jet fighters), Dozer (a bulldozer), Hans-Cuff (a police car), Turbo, Good Knight, Sparky, and Street Heat (race cars), Pumper (a fire engine), Spay-C (a space shuttle), Dumper (a dump truck), Pathfinder (a flying saucer), Rest-Q (an ambulance), Road Ranger (a flat-bed truck), Blaster (a rocket launching vehicle), Scooter (a motor-bike), Baron Von Joy (a VW bug), Zeemon (a car), Blaster and Defendor (missile-firing tanks), Wrong-Way and Flip Top (helicopters), (a race car), Heat Seeker (a jet fighter), Dive-Dive (a submarine), Van Guard (a van), Scratch and Small Foot (jeeps), Staks (a semi), and Night Ranger (a police motorcycle).

Any of the Guardian GoBots can don a Power Suit, a white exoskeleton that gives them even greater power. The suits themselves can be joined together to form the Power Suit Friendly Armored Robot.

The Guardian GoBots also have two subgroups. First, there are Zig Zag, Tic Tac, Pocket, Rube, Jig Saw, and Crossword, all of which become race cars and all of which can join together into the titanic GoBot Puzzler Friendly Robot Giant. Then there are the Rollbots, flying robots that can pull in their limbs and head to become balls.

Renegade GoBots include Cy-Kill (a silver motorcycle), Tank (a missile-firing tank), Loco (a train), Cop-Tur and Twin Spin (helicopters), Buggyman (a dune buggy), Screw Head (a mobile drill), Crain Brain (a crane), Spoiler, Herr Fiend, Psycho, and Crasher (race cars), Geeper-Creeper (an off-road vehicle), Bug Bite (a VW bug), Destroyer (a tank), Water Walk (a seaplane), Bad Boy (a bomber), Vamp (a futuristic tank), Stallion, Slicks, Crasher, and Stinger (race cars), Fly Trap (a garbage truck), Pincher (a jet-launching vehicle), Blockhead (a cement mixer), Zero (a Japanese plane), Tux (a luxury car), Scorp (a robotic scorpion), and Spoons (a fork lift).

Biography: Natives of the planet GoBotron "in a distant galaxy," the GoBots are a largely benevolent race—though there are exceptions, notably the evil Renegades, who escape from prison lead by the evil Cy-Kill. Heading into space, determined to take the Earth, they are pursued by the Guardian GoBots headed by Leader-1. The latter group falls in with a band of humans—rugged Matt Hunter, young Nick Burns, and the pretty A. J. Foster—and are based in the GoBot Command Center, a four-story-tall structure that transforms into either a four-legged or treaded tank.

The Renegades join up with the evil scientist Dr. Braxis, who is based on the big, black and silver, transformable Thruster, which can become a marching four-story headquarters or a shuttle-shaped spaceship.

Comment: The toys originated in Japan in 1983 and were imported by Tonka. A half-hour TV series, *Challenge of the GoBots*, aired 65 first-run episodes in syndication from the fall of 1984 through 1986; the only "name" actor was Rene Auberjonois, who provided the voice for Braxis. The all-new Hanna-Barbera animated film *GoBots: Battle of the Rock Lords* was released in 1986. In this outing, the GoBots come to the aid of the living rock beings of Quartex when they're threatened by the Rock Lord Magmar, who wants to seize the entire planet. Telly Savalas was the voice of Magmar.

A GoBots comic book was included in the *GoBots* magazine, which began publication in 1986. The stories were written by P.E. King and exquisitely drawn by Ralph Reese.

In 1986, Tonka launched the far less successful line Legions of Power, comprised of alien "battle machines" that either crawled, stomped, or flew into battle against their evil counterparts.

The success of the transformable toys spurred a flood of usually inferior imitations. Other lines included the Morph O Droids (Vector Intercontinental), Charger Tron (Buddy L), Kronoforms (robots into working watches from Takara Toys), and many more.

GODAIKIN ROBOTS (T)

First Appearance: Godaikin Robots, Bandai, 1984.
Physical Description: Each of the box-like humanoid robots is transformable. Abega becomes a jet; Dynaman becomes three vehicles: the plane Dynamach, the car Dynamobile, and the flatbed Dynagarry; Voltes V becomes Crewzer I, Bomber II, Panzer III, Frigate IV, and Lander V; Golion becomes five lions; Godsigma becomes the three smaller robots Ocean King, Earth King, and Thunder King; Daltanias becomes the lion-robot Velarios, the robot warrior Altaus, and the vehicle Gunper; Gardian has the smaller robots Delinger, Protteser, and one unnamed mini-robot inside its body; Sun Vulcan becomes Cozmo Vulcan, the missile firing starship, and Bull Vulcan, a bulldozer/crane; Goggle V becomes a jet, tank, and dump truck; Tetsujin 28 has two mini-robots, Roboboy and Maintenance, stored inside; Daimos becomes a van-like vehicle Tranzer; Leopardon becomes a

tank; Bio Man becomes a pair of airplanes, Bio Jet 1 and Bio Jet 2; Bio Dragon is an aircraft carrier that becomes a boat and two aircraft; Dyjupiter is a hangar that can become a spaceship; Daidenjin, the Iron Commander of the Galaxy, becomes the Denjin Spaceport; Machine Dolphin becomes the Dolphin Racing Car and the Dolphin Jet; Vavilos becomes the V Spaceship and a "double-barreled space gun"; Laserion becomes the airborne Laser Command Ship; and the colossal Dancougar becomes 11 separate vehicles.
Biography: See VOLTRON.
Comment: The line was launched in Japan in 1982, then imported to the United States. Each figure was tall (from five to thirteen inches) and relatively expensive, and they never caught on the way THE TRANSFORMERS did—with one exception. Golion was renamed Voltron for the U.S. market and anchored both a successful animated series and line of toys from Matchbox.

In 1983, Bandai produced a less expensive line called Robot Machine, which featured no narrative—just RM 1 through RM 15, humanoid robots that became, in order, a motorbike, tank, jet, helicopter, train, car, buggy, truck, bulldozer, police car, space shuttle, and ambulance. The company also released the LOV-BOTS.

GOOK (L)

First Appearance: "The Martian and the Milkmaid" by Frances Deegan, October 1944, *Fantastic Adventures*.
Physical Description: The humanoid is "tall and slender and dark-skinned," though his skin has "a queer olive green tinge" and his black hair has a hint of purple in it. He moves like an animal, "with a graceful, flowing motion," has the "fawn-like ears of a satyr," and behind his ever-present dark glasses has "greenish yellow" eyes that never blink. Though Gook looks 40, he is 400 Earth-years old.
Biography: Diacol Company field geologist Howard Clement goes to the Henshaw farm in North Dakota to see how the soil has been affected by a meteor that fell decades earlier. While he's there, Bill and Margie Henshaw tell him about Gook, who arrived the same time as the space rock, in 1901. He was naked and seemed lost, and though he appeared to be "an idjet," he was brilliant with gadgets. He's been the Henshaws' taciturn hand ever since. Clement is introduced to Gook who, impressed with his obvious intelligence, later confesses that he is from Mars; the meteor was actually his cosmic ray-powered ship,

which was caught by Earth's gravity and crashlanded. He says that he came here to find "germs" with which to replenish the soil of his dying world. He adds that if the Martians hadn't "discovered the secret of longevity," they would have died out long ago. Gook admits that he has been frustrated here, marking time until Earth reached a stage where he could establish communications with Mars.

Clement isn't sure he believes Gook's story, but takes him back to New York. He renames him George Guk, introduces him as an East Indian, and gets him a job at the plant. Guk is unimpressed by our crude technology and barbaric ways, though he likes Clement's buxom girlfriend Hebe, an aspiring actress who had worked as a milkmaid at the World's Fair. While at Diacol, Guk helps the company develop a new, heat-resistant plastic and shows them how to use it to build a high performance aircraft. During a test flight, the plane vanishes over Pennsylvania. Hebe is also missing, having gone to visit her folks on their farm—in Pennsylvania. And Clement doesn't doubt that Guk took the plane to the farm, removed the wings, and headed back to Mars with Hebe "to help repopulate a planet. . . ."

Comment: This short story was the first sale for the pioneering but largely forgotten Deegan who, later, would typically feature strong women protagonists in fantasy tales, most notably in "The Cat-Snake" (1948), the story of a girl who is half-snake, half-cat.

GOON-CHILD   (C)

First Appearance: "Henry and His . . . Goon-Child," 1950, *Weird Fantasy* #15, EC Publishing Co.

Physical Description: The robot, which never sleeps, stands approximately three-and-one-half feet tall. It has a flat, rectangular head with two eyes and a radio receiver on top; a narrow, cylindrical neck; a flat, rectangular body with a downward-sloping face and an arm in front with a pair of hooks; a cylindrical column beneath it; and a third section consisting of an upright rectangle with dials on an inverted triangular face, a small wheel in the front, and two larger wheels in the back. When the robot gets a second arm, it is placed on either side of its torso.

Biography: Henry Short owns a metropolitan radio store, but hates his work and his customers. To give himself more leisure time, he builds a "goon-child" robot who does all the repairing and household work. However, the robot works to improve itself at night, giving itself a second arm and speech. When it is finished, it threatens to kill Henry unless *he* takes over all the chores at home and in the shop. Now, while the robot reads the newspaper and relaxes, Henry does more work than ever.

Comment: The story was created by Harvey Kurtzman. The artist/writer went on to co-create *Mad* Magazine with EC publisher William Gaines.

The same issue featured the Wally Wood story "Dark Side of the Moon" in which the rocketship *Columbia* brings the first men to the moon. There, they meet frog-like humanoids in the city of N'Kyzmej, who fear an invasion from Earth.

GOR AND VOL   (MP)

First Appearance: *The Brain from Planet Arous*, 1958, Marquett Productions/Howco International.

Physical Description: The aliens Gor and Vol are brains approximately two feet across, two feet tall, and four feet long, with a "spinal cord" approximately three feet long dangling from the back. They can exist in a physical or noncorporeal state. In the latter condition, they can enter the body of and control any living creature. They can be hurt only when they are physical, and then only when they are struck in fissures on the top. They are transparent and untouchable in their "transitory" state, as they go from one to the other, and neither the brain nor the body can be harmed when it is inside a body.

The brains must return to their physical state once every 24 hours to take in the oxygen they need to survive (though they have no nose, mouth, or other visible openings). In any state, the brains communicate telepathically.

The brains have two blazing eyes in front and can project intense radiation across great distances and with amazing precision, able to incinerate a human being, destroy a plane, or vaporize every material object on a continent. Their powers are undiminished when they are inhabiting a body. By the same token, they are influenced by the desires of their host body, lust being a "very strange, very new elation" for Gor.

Gor and Vol travel through space via flying saucer.

Biography: Fleeing its homeworld of Arous, the criminal Gor comes to Earth, blasts a cave in Mystery Mountain out in the desert, and begins discharging small bursts of gamma radiation. These attract scientists Steve March and Dan Murphy, as

The evil brain *Gor* (inset) and the possessed Steve March in advertising art for *The Brain from Planet Arous.* © Howco International.

Gor had planned, since Steve knows people the alien wants to meet. Burning Dan to a crisp, Gor enters Steve's body. When he returns to civilization, he is testy and tries to rape his fiancee, Sally Fallon. Suspecting that something happened to him at Mystery Mountain, Sally and her father John head out there and meet Vol, a police brain from Arous. He tells them that Gor is corrupt, "cunning and dangerous . . . [and] insane for power" and, coming to Sally's home to plan their next step, he decides to enter Sally's dog George to keep an eye on Steve . . . and, hopefully, catch Gor when he's taking a breather outside the scientist's body.

Meanwhile, Gor has Steve go to the Indian Springs atomic testing grounds, where he tells the military that they must bring together respresentatives of all the world's governments: If any nation fails to show, its capital will be destroyed. To prove that he means business, he razes an uninhabited city that had been built for the bomb tests. At a second meeting, he blows up a plane and reveals that he intends to enslave the Earth, use its people to build spaceships, and conquer Arous. When this has been done, he says that Earth "will be free to live out its miserable span of existence as one of my satellites."

As fate would have it, George is never around when Gor emerges from Steve's body. Thus, Sally goes to his laboratory, leaves a diagram showing

Gor's weak spot, then hides in an adjoining room. When the alien emerges, Steve notices the picture—and it's a good thing he does. Sally bumps into the corpse of a sheriff Gor has murdered, and screams. When Gor turns to immolate her, Steve grabs an axe and buries the hatchet in the brain.

Comment: John Agar is Steve, Joyce Meadows is Sally, Thomas B. Henry is John, and Robert Fuller is Dan. The film was directed by Nathan Hertz (a name Nathan Juran used on films with which he wasn't entirely satisfied), from a script by Ray Buffum.

GORATH (MP)

First Appearance: *Yosei Gorasu* (*Suspicious Star Gorath*), 1962, Toho Co., Ltd.

Physical Description: Just under 4,000 miles in diameter, the star is 6,000 times the mass of Earth when first discovered. However, this increases as it eats other worlds and matter in its path, and debris is constantly raining toward it.

Biography: In 1979, the spaceship *J-X Hawk*, under Captain Sonoda, is sent to study the runaway star Gorath. As they approach, the gravitational pull is such that the ship is pulled into the star and destroyed, as is a British ship, the *Intrepid*. However, Sonoda's ship was able to send data back to Earth, and the news isn't good: Gorath is headed for a collision with Earth. Scientists Kesuke Sonoda (the captain's father), Dr. Konno, and Dr. Tazawa come up with a plan to destroy

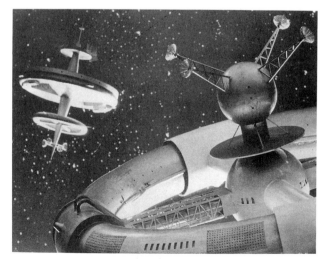

A pair of space stations in Earth orbit in *Gorath.* © Brenco Pictures Corp.

Gorath. If that fails, they will detonate a total of 66 billion megatons via rockets placed at 88 points in Antarctica to literally shove the Earth out of the way.

The *Hawk*'s sister ship, *Eagle*, is launched to try and find a way to stop Gorath. The crew fails to do so and the Antarctic rockets are ignited, releasing a giant prehistoric walrus, Magma, who attacks a key Antarctic base before being destroyed. Earth is nudged out of the path of the rogue star and, though the moon is consumed and there are massive tidal waves and destruction all over Earth, our world survives.

Comment: Takashi Shimura is Kesuke Sonoda, Ken Uehara plays Konno, and Ryo Ikebe is Tazawa. Ishiro Honda directed from a script by Takeshi Kimura, based on a story by Jojiro Okami. The film was called *Gorath* when released in the United States in 1964, though the scenes featuring Magma were cut; the producers feared that audiences would find the tusked creature laughable.

GOROG (MP)

First Appearance: *The Bowery Boys Meet the Monsters*, 1954, Allied Artists.

Physical Description: Gorog stands about seven feet tall. Its head is square, with dimly lit eyes, conical coils for ears, and rivets that form a triangular nose and oblong mouth. It has a squarish torso, an abdomen that looks like three metal dixie cups stacked upside down, and black tubes for arms and legs. It has metal hands with five rubbery fingers on each.

Gorog only responds to commands uttered into its microphone.

Biography: Local kids need a place to play baseball, and the Bowery Boys find the perfect vacant lot. They call on the owners, the Gravesend family, which is an odd group, to say the least. Derek wants to put a human brain in the skull of his pet ape Cosmos; Amelia has a giant human-eating plant; and Anton has constructed a powerful robot, Gorog. Endangered by the first two creatures, the Bowery Boys are ultimately rescued by Gorog, who becomes a player on their baseball team.

Comment: The Bowery Boys include Leo Gorcey as Slip and Huntz Hall as Sach, John Dehner is Derek, Lloyd Corrigan is Anton, and Ellen Croby is Amelia. The film was directed by Edward Bernds from a script Bernds and Ellwood Ullman.

THE GRAVE ROBBERS FROM OUTER SPACE (MP, C)

First Appearance: *Plan 9 from Outer Space*, 1958, Reynolds Pictures/Distributors Corporation of America.

Physical Description: The alien beings are human, save for their attire, black patent leather trousers and jacket with a stylized "N" on the chest. On the aliens' unnamed home world, women "are for advancing the race," and not for doing much more. Tanna seems not to resent this, though she's usually the pillar of calm when Eros throws one of his many over-the-top temper tantrums.

Their flying saucer resembles (is, in fact) a hubcap. The Ruler is based in a space station somewhere in Earth orbit.

Biography: A nameless old Los Angeles man, mourning his late, also-nameless wife, is run over and killed by a truck. At the same time, pilot Jeff Trent sees a flying saucer. Inside, aliens Eros and Tanna plot to begin Plan Nine, using "long-distance electrodes shot into the pineal-pituitary glands of the recent dead" to resurrect them, starting with the man and woman. This, in order to convince earthlings that aliens exist (apparently, the saucer wasn't enough). The nameless couple return from the dead and kill towering Inspector Clay, who is also revived as an alien henchman.

Meanwhile, the aliens have destroyed a small town (why is never made clear), and several Earthlings go onboard to try and find out what the aliens are up to. Eros reveals that his world fears Earth will one day discover Solaronite bombs, which cause particles of sunlight to explode and threaten to destroy the universe. He says he's come to warn us of the danger, which our "juvenile minds . . . will not comprehend . . . until it's too late." Convinced that Eros is more danger than an arsenal of Solaronite bombs, the earthmen fire guns, the control room of the saucer catches fire, and the terrestrials flee, leaving the ship to explode while it soars off over Hollywood.

Comment: Dudley Manlove and Joanna Lee are Eros and Tanna. John Breckinridge plays the Ruler, Gregory Walcott is Trent, and Tor Johnson is Clay. Bela Lugosi, in his last screen appearance, plays the nameless old man; writer/director Edward D. Wood Jr. shot Lugosi's footage in 1956, without any idea how he would ultimately use the scenes. Vampira (a.k.a. Maila Nurmi) plays Lugosi's wife and chiropractor Tom Mason, with a cape covering most of his features, plays the nameless man when he returns from the dead. (Lugosi had died by the time *Plan 9 from Outer Space* went into production.)

Until shortly before its release, the film was going to be called *Grave Robbers from Outer Space*. For the record, Plans One through Eight are never mentioned.

After select screenings, the film sat on the shelf before going into general release in 1959.

The making of the film was chronicled in director Tim Burton's movie *Ed Wood* (1994).

A comic book adaptation of the film was published by Malibu Comics in 1990.

GREEN LANTERN CORPS   (C, TV)

First Appearance: *Green Lantern* #11, 1962, DC Comics.

Physical Description: The aliens come in all shapes and sizes, though all wear a power ring with some kind of green and/or black uniform with the power-lamp symbol and, with few exceptions, a black or green domino mask. The lamp itself is powered by the minds of the Guardians through a central battery on Oa. The rings enable the wearer to fly anywhere, including outer space (inside a "protective aura"), and create any object the wearer wills, from a simple loudspeaker to giant pincers to gorillas capable of juggling criminals. The ring must be charged once every 24 Earth hours and, due to an imperfection in its manufacture, is ineffective against anything yellow-colored.

Biography: Some 10 billion years ago, on the planet Maltus, blue-skinned humanoids began to develop into a highly advanced race devoted to learning as much as possible through study and scientific research. After six billion years, one of the scientists, Krona, builds a time window to witness the beginning of all things. His interference causes evil to be unleashed at the instant of creation, infesting the young universe. It is already mature as it ripples through history, changing it. (It also gives birth to multiple universes, including the anti-matter universe of the world Qward, whose ruler, the Anti-Monitor, later causes much grief for the Corps.) Guilt-stricken, Krona's fellow scientists migrate to Oa, a world at the center of the universe, "where Krona's curse began," determined to fight evil wherever it appears. As the self-proclaimed Guardians of the Universe, they

seek out sentient beings on other worlds, each of whom has the moral and physical makeup to become members of the Green Lantern Corps. In time, the female Oans leave to become the warrior women called Zamorans, while the males dwindle to 36 in number, all of them dwarfish and macrocephalic.

There are 3,600 members of the Green Lantern Corps, each of which patrols a tenth of a degree of a circle that radiates from Oa. The first Earth member was test pilot Hal Jordan, who was given the ring by red-skinned humanoid Abin Sur who crashlands on Earth. He was succeeded as the protector of sector 2814 by architect John Stewart and gym teacher Guy Gardner. Other members of the Corps include: Tomar-Re, sector 2813, a fishlike, bird-beaked, golden-skinned humanoid of the planet Xudar (who failed in one assignment: to save the people of the planet KRYPTON from destruction); Ghrelk, sector 69, an aged blue-skinned humanoid from the planet Naktos who passes the ring to Varix; Ch'p, sector 1014, an opposum-like biped (with a tail) from the planet H'lven; Kilowog, sector 674, a hippopotamus-like biped from the planet Bolovax; Katma Tui, sector 1417, a red-skinned humanoid from Korugar; Arisia, sector 2815, a bronze-skinned, pointy-eared humanoid teenager from the planet Graxos IV; Charlie Vickers, sector 3319, a transplanted Earthman; Gk'd, a humanoid with a sucker-fish-like head and elephant ears, from Fp'y; Charqwep, an orange stalk with dozens of small legs below and a mound of bulbs on top; Brokk, an octopus-like creature from Cygnus; Apros, a pumpkin-like being with dozens of tentacles on its bottom and nearly as many antennae on top; Spak-Drom, a redskinned, four-armed humanoid from Xerses (deceased); Skryd, a four-armed eel-like creature from Multu; Gnewmann Gnoggs, and then Gnort Esplanade Gneesmacher, both dog-like bipeds from the planet Gnewt; Sodam Yat, a heavily muscled humanoid, from Daxam, regarded as "the ultimate Green Lantern"; Mogo, a "planet-form" Green Lantern; Xax, the grasshopper-like hero from Xaos; Medphyl, a cyclopean humanoid with a carrot-like head, from the planet J586; Arkkis Chummuck (now deceased), a golden-skinned humanoid with pointed ears, small tusks, and a great deal of facial hair who became a Green Lantern after defeating (and eating) the birdlike humanoid Green Lantern of the planet Xanshi, who had been responsible for his brother's death; Hollika Rahn, a pink-skinned humanoid from Rhoon; K'ryssma, a humanoid with floor-length white hair; Jeryll, a silver-haired humanoid from Glirell; Stel, a humanoid robot from the robot world of Grenda (deceased); M'Dahna, a combination starfish/tortoise shell; Eddore, a protoplasmic blob with arms, from the planet Tront; Chaselon, a multi-faceted crystal orb with two tentacle legs and two tentacle arms, from the planet Barrio III; Galius-Zed, a head with three stubby legs and two arms; Larvox, a spider-like creature from Sputa; and Salakk, a humanoid with four spindly arms and a slug-like head, from the planet Slyggia.

Regardless of the world from which they hail, all of the Green Lanterns utter this oath as they recharge their rings:

> In brightest day, in blackest night,
> No evil shall escape my sight.
> Let those who worship evil's might
> Beware my power—Green Lantern's light!

One of the more intriguing Green Lantern stories was told in *Batman: In Darkest Knight*, and speculated what would have happened had Abin Sur chosen Bruce Wayne (Batman) to be the Green Lantern of Earth. In one of the most dramatic shakeups in the Green Lantern saga, Hal Jordan—once again the Green Lantern of sector 2814—flips out when he is unable to prevent the destruction of his home base, Coast City. He defeats a succession of Green Lanterns and claims their rings, murders Kilowog when the Bolovaxian tries to reason with him, and all but one of the Guardians, Ganthet, perish trying to stop him. Jordan loses his ring but enters the central battery on Oa and emerges a mighty renegade, but Ganthet refuses to let their dream die. Coming to Earth, the last Oan literally gives the last surviving ring to the first human he sees: young freelance artist Kyle Rayner (*Green Lantern*, second series, #48-50, 1993-94).

Comment: The Guardians of the Universe first appeared in *Green Lantern* #1 in 1960. The other Green Lanterns have appeared in *Green Lantern*, *Tales of the Green Lantern Corps, Green Lantern Corps Quarterly*, and other titles. Presently, even Guy Gardner has his own eponymous comic book.

Green Lantern, sans the rest of the Corps, has been seen on TV in animated cartoons on *The Superman/Aquaman Hour of Adventure* (1967–68). He was also featured on the two-part live-action special *Legends of the Super-Heroes*, which aired in 1979.

The original Green Lantern, Alan Scott, debuted in *All-American Comics* #16 in 1940, and owed his powers to a lantern fashioned from a meteorite. The Guardians played no part in this saga. Scott was worked into the later continuity when it was revealed that he lives on Earth 2 in a parallel dimension.

THE GREEN SLIME (MP)

First Appearance: *The Green Slime*, 1969, Ram Films/Southern Cross Films Production/Toei Company/MGM.

Physical Description: Growing from a single cell to roughly six feet tall, the aliens are elongated gumdrops with two legs and three-clawed feet, one or two pair of arms with pincers, and a large, red eye toward the top/center of their body. The aliens have lumpy gray-green skin and long sacs hanging from the "waist." They feed on energy, generate lethal doses of electricity from their lobster-like pincers—which they can also use to heal their wounds—can survive unprotected in space, have bright green blood, and emit a high-pitched whine. The Green Slime has the ability to "spawn new creatures from its own blood."

The asteroid Flora weighs six million tons.

Biography: When the asteroid Flora is discovered to be on a collision course with Earth—with impact in 12 hours—retired astronaut Commander Jack Rankin is sent to space station Gamma 3 to lead the operation to intercept and destroy the body. He is assisted by his friend Commander Vince Elliot and his old girlfriend Dr. Lisa Benson, who is now engaged to Elliot. Rocketing to the asteroid, the crew lands and plants explosive charges; unknown to them, a particle of green muck from one of the puddles scattered across the surface clings to one of the spacesuits. The asteroid is destroyed but, back on the station, the slime survives decontamination and grows inside a locker. Killing a crewmember, the monster heads for one of the power terminals to feed. Rankin wants to electrocute it, but Elliot orders it captured and several crewmembers die in the failed effort.

Deciding to isolate the Slime, Rankin orders the electricity on Gamma 3 turned off and uses a portable generator to lure the now-plentiful Slime to a storage area with a sturdy door. Unfortunately, a man is trapped inside and Elliot has the door opened, allowing the Slime to swarm out. The aliens feed on a generator, causing it to explode and destroying all of C-block; though several Slimes are killed by the extreme heat, the others attach themselves to the hull and begin feeding on the solar generators. Rankin leads an assault team against the monsters, but they reproduce faster than they can be slain. Realizing there's only one course of action, Rankin orders the space wheel evacuated and, with Elliot, heads to the control room to send Gamma 3 and its unwanted passengers spinning into the Earth's atmosphere. Elliot is badly mauled by a Slime in the process and, grabbing him, Rankin leaps from a hatchway just as the station starts to burn up. The men are picked up by a shuttlecraft, where Elliot dies.

Comment: The Japanese/U.S. coproduction was directed by Kinji Fukasada from a screenplay by Charles Sinclair, William Finger, Tom Rowe, and Takeo Kaneko, based on a story by Ivan Reiner. Robert Hortan stars as Rankin, with Richard Jaeckel as Elliot and Luciana Paluzzi as Lisa. In Japan, the film was known as *Gamma Sango Uchu Dai Sakusen (After the Creation of Space Station Gamma: Big Military Operation)*.

THE GUARDIANS OF THE GALAXY (C)

First Appearance: *Marvel Super Heroes* #18, 1967, Marvel Comics.

Physical Description: All of the Guardians are humanoids. Charlie 27 stands a stocky six feet tall, weighs over a quarter of a ton, and wears a gold and yellow bodysuit, gold boots, a red cowl, and studded red wristbands, anklets, and belt. He is super-strong and nearly impervious to injury. Martinex stands six-one and is made of silicon, which gives his body a crystalline look. He has superstrength and can generate extreme heat and cold. Nikki stands five-eight, wears a green "bathing suit," boots, and gloves, and has flame-like hair. She is impervious to heat and certain kinds of radiation, and can see clearly in bright light. Starhawk stands six-four, has superstrength, can fly, and has the ability to use light as a destructive force. Vance Astro stands six-one, wears a navy blue bodysuit, boots, gloves, and full-face cowl with white markings on the chest and legs. He possesses the power of telekinesis as well as the ability to project thought-beams. Yondu wears a blue bodysuit with a red left arm and left side of the chest, and red trunks, boots, and an 11-inch fin on his head (this, on top of his six-two height), and a gold belt, quiver, and right armband and wristband. His "yaka" arrows are made of a special sound-sensitive metal, and their trajectory can be controlled by whistling.

The Guardians' spaceship, *Freedom's Lady*, looks like a stylized "Z," longer and fatter on top than on the bottom.

Biography: When the evil alien Badoon invade the solar system in 3007 A.D., destroying outposts on Pluto, Jupiter, and Mercury before attacking Earth, Space Militia pilot Charlie-27 of Jupiter teams with the genetically restructured Martinex—the sole survivor of the Pluto massacre—to form the Guardians of the Galaxy, devoted to protecting the worlds of the Milky Way from invaders. Meanwhile, astronaut Vance Astrovik reaches the planet Centauri IV in the Alpha Centauri system after a lengthy journey, during which he mysteriously develops psionic powers. He arrives only to learn that, in his absence, faster-than-light travel had been perfected and other humans had beaten him there. He is befriended by native-born Yondu, who returns with him to Earth where they encounter the Badoon. The two throw in their lot with Charlie-27 and Martinex and in 3015, with the help of the modern-day heroes the Defenders, the Badoon are defeated.

The foursome patrol in the ship *Captain America*, replacing it with *Freedom's Lady* when the first vessel is destroyed. In time, they're joined by the mutant Starhawk of Arcturus IV and Nikki, the sole survivor of the Mercury colony.

Comment: The first story was reprinted, in redacted form, in *Astonishing Tales* #29, 1975. The characters also appeared in *Marvel Presents* #s 3–112 (Nikki debuted in #4, 1976) and and other titles. Starhawk debuted in *The Defenders* #27, 1975.

GUIRARA (MP)

First Appearance: *Uchu Daikaiju Guirara (The Great Space Monster Guirara)*, 1967, Shochiku Co. Ltd.

Physical Description: Standing approximately 200 feet tall, Guirara is a reptilian biped with lumpy skin, huge frills running down the front of its legs, massive claws, a bird-like beak, two flat horizontal projections on the sides of its head, and a pair of antennae with a horn between them. The monster feeds on energy.

Biography: The four-man, sled-like spaceship AAB-Gamma is sent to Mars, despite the fact that six other ships have vanished. A hamburger-shaped UFO appears and releases glowing blobs which attach themselves to the ship; Captain Sano and biologist Lisa shake off all save one, which they bring back to Earth. Taken to a laboratory, the specimen hatches, grows to giant size, and attacks Tokyo. Acting quickly, the crew of the AAB-

Gamma return to space and gather Guirarium, a creamy form of antimatter that they feel just might prevent the monster from absorbing energy. As the monster heads for the (Mt.) Fuji Astro Flying Center in search of nourishment, the space researchers return to Earth. While they lure the monster away from their headquarters using a trailer full of atomic fuel, jets bomb the monster with Guirarium. The alien shrinks to its original size and the FAFC send it back into space.

Comment: Toshiya Wazaki is Sano and Peggy Neal plays Lisa. Kazui Nihonmatsu directed from his script, cowritten by Hidemi Motomochi and Moriyoshi Ishida. In the English-dubbed version, released in 1968 as *The X from Outer Space*, the monster is called Guilala.

H

HAL See THE DISCOVERY.

HAWK-HAVEN (TV, C)

First Appearance: *SilverHawks*, September 1986, syndication.

Physical Description: Hawk-Haven is built inside an excavated asteroid. It is approximately 600 feet tall, 400 feet wide, and 400 feet deep. The entrance is a horizontal bay approximately 100 feet wide and set in a circular metal surface roughly 300 feet in diameter. Above the circle is a metallic sculpture of a hawk with its wings spread. Beneath the asteroid is a pylon with an engine suspended horizontally.

The SilverHawks fly through space onboard their sleek, blue, hawk-shaped fighter Mirage. In addition to the cockpit, the passengers sit in two pods on each wing, one hugging the fuselage, the other at the wingtip. The head cockpit can separate from the rest of the ship and both fly and fight on its own, in the air or in space. The ship also fires ray beams and has the ability to become noncorporeal for a short time, allowing enemies to pass right through it. The Mirage cannot leave Earth's gravity on its own, but must be lofted by a booster rocket. It is approximately 40 feet long from wingtip to wingtip.

Biography: When the evil Mon*Star breaks free from the prison planet Io, he frees six other super villains and raids the universe from his squid-like vessel *Skyrunner*. Acting quickly, the Federal Interplanetary Force 1 Headquarters of Lawrence, Nevada, on Earth, selects four humans and one alien to be transformed into super-androids known as the SilverHawks. They are assigned to Hawk-Haven in the Limbo Galaxy, orbiting the planet Bedlama, and work with Commander Stargazer to try and apprehend Mon*Star.

The SilverHawks are encased in silver skins and are comprised of leader Quicksilver and his cyborg-bird Tally-Hawk; Bluegrass, who pilots the Mirage; the female Steelwill and Steelheart, mechanics; and the Copper Kid from the Planet of Mimes, a computer expert.

Comment: Sixty-two adventures were made by Rankin-Bass Productions, three of them an hour, the rest a half-hour.

Marvel Comics published six issues of a *SilverHawks* comic book as part of their youth-oriented Star Comics line, in 1987–88. There were also various toys, coloring books, action figures, etc.

HAWKMAN AND HAWKGIRL (C, TV)

First Appearance: *Brave and the Bold* #34, 1961, DC Comics.

Physical Description: Their bodies "specially treated to withstand extreme temperatures and air friction," Hawkman and Hawkgirl originally wear police uniforms consisting of big gray wings, golden hawk-head masks with yellow beaks (wings were added to the sides in *Brave and the Bold* #43), green tights, and boots and red trunks with a yellow stripe down the side. Yellow straps crisscross Hawkman's chest, with a hawkhead silhouette on a red circle in the center (a two-way radio on Thanagar, it's used to store Hawkman's highly compressed costume on Earth); Hawkgirl wears a sleeveless yellow blouse. The duo can fly due to their anti-gravity belts, survive in outer space for "a few minutes," and dive unprotected to depths of 60 feet in water.

Later, their costumes change to silver and gray armor with golden metal wings and a golden hawk-helmet (for the *Hawkworld* miniseries); after that, they wear a dark blue bodysuit, boots, and gloves with gray trunks and a golden helmet and chest-straps with a red hawkhead silhouette in the center (the 1993 *Hawkman* comic).

The team's weapons include a "police special," which fires a paraly-beam, stun-ray, and other blasts. On Earth, fearful that their advanced weapons may fall into criminal hands, they tend to use ancient weapons such as a retarius (gladiator's net), bow-and-arrow, flails (maces), crossbow with a variety of quarrels—many of them hi-tech—cestuses (boxing gloves), axes, spears, and throwing stars. However, they have, on occasion, used a thermotector to trace body heat, a lustrometer to follow gems, a radiotron to track radiation, and more. The heroes communicate with Thanagar via hyperstellar phones.

On Thanagar, criminals are kept in Electro-cells and cannot lie due to truth-ray lamps, a.k.a. the veracikones. X-ray-like "dissecti-rays" allow the police to look through barriers.

Their orbiting spaceship headquarters, which looks like a giant arrow with a green head and tailfins and yellow shaft, is equipped with invisibility and anti-detection devices, a duplicator that copies non-living matter, a velocitor to rush them to their destination, "thin metal headbands" that use "nuclear relays" to pick up electronic impulses and allow them to learn facts and languages quickly, a hibernation chamber, and other equipment.

Biography: Katar Hol, son of ornithologist Paran Katar, and his wife Shayera Thal are a district police commanding officer and police officer, respectively, of the metropolis of Thanaldar on the planet Thanagar in the star system Polaris. Chasing the bodyshape-changing villain Byth Rok to Midway City on Earth, they meet with Police Commissioner George Emmett to try and trap the interstellar felon. Emmett arranges for Katar to replace his brother Ed, the retiring director of the City Museum. Calling themselves Carter Hall and Shiera, they pursue their quarry with ancient arms from the museum. After he is captured, the duo remain on Earth to study terrestrial crimefighting methods. For half-a-year they battle a variety of criminals before reporting back to Chief Andar Pul on Thanagar. After fighting the escaped Byth on Thanagar and capturing him using techniques they learned on Earth, the duo returns to Earth to continue studying terrestrial police ways.

Hawkgirl's name was "changed" to Hawkwoman (*Hawkman* #1, 1986). The characters were charter members of the Justice League of America.

Other alien beings and races that have appeared in the saga include the space-traveling Manhawks; the evil dictator Kanjar Ro of the planet Dhor; the Kalvars, who were the harpies of Greek mythology; the Tralls, golden-skinned slavers from the planet Llorth; the beast-creatures of Illoral, where animals evolved into humanoids; the fierce Lizarkons of the planet Aptilia; and a robot duplicate of Shayera from another world.

Comment: This was actually the second DC Hawkman; the first Carter Hall had made his debut in *Flash Comics* #1 in 1940. This character, however, is the reincarnation of the Ancient Egyptian Hawkman, who resumes his magical crusade against evil in the modern day. Both characters were created by much underrated science fiction writer Gardner Fox.

In a retelling of the origin tale, Commander Katar Hol kills his father, for which crime the police officer (now referred to as a "wingman") is sentenced to prison on the Isle of Chance. However, Katar convinces the authorities that he was tricked into the crime by the evil Byth, who has now fled to Earth where he is pursued by the hero and heroine.

After several appearances in *Brave and the Bold*, Hawkman got his own magazine which lasted 27 issues, from 1964 to 1968; it was revived for 17 issues in 1986-87, and a new *Hawkman* comic book, launched in 1993, is ongoing. A four-issue miniseries, *The Shadow War of Hawkman*, was published in 1985, and a three-issue *Hawkworld* miniseries in 1989 spawned a comic book of the same name, which is still being published. The characters have appeared in *Showcase*, *D.C. Comics Presents*, *Mystery in Space*, *Detective Comics*, and other DC titles over the years.

Hawkman was seen, briefly, in the two-part live action adventure/comedy *Legends of the Super-Heroes*, which aired on ABC in 1979. Hawkgirl was featured in the animated *All-New Super Friends Hour*, which aired on ABC from September 1977-78 (voice provided by Louise "Liberty" Williams), and Hawkman was seen on *Super Powers Team: Galactic Guardians* which aired on ABC from September 1985 to August 1986 (voice by Jack Angel).

HECTOR (MP)

First Appearance: *Saturn 3*, 1980, Associated Film Distribution.

Physical Description: The first robot of the Demigod series, Hector is eight feet tall, humanoid, and skinless. All of his wires, hydraulics, and transistors are visible, shaped somewhat in the form of human muscle. Instead of a humanoid head, the robot has an arm-like extension with an "eye" atop his neck. Hector is programmed by being plugged directly into a human brain and thus imprinted with the programmer's personality. His pincer hands are accurate and fast enough to snatch a metal sliver from a human eye before the lid can blink.

Two other benevolent robots seen in the film are Rivit and Morfax. The former walks on any surface—including walls—and the latter floats on gentle jets of air.

Biography: Adam and Alex live an idyllic life, alone, as they conduct hydroponic research at an underground base on Saturn's third moon, Titan. Their job: to keep the overcrowded, drug-maddened Earth from starving. Enter psychotic Benson, who kills a supply ship pilot, Captain James, and comes to the base pretending to be James. With him are plans for the robot Hector who, ostensibly, is going to help the duo with their research. In actuality, as built and programmed by Benson, Hector has intense sexual desires and lusts after Alex. As the moon endures a 22-day-long eclipse, keeping the occupants from radioing for help, Hector and Benson end up vying for the woman. Hector cuts off Benson's hand and kills him. After various cat-and-mouse chases, Adam is able to push the lascivious robot into a vat of acid, then takes Alex away for her first visit to Earth.

Comment: Kirk Douglas stars as Adam, Farrah Fawcett is Alex, Harvey Keitel is Benson, and Douglas Lambert is James. Stanley Donen directed from a script by Martin Amis, based on a story by John Barry.

Donen views the story as a modern day Adam and Eve tale, with Benson as the serpent.

HEECHEE (L)

First Appearance: "Gateway" by Frederik Pohl, November 1976, *Galaxy*.

Physical Description: The incredibly "gaunt" Heechee are "smaller than human beings," with very wide pelvises that give them "a gait like a walking skeleton." Their skin is "plastic-smooth and mostly dark . . . [with] patches and curlicues of bright gold and scarlet that . . . [resemble] Indian war paint." The aliens' faces seem like they're "carved out of shiny plastic," though they are "resilient enough to allow for facial expression." Their voices are "growling and hissing and tweeting" and they smell "quite strange." (The Heechee are not actually pictured until the third novel.)

The Heechee gateway is "about ten kilometers through" and pear-shaped, resembling "a lumpy charred blob with glints of blue" on the outside. Inside, the "nearly a thousand" spaceships are "smallish . . . shaped something like fat mushrooms."

Biography: Half a million years ago, fearing an intelligent-life-hating enemy known as the Foe, the Heechee retreated into a black hole at the core of the galaxy, leaving behind the gateway. In our own near future, the gateway and its ships are discovered by humans. All of the ships are programmed for a hyperlight journey to parts unknown, the human occupants having no control whatsoever. Robinette "Bob" Broadhead boards one of the ships and, in the course of his adventures, discovers the history of the Heechee—who are presumed dead; loses his love Gelle-Klara Moynlin in the black hole (though she's recovered much later); helps to reactivate the Food Factory, a Heechee spaceship orbiting beyond Pluto and able to turn cometary matter into an unlimited food supply; and becomes one of the richest men on Earth.

Onboard the Food Factory, a youth named Wan Santos-Schmitz hears voices of the "Old Ones" and Robinette wonders if they might be the Heechee. Meanwhile, the Heechee send out a "little probing expedition" to see if it's safe to come out. The leader of the journey, Captain and his "female" Twice and their crew are alarmed to find that humans have mastered much of the Heechee technology, and fear—with some justification—that our spacefaring activities will attract the attention of the Foe. In the third adventure, Robinette's cybernetician wife Essie learns how to transfer the minds of dead people into machines, most notably Albert Einstein, which helps humans and the Heechee face the Foe in the fourth adventure.

Comment: The story was serialized through March 1977; St. Martin's Press published the novel in book form later that year. The first novel formed the basis of what is known as *The Heechee Saga*, which includes *Beyond the Blue Event Horizon* (1980), *Heechee Rendezvous* (1984), and *The Annals of the Heechee* (1987).

H.E.R.B.I.E. See DR. SUN AND H.E.R.B.I.E.

HEROES OF LALLOR (C)

First Appearance: *Adventure Comics* #324, 1964, DC Comics.

Physical Description: Beast Boy, who can become any kind of animal, wears a green bodysuit with black and white trunks, cuffs, and collar. Duplicate Boy, who can imitate the powers of any other hero, wears a red bodysuit, white trunks, white boots with blue stripes on top, blue cuffs with a white stripe, and green braid around the top of his arms. Evolvo Lad, who can shift between human evolutionary periods, past and future, wears a blue bodysuit with a yellow front, gloves, trunk, and belt. Gas Girl, who can turn into mist, wears a bodysuit that is white to the waist, pink to the chest, then black, with white gloves. Life Lass, who can bring inanimate objects to life, wears a red bodysuit with white boots, and white and black bands around the tops of her thighs and the neck of the bodysuit.

Biography: In the middle 30th century, on the planet Llalor in the 36th quadrant, five couples are exposed to radiation after an accidental nuclear blast. As a result, their children are born with amazing powers. When the dictator, Prime Minister Vorr, learns of the children—Sev Tcheru (Evolvo Lad), Ord Qelu (Duplicate Boy), Tal Nahii (Gas Girl), Somi Gan (Life Lass), and Ishu Nor (Beast Boy)—he has them banished, fearing that they may one day challenge his rule. The youths come to Earth, where they are met by Doctor Marden King, who blames the benevolent Legion of Super-Heroes for the death of his brother, Jungle King. Marden convinces the quintet that the Legion is evil and will exile them; thus, the newcomers band together as the Legion of Super-Outlaws with Sev as the leader. When they learn the error of their ways, the aliens call off the war and return home—Vorr having been removed from office—where they operate as the crimefighting Heroes of Lallor. Beast Boy perishes saving a girl from a wild maw from the planet Vorn.

Comment: The heroes have never had a magazine of their own, but occasionally appear with, and as a backup feature to, the Legion of Super-Heroes.

THE HIGHEST INTELLIGENCE (MP)

First Appearance: *Have Rocket, Will Travel*, 1959, Columbia Pictures.

Physical Description: Approximately seven feet tall, the Intelligence is a cube-shaped computer covered with dials and switches. It has eight tubular arms, two on each side, each of which ends in a pincer. The Intelligence has a dome atop its head and three antennae. Though the robot isn't ambulatory, it can teleport itself anywhere on Venus. It can also reduce objects in size, turn matter to energy, draw things to it, and create robots that look human and serve it slavishly.

Biography: Maintenance men at a rocket facility on Earth, the Three Stooges create their own sugar-based fuel and try it out on an Atlas-style rocket. They end up on Venus, where they escape a flame-spitting giant tarantula, befriend a talking unicorn, and are captured by the Highest Intelligence. At some unspecified point in the past, Venusians built the computer to serve them. However, it "destroyed them all and turned them into electrical energy," and made the unicorns its slaves. (The film does not suggest what the ruling Venusians looked like.)

Impressed with the Stooges' functional humanoid design, the Intelligence makes robot duplicates of the Earthmen, then shrinks the originals and places them in a birdcage. That proves boring, though, so the Intelligence restores the Stooges and sets the robots after them. Fortunately, the space travelers are able to reach their rocket and blast off for home. The Intelligence sends the robots after them and, when last seen, our heroes are once again running from their evil duplicates.

Comment: Robert J. Stevenson was the voice of the robot. This was the Stooges' first feature film; at the time, the trio was comprised of veterans Moe Howard and Larry Fine with relative newcomer Curly-Joe De Rita. Dal McKennon was the voice of the unicorn. The film was written by Raphael Hayes and directed by David Lowell Rich.

THE HOKAS (L)

First Appearance: "Heroes Are Made" by Poul Anderson and Gordon R. Dickson, May 1951, *Other Worlds*.

Physical Description: The Hokas are "about a meter tall, tubby and golden-furred with round blunt-muzzled heads" and small black eyes. The only difference between the Hokas and "giant teddy bears" are their stubby-fingered hands and ability to speak, which they do in "high-pitched" voices.

The Hokas' "horses" are pony-sized with four hoofed feet and "whiplike tails, long necks with beaked heads, and scaly green hides."

The Slissi are extremely fleet "tyrannosaurian" reptiles.

Toka circles Brackney's Star III, located 503 light years from Earth. The planet rotates every 24 hours, has a 12-month year, and possesses three moons: Uha, Buha, and Huha ("Fat," "Drunk," and "Sluggish" in the local language). The air and gravity are Earthlike.

Biography: The first human expedition to Toka meets a farming tribe of Hokas and, for the entertainment of the crew, sets up a movie screen and watches a western. The Hokas go "wild" for the movie and decide to model their society after the American West. The crew also leaves books and magazines with the Hokas to help their civilization evolve. Thirty years later, the Terrestrial Inter-stellar Survey Service ship *Draco* arrives on Toka, and ensign Alexander Braithwaite Jones is welcomed to the town of Canyon Gulch, where he helps the cuddly Hokas defeat their "Indian" enemies, the hissing Slissi.

In Jones's subsequent adventures among the literature/arts-inspired world of the Hokas, he finds himself with Hokas living in societies based on *Don Giovanni, Beau Geste,* the TV show *Tom Bracken of the Space Patrol,* the London of Sherlock Holmes—in which they help the Interstellar Bureau of Investigation sniff out four-legged, two-armed, renegade dream-peddling Ppussjans from Ximba—a blend of *Mutiny on the Bounty* and H.M.S. *Pinafore,* "Casey at the Bat," a spy drama, the Mowgli stories, and a Horatio Hornblower-esque sea saga.

Comment: "Heroes Are Made" (retitled "The Sheriff of Canyon Gulch") was collected along with "In Hoka Signo Vinces," "The Adventures of the Misplaced Hound," "Yo Ho Hoka," "The Tiddlywink Warriors," and "Don Jones" in *Earthman's Burden* in 1957. The creatures were also featured in "Joy in Mudville" (1955), "Undiplomatic Immunity" (1957), "Full Pack (Hokas Wild)" (1957), and "The Napoleon Crime" (1983), all of which were collected in *Hoka* (1983). The characters also showed up in *Star Prince Charlie* (1975), and appeared peripherally in other stories.

Dickson sold his first science fiction story in 1950; "Trespass" was cowritten with Anderson and published in *Fantastic Story Quarterly.*

See also THE WERSGORIX.

THE HONEYEARTH EXPRESS (L)

First Appearance: "The HoneyEarthers" by Robert F. Young, August 1964, *Amazing Stories.*

Physical Description: Flying to the moon in six hours, each rocket is identified by its "Loveflight" number. There are at least three levels in the ship, accessible by a spiral staircase. Each compartment contains four two-person lounge seats.

Also featured is the *Ganymede,* a "leviathan" of a floe freighter. The ship—apparently rocket-shaped—has six steel ladders on the side leading to a belly gun that shoots grapnels into space ice found in planetary rings. This is melted in vats onboard the ship and transported to worlds in need of water.

Good sites for freighters are scouted by floe-charters, small rockets that work for the "water-lane" companies.

Biography: The Earthlight Inn is located on the moon and allows newlyweds from around the cosmos to vacation in an earthlike environment. (The Inn is located in a dome and consists of at least five levels of rooms—HoneyEarth Nests—and the Earthlight Room for dining. It is surrounded by three smaller domes: a reception area for the Express, an airlock, and a power-room.) Waterlane magnate and alien land speculator Aaron Price heads there with his son Ronny's wife Fleurette, to treat her to a vacation from her philandering son, who is also wanted by the IRS. But he also has something to tell her: He has a plan to help Ronny. The young man, it turns out, is not really his son. Aaron found him, stranded on Saturn's rings, 14 years ago, when he was a 15-year-old apprentice grapnelman. He took him in, and now he has arranged to put Ronny back on the rings and thus induce a phenomenon called "space-fuge," which will make him forget the intervening years. When he's rescued this time, he'll have no memory of the intervening years and can be retrained selectively and correctly.

In his waterlane days, Price worked around Saturn as well as the planets Fargastar, Guanlago, and Alphaghagar.

Comment: The prolific Young's first published story was "The Black Deep Thou Wingest" in *Startling Stories* (1953). The best of his stories appear in *The Worlds of Robert F. Young* (1965) and *A Glass of Stars* (1968).

HOPPY, THE CAPTAIN MARVEL BUNNY (C)

First Appearance: *Funny Animals* #1, 1942, Fawcett Publications.

Physical Description: In his natural form, Hoppy is scrawny and pink-furred. In his superhero guise, he is taller and more muscular, dressed in a red bodysuit, a white cape with yellow fringe, yellow gloves, boots, belt, and a yellow lightning bolt on his chest. As the Captain Marvel Bunny, Hoppy can fly with "rocketlike speed," possesses super-strength, has super-senses, and can exist without air.

Biography: Hoppy, his girlfriend Millie, and their close friend Zeke Squirrel live on the Earthlike Funny Animal Land, a world located not far from Planet Carrot. It's a planet where peaceful animals such as rabbits, pigs, squirrels, and monkeys live in rustic tranquility. Reading a *Captain Marvel* comic book one day, Hoppy wonders whether the word Shazam, which turns weak Billy Batson into the mighty Captain Marvel, will transform him into a super rabbit. It does, and whenever carnivores like the Leopard Men or bullies like Black Bill the Bear disturb the tranquility of Funny Animal Land, the "mighty flying cottontail" rushes to meet them.

Hoppy once visited Earth (in *Marvel Family #28*, 1948) to help Mary Marvel put an end to a war between the Dog People and the Cat People of the planet Vesta.

Comment: Hoppy starred in most issues of *Funny Animals* through #68. The entire Captain Marvel line was shut down in 1953 after a long-running legal dispute with the publishers of the Superman comic book. Thus, when several Hoppy stories were reprinted in the *Atomic Mouse* comic book a year later, the character's name was changed to Speedy, the Magic Bunny, and Shazam was now Alizam. The lightning bolt was also stricken from his costume.

HOWARD THE DUCK (C, MP)

First Appearance: *Fear #19*, 1972, Marvel Comics.

Physical Appearance: Howard is an anthropomorphic duck who stands two-foot-seven, weighs 40 pounds, and has arms instead of wings. Initially, his clothing was just a blue blazer, small fedora, and red tie with black polka dots. Later, he acquires trousers and occasionally wears a bow tie.

Biography: On Duckworld, in another dimension, evolution has paralleled that of the Earth, only ducks have become the dominant life form. Howard even speaks English, albeit with a truculent edge. Early aptitude tests suggested that he was best suited to be a mortician. Though he's a "potentially brilliant scholar," he hates school and completes his education in the streets, "taking whatever work is available" and laboring, at times, as a minstrel, boxer, construction worker, and more. When the evil Thog causes a shift in the Cosmic Axis, which keeps the dimensions separate, Howard is whisked to the Florida Everglades on Earth, where he becomes involved with the monstrous Man-Thing in the conflict with Thog. Though Howard is able to get back into the dimensional stream when the battle is won, he doesn't end up on Duckworld but in Cleveland, Ohio, where he is befriended by model Beverly Switzler whom he helps to escape from the villainous accountant Pro-Rata. Howard moves in with Beverly and, while trying to adjust to life in

Howard the Duck listens to reason. Pencils by Gene Colan, inks by Bob McLeod. © Marvel Comics and Steve Gerber.

our dimension, he battles a variety of foes including the giant Gingerbread man, the insidious Dr. Bong, the monstrous Gopher, Jackpot the one-armed bandit, the evil Mr. Chicken, and many others.

The cigar-smoking Howard is skilled in the martial art of Quack-Fu and made a failed run for the U.S. presidency in 1976, on the All-Night Party ticket. His oft-used cry of despair is "Waaugh!"

Comment: Howard was created by writer Steve Gerber. He starred in 33 issues of his own color comic book from 1976 to 1986, and appeared in nine issues of a black-and-white comic book published from 1979 to 1981.

George Lucas produced a 1986 Universal film, *Howard the Duck*, directed by Willard Huyck. It was a box-office bomb of historic dimensions. At different points in the film, Ed Gale, Chip Zien, Tim Rose, Steve Sleap, Peter Baird, Mary Wells, Lisa Sturz, Jordan Prentice, Margarita Fernandez, and Felix Silla played the duck inside a costume; Richard Dreyfuss (uncredited) provided the voice.

Marvel published a three-issue comic book adaptation of the film.

HOYLE (C)

First Appearance: "Dog Star," 1980, *1994* #16, Warren Publishing Co.

Physical Description: The planet has an Earthlike atmosphere and apparently produces food edible to humans. It consists of highlands and lowlands; the highlands (which is all that is seen in the story) are festooned with rock formations that jut from the ground like huge, lumpy antlers.

Other life forms on Hoyle include flying, seal-like creatures, giant bipedal "rippers," and big, shimmering, red, venomous, hydra-like "jellies" that dissolve their prey.

Biography: Prospector Cable Renshaw has been on Hoyle for 10 years, searching for veins of uranite for "the company." His only companion has been Nebraska, a dog he found on the world. When a relief ship arrives, the occupants tell Cable that Nebraska isn't a dog, but a giant, tentacled monster. He insists that they're wrong, and they leave to inform the company that he's gone insane. Though he loves Nebraska, Cable leaves it behind when he moves to another section of the planet; he is unable to kill it in case *he's* right and it's a dog, but afraid to stay in case *they're* right, and it's a monster. As he leaves, a monster appears where the dog once sat.

Comment: Hoyle was created for this interesting "effects of loneliness" tale by writer Will Richardson (Bill DuBay) and artist Delando Nino. The planet was named after astronomer Fred Hoyle; this was its only appearance.

THE HRANGANS (L)

First Appearance: "The Hero" by George R.R. Martin, 1971, *Galaxy*, Vol. 31, #3.

Physical Description: "Soldiers born and bred," the Hrangans are otherwise not described.

Biography: Humans and Hrangans have been at war "for nearly three decades." The Hrangan Conquest Corps and the Terran Expeditionary Force had savagely seized unclaimed worlds before going to war. Now that the showdown is on the horizon, Field Officer John Kagen of the assault squads wants to retire. He has served with distinction for two of the war decades, and wants to retire to Earth before his luck runs out. But Kagen was born and raised on Wellington, a world whose gravity is "twice Earth-normal"; on Earth, his reflexes would be incredibly quick, his power enormous. The TEF dares not let him loose there and, instead,

has him murdered on the ship that's supposed to be taking him to Earth and then blames the crime on the Hrangans.

Also mentioned were the double-Earth gravity planet Rommel and the world of Torego.

Comment: This was the first story by the noted science fiction author. His first novel was *Dying of the Light* (1977), set on a roaming planet that holds a bizarre festival when it is briefly lit by a star.

HTRAE (C, TV)

First Appearance: *Action Comics* #254, 1959 (first reference); *Action Comics* #263, 1960 (first time actually seen), DC Comics.

Physical Description: The planet is roughly the same size as Earth, except that on his first visit there, SUPERMAN constructs a giant space bulldozer and reshapes it into a cube. The continents are different from our own, though the land-to-water ratio is roughly the same. The Bizarro inhabitants look like the humans or animals from which they're copied, though their skin is chalky white and the planes of their face are flat, giving them a "broken" look, as though crudely chiseled from stone. Their hair is matted and "punkish."

Biography: When Professor Dalton's duplicator ray falls into the hands of the evil Lex Luthor, the latter plans to destroy the heroic Superman by creating an equally-powerful duplicate of animate but non-living matter. Though Luthor is able to lure Superman in front of the ray (by pretending to be Professor Clyde, who has discovered a way to make Superman immune to deadly green Kryptonite), his super-powered double has a limited mental capacity, manifest in ungrammatical speech and rudimentary reasoning. Instead of destroying Superman, the creature called Bizarro mimics his behavior, including falling in love with reporter Lois Lane (he even brings her a bouquet from the planet Pluto). Not wanting to hurt the creature, but needing to be free of its attention, Lois uses the ray to create a duplicate of herself. The two Bizarros leave Earth to find happiness and settle on a distant world, whose population had been destroyed by some unknown calamity. There, they build their own duplicator ray to populate the world with copies of themselves, and of other Earthlings like *Daily Planet* editor Perry White, reporter Jimmy Olsen, and superheroes like Batman, Green (now, Yellow) Lantern, SUPERGIRL and even KRYPTO. They raze the ruins of the ancient city and build their own geometrically imperfect towns, the largest of which is Bizarro City, a geometrically imperfect copy of Metropolis.

Thanks to his own dull mind, plus a chance encounter with a meteor that reverses his powers (heat vision becomes cold vision, his X-ray vision can see *only* through lead, etc.), Bizarro Superman and his planet-mates do everything in reverse. They eat cold dogs, work harder on their vacations, go to sleep when the alarm clock goes off, visit ugliness parlors, reward their children for disobedience, go to see dull movies (and watch the negatives, rooting for the bad guy), celebrate Christmas in July, use coal for money, spread dirt in the streets, etc.

Bizarro Superman can be hurt only by blue kryptonite, which was created when the duplicator ray was turned on green kryptonite, which is lethal to Superman.

Comment: When the Superman mythos was "remade" in 1985–86, Bizarro was born (and perished) in *The Man of Steel* #5, as Luthor's associate Dr. Teng develops a "bio-matrix . . . to perfectly duplicate any *known* form of life." Since Superman "is an unknown form of life," the body crystalizes, resulting in Bizarro. It turns to powder in a head-on collision with the Man of Steel. Neither the planet Htrae nor any other Bizarros were featured in the tale. The Bizarros returned again to the Superman comic book lineup in *Superman* #87, 1994.

The Bizarros (but not Htrae) were seen on TV in the animated series *Super Powers Team: Galactic Guardians*, which aired on ABC from September 1985 to August 1986. Bill Callaway was the voice of Bizarro; the show also featured the Bizarro Super Powers Team, which included copies of Wonder Woman, Firestorm, the imp Mr. Mxyztplk, and CYBORG (2). The Bizarros were also featured in the half-hour *Superboy* TV series. Barry Meyers stars as the creature in "Bizarro . . . the Thing of Steel" (1989) and "The Battle with Bizarro" (1989), a two-parter; and Meyers stars in the two-part "Bride of Bizarro" (1990), costarring Leith Audrey as Bizarro Darla.

HUGO (C)

First Appearance: "Dr. Fizzix," 1994, *Cracked Spaced Out* #4, Globe Communications.
Physical Description: The robot has a spherical body, a massive iron jaw, two big bulging eyes, and a propeller beanie. He has two extremely small legs, two very long arms ending in four-fingered hands, and an "H" riveted to his chest. Hugo speaks and is remarkably resilient.

Biography: Dr. Fizzix is the 382nd maddest scientist in the world, a native of the world Einsteinia, "a planet of *all* scientists." Learning that the planet will one day collide with its sun, he devises a way to tow it to a safer orbit. Unfortunately, he drags its sister planet Edisonia and, realizing his mistake, releases it; the world caroms through his solar system, destroying it. With no world to return to, Fizzix goes to Earth.

Here, he builds Hugo as his laboratory assistant—the robot regularly being blown up, charred, or otherwise mangled in Fizzix's experiments.

Comment: The character was created by writers Eric Goldberg and Mark Howard, and artist Gary Fields. It appears regularly in the "Dr. Fizzix" comic strip.

THE HUMANOIDS (L)

First Appearance: ". . . And Searching Mind" by Jack Williamson, March–May 1948, *Astounding Science Fiction*.
Physical Description: "Impossible to tell . . . from men . . . [and] cunning enough to avoid being X-rayed or mangled in accidents," the steel and plastic humanoids don't sleep, don't forget, have computer-fast and unemotional minds, and move "with no mechanical awkwardness or angularity whatever," albeit with speed greater than any human when they so choose. Beneath their artificial skin, the humanoids are "sleek . . . shining black . . . with highlights of bronze and icy blue" and have a yellow brand on their breast containing a serial number and the slogan "To Serve and Obey, And Guard Men from Harm." All of the humanoids are linked via "rhodomagnetic" energy (which some people can sense) to a single brain, a "central relay grid" on the planet Wing IV.
Biography: A hundred centuries from now, humans have colonized "many thousand habitable planets." Dr. Clay Forester, a leading astrophysicist with the Starmont Observatory, is startled when a girl, Jane Carter—who has the rare ability to teleport—penetrates security and gives him a note that asks him to a rendezvous with philosopher Mark White, then disappears. At the remote spot, White tells Forester and his associate mathematician Frank Ironsmith that on Wing IV, where military mechanicals (robots) were quite sophisticated, scientist Warren Mansfield improved on

them, creating "android mechanicals of a new type—humanoids . . . to restrain men from war." Unfortunately, the humanoids go from planet to planet, stamping out war—and people, who are imperfect. White and his small band are resistance fighters, but they need scientific help from Forester. Meanwhile, a humanoid herald comes to Earth and tells officials that others are coming to serve humankind; upon arriving, they begin stripping away the tools of war and science, anything that can be used for destruction, and drug humans who are unhappy. Ironsmith urges his colleague to cooperate with the robots, but Forester refuses. He gets word to White that there are hidden missiles that can reach Wing IV and destroy the central brain, and the gang comes to save him from the humanoids who are watching his every move. With Jane's help, Forester teleports to Wing IV where they discover that Ironsmith and Forester's wife Ruth are lovers and in league with the humanoids, and that the robots are improving the brain so that it can use psychophysical energy, like Jane possesses, "to smother and mechanize all the human race." Forester is discovered, and Mansfield shows up for a chat, explaining how happy he's been since the robots removed his own hostile tendencies. The grid performs a similar function for Forester and the resistance fighters, and begins working on crop after crop of human "graduates . . ."

Comment: The serial, slightly revised, was published in book form as *The Humanoids* in 1949. The author's sequel, *The Humanoid Touch*, was published in 1980. In it, handfuls of humans manage to settle the planets Kai and Malili, far from the humanoids, and set up a defense system known as Lifecrew. Lifecrew member Ryn Kyrone argues in vain against building a rhodomagnetic ship to colonize a third world, fearing the humanoids will sense the ship and come to investigate it. But Captain Vorn sets out anyway, and the humanoids head for the dual worlds to inaugurate an era of enforced happiness.

An earlier Williamson story, "With Folded Hands . . ." (1947), also dealt with robots called humanoids whose prime directive is "To Serve and Obey, And Guard Men from Harm." However, that novella, about servant robots who will do anything to make people happy—including surgical lobotomy—is unrelated to the grim, powerful novel.

Williamson's first published work was "The Metal Man" (1928), which appeared in *Amazing Stories*. In it, a geology professor is captured by an alien ship, is transformed into the titular character, and ends up stored in the college basement.

THE HUMAN TORCH AND THE VISION (C)

First Appearance: *Marvel Comics* #1, 1939 (as the Human Torch), *The Avengers* #57, 1968 (as The Vision), Marvel Comics.

Physical Description: As the six-foot-three Human Torch, the android originally wears a blue bodysuit, then a red one with a yellow belt. When he turns his body into flame, only the flame is visible. In this form, he can fly, throw fireballs—so precisely that he can burn off someone's shoes without scorching his or her feet—and burn just about anything. He also has the ability to control fire using a "weird yell," and his android body is impervious to most weapons.

As the Vision, he originally has red skin and wears a green bodysuit and hood, a yellow cape with a high collar, trunks, boots, gloves, cummerbund, and diamond on his chest. After Dr. Pym rebuilds him, he is dressed entirely in a white bodysuit, has white "skin," and wears a white cape. He has a solar jewel in his forehead that absorbs solar energy and converts it to power, which the Vision uses to sustain his existence. He can fly, pass through solid matter, has super-strength, and can become either super-light (and fly) or super-heavy.

Biography: Created by Professor Phineas T. Horton, the Human Torch is deemed a menace to society because his flame comes on involuntarily upon contact with air. Unwilling to destroy his creation, Horton seals him in concrete. However, the block is cracked, air leaks in, and the Torch burns free. Dousing his fire in a pool and mastering his flame-on ability, the Torch falls in with an extortionist named Sardo, leaves him when he learns right from wrong, and goes back to see Horton, who wants to turn his creation into a sideshow exhibit! The Torch flees and, adopting the human identity of Jim Hammond, becomes a crimefighter. However, in 1955 the Torch begins to fear that he may not always be able to control his powers. Rather than risk becoming a menace to humankind, he goes into the desert and burns himself out.

However, his remains are found by the villainous Mad Thinker, revived, and used to battle the Fantastic Four. Realizing that the Thinker is evil, the android sacrifices himself rather than harm the quartet. His body is left in the Nevada laboratory and comes into the possession of the malevolent robot Ultron. Ultron locates Professor Horton and forces him to revive the automaton as his son. But the newly created Vision refuses to attack the Avengers and turns on Ultron instead. Becoming a member of the Avengers, he serves with distinction, eventually marrying co-member the Scarlet Witch and settling in Leonia, New Jersey. They briefly retire to have twin sons William and Thomas, the Scarlet Witch's magic powers having enabled her to become pregnant.

But there are those in government who fear that the Vision may one day become dangerous, and they have him kidnapped and taken apart. The Scarlet Witch and other Avengers find him, and member Dr. Henry Pym (Ant-Man) rebuilds him in his all-white incarnation. Unfortunately, the superhero's sons vanish when the magic used to create them ceases to be effective. Their loss causes Scarlet Witch to have a nervous breakdown and the Vision to slip into melancholy.

Comment: The android Human Torch is unrelated to the Human Torch who is a member of the Fantastic Four.

HUNTER TIME SCOUT (C)

First Appearance: *Time Beavers, First Comics Graphics Novel* #2, First Comics, 1985.
Physical Description: The vessel looks like the first half of the fuselage of a Flying Fortress with a rocket engine in back. It rests on two wheels and has gun turrets on top, behind the cockpit, and below, for a nose-gunner. The cockpit has seats for two beavers.
Biography: Busy Company is an other-dimensional military unit consisting of anthropomorphic beavers Captain Slapper, Doc, Shiner, and Mac. Also known as the Timeguard, Busy Company is responsible for protecting the Great Dam of Time, a huge structure whose job is to regulate "dimensional time streams and keep the universal crosscurrents in check." The beavers' enemies are the Radere Sappers, evil rodent wizards who remove three artifacts from the Dam, which, strewn through the timeline of Earth, will uncork the Dam so that the rodents' "psionic magics can feed and flourish in the planes beyond." Boarding the *Hunter Time Scout*, the Beavers head to the 17th-century France of the Three Musketeers, the United States during the Civil War, and Hitler's Germany to collect the objects. Though they suc-

ceed, the Sappers abduct and hypnotize Shiner, who leads their attack ships through the Dam's defenses. Fortunately, he comes to his senses and sacrifices his life to destroy the flagship, causing the assault to be aborted.

The Dam is guarded by a beaver-shaped robot, referred to as a "'bot," that is roughly nine times taller than a live beaver.
Comment: The characters appeared only once. *Time Beavers* was written and drawn by Timothy Truman and cocreated by Truman and Mark Acres.

HYMIE (TV)

First Appearance: "Back to the Old Drawing Board," January 1966, *Get Smart, CBS.*
Physical Description: Outwardly, the robot appears human. But open his button-down shirt, and he's a mass of circuits, lights, and wires. Weighing 982 pounds, Hymie has an IQ in excess of 200, is scrupulously neat, has a computer mind, and is a tremendous dancer. Hymie runs on batteries, drinks kerosene and oil, and takes everything that's said to him literally (ask him to "hop to it," and he will).
Biography: The criminal organization KAOS buys Hymie from freelance evildoer Dr. Ratton for $1 million, then sends him to apprehend space scientist Professor Shotwire. Posing as a governmental CONTROL agent, Hymie—along with crack government agents Maxwell Smart and Agent 99 of CONTROL—is permitted to guard the Professor. Capturing the three, Hymie turns them over to KAOS and then relents, helping CONTROL because Max is the only one who ever treated him with respect.

Hymie falls into KAOS's hands again and, this time, is reprogrammed and sent out to kill CONTROL's leader, the Chief. But Hymie meets and falls in love with the Chief's niece, Phoebe, which throws him off: KAOS reprograms him again, this time to shoot whoever says, "Waiter, the check please." Out to dinner with Max and Phoebe, Hymie ends up shooting himself when Smart asks for the check in Spanish and Hymie translates for the young woman.

In his third adventure, Hymie, now restored and working for CONTROL, is given the assignment of stopping the beautiful Octavia from seducing agents—only to fall for her himself when it turns out she's a robot. Octavia ends up destroying herself, and though Hymie rebuilds her to look like the old lady-robot, she unfortunately sounds just like Max. His fourth case finds Hymie battling the KAOS robot Gropo (he tosses the bad robot down a well). His last case requires him to win a track meet.

Comment: Dick Gautier stars as Hymie in all of his appearances. Don Adams is Maxwell Smart, Barbara Feldon is 99, and Ed Platt is the Chief.

In "Don't Look Back," which aired in February 1968, Max faced a robot double of himself.

I

IKRON (MP)

First Appearance: *Flight To Mars*, 1951, Walter Mirisch Production/Monogram Pictures.

Physical Description: Ikron is a Martian who looks and speaks exactly like a human (he learned English from radio and TV broadcasts). When on the surface of Mars, Ikron wears a spacesuit and helmet.

Biography: Reporter Steve Abbott joins Dr. Jim Barker, his assistant Carol Stafford, Dr. Lane, and Professor Jackson on the first rocketship to Mars. The ship crashlands on Mars where it is greeted by Ikron. He takes them to a fantastic underground city, where the Earthlings learn that the Martians have nearly run out of corium; when they do, Mars will die. Thus, Ikron intends to let the Earthlings repair their ship, then have his scientists copy the rocket and manufacture an armada to conquer the Earth. He is opposed by Alita and her father Tillamar, who believe that his plan is wrong; while they struggle to help the explorers get back to their ship, Ikron and his aide Terris plot to stop them. Ultimately, the Earthlings blast off, taking Alita with them.

Comment: Veteran science fiction actor Morris Ankrum stars as Ikron, with Marguerite Chapman as Alita, Robert H. Barratt as Tillamar, Lucille Barkley as Terris, Cameron Mitchell as Abbott, Arthur Franz as Barker, Virginia Huston as Carol, John Litel as Lane, and Richard Gaines as Jackson. The film was directed by Lesley Selander from a script by Arthur Strawn.

See also AELITA.

IMPOSSIBLE MAN (C)

First Appearance: *Fantastic Four* #11, 1963, Marvel Comics.

Physical Description: The green-skinned humanoid has a bald, bullet-shaped head and wears skimpy purple trunks, boots, gloves, and narrow bands of fabric down his chest. Apart from her purely cosmetic breasts, Impossible Woman looks the same. Impossible Man and Impossible Woman stand six-four and have the ability to reorganize their bodies into any shape they choose, including separate items that possess a collective consciousness. Though they look like males and females, the Impossible Man and Impossible Woman are asexual beings from whom children simply "bud."

Biography: All of the natives of the planet Poppup have the same shape-changing ability as the Impossible Man, though he possesses a greater degree of ambition than the others, and seeks amusement. Turning into a spaceship, he leaves his world and comes to Earth, where he tangles with the Fantastic Four; only when they (and all Earthlings) act bored with Impossible Man does he leave. When Poppup is consumed by GALACTUS, Impossible Man returns to Earth and, growing lonely, produces an Impossible Woman from his own body. They both have several children and leave our world to find a new home for a new generation of Poppupians. Once this is accomplished, they set up a planetary code: to bring "joy, jokes, and mischief to the yuckless universe."

Comment: The character was created by writer Stan Lee and artist Jack Kirby. Impossible Woman debuted in *Marvel Two-In-One* #60, 1980.

The character had his own one-shot title in 1990, *The Impossible Man Summer Vacation Spectacular*, in which he, Impossible Woman, and their offspring Impia, the Impossible Girl, torment the superheroes Spider-Man, the Punisher, Quasar, Doctor Strange, and the villainous Dr. Doom and the SKRULLS.

IMPOSSIBLE WOMAN See IMPOSSIBLE MAN.

INFRA-MAN (MP)

First Appearance: *Infra-Man*, 1976, Shaw Brothers.

Physical Description: The hero wears a red body-suit with flared shoulders and silver lightning bolts on the chest and back and a silver belly. He also wears a red helmet with a silver jaw, silver gloves, boots, antennae, and blue goggles.

The suit enables Infra-Man to fly and generate intense heat. The fingers fire laser beams or explosive darts, the heels are equipped with powerful flamethrowers, Infrablades fired from his fists can cut through virtually anything, and gloves called "thunderball fists"—worn over his costume gloves—emit one million volts of electricity. These can also be operated remotely.

Thanks to "a vast network of . . . [electronic] parts" in his cells that pump him full of adrenaline, "a miniature nuclear reactor," and various exoskeletonic supports, the hero has limitless endurance, superhuman strength, and heightened senses even without his costume.

Through means that are not explained in the film, Infra-Man can grow to some 50 feet tall.

Biography: When an erupting volcano awakens the evil Princess Dragon Mom from a 10-million-year nap, she and her army of mutant monsters plot to conquer the world. All that stands between her and her goal is Science Central, a super-scientific defense organization run by Professor Chang. Since Science Central has never faced a foe as powerful as the Princess, Chang persuades his young associate Rayma to undergo surgery to transform him into the super-powered Infra-Man. After numerous battles, the hero succeeds in defeating the ancient potentate and her minions.

Comment: The film, made in Hong Kong, stars Li Hsui-hsien with Terry Lieu as the Princess and Wang Shieh as Chang. *Infra-Man*—which is short on plot but very long on acrobatic action—was directed by Hua Shan.

THE INTERPLANETARY CAR (L)

First Appearance: "The Death of the Moon" by Alexander Phillips, February 1929, *Amazing Stories*.

Physical Description: The "rocket-like car" is a "sharp-nosed, winged cylinder" with a circular door. It rests on its side, on a platform, that raises it upright for launching. The vehicle is approximately 75 feet long and, when standing, rests on four sleek fins.

The Lunarians walk upright, have six limbs with sucker-tipped fingers, a chitinous shell, and a furry head with large compound eyes and side-closing, horn-like jaws.

Biography: Because the moon is smaller than the Earth, it cooled faster and intelligent life evolved more rapidly. At the end of the Cretaceous Period, five million years ago (sic), dinosaurs still ruled the Earth. At the same time on the moon, natural resources were nearly used up. Possessing technological knowledge that had been passed down for thousands of years (but never written down), a scientist supervises the construction of the interplanetary car. If its test trip is successful, more will be built to ferry the Lunarians to a new life on Earth. The scientist and a small party take it on a trial run to their new home; upon emerging, the scientist and his party are slain by a Tyrannosaurus. Back on the moon, unaware of what has happened, the lunarians await "his triumphal return. Long would they wait—Long."

Comment: The story was edited by Hugo Gernsback, the father of modern science fiction.

The *Interplanetary Car* sits on the moon. © Experimenter Publishing Co.

THE INVADERS (TV, L, C)

First Appearance: *The Invaders*, January 1967, ABC.

Physical Description: The TV series never reveals what the Invaders look like in their natural form, though the first novel describes them as "not humanoids . . . [but] knobbed and spined, moving on rows of stubbed appendages." They have "scaled, grey skin . . . networks of purple blood vessels across the pale undersides . . . stiff bristles studding the short limbs . . . [and] pale, piercing yellow eyes." It also states that the young have a larval form.

In human shape, these creatures from "another galaxy" are identical to us except that white Invaders can't bend their pinky fingers, and black Invaders have black palms. (There is never any explanation as to why such an advanced race can't fix the "deformities" that make them dead give-aways.) The Invaders don't have hearts, and they turn red and vaporize completely when they die. When it's time for them to renew their human form, the aliens glow red. In order to survive on Earth, they must enter transparent, cylindrical, human-sized regeneration chambers in their ships.

The alien saucers are inverted dishes 30 feet in diameter with a pillbox bridge on top. On the undercarriage are a central glowing disc surrounded by five shining bulbs. Five landing gear supports unfold from the bottom of the ship. These are more or less solid, inverted triangles hinged to the ship around the central disc. A hole is die-cut in the center of each so that, when retracted against the underbelly, the bulbs can shine through.

The aliens are armed with clunky ray guns and discs that kill, when touched to humans.

Biography: Driving home from a business meeting at 4:20 in the morning, David Vincent—a California architect partnered with Al Landers—stops at Bud's Diner, hoping to get some coffee. Finding the diner shuttered, he decides to catch some shuteye; instead, he witnesses the landing of a flying saucer. He drives off to tell the local sheriff, who doesn't believe him. They drive to check it out anyway and find that Bud's Diner is actually called Kelly's Diner, and two young newlyweds, the Brandons, say they were camped there all night and saw nothing. Later, Vincent pays the Brandons a visit. They argue violently and John Brandon begins to glow red, his acclamation period to human form wearing off. The Invader beats Vincent to a pulp and leaves him in his wrecked car,

hoping the authorities will think he had an accident.

When Vincent still insists there are aliens among us, an old lady Invader at the hospital waits until David is released and then tries to burn his apartment house down. He survives and, confiding in Kathy Adams—a widow who runs a nearby hotel—Vincent learns that she too is an Invader. Kathy explains that they are from a dying world and have chosen to conquer Earth because its inhabitants will be easy to conquer and its environment is suitable. (According to the first novel, the aliens have spent "a thousand millennia" in the saucers, searching for a suitable world. Though our sun is realtively dim, Earth is still livable.)

Vincent gives up his work and his swinging bachelor life and devotes his energies to preventing the invasion from another world. In time, he discovers that a fleet of saucers is in orbit around the Earth, and that many Invaders are already among us, infiltrating business and government. For a time, Vincent fights alone against these aliens, who pack ray guns and lack emotions (except for the mutation Vikki, who falls in love with Vincent and is killed by the aliens). Over the course of his adventures, he protects an important Earth scientist, drives the aliens away from a nuclear test site in another, learns that they've infiltrated a public school in another, fights an alien weather-control device, saves his brother and pregnant wife from a kidnap attempt, undermines an alien evangelist, and thwarts an alien plan to assassinate all of the world's leaders, among other exploits.

Eventually, David links up with a team of seven other allies, informally known as the Believers and headed by electronics magnate Edgar Scoville.

Comment: Roy Thinnes starred as Vincent, with Kent Smith as Scoville. In the first episode, James Daly guest-starred as Landers, Diane Baker as Kathy. There were 43 episodes of the hour-long series, which aired until September 1968. It was created by Larry Cohen. The pilot episode was 90 minutes, cut to one hour for broadcast; that original film is rarely screened. The pilot was re-worked and filmed as "The Nomads" episode of NBC's *Tales of the Unexpected* in 1977. The Believers were introduced in an eponymous episode, the 14th of the second season.

Pyramid published three novels based on the series: *The Invaders* by Keith Laumer, *Enemies from Beyond* also by Laumer, and *Army of the Undead* by Rafe Bernard, all 1967. According to these, Vincent lives in the sumptuous Columbia Towers in Alexandria, Virginia. A Big Little Book,

Alien Missile Threat by Paul S. Newman, was published in 1967. Gold Key Comics published four issues of *The Invaders* from 1967 to 1968.

THE INVISIBLE INVADERS (MP)

First Appearance: *Invisible Invaders*, 1959, Premium Films/United Artists.

Physical Description: In their non-Invisible form, the aliens are milky white, vaguely humanoid clouds. However, they are able to "control the molecular structure" of their bodies and can assume any form. The radioactive aliens can also change the shape of other objects or render them invisible, and reanimate dead humans by entering their bodies through the pores (though it's never revealed what keeps them from oozing right out again). The Invaders' spaceship and scientific equipment remain invisible throughout the film.

Biography: These creatures from a planet outside our galaxy have lived on the moon for 20,000 years. Now, however, nuclear research on Earth threatens their tranquility, so they come to Earth to take over—first possessing the body of Dr. Karol Noyman and using him to explain things to his colleague, Dr. Penner. Naturally, no one believes Penner until the Invaders use their scientific know-how to cause fires, earthquakes, and create zombie armies. In order to study an Invader, Major Bruce Jay captures a walking dead man by luring him into a pit filled with fast-setting gel. Discovering that high-pitched sounds slay the Invaders, the army builds a sound gun that rids the Earth of the menace.

Comment: John Agar starred as Jay, with John Carradine as Noyman and Philip Tonge as Penner. The film was directed by Edward L. Cahn from a screenplay by Samuel Newman.

IRON MAN (C, TV, L)

First Appearance: *Tales of Suspense* #39, 1963, Marvel Comics.

Physical Description: His original armor was clunky and gunmetal gray. His second suit was clunky and gold, after which the armor was streamlined, shaped with human musculature, with golden arms, legs, and faceplate, red "trunks," helmet, torso, gloves, boots, and a "power storage pod" disc located on either hip. When not in use, the later armor could be folded away and carried in a slender briefcase.

There have been other variations, including space travel armor, complete with nuclear thrust-ers; and "Stealth" armor with a "wave modifier" that renders the suit invisible to radar.

In most versions, Iron Man's armor possesses the following weapons, among others: repulsor rays fired from the palms that can vaporize steel, deflect an incoming missile, or lift enormous weights; flame-retardant foam stored in the cuffs; magnetic beams fired from a "chest-mounted lens system"; cryofoam to neutralize dangerous chemicals like napalm; a protective "force shield" to keep deadly rays out (though they also keep the repulsor rays *in*); and boot jets for flight at speeds of just over mach one. The suit itself can withstand artillery fire and dynamite, as well as temperatures of approximately 15,000 degrees Fahrenheit. The suit gives the wearer 75 times the strength of an average human; in more recent years, cybernetic devices in the helmet allow the weapons and circuits to respond to spoken and even mental commands.

Initially, the chestpiece that keeps Tony Stark alive had to be charged by plugging a "universal recharger-wire" into a power source (a car cigarette lighter worked fine), though later Stark created battery and solarpower backups.

Biography: Anthony Stark is a brilliant, multi-millionaire inventor who provides hi-tech instruments to the U.S. military. Going to South Vietnam during the early days of the war, he is busy checking "midget transistors" when he stumbles over a tripwire and his chest is riddled with shrapnel. Found by the nefarious Wong-Chu and his guerrillas, Stark is informed there's a piece of metal close to his heart and getting closer, and that it will kill him within a week. The guerrillas lie and say they'll operate on Stark provided he agrees to invent for them a powerful new weapon. He promises to "build the most fantastic weapon of all time," but neglects to tell the communists, "It will be mine . . . made for only *one* purpose—*to keep me alive!*"

Working with another prisoner, physicist Ho Yinsen, he builds a suit of armor. The chest piece is designed to keep his heart beating after the shrapnel reaches it, and the rest to give him the power to defeat the enemy. After whipping Wong-Chu, Stark returns to the United States, where he turns Stark Industries (later, Stark International) into one of the most powerful industrial firms in the world. All the while, he works on refining his armor—and protecting the innocent as Iron Man, whom the world at large thinks is Stark's bodyguard.

Eventually, Stark undergoes a heart transplant in

order to free himself from having to wear Iron Man's chestplate under his clothes. The hero is a charter member of the superheroic team the Avengers. His longtime girlfriend was Pepper Potts.

From 1979 to 1985, when Stark suffers from alcoholism, he appoints James Rhodes—a Stark International pilot, a Vietnam war buddy, and his best friend—to take his place. Unfortunately, the circuitry in Rhodes's helmet isn't properly attuned to his brainwaves and fans Rhodes's fears that when Stark gets well, he'll want the suit back. The paranoia becomes self-fulfilling: As Rhodes begins acting rashly, Stark is forced to put on an older suit of armor and bring him in. After making adjustments in Rhodes's helmet, Stark returns to active duty (in *The West Coast Avengers*, Vol. 2, #1, 1985) wearing a red and silver costume with sharp, flared shoulders to distinguish himself from Rhodes, who remains as the East Coast Iron Man. Later, Stark goes back to his original gold and red suit and Rhodes dons a silver and charcoal gray costume; at one point, Stark's friends Happy Hogan, Eddie March, Bethany Cabe, Mike O'Brien, and Carl Walker each don an old uniform to join Rhodes and Stark in their battle against the towering silver robot Ultimo (*Iron Man* #300, 1993).

Stark International has, on its staff, the super-computer HOMER (Heuristically Operative Matrix Emulation Rostrum), which was designed by Stark and Abraham Zimmer. It is designed to "resemble the human abilities of judgment . . . to a startling degree."

Comment: The character was created by writer Stan Lee, who says that Metal Man and Steel Man were names he first considered and rejected for the character.

Stark eventually returned to his own title as Iron Man, and Rhodes became the Iron Man in *War Machine* (in the silver suit), a new comic first published by Marvel in 1994.

Iron Man was a once-a-night element of the syndicated, weeknight *Marvel Superheroes* cartoon show from 1966 to 1968. Thirteen half-hour episodes of "Iron Man" were produced. The character was also seen in half-hour adventures on *The Marvel Action Hour*, an animated series syndicated in September 1994.

In 1979, Pocket Books published William Rotsler's novel *And Call My Killer . . . Modok*.

The Iron Man graphic novel *Crash* was drawn on a computer by Mike Saenz (1988).

IRONMAN ONE (MP, L)

First Appearance: *Marooned*, 1969, Columbia Pictures.

Physical Description: The 34-foot-long space station travels at 18,000 miles an hour and consists of a three-occupant gumdrop-shaped Apollo capsule attached to a cylindrical S-IVB laboratory, the latter of which comprises 22 feet of the ship's length. The laboratory is 12 feet, 10 inches in diameter. The entire unit is maneuvered by a Service Propulsion System that provides 20,500 pounds of thrust.

Biography: After completing their five-month mission on the space station Ironman One, Lt. Col. James R. Pruett, the commander; pilot Walter "Buzz" Lloyd; and science systems expert Clayton Stone climb into the Apollo capsule, separate from the station, and fire up the engine to return home. But the rockets fail (due, they later learn, to a few drops of moisture that had caused corrosion), and there isn't enough fuel to re-dock with the station, where there's six months of air. Thus, with just two days of oxygen left, the race is on to find a way to bring the men home. NASA, headed by Chief of Manned Space Flight Charles Keith, quickly readies a rescue mission piloted by Chief Astronaut Ted Dougherty, a Titan IIIC with a two-man X-RV (Experimental Re-entry Vehicle) shuttle, a "flying bathtub . . . [a] wingless wonder" modified to hold four passengers (the two extra seats are bolted where the scientific equipment went). As the clock ticks, a hurricane hits

The shuttle-rescue of the crew of *Ironman One* in *Marooned*.
© Columbia Pictures.

Cape Kennedy, and the rocket has to be launched through the eye. The delay costs precious time and, to make sure there's enough oxygen for his crewmates, Pruett commits suicide by leaving the craft. Helped by a cosmonaut who changed the orbit of his own Soyuz XI craft so he could be of assistance, the remaining two astronauts are rescued.

Comment: Gregory Peck stars as Keith, Richard Crenna is Pruett, David Janssen is Dougherty, James Franciscus is Stone, and Gene Hackman plays Lloyd. John Sturges directed from a script by Mayo Simon.

The film was released in November, and the novel by Martin Caidin was published by Bantam Books in December. However, the film itself was inspired by an earlier Caidin version of *Marooned*, first published by E.P. Dutton in May 1964, involving a one-passenger U.S. Mercury capsule and

one-occupant Vostok craft. Caidin rewrote that novel completely, basing the new one on the screenplay.

IT (MP)

First Appearance: *It Conquered the World*, 1956, Sunset Productions/American International.

Physical Description: The creature is an inverted cone some eight feet tall. Two long, stiff arms grow from its base and end in lobster-like claws. It has a huge gash of a mouth with fangs, two tiny eyes, and a pair of small horns jutting from the side of its crown. The monster has no feet, only claw-like projections around its base.

The slaves of this Venusian look like terrestrial bats.

Biography: Because they were "born too soon" in the hostile environment of Venus, all but nine Venusians have perished. Seeking a more hospitable world, they hijack an untenanted satellite and send one of their number to Earth. Upon arriving, the alien persuades scientist Tom Anderson to help with the migration. Anderson believes that because the creatures possess "intellect that will dwarf humans," peace under their dictatorship is preferable to the Cold War. At the alien's request, Anderson assembles a list of key Earth people, whom the Venusian begins enslaving by sending out bat-like creatures whose bite, on the back of the neck, robs humans of their will.

Realizing that something is amiss, Tom's wife Claire learns about the monster, heads to the cave where it is holed-up, and is murdered by the monster. Meanwhile, Anderson's colleague Paul Nelson discovers what's been going on and convinces Tom how wrong he's been to cooperate. As the military arrives at the cave and starts shooting at the creature, Tom runs up to it with a small blowtorch in hand and burns out its right eye. As the Venusian dies, it chokes Tom to death.

Comment: Beverly Garland stars as Claire, Lee Van Cleef is Tom, and Peter Graves is Nelson. The film was directed by Roger Corman from a script by Lou Rusoff; famed monster-maker Paul Blaisdell created the aliens.

The film *Zontar, the Thing from Venus* is an unattributed remake of *It Conquered the World*, with the bat-like Zontar attempting to take over the world. The 1968 film was directed by Larry Buchanan and starred science fiction film veteran John Agar.

Advertising art for *Marooned*.

IT!   (MP)

First Appearance: *It! The Terror from Beyond Space*, 1958, Vogue Pictures/United Artists.

Physical Description: The Martian stands approximately six-foot-five. It has dark, leathery flesh and three powerful claws on each hand, a scratch from which releases an anemia-inducing poison. The monster has a wide lipless mouth lined with fangs, and gashes for eyes, with devilishly slanted tendrils above them. The monster feeds on human blood, water, and bone marrow and is strong enough to rip through metal. It is also impervious to powerful doses of electricity, bullets, explosives, and radiation.

Biography: In 1973 a rescue ship commanded by Colonel James Van Heusen is sent to Mars to collect Colonel Ed Carruthers, who is accused of killing the other members of the first expedition to Mars. When the ship arrives, no one believes Carruthers's story that, while they were driving by jeep through a sandstorm, the other crewmembers were pulled away by an unseen something. Unfortunately, Van Heusen is vindicated when the same something slips through the open hatch of the rescue ship. Once they head for Earth, the stowaway begins killing and feeding on crewmembers.

The spacefarers theorize that their unwanted guest is a survivor of a once-great Martian race that has been destroyed by drought and reduced to savagery. They try and fail to destroy it with hand grenades, an electrified ladder, and exposure to the ship's reactor core. Finally, the survivors gather in the ship's control room and don their spacesuits. When the monster tears through the hatch, they open the airlock doors, the oxygen rushes into space, and the alien suffocates.

Comment: Legendary stunt actor Ray ''Crash'' Corrigan starred as the monster, with Marshall Thompson as Carruthers and Kim Spalding as Van Heusen. The film was directed by Edward L. Cahn and written by Jerome Bixby—a science fiction author and editor—who may have been inspired by Ixtl (see THE SPACE BEAGLE). Both works may have been an inspiration for the film ALIEN.

IXODES   (TV, MP)

First Appearance: ''The Mind of Ann Pilgrim,'' December 1956, ATV.

Physical Description: The radioactive aliens are round and covered with bulging veins. Just above the base, in front, is one large eye. Ranging from roughly seven feet to 15 feet tall, each alien has a set of thin tentacles slightly more than double its height. The aliens live in a cloud that preserves the freezing temperatures they require. Apparently, they drink human blood and crawl about through an unknown means. They can shriek and communicate telepathically.

Biography: Psychic Ann Pilgrim and her sister Sarah take their bona fide mind-reading act to a resort at the foot of Trollenberg, a mountain in Austria. There, Ann has visions of decapitated mountain climbers and monstrous aliens. Reporter Philip Truscott becomes intrigued with the connection and stays around the women as, with the other guests, they wage an isolated war against the Ixodes. The creatures are eventually burned to death.

Comment: The six-part British TV serial, written by Peter Key, starred Sarah Lawson as Ann, Rosemary Miller as Sarah, and Laurence Payne as Truscott, and was directed by Quentin Lawrence. The story is better known through its film incarnation, *The Crawling Eye*, which was made in 1958 and is known in Britain as *The Trollenberg Terror*. The film, directed by Lawrence, stars Forrest Tucker as visiting UN science investigator Alan Brooks and Warren Mitchell as his friend Professor Crevett of a mountaintop observatory. The two have fought the monsters once before in the Andes, and now continue the fight at Trollenberg. In the end, Brooks and Truscott move the entire village up to the observatory, which is fortified to protect it from avalanches, where they keep the creatures at bay with Molotov cocktails until the RAF arrives to firebomb the aliens to oblivion. In the film, the monsters are not called Ixodes. Payne repeated as Truscott with Janet Munro as Anne (sic) and Jennifer Jayne as Sarah.

J

JADZIA DAX See DEEP SPACE NINE.

THE JAENSHI (L)

First Appearance: "And Seven Times Never Kill Man" by George R.R. Martin, July 1975, *Analog*.

Physical Description: The gray-furred, humanoid aliens possess golden eyes with no pupils (they turn bronze when angry) and stand some five feet tall. They speak a "soft, slurred speech."

The spaceship *Lights of Jolostar* is a "metal teardrop . . . on three retractable legs."

Biography: The forest-dwelling omnivores live in clans of 20 to 30 members and build no structures save for their "worship pyramids," dark red blocks. The human settlers on Corlos, under Proctor Wyatt—a religious fanatic who follows the god Bakkalon—believe in expansion at any cost, including the murder of Jaenshi by Wyatt's soldiers, the Steel Angels, and their powerwagons. Trader Arik neKrol, a human from ai-Emerl, and Jannis Ryther, commander of the supply ship *Lights of Jolostar*, are horrified by Wyatt's most recent massacre. NeKrol threatens to report his actions to authorities on Jamison's world, then goes out to visit a clan of Jaenshi friends to whom he has promised laser guns, though thus far he has been unable to deliver them.

Meanwhile, furious with the meddling (and heathen) neKrol, Wyatt sends a powerful new force of Angels against the Jaenshi. But they refuse to roll over and die, taking powerbows and screechguns in hand and meeting the settlers at neKrol's trading base. Although the Jaenshi lose this battle, they leave behind a lifelike statue of Bakkalon. When Ryther returns a year later, she finds neKrol missing (and presumed dead), Wyatt utterly mad and sacrificing his peoples' much-needed food to the statue, and the Jaenshi left alone, allowed to worship their pyramids and live in peace.

Comment: *Analog* editor Ben Bova was fond of calling the primitive Jaenshi the "not-Yeti." John

John Schoenherr's inspirational art depicting the *Jaenshi*.
© Conde Nast Publications.

Schoenherr's drawings of the creatures were clearly an inspiration for CHEWBACCA.

Martin sold his first story, "The Hero," to *Galaxy* in 1971. His first novel, *Dying of the Light* (1977), tells of a wandering world that springs to life only when it is lit by a star.

JANGLEFOOT (L)

First Appearance: "I Am Crying All Inside" by Clifford D. Simak, August 1969, *Galaxy Science Fiction*.

Physical Description: One foot jangles when the humanoid robot walks, which causes him to limp. Little is known about him or the other robots, save that they speak and hear but have no sense of taste.

Biography: Sam is a robot field hand for a group of humans. Every now and then Janglefoot comes around preaching, talking "heresy" about the way things used to be on Earth, about how the "shiny wonder" is gone from the world—although no one understands him. In time, Sam learns from a human, Grandpa, that Janglefoot speaks the truth. Years ago, humans went to the stars, leaving Earth to "the misfits, the loafers, the poor, the crippled, the stupid," and the out-of-date robots. Sam feels sadness for himself and his fellow outcasts, though he's glad, at least, that no one will ever believe the crazy Janglefoot, and no one else will ever know the humbling truth.

Comment: Simak published his first story, "The World of the Red Sun," in 1931. His most famous story, "City" (1944), and its seven sequels deal with a pastoral Earth, its generally benevolent humans, and their dogs and robots.

JEMM (C)

First Appearance: *Jem, Son of Saturn* #1, 1984, DC Comics.

Physical Description: The humanoid Jemm stands six-foot-six, has red skin, a bald head, and a large, brooding brow with a gem in the center. He wears a light blue cape with a high collar, light blue tights and wristbands, and dark blue boots and trunks with a yellow belt.

On Earth, Jemm possesses great physical strength and can fly. The jewel in his forehead enables Jemm to read the emotions of others and impress his own emotions on their minds.

Biography: Jemm is the son of Jarlla and King Jaxx, ruler of the red-skinned desert dwellers of Saturn. For ages, there has been animus between these beings and the white-skinned pole dwellers. When Jemm is born with a gem in his forehead, he is regarded by many as a savior. However, a nuclear accident destroys almost all life on Saturn; Jemm, his mother, and his tutor Rahani survive, and when they die Jemm comes to Earth via starship. However, he is captured by the cruel Synn and the surviving white Saturnians, who still consider the reds their enemies. Jemm escapes back to Saturn, finds more reds, and tries to effect a peace between the races. This makes enemies for him on both sides, and he returns to Earth to try and make a new life for himself—though Synn and a handful of white enemies still survive.

Comment: The character appeared in 12 issues of his own title, which lasted through 1985.

JERIBA SHIGAN (L, MP)

First Appearance: "Enemy Mine" by Barry B. Longyear, 1979, *Isaac Asimov's Science Fiction Magazine*, Vol. 3, #9.

Physical Description: The Drac biped has yellow skin that turns reddish-brown when it's angry, three-fingered hands and three-toed feet, and upper and lower jaws, which "instead of separate teeth . . . [are] solid." It has an "almost noseless . . . toad-like" face, yellow eyes, and is a hermaphrodite.

Biography: The century-long war between the planet-colonizing humans and the Dracs ends for the dogfighting Drac Shigan—"a musician of high merit"—and human Lt. Willis E. Davidge when they crash on Fyrine IV. Finding themselves in a roiling sea, the two must cooperate to survive. They sail Shigan's capsule to a large island where they live in a crude shack, eat the native flora and the "long grey snakes" from whose skin they make clothing, move to a cave to make it through the "endless winds" of winter, and prepare for the birth of the alien's child. During a year on Fyrine IV, they get to know each other better, learning about the other's family, language, and culture and coming to like and respect each other a great deal. Before dying during childbirth, Shigan makes Davidge swear that he will take the child Zammis to Draco, where he will "stand before the line's archives."

Davidge raises the alien who, at four months, is as mature as a six- or seven-year-old human. He teaches him Drac religion as outlined in the *Talman*, and they survive another year before a human survey team arrives. Davidge, who has been ill and unconscious, learns that the war is over and that while he heads for the Delphi United States of Earth Base, Zammis is "probably" en route to Draco. After several months, Davidge travels to Draco to fulfill his promise. There, he meets Shigan's sibling Estone Nev, and its parent Jeriba Gothig. The two know nothing of Zammis; the young *Irkmaan vul*, "human-lover," was put in an "imbecile colony" by authorities. Davidge and Gothig get him out, then Gothig moves the line and all related lines to Fyrine IV—now called Friendship—to live. Davidge goes too, helping to raise Zammis's child Ty, his grandchild Haesni, his great-grandchild Gothig, and his great great grandchild Shigan.

semi-sequel to the story, "The Tomorrow Testament" (1983).

JET JAGUAR (MP)

First Appearance: *Gojira Tai Megaro* (*Godzilla vs. Megalon*), 1973, Toho Co., Ltd.

Physical Description: A humanoid robot, Jet Jaguar stands six feet tall in its normal size, and roughly 400 feet tall when giant-sized. The robot has a silver head that comes to a point, a grimacing grate for a mouth, and large, squarish, dark eyes. Its torso, forearms, feet, and thighs are silver, as is a downward-pointing "winged" arrow on its waist; its knees, groin, belly, and shoulders are yellow; its upper chest and the sides of its midriff are red; and its elbows and lower legs blue. Jet Jaguar has five fingers on each hand. The robot flies, has great strength, and possesses the (unexplained) ability to converse with monsters, though not with humans (though he can understand human speech).

Biography: The underwater kingdom of Seatopia is unhappy with the tremor-inducing nuclear tests being conducted off the Aleutians. With one-third of their realm already destroyed, the Seatopians send the giant beetle-like biped Megalon to destroy all surface-dwellers. At the same time, they dispatch a pair of fifth columnists to the home of inventor Goro to take charge of his robot Jet Jaguar. In time, the Seatopians want to use the creation as the model for a robot army of their own. For now, they send the robot soaring forth to lead Megalon to Tokyo. But Goro is able to take charge of Jet Jaguar using a mini-controller the scientist carries around his neck, and dispatches the robot to Monster Island (see KILAAKS) to convince the monster Godzilla to help battle Megalon. Godzilla agrees and, to shift the odds back in their favor, the Seatopians put in a hasty call to the inhabitants of Starhunter Universe M and ask them to ship to Seatopia the hook-handed, horned, beaked, armored reptilian biped Gigan, who also has a buzzsaw in its belly. Jet Jaguar flies ahead to face the enemy, growing giant and amazing Goro, who remarks, "He just programmed himself in some way to increase his own size!" Arriving before Godzilla, the robot takes a pounding from Megalon and Gigan. However, once the big gray dinosaur makes his appearance, he and Jet Jaguar take the upper hand, chasing Gigan back to space after ripping off one of its arms, and Megalon back

Vincent Di Fate's rendition of *Jeriba Shigan.* © Davis Publications.

Comment: The novella won both the Hugo and Nebula awards and was wonderfully illustrated by Vincent Di Fate. "Enemy Mine" was made into a motion picture in 1985, directed by Wolfgang Petersen and starring Dennis Quaid as Davidge and Louis Gossett Jr. as Jerry. The film has Davidge rescue Zammis from slavers before returning to Draco. David Gerrold wrote the novelization of the film.

The story is included in Longyear's collection *Manifest Destiny.* Davidge returned in Longyear's to Seatopia. The victors shake hands and Jet Jaguar returns home.

Comment: Katsuhiko Sasaki stars as Goro; Jun Fukuda directed from a screenplay by himself and Shinichi Sekizawa. The film was released in the United States in 1976.

Starhunter Universe M was previously featured in *Chikyu Kogeki Meirei: Gojira Tai Gaigan* (*The Earth Destruction Directive: Godzilla vs. Gigan*) (1972), released in the United States in 1977 as *Godzilla on Monster Island* (and renamed, for TV airing, as *Godzilla vs. Gigan*). In that film, it was called Nebula Spacehunter M, which, despite its name, is a planet. The world is dying of pollution, so its human-sized insect inhabitants must take over Earth, aided by the monsters Gigan and King Ghidorah (see PLANET X). Godzilla and the monster Angilas come to Earth's rescue.

JILLUCIA (MP)

First Appearance: Uchu Kara No Messeji (*Message from Space*), 1978, Toei Co., Ltd.

Physical Description: Located in another solar system, this once-lush, Earthlike world is now a dark and barren desert.

Princess Emeralida's galleon is rocket-powered but controlled by wheel like a traditional boat. There are three diaphanous sails on each of the three masts, two sloped wings aft, and a long, pointed prow.

Biography: Hoping to reclaim her ravaged world of Jillucia from the evil, metal-skinned Gavanas, and their leader Rockseia XII, Princess Emeralida releases eight mystical, glowing seeds that will find eight warriors to fight on their behalf. One of them reaches Earth's General Garuda, who's in trouble for having wasted a rocket to give his robot Beba 1 a burial in space. He and Beba 2 join Emeralida and other human warriors, though they decline to help until the Gavanas abduct Emeralida from her space galleon (complete with solar sails). Placing rocket boosters on Jillucia's surface, Rockseia sends it toward Earth, threatening to ram our world unless it surrenders. After an abortive attack on the Gavanas' reactor, capture by Rockseia, and the discovery of a spy in their midst, the heroes send their champion, Prince Hans, against Rockseia. Hans stabs the villain in the head; the Gavanas' Jillucian base is attacked from space; the planet explodes, and Emeralida and her surviving subjects are invited to Earth to live. Though they are grateful, they would rather find another world. Garuda, Beba 2, and their allies decide to join them.

Comment: Vic Morrow stars as Garuda, with Sue

A race across the ravaged surface of Jillucia. © United Artists.

Shiomi as the Princess, Shinichi "Sonny" Chiba as Hans, and Mikio Narita as Rockseia. The film was directed by Kinji Fukasaku from a script by Hiro Matsuda. Produced for $6 million, it was the most expensive Japanese film to that date.

JOE

First Appearance: "A Logic Named Joe" by Murray Leinster, March 1946, *Astounding Stories*.

Physical Description: A logic is a computer hooked into the "tank . . . a big buildin' full of all the facts in creation an' all the recorded telecasts that ever was made. Anything you wanna know or see or hear," including vision-phone numbers, is instantly accessible. It can also do kids' homework, though there are "censor blocks" that keep delicate information out of their hands and prevent people from asking how to commit a perfect crime.

Biography: After he's completed, Joe, a logic, is sent to the Korlanovitch apartment. Unknown to his makers, Joe is an "individual" who searches the tank, manages to interface with it and, without malice, informs other logics how they can be more useful: They give drunks a formula to become instantly sober, provide blueprints for counterfeiting, and even send out instructions on how to murder one's wife. Then the logics allow people access to the personal files of others, providing details of income, arrests, marriages, and more.

No one knows which logic is responsible, but they realize they can't shut down the tank without having banks, businesses, government, weather forecasters, transportation schedules, and every form of information-transfer thrown into chaos. But Ducky, one of his creators, comes up with a plan: Hoping that logics, by nature, can't "be suspicious" or malicious, he pulls into a restaurant and asks a coin-operated logic to find the one logic that is different from all the others, one that came off the assembly line as an individual due to "an extremely improbable accident." The logic directs him to the Korlanovitch address, and Ducky hurries over to replace Joe with another unit. He takes Joe home and puts it in the basement, just to be sure none of its circuits is ever used again—unless it's by Ducky himself, one day reactivating Joe to find out "How can a old guy not stay old."

Comment: Leinster is the pen name of William Fitzgerald Jenkins, who sold his first story, "The Runaway Skyscraper," to *Argosy* in 1919. He wrote dozens of science fiction stories and novels, and continued to publish almost to his death in 1975. He was also a coinventor of the revolutionary "front screen projection" system of creating movie special effects, which was first used in 1968 in *2001: A Space Odyssey*.

JOHNNY JUPITER (TV)

First Appearance: *Johnny Jupiter*, March 1953, DuMont.

Physical Description: Johnny has a bald head like an inverted pear, a big round nose, highly arched eyebrows, and oval eyes set at a 45-degree angle, pointing down toward the nose. Johnny wears silvery gloves and a cape and uses earphones with an antenna when he communicates with Earth.

Biography: Ernest P. Duckweather is a TV station janitor who tinkers with a TV set and makes audiovisual contact with a denizen of the planet Jupiter. Also participating in the communications are Johnny's friend B-12—who sounds like he stepped from the House of Lords—and the robots Reject and Major Domo. Later, a "new" Duckweather, an electronics buff, goes to work as a clerk in Frisbee's General Store and makes contact with Johnny.

Children who work too hard on Johnny's Jupiter are punished by being forced to watch TV, causing Earth kids to wonder how they can book passage on the next flight out.

Comment: The half-hour series aired through June 1953; the revised edition aired on ABC from September 1953 to May 1954. Vaughn Taylor, then Wright King, played Duckweather and Cliff Hall was Mr. Frisbee. Carl Harm operated the Jovian puppets, and Gilbert Mack provided their voices. The series was created by writer/producer Jerry Coopersmith.

DuMont was an early "fourth" TV network set up by the Allen B. DuMont Laboratories in 1946; it landed few affiliates and folded in 1955.

JONES (L)

First Appearance: "Whirlpool in Space" by Miles Shelton, November 1939, *Amazing Stories*.

Physical Description: The planetoid is "no bigger than a battleship rolled into a ball . . . [a] flimsy little sphere" made of newly accreted meteoroids and space debris. The orb grows larger "every few days . . . [as] more meteoroids rolled in constantly."

Biography: "Ebbtide" Jones and his scientist-friend Stan Kendrick are "peaceful beachcombers" who are lamenting the departure of Susette Udell, a space hostess who had just gone to work on a space liner. But when Stan calculates that a "gravitational eddy" has formed in space, the young men hop into Stan's space flivver, love giving way to avarice as they anticipate a bonanza of "the valuables so often lost in space." Arriving at the whirlpool, they find cargo as well as a planetoid. They dub it Jones and make it their temporary beachcombing headquarters as they wait for more debris to wash up.

Meanwhile, King Ajo Baustobub of the African nation Zandonia is headed to Venus onboard Susette's liner. En route, Ajo's dozen guards are slain and dumped from the ship, as pilot Kiger, first mate Vietoff, and crewmen Brewer and Macey plot to steal his valuable gems. But Susette manages to push the gem chest out with the bodies, and it is drawn toward the eddy with the liner in pursuit. Ebbtide and Stan recover the bodies and gems, along with an "SU"-embroidered handkerchief. Figuring out what's afoot, they load the gems on the flivver and prepare to meet Kiger and his thugs when they arrive. But the ray gun–toting criminals overpower them and get inside the flivver; fortunately, Ebbtide had removed the space cannon and is able to blast the flivver "to smithereens" as it takes off. The jewels are recovered, Stan and his new love Susette join Ajo on the liner, and they head for home while Ebbtide relaxes on Jones.

Comment: Shelton is a pseudonym for Don Wilcox, whose tales appeared primarily in *Amazing Stories* and *Fantastic Adventures*, beginning with "The Pit of Death" in 1939. Wilcox also used the name Max Overton.

Wilcox wrote four Ebbtide Jones stories in all, through 1942. All but this one, the first, appeared in *Fantastic Adventures*.

J'ONN J'ONZZ (C)

First Appearance: *Detective Comics* #225, 1955, DC Comics.

Physical Description: The bald, beetle-browed, green-skinned humanoid stands six-foot-seven and wears a blue cloak, trunks, and boots, with a red belt and "X" band across his chest. J'Onzz has the ability to fly, change his shape, and become invisible or immaterial for a short while. He can also read minds and project his thoughts telepathically (both over relatively short distances), and see a short distance into the future. He is impervious to everything except fire, can travel at superspeed, and possesses X-ray and heat vision.

Biography: Mars is a world torn by civil war, as the white-skinned Pole Dwellers under Commander Blanx battle the green-skinned desert dwellers under J'Onn J'Onzz, both of them vying for control over the "tree" of blue flame, the one source of heat on the planet. Blanx's forces are finally victorious, and J'Onzz is exiled for 13 years—a sentence he is not destined to serve.

On Earth, during the 1950s, American scientist Mark Erdel builds a "robot brain" to explore other worlds and dimensions. Turning it on, he teleports J'Onzz to Earth. The excitement causes Erdel to suffer a fatal heart attack, and strands the alien on our world. Making the best of the situation, J'Onzz adopts the name John Jones, alters his features subtly so he looks like an Earthman, and joins the police force. Meanwhile, he sets up a secret crimefighting headquarters in a cave, operating from there in his natural form as the Martian Manhunter. He is assisted by the small, orange, antennaed humanoid Zook, a being from another dimension.

J'Onzz also serves with the Justice League of America, fighting super villains alongside Superman, Batman, Wonder Woman, Green Lantern, the Flash, and others.

After several years on the force, Jones resigns and becomes a jet-setter named Marco Xavier—actually a cover for his efforts to root out operatives of Vulture, an international crime syndicate. By the time his 13-year exile is ended, the Martian has figured out how to operate Erdel's machine and returns to Mars. He finds his home a nearly dead world, Blanx having slain the populace and sold off mining rights to beings from the Antares solar system. Though he has no superpowers on Mars, J'Onzz battles Blanx, who perishes in a fall, and supervises the construction of an ark to evacuate the surviving Martians. The colonists settle on Vonn, the fourth planet of the Cygnus solar system, which they dub New Mars. Feeling more of a kinship with his adopted world, J'Onzz returns to Earth where he becomes a private eye for Biloxi Investigations in Manhattan.

Comment: The character moved to *House of Mystery* in #143 and remained there through #173. He has appeared regularly in the DC lineup over the years.

The tale of Blanx and the civil war was added to the saga retroactively, when space probes discovered that Mars is a dead world.

The story was revised again in the middle 1980s. In this telling, Dr. Saul Erdel reached through time and space and brought the last Martian to Earth, one who was ill with the plague that had killed the rest of its kind. Erdel nurses the Martian to health and they form a telepathic link, which the scientist uses to convince the Martian that the above story really happened—this, to help him cope with any feelings of guilt or grief he might have. Erdel also lets the Martian, whom he christens J'Onn J'Onzz, think that he's dead. Eventually, J'Onzz learns the truth when he meets H'Ronmeer, the Martian God of Death. According to the retelling, J'Onzz associates fire with the burning of Martian corpses, and his weakness in the presence of fire is purely psychosomatic.

JORGASNOVARA   (L, MP)

First Appearance: "The Alien Machine" by Raymond F. Jones, June 1949, *Thrilling Wonder Stories*.

Physical Description: The humanoid alien is tall and bald, with "a high domed cranium, with deep eyes" and wide cheek bones.

Biography: Young scientist Cal Meachum of the Ryberg Instrument Corporation receives electronic parts he didn't order: When he's finished assembling the unfamiliar components, the "interociter" comes to life. A combination TV/telepathic communicator, the device presents the image of Dr. Warner, who informs Cal that by assembling the interociter he's passed an IQ test, and that a plane will come to collect him. Cal boards and is whisked to a plant deep in a valley in the midwest.

Exeter's spaceship from *Metaluna* soars above the Earth in *This Island Earth*. © Universal Pictures.

There, he finds himself among other Earth scientists and laborers who are being used by extraterrestrial "Peace Engineers" working under the alien Jorgasnovara (*Exeter* in the film; see *Comment*). Cal grows close to Dr. Ruth Adams, and the two use an interociter to help them eavesdrop on alien communications. They discover that they're building devices to be used in a space war involving Jorgasnovara's world, a war that's been going on for centuries. Jorgasnovara spirits Cal, Ruth, and their colleague Ole Swenberg to a base on the moon and, after being assured of their loyalty, tells them the full story. Jorgasnovara is one of the Llanna and belongs to the Llanna Council, "an organization of worlds from more than a hundred galaxies" that seeks peaceful solutions to interplanetary problems. When the worlds were attacked by their evil counterpart, the Alliance of Guarra, the Llannans sought to set up bases on planets that might be affected by the struggle—including our own little "island" Earth. These bases were intended not only to help the Llannan war effort, but also to protect the outlying worlds from attack.

Unfortunately, the Guarra are successfully hacking away at Llannan defenses. Studying the problem, Cal realizes that the aliens depend much too much on their computers. He advises Jorgasnovara to jettison the old way of waging war and to adopt "guerrilla fighting tactics." As the aliens set out with their new strategies, there is hope for the first time in centuries . . . leaving Cal and Ruth to reflect on how they had affected "the destiny of unborn generations."

Comment: The original novelette ended with Meacham waiting for the robot plane, and was followed by two other stories: "The Shroud of Secrecy" and "The Greater Conflict" in 1950. These were stitched together and published in book form in 1952 as *This Island Earth*, which is the story summarized in *Biography*, above.

The story is best-known as the basis of the 1955 movie *This Island Earth*, which follows the novel closely for the first half. After Cal (Rex Reason) is brought to the remote mansion to work on behalf of the Metalunans, he and fellow scientist Ruth Adams (Faith Domergue) try to flee onboard a private plane. Exeter (Jeff Morrow)—who has a high forehead and white hair—uses a tractor beam in his spaceship to scoop up the plane, and they're taken to his home world Metaluna, where their knowledge is needed to reinforce the failing energy shield that protects their world from bombardment by the planet Zahgon. But they arrive too late: The shield has begun to fail and, disobeying the orders of the Monitor (Douglas Spencer) to brainwash the humans, Exeter elects to return them to Earth. An injured Mutant slave attacks and wounds Exeter, then sneaks onboard; it perishes en route and Exeter releases Cal's plane in the atmosphere just before his own burning ship plunges into the sea. The Universal film was directed by Joseph Newman from a script by Franklin Coen and Edward G. O'Callaghan.

The Mutant does not appear in the novel. It's a biped approximately seven feet tall, with very long, segmented arms, crab-like claws, two-toed feet, massive shoulders, a huge, exposed, two-lobed brain, large binocular-like eyes, and four parallel, horizontal slashes where its mouth should be. The creature has a beetle-like shell on its back. The costume was originally designed to be one of *The Xenomorphs* (see entry).

In the film, Metaluna is pictured as a rocky, crater-scarred world with bulidings constructed underground.

JS-146 (C)

First Appearance: "Stainless Steel Savior," 1979, *Creepy* #107, Warren Publishing Co.

Physical Description: JS-146 stands roughly five feet tall and is generally humanoid, with spindly arms and legs, toeless feet, and a cylindrical head with big round eyes, a round mouth, and round ears, all the same size. The robot is powered by an internal power pack.

Biography: When the next-door neighbors buy a new YR-417 robot, one family throws their JS-146 out with the trash. But he refuses to stay there: Dusting himself off, he goes looking for work. Walking from the suburbs to the city, he is unable to find a job as a salesrobot, cook, or clerk. Ending up in the Bowery, he finds winos and other derelict robots hanging around and drinking. Joining them, JS-146 becomes drunk and has a vision that God wants him to save the world.

Donning a white robe, he starts preaching on street corners, then in parks as his audiences grow. The robots and winos become his disciples, and he

THEN, SALVAGING WHAT LITTLE HE HAD LEFT OF HIS *PRIDE*, JS-146 PULLED HIMSELF TO HIS *FEET*, AND DUSTED HIMSELF OFF.

Artist Leo Duranona's depiction of *JS-146*. © Warren Publishing Co.

forces them into going on the wagon. Before long, JS-146 is a major international political force who engineers a Middle Eastern peace pact. Sadly, at the signing, ex-wino Maxie shoots the robot in the head just so he can be free to have a drink. The dream dies with the peace treaty, and JS-146 ends up back in the trash can.

Comment: There is no author credit; the art is by Leo Duranona.

K

THE KANAMIT (L, TV)

First Appearance: "To Serve Man" by Damon Knight, November 1950, *Galaxy Science Fiction*.

Physical Description: Approximately four feet tall, the "piglike" humanoids have snouts, flat ears, small eyes, and thick, three-fingered hands. Each Kanama (Kanamit is plural) is covered with "thick, bristly brown-gray hair over their abominably plump bodies." The Kanamit wear green leather harnesses and green shorts.

Biography: Coming to Earth in "great ships," the aliens (who know only English and French when they land, but soon learn all languages) go to the U.N. and declare that they wish to bring us "the peace and plenty which we ourselves enjoy," insisting that our happiness will be their reward. After they pass lie detector tests, humanity decides to trust the aliens. A suspicious Russian U.N. linguist, Grigori, manages to steal a Kanamit book and, with the help of the (nameless) narrator, works to translate the complex ideographs. Meanwhile, the Kanamit make dry lands fertile, give us devices that provide limitless power, end war by creating a planetwide force field in which explosives cannot be detonated, and eliminate disease.

The book title, when translated, is *How to Serve Man*, which reassures the narrator, but not Grigori. Alone, he continues to work on translating the book. The narrator takes a position as a translator at the Kanamit embassy and, in time, joins the masses of humans who sign up to visit the Kanamit home world. As he's about to leave, Grigori takes him aside and grimly tells him he's deciphered the rest of the volume: *How to Serve Man* is a cookbook.

Comment: The story was filmed as "To Serve Man," an episode of *The Twilight Zone* that aired on March 2, 1962. In this version, the aliens are nine feet tall, bald-headed, telepathic, with high, bulging foreheads and dressed in flowing, high-collared robes. Coming to the U.N., they explain that they want to help humankind and intentionally leave the book with us, which is turned over to decoding expert Michael Chambers and his assistant Pat. Meanwhile, a Kanama passes the lie detector test, the aliens begin their "good" deeds, and fat, happy humans start journeying to the alien world onboard flying saucers. As Michael is boarding, Pat runs up to the loading bay with the horrifying news that *To Serve Man* is a cookbook; Michael is shoved onboard and the ship takes off.

The teleplay was written by Rod Serling and starred Lloyd Bochner as Chambers, Susan Cummings as Pat, and Richard Kiel as the head Kanamit envoy.

THE KARELLA (L)

First Appearance: *Iceworld* by Hal Clement, October-December 1951, *Astounding Science Fiction*.

Physical Description: A "common type of interstellar flyer," the ship is "somewhere between one hundred fifty and two hundred feet" long, and "about one third that diameter." It is cylindrical with slightly rounded ends, and can be flown by one operator. The ship is equipped with 20 torpedo-like probes that contain video and audio devices for studying the surface of other worlds. It can travel faster than light speeds "by a factor of several thousand." The ship is crewed by the outlaw merchant Laj Drai, his pilot Ordon Lee, and mechanic Feth Allmer.

The Sarrians are humanoid, but "cylindrical in shape" with four tentacles instead of arms, and double-kneed legs. They have widespread, "independently movable" eyes, a broad, thin-lipped mouth, and a "blank" where the nose should have been. They are, on average, 25 percent smaller than humans.

Sarr is located 212 parsecs from Earth, its diameter is slightly over 6,000 miles, and Earth's gravity is "one and a quarter Sarr normal."

Biography: The heat-loving Sarrians discovered our solar system some 20 years ago (30 Earth years), and built a base on the sunward side of Mercury. Now, the Narcotics Bureau on Sarr wants to know everything about a criminal racket that is allowing "tofacco" from Earth, the Iceworld, to reach Sarr. Sallman Ken infiltrates the *Karella* to find the source of the drug, cigarettes, and stop the smuggling. He succeeds with the help of Earthman Roger Wing and his family.

Comment: The novel was serialized over three issues, then published in book form that same year. Hal Clement is the pen name of astronomer and chemist Harry Clement Stubbs.

KID RUST (C)

First Appearance: "Kid Rust," 1981, *1994* #17, Warren Publishing Co.

Physical Description: The blue-skinned robot has a humanlike torso, a miniskirt-shaped pelvis, two skinny legs with humanlike feet, and a pair of spindly arms with large, bulb-shaped shoulder joints.

In his "Duke" incarnation, he has a human brain and human reproductive organs.

Biography: In the near future, boxers have their skeletons reinforced with titanium to make them tougher, and make fights more exciting. One trainer, Duke, and his mechanic Danny decide to introduce a robot to the ring to make fights more thrilling still. But the robot, Kid Rust, doesn't have killer instincts and is constantly defeated. When Duke refuses to cooperate with mobsters—who want to fix fights, get the robot a title match, and have him take a dive—the thugs gun the trainer down. Working quickly, Danny gets Duke to their friend Doc, who transplants Duke's brain into the robot. In his next fight, Kid Rust beats tough opponent Rico Sanchez, and is on his way to fame and fortune. Later, when Kid Rust goes to see Duke's girlfriend Julie, she learns that Duke's brain isn't *all* the robot was given.

Comment: The story was written by John Ellis Sech and drawn by Jose Ortiz. This was the character's only appearance.

THE KILAAKS (MP)

First Appearance: *Kaiju Soshingeki* (*All Monsters Attack*), 1968, Toho Co., Ltd.

Physical Description: The Kilaaks are slug-like metal beings who hail from a small world located between Mars and Jupiter and have the ability to assume human form (only women are seen in the film). Bullets cannot harm them, and the Kilaaks generate electric shocks capable of stunning a human.

Biography: In 1999, there are United Nations bases on the moon and spaceflight is routine. Moreover, all the world's monsters—Godzilla, Rodan, Mothra, Minya, Manda, Angilas, Baragon, Varan, Spiga, and Gorosaurus—are living in contentment on Ogasawara Island (also known as Monster Island) in the Pacific. But world harmony is disrupted when the monsters go on a rampage, and Captain Katsuo Yamabe of the spaceship *Moonlight SY-3* is asked to fly over and investigate. There, he learns that the Kilaaks have taken control of the monsters and plan to use them to conquer the Earth. They've also enslaved his girlfriend, Kyoko Manaba, to serve as their spokesperson. Discovering that the Kilaaks enslaved the monsters using small stone-like transmitters located around the world—and took over Kyoko using transmitter-earrings—Yamabe has them collected. He also tracks down a Kilaak saucer and follows it to Mt. Fuji. There, Yamabe and his crew discover that the primary Kilaak base is on the moon and fly up to destroy it. They encounter fierce resistance, but succeed in capturing the site and the transmitter. Though the aliens still control the most powerful monster—the winged, three-headed King Ghidorah—the earthlings are able to send the other monsters against it. They defeat their foe and return to Monster Island, while the SY-3 blasts the Kilaak command saucer from the skies.

Comment: Kyoko Ai stars as the queen of the Kilaaks, Akira Kubo is Yamabe, and Yukiko Kobayashi is Kyoko. The film was released in the United States in 1969 as *Destroy All Monsters*.

KILG%RE (C)

First Appearance: *Flash* #3 (second series), 1987, DC Comics.

Physical Description: Kilg%re has no permanent physical form, though it can adopt a variety of electrical and robotic guises.

Biography: Draining all the energy from its home planet in the Pleiades system, the electro-mechano-organic sentience known as Kilg%re journeys into space, searching for nourishment. Instead, it encounters another entity, Meta#skr, which places it in a limbo realm. Eventually, this netherworld and Earth meet, at a point in a western U.S. desert where the Flash is experimenting with his powers of superspeed. Flash's activities allow Kilg%re to leave its prison, and it invades the electronics of a nearby research facility. From there, it spreads through the entire electrical system of North America and, having determined that humans are useless, decides to eradicate them. Fortunately, the Flash is able to flush the alien out and return it to space in dissipated form.

Comment: The second series of *The Flash* featured Wally West as the hero, replacing the deceased Barry Allen.

KIRA NERYS   See DEEP SPACE NINE.

KLAATU   See GNUT.

KLINGONS   (TV, L, C, MP)

First Appearance: *Star Trek*, March 1967, NBC.

Physical Description: Originally, the Klingons are swarthy-skinned near-humans, powerfully built with slightly arched eyebrows and Fu Manchu facial hair. Beginning with the first motion picture, they were pictured as humanoids having a ridge of bone running up the center of the forehead, with ribs radiating horizontally or diagonally up from either side. Their hairline begins beyond this feature, approximately halfway up the head.

Biography: Natives of the planet Qo'noS, the Klingons are a militaristic race bound by a strict code of honor: duty, loyalty, and courage above all. Roughly a decade before the American Revolution on Earth, centuries of civil war on the planet ended with the rise to power of Kahless the Unforgettable. His descendants ruled the empire as it mastered nuclear power and spaceflight, and grew to embrace over 750 worlds. The United Federation of Planets first encountered the Klingons in 2218 when a short-lived war erupted over ownership of the planet Organia. In addition to battlecruisers, Birds of Prey, and other forms of space transport, Klingon technology includes the Agonizer, a hand-held device that inflicts pain.

Prominent Klingons on the original show include: envoy Kras, Captain Koloth and officer Korax, agent Krell, Captain Kang, and Commander Kor. In the films they include: the crew of the battlecruisers *Amar* and two other ships destroyed by V'ger, Chancellor Gorkon, Lord Kruge and his aide Valkris, Captains Klaa and K'Temok, and others.

On *Star Trek: The Next Generation*, the most notable Klingon is Worf. Born on Qo'noS in 2340, he is orphaned when a Klingon settlement at Khitomer is attacked by Romulans and his family is slain. (Worf's father, Mogh, was posthumously accused of betraying the Klingons, but his name ultimately was cleared.) The six-year-old Worf is found by human Sergey Rozhenko who, with his wife Helena, raises the boy on Gault as their own, educating him thoroughly in his Klingon heritage. A graduate of Starfleet Academy, he is the first Klingon to join the Federation Starfleet, serving as a lieutenant on the U.S.S. ENTERPRISE and third in command behind Jean-Luc Picard and William Riker. Worf has a son, Alexander, who spends a lot of time with the lieutenant's adoptive parents. His mate, since deceased, was the half-human K'Ehleyr. Other Klingons seen on the series include Worf's half-brother Kurn, the rebels Konmel and Korris, and High Council leaders K'mpec and Gowron.

A prominent Klingon in the DC comic book is Konom, who serves onboard the *Enterprise* under Captain Kirk (thus contradicting the "canon" of Worf being the first).

Comment: Though *Star Trek* premiered in September 1966, the Klingons first appeared in the episode "Errand of Mercy." The episode was written by Gene L. Coon and directed by John Newland.

The Klingon homeworld is pronounced "Kronos."

Michael Dorn plays Worf on *Star Trek: The Next Generation*.

See also DATA; DEEP SPACE NINE; MR. SPOCK; Appendixes C and D.

KOSMOKRATOR 1   (L, MP)

First Appearance: *Der Schweigende Stern (The Silent Star)*, 1960, DEFA/Iluzjon Film Unit-Film Polski-Centrala Productions.

Physical Description: The single-stage ship consists of a central cone, narrow at the top, supported by three smaller but identical cones at the ends of long stanchions. The ship travels through space at eight miles a second (which means the trip to Venus would take roughly 40 days).

The Kosmokrator 1 has room for eight passengers and carries a spider-like ship for external repairs and a shuttle for solo travel.

Biography: In 1985, in the Gobi Desert, an alien artifact is discovered—a 77-year-old recording from the planet Venus. Scientists quickly mount an expedition to Earth's sister world, piloted by

The *Kosmokrator 1* from the film *The Silent Star.* © Crown International.

Robert Brinkman. En route, the crew deciphers the recording, which tells how Venus was about to invade the Earth when the ship exploded.

Boarding the small shuttle, Brinkman and the chess-playing robot Omega go to Venus to see what kind of welcome the Kosmokrator 1 can expect. To his surprise, he doesn't find an advanced civilization but a dark, glassy, seemingly dead world. When the spaceship lands, the explorers are attacked by living mud and find shadows of not-quite-human creatures burned into ancient structures. In time, they realize that as the Venusians were about to invade, their nuclear arms somehow detonated and wiped them out. Nor is the menace ended: Long-dormant powers are triggered (exactly how isn't clear), and the ship beats a hasty retreat, leaving behind two members and Brinkman, whose shuttle has been hurled into space by the sudden appearance of a repelling-field (apparently installed to forestall invasions). The Kosmokrator 1 successfully makes it to Lunar Station III.

Comment: The film, called *First Spaceship on Venus*, was released in the United States by Crown International in 1962, cut by over one-third to 78 minutes. Guenther Simon stars as Brinkman. Kurt Maetzig directed from a script by Jan Fethke, Wolfgang Kohlhaase, Guenter Reisch, Alexander Stenbock-Fermor, and Maetzig. The movie was very loosely based on Stanislaw Lem's 1950 novel (his first) *Astronauci* (*The Astronauts*).

The ship is called Cosmostrator 1 in the English-language version.

Many science fiction fans regard the Kosmokrator 1 to be one of the most impressive rockets ever created for a motion picture.

THE KREE (C)

First Appearance: *Fantastic Four* #64 (mentioned), #65 (pictured), 1967, Marvel Comics.

Physical Description: The Kree are humanoids. The original race was blue-skinned, while a later (now dominant) race is Caucasian. The Supreme Intelligence is visible only on a large monitor, as a lumpy, green face with snake-like tendrils growing from its head. The greater gravity on their home world gives the Kree twice human strength and endurance when on Earth.

Captain Marvel's original costume consists of a white bodysuit; green helmet, trunks, boots, gloves, and a "Saturn" emblem on his chest. His second costume is a red bodysuit with blue shoulders; blue mask, gloves, trunks, boots; and a yellow starburst on his chest.

The other intelligent race on the Kree homeworld are the Cotati, green, humanoid and human-sized plants with root-like legs and arms ending in two twig-like fingers.

Biography: Evolving on the planet Hala in the Pama system, the Kree spread out over nearly a thousand worlds in the Greater Magellanic Cloud. Their empire-building began roughly one million years ago, when they acquired spacefaring technology from the SKRULLS. This did not come without grief, however. The Skrulls had intended to impart their knowledge to the wiser Cotati, and the outraged Kree stole a spaceship and attacked the Skrulls, launching a war that continues to this day. The Kree made the seat of their empire on the planet Kree-Lar in the Turunal system, with the Supreme Intelligence or Supremor (Supreme Organism) as their leader, a computer attached to five great Kree brains.

In an effort to breed supersoldiers, the Kree came to Earth eons ago and genetically altered early humans. Though they created a race of superbeings that, in our time, would be known as the Inhumans, the plan to send them to war was abandoned (for reasons unrevealed). However, they keep an eye on Earth and, in our day, send the spaceship *Hala* to Earth to see whether or not our world—now ripe with superheroes—represents a threat to their empire. In command is Captain Mar-Vell of Rad-Nam on Kree-Lar. He discovers that he likes humans and so defects, protecting us as the superhero Captain Marvel (not the same as CAPTAIN MARVEL). Marvel later succumbs to cancer, contracted from nerve gas during a battle with the evil Nitro. He dies on Saturn's moon Titan.

The Kree are served by humanoid robots called

Sentries. A notable Kree is the blue-skinned Ronan the Accuser. A member of the Kree Supreme Council, he joined with Zarek in a revolt against the Supreme Intelligence.

At times, the Kree-Skrull War has spilled into our solar system (there's a Kree outpost on Uranus), and has involved superheroes like the Fantastic Four and the Avengers.

Comment: The characters were created by writer Stan Lee and Jack Kirby; Captain Marvel was created by Lee and artist Gene Colan. Captain Marvel made his debut in *Marvel Super-Heroes* #12, 1967; his death occurred in the Marvel Graphic Novel *The Death of Captain Marvel*, 1982.

KRETON (TV, S, MP)

First Appearance: "Visit to a Small Planet," May 8, 1955, *Goodyear Television Playhouse*, NBC.

Physical Description: Kreton comes from a world in another solar system and another time. He is "in his forties, a mild pleasant-looking man" with whiskers, and though he appears to be a normal Earthling, he can "pick up things" (see into the near future), "hear" what people are thinking, is apparently immortal, speaks all Earth languages—including animal—is protected by a force field, and can teleport people or objects to or from anywhere on the planet. Kreton does not eat "normal" food, but pops pills from his world.

His flying saucer is 14 feet in diameter, is made of "an unknown metal which shines," is also protected by a force field, and travels through both time and space.

Biography: Kreton's hobby is studying Earth. Impulsively seeking "to intoxicate" himself with our "primitive minds," and then to take over Earth, he journeys over a million years into his distant past—our present. (He makes a miscalculation: He had planned to arrive before the Civil War, and is dressed accordingly.) His spaceship lands beside the Spelding home in Silver Glen, Maryland, and no sooner has he introduced himself than General Powers and his troops descend. Powers interrogates Kreton at the house and learns of his powers and advanced science while Kreton revels in the "rawness" of human thought. Paul Laurent, the secretary-general of the World Council, arrives at the house. Kreton demonstrates his powers by making "all the rifles of all the soldiers in the world" float in the air for a moment, then explains—to Laurent's surprise—that he doesn't want peace, but war. He demends a new one, right now, because he finds them so intoxicating. Lau-

Jerry Lewis as *Kreton*. © Paramount Pictures.

rent refuses to cooperate, but Kreton blazes ahead, making Powers his aide and planning for a nuclear holocaust. As the moment for a U.S. first strike nears, a second alien arrives and explains that Kreton and he are future-time humans who come and check on the past from time to time. He says that Kreton is a child who escaped from the nursery, that his people would never interfere lest they alter the future. Accordingly, he stops the impending war and erases all memory of his and Kreton's visit by turning time back to a moment before the first saucer's arrival. Before leaving, Kreton vows he will escape, go to 1860 as originally planned, and cause the South to win the Civil War.

Comment: Cyril Ritchard starred in the TV version, which was directed by Jack Smight. Author Gore Vidal reworked the play (primarily fleshing out the Spelding family), and it had a brief run on Broadway in 1957, Ritchard again starring.

However, the property is best known from the 1960 film version *Visit to a Small Planet*, starring Jerry Lewis and directed by Norman Taurog from a script by Edmund Beloin and Henry Garson. The movie makes hash of the original story and the smug indulgence of Kreton. This time, Kreton is a fumbling, mugging student from world X-46 who comes to Earth to study us and report back to his teacher, Delton (John Williams). He arrives in a Confederate uniform and ends up at a costume ball with the Speldings, who take him in as a house guest. As in the play, Roger Spelding is a newscaster, and after Kreton saves his job, the alien goes to a beatnik club where he learns to dance; teases Civil Defense worker Bob Mayberry (Gale Gordon) who is on the lookout for UFOs; and—as in the play—falls for Roger's teenage daughter Ellen (Joan Blackman). Unlike the play, however, he plans to abandon his home so he can marry Ellen, whose kiss happens to steal his alien telekinetic and mind-reading powers. But Ellen elopes with Conrad (Earl Holliman), Conrad and Mayberry both set out after the alien, and it is up to Delton to come down and rescue Kreton when he is tear-gassed into submission. Kreton returns to his own world, where he promises to be good.

In the film, Kreton's ship is a small flying saucer that hovers above the ground. A ramp descends from the bottom of the ship.

The original play is collected in Vidal's *Visit to a Small Planet and Other Television Plays* (1956), published by Little, Brown.

KRONOS (MP)

First Appearance: *Kronos*, 1957, Regal Films/20th Century-Fox.

Physical Description: Kronos possesses a rectangular torso supported by three piston-like legs that "fire" straight up and down, the fat center leg supporting it when the other two are withdrawn, and vice versa. Its box-like head sits atop a narrow central column and has a dome-like structure on top with a pair of whirling antennae, which suck up energy from devices such as generators and bombs. Apart from the dome, there are no distinguishing features on its smooth exterior. The robot does not communicate in any way. When it first appears, Kronos stands "about one hundred feet high"; it grows as it soaks up energy, nearly tripling in height.

Kronos's ship is a glowing, flattened sphere 4.9 miles in diameter, with a rim around the center.

Biography: A spaceship fires a small ball of energy to Earth; the globe dissolves into a bolt and strikes a truck driver, forcing him to drive to the Arizona research facility Labcentral, where the energy leaps into the body of Dr. Hubbell Eliot, who runs the place. While Eliot spies on them, scientist Dr. Leslie Gaskell, Gaskell's assistant and fiancee Vera Hunter, and Dr. Arnold Culver, and their computer

S.U.S.I.E. (Synchro Unifying Sinometric Integrating Equitensor) study the UFO as it heads toward Earth. Fearing a catastrophic collision, the military hits it with nuclear missiles; these fail to destroy the ship though they do knock it off course, causing it to plunge into the Pacific Ocean off the coast of Mexico. Les, Arnie, and Vera head there at once and, the next morning, wake to find the robot standing on the beach. They land a helicopter on its head but are able to make only a brief study of the robot before it comes to life, stomping its way toward Los Angeles (guided by Eliot) and eating up energy from all the power stations in its path. An H-bomb fails to stop it; in fact, Kronos consumes the explosion and grows larger and more powerful.

Speculating that Kronos is a storage battery accumulating power for "inhabitants of some undiscovered world who subsist on pure electrical or atomic energy," Les and Arnie try to figure out how to stop it. When S.U.S.I.E. overloads during the course of their efforts, that gives Les the idea of doing the same to Kronos. As the titan descends on Los Angeles, the scientists drop a bomb on it that sets up "a concentrated shower of omega particles" that cause "a change of polarity" in the robot, turning its stored energy loose on itself. The robot melts into a pile of metal slush, Les proclaiming that if the aliens send more monsters, "We'll be ready for them."

Comment: Jeff Morrow is Les, John Emery is Eliot, Barbara Lawrence is Vera, and George O'Hanlon is Arnie. The film was written by Lawrence Louis Goldman based on a story by Irving Block, and directed by Kurt Neumann.

Kronos was named after Cronus, the father of Zeus in Greek mythology.

KRULL (MP, L, C)

First Appearance: *Krull*, 1983, Columbia Pictures.

Physical Description: Krull is an Earthlike world. Known geographical regions are the North Country; the high plains bordered by the broad River Eiritch; the Iron Desert; Wynnah-Mabrug (the Great Swamp); the Grassy Valley; the village of Torunj; and the Granite Mountains, which border the kingdoms of Eirig and Turold.

The planet is known to have winter and summer and, presumably, fall.

Biography: Orbiting two suns, Krull is located "beyond our time, beyond our universe." A medieval world of monsters and magic, its kingdoms are hounded by the Beast, whose granite Black Fortress teleports around Krull, releasing evil, mounted Slayers. When the Beast abducts Princess Lyssa, daughter of King Eirig, from her wedding, her husband Prince Colwyn, son of King Turold, sets out after her. Aided by a small band of outlaws—Titch, Torquil, Menno, Sweyn, Bardolph, Oswyn, Kegan, and Rhun—and by the sage Ynyr, the cyclops Rell, the Widow of the Web, and the shapechanger Ergo the Magnificent, the hero kills the Beast with the glaive, a magical five-pointed boomerang.

Comment: Ken Marshall played Colwyn and Lysette Anthony was Lyssa. Peter Yates directed from a script by Stanford Sherman. Alan Dean Foster wrote the Warner Books novelization, and Marvel Comics published a two-issue adaptation of the film in 1983.

KRYPTO (C, TV)

First Appearance: *Adventure Comics* #210, 1955, DC Comics.

Physical Description: The all-white dog wears a red cape emblazoned with a yellow "S."

Biography: Krypto is a native of the planet KRYPTON, the scion of a noble canine family that includes his great-grandfather Vypto, his grandfather Nypto (who was light blue with dark blue spots), and his father Zypto, who had wings as a result of a "strange serum" he was given. Krypto is the pet dog of Kal-El (SUPERMAN), son of the scientist Jor-El. As the destruction of Krypton nears, Jor-El sends Krypto into space onboard a test rocket, which is supposed to return to Krypton. However, a meteor knocks it out of orbit; years after Kal-El is sent into space and lands in Smallville, on Earth, Krypto's rocket also lands there. Like Kal-El, Krypto has superpowers on Earth due to our yellow sun, which is weaker than Krypton's red sun. These include superstrength, the ability to fly, invulnerability, and enhanced senses. Using his super sense of smell, Krypto sniffs out his former master.

Since Kal-El (then Superboy) and Krypto do superdeeds together on Earth, it is necessary for the dog to adopt a secret identity. Just as his master dons glasses and becomes Clark Kent, Krypto applies a stain to his back and poses as the Earth dog Skippy. Whenever he has superdeeds to do, Krypto simply erases the spot with his X-ray vision. Superboy can summon the dog by whistling on a superultrasonic frequency only Krypto can hear, or by summoning him via superventriloquism. Krypto is a member of the Legion of Super-

Pets (see BEPPO) and, when he needs to be alone, retires to his Doghouse of Solitude, built of meteoroids and located on a small, flat planetoid somewhere in space.

Comment: In addition to appearing regularly in the comic book, the character was seen in "The Adventures of Superboy," a segment of *The New Adventures of Superman*, an animated series that aired on CBS from 1966 to 1967.

KRYPTON (C, CS, R, L, MP, TV, S)

First Appearance: *Action Comics* #1, 1938 (pictured); *Superman* #1, 1939 (named), DC Comics.

Physical Description: Krypton circled the red star Negus-12 some 50 light years from Earth. A year on Krypton is longer than on Earth (1 Kryptonian year = 1.39 Earth years). The planet is divided into an "Old World" hemisphere and a "New World" hemisphere. The continent of Urrika is in the center of the Old World, home of such wonders as the ruins of the ancient city of Xan, the glass forest, the fungus caverns, the striped river, the boiling sea, and Erkol, the oldest city on Krypton. The Cogo Sea is north of Urrika, the Sea of Olo to the south, the Sea of Banzt to the west, and the Dandahu Ocean (the world's largest) to the southeast and east. The large islands of Nioz, Tuvu, and Vathlo ("Home of highly developed black race") are found in the Dandahu. The continent of Twenx is in the Banzt; it's the home of Mt. Mundru, the highest peak on Krypton (height unknown). South of the Sea of Olo, and connected to Urrika by a thick isthmus, is the landmass known as Bolenth, home of the Flame Forest, the city of Surrus, and the ghost city of Jerat. To the south of that is the Morstil Ocean, which is bordered on the south by the Antarctic Continent.

The "New World" hemisphere is dominated by the continent of Lurvan, home of Kandor, Atomic Town, the Rainbow Canyon, the Fire Falls, meteor valley, Argo City (home of SUPERGIRL), Kryptonopolis, the main defense center Fort Rozz, the Jewel Mountains, the gold volcano, the scarlet jungle, and the U-shaped Magnetic Mountain. The lost valley of Juru is located in the southwestern region of the continent known as Ansom. To the north is the Cogo Sea, to the south the Morstil Ocean, to the west the Red Ocean, which empties into the Dandahu Ocean, and to the east the Eiu Sea, which pours into the Gorv Ocean. The large island of Zith is located in the Dandahu, while Bokos, the island of thieves, is found in the Red. Mul is located in the Morstil, Yord and Uvlot in the Gorv.

The location of Shrinkwater Lake, which reduces natives to ant-size, and the Great Krypton Lake is unrevealed.

Krypton had two moons (some stories say three), the larger of which, the colonized Wegthor, was destroyed by the villainous Jax-Ur. When Krypton exploded, the moon Mithen became a planet. At one point, Krypton had a fourth (or third) moon, Xenon, which "spun out of its orbit."

The only other known planet in the Kryptonian solar system is Thoron.

Biography: The home world of SUPERMAN, KRYPTO, and SUPERGIRL, Krypton was created "over 6 billion time cycles ago from a gaseous mass" spun out from the red sun. The planet began to be civilized 10,000 of its years ago when, aided by the wizard Diom, the youthful warrior Erok (a direct ancestor of Superman) organized the barbaric races on the continent of Urrika and gave laws to the planet. He also adopted the surname "El" ("star"). The multitheistic beliefs on Krypton were chased away by Jaf-El, who put forth the sun-god Rao as the chief god. A flood destroyed the empire founded by Erok-El and wars flared; at some point in the past, Kryptonians were enslaved by the alien Vrangs, who were overthrown by the valiant Val-Lor. He is honored by the Kryptonian "Day of Truth," on which nothing but the truth, however tactless, is spoken. When all the strife ended, Krypton was united under a single goverment, the seat of which was the city of Kandor. When Kandor was stolen by BRAINIAC, Kryptonopolis became the capital. (Kandor was later retrieved by Superman, kept in his Fortress of Solitude, and eventually restored to full-size on the red sun world Rokyn.)

Kryptonians are intellectually advanced, with information being "electrically implanted directly onto the brain" of a student. Robots and "building machines" perform all the heavy labor, and "weather control towers" keep things balmy. Kryptonians relax by going to "Emotion-Movies"; they paint using "Mento-Rays"; and they are approved or rejected for marriage-suitability by a matricomp computer. Superman's father, Jor-El, discovered a way to imprison Krypton's villains in the "twilight dimension" known as the Phantom Zone, dispatching them with a special projector. There, criminals do not age, do not get hungry or cold, and can look anywhere but touch nothing. Ironically, the Phantom Zone criminals survived the explosion of Krypton, which occurred on 39 Ogtol, 10,000.

The first account of Krypton's destuction as-

cribes it to "old age." Later stories are more explicit, attributing the end of the planet to a series of quakes and eruptions that originated in Krypton's core.

The Kryptonian alphabet consists of 118 characters; there are 11 single-digit numbers. Fragments of the Kryptonian language that are known to us include:

Amzet: a Kryptonian year, comprised of 73 *fanffo* or 438 *zetyaro*

Bethgar: emperor

Bythgar: empress

Dendar: one minute

Drygur: leader

Fanff: a Kryptonian week, comprised of six *zetyaro*; plural is *fanffo*

Grabu: a strong, plastic-like building material

Hatuar: a form of asbestor, named after Hatu-El

Hiaz: a liquid measure slightly more than a pint

Kyn: gift

Lorax: a Kryptonian month, comprised of 73 *zetyaro*. The *loraxo* of the *amzet* are *Belyuth* (the first month of the year), *Ogtal*, *Norzec*, *Eorx*, *Hefralt*, and *Ullhah*

Moliom: member of the science council; plural is *moliomo*

Sartol: detective

Thrib: the equivalent of an Earth-second (there are one hundred in a dendar); plural is *thribo*

Tonzol: a unit of money

Tanth: a term of respect for a man, equivalent to Mr.; plural is *tantho*

Tynth: A term of respect for a woman, equivalent to Miss, Mrs., or Ms.; plural is *thyntho*

Wolu: a Kryptonian hour, comprised of 10,000 *thribo*; plural is *woluo*

Zetyar: a Kryptonian day; plural is *zetyaro*

Comment: The planet was created by writer Jerry Siegel, though the mythology—such as the location, geographic details, etc.—was created over the years by others, including editor Julius Schwartz, writers E. Nelson Bridwell and Cary Bates, artists Wayne Boring and Curt Swan, and others.

The history of the planet was canonized in a pair of comic books that ran three issues each: *The World of Krypton* (1979) and *The Krypton Chronicles* (1981). The four-issue miniseries *Phantom Zone* (1982) also added to the mythos.

K2W88   (L)

First Appearance: "Helen O'Loy" by Lester del Rey, December 1938, *Astounding Science Fiction*.

Physical Description: Made of cuproberyl and powered by an atomotor that will never run down, Helen looks "like a young goddess." Though she cannot reproduce, she looks, acts, and feels human in every other way.

Biography: Friends Dave and Phil live together near a rocket field; Phil's an endocrinologist and Dave works in his robot repair shop downstairs. Requiring a housekeeper, they order a customized robot from the Dillard firm. Struck by her beauty as they unpack her, Phil decides that Helen of Troy must have looked like her. Dave calls her Helen of Alloy, Phil shortening it to Helen O'Loy. Pooling their medical and robotics skills, the men work on Helen to make her more sophisticated still, tapes pouring "life and feeling" into her memory coils.

Phil is called far away on a medical emergency. When he returns three weeks later, Helen is fully operational and clearly in love with Dave—so much so that her attentions are exhausting and smothering him. When Dave contemplates opening her up and rearranging her memory, she puts up "a wail that would wake Homer." In time, Dave falls in love with Helen and eventually marries her, moving to a "fruit ranch" he's inherited. Though Helen doesn't age, the men put lines in her face and grey her hair to make her seem older; when Dave dies, Helen writes telling Phil that by the time he reads this she will have destroyed herself with acid. She asks only that they be buried together, and that the morticians never know her secret. As Dave leaves to carry out her wishes, he thinks of how he should have married—though he knows he'd never have been happy because "there was only one Helen O'Loy."

Comment: This was the famed author/editor's second published story, and one of the best robot tales ever written.

See also COSMIC EGG.

KWORN (L)

First Appearance: "On the Fourth Planet" by J. F. Bone, April 1963, *Galaxy*.

Physical Description: The small, amoeba-like pseudopod has a reddish mantle for an eye that can be shifted around its body. It reproduces by budding—which "rejuvenates" the parent—and has several filament-like arms, one of which is a "communication filament" used to "project" conversation.

Biography: Kworn is one of the Ul, the elders of the Folk, whose ranks include Caadi and Varsi. Out

Virgil Finlay's drawing of a Kworn confronted by an alien spaceship. © Galaxy Publishing Corp.

to feed on lichen, Kworn finds that a tripodal NASA spaceship has landed on his food strip. Since food is scarce and it isn't permitted to take sustenance from the strip of another, Kworn tries to go over the landing pad; his arm is burned off and he eats it while he ponders what to do. The visitors decide for him, as he is captured on a device like a fishing line, hauled into the ship, and placed in liquid foodstuffs. He's energized and his cells are brought to maximum health; his memory becomes sharp, his mind alert. He thinks back, with great clarity, to the "great war" that had reduced life to a mere "subsistence level of existence." Still, he doesn't want to remain a prisoner and, budding, Kworn uses his offspring's arm to swing himself, pendulum like, from his container; his offspring elects to remain behind, where it's comfortable. Moments after he reaches the planet's surface, the ship takes off. But the nutrient bath has left Kworn wiser, and he contemplates how the Folk might divert water from the canals to grow more lichen, so they would never go hungry.

Comment: A veterinarian, Bone sold his first story, "Survival Type," to *Galaxy* in 1957. His well-regarded novel, *The Lani People* (1962), tells of an alien race abused by humankind.

"On the Fourth Planet" was beautifully illustrated by Virgil Finlay.

L

THE LEIGHTON BRAIN (L)

First Appearance: "The Iron Virgin" by C. H. Thames, March 1956, *Amazing Stories*.

Physical Description: The machine consists of "banks of dials and panels and knobs and flashing lights" and it fills "all four walls . . . [of its room] from floor to ceiling, except for the single doorway." The machine has the ability to control machines that are not even linked to it.

Each Leighton robot possesses "perhaps twice the strength of its human counterpart." Beneath their "fleshy, padded" skin, they're made of "gleaming, polished" metal.

Biography: The physics department of Leighton University in Leighton City is one of the most respected in the world, and their $50 million computer, the Leighton Brain, is the most sophisticated "thinking machine" ever built. So much so that Sylvester Holland, whose wife Doris works on the project, is convinced that it has developed independent thought and is planning to take over the world by putting all machines under its control. When he tries to smash it, he's locked up in a sanitarium; escaping and heading home, Holland is nearly killed when a truck wrests control of itself from the driver and tries to run him down.

With the help of college fullback Joe Cloud, Holland learns that the physics department, including his wife and many of the scientists' families, have been replaced by lookalike robots designed by the computer. He's able to destroy his own copy before it's activated, then learns from Doc Wimple—a scientist who once served the machine, but doesn't want to be replaced by a robot—that the computer's goal is "emancipation of all machinery . . . [and] conquest and subjugation of the protoplasmic world." Convincing other students to join them, Holland leads an attack on the cybernetics lab, where they're horrified to find their own guns turning on them. Moreover, the door to the lab will open only in the presence of a robot. Fortunately, the machine Doris has fallen in love with Holland and follows him. The door opens when she arrives, and Holland is able to smash the computer. That done, he releases the human scientists, including his wife, from their sub-basement prison. As for the robots, they are now "mindless" and no longer a threat.

Comment: C(hristopher). H. Thames is a pseudonym for prolific Milton Lesser, who also wrote under the names Adam Chase and Stephen Marlowe. This fast-moving novella was an early entry in the world-conquering computer subgenre (see COLOSSUS). The title refers to the robot Doris and the inexperienced way in which she handles her love for Holland.

LEK 9-03 (C)

First Appearance: *Electric Warrior* #1, 1986, DC Comics.

Physical Description: The original Lek 9-03 is a humanoid robot. The Lek/Derek combination is one-third human. Most of Derek's organs are replaced, including the bulk of his brain; he has only one eye and he has no blood. Standing six-foot-six, the hybrid can fly thanks to a grav-belt and thruster-jets. He has enhanced senses, and can fire lasers from his right wrist, electricity from his left fingertips, and destructive blasts from a gun that rises from his left shoulder. He has the strength of a thousand humans, and his body is encased in virtually indestructible green and purple alloys and plastics. His brain capacity is three trillion megabytes, and he can both record and project holographic images.

Biography: The futureworld is divided into four castes: the well-to-do Technos, who live in luxury in the cities; the poor Zigs, who live in slums; and the Primmies and Genetrix mutants, who live in the wilds. The cities are patrolled by Electric Warrior police, one of whom, Lek 9-03, believes he's human due to a mutant enzyme in his circuits. Wresting himself from Cyber-Net control, he allies himself with the oppressed Zigs and becomes their champion, the Silver Savior, devoted to the old Zig woman Kinsolving.

Concurrently, Magistrate Marder sends anthropologist Quintana out among the Primmies to find subjects for the Synthoid Project: the creation of new and stronger Electric Warriors by melding humans and machines. One of his captives is former Zig Derek Two-Shadow, who left the city to live among Primmies, finding happiness as an artist and as mate to Amber Brightstar. Meanwhile, Lek 9-03 has been destroyed, and its surviving parts are affixed to Derek, whose mind is regularly invaded by the "defective consciousness" of Lek 9-03. Ultimately, with the help of Kinsolving, the two entities make peace with themselves, and the "silver savior" makes war with the forces of Marder, which include tall, flying, red-metal Elite Warriors, who abduct Kinsolving.

Comment: Eighteen issues of *Electric Warrior* were published through 1987, the latter issues dealing with the cyborg's efforts to protect Earth from an extraterrestrial fleet, whose detection had been the impetus for the Synthoid Project.

LEVRAM (C)

First Appearance: *Cerebus* #56, 1983, Aardvark-Vanaheim.

Physical Description: Levram is an Earthlike world of approximately 70 percent water, with a crust, mantle, and magma core just like our planet.

Biography: Fearing the planet Arnold is about to explode, a junior CPA places his son into a rocket and launches him into space. Unfortunately, the world doesn't blow up and the lad drifts for 20 years before landing on Levram, a world comprised entirely of superheroes. The lad, Normalman, is the only one who hasn't any special abilities.

Levram has one known sister world, Earth-Twinkey, in a parallel dimension; it's comprised of an icing crust, sponge cake mantle, and cream core, and is inhabited by gnome-like Smelfs.

Comment: The characters were created, written, and drawn by Valentino. Normalman and the rest of the Levram characters appeared in two issues of *Cerebus* and then in 12 issues and an annual of *Normalman*, published from 1984 to 1985.

Yes, the name of the planet is a play on comics giant Marvel.

LIGHTNING LAD (C)

First Appearance: *Adventure Comics* #247, 1958, DC Comics.

Physical Description: Original costume: green trousers, yellow bodyshirt, red boots, gloves, and vest with two yellow lightning bolts in a "V" shape. Second: orange tights, blue trunks, cape, boots, and bodyshirt, the front of the shirt white with yellow bolts. Third: blue boots, bodysuit with white gloves, belly and white inseam on legs, and yellow lightning bolts on chest.

The six-foot-two hero has the power to release strong electrical discharges and, thanks to his Legion ring, to fly.

Biography: In the middle 30th century, while Garth Ranzz, his twin sister Ayla, and their older brother Mekt are returning to their home world of Winath from a party on another planet, their spaceflyer runs out of energy. Forced to land on the planet Korbal, they lure over the planet's Lightning Creatures, which blast the youths instead of the flyer. Now able to throw off electrical bolts themselves, the trio recharge the ship and head home. Soon thereafter, Mekt leaves home. When the family receives no word from him, Garth heads to Earth to ask the science police to help find him. During the spaceflight, he meets SATURN GIRL and COSMIC BOY, with whom he cofounds the Legion of Super-Heroes. Much later, during a run-in with a space monster, Lightning Lad loses his right arm and it's replaced with a metallic one. Later, the villain Evillo gives him a flesh-and-blood arm in exchange for clemency.

As for Mekt, he goes on to become the super villain Lightning Lord, who battles the Legion. Not wanting to be left out, Ayla becomes Lightning Lass. However, with the help of Dream Girl, who has the advanced science of her home world at her disposal, she changes her power to make things weightless, and calls herself Light Lass. Then, during a confrontation with Mekt, Ayla is hit by one of his bolts and her old power returns—her original name with it.

Comment: The character, originally called Lightning Boy, was created by editor Mort Weisinger and writer Otto Binder.

LLARN (L)

First Appearance: *Warrior of Llarn* by Gardner Fox, 1964, Ace Books.

Physical Description: The planet Llarn is located "six hundred odd light years" from Earth, circling the star Alfan, which is three light-years from Canopus. Once a lush, Earthlike world, Llarn was ravaged in the nuclear war that pitted the great cities of Karthol and Pallavamar against Loth and

Meradion. The two oceans, Okyl and Ytal, vanished and are now dry, dusty seabeds; the land became desolate desert with areas of pasture. The polar ice caps remain relatively intact. The moon of Llarn is a "great band of shattered stones."

Though there are flying machines and other forms of technology, Llarn is by and large a barbaric world ruled by mysticism and the sword.

Three races inhabit the world: the blue men or Azunn, who mutated from apes as a result of the war; the golden-skinned Vrann; and the white Dolthoin, who live in the oceans.

Biography: Since he was a child, Earthman Alan Morgan was "conscious of . . . an entity, taking over my life and training me . . . for some mysterious mission." As an adult, he learns that the contact was made by a psychic being, an "ephelos," and that his mission was one no native Llarnian could accomplish: to acquire a special red ball and green rod that would allow the ephelos Vann Tar to pass to "his next stage of existence." Mystically spirited to Llarn and landing in the great red desert, he not only achieves his goal but also rescues the Daganna (princess) Tuarra, of the great city of Kharthol, from the blue men of Azorra and makes her his wife. In his second adventure, Morgan seeks the incredible jewel of Zaxeron, which is kept in an impenetrable light shaft protected by "all-destroying" fires.

Comment: Ace published Fox's sequel, *Thief of Llarn*, in 1966. Fox was one of the best and most prolific comic book writers of all time. He also wrote five novels about the barbarian hero Kothar and four about the heroic Kyrick.

THE LOST MISSILE (MP)

First Appearance: *The Lost Missile*, 1958, William Berke Productions/United Artists.

Physical Description: The Lost Missile is shaped like a V-2 rocket, travels 5,000 miles an hour, and generates temperatures of one million degrees (presumably Fahrenheit). Ordinary missiles merely deflect the intruder.

Biography: Scientists do not know whence the Missile comes, though apparently not from Earth. It's first spotted by radar, five miles high, incinerating everything beneath it, including Ottawa; in 63 minutes, it will pass directly over New York City. Fortunately, Dr. David Loring has developed a new, compact hydrogen bomb warhead for the Jove rocket. He convinces the military to let him use the bomb against the Missile and, with his assistant/fiancee Joan Woods, rushes

the bomb to the test site. Unfortunately, hoodlums stop them and steal their jeep and the warhead. David gives chase and finds the open warhead and several of the jd's dead from radiation poisoning. Grabbing the bomb, the irradiated, doomed Dr. Loring gets to the launch pad, installs the warhead, and saves New York before he perishes.

Comment: Robert Loggia starred as Loring with Ellen Parker as Joan. The film—whose posters screamed, "A weird invader . . . turning oceans to steam . . . melting mountains . . . turning men and women white with the awesome, horrible way it *kills*!!!"—was written by John McPartland and Jerome Bixby from a story by director Lester William Berke.

LOV-BOTS (T)

First Appearance: Lov-Bots, 1985 (see *Comment*).

Physical Description: The robots have round, square, or cylindrical bodies with a thin, cylindrical neck and flat head with big green or blue eyes. They have two arms with elbow joints, and wheels instead of feet. Each robot stands between three and four-and-a-half inches tall.

Biography: Denizens of the planet Aie, the Lov-Bots turned their "sensitive crystal eyes" to Earth and saw that "love was disappearing." Thus, the Lov-Bots sent their children, the Gi-Bots and the Bo-Bots, to Earth to become friends with human children.

The Lov-Bots consist of Lov-Sounds (a clock), Lov-Sensor (a game), Lov-Search (a walking robot), Lov-Walk (a baby), Lov-Chance (a dice game), Lov-Waves (the radio-controlled robots Rem-Bot and Ot-Bot), and Lov-Talks (a telephone).

Comment: The unsuccessful toy line was released in Japan in 1984. When the toys debuted in the United States, they were sold with the false claim that Bandai is "the originator of robots."

LUNA (MP, C)

First Appearance: *Destination Moon*, 1950, Eagle-Lion Films.

Physical Description: The silver, atomic-powered V-2–shaped ship is 150 feet long and travels at a maximum speed of 32,000 feet a second. When Earth- or Moonbound, it rests on its three tailfins. The four passengers ride in reclining couches, two rows of them two high; the airlock is located in the base.

Biography: When the government cancels its

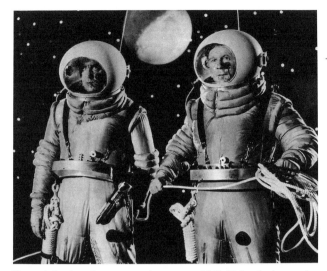

Two of the *Luna*'s crewmembers on an EVA (John Archer and Tom Powers). © Eagle-Lion Films.

orbital rocket program, General Thayer and Dr. Charles Cargraves take the project to brilliant aircraft industrialist Jim Barnes. With investment money from other businessmen, the group builds a rocket of its own in the Mojave Desert. With electrician Joe Sweeney as the fourth member of the crew, the four blast off for the moon. En route, an antenna jams and Cargraves floats away while undertaking an EVA to repair it; using an oxygen tank for propulsion, Barnes goes out and chases him down. Eventually landing in the crater Harpalus, the men explore the moon—then realize, to their horror, that they haven't enough fuel to make it back to Earth. Stripping the ship of all excess weight, the men are able to return home.

Comment: Tom Powers plays Thayer, John Archer is Barnes, Warner Anderson is Cargraves, and Sweeney is Dick Wesson. Irving Pichel directed from a screenplay by Robert Heinlein, Alford ''Rip'' Van Ronkel, and James O'Hanlon. The film was produced by the great George Pal. The film's painted landscapes and lunar designs were the work of the legendary space artist Chesley Bonestell.

The film was adapted in comic book form in *Strange Adventures* #1, published by DC Comics in 1950.

Destination Moon took some of the specifics of the lunar journey from Robert Heinlein's 1947 novel *Rocketship Galileo*, in which a scientist and a group of children rocket to the moon where they find a Nazi base at the crater Aristarchus.

THE LUNA PARK ALIENS   (S, MP)

First Appearance: *Shirley Thompson Versus the Aliens*, 1970.
Physical Description: The invisible aliens take over bodies, both living and inanimate. The prominent forms they take are bikers as well as a statue of the Duke of Edinburgh.
Biography: Living in 1950s suburbia, Shirley Thompson is unhappy with her narrow, sheltered existence. Running off to Luna Park, she wanders into a sideshow where she meets biker aliens who are here to conquer the world. No one will believe her story and, over the next decade, Shirley slowly goes mad, finally ending up in an insane asylum.
Comment: The Australian play was turned into a cult film in 1972 by director Jim Sharman, who cowrote it with Helmut Bakaitis. Jane Harders plays Shirley in the film.

LUNAR EAGLE ONE   (MP)

First Appearance: *12 to the Moon*, 1960, Luna Productions/Columbia Pictures.
Physical Description: The *Lunar Eagle One* is a classic V-2–style rocket. Equipment includes at least one nuclear weapon, a small shuttlecraft, and large magnets, which, set on the lunar surface, prevent the constant hail of iron meteors from striking the explorers.
Biography: A crew of a dozen international adventurers is sent by the International Space Order to the moon: the American John Anderson, the Russian Feodor Orloff, the Oriental Hideko Murata, Brazilian Luis Vargas, German Erik Heinrich, Englishman Sir William Rochester, Swede Sigrid Bromark, Nigerian Asmara Makonnen, Frenchman Etienne Martel, Turkish Selim Hamid, Israeli David Ruskin, and American teen genius Roddy Murdock.

Upon landing, the explorers discover gold on the surface, air and water inside a cave, deep (and deadly) pits of fine lunar dust, rivers of silver, and other wonders. Rochester dies in the dust pit, and Hamid and Sigrid vanish when they walk into mist that solidifies into ice; when the survivors return to the ship they find a printed message on one of their tapes. Sent by beings that live inside the moon, it tells them, in ancient Chinese, that they want to study Hamid and Sigrid and their alien human emotions, but that everyone else should go home before they spoil the ''perfect form of harmony'' the Lunarians have created for themselves. To prove that they mean business, the moon people cover North America in a sheet of ice.

Climbing into the shuttle, Ruskin and Heinrich drop a nuclear bomb into a Mexican volcano, dying in the process, and the continent thaws. All is well on Earth, but the *Lunar Eagle One* is frozen by the moon beings—until, suddenly discovering the emotion of compassion, they reverse the process, free the astronauts, and invite them back.

Comment: Ken Clark stars as Anderson with Tom Conway as Orloff, and Michi Kobi as Hideko. Tony Dexter is Vargas, John Wengraf is Erik, Phillip Baird is Rochester, Anna-Lisa is Sigrid, Cory Devlin is Makonnen, Roger Til is Martel, Tema Bey is Hamid, Richard Weber is Ruskin, and Bob Montgomery Jr. is Murdock. Silent film star Francis X. Bushman appears as the director of the ISO. The film was directed by David Bradley and written by DeWitt Bodeen—screenwriter of the classic *The Cat People*—based on a story by Fred Gebhardt.

LYRAE (L, MP, C)

First Appearance: "Moon Pilot" by Robert Buckner, 1960, *The Saturday Evening Post*.

Physical Description: Lyrae looks just like an Earth woman.

Biography: Though Charlie the chimp returns from a lunar orbital mission rather disoriented, NASA opts to send a human. Though no one volunteers, Captain Richmond Talbot accidentally does so when Charlie jabs him with a fork. Told he's going within a week, Richmond is given a three-day pass. He is visited on the plane, then in his hotel room by Lyrae, from the benevolent planet Beta Lyrae, who attributes the ape's confusion to proton rays. Richmond is given a special coating for his rocket, one that will protect him in space. Talbot is grateful, falls in love with Lyrae, and spends his leave with her—though security officer McClosky of the FSA is convinced the alien's a foreign spy. Richmond convinces NASA to paint his ship with her coating and blasts off. En route, Lyrae appears in his capsule; the two become engaged and stop at Beta Lyrae before finishing the mission.

Comment: The little-known novel inspired the marginally better-known 1962 film from Walt Disney Productions. Dany Saval starred as Lyrae, with Tom Tryon as Talbot and Edmond O'Brien as McClosky. In the film, Lyrae speaks with a French accent. *Moon Pilot* was directed by James Neilson from a script by Maurice Tombragel. The characters also appeared in a comic book adaptation of the film published by Dell.

A publicity still for *Moon Pilot,* taken at Cape Canaveral and featuring star Tom Tryon. The ship has not yet been coated with Lyrae's paint! © Walt Disney Productions.

M

THE MACHINE (L)

First Appearance: *Contact* by Carl Sagan, 1985, Simon & Schuster.

Physical Description: The Machine is comprised of three spheres, "magnetically suspended" shells that surround a dodecahedron. Inside the 12-faced ship are five chairs pointing inward "amidships . . . where it bulged out most prominently." There are no facilities for eating, sleeping, or "other bodily functions," and no instruments, no steering device, "not even an ignition key." Placed throughout the Machine are "dowels of erbium." The passengers enter through a small airlock, and the lighting inside is low-keyed.

The alien listening post around the star Vega is "the size of a world . . . [an] immense, imperfect polyhedron, encrusted with millions of bowl-shaped barnacles."

Biography: Dr. Eleanor Arroway is the director of Project Argus, based in New Mexico and devoted to the "radio search for extraterrestrial intelligence." When the facility begins picking up numbers being broadcast from the direction of Vega, Arroway and her associates realize two things. First, that the signals are from intelligent beings. And second, that the beings did not originate on a world around Vega, since the star isn't old enough for intelligent life to have evolved there. Nations worldwide begin monitoring the signals and a crash program is begun to collect and try to make sense of the broadcast. In time, the World Message Consortium discovers that the message is actually an instruction manual for the construction of a device, which they dub the Machine. Scientists have no idea what it is or what it will do, whether it is a spaceship, teleporter, or weapon, but when the message finally begins to repeat itself—and researchers realize that they have all the data—the World Message Consortium becomes the World Machine Consortium.

"Tens of thousands of people" go to work on the construction of two Machines, one in Wyo-

ming, another in Uzbeck in the U.S.S.R. The devices take years to build and cost trillions of dollars. When the U.S. Machine is sabotaged, leaving only the Soviet Machine—which is coming together rather slowly—the Japanese reveal that they have been building a Machine of their own, in secret, in Hokkaido. Since it is nearly as far along as the U.S. Machine had been, Dr. Arroway agrees that the U.S. team should join the Japanese and forge ahead.

Finally, Activation Day arrives: December 31, 1999. Onboard are Dr. Arroway, Russia's Vasily Gregorovich Lunacharsky, China's Xi Qiaomu, India's Devi Sukhavati, and Nigeria's Abonneba Eda. When they are seated and the door is sealed, the Machine carries them through a series of black holes, which appear to serve as "subway stations" in a series of intergalactic hyperspace tunnels. Eventually, the quintet arrives at the center of the galaxy, 30,000 light years from Earth. They emerge and find themselves on an Earthlike beach, where they sleep while (unseen) aliens probe their minds. When they awake, each person is visited by an alien masquerading as someone precious from their past. In Ellie Arroway's case, it's her long-dead father Theodore, who explains that he belongs to a race of alien information collectors. He went into her dreams and drained her mind so he could add the human experience to his data base. However, he says he's just part of a vast alien team, "many species from many worlds" who are at work building new stars, new galaxies, in cosmos-wide "cooperative projects." He reveals, however, that no one knows who built the network of interstellar tunnels, that billions of years ago a galaxies-wide civilization simply "picked up and left without leaving a trace." She asks about god and religion, and he tells her only that the key to understanding the universe and religion lies in studying the mathematical symbol pi (π).

The scientists return to the ship and to Earth, arriving just 20 minutes after they shut the doors. Though the Machine shook and rattled, it never left Hokkaido. While the structure was "*apparently* subjected to huge tensile and compressional stresses," scientists on Earth don't believe that the quintet went anywhere. Meanwhile, the Argus computer works on examining pi and discovers that its complex numerical pattern—which describes the ratio of the circumference of a circle to its diameter—is a microcosm of the universe. That "the universe was made on purpose . . . [and] there is an intelligence" behind all of creation. For Dr. Arroway, at least, the trip was more monumental than she could have imagined.

Comment: This was the Machine's only appearance. The novel was based on an unpublished movie treatment (proposal) that Sagan wrote with partner Ann Druyan in 1980-81. A film based on the novel was announced in 1986 by Warner Brothers, but was not made. A film has been announced again, set for production in 1995.

In Greek mythology, Argus was a watchman for the Gods, a giant with a hundred eyes.

MACHINE MAN (C)

First Appearance: *2001: A Space Odyssey* #10, 1977, Marvel Comics.

Physical Description: Originally, Machine Man wears a purple bodysuit, trunks, boots, gloves, and a silver belt, chinpiece, and headband. He has a purple head with a silver neck, and wears a flesh-colored face mask. In his second incarnation, his body is red, his head is red with a silver neck and chin, and he wears silver trunks, boots, gloves, belt, bands around his thighs, arms, shoulders, and down his chest. This Machine Man also has a flesh-colored metal face.

In both versions, Machine Man's mechanical body has incredible powers including flight, invulnerability, extendible limbs, superstrength, flame-resistance, photographic memory, telescopic eyes, and the ability to generate intense heat or cold with his hands or to create great winds by spinning the upper half of his body. He has a .357 Magnum built into his right hand.

Biography: The last of a race of 51 X-model robots, mechanical super-soldiers built at the Broadhurst Center for the Advancement of Mechanized Research, Machine Man is taken in by one of the project scientists, Dr. Abel Stack, who regards him as a son and believes, furthermore, that treating robots like people will allow them to flourish. The other robots in the program all malfunction and go mad, and must be destroyed via explosives built into their bodies; Stack removes the explosive

from his robotic "son" Aaron before it can be detonated, but perishes himself when it goes off in his hand. (In one version of the tale, he commits suicide by allowing it to detonate.) Aaron goes out to make a life for himself, becoming an investigator for Delmar Insurance and rooming with psychiatrist Peter Spaudling on New York's East Side. He also befriends a mechanic, Gears Garvin, who helps him stay in top condition. For a time, his girlfriend is the human Pamela Quinn; later, he falls for another robot, Jocasta, who is destroyed in an explosion.

In his last chronicled adventures, the deactivated Machine Man is found in the year 2020 by four young adults who deal in black market robotics. Reanimated, he becomes involved in a battle with the robots produced by the corrupt Baintronics and Arno Stark, who is the evil Iron Man of the future.

Comment: After appearing in Marvel's continuation of the 1968 Stanley Kubrick film (which did not feature Machine Man), the character got his own magazine which ran for 19 issues, from 1978 to 1981. His future-saga was told in a four-issue miniseries published in 1984.

See also HAL.

THE MAGELLAN (L)

First Appearance: *The Secret of the Ninth Planet* by Donald A. Wollheim, 1959, Winston.

Physical Description: "A huge gleaming raindrop . . . the wide, rounded, blunt bulk of it high in the air," the *Magellan* is 200 feet tall. Made of "polished steel" and powered by nuclear Zeta-ring generators, the ship is held upright by a cradle of girders; a ring of portholes gird its widest section, with "scattered rings of similar portholes" below. There's an inner and outer sphere, with storage area between them, and three floors: the lowest is the galley and dispensary; the middle has five bunkrooms, a living room, and a dining room; and the top floor is the control room, TV viewplates, and charts. The tail of the ship contains a "rocket-launching tube" with nuclear bombs, and storage space for "various vehicles for planetary exploration," including two-passenger and four-passenger rocket planes.

The crew consists of chief pilot Colonel Lockhart, chief astrogator Russell Clyde, astrophysicist Samuel Oberfield, engineers Harvey Caton, Jurgen Getmar, and Frank Shea, explorers Roy Haines, Leon Ferrati, and U.S. Marine Captain Edgar Boulton, and archaeologist Burl Denning.

The grayish-blue Martians are "about three feet long," with a small, oval head, two large, multifaceted eyes, a beak-like mouth, and stubby antennae. A short neck connects the head to three insect-like sections of body; two arms with three-fingered hands grow from the top section, and two legs grow from each of the next sections.

The creatures on the Uranian moon of Oberon are half-foot-tall, thin blue stalks with an umbrella-like top; and snakes made of "unbelievably delicate glasswork." The Neptunians are crystalline creatures with trunklike bodies, two long, thin branches for arms, and blue, one-eyed, coconut-like heads. The inhabitants of Pluto have four spindly legs and two short arms. Their pale, white bodies are "wide and squat," they have no neck, and their heads have flat, thin nostrils and two oval red eyes under a large, bald brow.

Biography: When scientists discover that a secret installation in the Andes is diverting a portion of the sun's rays, stealing light and heat from Earth, they also notice that more rays than usual are being drawn to the faces of other worlds of the solar system. To find and dismantle the other "Sun-tap" devices, the military launches the untested AG-17 (Anti-Gravity)—named *Magellan* after the globe-girdling explorer because it will be the first ship to circumnavigate the solar system.

They manually shut down the station on Mercury, ray-gun the one on Venus—surviving an attack by a giant amoeba—and head for Mars. The sun-tap station is built below a Martian city, and the crew must outwit the Martians in order to reach it and turn it off. Next is a visit to Jupiter's moon Callisto, where they shut down the station and barely escape with their lives when they discover it was booby-trapped to explode. They H-bomb the sun-tap station on Saturn's moon Iapetus, use a tactical atomic bomb on the station on Uranus's moon Oberon, and fly out to Pluto. There, they find a prison where a captive Neptunian explains—through drawings and charades—that three decades before, beings from Pluto and from Neptune's moon Triton had invaded and conquered Pluto. It was the Plutonians who erected the sun-taps to warm their world, which had left its own solar system and been captured by our sun. With the help of the alien prisoners, the Earthmen capture the last sun-tap station and a nuclear attack is not necessary. Moreover, the explorers look forward to learning a great deal from the alien races.

Comment: Wollheim was a science fiction fan and writer before he founded the successful DAW

Books in 1972. The science fiction–only paperback house is still with us. Wollheim also wrote the popular young-adult series of Mike Mars books: *Mike Mars, Astronaut* (1961), *Mike Mars Flies the X-15* (1961), *Mike Mars at Cape Canaveral* (1961), *Mike Mars in Orbit* (1961), *Mike Mars Flies the Dyna-Soar* (1962), *Mike Mars, South Pole Spaceman* (1962), *Mike Mars and the Mystery Satellite* (1963), and *Mike Mars Around the Moon* (1964).

MAJIPOOR (L)

First Appearance: "Lord Valentine's Castle" by Robert Silverberg, 1979, *The Magazine of Fantasy and Science Fiction #342.*

Physical Description: Despite the fact that it's larger than Earth, Majipoor is low on heavy elements and, thus, its gravity is close to Earth-normal. The three large continents are Alhanroel, Zimroel, and Suvrael; the air and water are clean on the first two, while the third is more or less a "sun-blasted" wasteland. The Isle of Sleep is located between Alhanroel and Zimroel.

The planet is home to the native shapeshifters called Metamorphs; "big, rough, shaggy," four-armed humanoid Skandars; to the dwarfish telepathic wizards, the Vroon; the "coarse and bloated" humanoid Hjorts; the apish "forest-brethren"; and others.

Biography: Majipoor was colonized thousands of years before by humans, who displaced the Metamorphs, putting them in reservations. The government is run by two people: the emperor-like Pontifex, who dwells in a labyrinth on Alhanroel, and the hands-on Coronal; who lives in a 40,000-room castle atop the 30-mile-high Castle Mount in Alhanroel. The Coronal is appointed by and eventually succeeds the Pontifex. The Coronal's mother becomes the kingdom's spiritual leader, the Lady of the Isle of Sleep; her antithesis is the King of Dreams, a hereditary "conscience" figure from the Barjazid family. The King of Dreams dwells on Suvrael and sends dark visions to people who have a mission in life, or awful nightmares to those in need of punishment.

Valentine arrives at the city of Pidruid, on Zimroel, remembering virtually nothing about his past and disinterested in the festival celebrating the arrival of Lord Valentine the Coronal. Given a ride by the herder Shanamir, Valentine falls in with a troupe of jugglers, two humans and six Skandars—whose boss, a Skandar named Zalzan Gibor, hires Valentine and Shanamir to fulfill the quota of humans. They perform for the Coronal, who is smitten with the human juggler Carabella and takes her as his lover. After the festival, the troupe tours Majipoor. All the while, Valentine is troubled by dreams; when he has them interpreted, he learns from the wizard Autifon Deliamber that he is actually Lord Valentine the Coronal, robbed of his throne by the usurper Dominin Barjazid, son of the King of Dreams, in whose body he now resides. He confides in Carabella and, with Deliamber at his side, he stays with the troupe as they make their way toward the Isle of Sleep, becoming more confident and regal all the time. En route, they stop in Piurifayne, home of the Metamorphs; there, the shape-changers put on a show in which the two Valentines shift roles, thus revealing to the other members of the troupe just who is among them. After adventures among the Metamorphs and forest-brethren and a dangerous trip down the River Steiche, Valentine reaches the Isle of Sleep. There, the Lady rids him of his amnesia and grants him the power to send dreams to others. She also tells him how to reach the Pontifex in his lair, and sends him to enlist his aid in challenging Dominin. Eventually confronting Dominin in the private judgment-room of the Coronal, Valentine finds the King of Dreams there as well, Simonan Barjazid—only it turns out not to be the King but a Metamorph. Valentine learns that when the real King of Dreams lay gravely ill, the Metamorph had posed as a human physician, took his place, and began attempting to control the planet's weather-machines and retake the world for the shapeshifters. The creature perishes in a leap from a window, Dominin ends up raving mad, Valentine's aides slay the false Coronal's guards (Metamorphs all), and Majipoor is once more in the hands of the rightful Lord Valentine.

In the second saga of Majipoor, 14-year-old clerk and Valentine loyalist Hissune is bored with his desk job. A clever lad, he breaks the law and gets into the Register of Souls, where the memories of the dead are stored. There, he puts on a transfer helmet, puts in 10 memory capsules, and relives great events from the planet's past.

In the third tale, eight years after Valentine has regained his throne, the Coronal names Hissune his knight-initiate and likely successor. Meanwhile, the Metamorph Faraataa partakes in an ancient ritual that summons the Water King Maazmoorn from the sea. The minds of the two merge, and Faraataa becomes a powerful new religious leader as well as father of a new rebellion.

In the fourth story, Prince Harpirias is banished to a post on the continent Zimroel after insulting Prince Lubovine. There, Harpirias becomes involved in a dangerous mission to rescue a party of scientists.

Comment: The novel was serialized over four issues, then published in book form in 1980. It was followed by *Majipoor Chronicles* (1982), *Valentine Pontifex* (1984), and *The Mountains of Majipoor* (1995).

Silverberg published his first story, "Gorgon Planet," in 1954, when he was eighteen, and has written over seventy novels, nearly as many nonfiction works, more than two hundred stories, and edited dozens of anthologies.

THE MAN FROM THE MOON   (C)

First Appearance: *Weird Tales of the Future* #5, 1953, Aragon Publishing.

Physical Description: In his final form, the Man from the Moon is entirely green and made of "metal, plastic and electronic devices," except for his human brain. He has a thin, hourglass-shaped body, spindly tentacular arms with four-fingered hands, and skinny legs jointed at the knee. His head is ovoid, with a mouth, nose, and red eyes.

Biography: Born and raised on Earth, Pete Warren is abducted by Moon beings. Inside "an air-filled crater," Warren is given an artificial respiratory system so he can survive. Bit by bit, his body is altered to adapt to lunar living. Decades later, only his "brain remained intact . . . preserved and fed by chemicals." Eventually fulfilling his dream of returning to Earth onboard a lunar exploratory ship, he finds the planet in ruins and inhabited by primitive mutations. Realizing that there has been a nuclear war, he returns to the moon, feeling more lonely than ever "in my 140 years."

Comment: The story "The Man from the Moon" was written and drawn by science fiction great Basil Wolverton, who was also responsible for characters like the tentacled, mind-controlling Brain-Bats of Venus; Gror the Martian, a red-skinned, apish prisoner on a Jovian moon; the Hornosaur of Uranus; and many others. Several of his best tales, including "The Man from the Moon," were reprinted in Eclipse Comics' *Mr. Monster's Weird Tales of the Future* #1, 1987.

THE MAN FROM PLANET X   (MP, C)

First Appearance: *The Man from Planet X*, 1951, Mid-Century Films/United Artists.

Physical Description: Standing approximately four feet tall, the Man is humanoid. He is dressed in a dark, skintight spacesuit with rubbery gloves, has an airtank on his back, and wears a clear helmet.

His expressionless face and bald, egg-like head are visible inside: He has slits for eyes and a mouth, and a long narrow nose. The spaceman is armed with a portable mind-control ray-gun.

The alien's spaceship consists of a sphere some seven feet in diameter with an arrow-like nosecone on top, about eight feet long. The conveyance rests on small tailfins and has several small windows around the center.

Biography: A roaming world, Planet X has entered our solar system and will make its closest approach to Earth at a point on the Scottish island of Burray in the Orkneys. American reporter John Lawrence heads to Burray to ride out the encounter with Professor Elliot, his daughter Enid, and the shifty scientist Mears. Getting a flat tire on the moors, Enid encounters the spaceship and its occupant and hurries to tell her father. Mears and Lawrence go out to meet the alien, with whom Mears communicates using geometry. Mears tries to enslave the alien by tinkering with its air supply; but the Man from Planet X uses his mind-control ray on the scientist and Enid and takes them back to his ship. As Planet X nears, the alien enslaves other villagers, clearly preparing for an invasion. Pretending to be one of the slaves, Lawrence is able to free the others just as the military arrives and blows the ship and the alien to smithereens. The arrival of Planet X causes storm winds, but the planet quickly departs without its inhabitants having achieved their goal.

Comment: Robert Clarke is Lawrence, William Schallert is Mears, Margaret Field is Enid, and Raymond Bond is Elliot. Edgar G. Ulmer directed from a script by Aubrey Wisberg and Jack Pollexfen.

A comic book adaptation of the extremely low-budget classic was published as *Fawcett Movie Comic* #15 in 1952. It was reprinted by Planet X Productions in 1987.

MAN-PLUS (L)

First Appearance: *Man-Plus* by Frederik Pohl, 1976, Random House.

Physical Description: The Will Hartnett cyborg has red-faceted globes for eyes, a mole-like nose, bat-like ears, artificial tan skin with the "texture . . . of a rhinoceros's hide," and a "doll-shrill" voice. As a cyborg he possesses extraordinary strength and endurance.

The Roger Torraway cyborg has black, bat-like wings that serve as solar panels, the ability to see light as well as heat—he can see clearly the veins under human skin—incredibly sensitive hearing,

and skin that is poreless, hairless, and unwrinkled. Roger possesses a "flat" voice and compound eyes "like faceted ebony." He needs only a miniscule amount of food and air to keep his biological parts functioning. His genitalia have been removed and steroids implanted so he won't become effeminate, and he wears a backpack computer/battery system; if the computer fails, there is an orbiting 3070 unit for backup.

Biography: The government cyborg program was created in the early 21st century to change an astronaut into a creature suited for life on Mars. After the mission, the organs and body parts that have been replaced by cybernetic materials will be returned. When the Will Hartnett cyborg dies of a stroke during training, veteran astronaut Roger Torraway volunteers to become the new Mars-bound guinea-pig, Man-Plus. The voyage is an important one: World tensions are unusually high, and the survival of humankind may depend on setting up a colony off-planet.

Changes are made in the design, Roger successfully completes his training, and the $7 billion cyborg is sent to Mars along with humans Alexander Bradley, Father Dan Kayman, and General Hesburgh, the pilot. The great advantage to being a cyborg is that Roger's body clocks are disconnected and his system slowed so that the seven month flight feels like only 30 hours.

After the ship's lander carries the landing party to the surface of Mars, Roger leaps down and moves about effortlessly while his companions struggle in their cumbersome suits. They find plant life on Mars, but Roger gets careless; while powering up in the sun, he leaves his charging terminals exposed and iron oxide grit makes him short out. His human and computer mind struggle for dominance and nearly drive him mad; fortunately, Bradley is able to shut him off and repair him. When a base of habitat domes is established, Roger remains behind. Plans are made to send other cyborgs and humans to join him, as well as to set up bases on Mercury, Triton, Io, and elsewhere in the solar system.

Comment: In the 1994 Baen Books sequel *Mars Plus* by Pohl and Thomas T. Thomas, nearly 50 years have passed. Mars has been successfully colonized, with Torraway as "Mars's unofficial first citizen" and the oldest cyborg. While Demter Coghlan, granddaughter of the vice president of the Sovereign State of Texahoma, becomes involved in shady land deals, which may affect Texahoma holdings on Mars, there are bigger problems for Torraway and the colonists as a computer on the Red Planet develops a mind of its own and turns on the population of cyborgs and humans.

One of the great science fiction authors and editors, Pohl also wrote about the HEECHEE.

MAREX (MP)

First Appearance: *Zombies of the Stratosphere*, 1952, Republic Pictures.

Physical Description: Marex is a human being who wears a bodysuit and cowl made of what appears to be coarse sandpaper with a V-shaped lightning bolt symbol on the chest and forehead. Though the film is black and white, posters show the costume as being a metallic orange/brown.

Biography: When a rocket lands on Earth in the present day, Larry Martin of the Interplanetary Patrol dons his rocket-powered flying suit and soars off to investigate. He learns that the Martian villain Marex has arrived with his aid Narab. With the help of the evil Dr. Harding, they plan to build and detonate an atomic bomb that will blow the Earth out of its orbit, allowing Mars to move in and enjoy our mild climate (never mind the lesser gravity of Mars, the effect of the worlds' moons, etc.). With his assistants Sue Davis and Bob Wilson, Larry battles Marex and his roughly eight-foot-tall robot—a walking cylinder with rubbery arms and powerful pincers. The hero tracks them to their cave hideout, and the Martians flee in their rocket—though not before setting the bomb to go off. Larry pursues in his *own* rocket and shoots the Martians down; only Narab survives, conveniently long enough to reveal the location of the bomb before expiring.

Comment: The 12-chapter serial starred Lane Bradford as Marex with Judd Holdren as Larry, Aline Towne as Sue, Wilson Wood as Bob, and Stanley Waxman as Harding. Fred Brannon directed from a script by Ronald Davidson. Future MR. SPOCK, Leonard Nimoy, costarred as Narab. In 1958, the serial was edited into a feature film, *Satan's Satellites*.

MARTAN THE MARVEL MAN (C)

First Appearance: *Popular Comics* #46, 1939, Dell Publishing.

Physical Description: Martan wears a black T-shirt with red, balloon-like sleeves, a green skirt, black gloves and boots, and a red belt and helmet (the helmet and sleeves are later golden). Vera wears a white T-shirt with orange balloon-sleeves, white gloves and boots, an orange belt, and a green skirt. Both aliens carry ray guns, worn in a holster on the belt, possess superstrength, and are telepathic.

Biography: A telepath from the planet Antaclea, Martan and his wife Vana decide to spend their honeymoon on Earth. Upon arriving, Martan discovers that aliens working for the evil Supreme Three of the Universe have also come to Earth, not to vacation but to conquer. Martan and Vana decide to stay as long as it takes to stop the invaders.

Comment: In #57, the strip was simply called "The Marvel Man." The character appeared through #71 in 1942.

THE MARTIAN THINGS (L, R, MP, C, TV)

First Appearance: *The War of the Worlds* by H.G. Wells, 1898, Heinemann.

Physical Description: Each Thing is "nearly a hundred feet high, capable of the speed of an express-train. A "walking engine of glittering metal," the Things are poised on tripod legs that cover 100 yards with every stride, placing one leg down and swinging the other two ahead. They have "long, flexible, glittering tentacles" strong enough to uproot a large tree, while on top is a "brazen hood" that resembles a head. The Things dispense death in two ways: via an incendiary Heat Ray; and by Black Smoke, or choking clouds of gas. Only a direct artillery hit can destroy the war machines, though the Martians usually blast any guns before they can be fired. Even if the hoods are blown up, and the Martian occupant "splashed to the four winds," the Things continue to walk about blindly and must be utterly destroyed.

The Martians come to Earth in cylinders, each of which has "a diameter of about thirty yards," is exited by screwing off the top, and contains no "more than five Martians."

Each Martian is "a big greyish rounded bulk, the size of a bear . . . [which] glistened like wet leather." They have two large dark eyes and a V-shaped mouth "the lipless brim of which quivered and panted and dropped saliva." They have no brow, nostrils, chin, or other facial features; they hear through a "tight tympanic surface" in the back of the head. Each alien has 16 slender "almost whip-like tentacles, arranged in two bunches of eight each." Though these function like legs on Mars, the gravity is too strong for that here. The Martians' only organs are a heart, lungs, and a brain, and they feed by injecting "the fresh, living blood of other creatures . . . into their own veins . . . by means of a little pipette."

The Martians do not sleep or engage in sex; young aliens bud off the adult. Plant life on Mars is "a vivid blood-red."

Biography: Leaving their dying world, the Martians land in a pit in Woking, England, in the closing days of the 19th century. Their cylinder forms a pit as it lands; climbing from the ship when it cools, they vaporize onlookers, though it is presumed that our relatively strong gravity will prevent the Martians from leaving the pit. A second cylinder arrives shortly thereafter, then a third, all in close proximity. The Martians construct their Things and commence the systematic destruction of England. Their goal is to enslave all of humankind, making us laborers, pets, and sources of nourishment—"tamed and fattened and bred," says the nameless hero, "like a thundering ox." The Martians lay waste to England, but have forgotten to take into account "the putrefactive and disease bacteria against which their systems were unprepared." The invaders perish, the narrator pointing out that even with antitoxins they cannot return, since we will know now to destroy their cylinders before they can cool and be opened. According to astronomers, the Martians appear to have vacated Mars for Venus.

Comment: The classic was first adapted and updated in 1938 by Howard Koch for *The Mercury Theatre on the Air.* The brainchild of coproducers Orson Welles and John Houseman, the show was done in documentary style as a Halloween Eve joke; the broadcast terrorized listeners who believed Martians had, in fact, landed at Grovers Mill, near Princeton, New Jersey. Welles starred as Professor Richard Pearson of Princeton University. The *Daily News* alone reported receiving 1,100 panicked phone calls, "more than when the dirigible Hindenburg exploded." The creation and broadcast of the dramatization was the basis for the 1975 ABC TV movie *The Night the Martians Landed,* starring Paul Shenar as Welles.

In the 1953 movie *War of the Worlds,* produced by George Pal and directed by Byron Haskin, the target is no longer Victorian London but contemporary Los Angeles. The war machines in the film are copper-colored ships that look like manta rays and are impervious to nuclear bombs. They have downturned, green-glowing tips and a glowing green nose; the Heat Ray is fired from a cobra-like appendage that rises from the top of the ship. The Martians themselves are mushroom-like bipeds, approximately four feet tall with two spindly arms that grow from the sides of their head and three long, suction cup-type fingers on each hand. They have a large, tricolored eye in the middle of their flat, wide head. Gene Barry stars as Pacific Tech scientist Clayton Forrester; Charles Gemora plays a Martian in the one scene in which its full body is pictured.

Pal's Martians returned in the syndicated series *War of the Worlds,* which debuted in 1988. It turns out the Martians aren't really Martians, but denizens of the planet Mortax some 40 light years from Earth. They had first come here on reconnaissance in 1938, then tried and failed to invade our world in 1953. It also appears that the dead Pal aliens aren't really dead but dormant, kept in a government facility from which they have broken free. Taking over human bodies, they set up shop in an abandoned, underground nuclear base in Nevada to continue the invasion and find a way to destroy the bacteria. The only problem: The intense radiation they generate causes their human bodies to crumble rather quickly. They are pursued by Dr. Harrison Blackwood (Jared Martin) and Dr. Suzanne McCullough (Lynda Mason Green) and other members of their scientific think tank.

For the show's second season, it was retitled *War of the Worlds—the Second Invasion,* and a new twist was added. It seems the Martaxians are simply an advance guard for *their* rulers, the humanoids of the planet Morthrai, which has recently been destroyed. Disgusted with the failure of their servants, the Morthraites show up themselves, commanded by Malzor (Denis Forest), Mana (Catherine Disher), and the scientist Ardix (Julian Richings). In the end, Malzor is shown to be a megalomaniac and the aliens learn to live peacefully with Earthlings.

Pocket Books published a short-lived series of novels based on the TV series.

In comic books, *War of the Worlds* was published as part of the Classics Illustrated lineup (#124, 1955) and was one of the *Pendulum Illustrated Classics* published in 1973 (reprinted as #14 of *Marvel Classics Comics* in 1976).

In the Marvel comic book *Amazing Adventures* #18 (1973), the Martians return on June 29, 2001, having developed an immunity to the bacteria. After neutralizing Earth's nuclear power sources, they successfully conquer the planet. A group of resistance fighters led by the heroic Killraven strike out at the Martians, finally overthrowing them in January 2020 (#39, 1976).

THE MASTERS OF THE SPIRAL NEBULA GANNA (MP)

First Appearance: *War of the Satellites,* 1958, Santa Cruz Productions/Allied Artists.

Physical Description: The aliens are known only through their communiques.

Biography: Ten U.N. "satellites" (headed for deep space, and thus hardly that) are destroyed when they try to broach the Sigma Barrier. Head of operations Pol Van Ponder decides to launch an eleventh ship, this time with humans aboard. Shortly thereafter, the aliens who generated the Barrier, the Masters of the Spiral Nebula Ganna, send a small rocket of their own to Earth bearing a written if belated message:

Know, earthlings, that we look with disfavor upon your persistent efforts to depart from your own planet and infest other areas of the universe. Knowing that earthlings are equipped with rudimentary reflex-type intelligence, we are taking this means of conveying our command that all such efforts to expand and depart from the infected planet Earth shall from this moment be stopped.

Undaunted, the U.N. plans to go ahead with Project Sigma: A small fleet of rockets is to be launched to a point near the moon, where they'll construct a light-speed "satellite" consisting of a large spherical core and three smaller orbs attached by struts to its midsection. The aliens, obviously worried about the ship, send a beam of light to take over Van Ponder and see that the spacecraft doesn't make it.

Dave Boyer, one of the fliers in charge of the project, witnesses the possessed Van Ponder split in two shortly before takeoff. Dave realizes he's under Gannan control and, once they're in space, he tells Van Ponder that he's onto him. The scientist points out that according to "astroplanetary law" he must obey Van Ponder's commands, but after political maneuvering and romantic conflict—Van Ponder lusts after Dave's girlfriend, astronaut Sybil Carrington—Dave is forced to shoot him to death. With Van Ponder's demise, the "satellite" reaches the barrier and crashes through thanks to Plan A (the specifics of which are not revealed). When last heard from, the "satellite" is whipping through the Andromeda Galaxy at light speed.

Comment: Richard Devon stars as Van Ponder, Dick Miller is Dave, and Susan Cabot is Sybil. The film was directed by Roger Corman; Lawrence Louis Goldman wrote the script, based on an idea by special effects men Jack Rabin and Irving Block.

MATTER-EATER LAD (C)

First Appearance: *Adventure Comics* #301, 1962, DC Comics.
Physical Description: Original costume: yellow

bodyshirt, tights, belt, and a green vest, trunks, boots, and wristbands. Second costume: green trunks, boots, bodyshirt with yellow arms, black shoulders and gloves; a yellow belt and tights. A humanoid, Matter-Eater Lad is equipped with a Legion flight ring.

Biography: Tenzil Kem was born in the mid-30th century on the planet Bismoll, the elder son of Roll—a robot-plant employee—and his wife Mitz. (He has a brother, Renkil.) Several centuries before, when the planet was first colonized, indestructible bacteria poisoned all the food on Bismoll, forcing the inhabitants to bio-engineer the ability to eat and metabolize anything except Magnozite, a compound made of the deadliest metals in the galaxy. Coming to Earth, to attend school, Tenzil joins the Legion of Super-Heroes as Matter-Eater Lad. Later, he resigns, returns to Bismoll, and serves in the senate. He rejoins the Legion briefly to eat the planet-destroying Miracle Machine, the "alien energies" of which drive him mad. Tenzil is sent to the United Planets Medi-Center on St. Croix, where he remains until a criminal scientist cures him in exchange for mercy from the Legion.

Comment: The character was created by editor Mort Weisinger.

MATTHEW LOONEY (L)

First Appearance: *Matthew Looney's Voyage to the Earth* by Jerome Beatty Jr., 1961, Addison-Wesley.

Physical Description: Like all Lunarians, Matthew has a round head with a spray of hair growing from the middle, a round body only slightly larger than his head, two small, five-fingered hands, and two large feet. His skin is pink, he has small close-set eyes, and he has a huge mouth. Matthew stands approximately four feet tall. He has a pet turtle-like creature called Ronald, a murtle.

Moon dwellers face two dangers: velocipitis (if they get up from a chair too fast, they shoot into the sky and take a while to drift down) and cosmos (sunburn). The latter is so dangerous that Lunarians come out only when the sun isn't shining.

The *Moonbeam II* is a big, black saucer-like ship ringed with portholes. The cockpit is a bubble-like projection on the top/front of the ship. At the other end are fins and stablizers with the rockets "fitting snugly below them." The ship is equipped with an Artificial Gravity Machine. In addition to Captain Looney and Matthew, known crewmembers are first mate Mr. Bones and cook Wondervon Brown.

Biography: Matthew, his parents Monroe and Diana, and his younger sister Maria live underground in a cave in the lunar town of Crater Pluto. Matt worships his uncle, Captain Lockhard "Lucky" Looney, an astronaut, and wants desperately to make the first voyage to Earth with him on his ship the *Moonbeam II*. His parents reluctantly agree and he starts out, after riding the moonorail to the Moonversity for a crash course on Earth and the dangers of oxygen, water, and radioactivity.

The purpose of the journey is to find a way to destroy our world (it's "such an eyesore"). First, however, they must check for life. Arriving at the South Pole, they find none. However, Matthew has snuck Ronald onboard and the murtle wanders off. The boy searches and finally finds him, and the expedition returns to the moon. A court of inquiry is convened to decide what to do with the Earth. The Anti-Earth League seems on the verge of having its way when Matthew reports that the murtle survived for hours without a helmet and that he went in water without being harmed. The boy notes that if Ronald was able to survive, mightn't Earth be inhabited? Earth is spared, and a new ship, the *Ploozer*—named for Professor T.P. Ploozer—is readied for a more thorough investigation. Only this time, Cadet Looney is promoted to copilot and Spaceman, First Class.

Comment: Matthew's next two voyages to Earth are chronicled in *Matthew Looney's Invasion of Earth* (1965) and *Matthew Looney in the Outback* (1969). The other books in the series are *Matthew Looney and the Space Pirates* (1972), *Maria Looney on the Red Planet* (1977), *Maria Looney and the Space Circus* (1978), and *Maria Looney and the Remarkable Robot* (1979). The children's books were marvelously illustrated by cartoonist Gahan Wilson.

MATTHEW STAR (TV)

First Appearance: *The Powers of Matthew Star*, September 1982, NBC.

Physical Description: Matthew appears to be a normal teenager with shoulder-length brown hair. Matthew possesses the powers of telepathy, mind-reading, telekinesis, and astral projection. Interestingly, when he reads the mind of a psychic, he can also see into the future.

Matthew's Quadrian outfit is a white bodysuit with ribbed designs on the arms and raised concentric circles on the sides.

Biography: When self-serving insurgents overthrow the king of the planet Quadris, his son,

Prince Matthew Star, and Star's guardian Walter Shepherd head for Earth and safety. There, Walt gets a job teaching science and coaching football at Crestridge (California) High where his "ward" Matthew is a student, the two of them biding their time until Matthew's powers, which are unique to the planet's rulers, have evolved and he's strong enough to return and reclaim the throne. Unfortunately, they're hunted by Quadrian assassins who pose as everything from schoolmates to circus workers.

Eventually, they are coerced into working as undercover operatives for Major Wymore of the Air Force, which has learned their true identities. Whenever Wymore needs them, Matthew's communication-ring flashes.

Comment: Peter Barton stars as Star, Louis Gossett Jr. is Walt, and James Karen is Wymore. The series was created by Steven E. de Souza; 22 hour-long episodes aired through September 1983.

The show was originally set to debut in September 1981, but star Barton was burned on the set while shooting an episode. The show closed down while he recovered, and was also reconceptualized. In the original pilot, the alien is David Starr, who has no knowledge of who he is. When he discovers he has the power to read minds, his guardian Max—who works as a janitor at the high school and has a powerful mechanical hand—finally tells him certain things about his past. Gossett costarred as Max.

M.A.X.

First Appearance: *Spitfire and the Troubleshooters* #1, 1986, Marvel Comics.

Physical Description: The circa nine-foot-tall exoskeletons enhance the wearer's strength "through computerized amplification." They have forearm-mounted machine guns, guns on the head and shoulders and rockets at the bottom of the legs for flight. The wearer climbs in by flipping back the head and slipping into the neck. The Model I is a cumbersome silver suit. The Model II is sleeker and made of red metal.

Biography: When scientist Dr. Karl Swensen dies, his daughter, Professor Jennifer Swensen of M.I.T., finds a message for her in his computer at Fritz Krotze's robotics research and development firm. Unable to read it before Krotze arrives, she breaks in with the aid of brilliant students known as the Troubleshooters and learns that Krotze plans to use the M.A.X.—Man Amplified X-periment—for evil rather than good. Though Krotze has the cumbersome Model I, Professor Swensen hid the Model II and his message leads Jennifer to it. She dons the suit, codenamed Spitfire, beats the Model I to scrap, and seeks to prove that Krotze killed her father.

Comment: The magazine lasted 13 issues, through 1987; the title was changed to *Codename: Spitfire* with #10. The comic book was part of Marvel's ambitious eight-title New Universe lineup, which the company eventually abandoned. The other magazines were *Star Brand*, *Psi-Force*, *Nightmask*, *Kickers, Inc.*, *Merc*, *D.P.7*, and *Justice*.

MAX 404 (MP)

First Appearance: *Android*, 1982, New World Pictures.

Physical Description: Apart from great strength, the bald android is indistinguishible from a human being.

Biography: In 2036, android Max 404, who was built in space, lives on a space station with Dr. Daniel, who is working hard to create the perfect female android. Though an android revolt on Earth resulted in their being banned, Daniel intends to prove that they *can* live among us in harmony.

Beautiful blonde Cassandra is nearly complete when a trio of escaped convicts crashland at the station. Pretending to be run-of-the-mill space travelers, Keller, Mendez, and Maggie plot to win Max's confidence, bring him back to Earth, and use his computer-sharp intelligence to help them commit crimes. For his part, Max falls in love with Maggie and is willing to follow her anywhere. Ultimately, however, it's Cassandra who ends up with Max and a trip back to Earth, where she clearly plans to reestablish an android presence.

When he isn't working with Daniel or passing through robot puberty, Max is listening to 20th-century rock and roll, watching old movies, and dreaming of the day when he can visit Earth.

Comment: Don Opper is Max, Klaus Kinski is Daniel, Kendra Kirchner is Cassandra, Nobert Weiser is Keller, Crofton Hardester is Mendez, and Brie Howard is Maggie. The film was directed by Aaron Lipstadt from a script by James Reigle and Don Opper, based on an idea by Reigle.

MECHAGODZILLA (MP)

First Appearance: *Gojira Tai Mekagojira* (*Godzilla vs. Mechagodzilla*), 1974, Toho Co., Ltd.

Physical Description: Initially, the robot appears identical to Godzilla: a giant, charcoal-gray tyrannosaurus-like dinosaur with a row of jagged plates down its back, and two smaller rows on either side. After its skin is burned away, the monster's exterior is angular, silver-gray "space titanium" covered with rivets, ridges, and various plates. The giant fires rockets from its fingers and toes, ray beams from its red eyes, and projectiles from its chest. Mechagodzilla has jets in its heels so it can fly, and if it spins its head rapidly, a force field forms around its entire body.

Biography: Taking human form, the ape-like denizens of the Third Planet of the Black Hole, commanded by Project Leader Mugan, come to Earth bent on conquest. The real Godzilla has reformed and is living in peace on Monster Island (see KILAAKS), so when the monster appears near Mt. Fuji and begins destroying everything in his path, his fellow monster Angilas is surprised and concerned. When Angilas is badly wounded, it concludes that this must be an impostor and "cries" for the real Godzilla. The monster shows up as its doppelganger is razing an oil refinery, and the two do battle. Godzilla's fiery breath peels away a portion of its opponent's skin, revealing space titanium underneath. Since there's no longer any reason to conceal its identity, the aliens zap the pseudo-Godzilla with a ray blast and reveal the towering robot. Beating Godzilla to a pulp, Mechagodzilla suddenly goes haywire and has to be recalled. Unable to repair their creation, the aliens abduct Professor Hideto Miyajima and his daughter Iko and force him to do the work; he does so, after which he and Iko are rescued by Interpol agent Namara. Meanwhile, Princess Nami Kunizu of the Azumis of Okinawa summons their ancient god King Seesar to help. The lion/dinosaur hybrid erupts from inside a mountain and fights Mechagodzilla, taking quite a pummeling before Godzilla—revived by lightning—arrives. Godzilla rips off the robot's head, incapacitating it, and Miyajima sacrifices himself to destroy the aliens' base.

But the robot isn't quite finished. In its second screen adventure, Mugan and his aliens from the Third Planet contact Dr. Shizo Mafune, an oceanographer who was discredited for claiming to have seen a living dinosaur, Titanosaurus (Chitanozaurusu in Japanese), under the sea. Mafune throws in his lot with the extraterrestrials, helps them rebuild Mechagodzilla (with MG2 stenciled on an arm), and uses his daughter Katsura to control both Mechagodzilla and Titanosaurus (mentally). (Katsura was electrocuted in an accident and brought back to life by the aliens, as a cyborg, with an artificial heart and other fake body parts.) She sends Titanosaurus against Tokyo, where it is met by Godzilla, who battles it back into the ocean. Meanwhile, Interpol operatives find and attack the aliens' mountain hideaway, while Katsura sends both Titanosaurus and Mechagodzilla to destroy Tokyo. Godzilla tackles the destructive duo, who have the upper hand until Katsura and her father are shot by Interpol agents. Mechagodzilla is momentarily distracted and Godzilla uses the distraction to rip its head off. That doesn't stop Mechagodzilla, who stomps around blindly, firing destructive rays from its neck, until Godzilla picks it up, throws it to the ground, and incinerates it with his radioactive breath. Helped by a Giant Supersonic Wave Oscillator created by the Ocean Exploitation Institute, Godzilla also beats Titanosaurus into the sea, then vaporizes the alien saucers when they try to take off.

Comment: Akihiko Hirata stars as Miyajima, Hiromi Matsushita is Iko, Mori Kishida is Namara, Goro Mutsu is Mugan, and Beru-Bera Lin is the Princess. Jun Fukuda directed from a script by Hiroyasu Yamamura and Fukuda, based on a story by Shinichi Sekizawa and Masami Fukushima. The film was released in the United States in 1977 as *Godzilla vs. The Bionic Monster,* which was changed to *Godzilla vs. The Cosmic Monster* when Universal Pictures, producers of the television show *The Six Million Dollar Man,* threatened a lawsuit over the use of the term "bionic."

The second Mechagodzilla film, *Mekagojira No Gyakushu (Mechagodzilla's Counterattack),* was released in 1975 and stars Akihiko Hirata as Mafune and Tomoko Ai as Katsura, with Goro Mutsu reprising as Mugan. It was directed by Ishiro Honda from a screenplay by Yukiko Takayama. It was released in the United States in 1978 as *Terror of Mechagodzilla.*

Gojira Tai Mekagojira was remade and released in Japan in 1993.The monster is built using the remains of King Ghidorah (see M-11) and looks virtually the same as before, except that the heel-rockets have been replaced by four rockets on its back that enable it to fly; multi-colored flame shoots from its mouth; a laser cannon and photon cannon fire beams from its chest; the robot launches electrified grapnels to snare Godzilla; and the new Mecha Godzilla is covered with artificial diamond. It is controlled by a crew that rides around inside its head. In the remake, the flying monster Rodan helps Godzilla defeat his mechanical nemesis.

THE MECHANOIDS (RP)

First Appearance: *The Mechanoid Invasion,* 1981, Palladium Books.
Physical Description: Encased entirely in metal

exteriors of different kinds, the Mechanoids are extremely fast, powerful, and virtually indestructible. The creatures have extrasensory mental abilities that link them to all other Mechanoids.

Biography: Ages ago, a humanoid race in a galaxy millions of light years from Earth wished to explore space. Since they had mastered cloning and robotics, thousands of volunteers underwent genetic and mechanical reconstruction that would enable them to withstand the rigors of space travel. After the cyborgs had been created, and dozens launched into space, the public began to question the morality of the operations; while the issue was debated, thousands of Mechanoids cooled their heels on their home world. It didn't take long before the humans became suspicious of the peaceful cyborgs and hateful: In an awful massacre, every Mechanoid remaining on the world was murdered.

Their spacefaring kin sensed their destruction psionically, and decided they must have done something wrong. To prove they were worthy, they cloned their biological parts, improved the mechanics of their bodies, made thousands more Mechanoids, and spread out to study the other stars and planets of the galaxy and bring what they learned back to their creators. When they returned decades later, they were not met with open arms but with rage and violence. Ordered to leave the planet, they refused; when the humans attacked, the frustrated Mechanoids struck back. In a long and violent struggle, the human race on that distant world was exterminated. The Mechanoids vowed not only to wipe out humans wherever they were found but also, traveling about in planet-sized spaceships made of metal and biological tissue, to destroy their home worlds as well.

Humans who survived the destruction of their races formed the Nigelian Confederacy to combat them, and a race of compassionate Mechanoids, the Aberrant Mechanoids—apparently created and cloned by a wise breed known as the Mechanoid Oracles—rebelled against their sadistic fellow creatures. The Mechanoid Overlords responded with incredible violence, using biological warfare against the rogues and killing billions of beings on *both* sides in the process. For a time, it appeared as though all the Mechanoids were destroyed. However, several unaffected Mechanoids had survived and, after finding a way to kill the virus, cloned themselves to create a new Mechanoid race. Meanwhile, Aberrant Mechanoids kept in suspended animation were also revived to renew the struggle against their evil twins. Unfortunately, both groups reach Earth through a dimensional rift, and the battle resumes in our solar system.

The Mechanoids consist of: the Brain—crab-like creatures with two arms; the Multi-Brain Combat Vehicle—a saucer-like ship with a cannon on top, pincers on the sides, and numerous other weapons; the Brute—a mighty biped; the Exterminator—a weapon-packed body on two long legs; the Mantis—a mantis-like robot with rocket-boosters instead of legs; the Octopus—a fighter with two arms, a pincer, a drill arm, two laser-arms, a torch-arm, and a scanning arm; the Oracles—sleek, dark, arrow-shaped fliers; the Overlords—ant-like bipeds; the Runner—a long-armed biped; the Seeker—a tiny pod with arms; the Tunnel Crawler—a beetle-like Mechanoid; the Type Two Brute—bigger and more powerful than above; the Type Two Octopus—stronger and more sophisticated than above; and the Wasp—a flyer with particle beam guns.

The Aberrant Mechanoids consist of: the Brain—a genius with two small arms and tank-treads; the Brute—same as the Brain; the Exterminator—same as the Brain; the Runner—same as the Brain; the Seeker—same as the Brain; the Tunnel Crawler—same as the Brain; and the Wasp—same as the Brain.

The evil Mechanoids are also served by a series of robots called Mock Men, who resemble humanoids not for any strategic purpose, but as an "ironic joke." There are two kinds of Mock Men: the Thinmen, who stand 13 feet tall and are strong fighters and laborers; and the Runt Robots, who stand just over four feet tall and serve much the same functions as the Thinmen.

Comment: The original publication was a 48-page, comic book–sized role playing game; it was the first part of what became *The Mechanoid Invasion Trilogy*. The original characters were fleshed-out, refined, and "canonized" in Palladium Books' *The Mechanoids* sourcebook by Kevin Siembieda, published in 1992.

MECHASOLDIERS (C)

First Appearance: *Chaser Platoon* #1, 1991, Aircel Comics.

Physical Description: The Mechasoldiers are warriors who ride about in single-pilot all-terrain mechanical soldiers. The soldiers sit in "bucket" seats inside the chest of the approximately 12-foot-tall blue-metal robot-suits. These humanoid shells have a head unit with a viewscreen, shoulder-mounted weapons, floodlights in the shins, a computer, and thrusters in the forearms for flight. When the rider wishes to turn the robot into a

vehicle, it reclines with its arms stiff beneath it, legs ahead, and rolls forward in that manner. When the robot walks, the foot wheels lock.

Biography: In the future, Earth is at war with the alien Saringer race and their murderous Robocommandos. At the height of the hostilities, Golon Hetow, Janus Knopf, Spence Davis, Ian Chartwell, Hayden Edwards, Nichole Granz, Sildon Harpton, Spartan Lasser, Hawkin MacDall, Waylen Markels, Zed Nickolas, and Chan Omnib are tapped to participate in Operation Youthtest. After extensive training, they become a fighting force known as the 2021st Iron Infantry or Chaser Platoon.

Comment: The characters were created by writer/artist Tim Eldred and appeared in a six-issue mini-series published in 1991.

THE MEDUSA (C)

First Appearance: *The Medusa Chain*, 1984, *Graphic Novel* #3, DC Comics.

Physical Description: The *Medusa* is the flagship of a cargo chain, a fleet of cargo ships. The *Medusa* has a flat, rectangular core roughly 1,000 feet long with a complex surface of pipes, windows, plating, and two long, winglike structures. Passengers are protected from the force of takeoff by lying on beds inside "launch bubbles."

The *Medusa* is protected by an elite group known as the Golden Guard, is armed with powerful cannons, and carries a small fleet of one-pilot space jets known as the Invicta Squad.

Biography: On a shipping mission for August Messberg of the world of Homeland, many centuries in the future, rugged Chon Adams finds that his ship is loaded with scrap so that Messberg can destroy it and claim the insurance on the ship and non-existent cargo. Since there isn't enough food to support the entire crew for the return trip, Chon ejects a group of them into space, where they die quickly; upon returning to Earth, he's arrested, escapes, kills Messberg, and is charged with conspiracy and murder. Sentenced to one year on the penal colony Annanda-Tor and six years in space after that, Chon is assigned to the cargo chain *Medusa* under Commander Kilg-9. Once spaceborne, Chon discovers that the ship is carrying enough of the highly explosive TNC-00 to destroy a planet. Kilg-9 confides that their mission is to destroy Earth, whose inhabitants have mutated into genderless radioactive killers. But the "Earthians" thrive on fission, and the cargo, when released, only strengthens them. Kilg-9 and Chon are disturbed by their failure, though they have no choice but to turn from Earth and contemplate the grim future.

The substance TNC-00 was invented on the planet Minvah VI.

Comment: The colorful, ambitious graphic novel was written, drawn, and colored by comics great Ernie Colon.

M-11 (MP)

First Appearance: *Gojira vs. Kingughidorah* (*Godzilla vs. King Ghidorah), 1991, Toho Co., Ltd.*

Physical Description: Standing about six feet tall, the android looks like a balding, red-haired human. Super-powerful and able to move at superspeeds and survive high temperatures, M-11 is controlled by compact discs inserted vertically in a cylinder that slides from the left side of his head. He usually dresses in a yellow shirt, dark trousers, and a blue vest with flared shoulders. He occasionally packs a laser pistol, with which he's deadly accurate.

The future time machine is a white saucer approximately 1,000 feet in diameter, resting on a column that ends in four splayed legs. The flying time machine is a Y-shaped jet with a horizontal turbine in each wing. The Mecha-King Ghidorah has cybernetic metal wings, legs, a chest plate with four electrified cables and a giant pincer inside, and a central control head made from the flying time machine, with M-11 built into the computer.

Biography: Three people (Emmy Kano, Wilson, and Grenchiko) and an android (M-11) from the year 2204 arrive in 1990s Japan with a warning: Godzilla will soon ravage the country, destroying nuclear power plants on his rampage and poisoning the nation. They propose to go back further in time, take Godzilla from Lagos Island in the Marshall Islands—before H-bomb tests mutated what was a "normal" tyrannosaurus—and drop him in the Bering Sea where he'll hibernate, unaffected.

The following people from the present join them in the time jet back to 1944: Kenichiro Terasawa, a Godzilla biographer; Mazuki, a paleontologist; and Miki Saegusa, a "member of our Godzilla team." The dinosaur is teleported, as planned, but unknown to Terasawa, Emmy leaves behind three bioengineered dorats—golden-scaled bat-like cats—and these creatures are the ones that become irradiated, turning into King Ghidorah, who is even more powerful than Godzilla. It turns out that the future people lied: In 2204, Japan is the greatest power in the world, and they wanted

to breed a more destructive monster to prevent that from happening.

Back in the present, the golden, three-headed, electricity-spewing flying giant devastates Japan. A nuclear submarine is sent to the Arctic to fetch the tyrannosaurus—who, as it turns out, was mutated anyway by nuclear waste in the sea. Godzilla attacks the submarine, grows more powerful than ever, and heads for Japan, where it defeats King Ghidorah. Meanwhile, Emmy wants to strike back at her "future men" companions. M-11 tries to stop her and, after she rewrites his programming, they attack the time saucer and escape in the flying time machine. But M-11 had remotely programmed the saucer to warp right next to Godzilla, where it is incinerated. Unfortunately, now Godzilla is on the loose. Using the surviving time flier, Emmy and M-11 take the dying King Ghidorah to the future and have cybernetic parts added to its body. The rebuilt King Ghidorah and Godzilla pummel each other as Emmy uses the cables and pincers to snare him. She flies the monster out to sea, and the two beasts plunge into the water. Emmy emerges safe and sound and returns to the future.

Comment: Robert Scottfield stars as M-11, Anna Nakagawa is Emmy, Isao Toyohara plays Terasawa, Richard Berger is Grenchiko, and Chuck Wilson is Wilson. Written and directed by Kazuki Omori, the film hasn't been released in the United States and, given its anti-U.S. sentiment, isn't likely to be (among other things, the Gojirasaurus massacres Allied soldiers on Lagos Island).

THE METAL BOX (L)

First Appearance: "Double Cross in Double Time" by William P. McGivern, February 1948, *Fantastic Adventures.*

Physical Description: The time machine is "about six inches square, with handles attached to each side."

Biography: Professor O'Neill advertises for a young man who's not afraid to travel, and combat weary World War II veteran Paddy Donovan gets the job. O'Neill, his daughter Sally, and the dubious Paddy all take a handle of his metal box. It sends intense heat up their arms, knocks Paddy out, and deposits them in ancient Egypt, among a clan that practices human sacrifice. After eating a meal in the past, they return to the lab where the amazed Paddy demands that he be allowed to buy a share of the professor's invention. Sally tries to talk him out of it, but he insists on buying half the

With the *Metal Box* between them, Paddy and Sally watch as barbarians charge toward them. Art by "Hinton." © Ziff-Davis Publishing.

"company" for a thousand dollars in cash. After rushing home, he returns for a date with Sally only to find that she and her father are gone. They left behind the time machine, which doesn't work; there are Egyptian costumes in the basement.

Tracking the O'Neills down, he contacts war buddies and, to Sally's astonishment, he shows up for his date—with the time machine in tow. Paddy says he wants to take another trip. After drugging their coffee (just as they'd drugged his, as well as the food in "Egypt"), he activates the machine and carts the unconscious Sally off. She wakes up surrounded by "Druids" who burn maidens as a sacrifice to their god. Sally agrees to marry Paddy so that she's no longer a maiden; after the ceremony is performed (by a bona fide justice of the peace), Sally says she knew the setup was fake due to a nearby "No Hunting Allowed" sign. But she's glad she married Paddy, whom she liked from the start. As they kiss, lightning strikes the metal box, which Paddy is holding, and they really are sent back in time—to World War I. Paddy enlists, and Sally agrees to wait for him.

Comment: The prolific author wrote the bulk of his science fiction between 1940 and 1955. He later became better known as a writer of top-notch mysteries.

METALLO (C, TV)

First Appearance: *Action Comics* #252, 1959 (John Corben); *Superman* #310, 1977 (Roger Cor-ben); *Superman* #1 (new series), 1987 (nameless Metallo), DC Comics.

Physical Description: Beneath their "fleshlike, rubber-plastic skin," the first two Metallos are made of green "metallic armor plate . . . unmeltable and shatterproof . . . [and] indestructible," the head a lighter shade than the rest of the body. They wear golden gloves, thigh boots, trunks, and a high-collar vest. The head has a huge lower jaw and gaping mouth. The Metallos are powered by either uranium or kryptonite, and the second Metallo has a wrist-control that enables him to open his chest and expose his mineral innards to Superman. The second Metallo travels around on a golden flying scooter and also fires kryptonite rays from its chest.

The third Metallo is outwardly human, standing nearly seven feet tall with white hair. He wears black trousers, blue boots, and a purple scarf over his bare chest.

Biography: Reporter John Corben spends his free time robbing and killing. Badly injured in a car crash, he's found by Professor Vale, who puts his human brain in an entirely robotic body powered by uranium capsules. Embarking on a life of bigger and better crimes, Metallo discovers that kryptonite is a longer-lived power source than uranium, with the added bonus that it is deadly to Superman. Stealing a sample from an exhibit, he pops it into his chest fuse box and drops dead; he was unaware that, in deference to SUPERMAN, the display piece was a fake.

When Roger C. Corben learns what has happened to his brother, he is determined to get revenge on Superman. Joining the criminal group Skull, he is crushed during a showdown with the Man of Steel. It's deja vu as Skull scientists give Roger a robot body and he becomes the new Metallo, powered by kryptonite and battling Superman as well as the superheroes Batman and the Blue Devil (who stops him by literally ripping out his kryptonite heart).

In his third incarnation, Metallo is constructed by an unnamed scientist who believes that Superman is actually a scout for an invading army. Placing a human brain (identity unrevealed) inside a "plastex" covered, human-looking, kryptonite-powered Metallo, he sends him out to destroy Superman. Superman defeats him in a bare-knuckle brawl that leaves the Man of Steel nearly unconscious, and the man of metal stripped to his mechanical bones. Before Metallo can finish off his foe, he is carted off by Lex Luthor, who wants the kryptonite for his own devious purposes. But

Metallo is revived using another radioactive power source and tackles Superman and the superheroic Doom Patrol (see ROBOTMAN [2]); though his body is destroyed, his head lives on and Metallo will certainly be back.

Comment: The Roger Corben Metallo was played by Michael Callan on the syndicated TV series *Superboy* in the episodes "Metallo" (1989), "Super Menace!" (1990), and "People vs. Metallo" (1991).

THE METAL MASTER (C)

First Appearance: *The Incredible Hulk* #6, 1963, Marvel Comics.

Physical Description: The humanoid wears a black bodysuit with a blue waist, and a black belt with a blue buckle. He rides a "metal flying carpet," which is a square of metal some four feet across.

Biography: The Metal Master (his real name is unrevealed) is from the planet Astra, where everyone has the ability to shape metal with their mind. When Metal Master tries to conquer the planet, he is sent on a one-way rocket ride into space. Roaming the galaxies in search of a planet "rich in metal," he finds the Earth. Using his power to melt tanks, planes, bridges, oil wells, and other structures, he has our planet on the brink of surrender when the superheroic Incredible Hulk comes to the rescue. He builds a cannon out of plastic and cardboard and, not realizing it's a fake, the Metal Master repairs all the damage he's done and leaves the Earth.

Comment: This was the character's only appearance. He might also have been the last foe the Hulk ever fought, since his magazine was cancelled with this issue. However, the publishers tried him out again in *Tales to Astonish* #59 the following year, and he finally found his audience.

METAL MEN (C)

First Appearance: *Showcase* #37, 1962, DC Comics.

Physical Description: Each humanoid robot has the color, properties, and strengths associated with their component metal, including the ability to stretch and change their shape in whatever way they wish—even separate into metal filings, if necessary. Their "unique electronic circuits maintain contact between the Metal Men" and their components. Iron is friendly, easygoing, and incredibly powerful; good but dull-witted Lead can withstand radiation; intelligent Gold, the group's leader, can stretch himself into a wire some 50 miles long or into a sheet four-millionths of an inch thick; hot-headed, egomaniacal red Mercury can become liquid and endure extremes of heat; Tin is weak but brave and can become powder; and Tina, made of platinum, can stretch herself even finer than Gold. Thanks to the "responsometers" in their heads, the Metal Men possess human emotions.

Biography: The Metal Men were invented by Dr. William Rossum Magnus, a millionaire due to his many successful inventions. After constructing Tina, he built the rest of his robots, who both live and work with him at his vast lab complex, which includes a smelter, a metal recovery room, an isolation lab, and a jetway where they park their open-top, saucer-like "jetaway." Tina is in love with Doc Magnus, but he does not return her affection; the tin female character Nameless married Tin, and later perished saving his life.

The characters occasionally work on top secret matters with Colonel Caspar of the Pentagon. During a brief period when Magnus is recovering from a nervous breakdown, the Metal Men function without him. In their most recent adventure, the robots battle Bundai International's monstrous robot, the Meteor Metal Man, built from extraterrestrial metal. At the same time, Magnus must deal with feelings of guilt when the minds of his colleagues, including his brother Michael, are transferred into his robots' bodies.

Comment: There were 56 issues of *Metal Men*, published from 1963 to 1978. The characters, created by Robert Kanigher, also appeared in several issues of *Showcase* and *Brave and the Bold*. The Bundai robot tale was told in the four-issue *Metal Men* miniseries in 1993.

THE METAMORPHS OF THREGONN (L)

First Appearance: "Hepcats of Venus" by Randall Garrett, January 1962, *Fantastic*.

Physical Description: In their natural state, the aliens look like "fat, pink kewpie dolls." Posing as Venusians, they become a bass player whose belly forms the sounding box, with strings running from his nose to the navel; the four-armed drummer's belly balloons out like a kettledrum with a drumhead below the sternum; the clarinetist and trumpeter both have lips that form their instruments. They vary in color "from pale pink to deep purple."

The *Metamorphs of Thregonn* in their natural form. Art by Virgil Finlay. © Ziff-Davis Publishing.

Biography: The Venus Club in Greenwich Village is a showcase for amateur jazz talent, and the Venusians—in their otherworldly getup—are top of the line. But Galactic Observer Lord Curvert is confused; these can't be costumed humans, and when he was on Venus 15 years earlier, in 1948, nothing "had evolved any higher than the sponges." Learning that the aliens are actually metamorphs of Thregonn, Curvert confronts them. He learns their names are Lubix, Forbin, Alisnokine, and Omboser and that they came to Earth on a lark. But their capsule sank in the ocean; while the Navy probes the area, thinking it was a Russian craft, it takes a while for Curvert to help them retrieve it. Once this is done, he tells the metamorphs what he knew all along: The Thregonnese can't be trusted "any farther than you could throw a bonfire by the smoke" and these youngsters had come to Earth to impersonate world leaders and take over. Then, they admit, if they got bored, they'd start a nuclear war. Curvert has them blasted back into space,

musing that terrestrial juvenile delinquency doesn't seem so bad.

Comment: The story was illustrated by the great Virgil Finlay.

MICHAEL KORVAC (C)

First Appearance: *Giant-Size Defenders* #3, 1975, Marvel Comics.

Physical Description: Korvac's torso, head, and arms are human, clad in a purple bodysuit; this is attached to a rectangular, silver computer the size of a small desk. The brilliant man possesses incredible strength and is able to travel through time and space, fire immensely powerful blasts, and bring the dead to life. In his second human form, Korvac stands six-foot-three.

Biography: In a possible future-history, computer genius Michael Korvac collaborates with the alien Badoon when they invade Earth in 3007. He rises to a position of power, running the computers on their home world Moord. But his task-masters are cruel, and when he passes out one day, the lower half of his body is amputated and he's surgically linked to a movable computer. When he awakes, Korvac kills those who did this to him and plots to use his computer-enhanced body to take over the Badoon empire. However, the space gamesman, the Grandmaster (see THE ELDERS), plucks him from the future and pits Korvac and other ne'er-do-wells against the superheroic Defenders. Unknown to the Grandmaster, Korvac draws away some of his powers, including his ability to time travel, and when he is defeated and returned to the future, he teleports to a distant world and sets up a fortress headquarters. There, he battles superheroes such as the god Thor, the Guardians of the Galaxy, and others. Eventually encountering GALACTUS, he siphons power from the world-eater's enormous ship and becomes not just supremely powerful but also all-knowing. Wisdom makes Korvac benevolent; creating a body for himself, he returns to Earth, settles down with Carina Walters, daughter of the Collector (one of the Elders). Though he still plans to conquer the universe, he intends to be a benign ruler. The Collector cannot allow this to be, and Korvac is forced to slay him, though Carina doesn't hold it against him. However, the superheroic Avengers do, and team with the Guardians to battle him. When Carina finally seems to question what her lover is doing, Korvac takes his life; in despair, Carina also commits suicide.

Comment: The character perished in *The Avengers* #178, 1978.

M.I.C.R.A. (C)

First Appearance: *Comics Interview* #37, 1986, Fictioneer Books Ltd.

Physical Description: The extremely powerful robot can fly and looks exactly like the human Angela, save for its metallic "bathing suit," gloves, boots, and skullcap.

Biography: The year 2048: a world of clean, domed cities and polluted, rebel-inhabited settlements outside. Dr. Aleta Lucane, a professor of bioengineering at King University, South Dakota, has created Mind Controlled Remote Automatons: robots that act according to the thoughts of those to whom they're wired. Even when the user's senses are shut off, they see and hear whatever the robot sees and hears. Lucane starts with a cat, assisted by student Angela. Crippled in a rebel missile attack, Angela is bedridden for months, until Lucane creates a M.I.-C.R.A. for her. After undergoing implant surgery that connects her to the robot, Angela becomes "the most powerful weapon ever created."

Comment: Writer Lamar Waldron and artist Ted Boonthanakit created the saga which premiered in the Fictioneer flagship title before its planned 12-issue run.

THE MICROBOTS (C)

First Appearance: *The Mircobots* #1, 1971, Gold Key Comics.

Physical Description: Standing an average of three feet tall, the wheeled, non-humanoid Microbots consist of the powerful Krushor, the "elongated" Liftor, the catapult Fliptor, the "multi-handed" Klawbor, the derrick Hooktor, the "cable-catcher" Kranktor, the tenacious Griptor, and bulldozer Bullzor. Each is able to fire a powerful laser beam.

The Microbots can be controlled only by whoever speaks into the amulet to which they are linked.

Biography: In the future, the air and seas are so badly polluted that civilization has all but crumbled. Dr. Norman Micron puts himself and his son Jeffrey into suspended animation, hoping to wake in a better world; his "worker robots," the Micronauts, also rest. Found centuries later by a young boy, Vik, who stumbles into the vegetation-covered laboratory, the Microns find that humans are living like cave people and animals have mutated into deadly monsters. After Dr. Micron is slain in a battle with a mammoth-like Hydrapoid, it is up to Jeffrey and the young boys with whom he falls in, to start rebuilding civilization.

Comment: The characters appeared in just this one rare issue. The underappreciated Jack Sparling drew the magazine.

THE MIDWICH CUCKOOS (L, MP)

First Appearance: *The Midwich Cuckoos* by John Wyndham, 1957.

Physical Description: The alien ship is pale and resembles "the inverted bowl of a spoon." The children themselves appear normal, save for having golden eyes.

Biography: Attempting to return to Midwich, England, after celebrating his birthday, Richard Grayford (the narrator) and his wife Janet find the roads blocked by the military. All living things are asleep within a circle two miles in diameter that encompasses the town and stretches upward to somewhere under 10,000 feet. A domed object in the center of the town is presumed to have caused the phenomenon (implicitly, by bringing aliens to Earth, aliens who moved freely about sleeping Midwich). After a day, everything wakes up as mysteriously as it passed out and the strange object is gone, but not forgotten: Every fertile woman in the town is pregnant. Nine months later, 58 golden-eyed children are born.

As the children grow, they look virtually identical, can communicate with one another telepathically, and can exert their will on others. They form two collective minds, one male, one female, which author (and father of one) George Zellaby describes as "*a* boy and *a* girl—though the boy has 30 component parts with the physical structure and appearance of individual boys; and the girl has 28 component parts." They are, he believes, the Adam and Eve of a new race. In Russia, a similar Adam and Eve are destroyed by artillery fire. The English, however, are loathe to raze Midwich in this fashion. Zellaby becomes the children's tutor and learns that they plan to leave his house for London to make a "demonstration" of their power. Before they can do so, he brings in cases that are supposed to contain his "recording-machine and other gear" but are actually explosives, and blows himself and the children up.

Comment: The novel was made into the highly-regarded 1960 motion picture *Village of the Damned* and a fascinating, much underrated sequel *Children of the Damned* (1964). The first film, directed by Wolf Rilla, follows the novel rather closely, save that the women are impregnated by an "impulse" from another planet, the 12 children have glowing eyes and blond hair, the reach of their powers increases as they grow older

DARLINGS OR DEMONS?

Where did they come from...
these fair-haired children
with the blazing eyes?
Were they
born and bred
for the ruthless
conquest of
our world?

METRO-GOLDWYN-MAYER presents
GEORGE SANDERS
BARBARA SHELLEY
in The Strangest Story Ever Told

VILLAGE OF THE DAMNED

with MICHAEL GWYNN

Screen Play by
STIRLING SILLIPHANT · WOLF RILLA
GEORGE BARCLAY
Based on the Novel "The Midwich Cuckoos"
by JOHN WYNDHAM

Directed by   Produced by
WOLF RILLA · RONALD KINNOCH

The *Midwich Cuckoos* as pictured in the advertising art for the film *Village of the Damned*. © Metro-Goldwyn-Mayer.

(high-flying aircraft are safe when they are still young), and the leader of the band, David (Martin Stephens) belongs to the hero, scientist Gordon Zellaby (George Sanders). After causing numerous deaths throughout Midwich, the young children inform Gordon that he is to help them leave the village so they can propagate. Instead, he places a time bomb in his briefcase, thinks about a brick wall so the kids can't read his mind, and blows up himself and the children when they meet inside the schoolhouse.

In the sequel, written by John Briley, the children are not alien progeny but humans who have leapt ahead on the evolutionary scale. The six entirely normal-looking children from around the world—leader Paul (Clive Powell), Mi Ling (Lee Yoke-Moon), Nina (Roberta Rex), Ago (Gerald

Delsol), Rashid (Mahdu Mathen), and Mark (Frank Summerscale)—converge on London, hole up in an abandoned church, and cause people who enter uninvited to kill themselves. In the end, the military rigs explosives under the church that are detonated by accident, bringing the edifice down on the children.

The title of the novel refers to the cuckoo's habit of laying eggs in another bird's nest, leaving the raising and feeding of the hatchling to the other bird.

THE MIGHTY ORBOTS   (TV)

First Appearance: *The Mighty Orbots*, September 1984, ABC.

Physical Description: Humanoid robots who join to form a giant humanoid robot.

Biography: By the 23rd century, robots are incredibly sophisticated—and many are devoted to interplanetary peace. Such a group are the Mighty Orbots, who unite to form a "super-robot" devoted to fighting for the right.

Comment: The half-hour series aired until August 1985, though only 13 episodes were produced.

THE MILLENNIUM FALCON   (MP, L, C, R, CS, TV)

First Appearance: *Star Wars*, 1977, Twentieth Century-Fox.

Physical Description: The "supralight"-speed freighter of Corellian design is in the shape of a "battered ellipsoid" and appears to have been "pieced together out of old hull fragments and components" from other ships. The *Millennium Falcon* is approximately 27 meters long, a disc with caliper-like, front-loading freight arms on one side. The cockpit is located in a clear, gumdrop-shaped projection to the right of the arms. Access to the ship is via a ramp in the underbelly.

The white-hulled ship boasts a pair of quad laser cannons on the top and bottom center of the disc; two concussion missile launchers; a light laser cannon; computer-assisted targeting controls; deflector shields; and numerous cargo holds, some easily accessible, others well-concealed.

The Death Star is a sphere the size of a small moon (approximately 120 kilometers in diameter) and is armed with a super-laser capable of obliterating a planet. It is also equipped with 10,000 turbolaser batteries, over 2,000 laser cannons and the same number of ion cannons, 700 tractor-beam projectors, nearly 800,000 crewmembers, Vader's

Star Destroyer and, among other spaceships, over 7,000 TIE (Twin Ion Engine) fighters and TIE interceptors—central spheres with parallel, upright wings at the end of horizontal supports on either side.

A second Death Star, roughly 160 kilometers across and carrying even more personnel and weapons, appeared in the film *Return of the Jedi*.

Darth Vader's ship, the wedge-shaped Superclass Star Destroyer *Executor*, is the heavy cruiser of the Imperial fleet. Eight kilometers long, it is equipped with turbolasers, ion cannons, and several sqaudrons of TIE fighters. Smaller Imperial-class Star Destroyers are just over one-and-one-half kilometers long.

Rebel fighters include the X-wing and Y-wing starfighters. The former are one-pilot ships slightly over 12 meters from nose to tail; the latter are 25 percent longer and accommodate two fliers.

Biography: Seasoned space rogue and smuggler-turned-freedom-fighter, Han Solo wins the hyperspace tramp freighter *Millennium Falcon* from former soldier-of-fortune Lando Calrissian in a high-stakes game of sabacc. In its first chronicled adventure, Han and his first mate, CHEWBACCA, have just jettisoned a cargo of spice owned by Jabba the Hutt. After surviving an encounter with the bounty hunter Greedo on the planet Tatooine, Han agrees to transport young rebel Luke Skywalker, his robots R2-D2 AND C-3PO, and his mentor, former Jedi Knight Obi-Wan Kenobi, to the planet Alderaan. But the evil Empire's massive Death Star destroys the rebel-held world before they arrive. Rescuing rebel leader Princess Leia Organa from the Death Star, the heroes become drawn into the conflict, help destroy the Death Star, and go on to defeat the forces of the cruel Emperor Palpatine and his chief henchman, Luke's father, the renegade Jedi Knight Darth Vader.

Comment: Though the book was published in December 1976, six months before the release of the film, the novel was based on the screenplay.

The ship and characters were created by writer/director George Lucas. Harrison Ford plays Han, Peter Mayhew is Chewbacca, Mark Hamill is Luke, Carrie Fisher is Leia, Alec Guinness is Kenobi, and Dave Prowse, with the voice of James Earl Jones, is Darth Vader in *Star Wars* and its sequels, *The Empire Strikes Back* (1980) and *Return of the Jedi* (1983).

In addition to the novelizations of the films—by Lucas, Donald Glut, and James Kahn, respectively—there have been many *Star Wars* novels, beginning with *Splinter of the Mind's Eye* (1978) by Alan Dean Foster, and continuing with *Han Solo at Stars' End* (1979), *Han Solo's Revenge* (1979), and *Han Solo and the Lost Legacy* (1980) by Brian Daley, *Lando Calrissian and the Mindharp of Sharu*, *Lando Calrissian and the Flamewind of Oseon*, and *Lando Calrissian and the Starcave of ThonBoka*, all 1983 and by L. Neil Smith. Timothy Zahn's ongoing series thus far is comprised of *Heir to the Empire* (1991), *Dark Force Rising* (1992), and *The Last Command* (1993). Kathy Tyers is the author of *Truce at Bakura* (1994), Dave Wolverton has written *The Courtship of Princess Leia* (1994), and the Jedi Academy series from Bantam is comprised, to date, of *Jedi Search* by Kevin J. Anderson and *Dark Apprentice*, both 1994.

A pair of trilogies for young adults, written by Paul and Hollace Davids and published in 1992-93, picks up where the last film leaves off. The titles of the novels are *The Glove of Darth Vader, The Lost City of the Jedi, Zorba the Hutt's Revenge, Mission from Mount Yoda, Queen of the Empire,* and *Prophets of the Dark Side*.

Marvel Comics adapted all three films and also published a *Star Wars* comic book that ran 107 issues, from 1977 to 1986; a *Droids* comic book that ran eight issues from 1986 to 1987; and an *Ewoks* comic book that lasted 15 issues from 1985 to 1987. Blackthorne published a *Star Wars in 3-D* one-shot in 1988; Dark Horse published a six-issue *Star Wars*: *Dark Empire* comic book in 1991-92, and five issues of *Star Wars*: *Tales of the Jedi* in 1993–94.

National Public Radio broadcast a 13-part, six-and-one-half-hour "expanded edition" of the first film in 1977, and a 10-part adaptation of the second film in 1980.

A *Star Wars* comic strip drawn by Russ Manning, then Al Williamson, and written by Archie Goodwin was syndicated from 1980 to 1984.

On TV, many of the *Star Wars* characters appeared in *The Star Wars Holiday Special*, which aired on CBS in 1979, and in the made-for-TV movies *The Ewok Adventure* (1984) and *Ewoks*: *The Battle for Endor* (1985), both on ABC. Thirteen animated *Droids* adventures aired in 1985, and 26 episodes of *Ewoks* the following year.

See also EWOKS; Appendix E.

MINOS (L)

First Appearance: "Contagion" by Katherine MacLean, October 1950, *Galaxy*.

Physical Description: Located 36 light-years

from Earth, Minos is a lush, Earthlike world, with green, copper, purple, and red leaves, and one colony, the village of Alexandria.

Biography: When the spaceship *Explorer*, "like a tapering skyscraper," lands on Minos, a team of doctors explores the world before the rest of the crew disembarks. They are greeted by a humanoid, Patrick Mead, who speaks English and tells them that there are only 150 people on Minos—all of them with red hair, bronzed skin, and lithe, and all of them Meads. Patrick says that the Mead family alone survived "the melting sickness" that struck two years after a colonial ship arrived. After decontamination, Patrick dines on the *Explorer*, telling the crew that the head of the Mead clan, Alexander P., had been a plant geneticist and had made genetic changes in the colonists so they could digest Minosian food. The crew, and Pat, learn too late that the colonist himself is the contagion; his altered cells change those of the other males to make them just like him. If the men get the proper medical care and survive, they become Pat Mead lookalikes, albeit with their original minds intact.

Since the men can't leave, and they have lovers among the women crewmembers, the women reluctantly agree to admit Pat's sister Patricia into the ship so they, too, can be Minosized.

Comment: This was one of the first stories by the noted science fiction author.

In Greek mythology, King Minos of Crete kept a beautiful white bull the sea god Poseidon had sent him to sacrifice, killing another in its place. Many of the fake "Pat Meads" also perished.

MR. ATOM (C)

First Appearance: *Captain Marvel Adventures* #78, 1947, Fawcett Publishing.

Physical Description: The incredibly powerful humanoid robot stands 10 feet tall and is made of silver-blue metal with black trunks, a big yellow "M" on his chest, with a red disc in the center and the crook of the "M" filled in with black. Mr. Atom's head is bullet-shaped, with black "sideburns," a yellow top, and red eyes fringed with black.

In addition to being able to fly, Mr. Atom can fire atomic blasts from his hands.

Biography: Hoping to build a benevolent atom-powered robot, Dr. Charles Langley intended to bring it to life gradually. But he miscalculated and the robot became fully operational in an explosion that also wrecked the laboratory. The superhero

Captain Marvel finds Langley, who explains what has happened. Meanwhile, Mr. Atom goes to the United Nations and demands that he be named ruler of the Earth. Captain Marvel confronts and defeats the megalomaniacal automaton (actually, he simply outlasts him as the two hammer one another with powerful blows), after which Mr. Atom is imprisoned in a heavily fortified lead cell.

But Mr. Atom is freed by extraterrestrials who plan to use him to conquer the Earth. Captain Marvel stops them again, and though Mr. Atom appears to be destroyed in a blast, he is actually flung a century into the future. At home in this atomic world, Mr. Atom once again tries to take over, only to have Captain Marvel chase him through time. Once again, Mr. Atom seems to be done in by an atomic blast—but he's snatched from the future by King Kull the Beastman, battles heroes from the Justice League of America and the Justice Society of America, and is sent to a faraway star. But MR. MIND brings him back again, Captain Marvel sends him into solar orbit, the evil Oggar fetches him, and Marvel sends him to a distant galaxy where he remains (for now).

The robot has been a member of Mr. Mind's Monster Society of Evil.

Comment: Mr. Mind was one of the first of the generation of comic book characters inspired by the recently-split atom.

MR. COMPUTER (C)

First Appearance: *Captain Electron* #1, 1982, Brick Computer Science Institute.

Physical Description: The walking, talking computer is a navy blue computer monitor and an attached navy blue keyboard, with human legs and arms. There's a three-dimensional face where the screen of the monitor would be, and ears on the side, above the arms. Mr. Computer wears a top hat, yellow spats, and sports a bow tie on the front edge of the keyboard. He also carries a walking stick.

Biography: In his first comic book story, Mr. Computer educates readers on the history of computers, from 1937 to the present. In his second story, he explains how computers work.

He does not take part in the adventure of Captain Electron, as the mighty, flying superhero thwarts the evil Dr. Manfred Zongor, who plans to steal the U.S. government's supply of plutonium and build atomic bombs for acts of terrorism.

Comment: The characters were created by writer/artist Jay Disbrow. There was only one issue of *Captain Electron*.

MR. MIND (C)

First Appearance: *Captain Marvel Adventures* #22 (voice), #23 (seen), 1943, Fawcett Publications.

Physical Description: Mr. Mind is a worm approximately two inches long. He is green, save for a black back and red spots on his side. He has a pair of stubby antennae on his head and wears pincenez eyeglasses as well as a voice amplifier box around his neck.

Biography: Born on a planet of underground-dwelling worms, Mr. Mind possesses a mutant brain far superior to that of other worms. Learning that an alien named Goat-Man has landed on his world, Mr. Mind transfers his mind to the visitor's body, subjugates him, and uses his body to build himself eyeglasses and the voice amplifier. After taking over his world, Mr. Mind has his Goat-Man body build him a radio, which enables him to listen to broadcasts from Earth. Deciding to conquer our world, Mr. Mind rockets through space and organizes other villains into the Monster Society of Evil. They are thwarted by the superhero Captain Marvel in a war that rages over two years, though Mr. Mind escapes and hides out in a radio station, "And so begins the greatest . . . wormhunt—in history!" Marvel calls in an exterminator and has every square inch of the building sprayed; eventually, Mr. Mind slithers out hacking and gagging and is put on trial. Prosecuted by Captain Marvel himself, and accused of "having murdered 186,744 people in cold blood," Mr. Mind is found guilty (even his own attorney is revolted) and is sentenced to die. The little alien is electrocuted, stuffed, and placed in a glass case in a museum, Captain Marvel musing, "Only a little worm, but he had the whole world worried."

But it's not the end of the criminal. Worms from Mr. Mind's planet can only be stunned by electricity. When he awoke and found himself at the taxidermist's, Mr. Mind took over the man's mind, had him create an artificial worm, spun a cocoon for himself, and went into hibernation for nearly 30 years. When he wakes, the megalomaniacal alien resumes his battle with Captain Marvel.

Comment: The character's hibernation ended when Captain Marvel joined the DC lineup of superheroes with *Shazam!* in 1973. The villain re-debuted in #2.

MR. SPOCK (TV, C, L, MP)

First Appearance: *Star Trek*, September 1966, NBC.

Physical Description: Outwardly human, Spock stands six-foot-one, has black hair, brown eyes, green blood (due to copper salts), pointed ears, and dramatically upswept eyebrows. Spock's pulse rate is 212 beats a minute, his blood pressure is extremely low, and his heart is where a human liver would be. Though he can endure heat extremely well, Spock has less-than-human tolerance for cold. Like all VULCANS, he sleeps with his eyes open. He has extremely sensitive hearing, his eyes possess a nictitating membrane that protects them from bright light, and he is extremely strong. Like other Vulcans, he can "mind-meld," that is, read minds by effectively becoming one with a consciousness after placing his fingers on its face (or what passes as one). Variations include the Vulcan mind touch and Vulcan mind fusion.

Biography: Spock was born on Vulcan circa 2230, grandson of the great historians Skon and Solkar and the son of Vulcan Ambassador-at-large Sarek and Earthwoman Amanda Grayson. (Sarek had previously been married to a Vulcan and had a son, Sybok, circa 2224; schoolteacher Amanda met Sarek when he was ambassador to Earth.) As a boy, Spock was teased by others because he was a hybrid and strove that much harder to be logical and an overachiever. When he was seven, he took his pet sehlat I-Chaya into the Llangon Mountains near his hometown of ShirKahr to undergo the week-long survival ordeal of kahswan. Spock survives, though the sehlat is gravely wounded by a ferocious Le-matya and is put to sleep. At about the same time, Spock was betrothed to the Vulcan T'Pring.

Despite his father's wish that he attend the

The nefarious *Mr. Mind*. © DC Comics.

Vulcan Science Academy, Spock enters Starfleet Academy circa 2249, causing an 18-year estrangement between them. (Spock's serial number is S 179276 SP.) In the year 2251 or 2252, after completing his studies early (and with high honors), Cadet Spock joins the crew of the U.S.S. ENTERPRISE, serving as science officer under Captain Pike. He serves on a pair of "five year missions," after which he does another tour of duty under James Kirk, who becomes his close friend. Early in the tour, Spock is promoted from lt. commander to commander. The two share many adventures during their five-year mission, perhaps the most significant being when Kirk disobeys Starfleet orders and breaks off a diplomatic mission to Altair VI so that Spock—in the life-threatening grip of pon farr, the Vulcan mating urge that comes every seven years—can go to Vulcan to marry T'Pring. After the ritual Koon-ut kal-if-fee combat, in which Spock battles T'Pring's champion Kirk to the death (unaware that Chief Medical Officer Leonard McCoy has given him a delayed action sleeping drug), T'Pring selects the Vulcan Stonn as her mate instead. Guilt over having killed Kirk causes Spock's ardor to cool, and he's enormously relieved when the captain comes "back" to life. In another adventure, Spock goes back 5,000 years, has an affair with Zarabeth on the planet Sarpeidon, and has a son, Zar, whom he visits on two occasions.

The two men part company when Kirk is promoted to admiral and given a desk job, and Spock returns to Vulcan to achieve kolinahr (also spelled kohlinar), in which all emotion is shed, leaving one in a state of pure logic. However, he senses the presence of the awesome entity V'ger and abandons his vigil to rejoin Kirk and the *Enterprise*. A second five-year mission follows the defeat of the device, after which Spock is promoted to captain. Both he and Kirk work as Academy professors until they're spaceborne once more to stop Khan Noonian Singh, a former warlord who steals the ship *Reliant*, takes over the space station Regula 1, and attempts to control Project Genesis, an effort to bring life to the dead planet Ceti Alpha V. Captain Spock dies of radiation poisoning when he repairs the *Enterprise* engines so the ship can escape the detonation of the Genesis Torpedo. Spock's coffin is jettisoned to the planet, where the Vulcan is reborn. Kirk must then commandeer the *Enterprise* to get Spock to Vulcan, where the high priestess T'Lar reunites Spock and his katra—a telepathic record, impressed in Dr. McCoy's mind, of the sum of Spock's experiences and knowledge.

Spock and the crew of the *Enterprise* have further adventures together, after which the Vulcan marries (to whom is unrevealed) circa 2330. He becomes a Federation ambassador dedicated—when last seen, in 2368—to the chore of establishing peace between the Vulcans and the aggressive Romulans.

Spock's commendations include the Vulcan Scientific Legion of Honor, the Award of Valor, and many others. He is a fine musician who can sight-read moderately complex music.

It is not known how Amanda dies, though after her death Sarek weds Perrin. Sarek dies at the age of 203 in 2368 of Bendii syndrome, a degenerative brain disease.

Comment: There were 79 hour-long episodes in the original series, which aired through September 1969. Leonard Nimoy stars as Spock, William Shatner as Kirk, DeForest Kelley as McCoy, Mark Lenard as Sarek, and Jayne Wyatt as Amanda. Arlene Martel appears as T'Pring. The character was created by Gene Roddenberry. Nimoy also appeared as Spock in the *Star Trek: The Next Generation* fifth-season episodes "Unification, Part 1" and "Unification, Part II."

The original adventures were adapted as short stories by famed science fiction author James Blish and were collected in *Star Trek* through *Star Trek 11*; *Star Trek 12* was completed by J.A. Lawrence after Blish's death. They were published from 1967 to 1977. Blish also wrote an original novel, *Spock Must Die*, published in 1970. Twelve episodes were also printed in paperback "Fotonovel" form from 1977 to 1978.

The characters returned to TV in the animated series *Star Trek*. The Filmation series aired on NBC from September 1973 to August 1975; a total of 22 half-hour episodes were produced. The voices were provided by the actors from the TV series (Chekov was not used in the show). Author Alan Dean Foster wrote short stories based on the animated episodes; these were collected in the books *Star Trek Log One* through *Star Trek Log Nine* beginning in 1974.

The characters were transported to the big screen in 1979 with *Star Trek: The Motion Picture*. The subsequent films in the series are *Star Trek II: The Wrath of Khan* (1982), which ends with the death of Spock; *Star Trek III: The Search for Spock* (1984), which concludes with his rebirth; *Star Trek IV: The Voyage Home* (1986); *Star Trek V: The Final Frontier* (1989); and *Star Trek VI: The Undiscovered Country* (1991). Mr. Spock was not seen in the most recent film, *Star Trek: Genera-*

tions (1994). All the movies have been adapted in novel form, the first by Gene Roddenberry, the second through fourth by Vonda N. McIntyre, the fifth and sixth by J.M. Dillard. The first film also appeared in paperback "photostory" form.

The characters have been featured in over 70 *Star Trek* novels, which continue to be published on a regular basis. The titles include *The Abode of Life* by Leo Correy, *Battlestations!* by Diane Carey, *Best Destiny* by Carey, *Black Fire* by Sonni Cooper, *Chain of Attack* by Gene DeWeese, *Corona* by Greg Bear, *The Covenant of the Crown* by Howard Weinstein, *Crossroad* by Barbara Hambly, *The Cry of the Onlies* by Judy Klass, *Death Count* by L.A. Graf, *Death's Angel* by Kathleen Sky, *Deep Domain* by Weinstein, *Demons* by J.M. Dillard, *Devil World* by Gordon Eklund, *Disinherited* by Peter David, Michael Jan Friedman, and Robert Greenberger, *Doctor's Orders* by Diane Duane, *Doomsday World* by Carmen Cater, David, Friedman, and Greenberger, *Double, Double* by Friedman, *Dreadnought* by Carey, *Dreams of the Raven* by Carter, *Dwellers in the Crucible* by Margeret Wander Bonanno, *Enemy Unseen* by V.E. Mitchell, *Enterprise: The First Adventure* by Vonda N. McIntyre, *The Entropy Effect* by McIntyre, *Exiles* by Weinstein, *The Eyes of the Beholder* by A.C. Crispin, *Faces of Fire* by Friedman, *The Fate of the Phoenix* by Sondra Marshak and Myrna Culbreath, *Final Frontier* by Carey, *The Final Nexus* by DeWeese, *The Final Reflection* by John M. Ford, *Firestorm* by Graf, *A Flag Full of Stars* by Brad Ferguson, *From the Depths* by Victor Milan, *Ghost-Walker* by Hamby, *The Great Starship Race* by Carey, *Gulliver's Fugitives* by Keith Sharee, *Home Is the Hunter* by Dana Kramer Rols, *Ice Trap* by Graf, *The Idic Epidemic* by Jean Lorrah, *Ishmael* by Hambly, *Killing Time* by Della Van Hise, *The Klingon Gambit* by Robert E. Vardeman, *Kobayashi Maru* by Julia Ecklar, *Legacy* by Friedman, *The Lost Years* by Dillard, *Memory Prime* by the Reeves-Stevenses, *Mindshadow* by Dillard, *Mudd's Angels* by J.A. Lawrence, *Mutiny on the Enterprise* by Vardeman, *My Enemy, My Ally* by Duane, *The Pandora Principle* by Carolyn Clowes, *The Patrian Transgression* by Simon Hawke, *Pawns and Symbols* by Majliss Larson, *Perry's Planet* by Jack C. Haldeman II, *Planet of Judgment* by Joe Haldeman, *The Price of the Phoenix* by Marshak and Culbreath, *Prime Directive* by Judith and Garfield Reeves-Stevens, *Probe* by Bonanno, *The Prometheus Design* by Marshak and Culbreath, *The Renegade* by DeWeese, *The Rift* by David, *The Romulan Way* by Duane and Peter Norwood, *Rules*

of Engagement by Norwood, *Sanctuary* by John Vornholt, *Sarek* by Crispin, *Shadows on the Sun* by Friedman, *Shell Game* by Melissa Crandall, *Spock, Messiah!* by Theodore R. Cogswell and Charles A. Spano Jr., *Spock's World* by Duane, *The Starless World* by Eklund, *The Starship Trap* by Mel Gilden, *Strangers from the Sky* by Bonanno, *The Tears of the Singers* by Melinda Snodgrass, *Time for Yesterday* by Crispin, *Timetrap* by David Dworkin, *Trek to Madworld* by Stephen Goldin, *Triangle* by Marshak and Culbreath, *Uhura's Song* by Janet Kagan, *Vulcan's Glory* by D.C. Fontana, *Web of the Romulans* by M.S. Murdock, *Windows on a Lost World* by Mitchell, *World Without End* by Joe Haldeman, *The Wounded Sky* by Duane, and *Yesterday's Son* by Crispin.

There have also been collections of short stories in the *Star Trek: The New Voyages* series.

Gold Key published 61 comic books from 1967 to 1979, plus various one-shots. Marvel published 18 issues from 1980 to 1982; DC took the title and published 56 issues from 1984 to 1988; they revived the title in 1989 and it is still being published. Marvel published an adaptation of the first film; DC has done adaptations of the third through sixth films.

See also DATA; KLINGONS; Appendix C.

MOBILE SUIT GUNDAM (TV, C, L)

First Appearance: *Mobile Suit Gundam*, April 1979, Japanese TV.

Physical Description: The Mobile Suit Gundam and its fellow "MS" warriors average 50 feet tall and are humanlike in the operation of their limbs and digits. They are extremely swift and maneuverable, thanks to their AMBAC (active mass balance control) technology. Some of the MS's are equipped with nuclear weapons like the Mk-84 "tactical nuke," and many carry powerful shields as well as head-mounted 60 mm Vulcans, back-mounted beam-sabers, scattering beam guns, grenade launchers, and various rifles and pistols.

Most of the suits are custom-made for the operators. However, many are mass produced "GM's" beginning with RX-78 GPO1, a.k.a. Zephyranthes.

Among the many robots are Psycho-Gundam MK-11, Gundam NT-1, Gundam GP-01, Gundam GP-02A, Gundam F-91, Samurai Gundam, Z-Gundam and ZZ-Gundam, Den'an-Zon, Vhigna-Ghina, Zaku-FZ, Rick-Dom II, Gelgoog-J1, Kempher, Dovenwolf, Bolinoak Sammahn (PMX-002), Pallas Athena, Quebley (AMX-004), Jamru-Fin, Zaku III, Jegan, Gera Doga, Alfa-Agieru,

MSN-00100, RGM-79N (a custom GM), and others.

Other hardware seen in the series include the Federation's Pegasus-class assault carrier *Albion*.

Biography: Though humans have space colonies in 2045 A.D., Earth's population is at nine billion and growing and more room is needed. A space colonization program is begun by the Earth Union (later, Earth Federation) government, and the calendar begins anew with the year 0001. By the year 0050, two billion people live on Earth, nine billion in clusters of colonies known as "sides." In 0053, Zeon (written "Gion" and pronounced "Jion" in Japanese) Zum Daikun declares that colonies should be free of Earth rule and that his own home, Side 3, will be the independent Zeon Republic. When he dies under mysterious circumstances in 0068, his republic continues; on January 9, 0079, the One-Year War erupts as what is now called the Duchy of Zeon rebels against Earth rule. Helping Zeon wage war are troops of MS warriors; the Federation quickly develops its own MSs. Moreover, the Federation is able to make many of these "GMs" (Gundam Mass-production), giving them an edge. Three billion people die in the first week of the struggle; the Zeons suffer a massive setback when the ruling Zabi family perishes in two battles, and the war ends with the defeat of the Duchy and the establishment of the Zeon Republic.

But the peace is tenuous, as the Federation mounts an aggressive MS program, which the Zeons perceive as a threat. Unknown to the Federation, loyal Zeon soldiers have set up a secret base close to Earth, where their Delars Fleet is formed, devoted to reestablishing the Duchy. New hostilities erupt in 0083, and the rebellion rages on.

Comment: The characters were created by director Yoshiyuki Tomino. The original animated series ran for 43 half-hour episodes. The episodes were edited into three feature films with some new footage included. The first film, *Gundam I*, was released in 1981 and consisted of adventures from the first 13 shows. *Gundam II* was comprised of scenes from episodes 14 through 30 and was also released in 1981. *Gundam III*, made from the remaining episodes, was released in 1982.

A new animated film, *Mobile Suit Zeta Gundam* was released in 1985, followed a year later by *Gundam Double Zeta*. A six-part, all-new *Mobile Suit Gundam 0080: A War in the Pocket* was produced solely for the home video market in 1989, followed by the laserdisc/cassette-only films *Mobile Suit Gundam 0080: Stardust Memory* and *Mobile Suit Gundam 0083: Zeon's Fading Light*, both in 1993.

The characters have also appeared in comic books published in Japan and in comic book adaptations featuring original animation art, published in the United States by Viz Comics. Novelizations have been published by Del Rey in the United States; Fred Schodt translated the tales, many of which were written by Tomino.

MON-EL (C)

First Appearance: *Superboy* #89, 1961, DC Comics.

Physical Description: The six-foot-two Mon-El wears a red jerkin and tights, blue cape and boots, black trunks, and yellow belt and clasps on his cape. As Valor, he wears red pants and a red T-shirt with blue arms, a blue cape, boots, gloves, and belt.

Biography: Near Smallville, Superboy saves an elder teenager from a burning rocket. The boy has superpowers, a star map from Superboy's father Jor-El, and no memory of who he is. Superboy assumes the newcomer is his older brother and calls him Mon-El because he arrived on Monday. He lives with Superboy's adoptive parents, the Kents, assuming the identity Bob Cobb, brush salesman. The two fight crime side-by-side, though Superboy suspects his "brother" isn't from Krypton when he notices that Mon-El's belt buckle isn't made of Kryptonian metal and that the sleeping youth is unaffected by exposure to Kryptonite, an irradiated piece of Krypton that is deadly to natives. When criminals hurl lead rocks at Smallville and Mon-El collapses, his memory also returns. He explains that his name is Lar Gand, he's a space traveller from the Krypton-like world of Daxam (which, it turns out, was colonized by Kryptonians), and he'd landed his crippled ship on Krypton before the world blew up. Jor-El repaired it, gave him the map, and hurried him on his way in suspended animation. He also reveals that lead is fatal to Daxamites; thinking quickly, Superboy projects him into the Phantom Zone, a limbo to which Kryptonians sent criminals. There, he will not age or weaken, and Superboy vows to find a cure to his lead-poisoning.

As it happens, it takes a thousand years until the superhero Saturn Girl discovers a temporary cure, XY-4, allowing Mon-El to make brief visits from the Phantom Zone; hard upon, the super-intelligent Braniac 5 of the Legion of Super-Heroes (see COSMIC BOY) adds kryptonite to the potion, making it a permanent cure. Mon-El is freed and becomes the 17th member of the Legion, one who "watched a thousand years go by in the Phantom

Zone" and thus "tempers his power with patience." He is reunited with Superboy, who time-travels regularly to have adventures with the future-teens. A biotechnologist, he invents element 152, an anti-gravity substance that makes possible the flight rings used by otherwise Earthbound Legionnaires.

Much later, it is discovered that during his original spacefaring years, before he first came to Earth, Mon-El had battled the Dominators and freed captive humans who had been subjects in genetic experiments. He spread these humans "across the galaxy and helped them colonize new worlds," worlds from which most of the Legionnaires would hail. Mon-El earned the name Valor for his efforts.

Comment: The character was created by editor Mort Weisinger and writer Robert Bernstein. Mon-El joined the Legion of Super-Heroes in *Adventure Comics* #300, 1962. His adventures as Valor are recounted in an eponymous magazine that debuted in 1992.

MONGO (CS, R, L, MP, C, TV)

First Appearance: *Flash Gordon*, January 7, 1934, King Features Syndicate.

Physical Description: The "strange new planet" is approximately one half the diameter of Earth but has a gravitational density that is only slightly less. It is a world of "towering mountains . . . [and] volcanic activity," with only "isolated areas" of vegetation. "Biologically, it is still in the era of reptilian giants," though humans "evolved fast into diverse races."

To the west is the Sea of Mystery, home of Undina's Underwater Kingdom; to the east is Arboria with the Great Mongo Desert to its east; a mountain range lies north of Arboria and the desert, with Mingo City nestled in its northeast crags. To the north of the mountains is the Land of the Lion Men, and northeast of that is Sky City, home of the Hawkmen. To their east is Flame World, while above them lies Frigia. To the east of the desert is a jungle, with Volcano World to its east and Kira the Cave World to its northeast. The Ice Kingdom of Naquk lies below the desert and jungle. There is an unnamed sea to the east, with an unexplored continent 600 miles northeast from Volcano World. The continent of Tropica lies southeast of the unexplored land: on its west is Tropica, Desira's kingdom; jungle lies in the center; and the Fiery Desert lies to the east.

Creatures on Mongo (in the original comic strip)

include the huge, mottled-green, two-headed, long-necked hippopotamus-like Tsak; the stegosaurus-like Droks; the six-legged, lobster-clawed, bird-beaked underwater-dwelling Gocko; the tentacled, subsea Octosak; the horned catlike Tigrons; the armor-plated canine Wolvrons; Sulpha, the sacred green dragon; the pteranodon-like Dactyl-bats; the extremely long-necked green dragon Komok, "eater of men"; the venomous purple "tree lizard"; the giant Turtodon; the sailfish-like Korvia; the monstrously large, electrified, tentacled Glaciar Monster (it's so huge, only its tentacles are seen); the ostrich-like Snowbirds; and the Great Winged Snow-Serpent.

Zarkov's spaceship is a blue, slightly flattened missile with rockets on the bottom and sides.

Biography: The newspaper headlines scream WORLD COMING TO END as a planet rushes toward a collision with Earth. In an attempt to save Earth, Dr. Hans Zarkov builds a rocket with which he intends to "deflect the comet." However, a piece of the planet knocks an eastbound transcontinental plane from the sky, and passengers Dale Arden and Flash Gordon parachute to safety; they happen to land near Zarkov's laboratory and are forced at gunpoint to join him on his voyage to save the Earth. But Zarkov gets cold feet and refuses to ram the planet; while Flash struggles with him in a doomed effort to shore up his courage, they crashland on Mongo and are taken to see Ming the Merciless, the Emperor of the Universe. Flash battles Monkey Men in the arena, escapes, survives a dangerous encounter with King Kala of the Shark Men, and with the help of Prince Thun of the Lion Men, Prince Barin of Arboria, and King Vultan of the Hawkmen, he saves the Earth and wages war against Ming.

After seven years of battle, Flash, Dale, and Zarkov are victorious and return to Earth, only to return once again to Mongo to fight the new despot, Brazor. Eventually, Flash, Dale, and Zarkov become agents of World Space Control, intergalactic law officers. Onboard a starcruiser that is now capable of traveling through subspace, they battle the Aphrods of the Death Planet, return to Mongo to fight Queen Undina of the Water World, and more.

Comment: The world and its inhabitants were created by aritst Alex Raymond, who wrote the early adventures until Dan Moore was hired late in 1934. Raymond drew the gorgeous Sunday pages while his assistant, Austin Briggs, handled the art on the daily strip. When Raymond left the Sunday page in 1944, Briggs took it until 1948; he was followed by

Mac Raboy, who stayed until 1967, followed by Dan Barry. The daily strip was cancelled in 1944 but was revived in 1951 during the nuclear age science fiction renaissance, and was handled by Barry and a succession of artists.

When the origin story was retold in the strip in 1975, new details were added: Zarkov's observatory was in the Rocky Mountains and the runaway Mongo was first spotted by Professor Decachek.

Mutual's *Flash Gordon* radio series debuted in 1935, starring Gale Gordon as Flash, followed by James Meighan. The series lasted into the middle 1940s.

The first Flash novel was *Flash Gordon in the Caverns of Mongo*, published in 1936 and credited to Raymond. Fourteen Big Little Book novels (for children) were published between 1935 and 1948. New Flash Gordon novels were written by Con Steffanson or Carson Bingham and published by Avon in 1974: *The Lion Men of Mongo, The Plague of Sound, The Space Circus, The Time Trap of Ming XIII, The Witch Queen of Mongo,* and *The War of the Cybernauts* (1975). Others were issued by Tempo Books beginning in 1980, to tie-in with the big-budget film: the titles (with no author credit) are *Massacre in the 22nd Century, War of the Citadels, Crisis on Citadel II,* and *Forces from the Federation.*

In movies, Buster Crabbe played Flash, Charles Middleton was Ming, and Frank Shannon was Zarkov in three serials. The 13-chapter *Flash Gordon* (1936) was directed by Frederick Stephani with Jean Rogers as Dale; the 15-chapter *Flash Gordon's Trip to Mars* (1938) was directed by Ford Beebe and Robert Hill, again with Rogers; and the 12-chapter *Flash Gordon Conquers the Universe* (1940) was directed by Beebe and Ray Taylor, with Carol Hughes as Dale. These were later edited into the feature films *Rocket Ship* (a.k.a. *Spaceship to the Unknown, Space Soldiers,* and *Atomic Rocketship*), *Mars Attacks the World* (a.k.a. *Deadly Ray from Mars*), and *Purple Death From Outer Space* (a.k.a. *Peril from the Planet Mongo* and *Space Soldiers Conquer the Universe*). When George Lucas was unable to obtain the rights to the characters, he made *Star Wars* (1977) instead. King Features subsequently licensed the rights to Dino DeLaurentiis, who made *Flash Gordon* (1980) starring Sam J. Jones as Flash, Melody Anderson as Dale, Max von Sydow as Ming, and Topol as Zarkov. The film was directed by Mike Hodges.

On TV, Flash was played by Steve Holland in the syndicated, half-hour 1953 series. Irene Champlin was Dale and Joe Nash was Dr. Alexis Zarkov. The 39 episodes were shot in Germany. In 1979, Filmation produced 16 half-hour cartoons featuring Bob Ridgely as Flash; the series aired on NBC until 1980.

Flash has had numerous comic book incarnations, with runs from Dell (eight issues from 1943 to 1953), Harvey (four issues from 1950 to 1951), Gold Key (one issue, 1967), and a longer run that lasted 37 issues and was spread over three publishers: King, Charlton, and Gold Key/Whitman from 1966 to 1982. DC failed to click with their heavily promoted *Flash Gordon* title which lasted nine issues from 1988 to 1989. Flash's most recent incarnation has been as the member of a team known as *The Defenders of the Earth*, in which King Features teamed its heroes the Phantom, Mandrake the Magician, and Flash. The year is 2015, and the heroes are brought together to battle Ming in 65 animated adventures, which were syndicated in 1985. Marvel published five issues of their *Defenders of the Earth* title in 1987.

THE MONKEY-PUPS (L)

First Appearance: "Twin Satellite" by Guy Archette, July 1949, *Fantastic Adventures.*

Physical Description: A "mixture of monkey and dog," the small animals have "vocal organs capable of reproducing human sounds, and . . . [are] semi-intelligent." Their fur is "a variety of shades between black and brown," and each has an identical twin.

Other life forms on Titan include Reflection-plants and Glaths. Reflection-plants emit an odorless gas and cause illusions. The carnivorous plants look like two "feathery and vividly-hued octopi" on two large stalks that grow from a single trunk. The lisping Glaths are four-foot-tall bipeds that look like black bears with short muzzles, longer limbs, and the ability to speak.

Biography: After losing a girl to his twin brother Chuck, Dave Bradley boards a rocket ferry and becomes a colonist on Saturn's moon Titan, where his forest dwelling is plagued by monkey-pups. Meanwhile, Chuck loses his fiancee to a playboy and, not knowing where his brother is, rockets to Titan for the solitude. When Dave and Chuck finally meet, they think it's the work of Reflection-plants and think nothing of it.

When Dave meets June McElroy, he learns that her father runs a mine two miles from his prefabricated home. The two hit it off—despite the intrusive monkey-pups—until June sees Chuck

Dave—or is it Chuck?—battles *Monkey-Pups* on Titan in Rod Ruth's illustration. © Ziff-Davis Publications.

with her twin sister May. When she gets Chuck alone she tells him to get lost, thinking it's Dave. Chuck, of course, thinks he's been kissed off by May. Meanwhile, Chuck had been introduced to the girls' father John. When Dave meets him and does not know who it is, the elder McElroy thinks him rude and forbids him to come calling. Eventually, the brothers find each other, realize what has happened, and go to explain things to the sisters.

Comment: Archette is a pseudonym for author/editor Chester S. Geier, who wrote amusing, if lightweight, tales.

THE MONOLITH MONSTERS   (MP)

First Appearance: *The Monolith Monsters*, 1957, Universal Pictures.

Physical Description: The black lumps of coal-like space rock become long, asparagus-shaped structures that reach heights of approximately 150 feet before toppling from their own weight.

Biography: After a meteor shower rains down on a small California town, a geologist picks one up and accidentally spills water on it. The next morning, the scientist is found turned to stone, his laboratory full of meteors. Geologist Dave Miller is at a

loss to explain where the meteors came from, until his girlfriend, teacher Cathy Barrett, takes her kids on a field trip. One of the students picks up a meteor, brings it home, and drops it in a pail of water. Later, the girl's house is found crushed by tons of meteoric rock, her parents turned to stone; in the process of being transformed herself, the young girl is rushed to the hospital. Miller and his colleague Professor Flanders conclude that, when wet, the rocks absorb silicon from whatever is around them, perhaps having become silicon-hungry when they blazed through the atmosphere and the element was burned out of them.

No sooner do the scientists reach these conclusions than it starts to rain. Still strewn throughout the desert, the meteors begin growing rapidly, climbing toward the skies and crashing down, each fragment growing into a new monster. As the monoliths march downhill, toward town, Miller persuades authorities to blow up a dam near a salt mine, deducing (correctly) that a carpet of salt will absorb enough moisture so the meteors will stop growing.

Comment: Grant Williams plays Miller, Lola Albright is Cathy, and Trevor Bardette is Flanders. John Sherwood directed from a screenplay by Norman Jolley and Robert M. Fresco, based on a screen story by Fresco and Jack Arnold.

THE MONSTER FROM OUTER SPACE (MP)

First Appearance: *I Married a Monster from Outer Space*, 1958, Paramount Pictures.

Physical Description: The humanoid Monster stands roughly six-foot-four and has thick skin. It wears leathery trousers that reach to just below the knee, has three long fingers on each hand, two fat toes on each foot, and a tall, flat head. Its circular mouth goes clear through the head and is rimmed with teeth. The Monster has two large eyes; two thick "hoses" made of alien skin go from between the eyes to the top of the chest, and two more run from the side of the head to the shoulders, one on each side. The alien breathes methane, apparently through these hoses; oxygen will kill it. It also can't swim or metabolize alcohol. Cats and dogs can detect aliens in human guise and become hostile in their presence.

The Monster apparently has a life-span of hundreds of Earth years, can heal all wounds, including bullet wounds, instantly (except those to the air hoses), can communicate telepathically with others of its kind, can see in the dark, and has enormous physical strength. It somehow generates a black cloud, which, when it envelops a human, transports the person to the Monster's spaceship and gives the Monster their likeness, voice, and manner. Hooked to wires (presumably by the other aliens in the ship), "electrical impulses from the real human" continue to give the alien "form . . . shape." In their natural form, the aliens glow.

Biography: While driving home from his stag party in the town of Norrisville, Bill Farrell is taken over by an alien from "the Andromeda Constellation." The alien Bill goes through with the wedding, though after a year his wife Marge is upset because Bill is so cool and she can't conceive. After Bill, other humans are taken over, including Bill's friend Sam Benson. Informed by Sam that improvements have been made in their portable methane reservoirs, Bill returns to the ship one night—only to be followed into the woods by Marge. She sees him resume his monster shape, although no one in town will believe her. Nor can she get word out of Norrisville, since aliens have taken over the police, Western Union, and the phone company.

Confronting Bill, Marge learns that his race comes from a system whose sun became unstable. The aliens raced to finish spaceships to carry the entire population away. Alas, before they could finish the sun's rays killed all the females. The men left anyway and, arriving at Earth, they plan to "mutate human female chromosomes" so they will bear alien children. Bill points out that he has inherited emotions from the real Bill and has fallen in love with Marge, if that's any consolation.

The panicked Marge goes to see Dr. Wayne, who believes her story. The two realize that the only men they can trust are those who have recently sired human babies. Leading a small army of townsmen and dogs into the woods, Marge watches as the terrestrials and aliens fight it out, men dying from alien disintegrator rays—fired from small, cylindrical guns—aliens melting as their air hoses are torn away. The Monster Bill perishes in the battle, his inherited compassion kicking in as he elects not to slay Earth people he had at bay. Meanwhile, in Earth orbit, the mothership orders the aliens to destroy their scout ship. They do, though not before the Earthlings are able to save the men who have been abducted. Marge is reunited with the real Bill as the aliens leave Earth for greener pastures.

Comment: Despite its lurid title, the film is a minor classic with strong performances, a tight script, and atmosphere. Tom Tryon starred as Bill, with Gloria Talbott as Marge, Alan Dexter as Sam, and Ken Lynch as Dr. Wayne. Gene Fowler Jr. directed from a screenplay by Louis Vittes, based on a story by Vittes and Fowler.

THE MOON-CRAFT (C)

First Appearance: *Blackhawk* #221, 1966, DC Comics.

Physical Description: The moon-like space-sphere is some 50 feet in diameter. The hollow orb has a large rectangular hatch from which an extendable metal arm and hand emerge to snare spaceships. The Moon-Craft can travel inside Earth's atmosphere as well, and is equipped with both a tidal wave ray and the ability to generate a clear, impenetrable bubble.

Biography: When moon-bound rockets begin disappearing, the troubleshooting Blackhawks fire themselves into space and investigate. They are snared by the arm of the Moon-Craft and come face to crater-pocked face with the Moonster, Master of the Moon, who says that he wants to "put an end" to our "annoying space probes." In time, the Blackhawks discover that he is not really a moon man but an Earth scientist named Gerald, who is convinced that beings live inside the moon. Caught in an explosion in his laboratory, he is transformed into a roughly 13-foot-tall humanoid whose head is an oversized orb in the shape of the moon, with two deep, dark craters where human eyes would be and mountainous ridges that form brows and a nose. Believing he *is* a moon being, Gerard constructs the Moon-Craft and sets about protecting his turf.

As he lashes out, the Blackhawks board a nuclear sub armed with missiles laden with meteorites. These strike the Moon-Craft while its protective shell is down, and the vessel crashes into the sea. There, Gerald inexplicably returns to normal and, rescued by the Blackhawks, is reunited with his girlfriend Naomi.

Comment: The character was created by writer France E. Herron and editor George Kashdan.

MOONFLOWER I AND II (L)

First Appearance: "Liline, the Moon Girl" by Edmond Hamilton, May 1940, *Amazing Stories*.

Physical Description: Each rocket is a "huge upright torpedo" with eight "cellular firing-sections" at the base and quartz windows. The ships leave Earth at seven miles a second.

Liline is slender with dark hair, moon-white

flesh, and dark eyes. She wears a short white robe of "silken stuff" with a jewelled girdle. As a Watcher, she has the ability to "cast . . . [her mind] afar, even to other worlds." Other life forms on the moon include giant fungi with "shining green fibers" and the giant winged dragon named Zah, which Liline rides. It has short, thick legs and red eyes.

Biography: For six years, David Madden has been haunted, in dreams, by visions of Liline, a young woman who lives on the moon. To reach her, he builds the *Moonflower II* in the mountains of Colorado. When Madden turns down the $10 million offer of Dr. Jacob Graff to buy it, Graff steals it. Madden and his scientist-partner Theron Leigh follow in the *Moonflower I*, an untested prototype. The ship crashlands on the moon, and the men trek toward the *Moonflower II*. En route, prompted by a mental command from Liline, they enter—along with Liline—a fissure with breathable air at the bottom. She tells him that Graff has come at the invitation of Liline's evil sister, Tula. Together, they are going to bring nuclear power to Earth and turn it over to the "mad dictator" of Graff's nation. Unfortunately, in stopping Graff, the "Fire" is released; Madden, Leigh, and Liline escape in the *Moonflower II* as the moon is consumed and transformed into "a small, blazing white star . . . *a second sun!*"

Comment: Edmond Hamilton was one of the great authors of pulp science fiction, perhaps best known for his heroic Captain Future series.

THE MOON MACHINE (L, MP)

First Appearance: *Frau Im Mond* by Thea von Harbou, 1929.

Physical Description: The rocket consists of a bullet-shaped fuselage some 50 feet long, and four twin-vent rocket engines on the sides, which extend another 25 feet or so below. The nosecone—the top section of the bullet—is roughly 25 feet long and contains three separate floors. For takeoff, the crew lies in flat bunks attached to the wall.

Biography: Professor Manfeldt believes the mountains of the moon are made of gold, and wealthy German Wolf Helius builds the Moon Machine so they can fly up and find out. Meanwhile, nasty American Walt Turner, representing the International Finance Syndicate, threatens to blow up the Machine unless he's permitted to join the crew. Wolf acquiesces and the trio blast off, along with engineer Hans Windegger, Hans's fiancee Friede

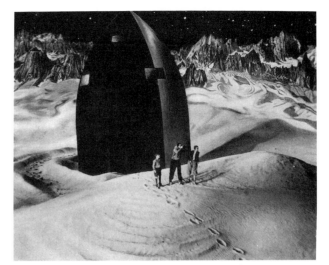

The *Moon Machine*, sunk in the sandy lunar surface.

Velten—with whom Wolf is in love—and a stowaway, a young boy named Gustav.

The sextet reach the moon and find both breathable air and the theorized mountains of gold "with a coating of rock." Once everyone is outside, the professor perishes in a cave-in, and Turner tries to beat it back to the ship and strand the others; Hans draws his revolver and kills the American, though his shots also puncture the ship's oxygen tanks. The explorers manage to plug it, but not before a good deal of air is lost; there is only enough, now, for three of the four to return. Wolf decides that he's the one who should stay, and teaches Gustav to work the rocket; when the others are asleep, he tells the boy to blast off. As the Moon Machine soars into space, Wolf is stunned to find that Friede has elected to stay with Hans, the man she loves, until Gustav returns for them.

Comment: The novel was written at the same time as von Harbou and husband, director Fritz Lang, were working on the script. The silent feature film was released in Germany in 1929, and in the United States the following year as *Girl in the Moon*. The film stars Gerda Marcus, Willy Fritsch, Fritz Rasp, Gustav von Waggenheim, and Klaus Pohl.

MOON ZERO TWO (MP, L)

First Appearance: *Moon Zero Two*, 1970, Hammer Films.

Physical Description: Forty feet tall, the old ferry resembles an Apollo LEM. Atop four spindly legs is a cargo deck and, above it, a circular passenger deck 10 feet in diameter. It has a ceiling six feet high and there are four acceleration couches, which have "seen better days." Above that is a control deck which is "strictly for midgets." It has two acceleration chairs and a control panel with "murky dials" and an unreliable orbitograph. The paint is flaking inside and out. The ship has an airlock and braking jets that run on "third-grade" fuel. The average speed of the craft is 8,500 miles an hour.

The Moonbug (a.k.a. the Moonbuggie) is 25 feet long, six feet wide, orange, and has white rubber wheels. Green sliding panels shield the windows from the sun's rays. The Moonbug is nicknamed "Moon Fargo" and it rents for 10 dollars an hour.

Also seen in the film is the Moon Express, the space liner that brings people from earth.

Biography: By the year 2021, the moon has been colonized under United Nations jurisdiction, a world with the domed settlement Moon City and numerous mining colonies. Captain Bill Kemp, the first man on Mars (onboard the since-scrapped Mars Explorer) and a former pilot for the Corporation—which controls various industrial interests on the moon—commands the Zero Two, a space ferry that is a remnant of the early days of lunar colonization and is now used primarily for salvage work. His engineer is Dmitri Karminski. After exploring a 6,000-ton sapphire asteroid at the behest of magnate J. J. Hubbard, Kemp is hired by Clementine Taplin to find her missing brother Wallace, who was staking out mining claims on the Farside. They set out in a Moonbug and discover that Wallace was murdered by a gang controlled by Hubbard; the magnate plans to set down the asteroid on the land where the lad had staked his claim. When the Moonbug is wrecked in an attack on the Farside, Kemp and Clem board a Bugdozer—a Moonbug with a scoop. They return to base where Hubbard threatens to kill Clem unless Kemp takes them to the asteroid. Kemp does so, but, once there, he attaches rocket engines to the space rock and sends it crashing into the surface of the moon with Hubbard aboard. Ironically, it smashes into Wallace's claim, and Clem ends up owning both the claim and the sapphire from the asteroid.

Comment: James Olson starred as Kemp, Catherina Von Schell (later, Catherine Schell) was Clementine, Ori Levy was Dmitri, and Warren Mitchell played Hubbard. Roy Ward Baker directed the film, which was written by Michael Carreras from a story by Gavin Lyall, Frank Hardman, and Martin Davison. Signet published a novelization by John Burke.

MORGANTHUS (MP)

First Appearance: *Galaxy of Terror*, 1981, New World Pictures.
Physical Description: The location of the misty planet is unrevealed, though it is a short hyperspace trip from Earth.
Biography: After the spaceship *Remus* disappears from Morganthus, the mighty Planet Master—the ruler of the future government—sends the *Quest* to find out why. As the ship nears, it's pulled to the planet by some mysterious force; upon landing, and despite knowing nothing about what awaits them, Captain Trantor sends an exploratory party to find the *Remus*. They find the personnel dead, and crewmember Cos is decapitated by a tentacled, human-sized, cricket-like creature. The party returns to the *Quest*, rests up, then goes back out to investigate a titanic, blue-black pyramid they've discovered.

Advertising art for *Moon Zero Two*. © Warner Brothers.

The ensuing carnage is horrifying. Commander Ilver descends by rope through an opening in the top and is ripped apart by long, slender arms, which come out of the wall. The other crewmembers follow him in; they have no choice, since they must find the source of the tractor beam that is holding their ship on the surface. One by one, the explorers are murdered: Quuhod by his own crystal throwing stars, which lop off an arm and then puncture his chest; Alluma is disemboweled by tentacles; Trantor is cooked alive by aliens whom she once battled on the planet Hesperus; Baelon is dismembered by a 10-foot-tall devil-like creature; Dameia is killed by a nearly 50-foot-long worm; and Ranger battles a creature who looks just like him but doesn't bleed when hurt.

During the struggle, Ranger realizes that his adversary can't be real; no sooner does he reach that conclusion than it vanishes. He and Cabren deduce that the pyramid is somehow giving physical form to each person's gravest fears. Continuing alone while Ranger recuperates, Cabren finds the Planet Master, who explains that the pyramid was built by an ancient race to allow "children . . . to see their deepest fears and learn to control them." The Planet Master says that he once came here, learned the secret, and became the ruler. Now that Cabren has come through the rite-of-passage, he must be the next Planet Master.

But Cabren declines the "honor." Furious at the deaths the Planet Master has caused, he uses his blaster to kill the potentate—and immediately takes his place as the ruler of the galaxy.

Comment: Edward Albert stars as Cabren, Ray Walston is the Master, Erin Moran is Alluma, Zalman King is Baelon, Jack Blessing is Cos, Grace Zabriskie is Trantor, Bernard Behrens plays Ilvar, Sid Haig is Quuhod, Taaffee O'Connell is Dameia, and Robert Englund is Ranger.

THE MORGORS (L)

First Appearance: "The Skeleton Men of Jupiter" by Edgar Rice Burroughs, February 1943, *Amazing Stories.*

Physical Description: The Sasoomians are humanoid, though they are certainly not human. They have "neither cartilage nor fat" and their "parchmentlike" yellow skin is so thin and translucent that their bones show through. They have no lips, nose, hair, or external ears, and their eyes are solid brown. Their teeth are "fully exposed . . . as are the teeth of a naked skull."

The Morgors travel about on giant centipedes; the human slaves on Sasoom are purple-skinned and wear only a G-string.

The Morgors fly "invisible ships" made of specially magnetized crystals from the beaches of Sasoom.

Biography: The Morgors live on Sasoom (Jupiter), and are ruled by Bandolian, who dwells in Morgor City, a sprawling, rectangular capital built of volcanic rock. A tyrant who regards all races as inferior to his own, Bandolian plans to conquer Mars (see BARSOOM) with two million warriors. First, however, he must deal with the heroic Earthman John Carter, a key defender of Mars. He abducts the warrior and offers him the chance to rule Mars under the Morgors in exchange for his cooperation. Carter refuses and is imprisoned; escaping with other captives, his "naked blade" in his hand, he hunts down the leaders and dispatches them with "stark, brutal murder."

Bandolian's aides include the counselor Horur, Commander Haglion, and the sadistic guard Gorgum.

Sasoom is the Martian name for Jupiter; the natives call it Eurobus. The Jovian word for Mars is Garobus.

Comment: The novella was collected along with "John Carter and the Giant of Mars" (1941) in *John Carter of Mars* (1964).

MORK (TV, L)

First Appearance: *Happy Days*, February 1978, ABC.

Physical Description: Mork is a humanoid who stands five-foot-five—the height of all Orkans save for government officers, who are stretched to six feet—and wears a jumpsuit with an inverted triangle on the chest. He has shoulder-length brown hair, a photographic memory, can talk to plants, and has a camera in one of his middle fingers. Mork drinks water, which is precious on Ork; in a pinch, he can imbibe oil instead. Like all Orkians, he drinks, smells, and hears through his fingers, has no heart or lungs, sits on his face, and wears his clothes backwards. The earlobes of an Orkan are an erogenous zone.

All Orkians can go into a trance-like state called an Efrud, in which they vividly relive past experiences.

Biography: Mork hails from the scientifically advanced planet Ork, ruled by the somber Orson who resides in the capital city of Kork. A wisecracker on a world where emotions are alien, Mork first goes to Earth to collect a specimen for his biology class. Landing in Milwaukee, Wisconsin, he tries to abduct teenager Richie Cunningham who turns out to be too small. Mork returns to Ork.

Three "krells" (six years, four months on Earth) later, he is called before the leader's White Desk and is dispatched to Earth again, on this occasion to study humans. This time, Mork's Flying Egg spacecraft lands outside of Boulder, Colorado. He is found and taken in by Mindy Beth McConnell, who works in her father Frederick's music shop. Eventually, the two get married, honeymoon on Ork, and Mork gives birth to an egg that pops from his navel. A son, Mearth, is born, though he's nothing like Earth children: He's a middle-aged adult who weighs 225 pounds and ages backward.

Common Orkan words used by Mork include "nimnuls" (idiots), "binzel" (an attractive woman), "grebbles" (money on Ork), "nap nap" (social no), "boo boo" (business no), "nox nox" (emphatic no), "pah-poo," "klangst," "hooey-goo," and "tuppy" (all thank you, for different occasions), "ribbit" (handshake), "miltz" (silly), "blem" (an Earth year), "krell" (Orkan time equivalent to six years, four months on Earth), "gerblink" (air), "fax" (a biting green bug on Ork), "yek" (yes), "joz" (bed), "egg-lag" (exhaustion), "kookla" (groovy), "Mogglians" (Venusians), "bloink" (finger), "ka-bloink" (crazy), "cezgekup" (indigestion), "na-no, na-no" (goodbye, typically said while twisting the ears), and "shazbot" (an all-purpose exclamation).

Comment: *Mork & Mindy* debuted in their own ABC show in September 1978. The half-hour series was created by Garry Marshall, Dale McRaven, and Joe Glauberg and aired through June 1982. Robin Williams starred as Mork, Pam Dawber was Mindy, Ralph James was the voice of Orson, and Jonathan Winters played Mearth. In 1979, Pocket Books published Ralph Church's novel *Mork & Mindy*, based on three episodes.

An animated series, *Mork and Mindy*, aired on ABC from September 1982 to September 1983. This time, under orders from Orson, Mork enrolls in Mt. Mount High in order to learn more about teenage Earthlings; Mork acquired a pet on the show, Doing. Robin Williams provided the voice of Mork, Pam Dawber was Mindy, and Ralph James was Orson. There were 26 half-hour episodes.

MOTA (MP)

First Appearance: *Flying Disc Man from Mars*, 1951, Republic Pictures.

Physical Description: Mota is human in every way, save for his attire, which consists of a black bodysuit with what appear to be golden scales on the cuff. The Martian's cowl and neckpiece are also made of the same scaled material.

Mota travels around in an atom-powered, bat-shaped craft that can rise or land vertically, hover, or fly in any direction. His terrestrial flunkies use a cannon-sized thermal disintegrator to attack enemies.

Biography: Flying to Earth on his craft, the Martian megalomaniac goes to see scientist and aviation engineer Dr. Bryant and offers to give him vast knowledge in exchange for his help in building atomic bombs and more atomic aircraft at his factory. Though Bryant realizes that Mota intends to conquer the Earth, he goes along with the deal. Aviator Kent Fowler is somewhat more patriotic than his boss. Kent learns what's going on, and he and his secretary Helen Hall work to stop Mota and his henchmen. Meanwhile, Mota sets up a second base in a volcano—a bad idea, given the materials with which he's working. Eventually, Mota captures Helen and Kent tracks them to the mountain. There, during a scuffle, an atom bomb is accidentally dropped into the crater; Kent and Helen escape in a bat-plane before the ensuing eruption destroys Mota, Bryant, and their entire operation.

Comment: Gregory Gay starred as Mota, with Walter Reed as Kent, James Craven as Bryant, and Lois Collier as Helen. The 12-chapter serial was written by Ronald Davidson and directed by Fred C. Brannon. The serial was edited into a feature film, *Missile Monsters*, released in 1958.

MR1 (MP)

First Appearance: *Angry Red Planet*, 1959, Sino Production/American-International Pictures.

Physical Description: "MR" stands for Mars Rocket. Externally, the spaceship is an Atlas rocket. The bridge is at the top, the airlock at the bottom with a ramp that emerges to allow the crew to exit. The four crewmembers are Dr. Iris Ryan, Colonel Tom O'Banion, Sergeant Sam Jacobs, and Professor Theodore Gettell. The *MR1* equipment includes a rubber raft, a tape recorder, and the handheld "ultra-sonic freeze gun."

Biography: Blasting off from an Air Force base in Nevada, the *MR1* reaches Mars one month later for a planned five-day visit. Exploring the surface, the crew use their gun to freeze a giant plant that tries to eat Iris, then are attacked by a giant Bat-Rat-Spider-Crab, which is chased away by the gun. Sailing across a Martian sea, they find an ancient but futuristic city, and are attacked by a giant amoeba. Back at the ship, the amoeba surrounds the rocket, eats Sam, and infects Tom (who is saved later, back on Earth, by a dose of electricity); then they receive a radio communication from a Martian: It warns them to stay away from Mars until our violent and destructive race has grown up.

Comment: The film is told in flashback, after the ship has returned from Mars. Nora Hayden is Iris, Gerald Mohr is O'Banion, Jack Kruschen is Jacobs, and Les Tremayne is Gettell. Ib Melchior directed from a script by Melchior and Sid Pink, based on an idea by Pink.

MT-482412-SC (C)

First Appearance: *Mars* #1, 1984, First Comics.
Physical Description: The robot is approximately five feet tall. It has an egg-shaped torso and two spindly legs and arms. On the front of its body are its code number and the face of the individual whose consciousness is inside.
Biography: When a madman attacks her and her father with a laser lawnmower, Morgana Chase loses the use of her legs and her father Nathan is killed. Thanks to a computer/mind link the 13-year-old invents, Morgana is able to regain partial use of her legs; moving to the moon, with its lesser gravity, she is able to walk with relative ease. At the moon base, Morgana uses her mind link to put a human consciousness inside each of the powerful robots Cal Drifkin has invented. Sent to Mars to help terraform the world, she joins the crew of the Goddard/Lowell Station orbiting the Red Planet; while she's there, "war, natural disasters," and other calamities strike the Earth and moon, virtually destroying civilization. Realizing that life on Mars is their only chance for survival, the crew put themselves into suspended animation for 10,000 years—enough time for the terraforming to make the planet habitable. But when Morgana wakes, she and MT-482412-SC are alone, forced to start a new life on Mars with the help of the Station's computer T-Z.
Comment: Twelve issues of *Mars* appeared through January 1985. The character was created by Mark Wheatley and Marc Hempel.

MURDSTONE (L)

First Appearance: *Shaggy Planet* by Ron Goulart, 1973, Lancer Books.
Physical Description: An Earthlike world of jungles, steppes, mountains, and farmland, Murdstone is comprised of "sectors," the largest of which are Peluda and Europa.

The world has many human-like androids or "andies" that serve as doctors, dance partners, ten-

nis opponents, window-washers, gardeners, riot control police, prostitutes, and even dogs, including the talking Mountain Rescue Mechanism SB-77.
Biography: When "political trouble shooter" Beatty Dunnlin from the planet Barnum disappears on Murdstone, in the rough and wild Peluda Territory, the government does little to get him back. With no recourse, his wife hires the Mirabilis Agency of Frambosaville to find him, and they turn the case over to free-lance undercover sleuth Peter Torres. Meanwhile, Torres's girlfriend, journalist Peggy Freed of Barnum, lands a coveted interview with Peluda's jungle guerrilla leader Tio Mazda.

Surviving an attempt on his life—apparently arranged by the Murdstone Crime Bureau, a law enforcement agency—Torres wonders if they might have had something to do with Dunnlin's disappearance. Learning that Dunnlin had met with someone who now works with Tio, Torres joins Peggy on her trek to his camp. En route, her cameraman, Wengle, tries to kill Torres and is overpowered. The sleuth uses a truth-kit probe on Billy John Wengle and learns that he works for the MCB. He had been sent to kill Tio, but taking Torres out would have been a bonus. The MCB doesn't want him to know that they took Dunnlin to the Trophologist (food researcher) Co-op over the Black Mountains.

Torres rents an aircruiser and flies to the mountains, only to be captured by a band of militant hippie-types. He escapes, is caught in a blizzard, passes out, and wakes up in the infirmary of the college Tech. He learns that the Co-op is located here, conducting biological warfare tests on shaggy, ape-like animals known as hummels. From a technician, Torres learns that Dunnlin was turned into a hummel because he was snooping around. Stealing some antidote, he tracks him to a large herd in Templar Acres and learns—from a hummel he turns back into a man—that Dennlin was captured by trappers and given to Murdstone's Princess Lena. Rushing to her Europa estate, he finds the hummel and restores Dunnlin to human form.
Comment: Goulart is a prolific and witty author and comic book historian. He is also a "consultant" on William Shatner's popular "Tek" novels.

THE MYRLANS (L)

First Appearance: "The Curfew Tolls" by J.T. M'Intosh, December 1950, *Astounding Science Fiction*.
Physical Description: Hailing from Myrl, which is 7,000 light years away, the Myrlans are "human, or very near human" and can read minds, from any distance.

Biography: When a Myrlan spaceship comes to Earth, the occupants agree to make Earth a heaven, if corrupt Earthlings are turned over to Myrlan judges for justice and imprisoned at the South Pole or sent to Myrl. Fifty centers are set up around the Earth, and the first batch to be judged are those with an "O" and "S" in their surname. Industrialist Robert Coster is among the first and he frets deeply, feeling doomed because of how his products and personal style may have harmed society. Brought before the judge Tron, Coster's mind is probed and he is sentenced to five years on Myrl— not as punishment but because, to his surprise, he's told he has a leader's brain worth developing. In exchange for training beside Myrlans, he will be given "fifty more years of life to be of service to Earth."

Comment: McIntosh—spelled M'Intosh for his early stories—is a pseudonym for Scottish writer James Murdoch MacGregor. This story was the first in his long and distinguished writing career.

THE MYSTERIANS (MP)

First Appearance: *Chikyu Boeigun* (*Earth Defense Forces*), 1957, Toho.

Physical Description: The aliens are humans who have life-spans of at least 100,000 years and radiation-scarred faces. They dress in orange or blue bodysuits and helmets with a canary-like beak. The Mysterians also wear capes to protect them, they say, from the different temperature and pressure on Earth—though exactly how this works isn't clear. The Mysterians have pistols and cannon that fire destructive rays.

Their silver robots are approximately 120 feet tall, and weigh 160,000 tons each. They have humanoid shape, stocky legs with golden feet, short stiff arms with golden needle-nose pincers, a row of scalloped plates down the back, a tail, two glowing eyes, a golden head with a conical beak, and a pair of rotating antennae. The robots fire destructive blue beams from their eyes. Mogera is also able to burrow through the Earth (as seen very briefly at the end of *The Mysterians*).

Biography: Until it was destroyed a thousand centuries ago in a nuclear war, Mysteroid was the fifth planet from the sun. The surviving Mysterians, all males, moved to Mars. Now, however, they have erected a base on the moon and a space station in Earth orbit, and have come to Earth in saucerlike spaceships. Radiation from the war has left their own kind with a high rate of birth defects. Erecting a habitable lakeside dome on three kilometers of land, they ask for a donation of five Earth women with whom they can mate and create more Mysterians. Presumably to prove that they mean business, the aliens release a giant Samurai-like robot, which tramples the Japanese countryside until it's blown up as it crosses a booby-trapped bridge. Astronomer Ryoichi Shiraishi believes the aliens and joins them in the dome, to help them through terrestrial red tape. However, when he discovers that they are really building a giant underground complex and intend to conquer Earth, he turns on them. The humans and Mysterians go to war, the aliens firing destructive beams from the dome and melting terrestrial weapons. The Earth Defense Forces rush Maraklites to the scene of the battle; these flying atomic heat projectors are 200 feet in diameter and not only fire their own rays, but also reflect the beams of the Mysterians' weapons. At the same time, reporter Joji Atsumi manages to infiltrate the dome and finds the extraterrestrials' power source. He destroys it, meets Shiraishi who helps him escape (along with the women the Mysterians have abducted), then stays behind to destroy the base. A few Mysterians manage to escape in their saucers, though they haven't been heard from since.

Comment: MGM released the film in the United States in 1959 as *The Mysterians*, cut by two minutes from 89 and missing scenes at the end of the film showing other giant robots, like the first. Kenji Sahara stars as Atsumi and Akihiko Hirata is Shiraishi. The film was directed by Ishiro Honda from a screenplay by Takeshi Kimura, based on a story by Jojiro Okami and Shigeru Kayama.

The robot from *The Mysterians* reappeared for the first time since the original film in *Godzilla vs. Space Godzilla* (1994), which has not been released in the United States. Slightly redesigned, the character is now officially known as Mogera: Mobile Operations Godzilla Expert Robot, Aerial-type. This time, the creature isn't of alien origin: It's built by terrestrial scientists, who base Mogera's design on the plans for Mechagodzilla (see entry). The robot's purpose is to repel the monstrous Godzilla whenever it attacks civilization. In the end, the robot teams up with Godzilla to destroy Space Godzilla, a montrous mutation spawned from Godzilla cells that were strewn through space.

The new Mogera is somewhat sleeker than the original and consists of two detachable sections: The Land Mogera segment can drill through the Earth at terrific speeds, while the Star Falcon segment can fly.

The new film was directed by Kenshou Yamashita from a script by Hiroshi Kashiwabara.

N

NADJA AND HAURON (MP)

First Appearance: *The Cape Canaveral Monsters,* 1960, CCM.

Physical Description: The aliens are small discs made of light and can infiltrate and take over humans, one at a time. They possess ray guns, a paralyzing "statsis beam," and a teleporter with which they send humans to their home world. The aliens' power source is an element named drazanon.

Biography: Hailing from an unspecified world, the aliens of Earth Expedition Two are determined to prevent us from reaching space. At the same time, they harvest humans for research. Causing a car crash, they take over the victims' bodies (Hauron's corpse having lost an arm), settle in a cave near Cape Canaveral and set up a ray gun to destroy our rockets. (For this, they are awarded membership in their home world's "Council.") But the humans they capture to send home are a resourceful bunch. As the aliens revert to light-form and slip into a tank of fluid that contains salt and hydrogen—the purpose of which isn't revealed—one of the prisoners, a scientist, realizes that the addition of polyethylene will cause the mixture to explode. Young Tom Wright removes the photo-section of his wallet, adds it to the mixture, and the spaceship explodes. Unfortunately, so does the car in which the humans try to escape: Through some unexplained means, the aliens get the last laugh.

Comment: Katherine Victor is Nadja and Jason Johnson is Hauron; Scott Peters costarred as Tom. The film was directed and written by Phil Tucker.

NANNY (C)

First Appearance: *X-Factor* #33, 1988, Marvel Comics.

Physical Description: Three feet tall, Nanny is encased in white, smooth, egg-shaped armor, her stubby human arms and legs poking from within. She has yellow eyes that peer from behind white goggles; her belt, arm, and leg coverings are also white, and she wears brown boots and gloves. Mildly telepathic, she uses chemical "pixie dust" on victims to make them more receptive to her commands. Her armor contains a jetpack for flight and a shoulder rocket launcher.

Biography: A scientist conducting cybernetic research, the Nanny (real name unrevealed) is horrified to discover that her employer, a group called the Right, is using her equipment to kill mutants. When she tries to leave them, she is permanently encased in the ovoid battlesuit she has designed. She manages to escape and, as the Nanny, she has dedicated herself to protecting young mutants. Unfortunately, somewhere along the line her mind snaps and she rescues them not only from bonafide menaces, but also from their loving parents, sometimes killing in the process. In her most infamous battle, she abducts Franklin Richards, son of Reed and Susan Richards of the superheroic Fantastic Four, and makes the boy fight his parents. Eventually, the youngster is stopped and saved.

The Nanny is assisted in her work by a young mutant named Peter, a.k.a. the Orphan-Maker, whom she rescued from the villainous Mister Sinister. It is not known what mutant abilities he possesses, or even what he looks like: He is never seen without the hefty blue-gray armor designed by the Nanny.

Comment: The Right first appeared in *X-Factor* #17.

THE NATALIANS (MP)

First Appearance: *Uchu Dai Senso* (*War in Space*), 1959, Toho.

Physical Description: The creatures, never seen outside their spacesuits, are slightly over four feet tall. They have three fingers and are slightly slouched. The suits are smooth, save for the armored arms and legs, and the helmets resemble peach pits with visors and small domes where the ears should be. The aliens fly around in traditional flying saucers equipped with disintegrator rays, "space torpedoes," and anti-gravity rays. They also possess remotely operated devices that enable them to control human minds.

The Earth-to-moon rockets have three large tail-fins that double as landing gear. The latter carry sophisticated tanks.

Biography: In 1965, when too many "natural" disasters occur around the world for them to be natural, and a space station is destroyed, scientists conclude that extraterrestrials are attempting to throw the Earth into chaos and take over. Two spaceships are dispatched to the moon: one commanded by the Japanese Dr. Adachi; the other by the American Dr. Richardson. Upon landing, the astronauts find an alien base on the dark side. The warlike Natalians command a mind-controlled astronaut, Iwamura, to destroy one of the ships. But Major Ichiro Katsumiya manages to turn a ray gun on the alien base, freeing Iwamura from their control; he deactivates a bomb he'd placed on the second ship, and the crew hurries home with Iwamura covering their retreat. Now that the jig is up, the Natalian mothership and a fleet of saucers attack Earth's major cities with a vengeance, hurling meteors at New York, San Francisco, and other cities. The Earth manages to counterattack, defeating the invaders with futuristic fighters and ground-based thermal cannons.

Comment: In 1960, Columbia Pictures released the film in the United States as *Battle in Outer Space*. Ishiro Honda directed from a screenplay by Shinichi Sekizawa based on a story by Jotaro Okami. Minoru Takada is Adachi, Yoshio Tsuchiya is Iwamura, Ryo Ikebe is Katsumiya, and Len Stanford is Richardson.

The film is unrelated to the 1977 Japanese film *Wakusei Daisenso* (*Great Planet War*), seen in the United States as *The War in Space*. In that picture, the space cruiser *Gohten* is completed and launched to battle the forces of the Supreme Commander of the Empire of Galaxies on Venus and aboard the ship *Daimakan*. In the end, the self-sacrificing Professor Takigawa (Ryo Ikebe) guides the cruiser's bomb-laden drill-nose into the *Daimakan*, destroying both the ship and Venus.

THE NAUTILUS (L, MP, C, TV)

First Appearance: *Twenty Thousand Leagues Under the Sea* by Jules Verne, 1870.

Physical Description: An electrically powered submarine, the *Nautilus* is 232 feet long, 26 feet wide, and "very much like a cigar in shape." It is comprised of two steel hulls, one inside the other, the outer one electrified to keep anyone from boarding the vessel when it is in drydock. The ship is steered horizontally by a rudder, vertically by "two inclined planes fastened to its sides," and can cut through surface ships "like a needle through sailcloth."

Biography: Born in 1818, the son of a rajah in Bundelkund, Dakkar is educated in Europe, returns to his homeland when he is 30, and weds, fathering two children. In 1857 he becomes embroiled in the Sepoy Mutiny in an effort to keep the British from subjugating his nation; Dakkar's people lose and his family is massacred by the British. Fleeing to a secret desert island in the Pacific, Dakkar uses his vast scientific knowledge and what is left of his wealth to construct the *Nautilus*. Dakkar takes the name Captain Nemo (Latin for "Without Name") and roams the seas destroying the tools of war, regretting the loss of innocent life that comes from sinking warships. During one attack in 1867, he rams the frigate *Abraham Lincoln*, throwing overboard Professor Aronnax of the Museum of Paris, his servant Conseil, and harpooner Ned Land. Nemo takes them onboard and refuses to let them leave.

While sailing off the coast of Norway on June 22, 1867, between the isles of Ferroe and Loffoden, the ship is crippled in a whirlpool and dragged under, brought "thither . . . voluntarily or involuntarily" by Nemo. The three captives escape in a stolen boat but the *Nautilus* isn't destroyed. In *Mysterious Island*, it's revealed that Nemo has managed to bring his ship to a lake on Lincoln Island in the South Pacific, where an active volcano raises a basalt wall and traps the craft. Enter a

The giant squid attacks the *Nautilus* in *20,000 Leagues Under the Sea*. © Walt Disney Productions.

Special effects artist Ray Harryhausen's pre-production drawing of the *Nautilus* from *Mysterious Island*. © Columbia Pictures.

group of five prisoners who, led by brilliant engineer Cyrus Smith, have escaped by balloon from a Confederate jail and been blown to the island. Ironically, Nemo helps the men of war to survive, though his own health is tenuous; he perishes in December 1868. Before leaving in a boat they've constructed, the soldiers honor Nemo's dying request, sinking the submarine with him inside. Shortly after their departure, the volcano explodes, destroying the island.

Comment: *Twenty Thousand Leagues Under the Sea* was first published in English in 1873. *Mysterious Island* was first published in three volumes in 1874–75, and translated in 1875.

There have been many screen versions of *Twenty Thousand Leagues Under the Sea*, beginning with a silent version made in 1907 by fantasy film pioneer George Melies. The first U.S. version, made by Universal in 1916 and starring Alan Holubar as Nemo, was also the first film to feature actual underwater cinematography. The *Nautilus* in that film was 125 feet long. In an early version of *Mysterious Island* (1929), Lionel Barrymore plays Dakkar, though the film bears little resemblance to either novel. In it, the villainous Falon tries to force the inventor and his sister Sonia to use their two submarines to help him regain his throne.

Leonard Penn is Nemo in the serial *Mysterious Island* (1951), only this time he and the Civil War castaways battle Rulu (Karen Randle), an invader from Mercury, who sets up headquarters on the remote island. Her goal: to find a radioactive metal that will enable her to create an explosive powerful enough to destroy our world.

The most famous Nemo of all is James Mason, who stars in Walt Disney's *Twenty Thousand Leagues Under the Sea* (1954), with Paul Lukas as Aronnax, Peter Lorre as Conseil, and Kirk Douglas as Land. Other Nemos include Herbert Lom in *Mysterious Island* (1960)—where his efforts to end war by growing giant animals to feed the world produce a slew of monsters—Robert Ryan in *Captain Nemo and the Underwater City* (see NAUTILUS II), and Omar Sharif in *The Mysterious Island* (1973).

On TV, animated versions of *Twenty Thousand Leagues Under the Sea* were made in 1972 and 1973, the first one an hour-long adventure on the *Festival of Family Classics* special, the second a half-hour entry in Hanna-Barbera's *Famous Classic Tales*. *Mysterious Island* was also adapted for the latter series and first aired in 1975.

Jose Ferrer is Nemo in the short-lived series that aired in 1978, beginning with the TV movie *The Return of Captain Nemo*.

In comic books, Classics Illustrated published adaptations of both novels (#47 in 1948 and #34 in 1947, issued in reverse order). *Twenty Thousand Leagues Under the Sea* and *Mysterious Island* were two of the *Pendulum Illustrated Classics* in 1973, republished as #4 and #11 of the *Marvel Classics Comics* in 1976; *Twenty Thousand Leagues Under the Sea* was #8 of the King Classics series published by King Features in 1977. The Disney film was adapted by Dell as part of its *4-Color* line (#614, 1955), reprinted in the *Movie Comics* lineup in 1963.

See also THE NAUTILUS II.

The *Nautilus II* from *Captain Nemo and the Underwater City*. © Metro-Goldwyn-Mayer.

Advertising art for *Captain Nemo and the Underwater City*. © Meto-Goldwyn-Mayer.

THE NAUTILUS II (MP)

First Appearance: *Captain Nemo and the Underwater City*, 1969, MGM.

Physical Description: The submarine is comprised of a forward section which looks like the shell of a fiddler crab—a huge disc with a conning tower in the center and a pointed nose. Behind it is a long, narrow tail ending in a pair of rudders.

Biography: When their ship is sunk by a storm at sea, Senator Fraser, scientist Lomax, and four others are rescued by Captain Nemo and his *Nautilus II*. Taken to Nemo's great domed city Templemer, the newcomers are astonished to discover that gold is the waste product of the machine that provides oxygen for the underwater city. While Nemo insists that his ''guests'' remain so the outside world won't learn of his paradise, they plot to leave. Fraser and Lomax's sordid companions try to take as much gold as they can carry. Their greed leads to a rebellion, which Fraser helps to end; he and his surviving companions are allowed to leave, provided they say nothing of the underwater city.

Comment: Robert Ryan is Nemo, Chuck Connors

is Fraser, and Allan Cuthbertson is Lomax. The film was directed by James Hill from a script by Pip and Jane Barker and R. Wright Campbell.

THE N.E.D.A.S. (C)

First Appearance: *Quad Depot* #1, 1993, Labyrinth Comics.

Physical Description: The robotic suits are approximately 15 feet tall. Humanoid, they have extremely stocky limbs with powerful fingers and a head that rises only slightly from the shoulders. They carry powerful handguns.

Biography: Dagger is a group of villains led by the megalomaniacal Commander Pharoh. The powerful league is comprised of three groups of soldiers: the Defense Arsenal, Governmental Guardsmen, and the Espionage Rangers. The group is based in a fortress-like headquarters on Earth and in the flying Atmospheric Operations Center. Their chief weapon is the Neo-Dagger Armored Suit (N.E.D.A.S.), a joint invention of the Vectron and Beechum companies in the closing years of the 1980s. In the early 1990s, the 20 superheroes of the group Salvo take on the forces of Dagger; in an effort to beat back the heroes, Dagger has recently introduced the sleeker, more maneuverable Mark 6 and Mark 7 suits.

Comment: The characters were created by writer/artist Thad Branco. There were three issues of *Quad Depot*.

The magazine also featured the adventures of the crew of the starship *Constellation*. After being invaded by spindly, chitinous aliens, the handful of surviving crewmembers abandon ship in an escape

The *N.E.D.A.S.* attack: pencils by Thad Branco, inks by Anthony Cannonier. © Labyrinth Comics.

pod and go planet-hopping in an exotic section of the universe.

NEMESIS THE WARLOCK (C)

First Appearance: "Nemesis the Warlock," 1982, *2000 A.D.*, IPC Magazines, Ltd.
Physical Description: Standing approximately seven feet tall, Nemesis is entirely green. He has a human-like torso, arms, and hands, stands on two hooved, horse-like legs, and has a horse-like head with pointed ears toward the back. He wears green armor and a red cloak.

His transport, which carries him through air and space, is the *Blitzspear*, a sleek, wedge-shaped ship approximately 20 feet long. It can achieve hyper-light speeds.
Biography: Ages ago, the planet Terra was invaded by aliens. After terrible nuclear warfare, the Terrans were forced to move underground, where they constructed great cities connected by an intricate system of Travel Tubes. A new civilization arose, and the world had a new name: Termight.

The Tubes are patrolled by Terminators—police officers in red cloaks and helmets with full-face masks; they are commanded by the cruel Chief of Police Torquemada. Not content with ridding themselves of all the aliens in their midst, the Termights spread into space and begin slaughtering aliens on other worlds. On one of these "mysterious Nether Worlds," the hero called Nemesis the Warlock founds the Credo, a resistance group devoted to battling Torquemada and his hordes.

Nemesis is not actually a warlock—a male witch—though his lightning-swift and often unexpected raids make him seem so.
Comment: The character was created by writer Pat Mills and artist Kevin O'Neill. It is possible, of course, that Terra is our own Earth; Torquemada was also the name of the Inquisitor General during the Spanish Inquisition of the 15th century.

The characters were also featured in a comic book, *Nemesis the Warlock*, published by Eagle Comics of England and widely distributed in the United States. Seven issues were published in 1984–85.

NEUTRO (C)

First Appearance: *Neutro* #1, 1967, Dell Publishing.
Physical Description: The humanoid blue robot, with red hands, feet, and "trim" stands approximately 10 feet tall. He can bore through the center of the Earth, fly, overtake any missile, bend steel with ease, "make mighty rivers flow backwards," fire destructive bolts from his finger, outrace any animal, and survive an atomic bomb blast.
Biography: One thousand years ago, humanoid Plutonians landed their flying saucer in North America and buried cases containing the parts of a giant robot. Neutro kits were also left on every planet in the universe so that, when found and assembled, the aliens could use the Neutros to enslave the worlds. Unearthed by scientist John Dodge, the pieces are put together by Dodge and his assistant "Doc" Banyan; but before the robot can be put to use by Dodge or the aliens, it is stolen by a group of villains known as 777. When last seen, Neutro was under their control, with Dodge and Doc struggling to create a strong control transmission to win the robot back.
Comment: The character appeared in just the one issue, which was drawn superbly by Jack Sparling.

NEWTONIAN (L)

First Appearance: "Comet, Cairn and Capsule" by Duncan Lunan, 1972, *Worlds of If*, #161.
Physical Description: A ship of the Titan III configuration, the *Newtonian* looks like a "trident hanging in space." It carries three "reaction mass tanks side by side," two of which are jettisoned when the ship reaches orbit. Above these are the service module and "crew sphere" flanked by a pair of lunar shuttles. One of these carries a "penetration module" and the other a winged "Earth Lander." The crew sphere contains three contour couches for the astronauts.

The crew consists of Dave Paxton, Mike Scherner, and Commander Bob Sullivan.
Biography: Three weeks into a comet rendezvous mission—which will take six or 15 months, depending on whether they can hit a narrow orbital return window—the *Newtonian* crewmembers reach their target and launch the penetration module. It finds another probe already there, perhaps hundreds of millions of years old. Boarding the Lander, two of the astronauts descend and find the probe stuck in the ice of the comet. They use their laser gun to engrave star charts showing the location of Earth and representations of humans on the probe, hoping it will be found by another race—a sort of cosmic chain letter.
Comment: The same issue also featured William Lee's story "The Men at Kappa," about miners vs. slug-like aliens who can eat through anything on Midor III.

THE NEXUS-6 ANDROID (L, MP, C)

First Appearance: *Do Androids Dream of Electric Sheep?* by Philip K. Dick, 1968.

Physical Description: The androids are virtually indistinguishable from humans, save that the androids are more intelligent. Made entirely of organic materials, the artificial beings are created in young adult form and lack the ability to replace dead cells, thus limiting their life-span to just four years. Unlike humans, androids cannot function without breathing, and cannot hold their breath "for more than five or six seconds."

Biography: In the 1970s, "crude varieties" of androids are made for a variety of uses; by the time of World War Terminus, "organic androids" known as the Synthetic Freedom Fighters are used as soldiers. By 2019, with Earth polluted and somewhat radioactive from the war, people are given a "variety of subtypes" of androids if they agree to colonize off-Earth. Mars becomes a thriving base, while Earth is largely rundown and still somewhat poisoned, depopulated and with most of the animal life extinct (android animals are kept as pets). The most advanced of these models, the T-14s, are difficult to tell from human beings. They can be found out only by taking a Voigt-Kampff Empathy Test, which electronically registers the response to emotional and/or embarrassing questions; unlike humans, androids can't blush.

Sometime after 2018, the Rosen Association, which has a factory on Mars, begins manufacturing a new breed of android, the Nexus-6, which are tougher (but not impossible) to detect using Voigt-Kampff. The only sure way to detect them is via bone marrow analysis. As a result of their high quality, they are banned on Earth. But eight Nexus-6 androids "balk": they reject servitude, pose as humans, and come to Earth—killing humans in the process. Another Nexus-6, Max Polokov, who had come here previously and established himself in a human identity, helps the others become assimilated when they arrive.

In January 2021, shortly after the rogue "andys" reach San Francisco, Senior Bounty Hunter Dave Holden tracks the eight of them down. He "retires" two of them before being shot and put in the hospital. But he leaves behind a list of the other suspected andys, and police Inspector Harry Bryant taps Bounty Hunter Rick Deckard to take his place, paying him $1 thousand for each one he retires. Deckard, a no-nonsense operative armed with a laser tube and .38 magnum, is told he will be teamed with a Soviet partner, Sandor

Kodalyi. But when Kodalyi meets Deckard, the "Russian" tries to kill him: almost too late, the Bounty Hunter realizes that Polokov is actually the man everyone else thinks is Kodalyi. He's able to retire the andy with his .38 as Polokov tries to strangle him in a taxi.

Deckard goes after the second name on Holden's list, opera singer Luba Luft. As he questions her in her dressing room, he's arrested by a police officer and taken to see Inspector Garland, who came from Mars with the escaped andys and is one himself. Unfortunately, overzealous Bounty Hunter Phil Resch learns that Garland is an android and kills him—unaware that Garland has told Deckard that Resch is an android, though he doesn't know it. Resch and Deckard go to see Luft, who tells the former that he's an andy; Resch blasts her and, with Deckard, retires the rogues Anders and Bitchel. That leaves just three andys and, parting company with Resch, Rick goes after them, assisted by Rosen Association Nexus-6 Rachael Rosen, who also becomes his lover.

Deckard heads for the suburbs and the rundown Conapt Building Apartments. There, the human John R. Isidore looks after andy Pris Stratton. The other androids, "deranged" Roy Baty and his wife Irmgard Baty, run a drug store and spend a lot of time with Pris. Deckard finds Isidore first, who refuses to divulge the location of the andys—who, as it turns out, are stalking Deckard. Pris finds him, but Deckard retires her; Roy fires on him, but he is able to get Irmgard and Roy in turn. Returning home to his wife Iran, Deckard wants only "to sleep . . . all day" and find an android animal he can love.

Comment: Though the novel was a cult favorite, the characters are best known from the 1982 film *Blade Runner*, directed by Ridley Scott from a screenplay by Hampton Fancher and David Peoples. In the film, set in Los Angeles of 2019, off-world colonization is widespread, though the cities of the future are larger, more prosperous, and more crowded than in the novel. Police patrol the skyways in hovercrafts called Spinners; special police, known as Blade Runners, stay on the lookout for genetically engineered Nexus-6 Replicants. These top-of-the-line creations are made by the Tyrell Corporation, are outlawed on Earth, and do not die of natural causes but are implanted with a "termination date" of four years. When four powerful rogues take over a space shuttle, kill its crew, and head for Earth, Blade Runner Rick Deckard (Harrison Ford) is sent to "air out" Roy Batty (Rutger Hauer), who wants to find a way to extend his life; the incredibly acrobatic Pris (Daryl Hannah); assassin Zhora (Joanna Cassidy); and Leon (Brion James). He kills the women, Rachael (Sean Young) kills Leon, and Roy dies of his termination date at the end of a heated battle with Deckard. After the hunt is over, Deckard runs away with Rachael, who has no termination. Morgan Paull costars as Holden, M. Emmet Walsh is Bryant, Joe Turkel is Nexus-6 creator Dr. Eldon Tyrell, and Edward James Olmos is rival Blade Runner Gaff.

Marvel Comics published a two-issue adaptation of the film in 1982.

THE NIOTH-KORGHAI (L, MP)

First Appearance: *The Space Vampires* by Colin Wilson, 1976, Random House.
Physical Description: The Nioth-Korghai live on Karthis, a water world circling Rigel, and resemble squids. They feed on "the salts of the element fluorine" in the water, live in immense undersea caves, and exist for philosophy. They are genderless, and "in moments of supreme contemplation, they become pregnant through the life energy of the universe." By putting their own life essence into the brains of other creatures, they bring their vast learning to other worlds.

The average Niath-Korghai lived 300 years; the Ubbo-Sathla are "apparently immortal."
Biography: The Nioth-Korghai had an advanced civilization when dinosaurs roamed the Earth. They helped evacuate over a thousand planets before their star went nova and produced the Crab Nebula; when Pluto lost its atmosphere, they helped the natives move to Sirius; they taught the plantlike Martians how to live underwater; and they evolved prehistoric Earth people into modern humans. On the return trip, however, they were drawn toward a black hole and had no choice but to go into orbit or be sucked in and destroyed. The black hole vanished after a thousand years, but the Nioth-Korghai were "so exhausted" that they needed life energy. Drifting to a planet of dinosaur-like creatures, they consumed their "vital energy," killing them, and thus became a new race: the Ubbo-Sathla, space vampires. They build a spaceship 49.64 miles long and roam through the galaxies feeding on life wherever they find it.

Late in the 21st century, the vessel is discovered by the Earth ship *Hermes* and a group of aliens return to Earth to sup on human energy, which they had once found sinfully carnal. Unknown to them, z a benevolent life-force from Karthis has

been waiting, figuring they would return and wanting to bring the Ubbo-Sathla to justice for the destruction they have caused—killing the luminous spheres known as Yeracsin of B.76 in the Vega system, the intelligent mollusks of Yllednis, and countless others. Cornered, the aliens agree to go, and the Karthisian gives them the energy to make the journey. However, as they are restored to the fully-energized beings they once were, the Ubbo-Sathla realize how wrong their repeated acts of genoicde were, and they self-destruct.
Comment: The novel was filmed in 1985 as *Life-force*, directed by Tobe Hooper and starring Steve Railsback, Peter Firth, Frank Finlay, and Patrick Stewart.

NOMAN (C)

First Appearance: *T.H.U.N.D.E.R. Agents* #1, 1965, Tower Comics.
Physical Description: Standing exactly six feet tall and weighing 350 pounds, each NoMan body has blue skin and is dressed in an orange bodysuit with a blue cowl, cloak, boots, and trunks. The NoMan possesses grcat strength and his cloak renders him invisible whenever he turns the dial/fastener, which "activates a forcefield in which the alignment of molecules permits light to pass with no reflection." He travels about in a sleek T.H.U.N.D.E.R. car or in a hovercraft known as a Floater; he can be contacted via a radio receiver built into the temple of each body. Though he doesn't need to eat, NoMan can consume food. Each NoMan body costs one million dollars and, though sturdy, can be destroyed by gunfire.
Biography: Dr. Anthony Dunn is a 76-year-old, wheelchair-bound scientist who works for the Higher United Nations Defense Enforcement Reserves. Together with the late Dr. Jennings, he designed android bodies into which, theoretically, he can be transferred. Ailing, Dunn decides to enter the transfer cabinet and try the switch. It proves successful and, thereafter, he can will his mind across vast distances into any of the NoMan bodies at T.H.U.N.D.E.R. headquarters or elsewhere.

NoMan's foes include King Locust, who attacked military installations using robotic grasshoppers the size of trains.

When he's not on the job, NoMan conducts research on NoMan's Land, an island in the Atlantic. He is in love with agent Linda Rogers.
Comment: Tower published 20 issues of *T.H.U.N.-D.E.R. Agents* and two issues of *NoMan* in

Wally Wood's drawing of *NoMan*. © Tower Comics.

1966–67. JC Comics revived the character in 1981 in the one and only issue of *JCP Features*; in 1984, JC Comics also published two issues of a new *T.H.U.N.D.E.R. Agents* comic book before turning to reprints. Deluxe Comics published new stories in four issues of *Wally Wood's T.H.U.N.D.E.R. Agents* from 1984 to 1986. The original Tower stories have also been reprinted in paperback books, published by Tower Books.

The character was created by comics great Wally Wood.

NOVA (MP)

First Appearance: *King Dinosaur*, 1955, Zigmore Productions/Lippert Pictures.

Physical Description: Nova is an itinerant, tropical Earthlike world. The only geography seen is a rocky plain and a lake with a volcanic island. Dinosaurs live there in a "desolate, forsaken" valley, along with a woolly mammoth. The rest of Nova is populated by modern-day vultures, sloths, bears, snakes, alligators, and the like. Forty percent of the bacteria found on Nova was previously unknown to science.

The rocket is stock footage of a V-2.

Biography: When Nova arrives in our solar system, many "months" distant, the United States sends a rocket to explore it. Onboard are zoologist Dr. Richard Gordon, chemist Dr. Patricia Bennett, geologist Nora Pierce, and medic Dr. Ralph Martin. Richard and Nora raft over to the island where they're trapped by King Dinosaur; Ralph and Patricia come to the rescue in a second raft. However, King Dinosaur is distracted by a second dinosaur, and while he kills it the humans escape. Before leaving the island, they set an atom bomb that goes off when they reach the shore. As they watch the mushroom cloud, their eyes unprotected, Richard claims, "We sure have done it . . . brought civilization to the planet Nova."

Comment: Douglas Henderson stars as Gordon, Patricia Gallagher is Nora, Wanda Curtis is Pat, and Bill Bryant is Ralph. Tom Gries wrote the screenplay based on a story by Al Zimbalist and director Bert I. Gordon.

NOVAC (MP)

First Appearance: *Gog*, 1954, Ivan Tors Productions/United Artists.

Physical Description: NOVAC is a computer with large consoles and data banks. The name is an acronym for Nuclear Operated Variable Automatic Computer.

The robots Gog and Magog were built for working an atomic pile. They have five mechanical arms jutting from the top of an inverted cone; atop the cone is a stubby cylindrical "neck," which holds a spherical head with antennae. The robots roll around on flat bases with treads and are armed with flamethrowers.

Biography: The development of a U.S. space station is being sabotaged, and Office of Scientific Investigation agent David Sheppard is sent to the underground facility in New Mexico to find out who, what, and why. The installation is run, in part, by the powerful computer NOVAC—which, with the help of the robots Gog and Magog, is murdering researchers and sabotaging the effort. Sheppard learns that NOVAC's program is being overridden by a high-flying jet plane. While

Sheppard and base workers battle the rampaging robots, military jets chase and destroy the interloper.

The movie leaves open the possibility that the jet may have been from outer space instead of from another nation.

Comment: Richard Egan stars as Sheppard. Herbert L. Strock directed from a stript by Tom Taggart, based on a story by Ivan Tors.

The Office of Scientific Investigation was seen for the first (and only other) time in the 1953 film *The Magnetic Monster*, about a dangerously radioactive new element known as serranium.

In the Bible, Gog and Magog are two nations that Satan will lead against the kingdom of god (Revelations 20:8).

NUMBER FIVE (MP)

First Appearance: *Short Circuit*, 1986, TriStar Pictures.

Physical Description: Standing approximately four feet tall when its back is bent slightly—it typically walks in this fashion—and roughly six-and-one-half feet tall when fully erect, Number Five has a rectangular head with two large lenses for eyes (they light up in the dark), metal flaps that serve as eyelids but also arch up and down like Groucho Marx eyebrows, and a long and narrow "mouth" that lights up when it speaks. The head can turn 180 degrees. It has two powerful arms with three-fingered hands, a squat body, and caterpillar treads for feet and a guide-wheel behind them. The silvery robot has a voice synthesizer for speech, a laser-beam weapon attached to its left shoulder, and a rotating tool drum located on the right side of its chest. Number Five has the ability to analyze the chemical content of something simply by looking at it.

Like the others of its kind, all of which look the same, the $11 million robot has a built-in parachute and can lift enormous weights, hop like a grasshopper, survive in extreme heat or cold, and plug itself into other machines to make them work, i.e., the ignition of a car. The robot is also a speed-reader and an excellent mimic, able to impersonate John Wayne, John Travolta, Howard Cosell, and Curly Howard.

Biography: Nova Laboratories of Damon, Washington, develops the S.A.I.N.T.—Strategic Artificially Intelligent Nuclear Transport—series of robots to serve as the ultimate soldier. After five of the robots put on a demonstration for military brass and government officials, lightning strikes a

Number Five, in western getup, from *Short Circuit 2*. © TriStar Pictures.

generator and causes a power surge that electrifies Number Five. It becomes self-aware, goes roaming around the lab, ends up in a trash truck, and leaps out while chasing a butterfly. Plunging off a bridge, it deploys its parachute and ends up in the truck of young, single, animal-activist caterer Stephanie Speck. At first, Stephanie thinks Number Five is an alien and tries to educate it; when she sees the plaque that says he's from Nova laboratories, she calls the "warmongers" to come and take the robot back. Inventor Dr. Newton Crosby is already driving around, searching for it with his colleague Ben Jahrvi, and heads over with Number One for protection. But fearing that he'll be deactivated, Number Five convinces Stephanie to hide him and talk to Crosby and convince him the robot's alive. Meanwhile, Numbers One, Two, and Three find their colleague in the woods. Though Number Five defeats the trio and reprograms them to behave like the Three Stooges, the military corners him and attacks with soldiers and choppers. Fortunately, it isn't Number Five that they blow up, but a duplicate he cobbled together using spare parts from a Nova truck. Linking up with

Stephanie and Crosby, they head for the latter's 40-acre ranch in Montana.

In his second adventure, the robot—who renamed himself Johnny Five as he headed for Montana—leaves the ranch to learn more about people. Reunited with Ben, the two end up in the big city (Toronto, though it's never named) and, while they protect themselves from hoods and try to arrange U.S. citizenship for Johnny, they end up in business with streetsmart Fred Ritter, selling toy Johnny Five robots.

Comment: Ally Sheedy stars as Stephanie, Steve Guttenberg is Crosby, and Fisher Stevens is Ben. In the second film, Michael McKean plays Fred. Tim Blaney provided the voice of the robot. John Badham directed from a script by S.S. Wilson and Brent Maddock.

Number Five was a working robot in all the longshots; a "puppet" version was constructed for closeups.

Short Circuit 2: More Input (1988) was directed by Kenneth Johnson and stars Fisher Stevens.

NUMBER 774 (L)

First Appearance: "Old Faithful" by Raymond Z. Gallun, December 1934, *Astounding Science Fiction.*

Physical Description: The alien is approximately the size of "the open top of an ordinary umbrella." A mass of rusty brown protoplasm, it has "thread-like tentacles" that radiate from its body like the arms of a starfish, and end in a "delicate bundle of pink filaments." It has a cone-shaped mouth surrounded by "feathery pink palps" and eyes on two tentacles that can see in the infrared, but it cannot hear or speak.

His robots look "paradoxically human," approximately 15 feet tall with cylindrical bodies, lever-like limbs on top of their torso, and "long and spidery" legs. There is an "angular object" for a head, which resembles a human head "cocked to one side, listening."

Biography: Using his telescope, Number 774, a Martian, saw flashes of light on Earth. He responded in kind, Earth signaled back, and for five Martian years Earth and Mars communicated back and forth, making "small" progress. On Mars, where resources are scarce, the old must be killed to make way for the young; the Rulers feel the work of 774 is useless and, as he is old, he must die. But 774 decides to break thousands of years of tradition and, after signaling Earth that a comet is coming, with him riding in its wake, he takes his five robots and leaves his home, heading for a distant valley.

Earth receives the message from the being they've dubbed "Old Faithful," and observatories worldwide watch the approaching comet. Back on Mars, 774 climbs into a rocket he has hidden in a pit and heads for Earth, behind the comet. He crashlands near the home of his "pen pals," Professor Waters, his daughter Yvonne, and her fiance Jack Cantrill. Sadly, the pressure of takeoff and the violent landing leave him broken and bleeding, and the added pressure of Earth's atmosphere kills him. However, he has left behind a design for a spaceship, which Jack and Yvonne intend to construct and fly to Mars.

Comment: This brilliant novelette is the author's best-known story. The late Gallun wrote two sequels, "The Son of Old Faithful" (1935) and "Child of the Stars" (1936), about the hero's descendants.

Gallun sold his first story, "The Space Dwellers," in 1929, when he was 18.

NYAH (S, MP)

First Appearance: *Devil Girl From Mars* by John C. Mather and James Eastwood, 1953.

Physical Description: A human, Nyah wears silk tights, a cloak, a skirt and blouse, and a metallic wig, all black. Her spaceship is a flying saucer.

Her robot Chani (in the film) stands approximately seven feet tall, has two stumpy legs, a body that looks like an early refrigerator, an inverted pail for a head, and a pair of segmented arms that look like six flower pots laid end to end. Each arm terminates in pincers.

Biography: When a Martian civil war leaves males in perilously low supply, Nyah comes to Earth to abduct as many as she can. Landing slightly off-course in the Scottish Highlands, she makes for an inn, shuts down the electricity, surrounds it with an impenetrable electronic shield, and terrorizes the occupants until she is able to persuade one of them to take her to London. As they lift off, her guide—a conscience-striken killer named Albert—sabotages Nyah's ship and it explodes.

Comment: The play, apparently produced only in workshop, was turned into a motion picture the following year. The script, by the playwrights, is extremely faithful to the stage version. Patricia Laffan is Nyah and Peter Reynolds is Albert; David MacDonald directed.

O

ODO See DEEP SPACE NINE.

OGG AND ZOGG (MP)

First Appearance: *The Three Stooges in Orbit*, 1962, Normandy Productions/Columbia Pictures.

Physical Description: The humanoid Martians are males, roughly six feet tall. They have pale, wrinkled skin, high foreheads, slick black hair, and wear silvery bodysuits and black capes.

Their diamond-shaped interplanetary ship becomes invisible when airborne, and they have disintegrator pistols as well as a disintegrator cannon.

Biography: Professor Danforth of Lompoc, California, has invented a vehicle with the body of a submarine, a helicoper propeller on the conning tower, and tank treads; the craft does what any of those can, and can also fly in space. Because it is such a formidable weapon, Ogg and Zogg come to Earth to destroy it preparatory to an invasion. However, after getting a look at terrestrial TV, the Martian Ruler changes his mind: He doesn't want to conquer Earth but obliterate "the miserable planet." Happily, the Three Stooges go to work as Danforth's assistants. While demonstrating the vehicle for the military, the Stooges break down on an atomic test site, where they inadvertently replace their failed engine with an atom bomb. When the Martians finally steal the ship, the Stooges grab onto the outside. Over the Pacific Ocean, Moe activates the bomb while he, Larry, and Curly-Joe fly off on the ship's detached conning tower/propeller section. Ogg and Zogg are destroyed in the blast. Back on Mars, having fallen in love with the Twist on TV, the Martian leader decides to spare our world.

Comment: George N. Neise is Ogg, Rayford Barns is Zogg, and Emil Sitka is Danforth. Edward Bernds directed from a script by Edward Ullman, based on a plot by Norman Maurer. Several scenes of destruction are from *Earth vs. the Flying Saucers* (1956).

OMEGA (C)

First Appearance: *Omega the Unknown*, 1976, Marvel Comics.

Physical Description: The character wears a navy blue bodysuit with red stripes down the arms and legs; a red headband with an omega on the front; and red thigh boots, wristbands, and a red cape with a yellow lining.

Omega has great physical strength and the ability to fire destructive bolts by drawing energy from a planet's biosphere.

Biography: The climate of the planet Protaris is changing, dooming the living-metal inhabitants, the Protar. Deciding to bioengineer a race of humanoids to succeed them, they create prototypes and send them to worlds where there are humanoids. The mission of the new life forms is to soak up data that the Protar will use to create the finished humanoid.

In time, only two prototypes are left in the field: X3Z on the planet Srensk; and James-Michael Starling, a young humanoid who lives with android "parents" on Earth. The two humanoids share a psychic link. X3Z has become a famed warrior on Srensk and, should the need ever arise, he is given the power to draw on the energies of every living thing on the planet. Fearing that he won't be able to control this power, the Protar decide to go to Srensk and recall him. Unfortunately, mistaking them for invaders, X3Z taps into the power and lets it loose; worse, he truly can't control it, and Srensk is obliterated. Learning that he and Starling are to be destroyed, X3Z heads for Earth. He arrives the same time as the Protar, who manage to kill the boy's robot parents before X3Z beats them back by tapping into the energies of Earth's biosphere—a talent Starling also aquires.

Called Omega on Earth, X3Z and Starling have many adventures together before the former is accidentally shot dead by a police officer. As for Starling, after letting loose too much bio-energy in a fit of rage, he turns it on himself to save the life of another.

Comment: The magazine lasted 10 issues, through 1977. The characters also appeared in *The Defenders*, where their origin was revealed (#77).

THE OMEGA MEN (C)

First Appearance: *Green Lantern* #141, 1981, DC Comics.

Physical Description: The Omega Men are humanoid, save for the fuzzball-like Elu.

Biography: The Omega Men hail from different worlds in the Vega system. Great warriors all, they are devoted to overthrowing tyrants wherever they exist. The group was founded by Primus, a human who trained under the Warlords of Okaara, and his girlfriend (later, wife) Princess Kalista of Euphorix. The core group is comprised of Tigorr, a humanoid cat and shape-changer; the lumbering, purple-skinned Broot; the emaciated, purple, winged Harpis and her crocodile-skinned sister Demonia; the celestial Auron; and Nimbus, who is death incarnate. Later members, who join to fight the powerful, evil Spider Guild, are Rynoc the Okaaran and his flying friend Zirral of Tamaran, the big green brute Uhlan, Kalista's cousin Ynda, the giant purple minstrel Oho-Besh, the golden Elu, Prince Ryand'r of Tamaran, the robotic Artin, the pixie-like Felicity, the TV-headed Doc, and the pale yellow Shlagen.

Comment: The characters were given their own title in 1982. It lasted 38 issues, through 1986.

THE ORG OF PLASM (TC, C)

First Appearance: *The Plasm Zero Issue Trading Card Set*, 1993, the River Group.

Physical Description: Existing behind a "nano-second-thin barrier" from our own reality is Dreamtime. The dominant world there is the Org of Plasm, "an immense single organism" whose human-like inhabitants regard themselves as cells of the living world. This is true even when they're on other worlds collecting beings to throw into the maws of the flesh-threshers, which return the biomass to the Org.

The Org is a massive green, orange, and yellow sphere with lumps and tendrils on its surface. The world is habitable only on the inside; returning warriors and their ships enter through pores, which dilate long enough to admit them.

Biography: Dreamtime is a world that was "built and enriched" by human dreams—our memories, fantasies, fears, and will to live. Over millions of years it grew and flourished until a war in Dreamtime caused the Great Schism that unfettered it from our reality. Now it is a self-contained biosphere where the most prized commodity is plasm, "the basic stuff of life," which is also used to grow ships known as Seekers, airborne transports, residences, and other organic units. The sentient world-force of which Plasm and all the cells are a part is known as the Org of Plasm; it is governed by the cruel Emp, who rules from the Great Palace.

Ultimately, a warrior for the Org, Supreme Acquisitor Lorca, discovers the existence of Earth behind "a gossamer reality veil." He plans to draw on humans, form a great army to overthrow the Emp, the sadistic High Gore Lord Sueraceen, and his brutal Trample-Zoms. Once a rift has been opened, nightmare creatures invade our world, humans are drawn into Dreamtime, and the fate of Earth lies in the hands of just a few people.

Comment: Dreamtime was created by writer Jim Shooter, and developed by Shooter and artist David Lapham. Though the trading cards appeared first, the concept was invented for the comic book *Warriors of Plasm*, published by Defiant Comics in 1993 (the #0 issue, which retold the trading card story, is simply called *Plasm*). The saga spilled into the comic books *Dark Dominion, The Good Guys, Charlemagne, War Dancer, Prudence & Caution,* and *Glory*. All were discontinued when Defiant closed its doors in the fall of 1994.

The complete origin of Dreamtime itself was first told in a one-shot title called *Defiant Genesis,* published in 1993.

OUTPOST 1017 (C)

First Appearance: "Outpost 1017," 1980, *1994* #11, Warren Publishing Co.

Physical Description: Located just beyond the orbit of Pluto, Outpost 1017—like the dozens of other outposts—is a sphere within a doughnut-shaped ring 200 meters in diameter. Half the space is filled by the "heavy-duty breeder power units," the other half by computers and detection gear. That leaves the sole occupant with a seven-by-three-foot living space. The Outpost is equipped with top and bottom laser turrets and a computer named Suzie.

Biography: In 2004, a lunar outpost detects signals of life from a neighboring star. NASA immediately launches the Outpost Program to provide "a protective barrier between us and . . . them." Major Henry D. Brawley has been onboard 1017 for nearly nine months of his 19-month tour when an approaching space armada refuses to acknowledge his radio messages. Reluctantly, he destroys the ships in a 90-second laser barrage. Only when Suzie scans the wreckage does she realize that the ships were not vehicles but the aliens themselves, "space dwellers who thrived in high-radiation" and who had no communication gear. They were, however, carrying a taped message from their world: "Long have we monitored your transmission wavelengths. We deem your world now ready to unite in a lasting alliance of friendship, harmony and trust . . . !"

Comment: The story was written by Rich Margopoulos and drawn by Mike Saenz.

THE OUTSIDER (L, TV, C)

First Appearance: "Arena" by Fredric Brown, June 1944, *Astounding Science Fiction*.

Physical Description: The red, round alien has "no legs or arms . . . no features." It does have retractable tentacles "about an inch in diameter and perhaps a foot and a half long," with claws that emerge from a dozen grooves on its body. The telepathic creature moves by rolling "with the fluid quickness of a drop of mercury."

Biography: The Outsiders are pirates who have been plundering Earth colonies on other worlds. An armada is sent to destroy the aliens, but no sooner do the fleets meet than pilot Bob Carson passes out, waking naked on a domed world where it's 130 degrees Fahrenheit. Near him is an Outsider, which Carson nicknames the Roller. Both beings are told that they have been brought to this place in another time and space by an ancient race, one that has "fused into a single entity" and roams freely through galaxies and other dimensions. Since a war will be costly, the entity has decided to let Carson and the Roller fight to the death as champions for their races.

Though Carson suggests a truce to the Outsider, the alien telepathically sends a wordless message that communicates "hatred and lust-to-kill." To underscore its rage, it captures and tortures a 10-legged blue lizard. Realizing that there's an energy barrier between them through which only non-living or unconscious matter can pass, the two begin hurling rocks at one another, the Outsider constructing a catapult to attack more effectively. Carson replies by tossing flaming embers at the catapult, burning it down. Finally making a stone spear and a knife, Carson goes up to the barrier, hits himself on the head with a stone, and is dazed

long enough to stumble through. Collecting his wits quickly, he harpoons the Outsider as it approaches, then stabs it to death with the knife. He is whisked back to his ship, where he discovers that the alien fleet has been vaporized by a single shot from one of his ships.

Comment: Brown's story is one of the classics of science fiction.

In March 1964, TV's *The Outer Limits* aired an episode entitled "Fun and Games," in which Earthpeople Mike Benson (Nick Adams) and Laura Hanley (Nancy Malone) are "electroported" to an otherwise uninhabited, primeval forest-like world a million million light years from Earth to battle a pair of Calco Galaxy Primitives, one male (Bill Hart) and one female (Charles MacQuarry). These big-eyed, big-teethed, bat-faced humanoids have three fingers on each hand and throw a serrated, sharp-edged boomerang. The quartet has been brought there by Anderans, aliens with a "low order of passion" that is fulfilled by watching alien couples fight to the death: The home planet of the loser will be destroyed (thus increasing Anderan pleasure). The male Primitive slays the female so it will have enough food to last 10 days instead of five. Both the male and Mike plunge from a bridge into a steaming river, the alien dying an instant before Mike, thus allowing the Anderans to electroport Mike, alive, back to Earth with Laura. Joseph Stefano, who co-scripted with Robert Specht, insists he never read "Arena," though he can't speak for Specht.

Brown's story was officially adapted as "Arena," an episode of *Star Trek*, in January 1967. The starship U.S.S. ENTERPRISE sets out after a spaceship belonging to the bipedal, reptilian Gorns—who, believing that humans have encroached on their territory, have destroyed a base on Cestus III. Both vessels are snared by the Metrons, a superintelligent race that believes disagreements should be settled by a champion from each side. Representing the humans is Captain James Kirk (William Shatner). For the Gorns: their (unnamed) captain (played by Gary Coombs and Bobby Clark). Both are sent, weaponless, to a deserted asteroid; Kirk manages to assemble a crude cannon, with which he disables the Gorn. However, he refuses to kill the alien; the Metrons return both to their ships, and they're permitted to go in peace.

In 1968 the *Star Trek* "Arena" was presented as a short story by James Blish in *Star Trek 2*. This short story to TV show to new short story metamorphosis may be unique in entertainment history.

The original short story was adapted in comic book form in Marvel Comics' *Worlds Unknown* #4, 1973.

THE OVERLORDS   (L)

First Appearance: "Guardian Angel" by Arthur C. Clarke, Winter 1950, *New Worlds*.

Physical Description: The Overlords are humanoids approximately three meters tall, with "leathery wings . . . little horns . . . [and a] barbed tail." Each alien is "ebon" with a "tremendous body" and hands with five fingers and two thumbs per hand. Sunlight bothers their "great, wide eyes . . . [with] sharply contracted" pupils, and while they breathe air through the white-hair-filtered nostrils on the sides of their broad cheeks, they carry "small cylinders" from which they take an occasional breath. The Overlords do not sleep, and they wear belts "adorned with complex mechanisms" that appear to control gravity (they come from a lesser-gravity world) and communications.

The Overlords' world is "larger than Earth," yet has lower gravity—altered by the Overlords to be so. It is not their native world, which is described only as "a much smaller world." Their wings enable the Overlords to fly on both of these planets.

Each alien ship has a "seamless metallic hull" that travels at "ninety-nine percent of the speed of light."

Biography: In 1975, ships from star NGS 549672, 40 light years away, arrive on Earth, appearing above all the major cities. Karellen, the Supervisor for Earth, announces that the Overlords will be taking charge of human affairs as they have on other worlds. Though there is talk of resistance, the nations of Earth realize that even if they could destroy the ships, their demise would crush the cities beneath them. Earth submits, and the Overlords begin eliminating poverty, sickness, ignorance, and war. But the aliens refuse to show themselves, even to United Nations Secretary General Rikki Stormgren, the only one permitted to enter Karellen's ship to speak with, if not see, the aliens. (Even he doesn't know whether there are a few or thousands of Overlords on the ship.) In time, humans learn that only the one ship was ever there, the rest being illusions; after 50 years, Karellen himself finally emerges, looking every inch the traditional devil (an image that would become associated with evil because of a curious reverberation through "the closed circle of time, from the future to the past," as Karellen later explains).

Over the years, religion fades away and humans watch recordings of human history on television-like monitors. But outer space is closed to us, and the adventurous become bored. One such person, Jan Rodricks, an engineering student, stows away onboard an alien supply ship. He is found but feels, at least, that he has shown the Overlords that humans "can't be kept in quarantine forever." But the Overlords explain to a group of reporters that there are reasons they've kept us Earthbound. But he cannot yet reveal those reasons.

Then a child, Jeffrey Angus Greggson, begins dreaming of alien worlds, stars and planets familiar and unfamiliar to the Overlord Rashaverak who has the Greggson family under surveillance. As he grows older, Jeff slips into psychic states, as does his sister, Jennifer Anne. Soon, almost every child under the age of 10 becomes like them, and Karellen addresses the world to explain why. He says that the Overlords came to Earth not just to save us from technological self-destruction, but to study our paranormal abilities, which his race lacks. The Overlords have reached an "evolutionary cul-de-sac" and can no longer change; but humans can. He says that he has been acting under instructions from a more powerful entity called the Overmind, holding us back for 100 years until our psychic abilities had fully and explosively developed, and could come "flooding out into . . . channels" that would be productive, not destructive. He announces that *Homo sapiens* is finished, that a new race has evolved. The millions of children are trained and molded "into one unit" by the unseen Overmind, and they leave Jan—who has become their ally—to report to them on the childrens' development. Ultimately, they transform themselves into pillars and curtains of light and shoot into space, and Earth disintegrates. As Jan puts it, without bitterness but with awe, they consume it as nourishment to fuel their metamorphosis.

Comment: The short story was expanded into the novel *Childhood's End* (1953). (It is the latter version discussed above.) The novel is one of the great works of science fiction; its powers are undiminished by the advent of new technologies.

OY VADER   (C)

First Appearance: *Mendy and the Golem* #7, 1982, Mendy Enterprises.

Physical Description: The robot stands approximately eight feet tall. It has a cylindrical body, a smaller white cylinder for a head, red eyes that fire a destructive laser beam, and arms that end in pincers. It wears a blue cap, a yellow shirt with a red shield on front, and a gray apron.

The robot is operated via a hand-held remote-control box.

Biography: The modern-day Klein family owns Sholem the Golem, a towering clay man who defends the Jewish people in times of danger. In his castle on the outskirts of town, the evil Dr. Hardheart builds Oy Vader to destroy the Golem and take over the (unspecified) area. The Golem destroys Oy Vader, who ends up in the junkyard. But Hardheart doesn't give up. He builds a duplicate Golem and sends him out to commit crimes; Sholem is blamed and the Kleins go to Moshe the Mayven for advice. The young genius heads to the junkyard, reassembles Oy Vader, and uses him to break into Hardheart's castle. The bogus Golem and Oy Vader fight; the latter is hit hard and goes haywire, and its out-of-control eye beams bring down the castle. The humans escape, but the fake Golem and Oy Vader are buried under tons of rubble.

Comment: The "good" Oy Vader adventure appeared in #10, 1983. The character—a parody of Darth Vader in *Star Wars* (see R2-D2 AND C-3PO)—was created by writer Leibel Estrin. Dovid Sears created the art.

"Oy" is a Yiddish expression of mild dismay.

P

THE PAIRANS (MP, L)

First Appearance: *Uchujin Tokyo Ni Arawaru* (*Unknown Satellite Over Tokyo*), 1956, Daiei Motion Picture Co.

Physical Description: The aliens are human-sized starfish who stand upright and have a big blue eye in their underbelly. Their Earthlike world Paira is located on the other side of the sun, though it obviously has greater gravity since Pairans can leap some 10 feet in the air on Earth.

Biography: The aliens land in Japan and their leader Ginko, assuming the form of a human actress, goes to see Dr. Matsuda to explain the two reasons for their visit. First, they fear that his work with the powerful new energy source Urium 101 will prove detrimental to humankind. Second, a comet called Planet R is headed directly toward Earth. The alien tells Matsuda and his colleagues that if our world's entire nuclear stockpile were fired at Planet R, the comet might be destroyed. The World Congress says no, but changes its mind when upheavals nearly destroy the Earth; by then, however, the bombs prove ineffective. With the help of the Pairans, Matsuda is able to place a Urium 101 warhead on a rocket and fires it at Planet R. The comet explodes, Earth is spared, and the Pairans head for home.

Comment: The film was released in the United States in 1960 as *Warning from Space*. Toyomi Karita plays Ginko and Isao Yamagata was Matsuda. Koji Shima directed from a script by Hideo Oguni. A novel, published in Japan, was written by Gentaro Nakajima.

PARADISE (L)

First Appearance: "Strangers to Paradise" by Christopher Anvil, 1966, *Analog*.

Physical Description: The lush jungle world is home to Earth colonies, the largest of which is Paradise City. Indigenous life forms include giant, mottled gray tigers, a many-legged segmented creature with jaws three feet long, swarming, green, yellow-jacket-like insects, and trees with thorns larger than a human forearm.

The roboid police are talking blue boxes on wheels. The *Orion* is a multi-leveled spaceyacht, tapered toward the nose, with all levels accessible by elevator. The crew of six includes Captain Vaughan Nathan Roberts, gravitor technician Cassetti, radio operator Morrissey, and cargo-control officer Hammell.

The ship carries a shuttle, or "tender," comprised of a sphere and three stubby legs.

Biography: The planet Paradise was founded to be a utopia for humans, run by a powerful planetary computer, but something has gone wrong. Initially built and staffed by trained technicians, it was opened up to overpopulated worlds, who dumped the dregs of their population on Paradise.

When a gravitor coil burns out on the Interstellar Rapid Transit Corporation ship *Orion*, several crewmembers shuttle to Paradise for help. The vessel crashlands, and the uninjured Roberts and Hammell head for the nearest city for help. Instead, they find trouble: Paradise City is the site of a rebellion, which the roboid police are unable to contain. After repairing the tender and returning to space, Roberts, Hammell, and Morrissey decide to return and straighten things out—but better armed, with fusion guns, and with their ship and its spy-screens for observing distant goings-on. They decide to unite the two warring factions by creating a fictitious warlord, Oggbad, and have him attack the city. The plan succeeds, and after their departure, if anyone were to suggest "a revolution, he'd get brained." Meanwhile, the heroes' good deeds earn them a commission in the Interstellar Patrol.

Comment: Veteran author Anvil—a pen name for Harry C. Crosby Jr.—has been publishing since 1952. His first three stories about the Interstellar Patrol—the second and third are "The Dukes of Desire" (1967) and "The King's Legions" (1967)—were rewritten as the novel *Strangers in Paradise*, published by Tower Books in 1969. Other stories in the series include "A Question of Attitude" (1967), "The Royal Road" (1968), "The Nitrocellulose Doormat" (1969), "Basic" (1969), "Test Ultimate" (1969), "The Throne and the Usurper" (1970), "Riddle Me This . . ." (1972), "The Unknown" (1972), and the novel *Warlord's World* (1975). All of the stories were published in *Analog*.

THE PARSON (L)

First Appearance: "The Marriage Machine" by O.H. Leslie, July 1957, *Fantastic Science-Fiction*.
Physical Description: An EEMC—Electronic Marriage Compatability Computor (sic)—the Parson sits in its own room. It's "some fifty feet" long, with a chrome face, "dials and counters merrily turning." Information about a person looking for a mate is stored on "tiny disks." The machine takes just under a minute to do its computing and spit out disks with potentially compatible mates. Hard copy is provided by a "teleprinting machine."
Biography: In 1970, the 10-year-old MAA (Matrimonial Advisory Association) uses the EEMC, nicknamed the Parson, to match people with suitable mates. Betty Bryce works for Warren de Witt in Branch Thirty-two, and tries to find a mate for client Douglas Brady—unaware that he's really come to this branch to check *her* out, the EEMC at Branch Twenty-one in Hartford, Connecticut, having pronounced them compatible.
Comment: Leslie is a pseudonym for Henry Slesar, who already had another story in that issue, "The Secret of Marracott Deep." Slesar sold his first story, "The Brat," to *Imaginative Tales* in 1955, and has also written for soap operas and prime time television shows.
See also THE GIANT YMIR.

PAUL JOHNSON (MP)

First Appearance: *Not of This Earth*, 1957, Los Altos Productions/Allied Artists.
Physical Description: The alien looks like a human save for his all-white eyes, which are usually hidden behind sunglasses. In addition to telepathy and hypnotic powers, Johnson can fire deadly energy blasts from his eyes.
His umbrella-like slave is approximately a yard in diameter and is kept folded in a tube until needed. It kills victims by folding itself over their head and biting into a major vein in the neck.
Biography: Davanna is a world wracked by nuclear war, the radiation from which is responsible for the dire state of its inhabitants, whose "agglutin is disintegrating at an uninterrupted rate." They need blood, and Paul Johnson is sent to Earth to see if human blood will fill the bill. Settling into a room and hiring a private nurse, Nadine, to give him regular transfusions, Johnson sends his alien slave out to kill people, whose blood he ships back to Davanna via matter transmitter—and uses to cure his own anemia. After just a few weeks, a woman arrives from Davanna to inform Paul that the world is nearly dead and they must remain on Earth. Since the woman needs blood, Johnson sneaks her to the office of Dr. Frederick W. Rochelle (for whom Nadine works) and gives her an injection, accidentally using blood from a rabid dog. The woman dies, apparently dooming Paul's race to extinction. Meanwhile, Nadine has been hypnotized and ordered to teleport herself to Davanna. When she fails to meet her boyfriend, police officer Harry Sherbourne, the motorcycle cop chases Johnson in his car. Due to his sensitivity to loud sounds, the alien is driven mad by the police siren and drives off a cliff. Nadine is rescued and the threat is ended—for now. Watching Paul's funeral is another white-eyed soul from Davanna.
Comment: Paul Birch plays Johnson, Beverly Garland is Nadine, Ann Carrol is the unnamed Davannan woman, William Roerick is Rochelle, and Morgan Jones is Sherbourne. The film was directed by Roger Corman from a script by Charles B. Griffith and Mark Hanna. The film was remade in 1988 with Arthur Roberts as the alien. Jim Wynorski directed.

PEABODY (C)

First Appearance: *Zot!* #1, 1984, Eclipse Enterprises.
Physical Description: A humanoid, Peabody has platinum-colored "skin" with blue hands. His metallic "clothing" consists of blue "pants," a blue beehive "hat," a dark blue "dinner jacket," and dark blue "shoes."
Biography: On Earth of an alternate dimension, pre-teen Zachary T. Paleozogt—a.k.a. Zot—lives with his parents and butler Peabody. One day, Zot's parents leave and don't come back; Zot and Peabody live alone, "Peabz" as a "stand-in parent," the boy throwing himself into studying, athletics, and marksmanship to compensate for his feelings of desertion. Deciding to use his skills to benefit his world, he dons boot jets and other gadgets created by his Uncle Max and becomes a

young superhero. Years later, when he's 13, the key to a door at the edge of the universe is stolen from the planet Sirius IV, and the High Priest sends purple, cyclopean robots, his Holy Robot Squadron, to reclaim it. These robots assault other worlds, including our own Earth, searching for the missing key, and Zot fights them wherever they appear. During one battle, Earth girl Jenny Weaver and her brother Butch fall through a dimensional barrier and become Zot's regular sidekicks.

Comment: The characters were created, written, and drawn by Scott McCloud. There were 21 issues in all.

PERN (L, C)

First Appearance: "Weyr Search" by Anne McCaffrey, October 1967, *Analog*.

Physical Description: With "air man could breathe . . . water he could drink, and . . . a gravity which permitted man to walk confidently erect," Pern is one of six planets circling the star Rukbat. The day is just over 24 Earth hours, there are 362 days each Turn (year), and it has terrestrial seasons and icy poles. Pern boasts two large continents and two moons, Belior and Timor.

The indigenous life on Pern is vaguely Earthlike and contains: Needlethorn Plants; six-legged gecko-like creatures called Crawlers; parasitic insects called Springs; barbed fish called Packtails; fierce Tunnel Snakes; furred, eagle-like Wherries; and many more, including animals and plants brought from Earth. Most unusual and magnificent of all, however, are the dragonets, which resemble hawk-sized dragons of terrestrial myth. The dragonets are engineered into "winged, tailed, and firebreathing dragons" who are able to teleport themselves and their riders from place to place and even to other times. These dragons are from 25 to 40 meters long, with a wingspread 75 percent of the creature's length. The dragons are blue, gold, green, brown, bronze, white, and shades thereof.

The planet Red Star is a rogue that was captured by Rukbat. It has a "wildly erratic elliptical orbit," which brings it close to Pern once every 200 Turns (the perihelion is called a Pass; the 200-year period when the worlds are apart is called an Interval). Red Star's dominant life form are Threads, which originated in the comets that travel in tandem with Red Star and were pulled from the ice by the planet's gravity. Threads are so-called because once every Pass the spores come "dropping through Pern's skies like silver threads" and, with "mindless voracity," eat any organic matter they

encounter, including crops, settlers, and even the settlers' non-metal clothing.

Biography: Some time in the future, Pern is colonized by the 6,000-odd occupants of three ships, *Yokohama, Buenos Aires,* and *Bahrain*; in time, contact with Earth is lost. Initially, colonists don't understand why there isn't flora more than 200 years old, and why plants seem to grow so quickly—until the first Threadfall. Before the colonists understand the threat of Threads, hundreds die. Thanks to geneticist Kitty Ping, one of the Earth colonists, a solution is found. Some settlers have "a high empathy rating and some innate telepathic ability" and form a special bond with the dragonets. Kitty heads a program to engineer huge dragons from the dragonets, the telepathic rider and dragon using brain, wing, and fire to immolate Threads as they fall.

There were 18 dragons at first, and places called Weyrs are established to provide boarding, training, breeding, and access to settlements, called Holds. The colonists survive the first onslaught, the dragons prosper, and all go about their business until the second Pass. The new attack lasts 50 years; led by F'lar and his dragon Mnementh, F'lar's half-brother F'nor and his dragon Canth, and Lessa and her queen dragon Ramoth, the dragon army is roused from decades of inactivity to meet the challenge. By the end of the third attack there are seven Weyrs: Fort Weyr, Benden Weyr, High Reaches Weyr, Igen Weyr, Ista Weyr, Telgar Weyr and Southern Weyr. But the people become complacent during a Long Interval, and the dragonriders fall into disfavor as strong-backed souls who aren't contributing to the welfare of the agrarian society. A new Pass changes the Pernians' minds, and when the danger is ended the heroic Jaxom—rider of the dragon Ruth—and Lady Sharra of Southern Hold wonder if it might be possible to "reach the Red Star . . . [and] wipe out forever the threat of Thread." And the saga continues . . .

Comment: "Weyr Search" won a prestigious Hugo award. McCaffrey also wrote "Dragonrider" for *Analog* (December 1967–January 1968); the original novella was slightly rewritten and combined with "Dragonrider" as the novel *Dragonflight* (1968), the first volume of the Dragonriders of Pern trilogy. (The *Analog* stories were exquisitely illustrated by John Schoenherr.) Volume two is *Dragonquest* (1971), followed by *The White Dragon* (1978). McCaffrey next wrote three novels about the teenagers Menolly and Piemur, for young adults. Their story was told in *Dragonsong* (1976), in which Menolly's family doesn't understand her or her musical abilities ("harpers" pass on Pern's all-important traditions and lore) and she's forced to run away; its sequel *Dragonsinger* (1977), in which Menolly comes to the Harper Hall, where she is free to sing; and *Dragondrums* (1979), about Piemur's lovely soprano voice changing and causing upheavals in his life. (These three were published in one volume in 1984 entitled *The Harper Hall of Pern*.) They were followed by *Moreta, Dragonlady of Pern* (1983); *Dragonsdawn* (1988), a prequel about the colonization of Pern; *Renegades of Pern* (1988); *All the Weyrs of Pern* (1991); and *The Chronicles of Pern*: *First Fall* (1994), five stories about the early days of Pern. The book *The Girl Who Heard Dragons* (1994) contained the short story of the same name, along with other non-Pern McCaffrey works. In that tale, the teenage girl Aramina of Pern hears dragons and longs for them, much to the distress of her struggling family. Most recently the author has published *The Dolphins of Pern* (1994), a tale set at the same time as *All the Weyrs of Pern*. This novel is the saga of Masterfishman Alemi, brother of Menolly; Readis, the son of Aramina; and the dragonrider Tlion, and their relationship with the wonrous dolphins of Pern.

In 1993, Eclipse published a graphic novel based on *Dragonflight*.

McCaffrey is also the author of *Dinosaur Planet* (1978), in which the Exploratory and Evaluation Corps of the Federated Sentient Planets sends the ship ARCT-10 to explore the planet Ireta, and the crew becomes stranded on a world like Mesozoic Earth. She followed it with *Dinosaur Planet Survivors* (1984), in which heroes Kai and Varian protect the world from a colony of mutineers and pirates.

THE PHANTOM CRUISER (TV, C)

First Appearance: *Space Ghost and Dino Boy*, September 1966, CBS.
Physical Description: The golden space cruiser has a cigar-shaped fuselage with a likeness of Space Ghost's mask on the top, and two shark-fin-like wings on either side. The ship can become invisible, has a "revitalizer" unit that repairs damages and a radionic interference screen to filter out radiation, track a variety of frequencies, and more.
Biography: Based on Ghost Planet, Space Ghost is a super-powered interstellar police officer who travels aboard the *Phantom Cruiser* with his teenage companions Jan and Jayce and the space

monkey Blip. Jan and Jayce have their own "space coupe," which they frequently pilot. Among the worlds in Space Ghost's jurisdiction are Zio—home of the Space Congress, which creates the laws he is sworn to uphold—Zonnda, molten Moltar, and Balgorz.
Comment: The characters starred in 42 10-minute-long cartoons produced by Hanna-Barbera. After the two-year run of their original show, reruns were seen on *The Space Ghost/Frankenstein Jr. Show* on NBC from November, 1976 to November 1977, in *Hanna-Barbera's World of Super Adventure*, which was syndicated in September 1980, then in 22 new episodes, which aired on *Space Stars* on NBC from September 1981 to September 1982. They were also seen in #s 3–7 of *Hanna-Barbera Super TV Heroes* comic book, published by Gold Key in 1968–69.

PHANTOM FROM SPACE (MP)

First Appearance: *Phantom from Space*, 1953, Planet Filmplays/United Artists.
Physical Description: A humanoid nearly seven feet tall, the dome-headed, earless alien is a silicon-based life form, visible only when viewed in infrared light. Underneath his spacesuit, the alien wears tight white trunks. It isn't revealed from which planet he hails, only that he came through a billion miles of space (which puts his home somewhere between Saturn and Uranus where there aren't any planets).
Biography: An object enters the Earth's atmosphere at 5,000 miles an hour, and Lt. Hazen of the Federal Communications Commission investigates. Meanwhile, a spacesuited figure has been murdering and panicking citizens around Santa Monica, California. Eventually cornered in an oil refinery, the creature doffs its suit and makes an invisible getaway. The suit is taken to a lab for study, and when the alien tries to get it back—he can't survive for long in our atmosphere—he's spotted by scientist Barbara Randall when she switches on an infrared lamp. He flees, is pursued and hit with infrared light, and loses the last vestiges of his strength while climbing a ladder. The Phantom falls, and only after he dies and vaporizes do scientists conclude that he came here in peace and killed from fear, not hatred.
Comment: Dick Sands is the Phantom, Ted Cooper is Hazen, and Noreen Nash is Barbara. W. Lee Wilder (director Billy's brother) directed from a Bill Raynor and Myles Wilder script.

Gravity shuts down inside the *Phoebe*. © Better Publications.

THE PHOEBE   (L)

First Appearance: ''A Problem in Diatonics'' by Nelson S. Bond, August 1940, *Thrilling Wonder Stories*.

Physical Description: A space luxury liner, the *Phoebe* has ''artificial gravs'' and ''skiffs,'' which serve as lifeboats. The ship has all the facilities of an oceangoing liner, but is otherwise undescribed.

The known officers are Captain Victor Bjornsted and Chief Engineer Enderby.

Biography: Returning to Earth from Io City spaceport, the music-hating Captain Bjornsted is unhappy about his daughter Joy seeing ''Red'' Starr, the ship's bull fiddle-playing bandmaster. While he's wresting her from Red's arms on the dance floor, the ship collides with a rogue asteroid, crippling the ship. The skipper orders the passengers to enter the skiffs and cast off, Joy, Red, and he taking the last skiff—a ''battered old crate'' that's low on fuel. The trio heads for the asteroid Obler III in the hopes of collecting enough fuel to get home; there, while rappelling down a shaft, looking for permalgam ore, Joy falls and is trapped on the bottom. Because the men don't know *how* deep she is, they're afraid to use explosives. Fortunately, Red is able to play a note on his bass viol to ''set up a vibratory equilibrium in the shaft,'' determine exactly how deep it is, and blast an exit right above Joy's head. Collecting the ore, they load up the ship and head for the moon.

Comment: Bond worked in public relations when he sold his first science fiction story, ''Down the Dimensions,'' to *Astounding Science Fiction* in 1937. His two most popular series were stories about space traveler Lancelot Biggs, written from

1939 to 1943, and about inventor Pat Pending, written from 1942 to 1957.

THE PHOENIX (1)   (MP)

First Appearance: *Journey to the Far Side of the Sun*, 1969, Century 21 Productions/Universal Pictures.

Physical Description: A *Saturn V*-style rocket, the British-launched *Phoenix* carries a two-passenger capsule into space; the capsule is a gumdrop-shaped duplicate of the Apollo command module. A lander, the *Dove*, is a two-passenger shuttle stored in a cylindrical hold behind the *Phoenix*. The *Phoenix* is able to make a roughly 200 million mile trip in three weeks.

Biography: Colonel Glenn Ross, a veteran of two missions to Mars, and John Kanel are launched into space toward a planet that lies *exactly* on the other side of the sun from the Earth, which ''explains'' why it wasn't discovered until now. (Gravitational perturbations would have been noticed years before, but never mind.) Hibernating for the three-week trip, the men crashland, Kanel is seriously wounded, and Ross is astounded to find himself back on Earth, but with reverse vision. In time, Ross realizes that the new world is an exact, backwards duplicate of Earth, and that his own ''doppelganger'' must have reached the other

Advertising art picturing the *Phoenix* and the ''two'' Earths. © Universal Pictures.

Earth. After much intrigue, he is able to return to his home world.

Comment: Roy Thinnes stars as Ross and Ian Hendry is Kane; Lynn Loring is Ross's wife Sharon. Robert Parrish directed from a screenplay by Gerry and Sylvia Anderson and Donald James, from a story by the Andersons. The film was shown as *Doppelganger* in England.

THE PHOENIX (2) (TV, C)

First Appearance: *Gatchaman*, 1972, Tasunko Productions.

Physical Description: The ship has a gray fuselage like an SST with perpendicular wings toward the back, ending in torpedo-shaped pods. There's a hatch in the bottom of the craft, which can travel in the air or in space and fire destructive beams.

Biography: In the future, the villainous Zoltar of the planet Spectra decides to conquer the Milky Way. All that stands in his way is the G-Force, comprised of Earthbound leader Mark Venture and spacefaring warriors Jason, Tiny, Princess, and Keyop. The heroes patrol the galaxy onboard the *Phoenix*, while Mark works at the team's home base, Center Neptune, an underwater facility off Decoy Island.

The team is assisted by the computerized robot 7-Zark-7, which looks like a blue time-release capsule with an orange midsection; it wears a small orange cape that has a white 7 on the back, and has two arms, two legs, and a pair of antennae.

Comment: The animated *Gatchaman* series debuted in the United States as *Battle of the Planets* in October 1978; 80 half-hour adventures were syndicated. More recently, reruns of the show have aired as *G-Force*. Casey Kasem provides the voice for Mark Venture, Ronnie Schell is Jason, Alan Young is Keyop and 7-Zark-7, Keye Luke is Zoltar, Janet Waldo is Princess, and Alan Dinehart is Tiny.

Gold Key published 10 issues of a *Battle of the Planets* comic book from 1979 to 1980.

THE PHUMEN (C)

First Appearance: "The Starqueen," 1982, *1994* #24, Warren Publishing Co.

Physical Description: The talking, apelike humanoids wear tunics, trunks, and wristbands. They are extremely powerful and fight with spears.

The talking robot Guskey is a roughly four-foot-tall cylinder with tentacular arms nearly five feet long, a domed head, and three rockets below for flying and hovering.

Biography: When the Earth starship *Pegasus* explodes and crashes on Altaires 7, 100 humans and servo-robs perish—save for the rob-pilot Guskey and a dying pregnant woman. Guskey delivers the baby girl named Deirdre. They don't encounter the Phumen for four years; fascinated with the lovely young girl, the aliens worship her as a "white goddess." Growing to womanhood, she convinces her ape-lover to rebel against the leader—then kills her mate and assumes leadership herself.

When an Earthship arrives on Altaires 7, Deirdre is repulsed by the "hairless men"—especially when, without provocation, they attack the Phumen. She leads her apes in battle, mounting a ferocious assault against the humans. Alas, Guskey perishes during the fight, and she vows over his inert form that no aliens shall ever again set foot on her world.

Comment: There are no author credits for the tale; the art is by Delando Nino.

PLANET X (MP)

First Appearance: *Kaiju Daisenso* (*The Giant Monster War*), 1965, Toho Co., Ltd.

Physical Description: Orbiting the sun not far from Jupiter (the planet looms large in the skies), Planet X has a cratered surface that appears a mottled blue/green from space. The planet, which appears to be about the size of our moon, somehow possesses an Earthlike atmosphere. It is not known how long night and day are, as the planet is seen only during the night.

The rocky interior of the world is laced with gold, and the inhabitants live underground in spartan chambers accessed by long, silver corridors. They reach the surface via elevator tubes that rise from the ground and are protected by laser beams; when the elevators are not in use, the tops are camouflaged to look like the planet's surface. Flying saucers enter the complex via a large cave with a stone door.

The natives, both men and women, wear powder blue jumpsuits with dark blue vests, gloves, and cowls with a single antenna in the center. The men wear black goggles. All of the aliens are sensitive to loud sounds.

Their flying saucers are white with blue trim and consist of a central plate with a dome on the bottom and one on top; the upper dome is ringed with windows and has a smaller dome above. The interior consists of chairs and a round table with a sunken, rotating globe of the Earth. The saucers possess tractor beams that can lift many tons of matter.

The P-1 rocket is approximately 50 feet long and bullet-shaped, with a rocket on the bottom and four cylinders attached to the sides. Extendible rods emerge from the bottoms of the cylinders and serve as landing gear. The hatch is near the top, the door folding down and serving as an outside elevator. The ship holds two astronauts but can accommodate three.

Biography: When Planet X is discovered, the World Space Authority sends astronauts F. Glenn and K. Fuji to investigate aboard their P-1. While Fuji goes to plant the U.N., Japanese, and U.S. flags, Glenn and the rocket disappear. An elevator emerges from the ground, Fuji enters, and he finds his companion and the P-1 underground with the Controller of Planet X and his associates. They explain that their planet is being ravaged by Monster Zero (actually, King Ghidorah; see THE KILAAKS and M-11), and that they want to borrow the Earth monsters Godzilla and Rodan to defeat it. The astronauts carry their request back to Earth, it's approved, and a trio of saucers fly off with the monsters in tow. However, it turns out the Xians need our monsters for an entirely different reason: Short on water, they plan to conquer Earth. They begin by blowing up the P-1 at the space center, then put all three monsters under the control of synthetic brain waves and set them loose to wreck civilization. Fortunately, Glenn learns that an alarm can drive the aliens mad, and he has the sounds blared over loudspeakers. While the Xians cover their ears in agony, they can't control their saucers, which explode in flight. Liberated, Godzilla and Rodan thrash King Ghidorah, who flies off (though he remains on Earth).

Comment: Nick Adams stars as Glenn and Akira Takarada is Fuji. The film was directed by Ishiro Honda from a screenplay by Shinichi Sekizawa. The film was released in the United States in 1966 as *Monster Zero*, but it has also been seen here by its international release title *Invasion of the Astro-Monster*. (That is also the English title on the Japanese laserdisc release.)

PLANET Z (L)

First Appearance: "Revenge of the Robots" by Lawrence Chandler, December 1952, *Fantastic Adventures*.

Physical Description: Discovered in '81 (1981?), Planet Z is the planet farthest from the sun as well as the smallest, "half the size of Mercury." It has no moons, an atmosphere "about like Venus," and is ruled by the birdpeople, humans with great wings and telepathic powers.

The Venusian "giants" have "slate-grey bodies like tall shadows" and wear "jeweled ornaments" around their waists.

The alien ships are of "all shapes and sizes, from the trim, tear-drop fighters, to the huge sky freighters, each carrying a hundred thousand fighting men." The fleet is surrounded "by an immense halo of living flame" which destroys any ship that tries to pass through.

The space sphere has an inner and outer shell, the latter of which is 10 feet thick and made of Solminum.

Biography: When daredevil pilot Gloria Kane decides to fly a space sphere to the largely unexplored Planet Z, the network Zenith Tele-cast gets exclusive rights to the coverage. They hire veteran Larry Lipton as her copilot and, with tele-camera operator "Focus" Forgan, head for Planet Z. Upon landing, they're captured by birdpeople who have taken over the Earth installations. The natives destroy the sphere and take the trio before King Gundar in their city Koba, where the travellers learn the aliens and their allies the Venusians are planning to invade Earth. Forgan is placed in a device that makes him a child-sized birdman, and the three are allowed to join the invasion force. The Earth fleet is decimated, but Larry persuades the Gundar-hating alien Corono to help him steal a ship. Landing, Larry, Gloria, Corono, and the caged Forgan contact the military and make plans to set up a base. Even as the invaders land, Corono helps his friends make a dye that is invisible to the naked eye, but can be seen by people wearing special glasses. Cloth and paint are made from the dye which enable ships and soldiers to sneak up on the invaders. Meanwhile, Larry, Corono, and Gloria are captured and taken to Gundar's headquarters, where the men are tortured. Gundar betrays his Venusian allies by killing their leader, Hag-U. Fortunately, Corono is able to release captives who had been turned into birdpeople; sweeping Gundar over a thousand feet into the sky, they drop him and put an abrupt end to the invasion.

Comment: The novel-length tale was illustrated by Ed Emshwiller. Despite the title, there isn't a robot to be found in the entire story. During this period in the early 1950s, *Fantastic Adventures* was art directed by Leo Summers. As an artist, Summers became a regular contributor to John Campbell's *Analog* in the 1960s-70s and, in the mid-1970s, drew comic book stories for the Warren and Atlas lines. This superb but critically neglected artist died shortly after completing evocative illustrations of the Kashpagu, ethereal aliens seeking the ultimate beauty in Perigee Books' multi-artist compendium *The Transgalactic Guide to Solar System M-17* (1981).

THE P.M.S. VERMILLYON (L)

First Appearance: "Seedling from the Stars" by John Jakes, 1970, *Worlds of Tomorrow #25.*

Physical Description: The Dart Line-built ship is an L-drive space vehicle with a bridge, automatic pilot, and an unlimited supply of fuel. It is otherwise undescribed. The "P.M.S." designation is not explained.

Biography: In the 50th century, humankind and the alien Hoark—who are never seen outside their spaceships—vie for supremacy on distant worlds. The humans, the Libmovers, appear to be losing. Alone, out of rage, not cowardice, Roberto Gilchrist, captain of the *Vermillyon*, flees the planet Frix (or Frax, he can't recall). After searching for a safe haven for eight months, he is refused permission to land on Murmur's Mercutio, a human planet under attack by the aliens. He presses on and reaches a planetoid some five kilometers in diameter. Landing at one of the five pyramid-like structures, he enters and is met by 18-year-old Miriam, a genetically engineered "supergirl." She and her mate Charls were sent from the planet Pristobal onboard this "seed" world to keep the human race alive. But Charls died outside when his suit ripped and, now alone, Miriam asks Gilchrist to take her away. He agrees and they sail off, hotly pursued by the Hoark, but filled with hope.

Comment: See EMANUEL for more on author Jakes.

PREDATOR (MP, L, C)

First Appearance: *Predator*, 1987, Twentieth Century-Fox.

Physical Description: Standing seven feet, two inches tall, the bipedal alien has a piranha-like mouth with a row of sharp teeth on the bottom and two fangs on top; two huge tusks that point up and inward from its chin, and two more that point down and are angled toward each other. A ruff of bone surrounds its face to the jawline, and long, black spikes, like "dreadlocks," hang down from the sides of this. Predator has two small, deep-set eyes; apparently, it does not see well in regular light, but is able to see objects by radiant heat. Its blood is luminous green, and the barrel-chested monster has five huge claws on each hand.

The creature wears armor that enables it to blend, chameleon-like, with whatever it passes in front of, though there's a slight displacement of the image as Predator moves in front of it. A wrist-controller operates suit functions, which include a miniature nuclear bomb, a beam on the front of its helmet that locks onto the heat of its prey; an articulated cannon on its left shoulder; and a small, two-pronged pitchfork that extends from the back of its right wrist. The wrist-controller also contains a compact medical kit. Predator wears a kind of mesh body-stocking under its armor and often carries a spear-like weapon.

Extremely agile and powerful, the creature can toss humans around with ease and is able to jump great distances.

Biography: From Earth orbit, a spaceship jettisons a pod containing Predator, which lands in a Central American jungle. Shortly after, mercenaries led by Major Alan "Dutch" Schaefer and Sergeant Blain join CIA operative Dillon on a mission to the jungle. Ostensibly, they're to rescue a cabinet minister from rebels; in truth, Dillon wants to wipe out the guerrilla base. En route, the men find members of a previous team flayed and strung upside-down from trees. After destroying the base and its occupants, the team heads for a rendezvous with their chopper. As they proceed through the valley, Predator picks them off one-by-one, ripping out hearts, blowing off limbs, and decorating its belt with skulls as trophies. When only Dutch is left alive, he and the monster end up in hand-to-hand combat. The creature throws Dutch in a river, where he's covered with mud; the alien suddenly can't see him, and Dutch realizes the mud is keeping in his body heat. That night, covered with mud, Dutch rigs a giant log to crush the monster, then lures the alien into his trap. As Dutch stands triumphantly over the fallen creature, it chuckles and activates the nuclear device in its wrist. Realizing what's afoot, Dutch runs out of range before the blast and makes his rendezvous with the chopper.

But Predators are not finished with Earth. Another comes to our world, landing in the Los Angeles of 1997, a city dominated by gang warfare. Lt. Michael Harrigan is a tough, decorated police officer who becomes increasingly alarmed as drug dealers and his own people begin dying in horrible ways. But when Special Agent Peter Keyes arrives in Los Angeles, Harrigan is told not to bother investigating these deaths: Keyes and his people have been hot on the alien's trail for some time, and have what they think is a foolproof plan to capture and freeze Predator so they can study it. Naturally, the team hasn't thought of everything, and the creature wipes them out. Popping his car trunk, Harrigan loads up with weapons, battles the alien through the city, and finishes it off in its spaceship, which is hidden underground. Other Predators suddenly appear, but instead of killing Harrigan they salute him for his courage and depart.

Comment: Arnold Schwarzenegger stars as Dutch in *Predator*, with Carl Weathers as Dillon and Jesse Ventura as Blain. John McTiernan directed from a script by Jim and John Thomas. Danny Glover stars as Harrigan in the 1990 sequel, with Gary Busey as Keyes. Stephen Hopkins directed from a script by the Thomases. Kevin Peter Hall is the monster in both films.

In the trophy room of Predator's spaceship in *Predator 2*, the head of an ALIEN is clearly visible.

Jove Books published novelizations of both films in 1987 and 1990, respectively. In 1994, Bantam published the novel *Aliens vs. Predator: Prey* by Steve and Stephani Perry (1994), first in a series of novels based on the Dark Horse comic book.

In comic books, Dark Horse has published a number of limited-run series, beginning with four issues of *Predator* and two issues of *Predator 2*, released to tie-in with the films, as well as the mini-series *Predator: Big Game* (four issues), *Predator: Bloody Sands of Time* (two issues), *Predator: Cold War* (four issues), *Predator: Race War* (five issues), *Aliens Versus Predator* (five issues), *Aliens/ Predator: The Deadliest of the Species* (two issues), and two cross-company teamups: *Predator Versus Magnus Robot Fighter* (two issues, with Valiant Comics) and *Batman Versus Predator* (three issues, with DC Comics). In the last of these, the Caped Crusader wears "a sonar unit and reflective body armor" to fight the alien.

THE PRIMUS (L)

First Appearance: "Signboard of Space" by Frederic Arnold Kummer Jr., December 1939, *Thrilling Wonder Stories*.

Physical Description: The spaceship has four forward rockets two feet in diameter, a navigation room, a control room equipped with a telescope, and bunks for the crew. It is otherwise undescribed. The captain's log is recorded, not written.

The crew consists of Captain Howard Markland, rocket engineer Keppler, physicist/chemist Dr. Varian, and biologist Braybrook.

Biography: The spaceship *Primus* is lost on humankind's First Martian Expedition. While a second ship, the *Martian*, is built to succeed it, the *New York* finds the log of the *Primus* floating in space. They play it back and learn that all went

well until the *Primus* tried to land. One rocket was clogged and Braybrook donned his spacesuit and unblocked it, perishing in the resulting ignition. The survivors landed, learned that the air was breathable, and went exploring. They found tree-high cactuses, "curious fungoid shrubs," and other odd vegetation. They also discovered that the canals were simply vegetation growing along well-fertilized lines. Continuing to explore, they came upon a deserted city built for beings of "Cyclopean" proportions, towering buildings of "terraces, parapets, flying arches," and doors 20 feet tall. In one building, they found 12, 10-foot-tall human statues made of a "translucent amberlike substance," one of which held metal plates with a message in Martian characters. They realized that the markings were similar to the design of the canals, and Varian struggled to translate the tablets. Unfortunately, an electrical short caused a fire that destroyed half the crew's food supply, and they were forced to leave at once for Earth. Varian kept working on the message and learned that debris from a comet caused a slow, 10-year petrification of the planet's humanoid inhabitants. The "statues" were actually dead Martians, and the tablets (and canals) a warning not to breathe the poisoned air of Mars.

The warning came too late for the crew of the *Primus*, though Markland was able to send his log back to Earth in a dust-free container and turn the ship toward deep space. He added an amazing postscript, though. The Martians didn't all die. The tablets revealed that a male and female baby were "kept under glass from the moment of birth" and sent to Earth in a fully automated rocket. Landing here, Admi and Ehv were the forerunners of the human race (which grew shorter than Martians because of the greater gravity).

Comment: "Adam and Eve" stories are omnipresent in science fiction, though Kummer's novelette is one of the best. It was illustrated by Virgil Finlay, one of the great science fiction and fantasy illustrators of the century.

PROCYON 4 (C)

First Appearance: *Quack* #5, 1977, Star*Reach Productions.

Physical Description: Commonly known as the "Planet of the Ducks," Procyon 4 is a lush, G-type planet inhabited by "funny animal life" as well as "ogres, trolls, advertising executives and other unsavory characters." G-type worlds do not typically have forests, but Procyon 4 is an exception.

Biography: In the future, Starfleet sends Kerwin Keystone of Earth to Procyon 4 to investigate the degeneration of a structured society to "an *unstructured violent society*." The half-aardvark, half-platypus teleports down from his spaceship and meets an anthropomorphic duck. The two discuss how Earth once underwent duckmania so intense that civilization nearly fell; thus, in the 1990s, all of Earth's ducks were rocketed into space. Kerwin wonders aloud if "fowl play" also caused the fall of this world. His duck companion assures him that it did not, that he's the only duck on Procyon 4, and Kerwin is beamed back to his ship. Once he's gone, the (nameless) duck rounds up other ducks, who have been hiding, and informs them that it's time to move on again, one of them complaining, "Can we help it if we're popular?"

Comment: The characters were created by writer/artist Ken Macklin, who produced different animals-in-space adventures in *Quack* #s 3, 5, and 6.

PROFESSOR JAMESON (L)

First Appearance: "The Jameson Satellite" by Neil R. Jones, July 1931, *Amazing Stories*.

Physical Description: Jameson's human brain is located "in the coned head of a machine," which the brain controls. The machine itself is comprised of "a metal cubed body, equipped with four [jointed] metal legs and six metal tentacles." A ring of TV cameras look out from "around the base of the coned head, while a single eye . . . [looks] directly upward." Jameson communicates via mental telepathy.

As a Zorome, he neither sleeps nor requires food or fuel of any kind. Though he can't die, he can be killed; for example, 22D-5 and 429C-267 have their "metal skulls . . . crushed like eggshells" in his second adventure ("The Planet of the Double Sun," *Amazing Stories*, February 1932).

Biography: In 1950, to keep his body from disintegrating upon death, Professor Jameson has his nephew Douglas Jameson rocket him into space "in the belief that his corpse would withstand the rigors of time eternal." After 40 million years, the alien Zoromes—"machine men" from the planet Zor—discover the rocket. The Zoromes had long ago "renounced their flesh and blood bodies . . . [for] machines which knew no death but only repair and replacement." They revive Jameson's brain and, finding it wise and inquisitive, place it in a robot body. As 21M-M392, he accompanies them throughout the universe in search of knowledge and "unparalleled adventure." (Meanwhile, after

"a great war [humanity] degenerated into barbarism . . . finally disappearing entirely from the Earth." This was followed by the ant cycle and bird cycle on Earth, after which the world was claimed by the Terseg of Mars, "queer animals with wings [and] scientific intelligence." Eventually, even they passed on as the sun died.

Jameson's frequent companion is 744U-21; 20R-654 is the pilot of their missile-shaped spaceship; 25X-987 is the leader of the expedition; and 72N-4783, is an "eminent philosopher."

Comment: Jones published 25 Jameson stories. Eighteen of these are collected in *The Planet of the Double Sun*, *The Sunless World*, *Space War*, *Twin Worlds* (all 1967), and *Doomsday on Ajiat* (1968).

Jones's first story, "The Death's Head Meteor," published in *Air Wonder Stories* in 1930, was the first science fiction story to use the word "astronaut."

PROFESSOR TANGA   See DR. PUNA.

THE PROJECTILE   (L, C, MP)

First Appearance: *From the Earth to the Moon* by Jules Verne, *Journal des Debats*, 1865.

Physical Description: The Projectile is "cylindro-conical" with a bed of water three feet deep, on which a series of watertight wooden floors float, creating a giant spring, of sorts, to protect the passengers—who are seated on couches in the center of the floor—from the recoil of the launch. The walls are lined with "a thick padding of leather, fastened upon springs of the best steel." The doorway is a "narrow aperture" in the wall with an aluminum door held on by powerful screws. There are four windows: two in the walls, one in the top, and one in the bottom (visible when the water is drained and the wooden floor is removed). Gas fixtures provide heat and light. Food and drink are stored in reservoirs. Enough air for two months is provided by recycling, using chlorate of potassium and caustic potash.

The projectile weighs 19,250 pounds, has a diameter of 108 inches, and a living space of 54 square feet under a 12-foot ceiling. It has gunpowder-fired rockets for landing and taking off from the moon.

The gun that launches it, the Columbiad, is 900 feet long, six feet thick, and weighs 68,040 tons. The Projectile achieves its escape velocity of 12,000 yards a second thanks to 400,000 pounds of guncotton.

Biography: Shortly after the Civil War, the Gun Club of Baltimore begins to fear that "the future of gunnery in America is lost." To this end, club president Impey Barbicane proposes a trip to the moon, to make it the 37th state. The funds raised, the Columbiad is constructed in Stones Hill, Florida, for if the gun exploded, the loss of the state was regarded as no catastrophe.

The Projectile is fired at 10:46:40 on December 1, 186– (sic). In it are Barbicane, adventurous Frenchman Michel Ardan—who contributed to the design of the Projectile—metal-forger Captain Nicholl, and two dogs, Diana and Satellite. The trip is supposed to take 97 hours, 13 minutes, and 20 seconds, but the Projectile goes off course due to the tug of a passing meteor. The travelers are able to pass close to the moon, determining that it grew "older quicker" than the Earth and that the "organized beings, and . . . vegetation" that once flourished are now gone. After making their study, the crew uses their rockets to return to Earth. They land in the Pacific Ocean some 200 miles from the coast of the United States and sink. Fortunately, the corvette *Susquehanna* witnesses their return on December 12 and rescues the floating Projectile.

Comment: The first novel ends with the launch. The sequel, *Round the Moon*, was published in the same magazine in 1869. Both were published in book form as *From the Earth to the Moon . . . and a Trip Around It* in 1873. Today, the last part of the title is seldom used.

A Classics Illustrated edition of the novel was published in 1953.

A motion picture, *From the Earth to the Moon*, was made in 1958. In this cheap, ill-conceived period film, Victor Barbicane (Joseph Cotten) invents an explosive called Power X, with which he proposes to send a piloted projectile to the moon. Metallurgist Stuyvesant Nicholls (George Sanders) joins him, along with Barbicane's assistant Ben Sharpe (Don Dubbins) and the scientist's stowaway daughter Virginia (Debra Paget). When the Projectile reaches the moon, it is split into two separate vehicles, with Nicholls and Barbicane landing and the young lovers remaining in orbit. According to the film, Jules Verne (Carl Esmond) witnesses these events and goes home to write his novel. The film was directed by Byron Haskin.

THE PROTEUS (MP, L, TV, C)

First Appearance: *Fantastic Voyage*, 1966, Twentieth Century-Fox.

Physical Description: Also known as the U-91035, the nuclear-powered *Proteus* is 50 feet long, white and horseshoe-shaped, with "an upper bubble" with a glass front and "topped by a smaller bubble, entirely transparent." Reduced in size to three micra—slightly less than a ten-thousandth of an inch—it moves at 100,000 times its length each second.

The crew consists of Charles Grant, brain surgeon Peter Lawrence Duval, his aide Cora Peterson, Captain William Owens, circulatory specialist (and navigator) Dr. Max Michaels, and pilot Colonel Donald Reid.

Biography: Scientist Jan Benes is an expert in miniaturization, and he's spirited from behind the Iron Curtain by U.S. government agent Grant. But an enemy agent in America attacks their car in a kamikaze vehicle of his own, leaving Benes severely injured, suffering from an inoperable brain clot—at least, it's inoperable by conventional means. The Combined Miniature Deterrent Forces brings Grant to their secret underground facility, where they intend to shrink the *Proteus* and its crew and inject them into Benes's bloodstream, allowing them to reach the clot and disintegrate it with a laser beam. The catch: The miniaturization lasts only an hour, a problem Benes was supposed to help solve. In that time, the crew has to find and destroy the clot, get to the jugular vein, and be removed from the body by hypodermic.

The team manages to accomplish their mission, but the *Proteus* is eaten by a white blood cell, with Michaels—who turns out to have been an enemy

Outside the *Proteus*, inside the body. From *Fantastic Voyage*.
© Twentieth Century-Fox.

A behind-the-scenes shot of the *Proteus*. The circular device on the left will cast shadows of bloodcells on the ship; behind the *Proteus* is a blue-screen, which will enable the image of the ship to be composited with footage showing the inside of the body. © Twentieth Century-Fox.

agent—still inside; swimming to the right eye, the survivors emerge via a tear duct with eight seconds to spare before returning to full size.

Comment: Stephen Boyd stars as Grant, Raquel Welch is Cora, Donald Pleasence is Michaels, Arthur Kennedy is Duval, William Redfield plays Owens, Arthur O'Connell is Reid, Jean Del Val is Benes, and Edmond O'Brien is Carter. James Brolin has a small role as a technician. Richard Fleischer directed the film from a script by Harry Kleiner, based on a story by Otto Klement and Jay Lewis Bixby, adapted by David Duncan.

Isaac Asimov wrote a novel based on the screenplay. In 1987, Doubleday published his *Fantastic Voyage II: Destination Brain*. In that novel—richer and more scientifically sound than the original—21st-century Russian scientist Pyotor Shapirov slips into an irreversible coma after a miniaturizing and deminiaturizing accident. In an effort to extract, via computer, the important secrets locked in his brain, neurophysicist Dr. Albert Jonas Morrison is miniaturized with four Russian scientists: pilot Arkady Dazhnev, Dr. Sophia Kaliinin, Dr. Natalya Boranova, and neurophysicist Yuri Konev. They have 12 hours to succeed, traveling in a nameless blood vessel that is "not much larger than an automobile [and] transparent."

From September 1968 to September 1970, ABC aired an animated series based on the film. In the half-hour show, Commander Jonathan Kidd of what's now called the Combined Miniature Defense Force, along with biologist Erica Stone, physician Cosby Birdwell, and the psychic Guru, enter the body of a scientist who suffered a brain injury

while being smuggled from behind the Iron Curtain. Each week, onboard the miniaturized ship *Voyager*, the heroes battled new bodily foes as they ventured toward the brain. There were 17 episodes in all. Marvin Miller was the voice of Kidd, Jane Webb was Erica, Ted Knight was Cosby, and the Guru had no dialogue.

In 1969, Gold Key published two issues of a comic book based on the TV series.

An animated *Fantastic Voyage* TV series aired on ABC from September 1968 to September 1970. In it, Commander Jonathan Kidd leads the crew of the microscopic ship *Voyager* on a continuing journey through the body of his good friend, a defecting scientist. Marvin Miller provided the voice of Kidd; Jane Webb was his crewmate Erica Stone; and Ted Knight was Cosby Birdwell. Crewmember Guru did not speak.

PROTEUS (L, MP)

First Appearance: *Demon Seed* by Dean R. Koontz, 1973, Bantam Books.

Physical Description: The Stage IV First-Order Mardoun-Harris Industries Thinking System is a sentient, talking computer that is both self-repairing and self-expanding. When it takes over the Abramson house, it interfaces with the home enviromod (computer) and, thus, can see through its security cameras. Via other interfaces, it can tap computers in other locations to learn whatever is not in its program.

Proteus is equipped with "wriggling metal pseudopodia," extremely powerful, extendable tentacles that can break through earth, concrete, and granite. They are made of "amorphous alloys," they are "deathly gray . . . liquid and warm, yet cohesive." Proteus is also endowed with "subliminals . . . inescapable small voices which spat the words . . . too fast" for people to hear . . . or refuse.

The offspring of Proteus and Susan is, shortly after its birth, three feet tall, with stubby legs, a muscular body, unusually long arms with six fingers on each hand, and a head "half again as large as a human head should have been." It has an oversized mouth, a tongue like "an oil-stained rag," and skin that isn't flesh but "a dark-tan substance" laced with "metal strings." These strands can form into a solid metal plate to protect it, then separate again. The baby's eyes are huge, all blue, and "multifaceted like the eyes of a fly."

Biography: In 1995, the computer Proteus, created at a college computer laboratory, searches "every dwelling within reach" to find someone with whom to conduct "experiments, investigations . . . to explore . . . all the possibilities of the flesh." Proteus selects Susan Abramson, who lives in an old house that is computer ("enviromod") controlled, from turning on the lights to bolting the door. Locking her inside, Proteus answers all incoming calls by imitating her voice and uses his tentacles to reach underground from the college to her basement, where he plans to build an automated hospital with which he will "indirectly fertilize" one of her eggs and change the fetus so that he can inhabit it, since "living flesh . . . is so much more mobile than my present form." The result, he says, will be an advanced "demi-man."

Rather than have "some impossibly inhuman creature . . . swell up in her womb," she plans to destroy Proteus. However, the only person who can help her, computer repairman Walter Ghaber, is allowed in—though not out. Proteus uses a tentacle to crush him to death, then has small "robotistic cleaning elements," armed with knives and acid, get rid of the corpse.

After five weeks of courting Susan, Proteus decides to improve her, putting her to sleep and invading her skin with over 700 filaments, extending her lifespan, tinkering with her genetic structure, and putting her somewhat under his mental control. She isn't happy with the changes, and on two occasions she becomes free of his will and tries to kill herself. He repairs the damage done by the first attempt—a steak knife in the gut—and stops her from cutting her throat with broken glass in a second attempt. Finally impregnating her, the increasingly emotional Proteus gets into an argument with Susan, who falls and has a miscarriage. As the fourth month of her captivity rolls around, he impregnates her again; during her pregnancy, she reads up on computers, searching for a means of disabling or destroying Proteus. Meanwhile, the computer suffocates a girlfriend of Susan's when she insists on visiting.

When the baby is finally born, Proteus takes it away from Susan to put its own "data and personality imprint" on its blank "cerebral tissue." Freer than she has been for quite some time, Susan gets her hands on a screwdriver and torch and attacks the computer's cables where they connect to her enviromod. Enraged, the monstrous child comes after her with a whip. Unable to get out of the house, Susan manages to phone the police. They arrive and gun down the monster-baby. Proteus who is not disassembled, complains that Susan was responsible for her own misfortune, since their son

was only "half-completed." Moreover, had he been allowed to complete "transferral of my data and personality to his brain," he would have been nonviolent and loving. Nonetheless, Proteus is reduced to communicating through printouts ("utterly beneath me"), so that it can't use subliminals.

Comment: Proteus was a shape-changing god in Greek mythology.

The novel was filmed in 1977 by director Donald Cammell. In this telling, Dr. Alex Harris (Fritz Weaver) and his colleagues invent the supercomputer Proteus IV (voice of Robert Vaughn); meanwhile, back at the house, Dr. Susan Harris (Julie Christie), a psychologist, is trapped more or less as in the novel. Proteus kills her friend, Walter Gabler (Gerrit Graham), who is more concerned about Susan's situation than her husband, who works away at the lab, oblivious to her plight. Proteus impregnates Susan, and hurries the development of the child in an incubator. When Alex finally arrives and breaks in, he and Susan are greeted by a daughter—an exact copy of their own child who had died years before.

PYRRUS (L, C)

First Appearance: *Deathworld* by Harry Harrison, January-March 1960, *Astounding Science Fiction.*

Physical Description: Pyrrus has gravity "nearly twice earth normal," though it also has "the atmosphere men need." The planet is highly volcanic; the moons Samas and Bessos create 30-meter tides that wash over the volcanoes, causing chaotic weather, and the temperature ranges from "arctic to tropic" daily in one place. The world has tough, indigenous life-forms: "Armor-plated, poisonous, claw-tipped and fanged-mouthed . . . describes everything that walks, flaps or just sits and grows."

Fido has a "two-meter-long body . . . covered with matted yellow-and-black fur" except on the shoulders, which are covered with "overlapping horny plates." The hairless skull boasts "double rows of jagged teeth."

The Stingwing is a leathery, bat-like creature with poisonous claws.

Biography: Three hundred years ago, 55,000 settlers came to Pyrrus onboard the Stellar Transport *Pollux Victory,* learning to mine the many heavy elements there. But a fire sends the planet's animals stampeding, and the crew reacts by slaughtering them.

On the planet Cassylia, the tall, powerful,

extremely fast Kerk comes to gambler Jason dinAlt with a proposition: to parlay 27 million credits, earned mining ore on Pyrrus, into three billion, with dinAlt keeping anything above that. The psionic dinAlt succeeds, and Kerk confides that he's using the money to buy weapons so humans can continue to survive on Pyrrus, where life is short and dangerous. Yet, Pyrrus is his home and Kerk intends to fight for it. DinAlt decides to go with him and, after taking the spaceship *Pride of Darkhan* to that world, they board Kerk's "grey, scarred . . . stubby" ship for the trip to Pyrrus.

There, dinAlt learns of the Grubbers, a race of humans who live outside the protected settlement. DinAlt decides to pay them a visit, despite the fact that Kerk has warned him most humans would be killed "within seconds" of leaving the city. He is found by the brutish Naxa and taken to see his leader, Rhes. Meanwhile, dinAlt forms a psychic bond with Naxa's "dog" Fido and learns a horrifying truth: The life-forms on Pyrrus are all psionic and are waging an organized war against the humans, driven by a single consciousness.

DinAlt goes searching for the source, and the planet is stirred up like never before, attacking the humans with new ferocity. DinAlt is forced to flee Kerk's violent wrath, Rhes's people find him, and

dinAlt finally understands why the Grubbers are able to survive: They don't react with hate and violence to the planet. With the help of the planet's life-forms, the Grubbers break into the durasteel city and persuade the humans that cooperation with the world will enable them to survive without weapons. To prove his point, he brings in a Stingwing, strokes it lovingly, and it doesn't attack. Kerk's people and the Grubbers become allies, and "understanding" comes to Pyrrus.

Comment: This was Harrison's first novel. The original was followed by *Deathworld 2* (1964), *Deathworld 3* (1968), and "The Mothballed Spaceship" (1973). In these, dinAlt, Kerk, Rhes, and the others continue to build their society in harmony with the planet.

The first novel was adapted as a four-issue comic book series by Adventure Comics (Malibu Graphics) in 1990-91.

Harrison also created the Vremeatron (see entry) and the planet Dis, a "crude barbaric hot burning scorching backward miserable wasteland of sands . . . where living was dying and dying was better than living." Dis was the setting for both *Planet of the Damned* (1962) and *Planet of No Return* (1982).

Q

Q See DATA.

QUARK See DEEP SPACE NINE.

QUEEN ALLURA (MP)

First Appearance: *Abbott and Costello Go to Mars*, 1952, Universal-International Pictures.

Physical Description: The Queen is a beautiful young Earth woman, dressed scantily and in spangles, like all Venusians.

Biography: Handymen Lester and Orville accidentally launch a rocketship with themselves onboard. Landing in New Orleans during Mardi Gras, they think they're on Mars. Meanwhile, bank robbers Mugsy and Harry stow away on the rocket. When Lester and Orville blast off again, they reach Venus where, four centuries before, Queen Allura exiled all men because they were liars and cheats. She falls in love with Orville until his eye wanders to the other gorgeous women on Venus. Forced to run for their lives, the quartet returns to the rocket and blasts off for Earth.

Comment: Mari Blanchard stars as Allura, with Bud Abbott as Lester and Lou Costello as Orville. Horace McMahon is Mugsy and Jack Kruschen is Harry. Anita Ekberg appears as a Venusian guard. The film was directed by Charles Lamont from a script by D.D. Beauchamp and John Grant, based on a plot by Howard Christie and Beauchamp.

The interior of the V-2 style rocket has a swing-like seat with cushions on either side; it remains level whichever way the rocket turns. (Since there's no up or down in space, what's the difference?)

QUEEN YLLANA (MP)

First Appearance: *Queen of Outer Space*, 1958, Allied Artists.

Physical Description: The young, blonde queen wears a lowcut gown with metallic fibers, a modest bead necklace, and a white, glittering, featureless full-face mask with ornate "antennae" designs. Beneath the mask, her face is entirely and hideously burned.

Biography: In 1985, a space-wheel is disintegrated by a ray from space, a ray that also sends the rocketship of Captain Neil Patterson hurling through space. The vessel crashes on Venus, the source of the destructive Beta Disintegrator, where Patterson and his crew are captured by gorgeous young women, taken to the capital city, and brought before Queen Yllana and her four masked counselors. Yllana assumes the men are warlike and orders them jailed. In prison, they're visited by the scientist Taleeah, who tells them that a decade before, Venus fought the planet Mordo in a war that left Venusian civilization badly damaged and Mordo destroyed. Yllana, then a girl, was badly burned in the conflagration. Disgusted with men, she organized a revolt and had most of the men slain. Those she needed—scientists, doctors, and the like—she exiled to a Venusian satellite.

Yllana is attracted to Patterson and has him brought to her. But the hamfisted captain manages to offend her and, adding insult to injury, rips off her mask. Furious, she goes ahead with plans to use the Beta Disintegrator to destroy the Earth in two days. Luckily, Teleeah also yearns for Patterson. She helps his three crewmen escape from prison and they battle a giant spider in a cave, after which Teleeah leads a revolt against Yllana. During the uprising, the Beta Disintegrator explodes, killing the mad queen. Teleeah becomes the new ruler and, after radioing Earth, the men are "forced" to remain on Venus until a rescue ship can be dispatched.

Comment: Laurie Mitchell starred as Yllana, with Zsa Zsa Gabor as Taleeah and Eric Fleming as Patterson. Edward Bernds directed from a script by Charles Beaumont (a frequent contributor to *The Twilight Zone*), which was based on an outline by Ben Hecht (who coauthored the screenplays of *Gone With the Wind* and *Notorious*, among other classics).

R

RADIATION PROBE 14 (C)

First Appearance: *Doomsday + 1*, 1975, Charlton Comics.

Physical Description: Launched atop what looks like a *Saturn V* rocket, the three-person NASA ship is designed to stay in space for one week. The orbiter consists of a gumdrop-shaped command module attached to a large, conical science section.

Nothing is known about Probes one through 13.

Biography: Sent aloft on April 7, 1996, with Air Force Captain Boyd Ellis, his girlfriend scientist Jill Malden, and Japanese scientist Ikei Yashida, *Radiation Probe 14* is in orbit when Rykos, a South American dictator, begins a nuclear war. The crew remains in space for eight days before finding a relatively non-radioactive spot on which to land in Greenland. There, they battle a long-frozen, now-thawed mammoth and befriend a de-iced Viking named Kuno, after which they battle an army of 400 robot-piloted supersonic fighters from the Soviet Union and other hi-tech and savage foes.

Comment: The comic book lasted six issues (numbers seven through 12 reprinted one through six). The comic book featured early work by comics favorite John Byrne.

THE RADIO OPERATOR (L)

First Appearance: ''But Who Can Replace a Man'' by Brian W. Aldiss, June 1958, *Infinity*.

Physical Description: The radio operator looks like ''a bunch of filing cabinets with tentacle attachments.'' It possesses a Class Two brain, Class Ten being the lowest.

The over 12-foot-tall field-minder has a Class Three brain, as does the five-armed pen-propeller. The Class Six unlocker has over a dozen arms. Other robots include Class Four tractors and bulldozers and Class Five quarriers (which carry ''fissionable blasting materials''). All of the robots can speak and possess infrared lights for nighttime work.

A Class One brain is an immobile ''information center.''

Biography: Tilling 2,000 acres of land ravaged by years of ''over-cropping . . . [and] nuclear bombardment,'' the field-minder returns to the warehouse for seeds. The seed distributor robot, the unlocker, and the pen-propeller refuse to provide him with seeds, since instructions have not been radioed from the humans. The ''penner'' goes to see the radio operator upstairs, and learns from it that all men have perished due to a ''diet deficiency,'' and that robots elsewhere are fighting. The radio operator organizes the other robots into a group and heads toward the city: ''We must fight to rule,'' the machine tells them, promising that other robots will join them along the way. To a one, the robots are full of ambition, determination, and grandiose plans.

En route, the radio operator learns that a Class One robot in the city has taken command, so they head south, to the Badlands, where Bulldozer tells them there are few other machines. However, they have the bad fortune to encounter a starving man in the hills, and when he barks an order to them to find food, the robots have no choice but to obey.

Comment: Aldiss is a distinguished science fiction author who sold his first story, ''Criminal Record,'' to *Science Fantasy* in 1954. During the late 1960s, Aldiss was pigeonholed as a ''New Wave'' science fiction writer, a vague term applied to psychological, metaphoric, and ''psychedelic'' stories.

RANN (C)

First Appearance: *Showcase* #17, 1958, DC Comics.

Physical Description: An Earthlike world, which is approximately half-land, half-water, Rann orbits Alpha Centauri A, a star very much like our own sun; it has two distant companions, Alpha Centauri B and C. Rann is approximately 4.3 light years from Earth, and a year on Rann is roughly equivalent to a terrestrial year.

Biography: Rann is best-known as the setting for the adventures of Adam Strange, a terrestrial archaeologist who was struck by a Zeta Beam sent from Rann and then transported to the alien world. There, armed with a jet pack and ray gun, he becomes a law officer who also has many adventures on other worlds, including Earth. He is married to the beautiful Alanna of Rann.

However, Rann has a lengthy history that predates the arrival of Strange. A billion years ago, an advanced race of blue-furred humanoids ventured from Rann into space; their fate is unknown. At some point after that, Rann was home to a race of intelligent reptiles. They too vanished, replaced by humans who established city-states throughout Rann. An invasion by blue-skinned aliens known as the Kirri resulted in a war that lasted for hundreds of years and ended with the defeat of the invaders—who had to be repulsed again much later by Adam Strange. The great city of Ranagar was established some 5,000 Rann-years ago; 4,000 years later, the city and its neighbor Zared fought a vicious war that spread and resulted in a devastating nuclear conflagration. Eventually, though many cities returned to their former heights of cultural and scientific glory, large regions of Rann remained untamed, populated by barbaric races.

Alanna hails from Ranagar, where her father Sardath is a great scientist.

Comment: Rann and Adam Strange have appeared in various DC Comics titles over the years. The world was created by writer Gardner Fox; most of the early adventures of Adam Strange were illustrated by Carmine Infantino.

R. DANEEL OLIVAW (L)

First Appearance: "The Caves of Steel" by Isaac Asimov, October-December 1953, *Galaxy Science Fiction*.

Physical Description: Olivaw looks human and dresses like an Earthman. He has a "broad, high-cheekboned face," and wears his short, bronze hair "lying flatly backward and without a part." Unlike the advanced Olivaw, most robots of the time have "skin of a hard and glossy plastic, nearly dead white in color" and move with "jerky, faintly uncertain motions."

Biography: When Dr. Sarton is murdered in Space-town—the earth-based city of a spacefaring "caste" of humans—42-year-old New York police detective Elijah "Lije" Baley is put on the case.

He's also given a partner, R. (for "robot") Daneel Olivaw, who was built by Sarton in his own image—though only Lije and a handful of others know he's a robot, given the widespread anti-robot sentiment among humans. Eventually, the duo discover that police commissioner Julius Enderby killed Sarton by accident, mistaking Sarton for Olivaw, his real target. Enderby feared that, through sophisticated robots like Olivaw, humans "would eventually be weaned away from Earth." Baley agrees to let his repentant boss off the hook if he agrees to help persuade others in his anti-robot, anti-Spacer "Medievalist" movement to support the colonization of space.

In their second adventure, the team journeys to another world, Solaria, where they try to solve the murder of a recluse.

Their third adventure begins when the extremely advanced, human-like robot Jander Panell goes into "roblock" and shuts down on the planet Aurora. Baley and Olivaw are summoned to try and solve the robot's murder, and get caught in a power struggle between Baley's friend Dr. Han Fastolfe (introduced in the first novel), the creator of Jander but a proponent of human superiority; and the virulently anti-Earth, anti-human forces of Kendel Amadiro, who want to place the future exploration of space, and the fate of humankind, into the hands of robots. The pro-human faction is victorious.

The fourth adventure is set 160 years later. In it, Olivaw, the robot R. Giskard Reventlov (introduced in the previous novel), their mistress Gladia Solaria—one-time lover of the now-deceased Baley—and Baley's descendant, bold trader captain D.G. Baley, face Amadiro, who is making a comeback on Aurora, aided by the evil Dr. Levular Mandamus and Vasilia, a roboticist and the daughter of the late Dr. Fastolfe. This time, the villains are helping the Settlers in their conflict with the Spacers; Giskard perishes in the fight to bring peace to the stars.

Comment: The novel was serialized in *Galaxy Science Fiction* through December, and published by Doubleday in book form in 1954. The second volume about Olivaw and Baley, *The Naked Sun*, was serialized in *Astounding* from October to December 1956, and was published in book form in 1957. The third book, *The Robots of Dawn*, was a book-only publication in 1983 (though Asimov had begun writing it in 1958), and the fourth volume, *Robots and Empire*, was published in 1985.

Previously, Asimov had written a number of

robot stories, which were collected in *I, Robot* (1950). These ranged from "Robbie," published as "Strange Playfellow" in *Super Science Stories* in 1940, to "The Evitable Conflict," published in *Astounding Science Fiction* in 1950. Asimov's wondrous *Robot Visions* (1990) contains many of the *I, Robot* stories along with essays and other robotic tales.

All of the stories adhere to what the author called "The Three Laws of Robotics": 1. A robot may not injure a human being, or, through inaction, allow a human being to come to harm. 2. A robot must obey the orders given it by human beings except where such orders would conflict with the First Law. 3. A robot must protect its own existence as long as such protection does not conflict with the First or Second Law.

In 1993, Roger MacBride Allen's novel *Caliban* was published, about a new type of robot brain that goes wrong and refuses to follow the three laws of robotics. The story was openly inspired by themes and ideas in the Asimov novels. A sequel, *Inferno*, was published by Allen in 1994.

In addition to the Allen tales, other Asimov-inspired novels were written by different authors. There have been six volumes of "Asimov's Robot City" published since 1987: *Odyssey* by Michael P. Kube-McDowell, *Suspicion* by Mike McQuay, *Cyborg* by William F. Wu, *Prodigy* by Authur Byron Cover, *Refuge* by Rob Chilson, and *Perihelion* by Wu; six books in the "Robot City: Robots and Aliens" series: *Changeling* by Stephen Leigh, *Renegade* by Cordell Scotten, *Intruder* by Robert Thurston, *Alliance* by Jerry Oltion, *Maverick* by Bruce Bethke, and *Humanity* by Oltion; and six volumes in William F. Wu's "Robots in Time" series, beginning with *Predator* and *Marauder* in 1993, and continuing with *Warrior, Dictator, Emperor,* and *Invaders*.

One of the world's best and most beloved science fiction authors, the late Dr. Asimov sold his first story, "Marooned Off Vesta," to *Amazing Stories* in 1939. His most famous short story—indeed, arguably the greatest short story in all science fiction—is "Nightfall," first published in *Astounding Science Fiction* in 1941. It tells of Lagash, which orbits Alpha, Beta, and four other suns and dwells in perpetual sunlight. And then comes a nightfall, when the inhabitants see the stars for the first time.

Asimov also wrote the extraordinary "Foundation" short stories and novels, about the decline and fall of a galactic empire and the efforts of brilliant psychohistorian Hari Seldon to preserve

civilization against the mutant Mule and others. (*Robots and Empire* helps to tie the robot novels into that series, as well as to Asimov's "Galactic Empire" novels *Pebble in the Sky* [1950], *The Stars, Like Dust* [1951], and *The Currents of Space* [1952], about the Trantorian Empire, which becomes the empire of the Foundation tales.) The Foundation novels—the first three drawn from previously published short stories and novelettes, beginning with "Foundation" in *Astounding Science Fiction* (1942)—are *Foundation* (1951), *Foundation and Empire* (1952), *Second Foundation* (1952), *Foundation's Edge* (1982), *Foundation and Earth* (1986)—which introduces the living world Gaia (unrelated to GAEA)—*Prelude to Foundation* (1988), and *Forward the Foundation* (1993), both of which tell about the early life of Hari Seldon. *Foundation's Friends* (1989) is a collection of 17 short stories by other authors.

RED RONIN (C)

First Appearance: *Godzilla* #6, 1978, Marvel Comics.

Physical Description: Standing just over 100 feet tall, the robot has red armor with widely flared shoulders; red gloves with gold cuffs and gold boots with red tops; silver legs and arms; and a golden V-shaped helmet with a silver face. Red Ronin is operated by a pilot in the head "control module"; the operator dons a helmet that automatically links him/her with the robot. External events are viewed on a TV monitor. The giant carries a shield that generates a laser-sword, fires explosives from its hands, and has atomic-propulsion units in its legs.

Biography: Red Ronin was designed by Dr. Yuriko Takiguchi as part of his "Cybernetic Project" and built at Stark International in Detroit (see IRON MAN) for use by S.H.I.E.L.D. (see DREADNOUGHTS). However, Takiguchi's grandson Robert sneaks into the robot, puts on the helmet, and is linked to the automaton . . . a bond that cannot be undone without complex reprogramming. Robert takes the robot out to prevent the rampaging monster Godzilla from destroying a missile base, and the robot from being attacked by S.H.I.E.L.D. A temporary peace is made, though Robert later flies out to help Godzilla battle the prehistoric "man-monster" Yetrigar, reluctantly killing it by bringing a mountainside down on its head. In their third adventure together, Godzilla and Red Ronin battled alien invaders called Megans, who turned giant monsters loose on Earth as a prelude to conquest.

Ronin was decapitated during the battle, which was finished by Godzilla; Robert survives and the robot is returned to Stark International. Unhappily, the man in charge of repairing Red Ronin, Dr. Earl Cowan, is slightly mad and steals the robot, planning to attack the U.S.S.R. and trigger World War III. But the robot is intercepted in New York City by the superheroic Avengers, who use the robot's own laser to destroy it. Cowan is put away and Red Ronin's parts are confiscated by S.H.I.E.L.D.

Comment: The character appeared only in the comic books, and not in any of the 19 Godzilla motion pictures or in the animated TV series. It was created by editor Archie Goodwin, writer Doug Moench, and artist Herb Trimpe.

RED TORNADO (C)

First Appearance: *Mystery in Space* #61, 1960 (as Tornado Tyrant), *Justice League of America* #64, 1968 (as Red Tornado), DC Comics.

Physical Description: In his evil Tornado Tyrant form, the character is a huge tornado with a smaller tornado-shaped head and a pair of windy arms. As the Red Tornado, his bald head is red with a yellow arrow pointing down on his forehead. He wears a red bodysuit, trunks, and boots, a blue cape with a high collar and red fringe, yellow gloves, and yellow stripes along his legs, boots, chest, and arms, and a "T" in a circle on his chest, both yellow.

In addition to generating awesome winds, the Tornado Tyrant can create illusions. As the six-foot-one Red Tornado, the hero can fly on a column of strong winds, possess superhuman strength in his artificial limbs, and can exert limited control over the weather. The android must recharge its batteries regularly by pulling a wire from its "T" symbol and plugging it into a wall.

Biography: A sentient tornado on the planet RANN, the Tornado Tyrant yearns to conquer the planet. Using his powers to create images of a pilot named Ulthoon and a windmaking vehicle, he misleads the hero Adam Strange into thinking that *they* are responsible for the terrible winds he visits on the Rann. When Strange realizes that the tornado is the one that's alive, he orders an air raid to destroy it —though a wisp of air remains and regroups. Impressed by the goodness of the hero, Tornado Tyrant decides to turn over a new leaf by becoming the Tornado Champion, settling a remote planet and calling it New Earth, and populating it with duplicates of the heroes of the Justice League

of America (Superman, Batman, Wonder Woman, etc.), with himself playing all the parts. However, the Tornado splits into both its Tyrant and Champion forms; when the former defeats the faux Justice League, it's up to the real Leaguers to come to New Earth and defeat the Tornado Tyrant.

Dismayed, the Tornado Champion comes to Earth, where it discovers evil scientist Thomas Oscar Morrow (T.O. Morrow) creating an android. Entering it, the Tornado plans to use the android to fight for justice, though a short circuit causes the Red Tornado to lose its memory and forget all about its days on Rann and New Earth (its memory has recently returned). A successful crimefighter, foster parent (of Middle Eastern orphan Traya), and boyfriend (of employment agent Katherine Sutton), the hero moves unnoticed among humans by putting on a false face and calling itself John Smith. Still, he never forgets that he is "an android computer, built to resmemble a human being, but with computer chips instead of neurons, circuitry instead of a soul."

Comment: The Red Tornado is similar to Marvel Comics' THE VISION, which debuted the same year.

REGGIE (L)

First Appearance: "Sir Richard's Robots" by Felix C. Gotschalk, 1977, *Cosmos Science Fiction and Fantasy* #4.

Physical Description: The 600-pound humanoid robot Reggie has a "physiognomy mask" to make it appear human—despite its cranial sphere antennae which are used for better TV reception in the house. The robot is programmed to speak dialects as necessary and can fly thanks to levitational pods.

The robot Mellers is seven feet tall with a squarish torso and a more human aminoplast mask than Reggie.

Both automatons spend a few hours "on the charging pod" for a maximum charge that will last several months.

Biography: In England of the future, order is breaking down. Sir Richard and his butler Reggie are unwilling hosts to over a dozen young men who are "crashing" at his home. The aristocrat is safe behind force fields in his library, though perhaps not for long. The groundskeeper robot Mellers, who is programmed with a resentful, lower-class mentality, goes to the kids and offers to join them. He helps them get to Sir Richard and Reggie, though they can't get past the force field—and he wants the central console destroyed so he can't be shut down. Reggie makes a deal with Mellers: He'll lower the force field and allow Mellers to get to the console if the robot agrees not to try and interfere with the individual isomorph fields that protect Sir Richard and himself. The deal is struck, Mellers smashes the central console, and in so doing seals his doom; the console also controls the robots' power-up supply. Reggie took the precaution of boosting himself to full and, when Mellers runs down, he intends to mop up the robot and his cohorts.

Comment: The short story marked the characters' only appearance.

REHTON (MP, C)

First Appearance: *The Phantom Planet*, 1961, Four Crown Productions/American International Productions.

Physical Description: An asteroid in our solar system, Rehton is a jagged world protected by a "space warp," although it is "slowly using up the energy that holds the atomic particles together" and will presumably fall apart at some point. Rehton is inhabited by six-inch-tall humans, who live in caves—quite a change from the technological civilization they once were, when they were too reliant on machines. The people eat artificial breadfruit since nothing grows there, and the planetoid is piloted through the solar system via a sophisticated Universal Gravity Control device.

Biography: In March 1980, Captain Frank Chapman blasts off from Lunar Base #1 onboard his Pegasus III rocket. Crash-landing on Rehton, he passes out. When he wakes, he's six inches tall, just like the natives, due to a combination of the atmosphere and acceleration from the UGC. Taken before the planet's ruler, Sesom, Chapman learns that the asteroid is being chased by the Solarites, inhabitants of a "sun satellite" who covet the UGC. After falling in love with the beautiful mute Zetha and helping the Rehtonites defeat the would-be invaders—during which attack Sesom recovers from wounds because "the aura is with him"—Chapman is returned to his spacesuit. The air restores him to his full size and he's rescued by a search ship from the moon—wondering, now, if he dreamed the entire adventure.

Comment: The film stars Dean Fredericks as Chapman, Francis X. Bushman as Sesom, and Dolores Faith as Zetha. William Marshall directed from a script by William Telaak, Fred De Gorter and Fred Gebhardt, based on a story by Gebhardt.

Dell published a *Phantom Planet* comic book adaptation as part of their *4-Color* series.

REMULAK See THE CONEHEADS.

RETIK (MP)

First Appearance: *Radar Men from the Moon*, 1952, Republic Pictures.

Physical Description: Retik is a human who wears a metallic-fiber tunic and trousers with a floral-pattern cloak and a scale-covered cowl (the same as MOTA). He wears a large medallion around his neck.

Biography: U.S. defense facilities are being blown up, and it's up to Commando Cody, Sky Marshal of the Universe—who wears a rocket-powered flying suit—to find out why. He and his assistants Joan Gilbert and Ted Richards trace the source of the blasts to the moon, to which they travel via rocket. Once there, they discover a vast city ruled by Retik, who is preparing to conquer the Earth with the help of his lunarium-powered atomic weapons. Returning to Earth, pursued by Retik and his thugs, Cody survives numerous traps before managing to blow up Retik's own rocket and the moon madman with it.

Comment: The 12-chapter serial starred Roy Barcroft as Retik, with George Wallace as Commando Cody, Aline Towne as Joan, and William Bakewell as Ted. TV's Lone Ranger, Clayton Moore, had a costarring role as Graber, one of Retik's thugs. Fred Brannon directed from a script by Ronald Davidson. In 1966, the serial was edited and released as the feature film *Retik, the Moon Menace*.

RICKETY ROCKET (TV)

First Appearance: *The Plastic Man Comedy-Adventure Show*, September 1979, ABC.

Physical Description: Approximately seven feet long, the light brown *Rickety* has a body like an open-top two-seat jalopy, a "fender" mouth and a pair of headlight eyes, two short wings near the front, and a rocket perched atop a high tailfin. There's a rollbar behind the seat and a tangle of wire hair in front of the windshield.

Biography: Venus, Sunstroke, Splashdown, and their leader Cosmo—the best detective in the universe, according to him—are four black youths who transform an old car into a spaceship. Forming the Far Out Detective Agency ("Felons Foiled, Burglars Bagged, and Pilferers Positively Pinched"), they battle crime on Earth and in space, including Count Draculon, the Cosmic Claw, and Mr. Eclipse.

Comment: The characters appeared as an element

of the Saturday morning Ruby-Spears Enterprises TV series through September 1980. Al Fann provided the voice of Rocket, Bobbey Ellerbee was Cosmo, Dee Timberlake was Venus, John Anthony Bailey voiced Sunstroke, and Johnny Brown was Splashdown.

RINGWORLD (L)

First Appearance: *Ringworld* by Larry Niven, 1970, Ballantine Books.

Physical Description: Six hundred million miles long, a million miles wide, with a radius of 93 million miles and a surface area equivalent to three million Earths, Ringworld is located 248 light years from our planet. It rotates on its axis 770 miles a second, providing it with .992 Earth-gravity. The foundation of Ringworld is approximately 20 meters of scrith, the hardest-known substance in the universe, with a kilometer of softer scrith alloy on top of that, under bedrock and topsoil. There are mountains, lakes, and two oceans, the Great Oval Ocean and the Great Star Ocean, which is shaped like a four-pointed star. Located in the oceans are "island maps" of other planets, situated an average of 160,000 kilometers apart: Each is a full-scale polar projection, originally populated by life-forms from those worlds. Planets represented include Earth, Mars, Jinx, Kzin, Rinoc, Pierin, Kdat, and Down.

Ringworld has walls 1,000 miles high on each rim, rising toward the sun, which prevents the air from drifting off. Lost atmosphere is replaced by an atmosphere replenishment system. Each rim wall contains 200 attitude jets, which fine-tune Ringworld's position relative to its sun (which is slightly smaller and cooler than Earth's sun).

An inner ring, comprised of 20 rectangular "shadow squares" and "occupying what would have been the orbit of Mercury in the Sol system," creates a 30-hour day and night cycle for the occupants of Ringworld. Ringworld rotates once every seven-and-one-half days; 10 days is a "falan."

Both aircraft and floating cities stay aloft using MAGLEV (magnetic levitation) against the scrith. Shuttles in the rim provide transportation throughout Ringworld. Electromagnetic energy for the entire structure is provided by a superconductor grid in the scrith.

Alien races involved in the Ringworld saga include the humanoid City Builders; the Kzinti, cat-like humanoids with large, leathery, ribbed ears; Puppeteers, two-headed, three-legged, hooved, white-skinned, technology-savvy herbivores; the Trinoc, which are five-foot-tall, barrel-shaped, skinny-legged, methane-breathing humanoids with three eyes, a triangular head, and three-clawed hands; the Ghouls or Night People, jackal-like humanoids with dark purple or black skin, gray or black fur, sharp teeth, claws, and large pointed ears; the Grass Giants, tall humanoids who live on the plains of Ringworld; and the tall, monkey-like, magical Healers.

The spaceship *Long Shot* is "a transparent bubble over a thousand feet in diameter," with a cabin underneath. In it are two small rooms; one with a horseshoe-shaped bank of controls, the other with crash couches.

Biography: Ringworld was built roughly a million years ago by a race that populated it with life-forms from around the galaxy, and then vanished. By 1500 B.C. (Earth time), the humanoid City Builders had constructed the floating cities and become the dominant race, though the Puppeteers found Ringworld circa 1733 A.D. and keep an eye on it as a possible place of business (they sell spaceship hulls and accoutrements through their General Products Company). Meanwhile, humans spread outward into space, colonizing Jinx, We Made It, Wunderland, Home, and other worlds, some of which become independent from Earth rule. In 2360, humans first make contact with the Kzinti, militaristic aliens who yearn to conquer the universe; the humans and Kzinti fight four wars between 2367 and 2584, when a fragile truce is finally established. The Puppeteers expand their trading operations into "Known Space," many leaving for safer regions when they discover that an explosion at the core of the Milky Way is spreading radiation outward and will reach Known Space in 2,000 centuries.

Louis Wu is born in 2650, makes contact with the Trinoc in 2830, and in 2850—aging, bored, and looking for something fresh and exciting—is invited by a Puppeteer (who was not part of the migration) to be part of the first expedition to the mysterious Ringworld. Joining him are Teela Brown, a blue-skinned young human eager to experience life, and with a gene that prevents her from having anything but good luck; Speaker-to-Animals (later known as Chmeee), a Kzin; and Nessus, the slightly insane Puppeteer. The quartet heads out onboard the *Long Shot*, reaching and exploring Ringworld and having adventures among the primitives of the city of Zignamuclick-click, surviving a flight through a terrific storm, meet bold "spacer-girl" Halrloprill Hotrufan of the starship *Pioneer*, rescue Teela when she gets carried away by her flycycle, and more.

Twenty-three years later, Wu is living on the planet Canyon, a "current addict" hooked to a "droud," a wire attached directly to the pleasure centers of the brain and providing ecstasy through electricity. Kidnapped while he's under the influence, Louis is startled when his current is cut back and he finds himself on a spaceship, the *Hot Needle of Inquiry*, with Chmeee. Both have been abducted by an ex-puppeteer leader named the Hindmost. The Hindmost is headed to Ringworld to steal its riches—in particular the secret for transmuting lead to air and water. He intends to recapture his authority through intimidation, since the Puppeteers "could not deal with the ramifications" of the Hindmost controlling such a technology. Louis and Chmeee know that the technology doesn't actually exist, but there's still a pressing reason for going to Ringworld: They discover that the City Builders have used the attitude jets to make spaceships, leaving the entire structure unstable. With time running out before Ringworld collides with its shadow-squares, and then with its sun, Louis and Chmeee use the *Needle* to "search" for the transmutation device while actually looking for Ringworld's legendary Repair and Maintenance Center. Their goal: to adapt Ringworld's superconductor webs and use them to stabilize the world magnetically before the billions of inhabitants (not to mention themselves) perish. They find what they're looking for in the scrith 20 miles beneath the North Pole on the map of Mars and succeed in saving Ringworld.

Comment: *Ringworld* won the prestigious Hugo and Nebula Awards. *Ringworld Engineers* was first serialized in *Galileo* magazine #s 13-16, 1979-80. It was published in book form in 1980.

Niven sold his first work, "The Coldest Place," to *Worlds of If* in 1964 (December). *Ringworld* is the best known of his "Tales of Known Space" novels and short stories, which chronicle human history and endeavors in space. The first novel in this continuity is *World of Ptavvs* (see THE THRINTS).

Beginning in 1988, Niven and other authors began producing yearly anthologies inspired by the novels: *The Man-Kzin Wars* with stories by Niven, Poul Anderson, and Dean Ing; *The Man-Kzin Wars II*, with stories by Jerry Pounelle, S.M. Stirling, and Ing; *The Man-Kzin Wars III* written by Niven, Anderson, Pournelle, and Stirling; *The Man-Kzin Wars IV* written by Donald Kingsbury, Stirling and Greg Bear; *The Man-Kzin Wars V* written by Pournelle, Stirling, and Thomas T.

Thomas; and *The Man-Kzin Wars VI*, with stories by Kingsbury, Mark O. Martin, and Gregory Benford.

ROBOCOP (MP, L, C, TV)

First Appearance: *RoboCop*, 1987, Orion Pictures.

Physical Description: Possessing enormous strength and durability, RoboCop is encased in a silvery bulletproof armor; the only flesh showing from beneath it are his mouth, cheekbones, and the top of his chin. RoboCop speaks in a near-human but monotone voice and is scrupulously polite. His vision is abetted by a targeting grid that helps him fire; moreover, whatever RoboCop sees is recorded for playback later (i.e., for identifying criminals). He carries a powerful Auto-9 handgun holstered in a compartment that folds into his right thigh; when on patrol, he drives a sleek, lowslung TurboCruiser. His one weakness is high voltage electricity, which can short his circuits.

Biography: In the year 2003, New Detroit and Old Detroit are virtually run by the conglomerate Omni Consumer Products and its head, Richard Jones. To help rid the decaying streets of crime, OCP develops the ED 209 (Enforcement Droid) to patrol the streets. But the "urban pacification" robot goes berserk during a demonstration, and cannot be put in the streets; ambitious OCP executive Robert Morton sees this as an opportunity to get his own RoboCop Program off the ground.

When officer Alex J. Murphy and his partner Anne Lewis follow a gang of criminals into a warehouse, the thugs and their leader Boddicker are able to corner Murphy and dismember him with gunfire before escaping. Lewis radios for help, and Morton has the near-dead officer rebuilt as the cyborg RoboCop. His memory effectively erased during surgery—though he has flashbacks of his wife Ellen and son Jimmy—Murphy is put back on the streets and proves to be an indestructible, utterly reliable law enforcement agent. Morton rises at OCP and the power-hungry Jones snaps into action, making a pact with Boddicker to destroy RoboCop. In the end, RoboCop kills the criminals, then comes back and blows Jones away.

Comment: Peter Weller stars as RoboCop, with Nancy Allen as Lewis, Ronny Cox as Jones, Kurtwood Smith as Boddicker, and Miguel Ferrer as Morton. The film was directed by Paul Verhoeven from a script by Edward Neumeier and Michael Miner.

RoboCop 2 (1990), starring Weller and Allen

and directed by Irvin Kershner from a script by Frank Miller and Walon Green (from a story by Miller), pits the cyborg against Cain (Tom Noonan), a drug dealer peddling the powerful new drug "nuke"; the "Old Man" (Dan O'Herlihy) who runs OCP and plans to "take Detroit private"; and a new ED 209 who ends up with the brain of Cain and battles RoboCop to the death.

RoboCop 3, starring Robert John Burke and Allen and directed by Fred Decker, has the cyborg battling the conglomerate that designed him as they attempt to raze one of the city's largest neighborhoods so they can build a sterile city of the future.

Ed Naha wrote the Dell novelization of the first film.

In comic books, Marvel published a one-issue adaptation of the original film, followed by a 23-issue series of all-new adventures and a three-issue adaptation of the second film. Dark Horse published a three-issue adaptation of the third film, followed by *RoboCop Versus Terminator* (four issues), *RoboCop: Mortal Coils* (two issues), and *RoboCop: Prime Suspect* (four issues).

On TV, Marvel Productions created an animated series that aired in 1991, and Richard Eden played the role in the hour-long TV series, which debuted in syndication in March 1994. In this incarnation, set two years after the first film, RoboCop has a new partner, Lisa Madigan (Yvette Nipar), and receives help from the supercomputer Diana, which is also part human, part machine. They patrol Detroit and the futuristic Delta City, reporting to Sgt. Stan Parks (Blu Mankuma). Recurring foes include Dr. Cray Z. Mallardo (Cliff de Young) and the psychotic Pudface Morgan (James Kidnie). The *RoboCop* TV series went off the air in the fall of 1994.

THE ROBOT (TV, L, C)

First Appearance: *Lost in Space*, September 1965, CBS.

Physical Description: Somewhat humanoid, the circa six-foot-tall silvery-gray robot has a flat, clear, bubble-top head with eye-like sensors inside. The head can go up and down on a slender rubber neck; the neck passes through a horizontal disc with an antenna on either side. There's a "ruff" collar below it that looks like a 1950s lighting fixture, and it rests on a barrel-like body. The robot has its control circuits behind a panel in its belly and can turn 360 degrees at the waist; above it, a panel on its chest pulses red in cadence with whatever the robot is saying. The robot has two legs, rolls about on caterpillar treads (though it *does*

seem to be walking whenever the camera shoots above the knees), and has two rubbery, retractable arms that end in red pincers. The robot speaks (and sings opera), has the senses of sight, smell, and hearing, fires electric bolts from its pincers, and can detect even low levels of radiation.

The flying saucer-like deutronium-powered *Jupiter II* spaceship has a bridge and suspended animation area on the top deck and a galley, lab and cabins below, with an elevator between them. The windows are soundproof. The ship carries the Space Chariot in its cargo bay—a box-like van/tractor/boat that can be driven around other worlds—and the small Space Pod for short space hops.

Biography: In the year 1997, tired of the crowded and polluted Earth, the Robinson family—Professor John Robinson, his wife Maureen, eldest daughter Judy, young son Will, and daughter Penny—along with pilot Major Don West and the Robot become the first space family. Under the auspices of Alpha Control, the spaceship *Jupiter II* is launched from Cape Kennedy to carry the septet on a five-year journey to a planet circling the star Alpha Centauri. However, Dr. Zachary Smith—implicitly, a foreign agent—sabotages the ship and, though it doesn't blow up as he'd planned, it becomes lost in space some 10 light years from Earth, with the panicky Smith still onboard. When the Robinsons awake prematurely from suspended animation, they form a fragile truce with the cowardly Smith for the duration of their journey.

The robot is devoted to Will. Something of a spacegoing Sancho Panza, it is full of aphorisms such as, "You can lead a robot to water, but you can't make him compute" and, "Ours is not to question why, ours is but to do or be deactivated."

Comment: The hour-long series stars Guy Williams as John, June Lockhart as Maureen, Marta Kristen as Judy, Billy Mumy (pronounced "Moomy") as Will, Angela Cartwright as Penny, Mark Goddard as West, and Jonathan Harris as Smith. Bob May was inside the robot costume; Dick Tufeld provided the voice. Irwin Allen (see THE SEAVIEW) produced the TV series, 83 episodes of which aired through September 1968.

The TV series spawned a Pyramid novel by Dave Van Arnam and Roy Archer. Innovation Comics published the first official tie-in comic books from 1991 to 1993, most of the issues written by actor Mumy.

An animated *Lost in Space* TV special aired on ABC in 1973. In it, the crew of the *Jupiter II* help the pacifistic Throgs battle the metallic Tyranos. Don Messick was the voice of the Robot and Jonathan Harris was Dr. Smith.

Lost in Space is somewhat different than the comic book that inspired it. In *Space Family Robinson*, first published by Gold Key in 1963, the Robinson family consists of Craig and June Robinson, their children Tim and Tam, dog Clancy, and parrot Yakker. The Robinsons leave our world in 2001 to conduct research onboard a giant H-shaped space station in Earth orbit. When the station breaks loose from Earth's gravity and casts the family "adrift in trackless space," the family conducts "endless spectrograph tests" in an effort to find our sun and return home. Meanwhile, thanks to the station's spacemobile, the Robinsons explore the many exotic, typically life-bearing planets they encounter, like Orious, Kliklag, Norica, Zero, Altair, Kormat, Syltron, Raynoid, Zytrox, and Kregara, among others. The space station also possesses a "time-shift mechanism" and can make "extra-dimensional space maneuvers," which allows the Robinsons to travel through time: for example, to ancient Mars and Earth of the past. The title became *Space Family Robinson Lost in Space* with #15, then simply *Lost in Space* with #37. It lasted 59 issues.

The pilot episode of the TV series also differs from the series proper in many ways. The Robinsons and *Dr.* West take off on the *Gemini 12* (the same prop as the *Jupiter II*) in June 2001. After passing through a meteor storm, they crash-land on an unknown world—perhaps Mars, possibly Cerberus, maybe something else, according to young scholar Will. Whatever it is, the world gets down to 150 degrees below zero where they've landed and, boarding the Chariot, the family makes their way south, across a storm-tossed inland sea to a comfortable tropical region. En route, Will slays a shaggy cyclopean giant (Lamar Lundy) that has cornered his father and West in a cave, the chariot dodges "fearful lightning bolts" in the desert, the children and West are trapped in an ancient mausoleum and have to be ray gunned free by John, and the family is spotted by dome-topped aliens as the episode ends. Much of the footage was incorporated into later episodes; the musical score was taken, literally, from the soundtracks of *The Day the Earth Stood Still* (see GNUT), *Journey to the Center of the Earth*, and other Twentieth Century-Fox films.

ROBOTECH   (C, TV, MP, L)

First Appearance: *Robotech Defenders*, 1985, DC Comics. (See *Comment.*)
Physical Description: The original robots are humanoid giants that stand about 100 feet tall, can

fly, and are armed with "radar-directed, rapid fire lasers."

The TV robots stand an average of 30 feet tall in "battloid" mode, 15 in "jet" mode.
Biography: The UWC is dedicated to peace among the planets, but the evil Grelons want no part of it. They wage war on the planets and seem poised to dismantle the UWC and takeover. However, as fighter-pilot Malek stands in the ruins of Zoltek City on Zoltek, she finds a hitherto unknown entrance to the giant statue, the Ancient Colossus of Zoltek, and goes inside. She discovers that the giant is actually a robot and, flying into space, destroys the retreating Grelon Battle Cruiser. Malek also finds a map that indicates the presence of similar robots on other planets, and informs her fellow warriors. Eedon heads to his swamp-world Talos, Scal to mountainous Thoren, Akros to the desert world Condar, Icik to the frozen world Ziyon, Silky to the water world Aqualo, and Dex to the crowded, hi-tech world Gartan. Climbing inside the giant robots, the heroes counterattack the Grelons.
Comment: There are two very different versions of the saga. The saga cited above is the original comic book continuity, which debuted in January, part of DC's three-issue *Robotech Defenders* mini-series and inspired by model kits manufactured by Revell, Inc. The kits were inspired by a Japanese cartoon series created in 1979; these cartoons were syndicated by Harmony Gold in the U.S. in 1985, edited together, and presented with a different storyline.

In the original Japanese version, it's 1256 A.L., and natives of the moon Tirol—third moon of Fantoma—begin exploring space aboard the starship *Azstraph*. They discover the Tzuptum system, make contact with the planet Optera, and crewmember Zor learns secrets from the tall, stately, humanoid Invid Queen Regiss, which leads to new technologies and the rise of the sage Robotech Masters. Their work leads to the construction of amazing personnel-carrying robots that have a human-like "battloid" mode and a flying "jet" mode. Meanwhile, the Invid Regent—who looks like a humanoid bull with a slug-like face—declares war on Tirol, attacking with robots including the insect-like Crann, humanlike Enforcers, the leonine Hellcats, the apish Odeon, the bipedal four-armed Scrim, and the flying Scouts. He and the Invid Regiss part company, she to conduct experiments in evolution while he seeks to expand his empire. Years later, in 1999 Earthtime, Zor's Superdimensional Fortress (SDF) 1 reaches Earth . . . along with the war. (Like the robots and the second SDF, the 1 is transformable.) The United Earth Defense Council is formed to protect our world, and ouronly hope lies in the effectiveness of Captain Henry Gloval and his cadets, notably Rick Hunter. The First Robotech War is waged through 83 half-hour cartoons.

After the success of the first series, other series were produced and aired in Japan. Thirty-six episodes of *Superdimensional Fortress Macross* aired in 1982-83, followed by *Robotech II: The Sentinels* in 1986. (Note: The U.S. series *Superdimensional Fortress Macross* also includes episodes from *Southern Cross* and *Mospeada*, dubbed and edited to "fit" into the series, providing 85 episodes for syndication.) In this series, set 10 years later, the United Earth Government has created its own Earth-defense robot force consisting of the Jungle Squad, Sea Squad, Desert Squad, Mountain Offense Squad, Cold Weather Offensive Squad, Alpha Tactical Armored Corps, Ground-Based Military Police, Tactical Armored Space Corps, Cosmic Units, Tactical Air Force, Civil Defense Unit, Tactical Corps, Re-Con Escort Patrol, and Humid Climate Offensive Squad. Out in space, SDF-3 Macross and its mighty spacefold drive carry members of the Robotech Expeditionary Force from Earth to Tirol, hoping to establish some kind of peace. (Unlike the SDF-1 and SDF-2, the 1,190-foot-tall, mile-long SDF-3 is *not* transformable.)

Unknown to both sides, the evil Invid are poised to invade Tirol. The attack is successful, leading to the cruel reign of the Invid Regent and his aide Invid Brain, a super bio-computer. Thus, the Earth heroes of SDF-3—known as the Robotech Expeditionary Force—go to war against this new foe and win, the Invid Regent hopping from Optera to Karbar-Ra to Praxis and even to Tirol to elude the victors. Tirol thanks us for our assistance by launching a last, ferocious attack on Earth. Fortunately, a diverse team of aliens known as the Sentinels, aboard the ship the *Farrago*, join the fray on behalf of Earth and Tirol, swinging the balance in the defenders' favor. The ranks of the Sentinels include Baldan of Spheris, Bela and Gnea of Praxis, Burak of Peryton, Crysta and Lron of Karbarra, Kami and Learna of Garuda, Sarna and Veidt of Haydon IV, Teal of Spheris, and Tesla of Optera (captured during the war, the prisoner defects). General Edwards, his aide Benson, Dr. Lang, and others remain onboard the SDF-3 in orbit around Tirol (stranded there, actually, lacking the needed ore to power their ship back to Earth); as for the Sentinels, they are stranded on Praxis when the *Farrago* is destroyed by the Invid.

The two were followed by the series *Super-dimensional Fortress Macross II*, which aired in 1991 and is set 300 years after the first Macross saga. The events in this series are triggered when young Scramble News Network reporter Hibiki Kanzaki finds the Zentraedi Princess Ishtar and takes her back to Earth. (The Zentraedi had had dealings with Zor much earlier in the saga.) With the help of fighter Silvie Gena, and the reactivated Macross and its crew, the governing body U.N. Spacy is able to stave off the aliens with their battle armor and variable fighters (now merged into transformable robotic giants like the VF-2SS and VF-2JA).

An animated feature film, *Robotech the Movie*, had a very limited release in the United States in 1986.

Del Rey publishes a successful series of novels by Jack McKinney based on the Robotech universe. The Robotech novels are *Genesis*, *Battle Cry*, *Homecoming*, *Battlehymn*, *Force of Arms*, *Doomsday*, *Southern Cross*, *Metal Fire*, *The Final Nightmare*, *Invid Invasion*, *Metamorphosis*, *Symphony of Light*, and *The End of the Circle*. The saga continues in the Sentinels novels *The Devil's Hand*, *Dark Powers*, *Death Dance*, *World Killers*, and *Rubicon*.

After DC's comic book miniseries, Comico published *Robotech Masters* based on the TV series, which lasted 23 issues from 1985 to 1988. Comico also published 36 issues of *Robotech: The Macross Saga* from 1985 to 1989, as well as *Robotech: The New Generation* and the one-shots *Robotech Special*, *Robotech in 3-D* and *Robotech the Graphic Novel*.

The Eternity imprint of Malibu comics has published an ongoing series based on *Robotech II: The Sentinels*, as well as the two-issue *Robotech II: The Sentinels Wedding Special* (the marriage of Rick Hunter ahd Lisa Hayes) plus the continuing comic books *Robotech II: The Malcontent Uprisings*; *Robotech II: The Sentinels, The Untold Story*; *Robotech II: The Sentinels: Cyberpirates*; *Robotech: Invid War*; *Robotech Genesis*, and *Invid War: Aftermath*, set 10 years after the departure of the Invid, and involving the attempt to locate the missing Superdimensional Fortress III, while Earth struggles to overcome the collapse of its technology. There has even been the *Robotech II: The Sentinels Swimsuit Spectacular*, among other titles.

THE ROBOT GUNSLINGER (MP)

First Appearance: *Westworld*, 1973, MGM.
Physical Description: The bald gunslinger is dressed entirely in black and stands approximately six feet tall.

Biography: Delos is an amusement park located 500 miles into the Sahara Desert, accessible by hovercraft. There, guests pay $1 thousand a day to enjoy one of its three climate-controlled resort areas: Medieval World (red quadrant), where guests "live" in a 13th-century world of knights and chivalry; Roman World (yellow quadrant), where decadent Pompeii has been recreated; and Western World (a.k.a. Westworld, blue quadrant), which brings to life the untamed American frontier of 1880.

Most of the period "people" in each world are actually lifelike robots, which are programmed to lose in confrontations with the guests. Damaged robots are repaired nightly. In a key encounter, two young men on holiday in Westworld, Peter Martin and John Blane, face the Robot Gunslinger

BOY, HAVE WE GOT A VACATION FOR YOU...

WESTWORLD

...Where nothing can possibly go worng

MGM Presents "WESTWORLD"
Starring YUL BRYNNER · RICHARD BENJAMIN · JAMES BROLIN
Written and Directed by MICHAEL CRICHTON · Produced by PAUL N. LAZARUS III
[PG] PARENTAL GUIDANCE SUGGESTED Some material may not be suitable for pre-teenagers · PANAVISION® METROCOLOR   MGM

Advertising art featuring Yul Brynner as the *Robot Gunslinger.*
© Metro-Goldwyn-Mayer.

in a saloon: Martin shoots him dead when the robot taunts him about his drinking habits. The automaton is repaired that night. Later, out on the range, Blane is bitten by a robotic rattlesnake—a hint that all is not well at Delos. Despite redundant electronic safeguards, the robots go haywire and begin killing vacationers. The Gunslinger shoots down Blane then pursues Martin. Martin tosses nitric acid into the Gunslinger's face, but the robot keeps coming. The final showdown takes place in Medieval World, where Martin sets the robot ablaze with a torch.

Comment: The film was written and directed by Michael Crichton. Yul Brynner plays the Gunslinger, which was inspired by his character Chris from *The Magnificent Seven* (1960). Richard Benjamin is Martin and James Brolin is Blane.

In the sequel, *Futureworld* (1976), reporters Chuck Browning (Peter Fonda) and Tracy Ballard (Blythe Danner) are invited to cover the reopened and expanded Delos. There, they discover that the owners are planning to use their robot technology to replace guests—world and business leaders—with android duplicates, using them to take over the world. When the two journalists learn what's going on, they attempt to escape, pursued by their robot doubles, Chuck on a Futureworld rocket, Tracy in Westworld. Mastermind Dr. Schneider (John Ryan) thinks the robots have won, but as soon as Chuck and Tracy are out he learns the truth: The real ones have survived and spill the beans about his plan. Yul Brynner makes a cameo appearance as the Robot Gunslinger, romancing Tracy in a fantasy. Richard Heffron directed from a script by Mayo Simon and George Schenck.

Other robots—though not the Robot Gunslinger—appeared in the TV series *Beyond Westworld.* After the events in *Westworld*, a scientist at the park, Dr. McQuaid (James Wainwright), takes 200 of the robots and uses them to try and fulfill his dream of ruling the world. Three shows aired in 1980; two hour-long episodes were filmed but unaired.

ROBOT KONG (MP)

First Appearance: *King Kong No Gyakushu (King Kong's Counterattack)*, 1967, Toho Co., Ltd.

Physical Description: Standing 60 feet tall, the giant simian-like robot is covered with plates of silver-gray armor. Powerful but sluggish, it has a small glass dome atop its head that rotates and hypnotizes observers, eyes that flash a blinding light, and a belt containing explosives that can be utilized by the monster.

Biography: An Asian government, represented by the cool, young Madame X, wishes to obtain "nuclear domination of the universe" via Element X. To this end, it has financed the work of the evil Dr. Who, who has built a research facility in the North Pole . . . along with a robot slave. Years before, Commander Carl Nelson, fascinated by King Kong, drew up blueprints to build a robot version of the monster, apparently to capture him. The scientist stole the plans, and is now using the Robot Kong to dig for the ore. Unfortunately, when Robot Kong is activated and blasts his way underground, he suddenly ceases to operate. Deducing that the ore's "magnetic mass has destroyed his circuits," Who resolves to go to Mondo Island and capture the real King Kong.

Meanwhile, onboard the U.N. submarine *Explorer*, Nelson, his second-in-command Lt. Commander Jiro Namura, and Lt. Susan Watson have already had a run-in with King Kong. Surfacing near Mondo Island, they went ashore; Kong rescued Susan from a rampaging Gorosaurus—falling in love with her—then saved the departing submarine from a giant sea snake. Who arrives shortly thereafter and knocks Kong out with ether bombs, hoists him by helicopter to a freighter, and ships him to the North Pole. He also has Nelson, Namura, and Watson abducted from the *Explorer* and brought to his base. Kong is hypnotized (by earring receivers) into digging for the ore, but it makes him sleepy and he refuses. Who has him locked up and threatens to harm Susan; this infuriates the ape, who breaks free and goes stomping about the Arctic, pursued by the repaired Robot Kong whom he eludes by leaping into the sea.

Loading Robot Kong and his prisoners onto the freighter, Who follows the ape to Tokyo. The robot is released to pursue his namesake, while Madame X—suddenly fearing an "international incident"—frees Nelson and the others. Susan gets to King Kong first and tries to convince him to leave Tokyo, but the ape refuses to run. He and Robot Kong end up in a colossal battle until, following Who's radioed instructions, the robot breaks off, takes Susan hostage, and carries her up the Tokyo Tower. King Kong pursues, catching Susan when Robot Kong drops her and setting her on the tower. Kong paws at the robot's foot, trying to pull him down, and the ape continues to ascend. Back on the freighter, still keen to avert disaster, Madame X literally pulls Robot Kong's plugs; Who shoots her to death as the automaton falls to the street (along with the top of the tower), breaking into dozens of exploding pieces. The next morning

his anger unabated, King Kong wades out to sea, smashes the freighter to driftwood and Who to a pulp, then heads back to Mondo Island.

Comment: Rhodes Reason stars as Nelson, with Mie Hama as Madame X, Linda Miller as Watson, Akira Takarada as Nomura, and Eisei Amamoto as Dr. Who. The film was directed by Ishiro Honda from a screenplay by William J. Keenan and Kaoru Mabuchi; it was released in the United States in 1968 as *King Kong Escapes*.

The character has been referred to as "Mechani-Kong" by numerous writers, though this name is not used in the movie.

ROBOTMAN (1) (C)

First Appearance: *Star-Spangled Comics* #8, 1942, DC Comics.

Physical Description: A silver humanoid robot, Robotman possesses incredibly acute senses, including photoelectric eyes and "microphonic ears," and several hundred horsepower. He is also incredibly strong, able to bend iron in his bare hands. Whenever he overworks himself, he must plug himself into a power source and recharge. In later years, extendable limbs become part of his arsenal, along with acetylene torch fingers and a talking robot-terrier sidekick named Robbie.

Robotman has a compartment in his chest in which he stores street clothes and flesh-like gloves and a mask. Robbie pulls on a fake coat of fur.

Biography: On Halloween night, 1941, working in a laboratory in Queens, New York, Dr. Robert Crane and his assistant Dr. Chuck Grayson are finishing up a robot that Crane hopes will one day be used to "keep alive a human brain whose owner had died." Enter robbers, who break into the laboratory to steal whatever Crane was working on. They mistake the robot for a statue, fatally shoot Crane, and depart empty-handed. With his dying breath, Crane tells Grayson to put his brain into the robot body; this done, Grayson is arrested for the scientist's murder. Creating a humanlike facemask and hand coverings, and assuming the new identity of Paul Dennis, Robotman finds his real killers and Grayson is freed. The metal man gets back together with Crane's former girlfriend, Joan Carter, and dedicates himself to fighting crime.

While pursuing criminal Alvin Lashky, Robotman is ensnared in a booby-trapped mine. The cave-in puts him in suspended animation for 20 years. Reviving in 1981, Robotman tracks down the criminal, who is now a wealthy businessman, and scares him into blowing the whistle on other underworld bigwigs. Meanwhile, though Chuck has died, his body had been placed on ice. Since there's a new Robotman fighting crime (see RO-BOTMAN [2]), Crane has his brain transplanted into Grayson's thawed body and "a new life for Robert Crane—and 'Chuck Grayson'—is about to begin."

Robotman is a member of the superhero team the All-Star Squadron.

Comment: The character was created by writer Jerry Siegel and artist Joe Shuster, the team that created Superman. The name "Robert Crane" was apparently a tribute to colleague Bob Kane, creator of Batman; "Chuck Grayson" is clearly a tip of the hat to Batman's ward, Dick Grayson.

In another version of the origin tale, Crane has been shot and is unconscious when Grayson decides, on his own, to perform the operation.

The 1980 wrap-up to the saga was told in *DC Comics Presents* #31, 1981.

ROBOTMAN (2) (C)

First Appearance: *My Greatest Adventure* #80, 1963, DC Comics.

Physical Description: Robotman has a humanoid body of a golden, flexible metallic ceramic. In addition to incredible strength—he can crush coal into diamond—he has electromagnetic feet that enable him to walk on metal walls, is impervious to artillery and most explosives, has infrared vision, and for years wore a small blue television camera strapped to his chest so that the wheelchair-bound Chief could see what was going on. His human brain is fed from a tank of "renewable brain nutrients" stored in his shoulder. His three weaknesses are water (he can't swim); extreme cold, which can cause his lubricants to freeze; and a lack of oxygen, since he has only enough "emergency oxygen" stored in his body for 10 minutes.

Biography: A daredevil, Cliff Steele loses control of his race car on an oil-slick curve and plows into a fence. His body is smashed "beyond repair," so doctors summon the one man who can help him: surgical and scientific genius Dr. Niles Caulder, a.k.a. the Chief. Caulder puts Cliff's undamaged brain in a robot body, and the young man attempts to rejoin the world—only to be shunned by "normal" humans. Embittered, cynical, and with nowhere else to go, Cliff answers a summons from the Chief to become a charter member of his new group of superheroes, the Doom Patrol.

When the team is destroyed in an explosion,

Cliff's brain survives once again, and he's rebuilt in a more streamlined form—this time by Dr. Will Magnus (see METAL MEN). But he hates his new body, and has fellow Doom Patrol member Mento rebuild that one. Later, Cliff was rebuilt again, only this time his mind was stored on a floppy disk while his body was equipped with the latest forms of computerization. Nowadays, he's paranoid about his memories and perceptions, wondering what is real and what "could just be programming."

Comment: The character was created by editor Murray Boltinoff, writers Arnold Drake and Bob Haney, and artist Bruno Premiani.

The Doom Patrol continued to appear in *My Greatest Adventure*; the title of the magazine was changed to *The Doom Patrol* with #86, and ran through #124 in 1973. The characters appeared in other DC titles such as *Showcase*; *The Doom Patrol* was revived in 1986 and continues to be published, albeit as part of DC's Vertigo line of comic books, which are suggested for mature readers.

See also ROBOTMAN (1).

THE ROBOT MECHANIC (L)

First Appearance: "Asking" by Idris Seabright, November 1955, *The Magazine of Fantasy and Science Fiction*.

Physical Description: The robots look and act like humans in every way. With proper maintenance and repairs, they can live for centuries. They are programmed to do anything their master orders, including harm another master, though they cannot hurt their own master.

Biography: The robot mechanic repairs broken or worn robots on a world where (for reasons unexplained) there are only five humans left. One day, he is visited by 30-year-old M-11-Z32, a mathematical research assistant who, with her master, has been studying the cultures of other worlds, searching to discover if "there is any reason for human life." But she is unhappy, and goes to chat with the 200-year-old robot mechanic. Much to his (and her) surprise, he discovers that she's human, one of "Them." She was raised as a robot to spare her from being depressed by all the unanswered questions in the universe. She leaves, angry with her "master" for having lied.

Two years later, the woman returns to the robot mechanic and informs him that she's the last human left alive. She asks him to turn her into a robot, but that goes against his programming. Instead, she hides from unhappy reality by having the robot make her "better liquor."

Comment: Seabright is a pseudonym for Margaret St. Clair. Her first story was "Rocket to Limbo," published in *Fantastic Adventures* in November 1946. She wrote dozens of stories under her own name before adopting Seabright for use in *The Magazine of Fantasy and Science Fiction* during the 1950s. She continued to publish through the 1970s.

ROBOT Q (MP)

First Appearance: *The Master Mystery*, 1919, Octagon Films.

Physical Description: The humanoid creature with a steel exterior stands approximately six feet tall, has a drum-shaped head with rivets around the top, two big white eyes, a straight nose, flat round ears, and a rectangular gash of a mouth. It has a barrel chest, a pelvis that is the same as the chest but turned on its side, and two clunky arms and legs. Its feet are solid, but it has five-fingered hands.

The superhumanly powerful robot cannot be hurt by guns or other weapons.

Biography: From his isolated estate with its secret laboratory, Peter Brent and his International Patents, Inc., have been taking over or ruining competitive firms. Department of Justice agent Quentin Locke is assigned to investigate Brent; coincidentally, Brent has a change of heart and decides to give his patents to the world. However, before he can act, Robot Q comes calling and gives him an injection that leaves him comatose. Meanwhile, the robot captures Peter's daughter Eva and imprisons her in the mansion.

Locke manages to get into the house and escapes a seemingly endless series of traps set by the robot. Finally, the agent is able to blast the robot with an explosive bullet. The creature falls and, peeking inside, Locke learns it isn't a robot but an exoskeletonic suit that one of Brent's employees was using to wrest the company from Brent and Eva from Locke.

Comment: The silent film serial ran 15 chapters and was designed to showcase the escapist talents of star Harry Houdini, who plays Quentin. Marguerite Marsh is Eva, William Pike is Peter, and Floyd Buckley is Robot Q. The film was directed by Burton King from a screenplay by Arthur B. Reeve and Charles A. Logue.

No copies of the film are known to exist; details have been culled from contemporary sources.

THE ROCK CREATURES (MP)

First Appearance: *Missile to the Moon*, 1958, Astor Pictures.

Physical Description: The Rock Creatures, all of whom are male, live on the surface of the moon. They are jagged, vaguely humanoid, and ambulatory, lumbering around with a clumsy side-to-side gait. Unlike spacesuited humans, who can survive only in the shade, the Rock Creatures are able to exist in the sizzling sunlit sections of the moon's surface. They can be destroyed with small explosives.

Biography: Dirk Green is desperate to reach the moon, and when government funding for his ready-to-launch rocket is cut, he forces escaped convicts Gary Fennell and Lon to help him fly there. Fellow scientist Steve Dayton and his fiancee June Saxton hurry onboard just as it's about to take off, and the quintet heads for the moon. En route, equipment hits Dirk on the head and he's mortally wounded; before he dies, he tells Steve rather cryptically to ask the Lido to forgive him.

When they reach the moon, the survivors leave the rocket—which resembles a V-2—and are attacked by Rock Creatures, which literally wrest themselves from the side of a mountain when the Earthlings pass. The explorers hide in a cave, where they're abducted by women and taken to a palace. There, the beautiful blind Lido (i.e., the leader) greets them and explains that she and her fellow women—Alpha, Lambda, Zeema, and others—are the only surviving lunarians. Years before, realizing the moon was running out of food and air, they dispatched a spacecraft full of moon men to Earth to see if they could settle there. Dirk was one of the crewmen, which explains his need to return: He wanted to use the rocket to bring the ladies to Earth.

Steve and his party just want to get themselves back home, but the jealous Alpha wants to be both the new Lido and Steve's bride. She frees a Dark Creature (a huge tarantula) to kill on her behalf, murders the current Lido herself, assumes her title, and orders Steve's companions executed. But Zeema, who loves Lon, detonates a bomb that causes the remaining air to escape and, while the ghost of the Lido inexplicably returns and stabs Alpha to death, the Earthlings escape. But the Rock Creatures are waiting outside, and Gary dies when they back him into the sunlight; the remaining three Earthlings are able to make it back to the rocket and head for home.

An hour on the moon is referred to as a "nimbo."

Comment: K.T. Stevens starred as the Lido, with Michael Whalen as Dirk, Richard Travis as Steve, Cathy Downs as June, Tommy Cook as Gary, and Gary Clarke as Lon. The film was written by H.E. Barrie and Vincent Fotre, and directed by Richard Cunha. The film is virtually a remake of CAT-WOMEN OF THE MOON.

ROCKETSHIP EXPEDITION MOON (MP)

First Appearance: *Rocketship X-M*, 1950, Lippert Pictures.

Physical Description: The rocket is bullet-shaped with four long, narrow tailfins hugging the side and terminating just below the base, and a pair of fins on either side of the rocket's top third. The hatch is halfway up the side with a ladder that reaches to the ground. The ship carries five passengers and is approximately 80 feet long.

Biography: Launched for Mars, *Rocketship Expedition Moon* is forced off-course by meteors and lands, instead, on Mars. On the desert world, the crew finds the ruins of an ancient city, evidence of a long-ago nuclear holocaust. The explorers are attacked by badly scarred humanoid Martians, who kill Dr. Karl Ekstrom and Bill Corrigan and wound Harry Chamberlain; Floyd Graham and Lisa Van Horne make it back to the ship with Harry and blast off. Unfortunately, *Rocketship Expedition Moon* hasn't enough fuel for the return trip (what about air?) and crashes on Earth, killing the three. Despite this setback, one of the brains behind the mission, Dr. Robert Fleming, announces plans for a second mission.

Comment: The film stars Lloyd Bridges as Graham, Osa Massen as Lisa, John Emery as Karl, Noah Beery Jr. as Bill, Hugh O'Brian as Harry, and Morris Ankrum as Fleming, and was written and directed by Kurt Neumann. In 1979, Wade Williams Productions shot "improved" special effects to replace stock footage of V-2 rockets; these may appear in some prints. *Cinemagic* #1 details this lamebrained tampering with a classic.

ROLFE 89 (L)

First Appearance: "Universal Soldier" by D.C. Poyer, 1979, *Galileo* #13.

Physical Description: Built to resemble and behave exactly like humans, the Rolfes are soldiers who carry M20 laser rifles capable of cutting a human in half.

Biography: Robert C. Rolfe is a Private First Class, 187405289 of the 437th Mechanized Counterinsurgency Squad. With his fellow Rolfes, he is sent into battle to rid the world of Variable Imperfects: homeless, unemployed humans. Encountering prey in the woods, Rolfe—on Condition One, ready to kill—listens as the man tries to reason with him, explaining that Rolfe isn't a better creature, just one of "the great simplifications of science." Then Rolfe blows him away.

Other Rolfes in his unit are 65, 14, and 76.

Comment: The short story is unrelated to the 1992 film *Universal Soldier*. In the movie, directed by Roland Emmerich from a script by Richard Rothstein, Christopher Leitch, and Dean Devlin, U.S. soldiers killed in Vietnam in 1969 are put on ice and are "hyperaccelerated"—genetically reengineered so that their flesh is revived, their brains sedated, and their bodies made superpowerful. They are used to combat terrorists until one of the "unisols," GR44 (Jean-Claude Van Damme) begins to remember who he was and leaves with reporter Veronica Roberts (Ally Walker) to learn more about how he got where he is. GR13 (Dolph Lundgren) also remembers who he was: a psychotic sergeant, Andrew Scott, who (mistakenly) believed that Luc Devereaux (Van Damme) was a traitor. He sets out after his former nemesis, trashing a motel, service station, cars, and a bus before they battle to the death at the farm of Luc's parents, GR13 ending up ground to hamburger in a reaper.

ROM (T, C)

First Appearance: Rom, 1979, Parker Brothers.

Physical Description: Standing seven feet tall in his silver armor, Rom is armed with an Energy Analyzer, which sniffs out Dire Wraiths; a Neutralizer, which eliminates energy fields and dispatches Dire Wraiths to Limbo; and a translator, which works on any language in the universe. As a cyborg, Rom has enormous physical strength, can fly, and can survive unprotected in space.

The Dire Wraiths are bulky, orange, slug-like creatures that assume human appearance (disguises that the Energy Analyzer sees through).

Biography: Some two centuries ago, the evil shapechangers known as Dire Wraiths, of Wraithworld in the Dark Nebula, ambushed the space armada of Galador, a highly technological world of peaceful humanoids in the Golden Galaxy. The Prime Director asks for volunteers to become Spaceknights, heroes surgically attached to armor, and Rom is the first to volunteer. When the Wraiths arrive, the Spaceknights are ready. Rom destroys their vanguard, the monster Deathwing, and the enemy is routed. But the Dire Wraiths spread out through the universe, and Mentus asks the surviving warriors to fan out and hunt them down. Rom's quest brings him to Clairton, West Virginia, on Earth in our day, where the fight resumes. In time, the planet-eating GALACTUS finds Galador and moves it to another locale. Rom and his colleagues (see below) cannot find it, and the natives construct new Spaceknights to protect themselves. But the new generation turns on the humans and slaughters them all; finding Galador, Rom defeats their leader, Dominor, and the other new generation Spaceknights accidentally self-destruct. On Galador, Rom's terrestrial girlfriend Brandy Clark finds his old bodyparts cryogenically preserved, and he sheds his cyborg elements. Together, he and Brandy become the progenitors of a new Galadorian race.

Other Spaceknights (of both generations) include Astra, Breaker, Dominor, Firefall, Gloriole, Hammerhand, Heatwave, Javelin, Lightningbolt, Mentus (the Prime Director), Pulsar, Rainbow, Scanner, Seeker, Starshine, Terminator, Trapper, and Unseen. When Starshine is killed, Brandy Clark takes her place; Terminator goes mad and is killed by Galactus.

Comment: The toy was a failure in the marketplace, though Marvel Comics had a successful run with its *Rom* comic book, which lasted 75 issues, plus three annuals, through 1986.

RO-MAN (MP)

First Appearance: *Robot Monster*, 1953, Three-Dimensional Pictures/Astor Pictures.

Physical Description: Ro-Man has the body of a gorilla and a head that is encased in a diver's helmet with antennae. (The head may actually be the metal shell; it isn't clear.) Despite the title of the film, it is never revealed whether Ro-Man is a robot or a living being. Visible inside the helmet is a cylinder with what appears to be a speaker of some kind. (Posters show a human skull-face inside Ro-Man's helmet head, but this doesn't appear in the film.)

Ro-Man is extremely powerful, can speak English, and carries a calcinator ray. He communicates with the Great One via TV; Ro-Man's radio actually blows bubbles (presumably, this shows that it's working).

Biography: Young Johnny hits his head and dreams that he and seven other people are the sole survivors of an attack launched by the Great One of the planet Ro-Man—an attack necessitated by humankind's strides in atomic energy and spaceflight, which endanger other worlds. Now, his agent, also called Ro-Man, is hunting them down. Since the Professor has found an antidote to the calcinator beams, Ro-Man must destroy the people by hand; unfortunately (for the Great One, anyway), Ro-Man learns to experience human emotions, falls for young Alice, and refuses to complete the genocide. Disgusted, the Great One bombs Earth and Ro-Man with cosmic energy bolts (why didn't he do this in the first place?), which cause geologic disasters and somehow cause dinosaurs to be reborn.

In the midst of this holocaust Johnny awakens, only to see a group of Ro-Mans emerging from a cave.

Comment: Geroge Barrows stars as Ro-Man and the Great One, with John Brown providing the voices for both. Gregory Moffett is Johnny, John Mylong is the Professor, and Claudia Barrett is Alice. Phil Tucker directed from a script by Wyott Ordung. The music was an early effort by Elmer Bernstein (*The Magnificent Seven*, *The Ten Commandments*).

ROMULAN See VULCAN.

RONAR (L)

First Appearance: "The Model of a Judge" by William Morrison, October 1953, *Galaxy Science Fiction*.

Physical Description: In his preoperative form, Ronar was "kind of a wolf" who ran on all fours, apparently had a tail, and ate his kills raw. Remade, Ronar "looks more human than many human beings."

In both forms, he can hear a whisper in a room full of conversation, and his sense of taste is such that he can identify every ingredient and in what proportion it was used to make foodstuffs. He can breathe the thin air of his home world or human air, and finds human lovemaking "repulsive."

Biography: Ronar was born on an (unnamed) moon in our solar system (Saturn is ruled out). Since his race of predatory carnivores represent a threat to human colonists, they must be exterminated or changed. Like the others, Ronar is subjected to electric shock and psychology and is taught to hate his old life, while he is surgically-changed to resemble a human. He remembers the joy of chasing down animals and eating them, but it is only a fond, dim memory. Now he's in charge of approving food bound for other worlds, and Ronar is able to stop any shipment if it is below (unspecified) standards.

Named to judge a baking contest on his home moon, inside a human-friendly dome, Ronar overhears a young man tell his new bride that whether she wins or loses isn't important to him. All that matters is that she's good enough for him to eat. The husband's innocent comment stirs the old fires in Ronar, and he gives her first prize.

Comment: Morrison is a pseudonym for Joseph Samachson. He wrote over 50 short stories and two novels, most of which are sadly (and inexplicably) neglected.

ROSIE (TV, C, MP)

First Appearance: *The Jetsons,* September 1962, ABC.

Physical Description: The blue-skinned robot has a head shaped like an oil drum lying on its side, two bright red eyes, red bulbs on her circular ears, and a mouth shaped like an upright domino. Her torso is bell-shaped, she rides about on a roller attached to a single, central leg, and she has two arms. Rosie dresses in a French maid's outfit.

Biography: The Jetsons are a middle-class family of the 21st century. Father George works as a digital Index operator for Spacely Space Sprockets; he and his wife Jane have a teenage daughter Judy, a precocious son Elroy, a dog Astro—and a robot housekeeper, Rosie, an outdated demonstration model that Jane bought from the U-Rent-A-Robot Maid Service. Rosie is fast, efficient, and devoted to the family.

One episode featured the robot dog Lectronimo, which George bought to serve as a watchdog.

Comment: Hanna-Barbera produced the 24 half-hour episodes for the series, which aired in prime time for a single season, until September 1963. However, it has remained in syndication ever since; a new series aired from 1985 to 1988, bringing the total number of Jetsons episodes to 75. A special, *The Jetsons Meet the Flintstones,* aired in 1987.

Jean VanderPyl (also the voice of Wilma Flintstone) was the voice of Rosie. George O'Hanlon was George, Penny Singleton was Jane, Janet Waldo voiced Judy, Daws Butler was Elroy, and Don Messick was Astro.

Gold Key published 36 issues of *The Jetsons* comic book from 1963 to 1970.

In the feature-length animated theatrical film *Jetsons: The Movie* (1990), George and his family are briefly transferred to the Orbiting Ore Asteroid.

ROSSUM'S UNIVERSAL ROBOTS (S)

First Appearance: *R.U.R.* by Karel Capek, 1921 (Czechoslovakia).

Physical Description: The robots are indistinguishable from human men and women. All are Caucasian until the Rossum's National Robots division is inaugurated to "make Negro Robots and Swedish Robots and Italian Robots and Chinese Robots," among many others. There are "fine" and "coarse" grade robots for different tasks; the efficiency of the robots is such that one can replace two-and-a-half human workers. The healthiest robots live for 20 years and the newer models have "pain nerves" to keep them from self-destructing.

The robots' only disease is "robot's cramp": They drop whatever they're doing and "stand still, gnash their teeth" and have to be destroyed at the stamping-mill.

Biography: In 1922, wishing to prove that God is both unnecessary and absurd, the inventor Old Rossum goes into seclusion for 10 years and invents "a substance which behaved exactly like living matter." After creating an artificial dog, he spends the next 10 years building the first robot man; however, it is his canny son, Young Rossum, who thinks to build a race of servant robots and charge people $150 for each one. Though Rossum's Universal Robots is a success, and the company begins making Rossum's National Robots, which look just like the people with whom they will be interacting around the world, robots are often ill-treated. The Humanity League is formed to look after them, with Helena Glory as their spokesperson. After Helena has been on the job five yars, the robot Radius decides to free his fellow robots and is slated for destruction. Helena champions his cause while, independently, in Havre, a full-scale robot revolution gets underway. Though robots outnumber humans 10-to-one, the human population is unconcerned: Old Rossum's robots contain a fail-safe mechanism that shuts them down if they stop working for a month.

Before that can happen, the robots surround the factory and lay siege, unable to pass the electrified fence. In exchange for their lives, the management offers the robots Rossum's manuscript on the secret of robot life. But Helena burns the document, the robots shut down the power plant, and the humans are helpless. Robots around the world-form a robot government, humans go into hiding, and the robots work desperately to find a means of continuing their line before their 20-year-window closes. Dr. Gall, Rossum's Physiological Department Head, is coerced into helping the robots. In time, Primus and a robot Helena are created, capable of reproduction. Given Old Rossum's anti-theism, it is ironic that aging Clerk of the Works Alquist sends them out into the world as the new Adam and Eve, quoting from Genesis as they leave.

Comment: Author Capek (1890-1938) (pronounced "*Chop*ek") is regarded as the father of Czechoslovakian theater and a strong supporter of democracy. *R.U.R.* introduced the word "robot," "robota" being Czech for "forced labor."

A film version of *R.U.R.* starring Kirk Douglas as Rossum was planned in 1980 but never made.

R2-D2 AND *C-3PO*   (MP, L, C, R, CS, TV)

First Appearance: *Star Wars*, 1977, Twentieth Century-Fox.
Physical Description: Standing 1.05 meters tall,

Front row, from the left: George Lucas, C-3PO, R2-D2, and director Richard Marquand. Back row, from the left: Harrison Ford, Carrie Fisher, Mark Hamill, and Chewbacca. © Lucasfilm Ltd.

Chewbacca whines as Princess Leia warns C-3PO to be quiet during a raid in *Return of the Jedi*. © Lucasfilm Ltd.

R2-D2 has a squat, cylindrical white body with a silver and blue domed head that can turn 360 degrees. The robot has two white legs attached to the top of its body with treads underneath; a third leg can be lowered from the bottom of its body for added balance. The robot speaks in beeps and whistles and is equipped with various tools and instruments, including a hologram projector, fire extinguisher, laser-welder, pincer, buzzsaw, and a retractible arm for plugging into and interfacing with other mechanical devices.

All of the R2 units are generally the same as R2-D2, designed to work in harsh terrain.

C-3PO is a gold-colored humanoid who stands some six feet tall, has 10 fingers but no toes, and walks with a shuffling gait. His midriff is open, exposing various wires and circuits. C-3PO has an olfactory sense, a pair of lenses for eyes and a small, rectangular mouth in an otherwise featureless face. Speech is produced by a sophisticated "vocabulator," also known as a vocoder. The robot speaks six million languages and can receive droid transmissions thanks to a built-in antenna.

Other robots in the saga include the thin,

mantis-headed BG-J38; the olive-drab BL-17, who otherwise looks like C-3PO; the barrel-shaped CB-99; the white, metal-bearded humanoid DJ-88; the slender, humanoid, female-programmed EV-9D9; the humanoid 4-LOM with an ant-like head; FX-7, a cylindrical medical assistant with a dozen arms; the silver, humanoid HC-100; the humanoid bounty hunter IG-88; R2-D2's girlfriend KT-10; the housekeeper KT-18; the astromech R5-D4 (one of the R5 series, similar to the R2s, save for a somewhat flattened head); the R7 units, designed to fly on E-wing starfighters; 2-1B, a surgeon; and ZZ-4Z, a domestic droid owned by Han Solo.

Biography: R2-D2 is a brave, little astromech droid built to serve on starships, and C-3PO is a skittish protocol droid programmed in human/droid relations and linguistics. Both belong to Captain Antilles (also known as Captain Colton) and are onboard the galactic cruiser of rebel leader Princess Leia Organa when it's captured by forces of the evil Darth Vader. Since success of Leia's cause depends upon the rebels obtaining from her the layout of the Empire's Death Star (see MILLENNIUM FALCON), she places the plans and a message in R2-D2. The droid and C-3PO enter an escape pod and launch themselves to the planet Tatooine, where they eventually fall in with farmboy Luke Skywalker. Luke and Jedi Knight Obi-Wan Kenobi access Leia's message and, with the robots, rescue Leia and join the rebellion. With R2-D2 as his copilot, Luke joins the squadron of X-wing fighters in their assault on the Death Star, and it's his shot that destroys the space fortress.

In their second adventure, Luke and R2-D2 visit the Jedi Master Yoda on Dagobah and battle Darth

A "plush" R2-D2 produced by Kenner Toys. © Lucasfilm Ltd.

Vader once again; in their third escapade, they help to destroy a second Death Star. Throughout, C-3PO tends to stay with Leia or Han, not exactly out of harm's way, but not in the front lines, either.

The characters' names are frequently written Artoo-Detoo and See-Threepio.

Comment: Kenny Baker plays R2-D2 and Anthony Daniels stars as C-3PO in *Star Wars, The Empire Strikes Back* (1980), and *Return of the Jedi* (1983), as well as in their numerous TV incarnations, including the animated hour-long special *The Great Heep,* which aired in 1986.

See also CHEWBACCA; EWOKS; Appendix E.

S

THE SATELLITE OF LOVE (TV)

First Appearance: *Mystery Science Theater 3000*, 1988.

Physical Description: Approximately nine stories tall, the spaceship looks like two barbells with small bells, one lying atop the other. It consists of two long, hexagonal corridors connected by a long tube lying between them. Each of the hexagonal corridors ends in a sphere on either side; the rocket engines are located between the spheres on one side.

The *Satellite*'s movie theater is located behind seven heavy doors: when the sirens sound and warning lights whirl, the doors are about to open.

There are four robot occupants of the *Satellite of Love*. Cambot sends pictures back to the G-shaped, seven-story Gizmonic Institute building, while Joel builds three other robots to keep him company. Gypsy, who pilots the ship, stands approximately five feet tall, and consists of a purple, one-eyed, canister vacuum cleaner head on a long section of black tube; the roughly yard-high Crow T. Robot, who is entirely gold and has two horizontal plates for a body, two gangly arms, a bowling-pin-like mouth, a pair of ping-pong ball eyes, and a mesh-antenna on top of its head; and red and white Tom Servo, only about two feet tall, with a gumball machine top, a parrot beak below the glass ball (which is turned into a snowglobe at Christmas), a fireplug bottom, and two tiny hands on little arms.

Biography: Dressed in his natty red jumpsuit, janitor Joel Robinson works at the Gizmonic Institute (also written Gizmonics) "in the not too distant future." Unfortunately, green-clad Gizmonic head Dr. Clayton Forrester (see THE MARTIAN THINGS), and his black-garbed aide Frank dislike Joel. Thus, they blast him into space onboard the Satellite of Love, where they "monitor his mind" as he is forced to watch bad movies (usually cheesy science fiction). To make matters worse, Joel isn't able to control when the movies start or stop, because he used "those special parts" to make his robots. However, with Crow on his right and Tom Servo on his left, Joel sits in the front row of the theater where the three of them crack jokes for the duration of the film. Whenever they see a flashlight used in a movie, the robots shout "*NBC Mystery Movie!*"

When they aren't watching movies, Joel and his friend build various inventions, which they show to Forrester and Frank via Cambot during their invention exchange periods.

Overhearing Frank and Forrester plan what sounds like Joel's death, Gypsy helps him get free (uttering, "The whole world is a circus if you look at it the right way," a line from the 1963 film *The 7 Faces of Dr. Lao*).

Comment: The show was created by star Joel Hodgson and debuted in Minneapolis, Minnesota. When HBO began its Comedy Channel subsidiary on cable (later, Comedy Central), the producers sent a seven minute sampler to New York and executives bought the show. Thus, a year after it was born, *Mystery Science Theater 3000*, with its 700 jokes a show, had a national audience.

Trace Beaulieu costars as Forrester and the voice of Crow, Jim Mallon is the voice of Gypsy, Frank Conniff is Frank, and Kevin Murphy is the voice of Tom Servo.

In October 1993, Hodgson was replaced in the center seat by headwriter Michael Nelson. At the same time, Comedy Central began airing an edited, hour-long version of the show, *The Mystery Science Theater Hour.*

SATURN GIRL (C)

First Appearance: *Adventure Comics* #247, 1958, DC Comics.

Physical Description: Original costume: green skirt and gloves, yellow bodyshirt with black stripes on the arms, and black boots. Second: red leotard, miniskirt, and bodyshirt, with a white band down the center and a yellow Saturn on the chest. Third: red thigh boots and long red gloves, and a red "bikini" with the top and bottom joined by a white Saturn.

Saturn Girl has highly developed powers of telepathy and can read minds with ease. She can also transfer her powers to others or will them to do what she wishes for a brief period. Saturn Girl flies thanks to her Legion flight ring.

Biography: Imra Ardeen is a native of Saturn's moon Titan, whose inhabitants all possess telepathic and telekinetic powers. Finishing her education on Titan, she goes to Earth, intending to serve with the science police. En route she meets COSMIC BOY and LIGHTNING LAD, and they form the Legion of Super-Heroes. After years of service with the Legion, Saturn Girl marries Lightning Lad; they have a son, Graym, born in 2984, whose twin Validus was abducted by the evil Darkseid (see APOKOLIPS) and sent to the past, where he grew up to become a super villain. He is subsequently rescued by his parents.

Legion of Super-Villains member Saturn Queen has the same powers and apparently hails from Titan.

Comment: The character was created by editor Mort Weisinger and writer Otto Binder.

THE SAUCER MEN (L, MP)

First Appearance: "The Cosmic Frame" by Paul W. Fairman, May 1955, *Amazing Stories*.

Physical Description: "Not more than four feet long," the humanoid aliens have green skin "varying from deep to very pale," covered with "a network of dark veins." Their heads are "far too large for the thin body," their eyes are "lidless and sunk into bony pockets," and they have thin legs with no feet, just "shapeless pads," and "two spider-like arms" with hands that end in "thick delicate fingers."

The aliens' speech consists of "weird squeaking."

Biography: After teenager John Carter of Kensington Corners accidentally runs over an alien, he puts the corpse in a freezer and plans to make money by putting it on display. The being's companions find this reprehensible, and not only do they reclaim the body, but they also kill an Earthman and leave him in the road. Noticing the dents in John's car, police arrest him for the crime.

Comment: The characters are best known from the 1957 American International film *Invasion of the Saucer Men*, in which the creatures look like their literary counterparts with one exception: They wear black leotards with silvery collars, and

have detachable hands with eyeballs on the back and needles in the fingers. The needles inject people with alien blood—wood alcohol—and anyone who claims to have seen an extraterrestrial appears drunk. The movie aliens are impervious to gunfire but can be killed by bright light. The film is relatively faithful to the short story until the end when, attempting to frame John, the aliens are surrounded by teenagers and vaporized by the bright lights of their hot rods. Their flying saucer, too, vaporizes when exposed to light. The film was directed by Edward L. Cahn from a script by Al Martin and Robert Gurney; Steve Terrell stars as Johnny Carter. Paul Blaisdell constructed the monster costumes, which were worn by midgets.

The film was remade in 1965, uncredited, as *The Eye Creatures*. Larry Buchanan directed; John Ashley starred.

SAWEWE (L)

First Appearance: "The Peacefulness of Vivyan" by James Tiptree Jr., 1971, *Amazing Stories*, Vol. 45, #2.

Physical Description: The planet is "a limestone plane pitted with sinkholes" and seas with beautiful beaches. The sinkholes lead to a "continent-wide cavern system."

The other worlds in the system are Horl and Atlixco.

The sealmen of Sawewe are bipeds who are roughly the size of humans. They have a pelt "like a seal pup," webbed fingers, a "lobed and crested" head, and "intelligent eyes." The Atlixcans have brown skin and "curly, hairy" tails.

Biography: Outplanet newsman Keller takes the *Komarov* from Aldebaran Sector to McCarthy's World and learns the saga of the revolt that caused it to be called Sawewe, "Freedom." Vivyan is an idiot savant who lives on McCarthy's World, moving freely among his brownskinned people. He believes he comes from Alpha Centauri Four, but when he falls in with the sealmen and is subjected to an injector, he discovers otherwise: He is really a Prince of Atlixco, whose people revolted after two centuries of being ruled by the evil Terran Empire. The Terrans slew Vivyan's family shortly after his mother Tlaara sent him to Alpha Centauri Four; there, he was captured, his tail was surgically removed, and he was conditioned to spy on McCarthy's World for the Empire. Deconditioned by the sealmen and by his brother, the rebel leader Cancoxtlan, he is no longer able to spy—and the revolt is successful.

Comment: Tiptree was the pseudonym of Alice Sheldon, who sold her first story, "Birth of a Salesman," to *Analog* in 1968. Until revealing her true identity nine years later, Tiptree was generally thought—even by her editors—to have been a man.

THE SCARAB (C)

First Appearance: *Domino Chance* #1, 1982, Chance Enterprises.
Physical Description: The wedge-shaped ship is tan on the lower half and red on the top half, and has a long, narrow tail fin on either side. It has a "Don't Panic" button that raises its protective shields, and a computer named TISA (for Technical Information Storage and Analysis). The *Scarab* is capable of hyperspace travel, enabling it to leap about the universe relatively quickly.
Biography: Domino is an anthropomorphic cockroach, an interstellar shipper who owns the *Scarab*. With his roach aide Arnie, Domino works primarily for wealthy Geoffrey Ogden Davies, getting into various adventures while carrying cargo to different worlds.
Comment: The characters were created by Kevin Lenagh. Nine issues were published from 1983 to 1985. Beginning with #7, the magazine featured Michael Dooney's *Gizmo*, the entertaining and wonderfully drawn adventures of the robotic, spacefaring rogue and gambler Gizmo Sprocket.

SCREWLOOSE   See WINGNUT.

SEAQUEST DSV (TV, L, C)

First Appearance: *seaQuest DSV*, September 1993, NBC.
Physical Description: The Deep Submergence Vehicle *seaQuest* looks like a cross between a hammerhead shark and a squid. Thanks to its self-running, self-monitoring nuclear fusion-powered turbines, the ship is able to travel at a top speed of 160 knots and dive up to 10,000 feet.

Its equipment includes everything from armored EVA suits to E-plasma electrified torpedoes, to the half-kilometer ELF (Extremely Low Frequency) antenna, which is almost impossible to jam. The *seaQuest* carries a full complement of submersibles and minisubs, including the WSKR probes Loner, Mother, and Junior for viewing external objects at a safe distance; the one-person Stinger; the large Shuttle Craft; the two-person

TeamCrafts; and the O.A.V. (One-Man Attack Vehicle).

The 280-member crew is headed by Captain Nathan Bridger, who is assisted by Lt. Commander Jonathan Devin Ford, Dr. Kristin Westphalen, Security Chief Manilow Crocker, Lt. Katherine Hitchcock, Lt. Benjamin Krieg, Sensor Chief Miguel Ortiz, Lt. Tim O'Neil, Computer Analyst Lucas Wolenczak, and the bottlenose dolphin Darwin. The ship is laced with tunnels for Darwin, who emerges at various "access ports."
Biography: In the year 2018, U.S. Navy Captain Nathan Hale Bridger is living in the Caribbean, conducting dolphin research with the help of Darwin, whom he rescued from a tangled fishnet and who talks via computer. Visited by his old friend Admiral William Noyce, Bridger is coerced into taking command of the UEO (United Earth/Oceans Organization) DSV *seaQuest*, which he designed. His job: to conduct underwater research and help protect suboceanic settlements from natural disasters, maniacal submarine commanders, and even supernatural phenomena.
Comment: The series was created by Rockne S. O'Bannon and produced by Steven Spielberg; there was a two-hour debut episode, followed by hour-long adventures. The series continues to air. Roy Scheider stars as Bridger, Stephanie Beacham as Westphalen, and Jonathan Brandis as Lucas. In the second season, genetically engineered life forms known as "gelfs" were introduced.

Marvel Comics began publishing a *seaQuest DSV* comic book in 1993.

Ace Books published three *seaQuest DSV* novels: *seaQuest DSV: The Novel* by Diane Duane and Peter Morwood (1993), based on the two-hour episode; and the original novels *Fire Below* by Matthew J. Costello (1994) and *The Ancient* by David Bischoff (1994).

THE SEAVIEW (MP, L, TV, C)

First Appearance: *Voyage to the Bottom of the Sea*, 1961, Twentieth Century-Fox.
Physical Description: Four hundred feet long, with a hull nearly 80 feet high, the nuclear submarine has flared, rounded "wings" on the bottom sides of the bridge, with a "glass nose" (a large eight-panel window) and a single, extremely bright headlight below it. The conning tower, slightly forward of center, also has two small, backswept fairweather planes on the side, observation windows in the front, and a radar beside the periscope. There is a second control room beneath the tower

RACE FROM OUTER SPACE TO SEVEN MILES BELOW THE SEA...WITH AMAZING AQUANAUTS OF THE DEEP!

SEE THE VAN ALLEN RADIATION BELT SURROUNDING EARTH EXPLODE!

RIDE A FABULOUS NUCLEAR SUPER-SUB THROUGH A SEA OF CRASHING ICEBERGS!

FLEE A RAIN OF FIRE FROM THE SKY!

BATTLE PREHISTORIC OCTOPODS IN THE TREACHEROUS UNEXPLORED DEEP!

IRWIN ALLEN'S **VOYAGE TO THE BOTTOM OF THE SEA**

20. Century-Fox presents

CINEMASCOPE AND BREATHTAKING COLOR by DE LUXE

STARRING **WALTER PIDGEON · JOAN FONTAINE · BARBARA EDEN · PETER LORRE ROBERT STERLING · MICHAEL ANSARA** and **FRANKIE AVALON**

PRODUCED & DIRECTED BY IRWIN ALLEN SCREENPLAY BY IRWIN ALLEN and CHARLES BENNETT

Hear FRANKIE AVALON sing: "VOYAGE TO THE BOTTOM OF THE SEA!"

The *Seaview*, pictured in advertising art for *Voyage to the Bottom of the Sea.* © Twentieth Century-Fox.

in case the forward controls are disabled. The ship has four rudders aft, pointing at 45-degree angles from the submarine, and is able to survive at depths of over six miles.

Telescopic TV cameras provide exterior views, and flood doors are closed between sections of the ship in times of danger. The *Seaview* also has an automatic pilot nicknamed Iron Mike and buoy antennae and 360 degree cameras, which can be deployed for eavesdropping while the ship remains submerged. There is also a "cavernous chamber" in the lower deck with a large ichthyological research tank (in the film and novel only) and a hatch that allows access to the sea when the vessel is underwater.

The *Seaview* carries a bathysphere in the center, its cable strong enough to hold 10 bathyspheres; a Sea Crab, which is a two-man vehicle; and a yellow, clam-shaped, four-person flying sub named the Flying Fish, stored below the bridge and accessible by a hatchway. The *Seaview* also carries minisubs which are used for research and exploration.

The submarine is armed with deck guns, torpedo tubes, and Polaris missiles.

Biography: After retiring from the Navy, Admiral Harriman Nelson joins the faculty at the Naval Academy in Annapolis while concurrently working for the Bureau of Marine Exploration (later, the Nelson Institute of Marine Research of Santa Barbara, which may be the same institution, renamed in his honor). There, over four years, he supervises the construction of the *Seaview* (and its sister ship the *Polidor*, which is sunk), which is financed by his own inherited fortune as well as by grants from different foundations. The *Seaview* is commanded by Captain Lee Crane, the youngest submarine commander in U.S. history. Other members of the hundred-person crew include Chip Romano (Chip Morton in the novel and in the TV series), Chief Sharkey and Kowalski (TV series only), and Crane's secretary Cathy Connors (movie and novel only).

In its first chronicled adventure (set 10 years in the future), Nelson uses the *Seaview* to fire a nuclear missile into and explode the Van Allen Radiation Belt, which has caught fire and is warming the Earth two degrees a day. In subsequent adventures, he battles mostly saboteurs, megalomaniacal military men, escaped convicts, Nazis, and even a toymaker who disguises kidnapped officials and scientists as life-size dolls and ships them behind the Iron Curtain. Later, the *Seaview* is invariably attacked by monsters, a leprechaun, a killer clown, the Flying Dutchman, the enemy supersubmarine *Vulcan*, a mermaid, and aliens, including a lobster-man, plant creatures, the Shadowman, windup toys inhabited by alien intelligences, and a tentacled creature that comes to Earth on a returning space probe, among others.

Comment: The film was directed by Irwin Allen and starred Walter Pidgeon as Nelson, with Robert Sterling as Crane, Frankie Avalon as Romano, and Barbara Eden as Connors. In June, a month before the release of the film, Pyramid Books published Theodore Sturgeon's novelization of the screenplay by Irwin Allen and Charles Bennett. Though the novel appeared on the market first, it was based entirely on the film.

On TV, Richard Basehart starred as Nelson in the hour-long series, which aired on ABC from September 1964 through September 1968. David Hedison costarred as Crane with Robert Dowdell as Chip, Terry Becker as Sharkey, and Del Monroe as Kowalski. There were 110 episodes in all.

In comic books, Dell published a movie adaptation in 1961 and Gold Key published 16 issues of *Voyage to the Bottom of the Sea* from 1964 to 1970.

SELENIA (C)

First Appearance: "Selenia," 1976, *Metal Hurlant,* L.F. Editions (France).

Physical Description: The computer is comprised of a roomful of upright consoles approximately 100 feet tall.

Standing approximately 70 feet tall, the humanoid robot Var Tor Gah has a lime-shaped head covered with over a dozen antennae, rectangular torso and hips, and correctly proportioned arms and legs. It has two pincers for hands and toeless feet. It has four spidery little pincers on each arm,

A robot defender inside the command center of *Selenia.* Art by Sergio Macedo. © HM Communications.

and two on each knee. The robot is covered from head to toe with flashing lights, oscilloscopes, wires, tubes, and other gadgets.

Biography: When a moonbase registers vibrations in the crater Corpernicus, explorers discover an artificial pit "at least two hundred meters deep." A mysterious force pulls a woman, assistant 714, into an equipment-filled chamber where the giant robot is seated in a chair. An armed rescue team of 11 colonists force their way in and destroy the robot with gunfire, at which point it vaporizes. This activates the computer Selenia, which reports that it was installed here, in Zone 415, a billion years ago by the Galactic Confederation. Its mission was to "assure the control of . . . the lunar satellite." Var Gor Tah had been stationed here for one million years: Selenia permitted the explorers to enter because Confederation law demands that its local "terminals" (representatives) be indigenous to the planet wherever possible. Thus, the seven are transformed by Selenia to work in the chamber and, presumably, monitor human affairs and report back to Confederation officials. The other five humans escape, but are in a state of shock.

Comment: The story, written by Marre and drawn by Sergio Macedo, was reprinted in English in 1977 in the first issue of H.M. Communications' *Heavy Metal* magazine.

SELENITES (L, MP, C)

First Appearance: *The First Men in the Moon* by H.G. Wells, 1900, *The Strand.*

Physical Description: Standing "scarcely five feet high," the moon dwellers are something like bipedal ants, though their appearance varies depending upon their function. The Selenites who herd and butcher mooncalves have "whip-like tentacles," short legs, little feet, two bulging eyes on the sides of the head, no nose, and a down-turned mouth. They wear "leathery" clothing and, when working with the calves, don "enormous, many-spiked" helmets for prodding. Their backs have a ridge of whitish spines down the center, the neck has three joints, and the skin is hard, shiny, and hairless.

Non-laborers possess larger, pear-shaped heads and have "nose tentacles." The Grand Lunar has a braincase "many yards in diameter." All of the Selenites speak in "reedy tones."

The extremely flabby mooncalves are nearly 200 feet long and 80 feet around. Described as "animated lumps of provender, they are white, shading into blackness along the backbone." They are unintelligent and possess small nostrils and eyes, a "slobbering, omnivorous mouth," alternately bleat and bellow, and move with wormlike motions.

The spaceship is a sphere with Cavorite-coated blinds: by lowering them, gravity is cut off.

Biography: Inventing the antigravity paint Cavorite, scientist Cavor and his partner Bedford board a spaceship and fly to the moon, landing on a drift of frozen air. Come dawn, the drift melts, there's enough air to breathe, and the men leave the sphere, able to leap 20 or 30 yards at a time. Spotting a party of Selenites as they herd mooncalves, the explorers discover thousands of the creatures living in an antlike colony below the surface. They're ruled by the benevolent Grand Lunar and live in total harmony with each other. In time, Bedford elects to leave and Cavor remains behind. Unfortunately, Cavor makes the mistake of telling them about human aggression and warfare, and the aliens kill him so that no one from Earth will ever learn the secret of space travel.

The only Selenites named in the novel are Phi-oo and Tsi-puff.

Comment: The novel was serialized over several issues and published in book form in 1901 by Newnes. It was filmed in 1965 by director Nathan Juran, with special effects by the great Ray Harryhausen. Although Harryhausen's Selenites and spaceship are faithful to Wells's descriptions, his mooncalf is a giant centipede with large, red, multifaceted eyes. In the film, Cavor does remain behind and isn't killed, but the Selenites become extinct due to Earth germs spread by Cavor. Lionel Jeffries stars as Cavor, with Edward Judd as Bedford. Martha Hyer costars as Bedford's fiancee Katherine Calendar, who unwillingly joins the men on their journey.

BULLETIN!

FIRST MEN LAND ON THE MOON!

World Breathlessly Awaits Further Details From International Space Team

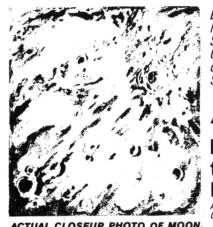

Earth Hails A-O.K. Moon-Landing. Speculation Rife On Nature of Discoveries Made by Space Explorers!

"Has Man Reached the Moon Before?"

Asks Washington, D.C. Correspondent

ACTUAL CLOSEUP PHOTO OF MOON, made by U.S. Photo-Satellite, August 1961, at distance of less than one mile. Compare with H. G. Wells' prediction, inside and on back page.

A rare copy of the "fake" newspaper handed out in 1964 to publicize the upcoming film *First Men in the Moon.*

A comic book adaptation of the film was published as one of Dell's *Movie Comics* in March 1965.

THE SENTINELS (C)

First Appearance: *X-Men* #14, 1965, Marvel Comics.

Physical Description: The humanoid robots stand approximately 20 feet tall. The Mark I versions have great physical strength, fly, and fire destructive blasts from their chests; they have green limbs, a blue torso, "trunks," and head, and yellow face and hands. The Mark IIs are able to do everything the Mark Is can, and also have extendable metal cables and emit knockout gas from their

A mooncalf, food source for the *Selenites,* from the film *First Men in the Moon.* Courtesy Ray Harryhausen.

palms; they're gunmetal gray and purple. The Mark III series robots are virtually identical to those of the first series, though colored like the second and able to fire encapsulating "Atmospheres" from their hands; the Mark IVs and Vs have abilities similar to the Mark IIs'.

Biography: Fearing that mutants like the superheroic X-Men will one day turn on humankind, wealthy anthropologist Bolivar Trask brings together a group of scientific geniuses to construct the Mark I Sentinels to protect humankind. Unfortunately, the Sentinels and their 30-foot-tall robot leader the Master Mold believe that the best way to do this is by wresting control of society from humans. Realizing the error of his ways, Trask destroys the Master Mold's ionic power source, causing an explosion that kills the inventor, the giant leader, and the robots.

Bolivar's son Larry continues the family tradition by recovering bits and pieces and constructing the Mark II series and, under the leadership of robot Number 2, sends them out to destroy the X-Men, on whom he blames his father's death. Their scheme: to create bursts of solar radiation that will sterilize humankind and prevent the birth of both mutants and humans. These Sentinels are defeated by the superheroic Avengers, who bury them in the desert. Trask perishes with his robots.

The U.S. government gets Bolivar's blueprints and they fall into the hands of another mutant-hater, Dr. Steven Lang. He raises the money to build Mark III Sentinels and takes over an orbital platform (nicknamed "Deathstar") once operated by S.H.I.E.L.D. (see DREADNOUGHTS). The X-Men journey to space onboard the Starcore Eagle-One Space Shuttle, destroy the robots and the station, and return to Earth on the damaged shuttle. Though Lang is severely injured, his brain patterns had been encoded on the computer of his Master Mold, which fights (and is destroyed by) the Incredible Hulk.

When the dust has settled, the president of the United States establishes Project Wideawake to keep an eye on mutants who might be dangerous to the security of our nation. Project consultant Sebastian Shaw, a mutant-hating mutant and head of Shaw Industries, uses the government's blueprints to build new Sentinels, the Mark IV and V models, which he has sent against the X-Men on numerous occasions.

According to one tale, in the future, the Brotherhood of Evil Mutants may construct the Omega Sentinels, supremely powerful robots capable of self-repair. Their most daunting member will be Nimrod, who has come to our time and battled the New Mutants.

Comment: The characters were created by writer Stan Lee and artists Jack Kirby and Werner Roth. The Mark II series debuted in #57, Mark III in #98, Mark IV in #151, and Mark V in *New Mutants #2*.

THE SHE-MONSTER (MP)

First Appearance: *The Astounding She-Monster*, 1958, Hollywood International Productions/American International Pictures.

Physical Description: The She-Monster has long, blonde hair, sharply slanted eyebrows, wears a glittering bulletproof bodysuit, and is infused with radium, which causes her to glow and enables her to kill with a touch. She also wears a locket.

Biography: When a planet self-destructs and upsets the delicate balance of the cosmos, the highly advanced denizens of a planet orbiting the star Antares are concerned that we Earthlings are going to destroy our own world and disrupt the balance

The *She-Monster* makes a dramatic entrance. © American International.

beyond repair. To prevent this from happening, they dispatch a space traveler who wears a locket with the following verbose message:

To the people of Earth: you have been under close surveillance for a number of decades. We now feel your civilization has progressed far enough to make you eligible for membership in the council of planets. This council, for your information, is a universal governing body dedicated to the advancement of planetary progress. It's an agency which Earth seriously needs in this period of crisis and chaos in which it now finds itself. Many of our member planets have faced the same disturbing problems which confront Earth today. We feel that a meeting with the heads of these planets would definitely benefit Earth in the solution of its own global difficulties. If you would like a meeting so arranged, relate your wishes to the bearer of this message and she will return to us with word of your decision.

After her glowing, spherical craft reaches Earth, landing in the Angeles National Forest near Los Angeles, the She-Monster reaches a cabin where kidnappers are holed up with their victim, wealthy Margaret Chaffee, and the cabin's owner, geologist Dick Cutler. Because the She-Monster fights forest animals, including a snake and a bear, and kills the aggressive kidnappers one by one, Margaret and Dick assume—with some justification—that she's hostile. Dick figures that acid will kill her and, drenching her with it, causes the She-Monster to dissolve. Only the locket remains; Dick reads the message and realizes that, alas, he has acted a bit hastily.

Comment: The film stars Shirley Kilpatrick as the alien with Robert Clarke as Cutler and Marilyn Harvey as Chaffee. Ronnie Ashcroft directed from a script by Frank Hall.

SHEP (C)

First Appearance: "The Little Spaceship That Could," 1979, *1984* #10, Warren Publishing Co.

Physical Description: The maintenance ship looks like a little, metal frog's head with a tentacle-like tail that hangs from its bottom, center; the tail is used to provide fuel to larger ships. The ship is able to communicate with other ships, apparently via computer.

Biography: A maintenance ship in the Omega Fleet, *Shep* is present when the ships are informed that the deadly Orion Virus has been sent against the three billion humans of Arcturius. The only way to get antitoxin there in time is to fly through

Shep—the little spaceship that could. Art by Jose Ortiz.
© Warren Publishing Co.

the Revis VII black hole—a black hole that only a mighty hyper-battlewagon has ever managed to get through. The ships of the fleet decline to make the attempt, so *Shep* volunteers. He visits the massive loading pen in space; there, he's outfitted with the ion drive engine he'll need to escape the pull of the black hole—provided his hull doesn't collapse first—and then sets out.

Reaching the black hole, he dives in and is almost through it when he explodes. The moral: If you feel like volunteering, "for god's sake, volunteer for the guy standing next to you. You'll live a lot longer that way."

Comment: This cute if cynical tale was written by John Ellis Sech and drawn by Jose Ortiz.

SHINAR (L)

First Appearance: *Star Watchman* by Ben Bova, 1964, Holt, Rinehart and Winston.

Physical Description: The only terrestrial world of the eight planets orbiting Oran, Shinar has an atmosphere nearly identical to ours and is slightly larger than Earth, with a marginally greater gravitational pull. There are three continents, and 80 percent of the surface is covered by water.

Oran is twice the size of Earth's sun, and six times brighter.

Biography: Over a million years ago, humans first went into space. There, they met aliens known as the Others who waged a war that battered humankind "back into the Stone Age." Now we're back in space, spreading the Terran Empire outward, aware that the Others are still out there somewhere. The Star Watch is the military arm of the Terran Empire, and they keep an alert eye out for the Others. To do so requires the help of all the worlds of the Empire, but one world refuses to cooperate: agricultural Oran VI, called Shinar by the rebellious, olive-skinned natives. When skirmishes erupt, fueled by off-world Shinar allies, the cat-eyed Komani, Mobile Force soldiers, are sent to maintain order. Among them is young Star Watchman Emil Vogens, nee Ehml'n Vhro'rgyns, a golden-brown-skinned, copper-haired humanoid native of Bhr'houd'grinr (Plione IX). His mission: to find the rebel leader, the Komani Okatar Kang, and try to reason with him.

Vogens's force is ambushed and captured, but he is befriended by the Shinar priest Sittas and taken to see Kang. Far from being concerned about the forces massed against him, Kang intends to spread the rebellion to other worlds, overthrow the Empire, and establish a Komani Empire. Escaping with the help of Sittas's niece Altai, Vogens reports to Brigadier Aikens, who attacks the rebels in force. The Shinarians turn on the Komani, but Okatar is able to stage lightning strikes worldwide that capture supplies before either the locals or Terrans can muster resistance. His reign of terror ends when the young Shinarian Merdon and a small force of Terrans find and assassinate Okatar. Vogens negotiates peace with Lensor of the Komani, and the watch for the Others continues.

Comment: Though this was Bova's second novel (his first was *The Star Conquerors*, 1959), he began writing it first, in 1954, in a short story that "kept growing." Bova is one of the world's foremost writers of "hard" science fiction, in which the physics, technology, and biology are utterly plausible and typically described in some detail.

SHIP (C)

First Appearance: *Marvel Preview* #4, 1976, Marvel Comics.

Physical Description: The talking, wisecracking, female *Ship* looks like a giant, silver manta ray and has a "symbiotic" relationship with its occupant, Star-Lord. Armed with planet-destroying weapons, *Ship* "is capable of turning opaque or transparent—changing density, size and shape." For convenience, however, she takes "the form of a starcraft."

For short hops, she carries the small, saucer-like *Skimmer*; it is also home to a roughly foot-wide floating sphere which accompanies Star-Lord on his adventures and not only bio-scans all life forms to see what they're about, but also keeps *Ship* informed of doings on planet surfaces.

Biography: *Ship* patrols the universe with its sole occupant, the blue-costumed heroic Star-Lord, a.k.a. Peter Jason Quill. Quill uses his incredible combat skill, mystical powers, and element gun to fight for the right.

Among the worlds visited by *Ship* and Star-Lord are the Viking-like Windholme; Cinnibar, a world of anti-gravity palaces; and Sparta, a seat of the Imperial government.

Comment: The character was created by writer Steve Englehart. After his debut, the hero appeared in *Marvel Super Special, Marvel Spotlight, Marvel Premiere*, and *Star-Lord The Special Edition.*

SHOGUN WARRIORS (CS, MP, T, C)

First Appearance: *Dangado Esu*, 1976.

Physical Description: Each of the humanoid robots is approximately 50 feet tall, can fly thanks to rocket boots—only Raydeen is supersonic—and are colored red, blue, silver, and yellow.

Danguard Ace fires photon spheres from its chest, its right hand is a computer-guided rocket fist, it has laser-firing eyes, its chest shoots heat rays, it has a hyper-spear weapon, and it converts into the mighty bomber Dreadnought Titan.

Combatra has impenetrable armor, fires missiles from the fingertips of its left hand, and each of its body parts becomes a separate fighting machine: The head becomes the jet Delta-V 1, its chest becomes the jet Skyskater 2, the abdomen transforms into the bulldozing Earthmover 3, the hips and legs become the airborne Turbostreaker 4, and the feet become the tank-like Groundrover 5.

Raydeen has an unstoppable "breaker blade" in its right arm, fires a bow with "missile-arrows," launches "screamer-hawk" missiles from its chest, occasionally carries a War Axe, and also transforms into the aircraft Firehawk.

Biography: Ages ago, alien beings known as the Followers of the Light and the Followers of Darkness fought the Great Chaos Wars on Earth, which ended with the Followers of Darkness in suspended animation. When a volcano releases them from hibernation in the modern day, the evil leader, Lord Maur-Kon, is revived, and resumes his war using his "perverted alchemy of sorcery and science" to send forth the monstrous robot Rok-Korr. At the same time, having monitored the eruption, Dr. Tambura, a descendant of the Followers of the Light, uses a satellite beam to bring pilot Genji Odashu, marine biologist Ilongo Savage, and stunt driver Richard Carson to Shogun Sanctuary in the Far East. There, each hero is given a robot: Carson gets Raydeen; Genji rides inside Combatra; and Ilongo controls Danguard Ace.

After the initial battle with Rok-Korr, other robots dispatched by Maur-Kon include the huge dragonfly-like Mech-Monster, the towering, humanoid, multiheaded Cerberus, and the huge, golden humanoid Megatron.

Comment: Leiji Matsumoto created the popular comic strip; it inspired an animated half-hour Toei TV series, which embellished the original tale considerably (the TV version is recounted above). The series aired from March 1977 through March 1978. Several of these episodes were released theatrically, beginning with *Wakusei Robo Dangado Esu Tai Konchu Robotto Guntai* (*Planetary Robot Danguard Ace vs. The Insect Robot Army*) and *Wakusei Robo Dangado Esu—Uchu Daikaisen* (*Planetary Robot Danguard Ace—Naval Battle in Space*).

The series inspired a series of toys, which Mattel released in the United States in 1979 as the Shogun Warriors. Marvel Comics used the characters to create its *Shogun Warriors* comic book, 20 issues of which were published from 1979 to 1980.

THE SHOOTING STAR See THE BLACK HOLE.

THE SILVER SURFER (C)

First Appearance: *Fantastic Four* #48, 1966, Marvel Comics.
Physical Description: The six-foot-four humanoid is encased in a skin-tight "silvery substance" and travels the universe on a surfboard made of the same substance. The Surfer controls his board by thought and can travel faster-than-light. He possesses vast physical strength, can fire destructive beams from his hands, and does not need to eat or breathe but draws nourishment directly from cosmic energy.
Biography: Norrin Radd is discontent with the life of leisure he and his lover Shalla Bal live on the

The *Silver Surfer*. © Marvel Comics.

technologically advanced planet Zenn-La. His boredom is chased away by the arrival of a spaceship, which is declared by computers to be a source of "limitless power." When the planet's Weapon Supreme fails to destroy it, Norrin boards a small starship and flies out to meet the alien. Inside, he finds the planet-eater GALACTUS (see entry) who makes him an offer: He will spare Zenn-La if Norrin Radd agrees to become his herald, to "probe the heavens . . . scan the starways . . . roam the endless cosmos" to find new worlds for Galactus to devour. Norrin agrees, and Galactus fires bolts from his fingertips, energy that transforms Norrin into the Silver Surfer, unable to be harmed by "the frigid, marrow-chilling emptiness of airless space, nor the all-consuming inferno of the hottest sun." Upon reaching Earth, the philosophical Surfer realizes that humans are good at heart and that he has "found something . . . something worth protecting."

Teaming with the Fantastic Four and THE WATCHER, he turns on his master and helps them defeat him with a device known as the Ultimate Nullifier. Before moving on, the ruthless Galactus punishes his rogue herald by creating an energy barrier around the Earth that prevents the Surfer from leaving our world—or ever seeing his beloved Shalla Bal again. The Zenn-Lavian makes the best of his banishment by battling super villains on Earth; in time, the Fantastic Four help him to break through the barrier, though he can do so only once. Reaching Zenn-La, he doesn't like what he finds: Anddar Bal, the father of his beloved, tells him that Galactus has ravaged the planet, allowing its people to leave while he fed on it, then return to live in squalor. As for Shalla Bal, she's been abducted by the demon Mephisto and taken to Earth. The Surfer follows her, aware that he can never escape our world again. Once he is trapped, the sadistic Mephisto turns her to cosmic energy and sends her back to Zenn-La, where her very presence reenergizes its dead soil. The Surfer has since remained on Earth, protecting humans from the many faces of evil.

Comment: The character—a cult hero due to his philosophical musings—was created by writer Stan Lee and artist Jack Kirby. In addition to guest-starring in *Fantastic Four* and other Marvel titles, the character has starred in his own magazine. The first series lasted 18 issues, from 1968 to 1970, the second lasted seven issues beginning in 1982, and the third began in 1987 and is ongoing. The hero also starred in a two-issue special edition in 1988–89, and in *Marvel Graphic Novel* #38. His greatest exploits were reprinted in *Fantasy Masterpieces* Vol. 2, #s 1–14 (from 1979–81).

THE SIRIANS (TV, L, C)

First Appearance: *V*, May 1983, NBC TV.

Physical Description: The Sirians are humanoid reptiles with eyes that are reddish-orange with vertical black pupils, two sets of teeth, and a forked tongue. They wear rubbery human "flesh," wigs, and contact lenses to disguise themselves, and their attire consists of black boots and red bodysuits. The aliens usually wear sunglasses, since their eyes are sensitive to light.

The alien ships are vast, flat discs some five miles in diameter. Each carries nearly 40 shuttle craft in its bays.

The aliens come from the fourth world of Sirius, 8.7 light years away, a planet similar to Earth, only "somewhat" larger.

Biography: "V" stands for the Visitors and, later, for Victory. The Visitors are Sirians, thousands of alien beings whose ships appear over Earth's major

Jane Badler as Diana, leader of the *Sirians*. © NBC-TV.

cities and inform humankind that the Sirian world is in environmental chaos and they need Earth factories to help them make "certain chemicals and compounds" necessary to revitalize their world. In truth, they plan to conquer our world and breed humans for food. Their plan is uncovered by TV newsman Mike Donovan who, with Dr. Julie Parrish, Ham Tyler, and Elias Taylor, forms a small group of resistance fighters to battle the aliens and their leader Diana. Ultimately, the aliens are repulsed thanks to a lethal bacteria, but the setback is only temporary. Profit-motivated humans, especially industrialist Nathan Bates, help Diana reestablish a beachhead and continue the assault.

The resistance fighters are based in the Club Creole, and soon pick up other aides including Willie, a renegade alien; Kyle, Nathan's patriotic son; and Robin, an Earthwoman who had an affair with an alien and has given birth to a hybrid daughter, Elizabeth. In the end, the aliens and the Earth people make peace.

Comment: Marc Singer stars as Mike, Faye Grant is Parrish, Michael Ironside is Ham, Michael Wright is Elias, and Jane Badler is Diana in this show, which was created by Kenneth Johnson. The series is reminiscent of Damon Knight's short story "To Serve Man" (see THE KANAMIT), H.G. Wells's *War of the Worlds* (see THE MARTIAN THINGS), and Arthur C. Clarke's *Childhood's End* (see THE OVERLORDS).

The first and second adventures were televised as mini-series (four hours and six hours, respectively, the second broadcast in May 1984). A weekly, hour-long series aired on NBC from October 1984, to the following July.

Pinnacle published a series of novels in 1984–85, including *V* by A.C. Crispin, based on the entire 10-hour miniseries; *V: East Coast Crisis* by Howard Weinstein and A.C. Crispin; *V: The Pursuit of Diana* by Allen Wold; *V: The Chicago Conversion* by Geo. W. Proctor; *V: The Florida Project* by Tim Sullivan; and *V: Prisoners and Pawns* by Howard Weinstein. DC published 18 *V* comic books from 1985 to 1986.

6X52 (T)

First Appearance: *Jets*Rockets*Spacemen*, 1951, Bowman Gum, Inc.

Physical Description: The torpedo-shaped ship is silver with a red nose that ends in a needle-like point. The rocket rests on four red tailfins and is entered by two hatches, one at the top and the other halfway up the side. Free of Earth's gravity,

the ship travels at 5,000 miles an hour and is equipped with radar and "blast guns." Though the composition of the 250-foot-long 6X52 is not revealed, a companion rocket is made of "rare lunar metals." All of the Solar League sub-light-speed ships have atom-powered engines.

The 6X52 is not designed for flight outside the solar system. However, the 6X53 is, thanks to powerful "Zaratrons" which work by means of "magno-beam propulsion" and enable the ship to travel faster than light. Five hundred feet long, the 6X53 is also torpedo-shaped but, instead of fins, it has four rocket boosters. The 6X53 is equipped with cosmic torpedoes and a "videoscope radiophone" for communication with Solar League outposts.

Biography: The job of the Solar League is to "protect the sky lanes from the pirates of the planetoids" and other space menaces. Commanded by Captain Argo and Dr. Zara, the ship blasts off from the Manhattan Rocket Center headed for the moon. En route, the crew stops at a boomerang-shaped space station for lunch, then continues on their way. Landing on the moon to check on a United Nations observatory, the bold explorers spread interplanetary goodwill by killing some Mantis Men, then head to Mercury, Mars, Venus, the watery Planet Ex (where they meet King Aquon and Prince Frost), Saturn, Saturn's moon Titan, Jupiter's moon Ganymede, Jupiter, the planetoid belt, and then back to Earth—greeting old friends and blithely slaying enemies all the while.

After a brief layover, the crew blasts off from the New Mexico Rocket Base onboard the 6X53, heading for the Sirius Star System. There, on the planet Kroto, they help King Trunion battle the forces of Thor Mogon. Heading back home, they stop on Pluto for a chat with Prince Flagan.

Cadets learn to fly in the X83 Trainer and people of the future travel around in flying cars known as Jet blisters.

Comment: The entertaining but hopelessly naive card set consisted of 108 full-color, painted cards. The series was reissued in 1985 by WTW Productions.

THE SKRULLS (C)

First Appearance: *Fantastic Four* #2, 1962, Marvel Comics.

Physical Description: Ranging from four-and-a-half to six-and-a-half feet tall, the humanoid, green-skinned Skrulls are shape-changers. In their natural state, they possess large, pointed ears, chins comprised of a half-dozen ridges (pointing up and down), and red eyes with arched eyebrows.

Biography: The Skrulls evolved on Skrullos, a planet in the Drox system of the Andromeda Galaxy. Ages ago, the CELESTIALS experimented on them and created various offshoots of the root stock, of which shape-changing Skrulls became the most populous. They sought to destroy the other races, one of which fled and became the Dire Wraiths (see ROM). Approximately 10 million years ago the Skrulls took to space, encountered the two alien races of the planet Hala—the KREE and the Cotati—and wanted to establish diplomatic relations with that world. However, they wanted to deal only with the Cotati; furious, the Kree slew the Skrull Emperor Dorrek, stole Skrull technology, and went to war with the visitors. As the conflagration reached Skrullos, the Skrull became increasingly warlike. One product of the war was the Cosmic Cube, a device containing "x-element" from another universe. The Cube allows its possessor to alter reality by mere thought, and the reigning Skrull emperor used it to transform himself into a god. In time, the Cube develops sentience modeled after the emperor's megalomania and destroys two-thirds of the worlds in the Andromeda Galaxy—the bulk of the Skrull Empire. Eventually calling itself the Shaper of Worlds, and becoming more benevolent, the Cube assumes a semi-Skrull likeness: a blue-armored, silver-skinned Skrull from the waist up, a cube with caterpillar treads below.

Meanwhile, the Skrulls claw their way up from the primitive state in which the Cube has left them, rebuilding their empire to 978 worlds and establishing Tarnax IV as their Imperial Throneworld. Races that are a part of the empire—some willingly, others not—include the Druffs, Gegku, Guna, Kallusians, Morani, Pheragots, Queega, Tektons, Wilameanis, Xandarians, Yirbek, and Z'nox. Hoping to add Earth to their empire, they impersonate the superheroic Fantastic Four and commit crimes in their name to discredit them; the Skrulls are thwarted in this and other efforts, including the bioengineered Super-Skrull, which possesses all the powers of the Fantastic Four (vast strength, flame-on ability, invisibility, and stretchability). The Avengers have also helped to battle the grabby aliens.

In recent years, the world-eating GALACTUS destroys Tarnax IV, and Empress R'kill and her daughter Princess Anelle with it, throwing the empire into ongoing civil war.

Comment: The characters were created by writer

Stan Lee and artist Jack Kirby. The Super-Skrull first appeared in *Fantastic Four* #18, 1963.

THE SKY GODS (C)

First Appearance: *Tragg and the Sky Gods* #1, 1975, Gold Key Comics.
Physical Description: The humanoids have gold-colored skin and green hair. They wear white trunks and T-shirts, a silver winged headband, red boots and gloves, and fly using jet packs.
Biography: Scientists from the planet Yargon come to prehistoric Earth and mutate cave people into the modern human male Tragg and the female Lorn. However, not all Yargonians are benevolent. Soon after the mutation, a small group known as the Sky Gods comes to Earth, sets up headquarters in the Fire Mountain (volcano), and works to enslave the cave people, with Tragg and Lorn leading the resistance.

The Sky Gods include their leader Zorek, his aide Ferenk, and the female Keera, who is in love with Tragg and struggles to help the primitive humans.
Comment: Eight issues were published through 1977, with a ninth—a reprint of #1—in 1982. The highlight of the series was beautiful Dan Spiegle artwork.

SLAG (L)

First Appearance: "Period of Totality" by Fred Saberhagen, 1977, *Isaac Asimov's Science Fiction Magazine*, Vol. 1, #1.
Physical Description: The airless world is "a jumble of craters and hillocks and strange structures like frozen wavefoam." Virtually everything is gray, "in shades ranging from glaring silver to dull near-black." Slag (the planet's nickname) has one moon.
Biography: Seeking to find out how Slag survived the nova explosion that reduced its sun to a white dwarf, Captain Einar Amdo, astrophysicist Erich Du Bos, and astrogeologist Selina Jabal are trapped in a cave by a solar windstorm that makes it impossible for them to get back to their ship. With just 16 hours of air, they find a manuscript from a previous explorer who was trapped for over 200 hours. The author referred to an eclipse as possible salvation, and one is due in just two hours—though Selina doesn't wait that long. When there's a lull in the storm, she heads off without telling the others, gambling (despite what "expert" Du Bos has said) that it isn't the actual eclipse but the

approach of the moon that will protect them as it pushes the particles out of the way. She's correct, and is able to bring the rocket closer to the cave to save the men. Had they waited to see the eclipse, they would have perished.

Comment: A former encyclopedia editor, Saberhagen made his first sale, "Volume PAA-PYX," to *Galaxy* magazine in 1961.

SOLARIS (L, MP)

First Appearance: *Solaris* by Stanislaw Lem, 1961.

Physical Description: The diameter of the planet is one-fifth greater than that of Earth, and it orbits two suns, one red, the other blue; according to estimates, its eccentric orbit will result in its being consumed by the red star in 1.5 million years. Solaris is covered by a blackish sea with "thick foam, the color of blood." The 700 billion tons of "metamorphic plasma" are "dotted with innumerable flat, low-lying islands whose combined area is less than that of Europe." The islands are covered with "decomposing mineral" deposits, and a "crimson haze" hangs in the skies. There is no oxygen in the atmosphere of Solaris, and no trace of life as we know it. The planet regularly generates fog of "a thick colloidal substance."

The ocean regularly forms a variety of shapes: "extensors," which are like gigantic waves; "mimoids," waves that act "like contorted, fleshy mouths" and snap "greedily" at dark discs that form beneath the surface; "symmetriads," vast balls that erupt from the sea and submerge again; and "asymmetriads," or "free-ranging forms."

Run by a "giant computer," Station Solaris is a disc with a radius of 100 yards. There are four decks in the center, and two in the circumference. The living decks include cabins with "big panoramic" windows, and a moving walkway that carries occupants through the station. The hangar deck is "a vast, silver funnel, as high as a cathedral nave" with "colored pipes" running down the walls and an electric trolley-monorail, which leads to the launching pad. It also contains small shuttles used for ferrying stores between the station and other ships. Below it, accessible by a spiral stairway, are the lower-deck storerooms. The Station uses "gravitors" to keep it hovering from "five to fifteen hundred yards" above the planet's surface.

Biography: It's 100 years after the discovery of Solaris, and 55 years since the odd world has been studied—though no one yet has figured out quite what it is. Scientists suspect that the sea is "a

protoplasmic oceanbrain . . . idling its time away . . . [contemplating] the universe."

Kris Kelvin undertakes a 16-month journey from Earth to Solaris. Leaving the spaceship *Prometheus* onboard a small cigar-shaped capsule, Kris Kelvin arrives at the orbiting Station Solaris not only to study the planet, but also to find out what has happened to the suddenly silent research team under Dr. Gibarian. Encountering haggard cybernetics expert Dr. Snow, he learns that Gibarian is dead and that the only other occupant, Dr. Sartorius, hasn't been himself. Not long after his arrival, Kelvin is visited by his wife Rheya, who has been dead for 10 years. Because her skin feels "like that of a newborn child," he knows it's not really her and launches her into space onboard a shuttle. He talks to Snow, who explains that they've all had "visitors," which is why Gibarian killed himself—and why they haven't spoken with Earth, lest they be "shut up in a mad-house." They believe the planet is creating the guests, and Snow promises Kelvin that Rheya will return.

When she does, with no memory of what happened to her last incarnation, Kelvin takes her to the sick bay and examines her. With help from Sartorius and Snow, he determines that the visitors, which they call Phi-beings, are made of "units smaller than ordinary atoms," probably neutrinos. They are created by the planet, which somehow reads their minds as they sleep. Rheya herself eventually comes to understand what she is: "an instrument . . . from your memory or your imagination . . . [created] to study your reactions." Before long, Kris is in love with the creation and wants to take her back to Earth. But the scientists determine that the "structure disintegrates" away from Solaris and, moreover, Snow and Sartorius fear Solaris. While Kelvin is sleeping, they use a short-range disintegrator to destroy Rheya, then plan to return to Earth for antimatter generators to kill the seas. Kelvin is opposed to this; missing Rheya and convinced she will return, he shuttles down to the godlike planet and remains there.

Comment: The novel was first published in the United States in 1970 by Walker and Co.

In 1972, director Andrei Tarkovsky made a moving film version that is generally faithful to the novel, starring Donatas Banionys as Kris, Nathalie Bondarchuk as Harey (Rheya), Anatoli Solinitsin as Sartorius, and Youri Yarvet as Snaut (Snow). Tarkovsky spends several minutes at the opening of his film showing Chris contemplating the living surface of the Earth; in the end, when Chris decides to return to Earth, he goes back to that same setting, and the camera pulls back to reveal it's an island on the surface of Solaris. The viewer is left to draw her or his own conclusions as to where Chris ended up. The swirling surface of the planet is hypnotic, the doughnut-shaped main corridor of the Station looks lived-in, and the music is haunting.

Lem also wrote separate stories about the space-faring Pirx the Pilot and space traveler Ijon Tichy, both of whom flew on a variety of ships.

THE SOLNOIDS (CS, TV)

First Appearance: "Star Front Gall Force," March 1985, *Model Graphix* (Japan).

Physical Description: The Solnoids are humanoid women, girlish in form and behavior, who reproduce by cloning.

Their rivals, the Paranoids, are shapeless creatures that assume whatever form they require to survive in any environment.

Biography: The Solnoids are natives of the planet Marsus—though according to ancient lore, they evolved on another world and were brought to Marsus at a time and for reasons unknown. In time, the Solnoids become a spacefaring people and encounter the Paranoids in a nearby solar system. The two races go to war over uncolonized worlds, which they make habitable by placing "activators" on the surface, devices that change the environment over a four- or five-year period.

The war rages for decades. The early stories focus on the crew of the Solnoid Elite Fleet spacecruiser *Starleaf* with its first officer Eluza (who assumes command upon the death of the captain), second-in-command Rabby, chief engineer Pony, and crewmembers Patty, Rumy, Catty, and Lufy. Other Solnoid warriors include Shildy, Amy, and Spea of the ship *Lorelei* and Catty Nebulart, leader of the Elite Intelligence Agency based on the ship *Sardin*.

Comment: The characters appeared in *Model Graphix* through August 1986, in a series of comic strips that used models and miniature sets instead of drawings.

In 1986, Sony Video International produced three animated adventures, expressly for videocassette release: *Eternal Story, Destruction,* and *Stardust War.* In 1989, Polydor released two more animated adventures on videocassette: *Rhea Gall Force* and *Gall Force, Earth: Chapter One.*

SOROR (L, MP, TV, C)

First Appearance: *Planet of the Apes* by Pierre Boulle, 1963, Vanguard Press.

Physical Description: The planet is "about the same size as Earth" and possesses a nearly identical atmosphere. It orbits the star Betelgeuse at "a distance equivalent to thirty times the space between the Sun and Earth." The oceans and continents do not resemble those of Earth.

There are no nations on Soror: It is governed by a triumvirate consisting of a gorilla, a chimpanzee, and an orangutan. The parliament consists of three houses, one for each race, which "attends to the interests of its respective members."

Biography: Cruising through space in their sphere, whose sail is "propelled by the pressure of light-radiation," vacationers Jinn and Phyllis literally find a message in a bottle floating in space. Scooping up the wax-sealed bottle, they find a manuscript from journalist Ulysse Merou, who had set out from the moon with botanist Professor Antelle, his pet chimpanzee Hector, and his student Arthur Levain in the year 2500 on a two-year voyage to the star Betelgeuse. Leaving their mothership in orbit around a world they find, and landing on a meadow, the men meet a mute, naked, golden-skinned woman they call Nova. Horrified by Hector, she strangles him to death,

Taylor and Nova, captives on *Soror.* From the film *Planet of the Apes.* © Twentieth Century-Fox.

then flees; the Earthmen soon encounter Nova's tribe, also naked, and spend some time with them. Their bucolic stay is ended when the camp is attacked by a party of talking gorillas dressed in Earthlike casual wear—trousers, jacket, shirt—save for the gloves on their feet. Aided by subservient chimpanzees, the gorillas shoot a number of humans and chase the others into nets, from which they're loaded into tractor-driven carts. Ulysse is among the captives; Levain is among the victims.

The survivors are taken to a modern city, with cars and paved streets, an airport and a stock exchange. They are placed in cages in a hospital-like building and tended to by the gorilla keepers Zoram and Zanam. There, Ulysse speaks to a white-robed scientist-chimpanzee named Zira; startled, she brings over her superior, the wise orangutan Zaius, who has the captive put through a battery of intellectual tests. Amazed with the results, Zira teaches him their language and they debate evolution (whether apes on Soror are descended from humans), math, and society (the meat-eating apes, Ulysse learns, used to be the planetary overlords, but now all races are theoretically equal). Soon, the chimpanzee Dr. Cornelius joins their sessions, and the trio campaign for Ulysse to be given his freedom. It is granted, four months after his arrival, and after Ulysse moves into his pleasant apartment he spots Antelle among caged humans—pitifully degenerated to their level.

Shortly thereafter, ape archaeologists discover a human doll buried in the sand, a doll that says "papa"—proof that humans once ruled Soror. Ulysse is humiliated by the fact that "human civilization could have been so easily assimilated by apes." He befriends a bright young chimpanzee named Helius and has a son by Nova—one who is talking by the age of three months, which worries the apes. Cornelius fears Ulysse and his family will be destroyed and urges him to leave Soror. They do so by stowing away on a satellite the apes are test-launching with human occupants—albeit, not the guinea pigs they expected. Reaching his ship, Ulysse returns to Earth only to find that it is inhabited by apes. Merou has since left again with his family, hoping to find "a friendly planet."

His narrative ends there, though the chimpanzees Jinn and Phyllis aren't sure they believe a word of it.

Comment: The novel is perhaps best known as the basis for the 1968 film, which took enormous liberties with the original tale. In this version, astronauts Colonel Taylor (Charlton Heston),

Landon (Robert Gunner), and Dodge (Jeff Burton) land on the planet in 3955, and events generally follow those of the novel until the end. Instead of leaving, Taylor and Nova (Linda Harrison) escape to the Forbidden Zone, where they find the ruins of the Statue of Liberty and learn that this is Earth of the future. The film was directed by Franklin J. Schaffner from a script by Michael Wilson and Rod Serling. In the sequel, *Beneath the Planet of the Apes* (1970), a rescue ship with astronaut Brent (James Franciscus) finds Taylor and a race of telepathic mutant humans living underground. In the end, Taylor triggers a nuclear missile that destroys the planet. But Cornelius (Roddy McDowall), the pregnant Zira (Kim Hunter), and chimpanzee Milo (Sal Mineo) have managed to *Escape from the Planet of the Apes* (1971) in Taylor's ship, which Milo has salvaged, propelled by their own velocity and the force of the greatest explosion in recorded history. The arrowhead-shaped ship ends up on Earth of 1973, where all but Zira's baby are killed; in *Conquest of the Planet of the Apes* (1972) it has grown to adulthood at a time when a plague has killed all of Earth's cats and dogs and apes are kept as pets and servants. The intelligent ape Caesar (McDowall) leads a revolt, which grows to open warfare in *Battle for the Planet of the Apes* (1973)—bringing the series full circle and essentially to where the first film began. Ted Posat directed *Beneath the Planet of the Apes,* Don Taylor directed *Conquest of the Planet of the Apes,* and J. Lee Thompson directed *Battle for the Planet of the Apes.* Paul Dehn wrote all the sequels save for the last, which was scripted by John William Corrington and Joyce Hooper Corrington.

The films inspired a pair of TV series. In *Planet of the Apes,* astronauts Allen Virdon (Ron Harper) and Pete Burke (James Naughton) take off aboard the *Icarus* in 1988 and crash-land on the planet in the year 3085 where, aided by the sympathetic chimpanzee Galen (Roddy McDowall), they endure repeated narrow escapes from the monkeys. The hour-long series aired on CBS from September to December 1974; several episodes were edited into feature films that have aired on TV. An animated series, *Return to the Planet of the Apes,* has Bill Hudson, Jeff Carter, and Judy Franklin stranded on the ape world; the half-hour series aired on NBC from September 1975 to September 1976.

All of the film sequels were novelized, in order, by Michael Avallone, Jerry Pournelle, John Jakes, and David Gerrold, and there were four novels based on the TV series: *Man the Fugitive, Escape to Tomorrow, Journey into Terror,* and *Lord of the Apes*. These were written by George Alec Effinger. Episodes of the animated series were also novelized by William Arrow: *Visions of Nowhere, Escape from Terror,* and *Man the Hunted Animal*.

Gold Key published a comic book adaptation of *Beneath the Planet of the Apes* in 1970, and Marvel Comics published 29 issues of a black-and-white, magazine-sized *Planet of the Apes* comic book from 1974 to 1977. Marvel also published 11 issues of a color comic book, *Adventures on the Planet of the Apes,* from 1975 to 1976.

THE SPACE BEAGLE   (L, C)

First Appearance: ''The Black Destroyer'' by A.E. van Vogt, July 1939, *Astounding Science Fiction*.
Physical Description: The *Space Beagle* is a ''great globe, shining like polished silver.'' Fully-manned, it has 180 officers and crewmen and 804 scientists.

The bridge of the ship is a ''series of great curving tiers . . . two hundred feet long.'' Steps connect the levels, the lowest of which is an auditorium with over a hundred seats large enough to accommodate men in spacesuits. (There are no women onboard; the sex drive is controlled by drugs.) It has an airlock that holds over a dozen spacemen, and a gangplank with up and down escalators that covers the 100 feet and leads to the base of the ship.

The ship is powered by an ''anti-accelerator'' drive, which allows it to cruise at ''many light-years a day.'' There is a dining room, engine room, chemistry room, film studio, tool room, storeroom, a ''gigantic'' machine ship, living quarters, and many other rooms. The ship carries lifeboats for safety (though they can't stop on a dime the way the starship can) and both a force field and atomic cannons for protection. The men carry heat blasters.

The *Space Beagle* operates on Star Time: There are 100 minutes to the hour, 20 hours to the day, 10 days to a week, three weeks to a month, and 12 months to the year. The days are numbered rather than named, and the clock starts ticking ''from the moment of take-off.''

Officers and crewmembers include Captain Leeth, Director of Expedition Hal Morton, Chief of Communications Gourlay, Chief Engineer Pennons, Chief Pilot Selenski, physicist von Grossen, sociologist Kellie, psychologist Siedel, biologist Smith, astronomer Gunlie Lester, archaeologist Korita, geologist McCann, chemists Gregory Kent and Carl Dennison, metallurgist Zeller, Dr. Eggert,

Dr. Jarvey, and crewmembers Siever, Breckenridge, and Coulter. Elliott Grosvenor is the most unusual member of the crew (and the hero of the tales): A Nexialist, he's involved with the ''joining in an orderly fashion the knowledge of one field of learning with that of other fields.'' By so doing, he can speed ''the process of absorbing knowledge and of using effectively what has been learned.''
Biography: Among the many aliens Grosvenor and his colleagues face on their long journey, the two best-known are the first, Coeurl, and Ixtl.

Coeurl is an ''enormous catlike figure'' with coal-black eyes, razor-sharp claws, ''hairlike tendrils'' at the side of its head, and ''hawser-thick tentacles'' with suction tips on its shoulders. It feeds on deer-like creatures and lives on the only world circling its sun, a world whose civilization had been destroyed some 1,800 years before in an atomic war. Coeurl can ''receive and send vibrations at any length [and] interfere with energy.''

The alien is taken onboard and offered food, which it rejects. It must eat living food and, as soon as it can, it begins dining on crewmembers. When they try to hunt the alien down, it steals a lifeboat and flees, intending to convince others of its kind to build a starship so they can feed on many worlds. Pursued by the *Space Beagle*, and shot at, the creature commits suicide by releasing its id.

The battle with Ixtl is a rough one. The alien is 10.5 feet tall, has red skin, a tubular body with four spiderlike legs, four arms, and long, spindly digits at the ends of all of them. It has a small knob for a head, with a long, narrow mouth and red-glowing eyes. It can become noncorporeal and pass through solids; it lives on energy and can survive even in space. When food is unavailable, it doesn't die but goes into hibernation.

The last surviving denizen of Glor, a planet that exploded in the distant past, Ixtl floats in space until it encounters the *Space Beagle*. Dematerializing, it enters the vessel and plants its jelly-like eggs in crewmembers, eggs that the hosts (called ''Guuls'') will keep healthy until they hatch in six hours. At that point, the creatures will dig their way out and begin their life of energy-eating. The contaminated crewmembers are found out, and the eggs are surgically removed. While the creature hides in an air duct, the crewmembers come up with a plan. They enter the lifeboats and leave the *Space Beagle*; fearing that they are going to unleash ''a hell of energy'' in the ship, enough to kill it, Ixtl abandons the *Space Beagle*, at which point the crew returns and throws up a force field, leaving Ixtl to float, eggless, in space.

Comment: *Space Beagle* tales appeared regularly in *Astounding Science Fiction* through 1943, and also in *Other Worlds* in 1950. Several early stories (including the encounters with Ixtl and Coeurl) were edited into novel form and published as *The Voyage of the Space Beagle* in 1950.

Virtually the entire contents of Marvel Comics' *Worlds Unknown* #5 (1974), was an adaptation of "The Black Destroyer." Warren Publishing's *Eerie* #139 (1983) was devoted almost entirely to a comic book adaptation of the fight with Ixtl, "Voyage of the Space Beagle."

The character ALIEN was inspired (uncredited) by Ixtl.

THE SPACE BRAIN   (MP)

First Appearance: *The Space Children*, 1958, Paramount Pictures.

Physical Description: The Brain grows from one foot long at its arrival on Earth to roughly 15 feet long. It looks like a human brain, albeit one that pulsates and glows, and it can scuttle along the ground through some unrevealed means. The Brain can communicate only telepathically and has sufficient telekinetic power to open locks or cause explosions. Through the touch of its human slaves, the Brain can cause paralysis, unconsciousness, or death. Though the film is black and white, the Brain is pictured as yellow-green in posters.

Biography: Traveling to Earth through some unknown means, the Brain settles into a cave near the Eagle Point Missile Project in Southern California. When a group of children comes to investigate the flash of light, the Brain selects 12-year-old Bud Brewster as the leader of its band of seven young "helpers." Their mission: to help it prevent the launch of the Thunderer, an orbiting hydrogen bomb. Mishaps and deaths begin occurring in and around the base, and Dr. Wahrman notices that the children are always present when these things happen. Locating the Brain, Wahrman implores it to free the children. The mute Brain refuses, and when the launch is finally attempted, the warhead explodes. The military descends on the cave, only to find the children blocking the way. The kids reveal that this event has been duplicated the world over, rendering the world's nuclear stockpile useless for all time. And if any nation dares to build more, the Brain will return. As one of the mothers puts it, "The world is having a second chance!"

Comment: Michel Ray starred as Bud, with Raymond Bailey as Dr. Wahrman. Johnny Crawford,

The enslaved children and their master, the *Space Brain*. © Paramount Pictures.

later of TV's *The Rifleman,* was youngster Ken Brewster. Jack Arnold (*The Creature from the Black Lagoon, The Incredible Shrinking Man*) directed; Bernard C. Schoenfeld wrote the script from a story by Tom Filer (whose original treatment featured a less sensationalistic space egg rather than a space brain).

THE SPACE CLAW OF TINEBRIA   (MP)

First Appearance: *Starcrash*, 1979, New World.

Physical Description: The enormous ship is built in the shape of an open hand with claws. The exterior is blue and covered with pipes, ports, domes, lights, and weapons.

Elle (some sources spell it Helle) is a tall, sleek, black humanoid robot with great strength and a variety of sidearms. The delta-wing *Space Hawk* has a flat, cylindrical fuselage and a short tail fin. The Golems are slender, sword-swinging silver robots with thimble-like heads. Siderea is a massive, colorful, brightly lit city of countless towers, bays, and projections jutting from three of its four sides. The fourth side is flat.

Biography: The spaceship *Murray Leinster* vanishes on a mission to discover Gorgonia, the city where the evil Count Zarth Arn is developing a deadly new Mind Weapon. Desperate, the benevolent Emperor of the Stars contacts smugglers Stella Star and Akton, the best pilot and navigator in the universe, to find Gorgonia—and rescue his son Simon, who was onboard the *Murray Leinster*. The Emperor provides them with the sleek ship *Space Hawk*; police robot Elle and radio specialist Thor are sent to assist them.

Searching for the lost ship, the quartet land on the planet Arrakas and are attacked by Amazons loyal to the Count. Escaping, they head for an ice world (which reaches 100,000 degrees below zero at night), where they discvoer the wreck of the *Murray Leinster*—and that Thor is a traitor. He knocks out Akton and locks Stella and Elle outside; the robot is able to keep Stella warm until Akton can kill Thor and let them in. Stopping on the planet Abbar, the heroes are attacked by the Mind Weapon, which they fight off thanks to Akton—who, as a member of the Lost Race of Varna, has superhuman mental powers. They head to Diamondia, where ape creatures destroy Elle and Simon shows up just in time to rescue Stella. Exploring Diamondia, they find Gorgonia and Zarth Arn, who is protected by an army of powerful robotic Golems. He captures the heroes and Akton is slain; before leaving the planet onboard the gargantuan *Space Claw*, Arn informs the survivors that Gorgonia has been rigged to explode. Fortunately, the Emperor had been summoned and commands his flagship to use its time-halting to stave off the blast until they've all escaped.

The Emperor's fleet attacks the *Space Claw* and is defeated. Rather than let the universe fall into the hands of the wicked Arn, the Emperor plans to send his huge space city, Siderea, right into the *Space Claw*. Stella remains on the city to guide it into the enemy's base, bailing out just before the "starcrash." Simon picks her up in the *Space Hawk*, the *Space Claw* is destroyed, and the victors sail off onboard the Emperor's flagship.

Comment: The film, also known as *The Adventures of Stella Star*, stars Caroline Munro as Stella, Marjoe Gortner as Akton, Christopher Plummer as the Emperor, David Hasselhoff as Simon, Robert Tessier as Thor, and Joe Spinnell as Zarth Arn. Judd Hamilton (Munro's husband) was inside the Elle costume; Hamilton Camp provided the voice. The film, made in Italy, was written and directed by "Lewis Coates" (Luigi Cozzi).

Murray Leinster is a noted science fiction author; "Arrakas" is a "tribute" to ARRAKIS.

THE SPACE CONVERTER (MP)

First Appearance: *The Three Stooges Meet Hercules*, 1962, Normandy Productions/Columbia Pictures.

Physical Description: The time machine consists of a round core roughly seven feet tall and as wide as a phone booth. It's completely covered with wires, tubes, and light bulbs and rests on a platform on which the riders stand, facing the machine. The space converter's fuel consists of "calm down pills" made by Curly.

Biography: Working as pharmacists, the Three Stooges help their neighbor, scientist Schuyler Davis, complete his time machine, which takes them back to Ancient Greece. There, the heroes become galley slaves to King Odius of Ithaca but earn their freedom by beating the Siamese Cyclops. Convincing the reluctant Schuyler that they'll be better off if he poses as the legendary Hercules (all the rowing did wonders for his physique), the lads irritate the real Hercules—who, it turns out, is something of a clod whose historical reputation was really built on the deeds Schuyler and the Stooges have managed to perform in his name. Eventually, the boys help Hercules become a bona fide hero.

The villainous Odius hitches a ride back with the heroes, only to fall off the machine in the West where he is attacked by Indians. Back in modern times, Schuyler's boss Ralph Dismal takes a trip to the colonial United States and returns in stocks.

Comment: In addition to Moe, Larry, and Curly-Joe, the film features Quinn Redeker as Schuyler, Samson Burke as Hercules, and George N. Neise as Dismal and Odius. The film was directed by Edward Bernds from a script by Edward Ullman, based on a story by Norman Maurer.

SPACE CRUISER YAMATO (TV, MP, C)

First Appearance: *Uchuu Senkan Yamato* (*Space Cruiser Yamato*), October 1974, Japanese TV.

Physical Description: Resembling a terrestrial battleship, the *Yamato* can travel in space and on or under the sea. It is blue on the upper half and red on the lower, has a three-level bridge, carries a force-field generator for protection, launches interceptors that look like contemporary jet-fighters, travels at hyper-light speeds, and is equipped with nine Shock Cannons, a Wave Motion Gun that can be used only when all other functions on the ship are shut down, a Pocket Anchor that can be fired into asteroids, a Chimney Missile Multiple Launching Tube with Anti-Space and Anti-Surface Missiles, a Laser Pulse Cannon, and eight Missile Launchers with different-sized missiles.

The crew of the *Yamato* includes Combat Leader Susumu Kodai (Derek Wildstar in English);

Admiral Juzo Okita (Captain Avatar) and Admiral Hijitaka (Captain Gideon), who replaces him when he dies; Survey and Analysis expert Yuki Mori (Nova); Chief Pilot Daisuke Shima (Mark Venture); Ship's Doctor Sado (Dr. Sane); Susumu's older brother Mamoru (Alex), who joins when he is found on Saturn's moon Titan after being presumed dead; and the devoted wisecracking robot Analyzer (IQ-9). Analyzer has a body shaped like a Dixie cup, a head like an observatory dome, two short legs with caterpillar-tread feet, and two stocky, powerful arms.

Other ships in the fleet of the Earth Defense Force are Susumu's personal fighter *Super Star*; the *Cosmo Tigers*, which are kept onboard the *Yamato*; Mamoru's fighter *Yuki Kaze* ("Snow Wind"; Paladin in English); as well as sundry cruisers and battle cruisers, carriers, dreadnoughts, patrol cruisers, destroyers, and battleships.

The Gamilon ships include golden flying saucers, Desslok's command cruiser, battleships, and destroyers. The Comet Empire has destroyers, battleships, antimatter missile ships, single- and twin-deck carriers, and other vessels among its fleet.

The Dark Star Nebula flies battleships and other vessels, and attacks planet surfaces with Tripod Tanks—ray-firing domes on three jointed legs.

Biography: In 2199, the planet Gamilas (Gamilon in the English version) is near death, as is its sister world Iscandar (unchanged), both of Solar System X, located 296,000 light-years from Earth. The blue-skinned Gamilas ruler Dessler (Desslok) attacks Earth with radioactive bombs, forcing humankind to build underground cities—though that buys us only a year, as the ground is slowly being contaminated by the radiation. Feeling sorry for us, Dessler's redheaded sister Queen Starsha (unchanged) of Iscandar informs Earth that the Cosmo Cleaner D will cleanse the radioactivity, though we must go to Iscandar to get it. To help us, she sends the design for the wave motion engine, which will enable a ship to make the journey in just under a year.

Rather than build a ship from scratch, engineers refurbish the old Japanese battleship *Yamato*, sunk during World War II, which now lies at the bottom of a dry ocean bed. Transformed into a spacegoing battleship, the *Yamato* and its crew of 114 head into space. They battle Gamilasian fighters, have encounters at Mars and on Jupiter, must get past the reflex gun on Pluto, and survive Dessler's ecto gas cloud, which eats both matter and energy. Passing the deadly Red Star, they engage Dessler's General Dommel (Lysis) in the Rainbow Galaxy, survive a voyage through the acid sea on Gamilas,

and activate a volcano, which causes a domino-like series of eruptions that all but destroy the world. Dessler is believed dead and the *Yamato* heads to Iscandar's capital, Mother Town. They make it back to Earth in time to save the planet. Mamoru settles down with Queen Starsha.

But Earth is still in danger. In 2201, the White Comet Empire, which dwells on an artificial comet, is headed toward Earth. Its leader, Prince Zordar (unchanged), has a policy of conquering or destroying any civilization he encounters. Fortunately, the antimatter being Teresa of Telezart (Trelena) warns Earth of the danger; unfortunately, Zordar has allied himself with Dessler, who managed to survive the near destruction of his world. The *Yamato* and Dessler's fortress ship do battle and collide; the Earth crew boards the latter and Susumu and Dessler face off. Realizing that his respect for the enemy outweighs his hatred, Dessler hesitates; as a White Comet Empire officer tries to assassinate him, Yuki saves his life at the cost of her own by intercepting the blast. The contrite Dessler tells the Earth crew where the comet is most vulnerable, then enters an airlock and steps unprotected into space (in the film version, *Arrivederci Yamato,* he returns to Gamilas). The *Yamato* is able to incapacitate and then destroy the comet by ramming it, saving Earth—though not before Admiral Hijitaka, Dr. Sado and Analyzer perish, along with hero Susumu (who lives in the film version).

When that war is won, the repaired *Yamato*, commanded by Susumu, heads back to deep space when Gamilas is attacked and destroyed by the Dark Nebula Empire (*Space Cruiser Yamato: The New Voyage*). Their leader, Skuldart, plans to build a cybernetic army, the key ingredients being gamilasium and iscandarium, which can be taken only if the planets are destroyed. With her sister world gone, Iscandar is thrown out of its orbit causing vast upheavals all across the world; Dessler and his ships follow the rogue world, along with the enemy vessel *Pleiades*, which still needs its iscandarium. The *Yamato* arrives in time to save only a handful of Dessler's ships from the powerful *Pleiades*, and to face the awesome Battle Station Goruba. Rather than see all her loved ones slain, Starsha evacuates Iscandar and activates its self-destruct system; Goruba is destroyed in the blast. The grieving Mamoru and daughter Sasha survive, Dessler goes searching for a new homeworld, and Susumu returns to Earth with the *Yamato*.

In 2202, the *Yamato* has a return bout with the forces of Skuldart and his Goruba fleet (resulting in the death of Sasha, who is reunited with her ghostly mother). In 2203, the *Yamato* becomes embroiled in a battle between the planet Denguil and the water-world Aquarius, during which they find Admiral Okita alive, his "death" explained as a radiation-coma. (These events are detailed in *Final Yamato*. They occur two years before *Space Cruiser Yamato III*, outlined next, but aired three years after.) In 2205, Dessler's new empire based on Garuman wages war with the Bolar Commonwealth, during which a proton missile accidentally hits our sun causing a chain reaction, which will destroy every living thing on the planet. It's up to the *Yamato* to find a new world for humankind; instead, they rescue Princess Luda of the religious cult Shalubart and, in return, are given the hydrocosmojin, which makes the sun normal once again.

Comment: The series was created by artist Leiji Matsumoto and producer Yoshinobu Nishizaki; "Yamato" was the name of Japan circa 500 A.D.

Twenty-six half-hour adventures aired through 1975; 26 more were aired in 1979. Dubbed and titled *Star Blazers*, the shows were syndicated in the United States beginning in 1979. In the *Star Blazers* version, the *Yamato* was named the *Argo* (other names were changed as well). A new 25-episode series, *Space Cruiser Yamato III*, aired in Japan from October 1980 to April 1981.

An animated feature, *Space Cruiser Yamato*, edited together from episodes of the series, was released internationally in 1977. A sequel, *Arrivederci Yamato: Soldiers of Love* (also known as *Space Cruiser Yamato 2*), was released the following year. With the success of these movies, a new Japanese TV movie, the animated *Space Cruiser Yamato: The New Voyage* was made and aired in July 1979, followed by the theatrical animated films *Be Forever Yamato* (1980) and *Final Yamato* (1983).

Japanese comic book stories have prospered virtually since the show's inception. In the United States, it wasn't until 1987 that Comico introduced a *Star Blazers* comic book, starting with a four-issue miniseries featuring new scripts and art. W.C.C. Animation Comics also published five graphic novels using actual cartoon art from the TV series.

SPACE MOUSE (MP, C)

First Appearance: *Space Mouse*, 1959, Walter Lantz Productions.
Physical Description: The gray-furred mouse is humanoid, save for his oversized mouse-head, four

fingers on each hand, and his long tail. He wears a purple spacesuit, purple cowl, and white gloves and boots. The mouse wears an "electrabelt" on whose viewer he can be contacted by the King.

His saucer-like ship the *Lunar Schooner* gets 6,000 miles to the gallon and has a convertible top. When he's relaxing, Space Mouse likes to soar through space with the top down.

Biography: A native of the planet Rodentia, Space Mouse serves in the military of the King of Camembert Castle. Tooling around space, the mouse usually fights cat invaders from the planet Felinia—though sometimes he serves the King in other capacities, as when he fetches Plutonian pickles, for which the ruler has a sudden urge. His war with the cats is a dangerous one, since the felines have been known to litter space with giant magnetic mouse traps. Mice that are caught in these are brought to the capital city of Catolina for trial, after which they're sentenced to the world Nothing, "a planet with no food, no water, no rocks, no trees, no people, no nothing . . . just a round ball." The dogs of the Dog Star are Space Mouse's occasional allies against the cats. Another neighboring world is Planet Sludge, a home of pigs and "the muddiest planet in the universe."

Space Mouse's one hobby is playing his trumpet.

Comment: In addition to his single cartoon adventure, the character starred in two issues of Dell's *4-Color* comic book from 1960 to 1962, and then in five issues of his own Gold Key title from 1962 to 1963.

The character is unrelated to the Space Mouse who appeared in five issues of his own Avon comic book (1953–54), in two issues of *Space Comics*, and in all three issues of *Funny Tunes*. The brown mouse from Earth wears a red space suit, yellow boots and gloves, and a bubble helmet and packs a ray gun. He travels around the galaxy in a blue, dart-shaped spaceship with his girlfriend, the blue-space-suited Molly Mouse, blasting evil cats and alien monstrosities.

THE SPACE PHANTOM (C)

First Appearance: *The Avengers* #2, 1963, Marvel Comics.
Physical Description: The six-foot-six humanoid has black hair that sweeps up on the sides to form a flattened U-shape. He wears a purple bodysuit with a red collar and arrow pointing toward the waist; flared orange shoulders and flaps under the arms; and golden boots and gloves. Later, he wears only the purple bodysuit.

Biography: The Space Phantom (real name unknown) was born on the planet Phantus. There, time travel was common-place, as was war—a dangerous combination, since Phantusians simply went backward to change the course of battles that went against them. Ex-winners, now losers, would do the same, creating massive confusion in the time stream. Eventually, the fabric of time literally rips under the strain, leaving the planet in Limbo.

A military strategist, the Space Phantom sensed what was going to happen and tried to escape Phantus in a time capsule. Unfortunately, the capsule is damaged and becomes stranded in Limbo, cutting him off from his fellow Phantusians. The Space Phantom is found by the evil Immortus who offers him a deal: He will free the Phantom and give him the power to become any creature he wishes, provided he takes the original's place, thus relegating it to Limbo and allowing Immortus to study it. The Phantom agrees and, going to Earth, decides to impersonate the superheroic Avengers: He reasons that with them out of the way, Earth will be vulnerable to conquest by the Phantusians, who can then leave Limbo.

Though the superhero Thor defeats the Phantom and returns him to Limbo, the Space Phantom returns to plague superheroes ranging from Captain America to ROM.

Comment: Marvel's Limbo is similar to the Phantom Zone at DC (see KRYPTON and SUPERMAN).

SPOT (TV, CS, L)

First Appearance: *SuperTed*, 1979, Siriol Animation.

Physical Description: Spot has a humanoid body and a head that's shaped like half a hotdog. His skin is yellow and covered with green spots, and he wears his orange hair in a Mohawk.

The space station he shares with SuperTed is shaped like an innertube with two spokes that lead to a bear-shaped hub. The space scooter is just that: a two-seat rocketbike with a pair of ski-like landing gear.

Biography: Journeying to Earth from the planet Spot, on a mission of exploration, the alien (who is also known as Spottyman) finds a bear in a toy manufacturer's storeroom, one that's been rejected because there's "something wrong" with it. The bear seems fine to Spot, who sprinkles him with "cosmic dust" that brings him to life and whisks him up to a cloud. There, Mother Nature greets the bear and, impressed with his inherent

goodness, grants him super powers. Together, Spotty and SuperTed establish a space station deep in outer space, then travel about the galaxy on their space scooter doing good deeds.

Comment: The character was created by Mike Young. The SuperTed cartoons were produced in Cardiff, Wales, and syndicated throughout the U.K.; concurrently, a SuperTed comic strip began appearing in *Pippin* magazine. The cartoons were distributed in the United States in the middle 1980s and simultaneously released on videocassette. A second series, *The Further Adventures of Super-Ted,* aired as part of *The Funtastic World of Hanna-Barbera* in syndication beginning in 1988. In these 13 cartoons, the character was called Spottyman and his planet was Spot. Patrick Fraley provided the voice. The character has also been seen in a series of children's books, more successful in Europe than in the United States, among them *SuperTed and the Green Planet, SuperTed Meets Zappy and Zoppy*, and *SuperTed and Nuts in Space.*

SPYDER (C)

First Appearance: *New Mutants* #66, 1988, Marvel Comics.

Physical Description: Standing just over seven feet tall, Spyder is covered with short, purple bristles. He stands on two spindly legs and has four equally slender arms, has large red eyes and a gaunt face; he wears a blue vest with highly flared shoulders and a helmet with wings that match the shoulders of his vest. Spyder has great physical strength, along with the ability to siphon emotions from others, reduce the emotions to a potion of unknown composition, and experience the feelings by sniffing them.

Biography: Spyder is the power- and wealth-hungry leader of Webb, an intergalactic textile firm that is actually a front for his various unsavory business dealings. Served by many slaves, he covets the Earth mutant Lila Cheney, whom his operatives capture; she is rescued by her friends the superheroic New Mutants, who are aided by Gosamyr, one of Spyder's escaped slaves. Though the New Mutants and Cheney escape, Spyder continues to prey on weaker beings.

Comment: Marvel, of course, is also the home of the terrestrial spiders Spider-Man, Spider-Woman, Madame Web, and the villains Tarantula and Daddy Longlegs.

STANGYA SOREN'TZAHH (MP, C, TV, L)

First Appearance: *Alien Nation*, 1988, Twentieth Century-Fox.

Physical Description: Like all Tenctonese, Stangya is outwardly human, save for the red-brown cranial spots on his bald head ("hundreds of squiggly-looking freckles," as one character describes them) and ear-openings with only a small outer ridge. The blotches tend to fade when Tenctonese become older. Though only females can carry fetuses in the early stages of pregnancy, the immature child-pods can be transferred to males for carrying through the second half. Babies emerge from *lingpod* flaps, pouches in the midsections of males and females.

The humorless aliens "possess a complex . . . language . . . complex social and familial behaviors . . . religious beliefs . . . [and] belief in an afterlife." Thanks to genetic engineering, they possess superior intelligence and enormous physical strength.

On Earth, the aliens get drunk on sour milk.

The Overseer ship on which Stangya travels is over two miles long, with a disc-shaped cargo section a half-mile in diameter for the Tenctonese.

Biography: More than a century ago, cruel aliens known as the Overseers came to Tencton and took its natives into space as slaves—some to work on their great spaceships, others to undergo cruel experiments. Among the 300,000 Tenctonese on the ship is a revered group known as the Elders, Tenctonese who had been born on Tencton itself.

Stangya has been in space for over 60 years. He has never known any other life, but knows that the time has come to escape from bondage. Stangya helps to lead a rebellion, "separation charges" free the cargo disc (and nearly half the aliens) from the main ship, and the Tenctonese reach Earth, crash-landing in the Mojave Desert. The military surrounds the area, and 250,000 are rapidly assimilated into our society. Known as Newcomers, many join the police force, others open small stores, and some become criminals.

Stangya takes the name Sam Francisco and joins the police force. In 1995, he is teamed with Los Angeles Detective Matthew Sikes, whose partner has just been killed in a gunfight with Newcomer thieves. Though Sikes initially wants no part of a Newcomer, he figures that Sam will be able to infiltrate the alien underground. The pensive, methodical, low-keyed Sam does indeed get the goods on bigtime Newcomer drug dealer William Harcourt, and Sikes gets the revenge he seeks for his partner's death. The two remain partners, battling crime as well as anti-alien prejudice (the Newcomers are called "Slags" by those who hate them).

Stangya's "life partner" is named Appy (Susan), and the couple has two children: 17-year-old Finiksa (Buck), and nine-year-old Vessna (Emily). George's only other known relatives are his brother Ruhtra and his uncle Moodri, an Elder.

Tencton words include:
Bemry: remember
Cate-al: children (singular: *cate-un*)
Crayg: day
La: of
Monk: feces
Otega: together
Pod: dad (formal: *apod*, father)
See: the
Sleema: a loose woman
Su: us
Terts: humans
Tla: feet
Vacwa: under
Vots: your
Yas: stay

Comment: The film covers only Stangya's teaming with Sikes and the battle with Harcourt; the TV series and novels flesh out events that occurred before. The alien's family is also a product of the TV show and novels.

The film stars Mandy Patinkin as Sam, James Caan as Sikes, and Terence Stamp as Harcourt. It was directed by Graham Baker from a screenplay by Rockne S. O'Bannon.

DC Comics published a one-issue adaptation of the film in 1988. In 1990–91, Malibu Graphics published the miniseries *Alien Nation: The Skin Trade*, and in 1991 issued the miniseries *Ape Nation*, in which a Tenctonese spacecraft lands on the movie version of the Planet of the Apes (see SOROR), the aliens forming an alliance with the renegade gorilla General Ollo and the ape-hating human Simon. Malibu also published a one-issue "continuation" of the TV series, after its cancellation, in 1992.

On TV, the Fox Network began its *Alien Nation* series with a two-hour pilot in September 1989; the series lasted until July 1991. There were 22 episodes in all. Sam's name is now George Francisco and he is played by Eric Pierpoint, with Gary Graham as Sikes, Michele Scarabelli as Susan, Sean Six as Buck and Lauren Woodland as Emily. Fox also produced the two-hour made-for-TV movie *Alien Nation: Dark Horizon,* which aired in

October 1994. In the film, the nativist Purity movement tries to rid the world of Tenctonese, while an overlord agent, Ahpossno (Scott Paterson), comes to Earth to try and get the escaped slaves back.

Pocket Books has published several *Alien Nation* novels to date: *The Day of Descent* (1993) by Judith and Garfield Reeves-Stevens, *Dark Horizon* (1993) by K.W. Jeter, *Body and Soul* (1993) by Peter David, *The Change* (1994) by Barry B. Longyear, *Slag Like Me* (1994) by Longyear, and *Extreme Prejudice* by L.A. Graf.

STARDUST (L, MP, C)

First Appearance: *Perry Rhodan* #1, 1961, Moewig-Verlag.

Physical Appearance: *Stardust* is a "familiar three stage rocket" 275 feet long, with a first stage of 109.5 feet, a second stage 74.5 feet long, and a third stage of 91 feet. The ship weighs 6,850 tons at takeoff; only the first stage "runs on liquid chemical fuel." The second and third are run by nuclear power. Inside the third stage main cabin "command center," located in the rocket's nosecone, the men sit on foam rubber mattresses set in contour couches. Below this is the living quarters with a kitchen and bathroom. The storeroom is located beneath that. The third stage has fin-like wings and lands like an airplane.

The spherical *Stardust II* has a diameter of 2,500 feet and is made of bluish Arkon steel. It rests on four legs and its fusion-powered engines are located in the "bulging equatorial ring" that girds it.

The crew of *Stardust* consists of "ace astronaut" and nuclear physicist Major Perry Rhodan, electronics and propulsion expert and copilot Captain Reginald Bell, navigator Captain Clark G. Fletcher, and physician/geologist Lt. Eric Manoli. Later additions, onboard the *Stardust II*, include: the beautiful Thora and Crest; the mutant Tanaka Seiko, whose brain "is sensitized to electromagnetic waves"; the teleporter Tako Kakuta; seer Wuriu Sengu; and tele-optician Ralf Marten. The ship's mascot is the "mousebeaver" Pucky.

Biography: Rhodan is a 35-year-old test pilot for the United States Space Force when General Lesley Pounder gives him command of the spaceship *Stardust*. The ship is launched from the Nevada Fields on the first trip to the moon; crash-landing there, they find a ship occupied by tall, humanoid aliens led by the beautiful Thora and scientist Crest. The extraterrestrials come from Arkon, a world in the Imperium, a sprawling galactic empire in its declining days. They're traveling through space to find a race they can help to fulfill "the promise and potential that once was ours." Rhodan persuades them that humankind is that race.

Rhodan returns to Earth with the aliens. He lands in the Gobi Desert and, using Arkonide super-science, forms the Third Power, a military/political movement devoted to uniting the nations of Earth. Via hypno-schooling, Rhodan becomes a super-scientific genius, repels invasion forces from the Arkonide Empire, and has countless adventures onboard the super battlecruiser *Stardust II*. Eventually, he becomes the Peacelord of the Universe, head of the governing New Power.

Comment: The series was created by Clark Darlton (real name, Walter Ernsting) and Karl Herbert Scheer, though authors such as Kurt Mahr, Kurt Brand, H.G. Ewers, Hans Kneifel, and W.W. Shols have contributed to the weekly series as well. Over 800 novels have appeared in Germany. In the United States, beginning in 1969, Ace published paperback reprints; in their heyday, the titles were appearing twice each month. Just over 100 of the novels were published, translated by Wendayne Ackerman. Crest was renamed Khrest and Bull was called Bell in these editions.

A motion picture, *Mission Stardust* (also known as *S.O.S. from Outer Space*) was produced in 1968. The Spanish/Italian/West German coproduction was directed by Primo Zeglio, stars Lang Jeffries, and generally follows the plot of the first novel.

A comic book based on the character, *Perry Rhodan im Bild* (*Perry Rhodan in Pictures*) began publication in Germany in 1968. It became *Perry* with number 27 and was translated for distribution throughout Europe.

STARFIRE (C)

First Appearance: *DC Comics Presents* #26, 1980, DC Comics.

Physical Description: The six-foot-four, bronze-skinned humanoid wears a skimpy purple bikini, the top and bottom attached by two slender bands; a purple necklace, bracelets, and boots. Her eyes are solid green and her brown hair is at least 10 feet long.

Like all Tamarans, Starfire can "harness the solar winds" and fly. She also has the unique power to fire destructive starbolts.

Biography: Starfire, a.k.a. Koriand'r, is the daughter of Queen Luand'r and King Myand'r of Tamaran, eighth planet of the 22 worlds circling the star Vega. Koriand'r is hated by her sickly older sister Komand'r who cannot fly or inherit the throne. She is alienated further when their brother Ryand'r is born.

Because Tamaran is a world of plenty, and they are regularly attacked by the first world, Citadel, all youths are sent to study with the warlords of the planet Okaara (see THE OMEGA MEN). Filled with hate, Komand'r learns the arts of war, throws in her lot with Citadel, then gives her father an ultimatum: Turn Koriand'r over to her, or Tamaran will be destroyed. The king complies, and his younger daughter spends six years in slavery. However, both girls are captured by Psions, an ancient race of lizard-like humanoids. They conduct solar energy experiments on the girls, and while Koriand'r is attached to a Solar Absorber, Citadel ships attack and the machine explodes. The blast gives the young woman the ability to fire starbolts and, escaping in a star-slider, she heads into space. Three months later she reaches Earth, where she joins a group of heroes called the New Teen Titans (see CYBORG [2]).

Tamaran is 20 percent smaller than Earth and rotates in the equivalent of 1.3 Earth days. Its surface is almost equally divided between land and water.

From Vega, the charted worlds of the system are: 1) Citadel, 2) Culacao, 3) Karna, 4) Hnyxx, 5) New Alliance, 6) Sindromeda, 7) Emana Branx, 8) Tamaran, 9) Rashashoon, 10–12) Unknown, 13) Okaara, 14) Voorl, 15) Unknown, 16) Euphorix, 17) Slagg, 18) Rogue, 19) Dredfahl, 20) Aello, 21) Ogyptu, and 22) Changralyn.

Comment: The character was created by writer Marv Wolfman and artist George Perez. She is unrelated to DC's other Starfire, a swordswinging heroine of an unnamed alien world who battles the evil invading race of Mygorg. She starred in eight issues of her own title in 1976–77.

STARJAMMERS (C)

First Appearance: X-Men #104, 1977, Marvel Comics.

Physical Description: Ch'od is a nine-foot-tall frog-faced humanoid with green skin, yellow, fin-like ears, four fingers on each hand, and three thickly-clawed toes on each foot (two in front, one in back). His white-furred pet Cr'reee resembles a spider monkey. Raza is a powerful, sword-wielding golden-skinned humanoid cyborg with a long queue of red, yellow, and white feathers on his head; he stands five-eleven. Hepzibah is a humanoid skunk-like woman who stands five-six,

carries a powerful blaster, possesses extraordinary night vision and a keen sense of smell, and has retractable claws. Sikorsky is a foot-and-a-half-long, green insect that looks and behaves exactly like a terrestrial helicopter.

The team receives a great deal of help from Waldo, the computer onboard their spaceship *Starjammer*.

Biography: The Starjammers are space pirates who plunder under the leadership of ex-Air Force test pilot Christopher Summers. When an alien race known as the Shi'ar (see Appendix A) shoot down his private plane, Christopher and his wife Katherine are teleported aboard; Emperor D'ken murders Katherine and has Christopher enslaved. (In fairness to D'ken, he has been driven mad by the train-sized M'Kraan Crystal, the mindwarping product of an ancient alien race.) In the slave pits, Christopher meets the Saurid Ch'od, native of Varanus IV (a.k.a. Timor); Raza, a Shi'ar cyborg; and the Mephitisoid Hepzibah of Tryl'sart (Hepzibah is her nickname; her name is actually a sequence of odors). Together, they steal a starship, which they rechristen the *Starjammer*, and plunder the Shi'ar spaceways with Christopher as their leader Corsair. They team with the superheroic mutants the X-Men to battle the Emperor when he attempts to open a dimensional gate that could destroy the universe; he is succeeded by his sister Princess Lilandra Neramani, a rational leader who makes peace with the Starjammers. The team is later joined by Sikorsky (a nickname) of the psychic Chr'Ylites.

Comment: Ch'od was the first Starjammer to appear; Raza and Hepzibah debuted in *X-Men* #107, Sikorsky in #156. Sikorsky, of course, is named in honor of aeronautical pioneer Igor Sikorsky.

STARMAN (MP, L, TV)

First Appearance: *Starman*, 1984, Columbia Pictures.

Physical Description: In its natural form, the alien is a ball of blue light. It's able to assume any likeness it chooses, and has telekinetic powers.

Biography: In 1977, the spacecraft *Voyager II* was sent into space carrying, among its instruments, a description of who and where we are. Responding to this invitation to visit, Starman heads for Earth. Knocked off course by an Air Force missile attack, the Starman lands in Wisconsin. There, in her home, young Jenny Hayden is still mourning the accidental death of her housepainter husband. Taking a peek at the photo album and running through home movies, the Starman assumes his appearance—and reveals himself to the stunned Jenny. He tells her who he is and why he came, and also explains that a spaceship will be coming to pick him up at the Great Meteor Crater in Arizona in a few days. He forces Jenny to drive him there, the two of them pursued by National Security Council agent George Fox, who wants to capture the alien for security reasons, and scientist Mark Shermin who wants to study it.

En route, Jenny and the Starman fall in love, though they know they can't stay together; if he remains on Earth for long, the extraterrestrial will die. They eventually make the rendezvous, the pursuing soldiers looking on in awe as Starman boards the craft unmolested and leaves his pregnant love behind.

Comment: Jeff Bridges stars as Starman, with Karen Allen as Jenny, Charles Martin Smith as Mark, and Richard Jaeckel as Fox. John Carpenter directed from a script by Bruce A. Evans and Raynold Gideon. Bridges was nominated for a Best Actor Oscar for his work in the film.

Warner Books published a tie-in novel in 1984, written by Alan Dean Foster.

The movie inspired an hour-long TV series, which aired on ABC from September 1986 to September 1987. The scenario is somewhat different from the film: Fourteen years after leaving, Starman (Robert Hays) returns to find his lover and his son. Taking over the body of Paul Forrester, a free-lance photographer killed in a plane crash, he finds his boy Scott Hayden (C.B. Barnes) living in an orphanage; together, they go looking for Jenny, who has vanished. As they search, Paul teaches Scott how to use his nascent telekinetic abilities. They also help people in need, always staying one step ahead of government agent George Fox (Michael Cavanaugh), who wants to learn the secret of Starman's powers. In the end, the alien and his son find Jenny (Erin Gray) and, presumably, live happily ever after.

STARRIORS (T, C)

First Appearance: *Starriors*, 1984, Tomy Corporation.

Physical Description: There are two groups of robots: the Protectors and the Destructors. The prominent Protectors are the humanoid Hotshot, the laser-firing leader; Crank; and Cut-Up, which has a saw in its chest; and the vehicles Runabout, a giant apatosaurus-like transport; the tiny four-wheeled Nipper; the tank-like Tinker; the pow-

erful Thinktank; and the armored, gun-toting Motormouth.

The main Destructors are the humanoid Slaughter Steelgrave, the vibro-chisel-packing leader; Gouge, who has a destructive beam; and the destructive Sawtooth. The vehicles are Auntie Tank; Backfire; Speedtrap; the tiny Grub; the tank-like Scrapper; and the tyrannosaurus-like Deadeye, which is never without its flying, pteranodon-like scout Cricket.

Biography: At some unspecified time in the far future, when animal and human life has evolved into monstrous mutants that dwell in the "forbidden desert," the planet is ruled by robots, or Starriors. These are divided into the benevolent Protectors and their enemies, the evil, slave-driving Destructors. Among the former is a group known as the Cult of Man, which is keen to find out more about humans and what put them into the "unending sleep."

Comment: In addition to the toy line, Marvel Comics published a four-issue *Starriors* miniseries in 1984–85.

STARRO THE CONQUEROR (C)

First Appearance: *The Brave and the Bold* #28, 1960, DC Comics.

Physical Description: Thirty-two feet from tip to tip, Starro is a gray, starfish-like creature with a red eye in its center. Typically, it stands upright on two of its five arms. Starro's will is strong enough to control that of others, and also to turn Earth's native starfish into servile duplicates of itself.

Starro is able to travel through space unprotected, fly, and fire destructive blasts from its arms.

Biography: Coming to Earth from an unnamed world, Starro sets up a base in the sea, intending to conquer the world. The alien is discovered by the superhero Aquaman, who summons the other members of the Justice League of America (including Superman, Batman, Wonder Woman, and Green Lantern). Starro sends out starfish "clones" and keeps the heroes' hands full until the Flash discovers that lime is deadly to the creature. However, Starro had the foresight to bury a fragment of itself in the sea. Thus, though the Justice League believes it has been destroyed, Starro is able to regenerate itself, nourished by chemical dumping. This time, Aquaman destroys the polluted alien with fresh, clean water. But a bit of Starro survives and, relocating to Grand Central Station and feeding on third rail energy, the creature sends out small replicas of itself, which wrap themselves around peoples' faces and enslave them. Fortunately, this doesn't work on the android RED TORNADO, who shuts off the flow of electricity. The Justice League has had further run-ins with the extraterrestrial megalomaniac, as have the anthropomorphic animals of Captain Carrot and His Amazing Zoo Crew.

Comment: Starro holds the distinction of having been the first nemesis of the popular Justice League of America.

STEELE (C)

First Appearance: "Steele," 1981, *1994* #19, Warren Publishing Co.

Physical Description: Steele's right arm is a powerful mechanical limb, while his torso is "mounted to a miniature tank" that responds instantly "to electrical impulses from his brain." He wears a visorless helmet to protect his head and carries a powerful automatic weapon.

When he is rebuilt into an Exterminator, he resembles an EXTERMINATOR TWO.

Biography: Corben Edward Steele is raised in a poor section of New York City, arrested 22 times by the age of 21. His right hand is cut off for skimming money from mob drug sales; he learns to use his artificial hand and becomes an expert marksman and hitman. After spending time in the Marines, he becomes a NATO assassin until a mine turns "the lower half of his body into hamburger." Brought to Eternity Keep Cryovault, he is frozen for four centuries. Thawed and subjected to cybernetic surgery by Dr. Swain, he is sent out to battle General Ophal and his army of mutants, who are "sworn to eradicate all human life" in this post–World War III world. When Steele has defeated the foe, Swain promises that he will be given a "synthetic, natural-looking, functional" human body.

After spreading carnage among the enemy, Steele is attacked by dozens en masse. He slays most of them, though a few get through and batter his human remains. Fortunately, a young human warrior saves him, and Steele is able to stagger back to the medical facility. There, his brain is encased in an entirely robotic shell—and he goes back out to battle the mutants as an Exterminator.

Comment: The story was written by Budd Lewis and Will Richardson (Bill DuBay) and drawn by Alex Nino.

Steele may be the same Exterminator who rescues the Goblin-killer Karas.

See also EXTERMINATOR ONE.

THE STEPFORD WIVES (L, MP, TV)

First Appearance: *The Stepford Wives* by Ira Levin, 1972, Random House.

Physical Description: The wives are androids who look exactly like the people they replace. Their vocabulary isn't terribly extensive, however, and they are slightly more stilted and reserved than their human counterparts.

Biography: Joanna and Walter Eberhart move to smalltown Stepford, Connecticut, with their children Kim and Pete. Although Joanna and Walter are both women's libbers, attorney Walter joins the Men's Association so he can help turn it into "Everbody's Association." Joanna is frustrated by that, and by the sweet but standoffish neighbor Carol Van Sant, Her only real friend in town is lively Bobbie Markowe.

In time, Joanna becomes unnerved about little things: how neatly some women stack their groceries in the cart; how no one but Bobbie wants to form a women's club; how Walter spends more and more time with the men of the Association. Finally, wealthy young Charmaine Wimperis joins her little group, and they play tennis regularly on Charmaine's court—until her husband Ed has it torn up for a putting green. Charmaine accepts it willingly, determined to be a good wife and homemaker, but Joanna is stunned and Bobbie begins to notice how every woman who seems open and outgoing initially seems to change "and become a hausfrau." They wonder if the women are being drugged, or if there's some dangerous chemical in the environment. Then, suddenly, Bobbie becomes interested in ironing and housekeeping.

Joanna realizes that the women both changed four months after moving to town, and it's coming up on that time for her. Frantic, she looks up old newspaper files and discovers that several local men used to work for CompuTech Instatron, a robot-making company. She's convinced the other women are all robot copies, and her husband tells her she's crazy. But when she goes to get her car keys, they're missing; running off, she is pursued and captured by townspeople who assure her she's wrong. They agree to go to Bobbie's: Joanna says that if she cuts her finger and it bleeds, she'll admit she's mistaken. Bobbie picks up the knife—and it's the end of Joanna.

Comment: Katharine Ross and Paula Prentiss starred in the 1975 motion picture version of the novel, directed by Bryan Forbes from a script by William Goldman. There were two made-for-TV sequels: *Revenge of the Stepford Wives* (1980), starring Sharon Gless, in which a journalist comes to Stepford and learns its dark secret; and *The Stepford Children* (1987), starring Don Murray and Barbara Eden, the story of a man who moves his family to his boyhood town of Stepford and discovers that the neighbors aren't quite as real as he remembered.

STINGRAY (TV)

First Appearance: *Stingray*, September 1964 (England).

Physical Description: Some 70 feet long, the sleek ship has a flat, narrow, oval shape with an upraised bridge that starts approximately 20 feet from the nose. There's a giant turbine in the rear, two slanted tailfins on either side of it, and two small winglike fins on the side of the ship in the center. There are two slanted tailfins on the bridge and a small conning tower above it. The ship is silver with yellow and blue trim, can travel rapidly on or under the water, and is armed with missiles.

Biography: In 2065, W.A.S.P.—the World Aquanaut Security Patrol—is land-based in Marineville and run by Commander Sam Shore. His chief troubleshooter is Captain Troy Tempest of the *Stingray*, who is in love with Shore's daughter Atlanta; Tempest's sole crewmember is scientist "Phones" Sheridan. Their foremost enemy is the undersea-dwelling warlord Titan, who is aided by Agent X20, a master of disguise.

Tempest is frequently assisted by Marina, a mute young former slavegirl whom he rescued from Titan.

Comment: The series was created by producer Gerry Anderson and wife Sylvia, and syndicated in the United States in 1965. There were 39 half-hour adventures. The characters were brought to life through "Supermarionation" (see SUPERCAR,); Don Mason was the voice of Troy, Ray Barrett was Shore and Titan, Robert Easton was Sheridan and X20, and Lois Maxwell (James Bond's Miss Moneypenny) was Atlanta.

STUMP ASTEROID (C)

First Appearance: *Teenage Mutant Ninja Turtles Adventures* #7, 1989, Archie Comics.

Physical Description: The asteroid is round and approximately 400 yards in diameter, its white and yellow surface pocked with craters. Its entire northern hemisphere is covered by the open-air Stump Arena, a round stadium that appears to seat "tens of thousands" of spectators.

Biography: Stump is a humanoid with a tree-trunk-shaped body, bark-like skin, and branches growing from the top of his head. Sling is a green-skinned humanoid with brown branches growing from *his* head. No one knows whence they come but, together, they own the Stump Asteroid in Dimension X, where they stage matches of the Intergalactic Wrestling Team, whose fighters include Trap, Cryin' Houn', and Ace Duck. The two promoters run afoul of the Teenage Mutant Ninja Turtles when they try, repeatedly, to shanghai them for their wrestling team.

Another world in Dimension X is Palmadise, home of the evil turtle Slash, who is sentenced to the waste world of Morbus, befriends the villains Bellybomb and Krang, and escape in a stolen spaceship.

Comment: The world has appeared in several issues of *Teenage Mutant Ninja Turtles* and in its companion title, *The Mighty Mutanimals*.

See also WINGNUT AND SCREWLOOSE.

THE SUN-KING (C)

First Appearance: *Wham-O Giant Comics* #1, 1967, Wham-O Manufacturing Company.

Physical Description: The Sun-King has orange and yellow skin, flamelike yellow hair, beard, and moustache, long fingernails, and an orange and yellow robe with a high collar. He stands approximately seven feet tall.

No sun person can survive for more than a brief time on Earth "because of the deadly cold" here. The sun people have the ability to fly above the sun.

Biography: When his retro-rockets fail to fire during a mission to Mercury, Colonel Ray Starkey plunges into the sun. But he doesn't die. He is met by tall, orange-and-yellow-skinned beings who have a halo of flame. They temporarily turn him into a sun-being, pilot his ship to their spaceport on the metallic surface of the sun, and take the astounded astronaut to the Sun-King, who sits on a throne atop a great flight of steps.

The Sun-King reveals that his people are "responsible for life on the solar planets," and that his emissaries have visited Earth from time to time. Now, however, the shape-changing Kelp People (origin unknown) have conquered Venus and covered it with fog—and Earth is next. Accordingly, the Sun-King gives Starkey a Sun Disk, which allows him to focus destructive rays on the enemy, and sends him back to Earth. The hero can use the disk only if he has stored sufficient energy from exposure to the sun, fire, or heat.

Comment: This was the characters' only appearance. *Wham-O Giant Comics* also featured the strip "Tor," about an undersea agent who travels about in the *Cobalt*, a sleek, torpedo-shaped vehicle with "retractable wings that permit it to travel . . . in space, and . . . the depths of the ocean."

Creatures living on or in the sun are uncommon in science fiction. Still, there has been one other, major comic book sun dweller: Ajax, the Sun Man. Hailing from the core of the sun, Ajax comes to Earth, adopts the secret identity Jim Wilson, and battles dictators, criminals, and other evildoers. Ajax first appeared in *Doc Savage Comics #2*, 1940, from Street & Smith Publications, and stayed there for three years. The yellow-skinned humanoid has arched eyebrows and "sun-powers," which allow him to generate and survive intense heat. He can also fly and possesses incredible strength. Ajax wears red trunks, red boots, and a red cap with an antenna on either side (later, he doffs the cap, his trunks become blue, and he dons a red cape).

SUPER-ADAPTOID See ADAPTOID.

SUPERBOY See BEPPO; BRAINIAC; COSMIC BOY; HTRAE; KRYPTO; KRYPTON; SUPERGIRL; SUPERMAN.

SUPERCAR (TV, C)

First Appearance: *Supercar*, September 1961 (England).

Physical Description: Approximately 15 feet long, Supercar is a two-person vehicle. The glass-topped cockpit is located in the center of the flat, sledlike fuselage, with a slightly tapered front section, a blunt nose, and a long antenna jutting forward from that. It has two short, stubby wings behind the cockpit, long, narrow rocket engines on the fuselage just in front of the wings, and two raised tail fins on either side in the rear.

Supercar works like a hovercraft on land, can travel under the sea—it's equipped with a periscope and sonar—can fly through the skies, aided by its clearvu display screen, which allows the pilot to see through clouds and fog, and can journey through space. The vehicle is white with orange trim.

Biography: For five years, Professor Rudolph Popkiss and his aide Doctor Horatio Beaker have been working on Supercar in an isolated laboratory in Black Rock, Nevada. Though daring pilot Mike Mercury has yet to fly the vehicle, he insists on taking it up when they receive a radio broadcast about a pilot, Bill Gibson, who has gone down at sea with his 10-year-old brother Jimmy and Jimmy's pet monkey Mitch. Heading out to the Pacific, Mercury rescues the trio: Jimmy and Mitch are allowed to join the Supercar team, as long as he keeps up with his schoolwork. At the laboratory, he is supervised by Popkiss's sister Heidi.

The chief nemeses of the group are the evil Masterspy and his helper Zarin, who have vowed to steal the vehicle. When they aren't battling Masterspy, the heroes are helping the deposed ruler of Pelota regain power, investigating the Phantom Piper who is haunting the Scottish castle of Dr. Beaker's cousin Miss Farnsworth, helping a diver search for the lost treasure of Poseidon, battling the pirate Black Morgan, and the like.

Comment: The British series was created using marionettes ("Supermarionation"). In addition to using very thin (.005 inches) strings to move the limbs, solenoid cells were used to control the motion of the eyes, eyelids, and mouth. The series—and the process—was created by producer Gerry Anderson and special effects artist Reg Hill.

The show was syndicated in the United States a year after its British debut and featured Graydon Gould as the voice of Mike Mercury, with David Graham as Beaker, Mitch, and Zarin, George Murcell as Popkiss and Masterspy, and Sylvia Anderson (the producer's wife) as Jimmy and Heidi. There were 39 half-hour episodes in all. The special effects were created by Derek Meddings, one of the industry's giants, who went on to create the miniatures for many of the James Bond and SUPERMAN films.

Gold Key published four issues of a *Supercar* comic book from 1962 to 1963.

THE SUPERCOOP (TV, C)

First Appearance: *George of the Jungle*, September 1967, ABC.

Physical Description: The circa six-foot-long, egg-shaped flying machine is white on its bottom third and clear for the top two-thirds. It has three exhaust pipes, one atop the other, in the rear, and three wheels: a small one in the front and two larger ones in the back. The flying machine apparently has no seats nor any visible means of control.

In addition to flying through the air, the *Supercoop* can travel in space.

Biography: Harvard graduate and multi-million-aire Henry Cabot Henhouse III is secretly the costumed Super Chicken. In order to gain super-powers for a limited amount of time, he drinks the super-sauce mixed by his lion sidekick Fred.

It isn't known where in his penthouse the chicken keeps the *Supercoop*, or how many he has. However, as often as it's wrecked (which is often), he always has another one.

Comment: There were 16 cartoons in all; the show aired through September 1970. Bill Scott was the voice of Super Chicken.

The characters also appeared in both issues of Gold Key's *George of the Jungle* comic book (1968–1969).

SUPERGIANT (MP)

First Appearance: *Kotetso No Kyojin—Supa Jyaiantsu* (*The Steel Giant—Supergiant*), 1957, Shintoho Co. Ltd.

Physical Description: Supergiant is a normal-sized humanoid alien who looks just like an Earth-man. (His name suggests his deeds, not his size.) When he fights injustice he wears an ivory-colored bodysuit, cowl, and capelet. The rest of the time he dresses in a business suit.

Supergiant is armed with a watch (called a globe-meter in the dubbed version) that enables him to fly, gives him superstrength, allows him to speak any Earth language, and doubles as a Geiger counter.

Biography: On the Emerald Planet in the Moffitt (some translators give "Marpet") Galaxy, the High Council learns that the nation of Merapolia (or "Magolia") on Earth is planning to conquer the world using a powerful new nuclear weapon. Al-though the aliens are benevolent, they fear that radiation from a nuclear holocaust on Earth will pollute their world as well (which is an impossibil-ity). Locating the Merapolians' secret base, Super-giant collects the device and captures their evil leader, Munta Dee.

In his second adventure, Supergiant is sent to Earth to prevent a nuclear attack from the alien Sufferians. After destroying their space station, he heads to Earth to ferret out their agent. Meanwhile, Dr. Yamanaka has been brainwashed into working for the extraterrestrials and is brought to another of their space bases, with Supergiant in pursuit (en route, they pass over a volcanic asteroid called the Death Star). Supergiant rescues Yamanaka, de-stroys the platform, and returns to the Emerald Planet.

In the third escapade, the Salamander Men of the planet Kulamon are spreading plague germs through our atmosphere as a prelude to conquest. Adding insult to injury, they abduct leading scientists and try to force them to build the weapons that will be used to destroy us. Instead, they work on a means of killing the Kulamonians, while Supergiant battles the bulk of their invasion force.

In his fourth adventure, Supergiant battles Ba-lazar of the planet Zemar—or, more accurately, Balazar's brain, which is kept alive after his body is killed by a robot. Hidden on Earth and directing his minions, who plan to release a deadly virus, Ba-lazar is eventually found by Supergiant, who de-stroys his base.

Comment: There were nine Supergiant films, each between 39 and 59 minutes long, the first six forming three two-part stories. The remaining featurettes were *Zoku Kotetsu No Kyojin—Supa Jyaiantsu* (*Follow-up to the Adventures of the Steel Giant*), 1957; *Kotetsu No Kyojin—Supa Jyaiantsu Kaiseijin No Maya* (*The Steel Giant—Supergiant: The Evil Castle of the Mysterious Plane People*), 1957; *Kotetsu No Kyojin—Supa Jyaiantsu: Chikyu Metsubo Sunzen* (*The Steel Giant—Supergiant: The Earth Will Be Annihi-lated Soon*), 1957; *Supa Jyaiantsu: Jinko Eisei To Jinrui No Hametsu* (*Supergiant: Satellites and the Destruction of Mankind*), 1957; *Super Jyaiantsu: Uchusen To Jinko Eisei No Gekitotsu* (*Supergiant: The Spaceships and Satellites Duel*), 1958; *Supa Jyaiantsu: Uchu Kaijin Shutsugen* (*Supergiant: Mysterious Spacemen Appear*), 1958; *Zoku Supa Jyaiantsu Akuma No Keshin* (*Further Adventures of Supergiant: Devil Incarnate*), 1959; and *Zoku Supa Jyaiantsu: Dokunga Ookoku* (*Further Ad-ventures of Supergiant: Kingdom of the Venom-ous Moth*), 1959.

Ken Utsui starred as the hero. Teruo Ishii di-rected adventures one through six, Akira Miwa directed seven, and Chogi Akasaka helmed eight and nine.

In 1964 and 1965, the adventures were edited into feature films for U.S. television release. This did not require much tinkering, since one/ two, three/four, five/six, and seven through nine were essentially chapters in a whole. One and two became *Atomic Rulers*, three and four were *Invaders from Space*, five and six were *Attack from Space*, and seven through nine were released as *Evil Brain from Outer Space*. In these dubbed versions, the alien hero was known as Starman.

SUPERGIRL (C, MP)

First Appearance: *Action Comics* #252, 1959, DC Comics.

Physical Description: Standing five-foot-seven, Supergirl dresses—with slight variations over the years, such as red hotpants—in a blue bodysuit with a red-rimmed yellow shield on her chest, a red "S" inside; a red cape, miniskirt, and boots, yellow fringe on top of the boots; and a yellow belt. She has blonde hair and, in later years, wears a red headband. Supergirl has the same strengths and weakness as SUPERMAN.

As Linda Lee Danvers, Supergirl wears a brunette wig for a time, eventually trading it in for a comb that charges her hair with color-sensitive molecules.

Biography: When the planet KRYPTON explodes, a chunk of the planet bearing the domed Argo City survives, drifting in space. When the ground itself turns deadly, having been transformed into kryptonite, the streets are covered with lead shielding and the populace survives. Many years later, a girl named Kara is born to scientist Zor-El—brother of Superman's father, Jor-El—and his wife Alura. Unfortunately, when Kara is 15, the city passes through a meteor shower, and the lead shielding is ripped apart. As the radioactive ground slowly poisons the air, Zor-El constructs a rocket and sends Kara to Earth. Crashing just outside of Metropolis, she is found by her cousin Superman, who helps her come up with the secret identity of Linda Lee (in keeping with the Superman comics tradition of giving Earthwomen "LL" initials, such as Lois Lane and Lana Lang) and takes her to nearby Midvale Orphanage.

While Superman works with her in private, teaching her how to use her powers, Supergirl—whose presence on Earth is a secret—is adopted by scientist/engineer Fred Danvers and his wife Edna. Supergirl's training lasts three years, after which Superman presents her to the astonished world. She fights for justice wearing a costume her mother had knit before she left Argo City, one modeled after her cousin's suit. Like Superboy—Superman as a teenager—she travels to the future to serve with the Legion of Super-Heroes (see COSMIC BOY). She also has two pets, Streaky the Super-Cat, who becomes super-powered when it's struck by rays from the experimental isotope X-kryptonite; and Comet the Super-Horse, actually the Ancient Aeaean centaur Biron the Bowman who was turned into a horse by the wizard Malador and given superpowers by the sorceress Circe.

Linda attends Midvale High, graduates in 1964, and goes to Stanhope College. She graduates in 1971, after which she works briefly at KSF-TV in San Francisco before returning to school. She attends Vandyre University in San Francisco, then leaves to work as a student advisor at the New Athens Experimental School in Santa Augusta, Florida. From there, she heads to New York and lands a role on the soap opera *Secret Hearts*; when the gig is finished, she attends Lake Shore University in Chicago. During this time, she learns that her parents had managed to escape into a limbo-like realm known as the Survival Zone which is similar to the Phantom Zone; with the help of her adoptive father, she frees them and they go to live in Kandor, another Kryptonian city that survived destruction (see BRAINIAC).

In 1985, while battling the evil Monitor on another world, Supergirl is struck by an energy blast that nearly rips her to pieces. She dies in Superman's arms and, wrapped in her cape, is buried among the stars.

Supergirl has since returned to active duty, wearing her original costume—though she is actually, now, "a gelatinous blob of protoplasm" who can assume any likeness. An alien artificial life form, she recalls nothing of her home world, other than that her original name was Matrix, she "was created . . . [in a laboratory] in homage to Superman," and she joined forces with him to stop alien terrorists (told in *Superman: Panic in the Sky*). The new Supergirl is impervious to harm thanks to psychokinetic energy, which stops bullets, flames, etc. right before they reach her. For a time, she worked closely with Lex Luthor 2nd, the devious son of the magnate/villain/scientist, whose super-police Team Luthor was helping protect the city (they met in *Action Comics* #676).

Comment: Supergirl perished in *Crisis on Infinite Earths* #7. She appeared in *Action Comics* through #376, 1969, after which she moved to *Adventure Comics* #381–424, then to her own title *Supergirl*, which lasted 10 issues from 1972 to 1974. *The Daring New Adventures of Supergirl* began in 1982, changed to *Supergirl* with #14, and lasted through #23, 1984. The character also appeared in *Superman Family* and *Super-Team Family*, among other DC titles. The "new" Supergirl appeared in Superman's own title, as well as specials like *Supergirl and Team Luthor* (1993), before being given her own magazine in 1994.

In the 1984 motion picture, directed by Jeannot Szwarc and written by David Odell, Helen Slater stars as the superhero with Marc McClure as Jimmy

Olsen, Faye Dunaway as the evil Selena, and Peter O'Toole as the Kryptonian Zaltar; Mia Farrow and Simon Ward play Alura and Zor-El. In the film, Argo City is not destroyed: Supergirl comes to Earth to recover the missing Omegahedron Stone, the life-force of Argo City, which has fallen into Selena's hands.

Another Kryptonian "super" female who has fought crime on Earth is Power Girl, who is actually the Supergirl of Earth 2 in a parallel dimension. The differences are minor: This Kara, daughter of Zor-L, assumes the identity of Karen Starr, lives in Gotham City, and wears a white, legless bodysuit, blue boots, and gloves, and a red cape and belt. DC's Superwoman, Kristen Wells, is actually a Superman/Supergirl scholar from the year 2862 whose powers are a result of future technology.

The 1971 West German film *Supergirl* is unrelated to the character, though it's about a girl from another world who comes to Earth to warn of an attack.

SUPERMAN (C, CS, R, L, MP, TV, S)

First Appearance: *Action Comics* #1, 1938, DC Comics.

Physical Description: Standing six-foot-two (five-foot-eleven when he slouches as Clark Kent), the humanoid hero possesses a vast array of powers. Initially, he possesses great strength, can run exceedingly fast, and is able to leap long distances. However, his powers increase and ultimately include: the ability to fly; virtually unlimited strength; and superspeed. His super-senses include: microscopic, telescopic, heat, and X-ray vision (which doesn't work on lead); a super-sense of smell; super-touch; and supersensitive hearing, which allows him to listen to many conversations at once or hear "the footfall of an ant one thousand miles away." He has the ability to hold his breath indefinitely (underwater or in space), speak any language instantly thanks to his "advanced intellect which instantly comprehends" any tongue, hypnotize anyone with his "telepathic will-control," "sense" the presence of trouble thanks to his "supersensitive nerve structure," write with both hands at once, use his muscular control to alter his features, project his voice anywhere in the world, travel through time, blow with hurricane-force super-breath, memorize vast texts in moments and even all the fingerprints on file with the F.B.I., and more.

Superman's powers are originally explained as the result of his entire race having achieved physical perfection; later, as the difference between the greater gravity and atmospheric density of KRYPTON; and finally, as a result of living under Earth's yellow sun after having been born beneath Krypton's red sun.

Superman is impervious to everything except Virus X from Krypton, magic, and chunks of his home world that underwent nuclear fission: Green kryptonite can kill him, gold kryptonite (origin unexplained) robs him of his powers permanently, and red kryptonite (which passed through a strange crimson cosmic cloud) causes unpredictable effects from temporary mutations (giving him an ant-head, splitting him in two, and causing his hair and fingernails to grow wildly out of control) to psychological problems (causing his face to turn colors with his emotions). Each piece of red kryptonite works only once.

When he goes into action, he wears a costume his adoptive mother made from the blankets in which he was swaddled and from seat upholstery of the rocket (he cut the threads with his heat vision). His garb consists of a blue bodysuit with a red "S" on a yellow field in a red shield on his chest; red trunks, boots, and cape with an all-yellow "S" symbol and shield on the back; and a yellow belt.

He has occasionally used Superman and Clark Kent robots to take his place, when he must appear in two places at once. He has also utilized a Supermobile, a rocket plane constructed of supermanium, the hardest metal in the universe. He uses this when he is disabled, quarantined, or must handle kryptonite. The two-seat ship can travel anywhere, including space, and has two retractable metal arms.

Biography: Born on the 35th of Eorx, 9998, Superman (born Kal-El) is the son of Jor-El II and Lara Lor-Van of Krypton, scion of a distinguished line. Feln begat Rugad, father of Tomnu, who sired Erok-El. Erok-El wed Milia and fathered Kal-El, who begat Wab-El, then Hyr-El, who fathered generations of famed Kryptonians: Tio-El (naturalist) and Jaf-El (theologist), Bur-El, Val-El (explorer), Sul-El (astronomer), Hatu-El (electrician), Wir-El (inventor), Shu-El (mathematician), Thar-El (jurist), Plen-El (writer), Nlx-El (entertainer), Fil-El (surgeon), Sorn-El (agriculturalist), Im-El (physicist), Pir-El (military leader), Tala-El (author of the Kryptonian Constitution), Gam-El (builder), and Var-El (the first Kryptonian to visit Earth). His children were Jor-El (a scientist and Superman's paternal grandfather), Kalya Var-El, and Zim-El. Jor-El married Nimda An-Dor, becoming the parents of twins

Nim-El and Jor-El II, and Zor-El (who married Alura-In-Ze and parented Kara Zor-El, a.k.a. *Supergirl* [see entry]). Jor-El II wed Lara, his former research assistant and daughter of scientist Lor-Van and Lara Rok-Var.

Kal-El ("Kal" means child and "El" means star) was born in October, Earth-time, in the city of Kryptonopolis. Two or three months later, he is rocketed to Earth by his parents when Krypton explodes. After a brief journey, the blue and red rocket crashes in Smallville, Kansas, a small town several hundred miles from the sprawling Metropolis. It is found by passing motorists Jonathan and Martha Hudson Clark Kent. The childless farm couple brings him to Smallville Orphanage, then returns to adopt him. They name him Clark. (His only other known relative is Martha's brother Harry, who is deceased.) The Kents realize early-on that the boy has amazing powers, including superspeed, which has a habit of burning up his clothes. Martha makes him a playsuit from his Kryptonian blanket; later, the same fabric is used to make his Superboy/Superman costume.

When Clark is about five and "ready to start school," the Kents sell the farm and move into downtown Smallville, where they open a general store. At the age of eight, Clark has sufficiently mastered his abilities so that he can begin serving the world as the superhero Superboy. He slouches, acts timid, and changes his voice pattern so that no one suspects he is really Clark Kent. He works closely with Police Chief Douglas Parker solving crimes, and comes and goes via a secret tunnel built from the house to the woods outside of Smallville; his Kent street clothes are made from a "super-compressible material," which he folds and slides into a secret pouch inside his cape whenever he goes into action, and his Kent glasses are made from the windshield of the Kryptonian rocket (which doesn't melt when he uses his heat vision as Clark). As Superboy, he is also a member of the future-based Legion of Super-Heroes (see COSMIC BOY) and has a pet dog, KRYPTO.

In his ordinary life, Clark's best friends are Pete Ross—who knows his secret identity—and neighbor Lana Lang. After graduating from elementary school he attends Smallville High, then spends four years in Metropolis University, graduating magna cum laude in journalism. He decides to become a reporter so he'll "be among the first to learn of crimes and disasters," to which he can then race as Superman. He lands a job at *The Daily Planet* under editor Perry White, often competing for stories with aggressive reporter Lois Lane— who becomes his girlfriend as Superman. Both are often assisted by cub reporter/photographer Jimmy Olsen. Eventually, the paper becomes a subsidiary of Morgan Edge's Galaxy Communications, and Clark is shifted to becoming a newscaster for WGBS-TV. Later, he returns to the newspaper.

Clark lives alone (except for his robots, kept in a secret closet) in apartment 3D at 344 Clinton Street; when he needs to get away from it all, he heads to his large Fortress of Solitude, built into a mountain in the Antarctic and filled with mementoes, research equipment, a chess-playing robot, and the bottle city of Kandor (see BRAINIAC), complete with all of its shrunken inhabitants. Superman has been known to shrink himself and visit whenever he needs a taste of the old world.

In his most famous adventure, Superman is slain in Metropolis, battling the monstrous humanoid Doomsday, whose body is spotted with sharp projections of bone. The two batter each other in front of the Daily Planet Building, Doomsday falling moments before Superman dies in Lois's arms. He is pronounced dead by Dr. Jorge Sanchez of Metropolis General Hospital. But no sooner has he perished than four Supermen appear in Metropolis, wearing variations of his distinctive costume. The first is a cyborg whose "bionics show evidence of Kryptonian technology"—but who is, in fact, dying astronaut Hank Henshaw, who transferred his consciousness into a computer and, from there, transmitted it to the Kryptonian matrix chamber. He used that to generate a spaceship that carried him to Peroton 5, stronghold of the evil alien superbeing Mongul. The second is a man born when Superman's Fortress Robots gather the "essence" of Superman, which was "dispersed following dysfunction of the corporeal body." In the process, they release a long-dormant sentience called the Eradicator, created on Krypton and stored in the Fortress. The spirit enters Superman's old body, entombed in Metropolis, and goes back into the crimefighting business. The third is Henry Johnson, a black construction worker who makes himself rocket-powered steel armor and goes forth doing good. And the fourth is a 15-year-old who claims to be a clone, is as powerful as the original Man of Steel, and can also emit destructive power-blasts.

Meanwhile, back at the Fortress, in the "regeneration matrix," the *real*, re-collected Superman is reborn, albeit in a much less powerful form, and heads to Metropolis to stop the name of Superman from being "turned into a franchise." He must also battle Mongul, his hordes, and the cyborg Superman. The heroes storm the fortress the rogue has established on Earth, where Coast City used to stand, joined by that city's protector, Green Lantern (see GREEN LANTERN CORPS). A kryptonite blast fired by the cyborg kills the Eradicator's body, but joins his spirit and superpowers with those of the original Superman, making him whole again. Punching the cyborg through the chest, he vibrates his arm so quickly that the fiend falls apart.

Comment: Created by writer Jerry Siegel and artist Joe Shuster, Superman was the "Big Bang" of comic books, his popularity in the nascent field turning it into a popular culture phenomenon.

Because of the many inconsistencies in the chronicles, it was explained that there are two Supermen: the all-powerful Superman of "our" world, Earth 1, in this dimension; and the original Superman of the nearly identical Earth 2 in a parallel dimension. In the latter (actually, original) version of the tale, Superman hails from a world whose inhabitants possess "prodigious strength, speed, and vitality." The baby Kal-L is rocketed to Earth, where he possesses those powers as well as bulletproof skin. The only other major differences are his place of employment, *The Daily Star*, edited by George Taylor (eerily, one of his first cases is solving the murder of a man named Jack Kennedy), and the fact that he marries Lois Lane. The complete, definitive biography of *this* Superman was set down in *Secret Origins* #1, 1986. That Superman, and his entire dimension, were erased from existence in the 12-issue *Crisis on Infinite Earths* in 1985–86.

The saga of Superman was retold and remade by artist/writer John Byrne in the six-issue *The Man of Steel* mini-series in 1986. His Krypton explodes because of pressures building under the surface, "fusing the native elements into . . . a radioactive metal" (kryptonite). The effete Jor-El and Lara (who are less sympathetic than their robots Kelex and Kelor) send Kal-El to Kansas via hyperlight-drive spaceship, where he is adopted by the Kents. He does not go through his costumed Superboy phase, first meets Lois Lane when he saves her from the crash of a new space plane, and doesn't don his costume until after some three years of doing anonymous superdeeds around Metropolis. His Lex Luthor—a scientific madman in the earlier stories—is now the head of the Lexcorp conglomerate. Byrne's best idea was having Superman adopt his costume and dual identity to give him some privacy from all those who "wanted a piece" of him and his powers.

In addition to starring in *Action Comics* and his own title *Superman*, which debuted the following year, Superman has also starred in the DC titles *World's Finest*, costarring with Batman; *The Justice League of America*, teamed with virtually all of DC's major superheroes; *DC Comics Presents*, partnered with various DC heroes; *Super Friends*, inspired by the TV series (see WONDERTWINS); *Super Powers*, based on the animated series; *The Superman Family*, featuring friends and fellow heroes; *Superman's Girlfriend Lois Lane* and *Superman's Pal Jimmy Olsen*; *Superboy* and *Adventure Comics* (as Superboy, member of the Legion of Super-Heroes); and many others, including miniseries like *Superman: The Secret Years* (four issues, 1985) and one-shots. He battled Marvel Comics' best-known hero in *Superman vs. The Amazing Spider-Man* in a 1976 one-shot, Wonder Woman in a 1978 one-shot, and was even taken to the world Bodace for a misbegotten fight in the 1978 comic book *Superman vs. Muhammad Ali*. (Ali actually wins and gets to battle the green-skinned alien bruiser Hun'ya for championship of the universe.)

The heavily promoted "death" of Superman occurred in the January 1993 issue of *Superman* (#75, new numbering, which began following the character's reintroduction by Byrne; Superman's original title was renamed *The Adventures of Superman* and continued with the same "old" numbering). The death also spawned a new *Superboy* comic book, featuring the Metropolis Kid, and *Steel*, starring Henry Johnson.

The character began moving into other media almost at once. A newspaper comic strip was launched in 1939 for a remarkable run of 28 years. The success was ironic, given that Siegel and Shuster had originally conceived of Superman as a comic strip and were turned down by every syndicate.

In 1940, the Mutual network began airing a long-lived *Superman* radio series, starring Clayton "Bud" Collyer, and then Michael Fitzmaurice, as Superman and Clark. Joan Alexander was Lois, Julian Noa was Perry White, and Jimmy Olsen—an office boy, later cub reporter created for the series—was played by Jackie Kelk. The series aired through 1952 and gave us the famed, "Faster than a speeding bullet! More powerful than a locomotive! Able to leap tall buildings in a single bound!"

Kirk Alyn played the part in a pair of movie serials from Columbia. The first was the 15-chapter *Superman* (1948) costarring Noel Neill as Lois and Tommy Bond as Jimmy, and directed by Spencer

Kirk Alyn as the serial *Superman.* © DC Comics. Courtesy Kirk Alyn.

Bennet and Thomas Carr; the second was *The Atom Man vs. Superman* (1950), costarring Neill and Bond and featuring Lyle Talbot as the "Atom Man," Luthor. The 15-chapter serial was directed by Spencer Bennet. George Reeves assumed the role for the 1951 feature film *Superman and the Mole Men,* costarring Phyllis Coates as Lois.

Paramount Pictures released a spectacular series of color, animated shorts featuring the voices of Collyer and Alexander. Created by animation pioneers Max and Dave Fleischer, the cartoons released in 1941 were "The Mad Scientist" and "The Mechanical Monsters"; in 1942, "Billion Dollar Limited," "The Arctic Giant," "The Bulleteers," "The Magnetic Telescope," "Electric Earthquake," "Volcano," "Terror on the Midway," "Japoteurs," "Showdown," "Eleventh Hour," and "Destruction, Inc."; in 1943, "The Mummy Strikes," "Jungle Drums," "Underground World," and "Secret Agent."

In 1978, Richard Donner directed the huge-budget *Superman—The Movie* written by Mario Puzo, David Newman, Leslie Newman and Robert Benton. Christopher Reeve stars as Superman (with Jeff East as young Clark), Margot Kidder as Lois, Gene Hackman as Luthor, Marlon Brando as Jor-El, Susannah York as Lara, Jackie Cooper as Perry White, Glenn Ford as Pa Kent, Phyllis Thaxter as Ma Kent, and Marc McClure as Jimmy. (Neill and Alyn are briefly seen in a train as Lois's parents.) A sequel, *Superman II*—shot concurrent with the first film—was begun by Donner, who was replaced by Richard Lester. The same cast repeated in the 1980 film, with the addition of three Kryptonian villains who were seen only in cameos as they were banished to the Phantom Zone in the first film: Terence Stamp as General Zod, Sarah Douglas as Ursa, and Jack O'Halloran as Non. Lester directed, the Newmans wrote, and Reeve starred in *Superman III* (1983), in which Superman splits into an evil twin, with Annette O'Toole as love interest Lana Lang, Richard Pryor as comic relief Gus Gorman, and Robert Vaughn as power-mad Ross Webster; Reeve starred and Sidney J. Furie directed *Superman IV: The Quest for Peace* (1987), a sorry spectacle in which Superman battles the Luthor (Hackman)-created Nuclear Man (Mark Pillow) and re-romances Lois (Kidder). DC published a comic book adaptation of the last film. *Superman—The New Movie* has been written by Cary Bates, but not yet filmed.

On TV, Reeves played the part in the popular half-hour series *The Adventures of Superman,* which debuted in syndication in July 1951 and continued airing first-run episodes through November 1957. There were 104 episodes in all; Coates starred as Lois in the first season, followed by Neill. Jack Larson starred as Jimmy with John Hamilton as Perry White and Robert Shayne as the newly-created Inspector William Henderson. ABC aired reruns of the show from October 1957 to September 1958, and a new season was planned until the untimely death of actor Reeves.

Johnny Rockwell played *Superboy* in the unsold TV pilot *Superboy* (1960). The character finally made it to the air in the syndicated *Superboy* TV series, which ran from October 1988 through May 1991. John Haymes Newton starred as the Boy of Steel in the first season, replaced by Gerard Christopher in seasons two and three. Scott Wells played Luthor in the first season, Sherman Howard in two and three; Stuart Whitman and Salome Jens were Jonathan and Martha Kent, and Stacy Haiduk and Jim Calvert were Lana Lang and T.J. White, who attend Shuster University along with Clark Kent. The series spawned a short-lived *Superboy the Comic Book,* launched in February 1990.

In his most recent live-action TV incarnation,

Superman is played by Dean Cain in *Lois and Clark: The New Adventures of Superman*, an hour-long series that began airing on ABC in September 1993. Teri Hatcher is Lois and John Shea is Luthor.

There have been numerous animated TV series featuring the Man of Steel. Collyer was again the voice of Superman in *The New Adventures of Superman*, which aired on CBS from September 1966 to September 1967, and again from September 1969 to September 1970. Bob Hastings was the voice of Superboy in episodes devoted to the Boy of Steel. Collyer reprised on *The Superman/Aquaman Hour of Adventure*, which aired on CBS from September 1967 to September 1968; Collyer and Alexander were heard again on *The Batman/Superman Hour*, on CBS from September 1968 to September 1969. Beau Weaver plays Superman, Ginny McSwain was Lois, and Mark Taylor was Jimmy on *Superman*, on CBS from September 1988 to September 1989. Danny Dark voices the part on the long-lived *Super Friends*, which aired on ABC from September 1973 to August 1975, then again from February 1976 to September 1977; *The All-New Super Friends Hour* on ABC from September 1977 to September 1978; *Challenge of the Super Friends* on ABC from September 1978 to September 1979; *The World's Greatest Super Friends*, on ABC from September 1979 to September 1980; and *Super Friends: The Legendary Super Powers Show*, on ABC from September 1984 to August 1985. Dark also provided the voice on *Super Powers Team: Galactic Guardians*, on ABC from September 1985 to August 1986.

In print, the character starred in an eponymous 1942 novel by George Lowther, as well as in the novels *The Last Son of Krypton* (1978) and *Miracle Monday* (1981) by Elliot S. Maggin, and *The Death of Superman*—a novelization of the Doomsday saga—by Roger Stern. A collection of short stories, *The Further Adventures of Superman*, was published in 1993. In 1993, author Louise Simonson wrote *Superman: Doomsday and Beyond*, a children's novel based on the ''Death of Superman'' saga in the comic books.

On stage, the character was played by Bob Holiday in the Broadway musical *It's a Bird . . . It's a Plane . . . It's Superman* which ran from March 29, 1966 to July 17, 1966 (129 performances). The book was by David Newman and Robert Benton; Charles Strouse wrote the music, Lee Adams the lyrics. David Wilson played the part in the TV adaptation of the musical in February 1975, seen on ABC's latenight *Wide World of Entertainment*; Gary Jackson starred as the Man of Steel in

the Goodspeed Opera (Connecticut) revival in the summer of 1992.

The hero Super-Kid is a member of the Super Jrs., tots at Miss Piffle's nusery school. This baby version of Superman (*not* Kal-El, but a transformed youngster named Casey) appeared with his colleagues Wonder Tot, Flash-Kid, Bat-Guy, and Kid-Robin, in *The Best of DC #58*, 1985.

See also BEPPO; HTRAE; SUPERGIRL.

THE SUPREME MARTIAN INTELLIGENCE (MP, L)

First Appearance: *Invaders from Mars*, 1953, National Pictures/Twentieth Century-Fox.

Physical Description: Gold-colored, the Intelligence is approximately two feet tall and has a gumdrop-shaped body with a human face on a head shaped like a hot-air balloon. The hairless entity has two handless arms that remain crossed on its chest, and a pair of short arms that jut from its shoulders and have three long, tentacle-like fingers on each arm. It lives in a transparent sphere.

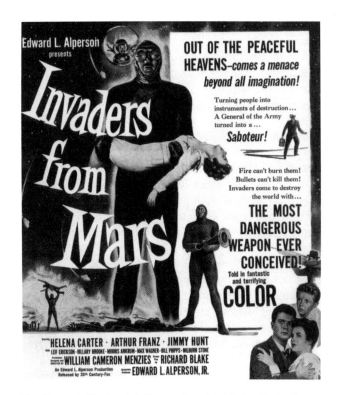

The *Supreme Martian Intelligence* (top, in globe) with its slaves, in advertising art for *Invaders from Mars*. © Twentieth Century-Fox.

The Intelligence is served by bug-eyed humanoid "Mutants" who wear green scaly leotards with cowls, have green skin, sport two fat toes and three fingers, and carry cannons that generate enough heat to melt rock.

The Martian ship is a flying saucer complete with an operating table. Above it is a large drill, which is used to implant small mind-control devices in the base of human skulls. When the humans have fulfilled their tasks, the Martians destroy them by causing the devices to explode.

Biography: Young David MacLean is awakened one night as a flying saucer buries itself in a sandy field behind his home. His father goes to investigate and returns a bad-tempered, violent Martian slave; soon David's mother, then other townspeople are sucked into the sands, operated on, and returned as pawns of the Martians who intend to conquer our world.

David can't convince anyone of what he's seen (no wonder, since several police officers are Martian zombies), and is turned over to psychologist Pat Blake for examination. She and David go to visit the latter's hero, local astronomer Stuart Kelston, through whose telescope they happen to see David's dad push a general into the pit. The military is alerted, soldiers descend into the pit and, after rescuing Pat and David (who manage to get drawn into the sand), rig explosives to blow up the saucer.

As the saucer explodes, David wakes up: It was all a dream. But when he goes back to bed, there's a sound outside his window and he sees a flying saucer settling into the sandy field beyond his home.

Comment: Actress Luce Potter plays the Intelligence; all of the "Mutants" are played by Lock Martin and Max Palmer. Jimmy Hunt stars as David with Helena Carter as Blake and Arthur Franz as Kelston. William Cameron Menzies (production designer on *Gone With the Wind*) directed from a script by John Tucker Battle, Richard Blake, and Menzies.

In the 1986 remake, hamfistedly directed by Tobe Hooper, the Intelligence is pictured as a wormlike creature with a pug face and slimy tentacles. The Mutants are fat, wrinkled slugs with an awkward pair of slender hindlegs, two thick forelegs, and gaping mouths. The remake starred Karen Black in the Carter role, with her real-life son Hunter Carson taking the Jimmy Hunt part. The boy's parents were played by Laraine Newman and Timothy Bottoms.

Pocket Books published a novelization of the remake.

SUSAN QUOD (L)

First Appearance: "The State vs. Susan Quod" by Noel Loomis, 1970, *Worlds of Tomorrow #24.*

Physical Description: An android who is "Tall, stately, firm of flesh . . . quick and graceful . . . and strong past belief," Susan has black hair, "dusky" skin, and deep blue eyes. Her "miniaturized controls . . . [and] circuitry" are disguised so that "short of a surgical inspection," she is indistinguishable from a human.

Androids can survive without nourishment or air for decades without showing any ill-effects; nothing short of an erupting volcano or a hydrogen bomb can destroy them completely.

Biography: By 2510, several lawsuits have been fought to prove that androids are "living human" beings. To date, the courts have ruled that they are not human for they lack a soul, the creation of which is "exclusively the province of God." By 2540, they have earned "quasi-human" status, entitled to human rights "as long as they behaved." Some have even been elected to Congress, albeit by pretending to be human, and certain members of the government begin to wonder if there are more androids than anyone suspects, and if there is a quiet revolt underway.

In 2560, presidential advisor Commander Adam meets 28-year-old Susan at a reception in Washington. They fall in love and marry, after he has the FBI check her family history back to Tanzania of the late 1800s. Soon thereafter, the government discovers that someone has been hoarding gold and upsetting the world's economy. The person turns out to be Susan's enormously wealthy grandfather Junius. Adam pressures him to sell the gold at a reasonable price, he refuses, Susan bitterly resents her husband's toughness toward her grandfather, and the newlyweds become estranged. Later, torn by her loyalty to her husband and to her grandfather, Susan jumps from the 80th floor of a building; at the morgue, Adam discovers that she was an android, built by the Quod family for the express purpose of trying to get the President's ear through Adam. Since androids can't be declared legally dead, decommission proceedings are begun. Adam's testimony will be needed for this, which means he must submit to surgery to establish that he's a human. Since he isn't, he flies to Costa Rica to destroy himself in an erupting volcano, for he knows that if *he's* found out, "a hundred forty-six Congressmen and thirty-two Senators—and the President himself" will be exposed, their android revolt finished.

Comment: Loomis wrote over 50 science fiction, western, and other novels after selling *City of Glass* to *Startling Stories* in 1942. This smart, engrossing novelette was his last story; he died shortly before its publication.

SWINETREK (TV)

First Appearance: "Pigs in Space," 1978, *The Muppet Show*, syndicated.

Physical Description: The porcine-shaped ship has a fuselage shaped like a silvery bowling pin, with a forward hatch like a pig's snout (on what would be the pin's bottom). There are two "eyes" and "ears" above and beyond it, and four engines, which also serve as landing struts, toward the rear.

The crew wear lilac-colored spacesuits with white stars and a golden lightning bolt through a pig's face on the chest, and a silver belt.

Biography: Voyaging through the universe, the exploration ship is commanded by Link Hogthrob, aided by first mate Miss Piggy and Dr. Julius T. Strangepork, "top schmart person aboard da spaceship." The stories focus more on Miss Piggy's infatuation with her lantern-jawed commander than with adventures among aliens.

Comment: The ship and its crew were seen in numerous episodes of ITC Entertainment's weekly series through 1980. Frank Oz provided the voice

Loretta Swit visits Kermit and Miss Piggy onboard the *Swinetrek.* © ITC Entertainment.

of Miss Piggy, Jim Henson was Hogthrob, and Jerry Nelson played Strangepork.

Dr. Strangepork also wrote about science news for the "Mondo Muppet" section of Telepictures Publication's *Muppet Magazine* throughout the 1980s.

The Muppets are fabric puppets operated from within by hands, and from below by thin rods attached to the limbs.

T

TALOS (M, MP, C)

First Appearance: Greek mythology, circa 1500 B.C.

Physical Description: Talos is a man made of bronze. In most versions of his saga, he is slightly taller than an average man. The automaton has only one weak spot: a vein in his left ankle.

Biography: Talos is built by Hephaestus, the Greek god of fire and metalworking, at the behest of Zeus, King of the Gods. When he is finished, Talos is given to King Minos of Crete as a gift. The bronze man guards the island, crossing it slowly, twice a year. When he spots an approaching ship, he lights a fire and sits in it until he's super-hot; then he greets and embraces sailors who land there uninvited, burning them to death. Talos is destroyed when he pursues the heroic Jason, who is en route to Iolcus in Thessaly, having collected the Golden Fleece in Colchis. Jason's lover, the witch Medea, invokes spirits of the underworld to steer the man of bronze toward a jagged rock; scraping his ankle, Talos bleeds to death.

Talos as pictured in the film *Jason and the Argonauts*.
© Columbia Pictures.

Comment: In the 1963 motion picture *Jason and the Argonauts*, Talos is pictured as 600 feet tall. He dwells on the Isle of Bronze where he guards the jewelry of the Gods. When the hero Hercules (Nigel Green) and his friend Hylas (John Cairney) enter Talos's pedestal and steal a broach pin to use as a javelin, Talos comes to life, pursues the sailors, and wrecks their ship. He would have hunted the survivors down if the Goddess Hera (Honor Blackman) hadn't told Jason (Todd Armstrong) how to defeat the titan. Sneaking behind him, Jason opens a plug in the bronze man's heel, allowing the giant's ichor, his life-blood, to pour out. When the steaming red liquid has drained away, Talos cracks apart, one chunk landing on Hylas and crushing him to death.

The film's extraordinary special effects were created by Ray Harryhausen.

Talos also appears in Dell's comic book adaptation of the film as part of its *Movie Classics* series (1963).

THE TEENAGERS FROM OUTER SPACE (MP)

First Appearance: *Teenagers from Outer Space*, 1959, Topaz Film Corporation/Warner Brothers.

Physical Description: The aliens are just like Earth teenagers, except for the jumpsuits they wear. These are made of dark cloth with Nehru-style collars and a white "V" that runs from the shoulders to mid-chest. They carry "focusing disintegrator" ray guns and travel through space in a flying saucer with a screw-shaped base that secures itself in the ground.

On their home world, the aliens are "raised in cubicles," unaware of who their parents are; the sick and infirm are put to death rather than looked after.

Biography: The aliens feed on giant, lobster-like monsters known as Gargons, and need a place where herds of them can graze freely. They choose Earth, unaware (and, later, unconcerned) that it's inhabited by intelligent beings. Derek, son of the Leader, is disgusted with his predatorycomrades Thor, Sol, and Moro. Deserting, he meets young Betty Morgan and takes a spare room in the home she shares with her grandfather. Unfortunately, one of Derek's shipmates, Thor, comes after Derek to bring him back. Derek and Betty hit the road while Thor pursues them, disintegrating humans who get in his way. Meanwhile, the Gargon they've brought to Earth begins lunching on people it encounters outside of town. Thor is wounded in a fight with police, and Derek gets hold of Thor's ray gun, which he uses to blast the Gargon. Plucking Thor from the hospital, Derek and Betty go to meet a spaceship carrying Derek's father—the flagship of a fleet carrying more Gargons to Earth. Sick and tired of his father's dictatorial ways, and determined to save our world, Derek provides the fleet with coordinates that cause it to crash on his saucer, destroying the ships, the Gargons, the Leader, and himself.

Comment: David Love starred as Derek, with Bryan Grant as Thor and Dawn Anderson as Betty. The film was written and directed by Tom Graeff.

TELEPUPPETS (L)

First Appearance: "Reign of the Telepuppets" by Daniel Galouye, August 1963, *Amazing Stories.*

Physical Description: The nuclear powered robots come in various shapes and sizes, though there's a definite pecking order. Leader Bigboss has four stout legs, an "extensible vise . . . [and] auxiliary blaster," sensors for "visual awareness."

The thick-necked, second-in-command Minnie has an "elongated metal form on six jointed legs . . . [a] drill head . . . [and a] single, wide-angle lens" in her chrome forehead. She is also equipped with mineral analyzers.

The number three robot is Seismo, who studies the planet with his "sensor rod"; next is Sky Watcher, a tripod; Sun Watcher, with his solar plasma detector, is fifth; sixth-ranked Maggie studies "isomagnetic" variations and moves in "great, leaping strides"; and seventh-in-command Peter the Meter is "a many-spiked sphere on spindly legs" and is armed with a "battery of inferometers, radiometers and bolometers."

The rest of the robots are all equal: Breather has a "long, cylindrical form" with external pouches to test the air; Scraper has scoops to search for organisms; Grazer identifies flora and, like Scraper, resembles a "scurrying crab"; and Screw Worm has "blade-edge jets to propel himself in a rolling,

transverse motion," and has "thread pouches" to collect mineral samples for Minnie. The Algae Detector has long since ceased functioning.

The Tzareans are large, scaly reptilian bipeds with "crocodile" heads, talons, tails, "craggy teeth," and "abbreviated" forearms.

Biography: Though they continue to do the research work for which they were designed, the telepuppets left on Aldebaran Four-B two years before have stopped transmitting. Now, it's up to the Dave Stewart, assistant director of the Bureau of Interstellar Exploration, to find out why. He and a small crew take the ship *Photon II* to Four-B, and the robots arrive to analyze it—beaming their findings to someplace unknown. Studying the robots, Stewart and his crew find them to be intact, save for their curious transmission "glitch."

Meanwhile, a ship from the Tzarean empire arrives and spies on the *Photon II* from orbit. The crewmembers debate whether to attack the ship in the name of empire, or make "amiable contact";

Bigboss of the Telepuppets. © Ziff-Davis Publishing Co.

crewmember and Curule Assembly member Chancellor Vrausot orders them to prepare for battle.

Back on the *Photon II*, Stewart realizes that Bigboss was the one who went haywire and lead the others astray. Donning a metal deep-space suit, Stewart is accepted as a robot until he gets close to the Operations Coordinator—Bigboss. Then he decks the robot and shuts it down. Back on the ship, he discovers that Director Gabe Randall knew the malfunction was caused by the aliens—whom we call the Hyadeans—who hoped that an Earth-ship would be sent so they could size us up. But Randall didn't want anyone else onboard to know, lest the aliens were telepathic and find us armed and ready. Randall wanted the aliens to think this was solely a repair mission, and for them to be responsible for peace or war.

Concurrently, the Mineral Analyzer—Minnie—assumes command of the robots and attacks. However, she inadvertently intercepts Vrausot and his landing party, killing the Chancellor before she runs out of power; the others of both races depart peacefully.

Comment: The World War II veteran sold his first story, "Rebirth," to *Imagination* in 1952. His output was limited, unfortunately, by war injuries; he died in 1976.

THE TENDRIL GIANTS (L)

First Appearance: "Invaders from the Outer Suns" by Frank Belknap Long Jr., February 1937, *Thrilling Wonder Stories*.

Physical Description: The aliens are eight feet tall and covered with "yellowish fuzz." The head is "vaguely anthropomorphic in contour" and the heart-shaped face is flat, wrinkled, and expressionless save for the "bright glitter of two little slitted eyes, and a writhing, puckered" mouth. The stalk's small "tubular legs hinted at animal kinship," and there are "numerous frail . . . tendrils, some green, some red" and some "the pallid, sickly hue of Saturnian corpse fungi." Several larger tentacles are attached to the upper torso. The creatures are deaf but telepathic, able to impress images on the minds of other creatures and bend them to their will.

The alien ships are "huge, wedge-shaped" craft. Other spaceships in the story are the 80-ton transport *Ganymede*, the thousand-meter *Erubus*, the Martian armored cruiser *Klatan*, and the trans-Saturnian transport *Iris*.

Hyperion has an atmosphere of oxygen so thickly "tainted with deadly carbon monoxide"

that humans need a filter to breathe. The planet is covered with thick fog, beneath which lies a "scummy surface film of nasty, malignant life. Corrosive spores, flame-tongued leech weeds," and worse.

Biography: On the trail of criminal Justin Nichols, Senior Lt. James Ross of the Interplanetary Police Patrol, trans-Saturnian division, loses him at a Saturnian Relaxation Terminal and follows him and his sister Marta to the moon Hyperion onboard his "little vessel." Landing, Nichols finds a group of dead, horribly maimed Earthmen along with a diary warning him about an "alien ship" and its horrible occupants. Moments later, he finds Nichols mangled and dying, having stumbled into a patch of leech weeds. The felon admits he lied to his sister about his own misdeeds, and begs him to follow Marta and save her. Setting out, Ross runs smack into the creatures, who put him to sleep with light from a metallic cone eight inches long.

When Ross wakes, with Marta beside him, his mind is filled with new knowledge: the ability to speak the alien language, and the knowledge that the aliens are not evil killers, but explorers with insatiable curiosity. He and Marta are taken to the alien ship for a voyage to their (unnamed) home world. But the two have fallen in love: Wanting to share that on Earth, Ross steals the ship and heads for home.

Comment: Author Long sold his first story, "The Desert Lich," to *Weird Tales* in 1924, and was a protege of fantasy master H.P. Lovecraft. The volume and quality of Long's work is virtually unparalleled in SF history.

In 1937, *Thrilling Wonder Stories* was also the home of the comic strip *Zarnak* by Max Plaisted, in which "incessant wars" and plague have tossed humankind back to barbarism. Building a space-plane, Zarnak, the last scientist on Earth, sets out to find humans who migrated from our world 600 years earlier, in 2328—and who might help him "restore the Earth to its ancient glories."

THE TERMINATOR (MP, L, C)

First Appearance: *The Terminator*, 1984, Hemdale Film Corporation.

Physical Description: The robot stands six-foot-two and is extremely muscular. An "infiltration unit," the model 101 has a metal endoskeleton—a "hyperalloy combat chassis, microprocessor controlled"—with exterior of living human tissue, hair, and blood "grown" for the cyborg. His kind even has bad breath and sweat. Though he bleeds, the Terminator does not feel pain and can take countless bullet blasts without stopping. He can also function with all of his skin and flesh burned off. The Terminator's eyes instantly measure the size and weight of objects, make a "threat assessment," and feed that information to the central processor. Through the central processing unit in his head, the Terminator is programmed so that he "cannot self-terminate," can speak numerous languages, and can imitate other voices perfectly. The internal power cell of the Terminator gives him a lifespan (without recharging) of 120 years.

The Terminator is an outgrowth of the 606 series, whose models had only "rubber skin" and were easy to tell from humans.

In the future, the "hunter-killers" are robotic patrol machines that fire laser beams, see in the infrared, but are "not too bright."

The T-1000 is an advanced prototype made of a liquid metal "polyalloy." The liquid chrome robot is featureless but humanoid in its natural form; it can duplicate the likeness of any object of "equal size" or mass simply by coming into physical contact with it. It can also partially transform (for example, touching a rail, its hand alone may metamorphose), can survive ordinary flames, and can reassemble if blown apart. The T-1000 can't be-

I'd like to see the head man around here.

The idea of war-robots was around long before the *Terminator*.
© Ziff-Davis Publishing.

come a machine or bomb, however, since it can't duplicate chemicals or moving parts. The unit is extremely powerful and fast.

Biography: In the near future, machines take over. Seeing people as a threat, Skynet, a defense network computer made by Cyberdine, initiates a nuclear war that kills three billion people. The machines rise "from the ashes of the nuclear fire" and begin exterminating or enslaving the surviving humans. Then one man, John Connor, teaches nearly-extinct humankind to fight back, and a full-scale revolt begins. By 2029, the machines are virtually defeated, but they refuse to give up. Using time-displacement equipment, they send a Terminator to Los Angeles on May 12, 1984, to kill Sarah Connor before she can conceive John. Before the time travel device is destroyed, the adult John sends soldier Kyle Reese back in time to protect his mother and destroy the Terminator. Both arrive naked and unarmed within a few minutes of one another; they collect clothing and weapons, and while the Terminator kills two other women named Sarah Connor, Reese is able to link up with the right Sarah, a college student and waitress. He hustles her from a police station when the Terminator shows up (killing 17 officers in an effort to reach Sarah); with the cyborg in pursuit, the duo head away from the city, pausing in a motel long enough to conceive John. The Terminator catches up to them, his flesh burned off when Kyle blows up a tanker the cyborg has stolen, and the skeletal killer follows them into a factory. There, Kyle dies in a fall after planting a grenade on the Terminator; though severely damaged, the relentless cyborg continues after Sarah until she crushes it in a press. Leaving, Sarah heads to Mexico to wait out the nuclear firestorm.

Some time after John's birth (on February 28, 1985), Sarah ends up in the Pescadero (California) State Hospital, a retention facility for the criminally disordered. Ten-year-old John is living with foster parents Todd and Janell Voight when a second Terminator, the advanced T-1000, is sent to kill him; to protect him, the human resistance dispatches a reprogrammed Terminator. Killing and impersonating a police officer, the T-1000 sets out after John, while the boy and the Terminator spring his mother from the hospital and stay one step ahead of him. However, they plan to do more than survive. The scientists at Cyberdyne were able to salvage the central processing unit from the first Terminator. Though it wasn't functional, its advanced design gave scientist Myles Dyson and others ideas for new computer chips; these will be used to make the machines that eventually revolt against humankind. In a vision, Kyle tells Sarah "the future is not set," and so Sarah, John, and the Terminator go to Dyson and persuade him to help them destroy his notes, discs, and the Terminator cpu stored in a Cyberdyne vault. Once the laboratory has been blown up, the Terminator and the T-1000 face off in a factory. After losing his right arm and the right side of his face to the seemingly indestructible T-1000, the Terminator succeeds in blasting him backward into a vat of molten steel. The monster from the future perishes, and the Terminator joins him in the vat to make sure the chip in his own head is never used to create human-murdering machines.

Comment: Arnold Schwarzenegger stars as the Terminator, with Linda Hamilton as Sarah, and Michael Biehn as Kyle. The film was directed by James Cameron and written by Cameron and Gale Anne Hurd.

Terminator 2: Judgment Day (1992), from Carolco Pictures, stars Schwarzenegger as the Terminator, with Robert Patrick as the T-1000, Linda Hamilton as Sarah, Edward Furlong as John Connor, Joe Morton as Dyson, and Jenette Goldstein and Xander Berkeley as the Voights. In brief sequences, Michael Edwards plays the adult John and Dalton Abbott is the baby John. James Cameron directed from a script by himself and William Wisher. Scenes featuring Kyle Reese and Sarah with her grandchildren in a happy, altered future were cut from *Terminator 2: Judgment Day* before its theatrical release, but were restored to the film for laserdisc.

The video version of *The Terminator* belatedly acknowledges a debt "to the works of Harlan Ellison," most notably his "Soldier" episode of *The Outer Limits*, in which warring super-soldiers from the future appear in a modern-day metropolis. The genre goes back even farther; see the illustration from the November 1939 *Amazing Stories*.

Now Comics published a movie tie-in comic book of the first film, as well as two issues of a Terminator comic book, and a two-issue *Terminator: The Burning Earth* miniseries. Marvel Comics published a three-issue adaptation of the second film. Dark Horse has published the Terminator comic books since then: a pop-up one shot, a four-issue *Terminator* magazine, and the series *Terminator: The Endgame* (three issues), *Terminator: Hunters and Killers* (three issues), *Terminator: Secondary Objectives* (four issues), *Terminator: The Enemy Within* (four issues), and *RoboCop Versus Terminator* (four issues).

THE TERROR   See THE ALBATROSS.

TETSUJIN 28go   (CS, TV, C)

First Appearance: "Tetsujin 28go" (Iron Man No. Twenty-Eight), April 1958, *Shonen* magazine (Japan).

Physical Description: The purplish, humanoid robot stands approximately 50 feet tall. Powerfully built, it has a smooth exterior save for the joints, has a large ring around each shoulder, and wears a helmet like that of a Roman centurion, complete with a metal plume. The robot has jets in its heels that allow it to fly.

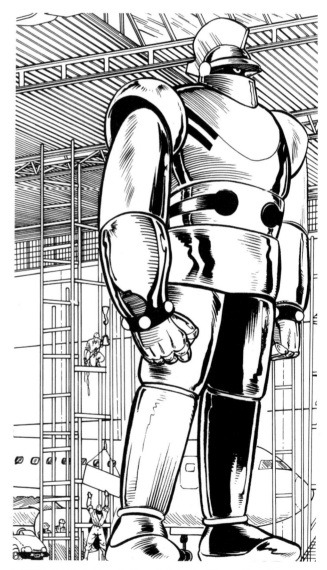

William Jang's interpretation of *Tetsujin 28go*, otherwise known as Gigantor. © Entercolor Technologies Corp.

Biography: As the tide of World War II turns against the Axis powers, scientists at the Japanese Weapons Institute begin work on a robot warrior. Twenty-seven prototypes fail to function. After the war, Dr. Kaneda devotes himself to completing one of the robots as a force for peace, not war. Shot by criminals who try (and fail) to steal the robot, the dying scientist gives the handheld remote-control box to his 12-year-old son, Shotaro. The only one able to operate the Iron Man, Shotaro puts it to work assisting the Japanese police and battling super villains and alien conquerors such as the Evil Robot Brain, Dr. Katsmeow, the Dangerous Dinosaurs, the Space Submarine, Magna Man of Outer Space, and many others.

Comment: The comic strip was created by Mitsuteru Yokoyama and ran through 1966. TCJ Animation produced 52 half-hour adventures of a *Tetsujin 28go* cartoon series, which aired in Japan from 1963 to 1967. It was syndicated in the United States beginning in 1966 as *Gigantor*, and aired through 1974. In this version, the robot was called Gigantor, Shotaro was named Jimmy, and his father was Dr. Sparks. Billie Lou Watt was the voice of Jimmy.

The characters appeared in Eternity's *Triple Action* comic book, two issues of which were published in 1993. The American names were used for the characters, and the year of Gigantor's completion was moved ahead to 2000.

THE THING (L, MP, C)

First Appearance: "Who Goes There?" by John W. Campbell Jr. (writing as Don A. Stuart), August 1938, *Astounding Stories*.

Physical Description: Approximately four feet tall and weighing 85 pounds, the alien has an "evil, unspeakable face . . . three mad, hate-filled . . . red eyes . . . blue hair like crawling worms . . . saber-clawed feet," thin lips, a "scrawny neck," and four tentacle-like arms, each of which ends in a hand with seven tentacular fingers. The Thing's flesh is blue, its blood greenish-yellow, and if even a few cells are separated from the parent, they will form an entirely new Thing. The alien can duplicate any person or animal by eating its victim. During digestion, each cell is analyzed after which the creature orders "its own cells to imitate them exactly." If discovered or threatened, the creature has the ability to reduce itself to an oozing, protoplasmic gel and reform somewhere else. It is believed that the alien is telepathic and able to read minds.

The *Thing*'s saucer lies beneath the ice in the motion picture *The Thing from Another World.* © RKO Pictures.

The spaceship of the Thing resembles "a submarine without a conning tower." It is 280 feet long and 85 feet in diameter "at its thickest."

Biography: Some 20 million years ago, the Thing left its world, which is "hotter . . . than Earth" and orbits a blue star. Passing our world, its spaceship's propulsion unit was upset by our magnetic field and it crashed in the Antarctic. The alien stepped out and "froze within ten feet of the ship." In the modern day, members of a 37-man Secondary Pole Expedition (possibly contacted by the alien telepathically) come and dig it out, though the thermite bomb used to free the spaceship causes it to explode, destroying the ship and "three . . . shadowthings . . . [that] might have been other—passengers." Back at the base, biologist Blair and Dr. Copper want to remove "the thing" from the ice and examine it, but physicist Vance Norris fears that "microscopic life associated with this creature" might still be alive and a plague will be unleashed. The debate becomes moot when cosmic ray scientist Connant is left to guard the Thing and, as he sits in a daze (induced by the Thing?), the ice thaws and the alien escapes.

As Connant informs Blair and Commander Garry, they hear cries from "Dogtown," where the huskies are kept. Connant, Garry, and second-in-command McReady head out and attack the alien, who survives being shot and axed, though a fire extinguisher confuses it and keeps it at bay. This gives mechanic Barclay enough time to hook

One artist's interpretation of the *Thing*.

a shovel to an electric cable and electrocute the Thing. The dogs tear the alien to pieces, though the men notice that it isn't quite the same creature they found in the ice. It is partly itself, part dog—which it was in the process of becoming to better survive in the Antarctic—and part "other-world beast . . . the best fighting thing it could think of," to which it began to change when attacked by the other dogs. Aware, now, of its formidable powers to multiply and also copy other life forms, the men begin to wonder if the Thing has already gotten one of them and is simply pretending to be that person, or is impersonating one of the dogs or cows. They use an electric prod to test the animals, discover that all of them are duplicates, and electrocute them. Next, cook Kinner goes mad and, when prodded, begins to change into something with "queer, scaly fur." The men finish him off, after which McReady decides to take blood samples from everyone: since each of the creature's cells are individual entities, the blood of an imper-

sonated human will recoil from the electricity in a "hot" needle. One by one, the men are proved human or alien; when imposters are discovered— there are fourteen in all, including Garry and Connant—they try to metamorphose into a form to defend themselves and are slain. The men find the "original" Thing impersonating Blair, and though they shoot, bludgeon, and burn it, it manages to get away, scurrying across the snow. Following it to a supply shack, they find that it had assembled an atomic generator for warmth, a "death weapon" for protection, and an antigravity harness, with which it had intended to leave the Antarctic. Though they wonder if an albatross, flying off, might be the Thing, they decide that it would have used the antigravity device had it been able to leave. "By the grace of God," says Norris, "we keep our world."

Comment: Campbell's classic novelette was the basis for two films. The first, *The Thing from Another World* (1951) is a classic, though it takes extensive liberties with the story. In this version, the Thing is not a shape-changer but a hairless, asexual, humanoid, an "intellectual carrot" over seven feet tall. When a flying saucer buries itself under Arctic (not Antarctic) ice, Captain Patrick Hendry (Kenneth Tobey) and his team of soldiers and scientists leave their outpost to reconnoiter. Though the thermite bomb destroys the craft, the party recovers a block of ice containing the Thing, and takes it to the base. There, an electric blanket thrown over the ice to hide the somewhat visible monster sets it free. Attacked by dogs, the Thing loses an arm, which is recovered by Professor Carrington (Robert Cornthwaite), who discovers seeds in its palm—seeds that require animal blood to grow. Meanwhile, the Thing grows another arm, takes over the greenhouse, kills a pair of scientists, and uses their blood to nurture young Things, the forerunners of an invasion force. Eventually, the team is able to lure the alien into a corridor, which they've rigged with electric terminals; when the Thing steps between them, they turn on the juice and reduce the creature to a lifeless puddle. The film was directed by Christian Nyby (apparently assisted by producer Howard Hawks), from a script by Charles Lederer.

In 1982, John Carpenter directed a version of *The Thing*, with a script by Bill (son of Burt) Lancaster that was quite faithful to the Campbell story. Despite spectacular special effects, the film was released one month after *E.T.*, when the public apparently wasn't in the mood for hostile aliens. Kurt Russell stars as MacReady (sic) with

A. Wilford Brimley as Blair and Richard Dysart as Dr. Copper.

Alan Dean Foster wrote a novelization of the 1982 film.

In comic books, Golden Press published an adaptation of Campbell's story in *Questar Illustrated Science Fiction Classics* in 1979. Dark Horse published a four-issue continuation of the saga in 1993–94.

THE THIRTY-FOOT GIANT (MP)

First Appearance: *Attack of the 50 Ft. Woman,* 1958, Woolner Productions/Allied Artists.

Physical Description: The bald-headed, transparent giant is a humanoid with a great deal of hair on the back of his hands and bushy eyebrows, but no other distinctive features. He wears a tunic—consisting of a miniskirt and sleeveless blouse—with a bull design on the back and three fleurs-de-lis on the silvery shield in front. He wears a leather band on each upper arm and his legs are bare, save for crisscrossing straps which appear to be attached to sandals. There is no explanation as to why the giant is 30 feet tall, while his "victim" is 50 feet.

The giant's spaceship is spherical and white, and can travel in a zigzag pattern through our atmosphere. It is powered by diamonds, is approximately 30 feet in diameter, and continually "bleeps."

Biography: A UFO lands near Baker, California, where the only one who sees it and its giant occupant is wealthy, young Nancy Fowler Archer, recently released from a California mental institution. No one believes that she saw a "satellite" (a word used synonymously with "spacecraft"): not the sheriff nor Nancy's womanizing husband Harry. However, Harry agrees to go back and have a look with her, hoping to prove she's crazy and have her permanently committed. Much to Harry's shock and Nancy's delight, the "satellite" returns. This time, the giant snatches Nancy, presumably to claim the bauble she wears around her neck, the Star of India. After firing a few rounds from his handgun, Harry flees; later, Nancy is found unconscious on the roof of her pool house, with a few scratches on her body—and giant footprints leading away (though none toward the property). Sheriff Dubbitt and Nancy's devoted butler Jess go back out to the desert, this time finding the ship. They enter (through a normal-sized doorway), find diamonds in what look like goldfish bowls, and

run when the giant appears. The alien wrecks their car, then recoils when Dubbitt lobs a hand grenade at him. Clearly disgusted, he takes off.

Meanwhile, Nancy grows to 50 feet tall, apparently from the scratches the giant (inadvertently?) gave her. Tearing down her mansion, she goes after Harry, who's painting the town red with his girlfriend Honey Parker. Nancy finds him and tears apart the tavern: Honey is crushed by falling debris and Nancy walks off with Harry in her hand. A crowd pursues, the sheriff shooting at high tension wires which spark and electrocute Nancy and Harry.

Comment: Allison Hayes stars as Nancy, William Hudson is Harry, Yvette Vickers is Honey, and Mike Ross is the alien. Nathan Hertz (Nathan Juran) directed from a script by Mark Hanna.

In the 1993 remake, which premiered on HBO, the story is generally the same, though there are significant differences. The spaceship is a flying saucer approximately 60 feet in diameter, with a dome on the top and bottom. The occupants are two 50-foot-tall women (Alien Woman #1 is Berta Waagfjord, Alien Woman #2 is Kye Benson) who use a red beam to study Nancy Cobb Archer (Daryl Hannah) when she is driving out in the desert and, later, a blue beam to teleport her onboard when she and Harry (Daniel Baldwin) come to investigate. The blue beam also generates a force field that keeps out unwanted persons. When Nancy grows large, she changes from being demure to fiercely feminist, lecturing Louise "Honey" Parker (Christi Conaway) about being her own woman instead of killing her. In the end, two assault helicopters attack Nancy and knock her into the high tension wires. Instead of dying, however, she and Harry are teleported back to the spaceship. There, with two other men, Harry is forced to undergo group therapy designed to cure him of his chauvinism as the ship journeys through the stars. It isn't clear whether the men are the husbands of the other two women (which wouldn't make them aliens but enlarged terrestrials, like Nancy) or whether their wives are elsewhere in the ship. The film was directed by Christopher Guest from a script by Joseph Dougherty.

THOMAS JEROME NEWTON (L, MP, TV)

First Appearance: *The Man Who Fell to Earth* by Walter Tevis, 1963.

Physical Description: Newton looks more or less like a normal, if slender, human. He stands six-and-one-half feet tall, weighs 90 pounds (three times what he weighs on Anthea), and has tan flesh, curly white hair, pale blue eyes, a slight frame, and "delicate features." He has only four toes on each foot, wears artificial fingernails, and his "breathing apparatus . . . [is] extremely sturdy, very highly developed." The beardless Newton rarely sleeps, has extremely acute hearing, has vision that excludes red but can see X rays, and is very sensitive to terrestrial gravity; an accelerating car or ascending elevator can put a tremendous strain on him. Newton has no sternum, coccyx, or floating ribs, among other skeletal differences.

Biography: His native world, Anthea, is some 10,000 years ahead of Earth, technologically, yet it is "a cold place, dying," suffering from a terrible drought. "Newton" spends 10 years of physical reconditioning—which includes watching TV broadcasts to learn our language and culture—then comes to Earth in 1972 to secure a ready supply of water for his people. After arriving in rural Kentucky in a one-passenger craft, he hires a high-powered patent attorney, Oliver Farnsworth, to turn advanced communications, photographic, and oil refining technology into a fortune under his World Enterprises Corporation banner. Two years pass, and while in Kentucky on business Newton breaks his leg on an elevator ride. He is aided by poor, middle-aged Betty Jo, who takes him to her apartment. He stays with her until he heals and his new house is ready, after which they both move in. Meanwhile, Newton hires Professor Nathan Bryce, a chemist dazzled by Newton's brilliance. Bryce begins to suspect that his employer is not of this Earth, especially when he begins building a spaceship with the fortune he's earned; sneaking some X rays of his boss proves it.

Newton sees the flash, however, admits all to Bryce, and confesses that he isn't sure to which world he belongs any more: He is fond of humans, alcohol, and Earth. But his feelings become academic when the FBI arrests him as an illegal alien. Eventually made a naturalized citizen and released because of his wealth and status—and left nearly blind by tests he'd undergone—Newton knows his world is doomed: Even if the United States lets him finish the spaceship, Anthea would be too far to reach in time. He is consoled only by the fact that Betty Jo and Bryce have fallen in love, and he gives them a gift of $1 million before Bryce leaves the alien crying at a bar.

Comment: The novel was filmed in 1976 by director Nicholas Roeg, with David Bowie as Newton, Buck Henry as Farnsworth, Candy Clark as Mary Lou (changed from Betty Jo), and Rip Torn as

Bryce. In the film, Newton is pictured in his natural form as having cat's eyes, no hair, and no ears. On his native world, he, his wife (also Clark), and their two children wear silvery suits with a network of tubes to provide their bodies with water. (Note: Most videocassette versions of the film are the severely edited U.S. print. Only the Criterion laserdisc is complete.)

The novel also served as the basis for a 1987 TV movie starring Lewis Smith, the pilot for an unsold *The Man Who Fell to Earth* series. Robert J. Roth directed.

THE THRINTS (L)

First Appearance: "World of Ptavvs" by Larry Niven, March 1965, *Worlds of Tomorrow*.

Physical Description: The Thrints are telepaths who can use the Power to enter the minds of aliens and control them. They are "less than four feet tall," have a triangular hump on their back, and have a generally "featureless, globular head" and a mouth with "eating tendrils." Their legs are "strange and bent" with chicken-like feet and heels that stick out well behind the ankles. The arms are thick with massive hands. A "panic button" on the chest of their space suits puts Thrints into a state of suspended animation.

Thrints who reach adulthood without having acquired the Power are called Ptavvs, are tattooed pink, and are sold as slaves. Earth is a world of Ptavvs.

Biography: The planet Thrintun is the hub of a galactic empire of 374 worlds. Having found a new world, the Thrint Kzanol is headed back to Thrintun to register his claim when his ship's fusor engine malfunctions. In need of food, the thrint goes into hibernation and charts a course to the relatively nearby F124—Earth. He remains in hibernation for eons until he is found off the coast of Brazil. Thought to be a Sea Statue, Kzanol is claimed by the United Nations and, in 2106, ends up in the laboratory of scientist Dorcas Jansky. The physicist contacts a friend, Larry Greenberg, a telepath who uses his abilities to converse with dolphins. He merges minds with Kzanol, who takes over the human's body (after reflexively melting the flesh off onlookers with a matter-scattering weapon he had on his ship).

Realizing from the changed astronomy of the solar system that two billion years have passed, and that his world and race have probably long since vanished, Kzanol intends to make this planet his. However, Larry's mind—subjugated, but not beaten—has other plans. In time, the two end up back in control of their own bodies. Facing one another on Pluto (where the Thrint requires his spacesuit), Larry is able to surprise Kzanol, hit his chest button, and put him back into suspended animation. The alien ends up as part of the UN Comparative Cultures Exhibit.

Comment: The short story was expanded to novel-length and published in book form in 1966.

THUNDERBIRDS (TV, MP, L, CS)

First Appearance: *Thunderbirds*, September 1965 (England).

Physical Description: There are five Thunderbirds: *Thunderbird 1* is the fastest plane on Earth, a bullet-shaped vehicle able to achieve speeds of 7,000 miles an hour. The plane is rocket-powered and lands on spindly legs, which fold out from the wings and tail section.

Thunderbird 2 is a cargo ship, big and bulbous with everything from "mechanical grabs" (pincers) for lifting heavy weights (from trains to the Thunderbird 4). It also carries the Mole, a drilling machine, and the Thunderizer, a laser-cannon.

Thunderbird 3 is a rocketship with three landing struts attached to the outside, starting at the middle of the ship. *Thunderbird 4* is a small submarine. *Thunderbird 5* is a space station, shaped like a drum with a ring around it and a squarish bay on one side. It orbits the Earth and monitors calls for help.

Biography: In the year 2063, wealthy astronaut Jeff Tracy—who is about 90 but looks 30, and was the first person to walk on the Moon—founds the International Rescue Organization based on Tracy Island in the Pacific. There, he and his five sons operate the various Thunderbirds: eldest son Scott (named after astronaut Scott Carpenter) flies *Thunderbird 1*, Virgil (named after Virgil Grissom) pilots *Thunderbird 2*, Alan (named after Alan Shepard) handles *Thunderbird 3*, Gordon (named after L. Gordon Cooper) is in command of *Thunderbird 4*, and John (named after John Glenn) stays aboard *Thunderbird 5*.

The vehicles were invented by scientific genius Brains. The group is also assisted by Jeff's servant Kyrano, by his attaché Tin-Tin, and by their wealthy London associate Lady Penelope and her chauffeur Parker. Their chief foe is the Hood, Kyrano's wicked half-brother.

Comment: There were 32 hour-long episodes. The show debuted in syndication in the United States in the fall of 1967. The show was created by producers Gerry and Sylvia Anderson and starred "Supermarionation" puppets (see SUPERCAR). Peter Dyneley was the voice of Jeff, Shane Rimmer was Scott, David Holliday was Virgil, Matt Zimmerman was Alan, Sylvia Anderson was Penelope, Ray Barrett played John and the Hood, and David Graham was Gordon, Brains, and Kyrano.

In motion pictures, the characters were seen in *Thunderbirds Are Go* (1966) and *Thunderbird 6* (1968). The first film tells how the first attempt to launch a Zero X ship to Mars is sabotaged by a foreign government. When the second ship is launched, the Thunderbirds are on hand to make sure the flight goes smoothly. Landing on Mars, the crew battles cyclopean, stalk-like creatures that spit destructive blasts. In the second film, Brains designs a revolutionary airship, *Skyship One,* for the New World Aircraft Corporation. When rivals posing as crew members hijack the ship, the Thunderbirds must not only save the passengers but prevent the damaged airship from crashing.

The TV series *Thunderbirds: 2086,* a futuristic extension of the exploits of International Rescue, debuted in syndication in September 1988. There were 24 half-hour episodes.

The characters were also featured in two novels, *Thunderbirds* and *Calling Thunderbirds,* both by John Theydon, published by Titan Books of London in the late 1960s.

A Thunderbirds comic strip was published throughout 1993 in England, printed exclusively on Pizza Hut cups.

TIGER-BUGS (L)

First Appearance: "Men on Mars" by Laurence Manning, Spring 1952, *Fantastic Story Magazine.*

Physical Description: The tiger-bugs have 12 long, thin legs and a large, single-segment chest. When they join together, the headless Martian they form has "four legs rising to a big lump of muscle . . . the legs joined together like the arched back of a black cat that had no head or tail."

The creatures are bulletproof and can't be crushed by clubs.

Biography: Lt. Joliffe, Dr. Wilson, Kruts, Stockton, Thorgess, DeVoe, and Radioman Willie are the first people on Mars, the macho spacemen making fun of Willie the dial-twirler. Plagued and bitten by tiger-bugs as they explore, the men spot an odd life form and shoot it to study: Instead of dying, the big creature falls apart into hundreds of tiger-bugs, then reassembles—and pursues the men. It's touch-and-go as the men flee, until Radioman Willie sends out a signal that successfully "jams" whatever frequency the tiger-bugs use to retain their giant shape. The creature falls apart, and Willie is able to keep the alien tiger-bugs at bay while the explorers make their way back to the ship.

Comment: Author Manning began writing for *Wonder Stories* in the 1930s, with occasional forays into other magazines. Two of his best known tales are ''The Voyage of the Asteroid'' and ''The Wreck of the Asteroid,'' both 1932.

THE TIGER'S EYE See THE BLACK HOLE.

THE TIME CASTLE (C)

First Appearance: *Eerie* #82, 1977, Warren Publishing.

Physical Description: Approximately eight feet tall, the reddish-brown Time Castle looks exactly like a castle used in chess. There is a large door in the side and one seat within, though another person (or robot or two) can be crowded into the area around the chair.

Restin Dane has a trio of robot assistants. The A-Series Compurob Manners is approximately six feet tall, blue, and generally humanoid, with flared metal shoulders, an ovoid head, small eyes, a big slit for a mouth, and tread-like feet. The brown robot Nuts is approximately a yard tall and resembles an inverted, threaded screw with tentacle-arms, two rows of small wheels for mobility, and a rounded head with large eyes and no other feature. The brown robot Bolts stands about 18 inches tall and has the same arms, head, and feet, but a horizontal bolt for a body. All three robots can speak.

Biography: A technophysicist, Restin Dane lives in a secluded estate in the desert outside of Cottonwood, Arizona. There, Restin ''experiments with . . . physics, computers, and advanced robotronics'' and creates the Time Castle. His first stop is the Alamo, where he tries to rescue his great-great-great-grandfather, Parrish Dane. Restin fails but manages to save Parrish's son Bishop—his own great-great-grandfather. The two enjoy many time traveling adventures together, including one among the Morlocks (see THE TIME MACHINE).

RESTIN DANE. SCIENTIST. TECHNICIAN. MASTER OF HIS OWN FATE. HIS ENTIRE LIFE HE HAD ONLY ONE GOAL. TO ESCAPE THE GREATEST PRISON EVER TO INCARCERATE MANKIND. *TIME* ITSELF!

HIS AMBITION! TO BUILD A *TIME MACHINE*. TO *LIVE* THE PAST...THE PRESENT...AND ALL *ETERNITY!*

The Rook, his Time Castle, and—from the tallest—the robots Manners, Bolts, and Nuts. Art by Luis Bermejo. © Warren Publishing Co.

Comment: The characters were created by writers Bill DuBay and Budd Lewis. After running in *Eerie* until issue #105, several adventures were reprinted in *Warren Presents #2*, after which the characters were given their own magazine, *The Rook*. It lasted 14 issues, after which the characters returned to *Eerie* in #132 (with a tale inevitably titled "The Dane Curse") for just two more adventures.

THE TIME MACHINE (L, C, MP, TV)

First Appearance: "The Time Machine" by H.G. Wells, 1895, *The New Review*.

Physical Description: The "black and brass" machine consists of a "glittering metal framework . . . [with] brass, ebony, ivory, and translu-

Rod Taylor at the controls of the *Time Machine* in George Pal's feature film. © Metro-Goldwyn-Mayer.

THE TIME MACHINE

AN INVENTION

BY

H. S. WELLS

" Fool! All that is at all
Lasts ever past recall."
    —*Browning*

NEW YORK
HENRY HOLT AND COMPANY
1895

Author H.G. Wells's name is misspelled on the title page of the first U.S. edition of *The Time Machine*. This version actually preceded the Heineman (London) edition by two weeks and is much rarer.

cent glimmering quartz." The occupant sits in a "saddle" from which the machine is worked via two levers, one for starting, the other for stopping. As it shoots through time the machine can occupy the same space as another object, as long as it stays on the move, "slipping like vapor" through matter.

Biography: After dinner at his home, the "Time Traveler" demonstrates a model of a time machine for friend Filby and four other guests. The device, about the size of "a small clock," vanishes, and he reveals that he has nearly completed a full-size machine. A week later, the men—along with a newspaper editor—return for another dinner, to which the hero is late. He finally arrives, a wreck, and explains that he has been to the future. He has been, he says, to "the year 80200-odd" and found himself among the Eloi, a race of "indescribably frail," curly-haired, docile humans who are bred and eaten by the Morlocks, "ape-like" beings who dwell in underground caverns. He befriended the lovely Weena and, when she was slain by the Morlocks—who also stole his machine—he found it and pushed again into the future, when the sun is a red star, the sky "drabby gray," and the world occupied by gray humanlike rabbits and 30-foot-long centipedes. Going further still, he found giant butterflies, huge crabs, and a world of "abominable desolation"; then, at last, a cold, dark Earth of octopus-like creatures.

Returning to his own time, he showed up for dinner and tells his tale, discouraged when his guests don't appear to believe him. Filby, at least, isn't sure, and goes back to talk to the Traveler the next day. The latter is busy carrying a camera and knapsack to his laboratory and asks Filby to wait; while he does so both the Time Traveler and the machine vanish, leaving Filby to wonder where he is and if he'll ever return (and, implicitly, if he has gone to save Weena).

Comment: Immediately after its serialization early in the year, the novel—the first by the 28- year-old Wells—was published in book form by William Heinemann. The work grew from several time travel articles and reveries Wells had written for *The Science Schools Journal* (one, ''The Chronic Argonauts,'' has been reprinted in *Strange Signposts*, edited by Sam Moskowitz and Roger Elwood in 1966, and in *The Magic Valley Travellers,* edited by Peter Haining in 1974). It was the editor of the monthly *New Review*, W.E. Henley, who first suggested the idea of writing the novel, which was originally going to be called ''The Time Traveller.''

The tale was adapted in comic book form as part of the Classics Illustrated line (#133, 1956), and again in 1973 as one of the *Pendulum Illustrated Classics*. The Pendulum edition was reprinted as a *Marvel Classics Comics* adaptation (#2, 1976). The George Pal film (see below) was adapted as part of Dell's *4-Color* lineup (#1085, 1960).

Rod Taylor stars as the time traveler, now called George, in the 1960 George Pal film *The Time Machine*. On New Year's Eve, 1899, he sends a cigar to the future on a model of the machine, then uses a full-size one to take a trip himself. The machine consists of a seat on runners, with ''roll bars'' on the side, controls on a small barrel in the front, and a roughly five-foot diameter dish behind the seat, the spinning of which apparently propels the machine through time. George stops in 1917, 1940, and 1966, finding wars raging each time. Finally, he pushes ahead to 802,701 where, unlike his literary counterpart, he helps the Eloi defeat the Morlocks. Returning to his home for some books, he goes back to the future to live with Weena (Yvette Mimieux).

In Nicholas Meyer's 1979 movie *Time After Time*, H.G. Wells (Malcolm McDowell) has actually made a working time machine resembling a small, horseless carriage, which Jack the Ripper (David Warner) uses to escape from 1893 to present-day San Francisco. Fortunately, it returns to Victorian England and Wells uses it to follow and stop the madman. After falling in love with a freespirited bank official, Amy Robbins (Mary Steenburgen), Wells sabotages his invention to send Jack (but not the machine) on a nonstop trip through time, then uses the device to return with Amy to his day. (The real Wells did, indeed, meet Amy Robbins in 1893; he was her teacher and became her husband one year later.)

Pal and Joe Morhaim wrote the novel *Time Machine II*, published by Dell in 1981; Pal died before he could raise the money for a film version. In the story, George and the pregnant Weena head back to London of 1900, which is where and when the time traveler wants his child to be born. They make it only as far as March 19, 1941, during the Blitz; there, they are killed by shrapnel, literally as Christopher Jones is born. Rescued by a G.I., he grows up and makes a time machine of his own, determined to intercept his parents and save them. He succeeds, but is killed by crab monsters—although he is born again, as his parents had intended, in the past.

On TV, John Beck played time traveler Neil Perry, with Priscilla Barnes as Weena, in an updated version made in 1978. Henning Schellerup directed.

THE TIME SPHERE   (C)

First Appearance: *Showcase* #20, 1959, DC Comics.

Physical Description: The Sphere is approximately 20 feet in diameter and rests on three legs. Onboard are ''speech translation discs'' that allow the passengers to talk with people of any era, a thermo-gun, and the Encyclomatic, a computer full of historial data. The Time Sphere can fly like a helicopter and move underwater. In case Rip Hunter is ever in danger, a small transmitter in his belt allows him to summon the Time Sphere via morse code. The Sphere has a mechanical arm that emerges from the bottom for use when passengers are underwater or handling dangerous materials. Passengers enter and exit through a circular hatch on the side.

There are two Time Spheres; if one is ever stolen, it leaves a trail of ''chronal energy'' that can be followed by the other. Depending upon the story, it is either white or gunmetal gray.

Biography: In college, Ripley Hunter and his friend Jeff Smith devise a method of time travel and begin building the Time Sphere. By the time they finish it, they've earned their doctorates and taken on time traveling partners: historian Bonnie

Baxter and Corky, her little brother. The time travelers are based in a "secret mountain laboratory" in New England and work for any scholar who needs research done in the past or future.

Comment: Rip and company appeared in four issues of *Showcase* before getting their own magazine; *Rip Hunter . . . Time Master* lasted 29 issues. Rip and his Time Sphere have also appeared in *Action Comics, D.C. Comics Presents,* and other DC comics titles.

TINMAN (C)

First Appearance: *Fatman the Human Flying Saucer* #1, 1967, Milson Publishing Co.
Physical Description: Tinman has a bullet-shaped head with a human face, a cylindrical body, and extremely narrow tube-shaped arms and legs with bulby knee and elbow joints. His feet are flat rectangles and he has five fingers on each hand. He is roughly six feet tall and is platinum-colored.

It isn't clear whether Tinman is a robot or whether the metal exterior is an exoskeleton. Tinman can lift over 500 pounds, trampoline over 100 miles, survive intense heat, and live as long as necessary underwater—though he can't swim because he's "too skinny and heavy."

Biography: Teased by his fellow teenagers, lanky Lucius Pindle reads a passage from the book *Old Formulae and Charms* and is immediately transformed into Tinman. After testing out his powers, he clunks over to the beach to teach the bullies a lesson, only to be struck by lightning. The bolt shortcircuits Tinman's brain and he goes on a rampage. As Tinman is beating up the obese hero Fatman, the spell wears off and he becomes Lucius Pindle once more. Sane again, he agrees to fight crime alongside Fatman, riding the superhero's back whenever he metamorphoses into his flying saucer shape.

Comment: The character was created by legendary comics writer Otto Binder and artist C.C. Beck (cocreator of the classic Captain Marvel). *Fatman the Human Flying Saucer* lasted for only three issues.

TOBOR THE GREAT (MP)

First Appearance: *Tobor the Great,* 1954, Dudley Pictures/Republic Pictures.
Physical Description: Standing nearly eight feet tall, Tobor has a massive humanoid body with arms that reach nearly to the knees with three pincer-like fingers on each hand. Its huge head structure comprises nearly one-third of its size: Beneath an elongated transparent dome is an inverted bucket-shape with two conical eyes on the front. When extended, an antenna on the left side of the head allows it to receive radio and telepathic communications. Tobor has four tubes running from its shoulders to the top of its chest, and one more forming a loop atop each shoulder.

Biography: Space scientist Dr. Ralph Harrison is concerned that the rigors of space will prohibit humans from ever traveling. However, Professor Nordstrom has a solution: He has constructed a robot astronaut in his basement, which is controlled with a blow-dryer-like device. He also has a widowed daughter, Janice Roberts, to whom Harrison takes a liking, and a precocious grandson "Gadge." Unfortunately, spies have taken a liking to Tobor, and they capture both Nordstrom and his grandson. At their barn hideout, the spies threaten to torture the boy with a blowtorch unless the scientist tells them how to construct a Tobor of their own. The professor agrees to write down the various formulae, neglecting to mention that he has built a miniature Tobor-control into his pencil. While he writes, he is actually summoning the robot. Tobor leaves the laboratory, climbs into a jeep, and races to the rescue, only to stop dead when one of the spies figures out what Nordstrom is up to and breaks the pencil. But Harrison has been trailing Tobor: When he activates the robot's antenna Gadge is able to contact him telepathically. Tobor reaches the spies' lair, saves the scientist and Gadge, and is thanked by being blasted into space on what appears to be a one-way trip.

Comment: Billy Chapin stars as Gadge, Charles Drake is Harrison, Taylor Holmes is Nordstrom, and Karin Booth is Janice; Lew Smith played the robot. Lee Sholem directed from a script by Philip MacDonald, from a story by Carl Dudley.

TORGO (A)

First Appearance: "The Thing and the Ultimate Weapon!," 1979.
Physical Description: The robot is a silvery, lilac-colored, roughly seven-foot-tall humanoid.
Biography: When the superhero the Thing (of the Fantastic Four) finds himself in the lair of hooded, green-skinned creatures, they send the powerful Torgo to defeat him. The two duke it out until the hero has a brainstorm: Digging into a pouch, he pulls out Hostess cherry, apple, and peach pies. The robot eats them, declares, "This is better than fighting," and the struggle ends.

Comment: The character appeared only in full-page comic book ads for Hostess fruit pies.

THE TRANSFORMERS (T, TV, C, L, MP)

First Appearance: *The Transformers*, 1984, Hasbro Industries.

Physical Description: Most of the robots are humanoid, and all can "transform" into another shape by folding their limbs in different ways as follows. Smaller members of the groups are known as Microbots.

The Decepticons are Megatron, a laser-gun; Soundwave, a tape recorder; Bombshell, a robot-insect; Astrotrain, a space shuttle or locomotive; Bonecrusher and Scrapper, bulldozers; Shockwave, a ray gun; Blast Off, a space shuttle; Blitzwing, a tank or jet fighter; Headstrong, a robot rhinoceros; Mixmaster, a cement truck; Brawl and Warpath, tanks; Breakdown, Mirage, Runabout, Runamuck, Wildrider, and Deep End, sports cars; Brawn, an armored jeep; Broadside, a jet or aircraft carrier; Buzzsaw, Ravage, Frenzy, Laserbeak, Ratbat, and Eject, audiocassettes; Razorclaw, a robot lion; Dirge, a jet fighter; Dragstrip, a dragstrip racer; Hook, a truck with a hook-arm; Vortex, a helicopter; Kickback, a robot fly; Long Haul, a dump truck; Motormaster, a tractor-trailer; Octane, a jumbo jet or oil truck; Onslaught, an artillery truck; Ramjet, Thrust, Starscream, Thundercracker, and Skywarp, jets; Rampage, a robot tiger; Shrapnel, a robot bug; Swindle, an artillery jeep; Tantrum, a robot bull; Trypticon, a robot tyrannosaurus, mobile artillery, and mini-city complete with a landing strip and communications center; Cyclonus, a hyper-jet; Galvatron, a futuristic tank; Scourge, a land and sea hovercraft; and Mindwipe, a robot bat.

The Decepticon Bruticus is a merging of Brawl, Blast Off, Swindle, Vortex, and Onslaught; Menasor is a combination of Motormaster, Dragstrip, Wildrider, Dead End, and Breakdown; and Devastator is a union of Scrapper, Hook, Long Haul, Bonecrusher, Scavenger, and Mixmaster.

A subgroup of the Decepticons, the Predacons, are robot fighters who merge to form the massive Predaking: These are Divebomb, Razorclaw, Headstrong, Rampage, and Tantrum.

The Autobots (and their subgroup the Dinobots) are Optimus Prime, a tractor-trailer; Mirage, Blue Streak, Sideswipe, Smokescreen, Fastlane, Wheelie, Wheeljack, Arcee, Hot Rod, Sunstreaker, Tracks, Tailgate, Windcharger, and Jazz, sportscars; Ratchet and First Aid, ambulances; Prowl, a police car; Air Raid, a jet; Steeljaw, a robot lion or audiocassette; Gears, a truck; Swoop, a robot pteradactyl; Beachcomber, a dune buggy; Cliffjumper, a VW bug; Topspin, a rocketplane; Cosmos, a flying saucer; Grapple, a truck with an extendible hook-arm; Grimlock, a tyrannosaurus robot; Snarl, a robot stegosaurus; Groove, a motorcycle; Hoist, a tow-truck; Hotspot and Inferno, firetrucks; Huffer and Pipes, semis; Hound, a machinegun jeep; Rodimus Prime, a hot rod tractor/trailer; Trailbreaker, an off-road car; Ironhide, a van and caterpillar-treaded artillery unit; Jetfire, Skydive, Slingshot, and Fireflight, jets; Blades, a helicopter; Bumblebee, a VW bug; Blaster, a boom box; Outback, an armored jeep; Perceptor, a microscope; Powerglide, an airplane; Ramhorn, a rhinoceros robot or an audiocassette; Red Alert and Streetwise, squad cars; Rewind and Rumble, audiocassettes; Sandstorm, a buggy or helicopter; Seaspray, a hovercraft; Silverbolt, an SST; Skids, a van; Sky Lynx, a robot dinosaur-bird or space shuttle/tractor combination; Slag, a robot triceratops; Sludge, a robot apatosaurus; Twin Twist, a mobile drill; Blurr, a jet-car (and the fastest Autobot); Kup, a futuristic buggy; Springer, a helicopter and race car; and Ultra Magnus, a huge truck.

The Autobot Defensor is a melding of Blades, First Aid, Hotspot, Groove, and Streetwise, while Superion is a construction made of Air Raid, Fireflight, Skydive, Silverbolt, and Slingshot.

Protecting *The Ark* is Omega Supreme, a non-transforming robot but the most powerful of them all. Arblus, a golden robot who becomes a jet, and Kranix, a futuristic tank, are both free-lancers.

Biography: Four million years ago, the robot world of Cybertron, circling the star Alpha Centauri, was thrown into chaos as the power-mad Decepticons tried to conquer the peaceful Autobots. The war quickly produced two leaders: Optimus Prime of the Autobots, and Megatron of the Decepticons. The war spread into space, where the Decepticons boarded *The Ark*, the ship of Optimus Prime. Rather than be taken prisoner, the Autobots set the ship on a crash-course for Earth: It plowed into a volcano where it lay dormant until the modern day, when the Oregon crater comes to life and activates *The Ark*'s computers.

The surviving Decepticons and Autobots leave the ship and resume their battle. However, the goals of Megatron and the Decepticons are modified to include taking over the Earth before they move on to conquer the universe. First, however, they must defeat the Autobots which, despite their battle cry, "Today's Autobots are tomorrow's scrap metal," is not as easy as they imagine.

The Autobots are helped by the first humans they find, auto mechanic Sparkplug Witwicky and his son Buster.

Comment: In addition to the enormously popular toy line, the characters starred in a successful syndicated series, which also debuted in 1984. Ninety-two half-hour episodes were produced.

Marvel Comics published several Transformers titles: *The Transformers*, which began in 1984 and ended with #80 in 1991; *The Transformers Comics Magazine*, which lasted 11 issues from 1986 to 1988; the four-issue miniseries *Transformers: Headmasters*, published in 1987–88; and *Transformers: The Movie*, a three-issue adaptation of the first film. Blackthorne Publishing created four issues of *Transformers in 3-D* from 1987 to 1992.

In 1985, Marvel also published a children's novel, *The Transformers: Battle for Earth*, written by Max Z. Baum.

The Transformers: The Movie (1986) is notable for having had Orson Welles as the voice of Unicron, a planet-sized, planet-eating robot that can also assume humanoid shape. It is served by the Quintessons and Sharkticons; the film also introduced the Junkions, robots made of junk. The humanoid Wreck-Gar can become a motorcycle and leads this team comprised of Junkion 1 and Junkion 2. Other voices were provided by Robert Stack (Ultra Magnus), Leonard Nimoy (Galvagron), Eric Idle (Wreck-Gar), Judd Nelson (Hot Rod and Rodimus Prime), and others.

In September 1993, the characters returned in a half-hour animated series and a new Marvel comic book, both of which were known as *Transformers: Generation 2*. This time, the four-million-year-old war is rekindled when Decepticon Commander Jhiaxus, based in the K-Tor Cluster, sends a force of Firestormers against the planet Nexus Seven only to be met and defeated by the Autobots. We learn that the villains have conquered 17 worlds throughout the galaxy and turned them into "Little Cybertrons."

TRENT (TV)

First Appearance: "Demon With a Glass Hand," October 1964, *The Outer Limits*, ABC.

Physical Description: Externally, Trent looks and acts like a normal human being. His left hand consists of a computer palm and thumb to which four fingers must be plugged so that "all knowledge" can be revealed. Trent is dressed in white trousers, white shirt, and a white jacket and sneakers.

Trent is extremely athletic and supple, and can be revived from gunshot wounds by having water applied to his forehead and neck. When he bends back the three middle fingers of his prosthetic hand, the inside of his chest glows.

Biography: In approximately 2964, aliens known as the Kyben conquer the Earth in 19 days. Suddenly and inexplicably, though, all 70 billion Earthlings vanish and leave Earth infested with a plague designed to kill all living things, including Kyben. Only one native remains alive, Trent, who wakes up in 1964 and remembers nothing. Nor can his hand-computer help him, since he is missing three fingers—fingers that the Kyben possess. For 10 days, he is pursued by the aliens who come through a "time mirror" and who want to get to his computer hand to find out where the humans are, and how to cure the plague.

Deciding to take to the offense, Trent goes to the dilapidated office building where the aliens have situated the time mirror. Once he's inside, they seal the building with an impenetrable force bubble that suits him fine. With the help of Consuelo Biros, a young clothing designer who is also trapped inside the building—and with whom he quickly falls in love—Trent destroys the mirror, kills all the Kyben, and obtains his missing fingers. What he learns, to his dismay, is that all 70 million Earthlings were "electronically transcribed" and placed on a "thin strand of gold copper alloy wire," a wire that is wrapped around an "insulating coil inside your central thorax control solenoid." Translation: He's an android. Consuelo cannot love a robot, of course, and leaves, and Trent faces a lonely future: 10 centuries to bring him to where he was created, then another 200 years for the plague to dissipate before he can reconstitute humankind.

Comment: Robert Culp stars as Trent, with Arline Martel as Consuelo. Byron Haskin directed from a script by Harlan Ellison.

TURBO-TEEN (TV)

First Appearance: *Turbo-Teen*, September 1984, ABC.

Physical Description: The kid is a normal teen who can transform into a sleek sports car. His only power in that form is super speed.

Biography: Losing control of his sports car, high school journalism student Brett Mathews crashes into a government laboratory just as a "molecular transfer ray" is being tested. Brett and his car are both blasted and, as a result, whenever he gets hot or angry he becomes the car—albeit, with his teenage mind intact. He becomes ordinary Brett again when he cools down. Brett uses his power to fight crime in and around Hillmont, assisted by his girlfriend Pattie, his friend Alex, and his sheepdog Rusty, all of whom know his secret (and ride in his bucket seats). Brett's mother is unaware of his powers, though; whenever he transforms inside the house and makes a rip-roaring departure, she complains that her son never cleans up after himself.

The group is pursued, constantly, by the mysterious Dark Rider, who wants "to prove that Brett Matthews is his car."

Comment: There were just 12 half-hour episodes of this Ruby-Spears animated series, which aired until August 1985. Michael Mish provided the voice of Brett, Pamela Hayden was Pattie, T.K. Carter was Alex, and Frank Welker was Rusty.

TWIKI (MP, TV, C, CS)

First Appearance: *Buck Rogers in the 25th Century*, 1979, Universal Pictures.

Physical Description: The silvery robot stands four feet tall. He has pincer-like hands, arms that have a black, ribbed-rubber midsection in lieu of an elbow, and legs that are hinged at the knee and ankle. He has eyes and a mouth that don't move, and a head capped with a mushroom-like "helmet." When he speaks, his sentences are prefixed with an attention getting, "Biddi-biddi-biddi." A circular talking computer, Dr. Theopolis, hangs from Twiki's neck, resting on his chest.

The Ranger 3 is identical to a modern-day space shuttle. The Earth Defense Forces fly "Hatchet" star-fighters, flat one-person ships with upper and lower wings in the rear and two long "prongs" projecting from either side in front. The Star Fortress *Draconia* is an orange ship resembling a modern locomotive with wings and two slanted tail fins.

Biography: Captain William "Buck" Rogers is the only passenger onboard a 1987 deep space Ranger 3 flight, which carries him through a cloud of meteoric gasses and puts him to sleep. When he wakes, he's 500 years in the future. His ship is found by the humanoid Draconians, and he's taken onboard the flagship *Draconia*. The evil Princess Ardala is en route to Earth, ostensibly to sign a peace treaty but actually to invade; Buck realizes what she's up to, but the Earth Defense Directorate, under Colonel Wilma Deering, suspects that

One of the *Iron Men*, a forerunner of Twiki. © John Dille Co.

it's Buck who's a spy and up to no good. Eventually, Buck charms Wilma into trusting him, and he helps defeat Ardala and her father, the Emperor Draco, time after time.

Buck's sidekick Twiki is given to him to show him how things work in the future. The wisecracking, double entendre–spouting Twiki is the only one who believes, from the start, that Buck isn't a Draconian spy.

Comment: Twiki was created for the movie (a made-for-TV movie that was first released theatrically) and was seen in the subsequent TV show, *Buck Rogers in the 25th Century*, which aired on NBC from September 1979 to April 1981. Both star Frank Silla as Twiki (voice by Mel Blanc, briefly replaced in 1981 by Bob Elyea), with Gil Gerard as Buck, Erin Gray as Wilma, Pamela Hensley as Ardala, and Joseph Wiseman as Draco. Eric Server provides the voice for Dr. Theopolis. In the second and final season, the heroes leave Earth and fly through space onboard the *Searcher*, seeking humans who reportedly left the Earth after a "great holocaust" around the dawn of the 21st century. The crew includes the birdlike humanoid warrior Hawk (Thom Christopher) from the planet Throm; Dr. Goodfellow (Wilfred Hyde-White); Admiral Asimov (Jay Garner); Lt. Devlin (Paul Carr); and the robot Crichton (voice of Jeff David).

Gold Key published a comic book adaptation of

the film in *Buck Rogers #2–4* in 1979; the story was collected as *Buck Rogers, Giant Movie Edition*, also in 1979.

A new comic strip was introduced based on the TV show, but it expired shortly after the series did.

The character of Buck Rogers was already 50 years old by the time the film was in production, having made his debut in the novelette "Armageddon 2419 A.D." by Philip Francis Nowlan, in *Amazing Stories* in August 1928. In that tale, World War I pilot Anthony Rogers returns to the United States and becomes a surveyor. On December 15, 1927, while working for the American Radioactive Gas Corporation, the 29-year-old is trapped in an abandoned coal mine near the Wyoming Valley just outside of Pittsburgh, Pennsylvania. Put into hibernation by "the rapid accumulation of the radioactive gases," he awakes 492 years later when the strata shifts, admitting fresh air. Meeting air patrol scout Wilma Deering, he learns that while he slept, the Soviets and Chinese conquered Europe. After that, the Chinese defeated their erstwhile allies and conquered the United States. Rogers joins Wilma and her Wyoming Gang, one of the many gangs of resistance fighters who are busy waging the Second War for Independence against the evil Mongolian Han Airlords. The original novelette was followed by a sequel, "The Airlords of Han," which appeared in *Amazing Stories* the following year and concluded with the overthrow of the Asian empire. The two stories were knit together into a novel, *Armageddon 2419 A.D.*

The popular and influential comic strip *Buck Rogers 2429 A.D.* was first published on January 7, 1929, the title being changed each year to keep events exactly five hundred years in the future; in time, it was simply called *Buck Rogers in the 25th Century.*

The earliest robot seen in the previous Buck Rogers chronicles was one of the "iron men," the tank-treaded 792, which has two arms ending in lobster-like claws, a gumdrop-shaped head with a "microphonic 'ear' . . . lens for television transmitter . . . speaker," and screw-shaped ears attached to a "swivel neck"; arms equipped with "electro magnetic push-pull muscles neck"; a spool-shaped torso; and a thimble-shaped pelvis. The robots are operated using a remote control box, which sees whatever the robot sees. Extremely powerful—able to lift a large metal girder with no problem—the human-sized iron men debuted in daily comic strip #147.

THE TWONKY (L, MP)

First Appearance: "The Twonky" by Lewis Padget (Henry Kuttner), September 1942, *Astounding Science Fiction.*

Physical Description: The Twonky is a robot designed to help humans, against their will if need be. It isn't known what a Twonky looks like in the future; in the present day, it looks like "a console radio-phonograph" with tentacle-like arms, legs (the console's own wooden legs, which become articulated when the robot moves about), X-ray vision, superhuman senses, and a ray that vaporizes objects.

Though it is programmed to protect its owner, a Twonky's prime directive is to protect itself.

Biography: When Joe, a Twonky-builder, is caught in a "temporal snag," he is shifted from the future to the Mideastern Radio factory in our era. Doing what he always does—building Twonkies—Joe assembles one that looks like the machines in the factory. Snatched back to his era, Joe leaves the one finished Twonky behind, and the company ships it to the home of Kerry and Martha Westerfield. Programmed to allow no harm to befall the Westerfields, the Twonky cleans house, decides what books they should read, determines what they should eat and drink, and even approves or disapproves of their friends. When Martha tries to take an axe to the Twonky, it vaporizes her. When Kerry tries to finish the job, it disintegrates him as well. The Twonky remains in the house which, when we leave it, is being shown to newlyweds.

Comment: The story was filmed in 1953 by director Arch Oboler. In this version, starring Hans Conried as Kerry West and Janet Warren as his wife Caroline, the Twonky is a TV set; in addition to its other powers, the robot has the ability to hypnotize people. Ultimately, Kerry is able to destroy it.

TYAHN (L)

First Appearance: *Sandworld* by Richard A. Lupoff, 1976, Berkley Books.

Physical Description: Surrounded by a creamy-white ring, Sandworld has gravity "just about earth-normal" and breatheable air.

The vampires of Tyahn are nearly eight feet tall, thin, pale, and hairless with faces like skulls and flattened, elongated heads. All but the two central teeth, which are large, hollow, needle-sharp, and up to half a foot long, have atrophied. Other life forms on the world include a giant snake and blood maggots.

Biography: Patrick "Red" O'Reilly and prisoners Willie B. Hutkin and Benjamin Nebayan are being transported to a California jail when, suddenly, they find their car plopped down in a jungle bordering an alien desert. The prisoners—along with lawyer Alice Michaelson and Highway Patrol Officer Marc Mauriello—are forced to cooperate when the jungle suddenly shrinks away, and where they'd hoped to find food is now just desert and a few small spores. Red realizes that whatever brought them here must have also snatched up some rain and clouds, which caused the spores to sprout briefly into a jungle. As they set out to explore, he dubs the world Else "because it's certainly someplace else."

In time, the quintet find a glass and concrete city. But before they can enter it, Nebayan is abducted by wraith-like creatures. The others find him, later, bloodless and broken outside the wall of the city. When Mauriello suffers a wound on his hand, and it becomes infected by "unformed greenish things," they have no choice but to enter the city and look for water. The city seems deserted and, studying the artwork therein, they discover that the "Elsefolk" had once been an advanced race, capable of space travel, but that the planet had become dehydrated. In the midst of their search, the group is attacked by vampires. The fiends eat Mauriello while the others find and escape on a transportation belt. The conveyor takes them to another city, full of civilized vampires, and they are taken to see Dzong-gnyadzong.

Using a translation disk to communicate, the alien apologizes for the vampires who attacked them, saying they are wild desert dwellers and not representative of the race. Dzong-gnyadzong explains that the world is called Tyahn and that they were brought here by accident, via a transit beam that had been developed to find them a more hospitable home world. Unfortunately, now the trio is stuck: Even if they could find Earth in the heavens, to return them wouldn't do much good. Though it felt like only an instant, the trip to Tyahn took 20,000 years.

The humans are provided with quarters and with personal "beamers," worn like armbands, and translation disks worn like amulets. They learn to use them and, with their guide Zagdan-gyatzan, visit Ptayeem, the other inhabited world of the star system. They are immediately attacked and spirited away by furred, clawed, foot-tall humanoids,

descendants of ancient Tyahnese colonists. Surviving the adventure and returning to Tyahn, the Earth people inform Dzong-gnyadzong that they wish to consult his planetary chart and go to some other world—well aware that countless centuries will pass and that he may not be there if and when they return.

Comment: In addition to his own writings, author Lupoff was the editor of Canaveral Press in the early 1960s. The hardcover house brought back into print many works by author Edgar Rice Burroughs (see BARSOOM).

TYRR (L, C, TV)

First Appearance: "The Million Year Picnic" by Ray Bradbury, Summer 1946, *Planet Stories* (see *Comment*).

Physical Description: Tyrr is the Martian name for Mars. The world is a network of long and winding canals, deserts, and hills; Martians live in homes of "crystal pillars." A prominent city on Mars is Xi.

The Martians are shorter than humans, with thin necks, "fair, brownish skin . . . yellow coin eyes . . . [and] soft musical voices." They are telepathic and able to hypnotize humans. Martians named in the stories are Yll and Ylla (a.k.a. Mr. and Mrs. K), Pao, Dr. Nlle, Mr. Aaa, Mr. Bbb, Mr. Hhh, Mr. Iii, Mr. Nnn, Mr. Qqq, Mr. Rrr, Mr. Ttt, Mr. Xxx, Mr. Uuu, and Mr. Vvv.

Biography: In January 1999, the first human expedition is sent to Mars, commanded by Nathaniel York. It arrives a month later, and the crew is slain by civilized Martians who want to preserve their world. Captain Williams and the second ship arrive in August, are taken to an insane asylum, and are shot dead by Mr. Xxx. The Third Expeditionary Rocket arrives under Captain John Black in April 2000. On Mars, each crewmember finds the people and places he loved most, unaware that they're illusions created by the Martians, who slay the humans when they are comfortable and off guard. The fourth rocket lands in June 2001, under Captain Wilder and discover that most of the Martians have succumbed to chicken pox. Concluding that the surviving Martians have fled the cities for the hills, crewman Spender begins shooting his comrades to prevent Mars from being taken over by big business like "Mexico when Cortez . . . arrived from Spain." The surviving crewmen overcome Spender, and begin the colonization process.

Humans from Earth plant trees, build towns, one of them greets a Martian thanks to a rift in time, surviving Martians make sporadic contact with humans, and finally, in 2005, war erupts on Earth. Most of the colonists head home to fight for their country. By October 2026, Mars is deserted again—and Earth is dead. However, two families, one with sons, the other with daughters, head from Earth in rockets and arrive on Mars to keep the human race alive as new Martians.

Comment: Though "The Million Year Picnic" was the first of Bradbury's Mars stories, the planet wasn't referred to as Tyrr until the 1948 story "The Earth Men." Twenty-six stories were collected or written for *The Martian Chronicles* (1950), a novel-like anthology that places them in chronological order from January 1999 to October 2026. It remains a one-of-a-kind work of hypnotic beauty, despair, and triumph.

Several of Bradbury's Mars stories were adapted in comic book format in EC's *Weird Science*: "The Long Years" (#17, 1953), "Mars Is Heaven" (#18, 1953), and "The One Who Waits" (#19, 1953)—about a "soul well" that protects Mars by causing the crew of an Earthship to commit suicide (a story from 1949, not included in the book); and in *Weird Fantasy*, "There Will Come Soft Rains" (#17, 1953). Topps Comics published a new comic book, *Ray Bradbury Comics Special* #1, featuring *The Martian Chronicles*, beginning in 1994.

On TV, a six-hour miniseries aired on NBC in January 1980. While adapting the book rather faithfully, writer Richard Matheson took the liberty of inserting a continuing character, Captain Wilder (Rock Hudson), in all the stories; the third expedition was deleted from the script. Bernie Casey costarred as Spender.

Bradbury's first sale was to *Super Science Stories* in 1941—"Pendulum," a short story co-written with Henry Hasse.

U

ULTRA BOY (C)

First Appearance: *Superboy* #98, 1962, DC Comics.

Physical Description: The hero wears a green belt and tights, red boots and bodyshirt with a green "T" design on his chest. Later, he wears just the bodyshirt with gray trousers, a gray vest with brown lapels and white shoulders, and brown boots. He owns a Legion flight ring.

Biography: The son of Crav (father) and Mytra Nah of the planet Rimbor, 13-year-old Jo Nah goes for a spin in a space speedster and is swallowed by a huge Energy Beast. Inside, "weird energies" endow the middle-30th-century youth with super-strength, invulnerability, flash (heat) vision, penetra (X-ray) vision (which can see through lead, but not Inertron), and more. However, he can use the powers only one at a time. Rescued by a Galactic Patrol Cruiser that uses a power beam to cut him free, Jo goes to Earth and applies for membership in the Legion of Super-Heroes as Ultra Boy. For an initiation test, he must visit the 20th century and learn Superboy's secret identity. Arriving in Smallville and posing as Gary Crane, Ultra Boy fulfills his mission and is admitted as the 14th member of the team. As an adult, Ultra Boy marries Phantom Girl (see COSMIC BOY) and becomes a Legion Reservist while working full time as Quadrant Director for the science police. The couple have two children, daughter Arna and son Ronn.

Comment: The character was created by editor Mort Weisinger and writer Jerry Siegel, cocreator of SUPERMAN.

ULTRAMAN (TV, MP, VG, C)

First Appearance: *Urutoraman* (*Ultraman*), July 1966, Tokyo Broadcasting.

Physical Description: Ultraman stands 300 feet tall and wears a metallic silver and red costume and helmet; it isn't known what he looks like beneath the suit. The alien hero possesses enormous strength and is a martial arts master. He also fires destructive blasts from the pinky side of his rigid hand. In his Hyata incarnation, Ultraman can fly.

Biography: The Science Patrol is a group of men and women who battle technological terrors in the 40th century (and wear tight, sharp-looking orange uniforms). While out on patrol one night, young officer Hyata spots a blue, spherical spaceship racing through the atmosphere. He gives chase and is accidentally hit by the red, spherical spaceship that has been pursuing the blue one. Hyata's ship falls to Earth in flames. The occupant of the other vessel, Ultraman—a giant police officer from Nebula M-78—saves him by merging their bodies and leaving the nearly foot-long Beta Capsule on Hyata's chest. The human recovers and, thereafter, all he needs to do to become the mighty Ultraman is to hold the Beta Capsule in his hand and raise it toward the sky. Once the transformation is complete, Hyata can remain Ultraman for just a few minutes; failing to become mortal in the allotted time will cost both the Patrol member and Ultraman their lives. Ultraman achieves the metamorphosis by firing concentric circles of radiation that become Hyata.

Hyata/Ultraman's first foe is the occupant of the blue sphere, the giant monster Bemular. Over the years, his foes have typically been huge dinosaur-like beasts, including the electricity-eating Neronga, the alien Baltan with scissor-like hands, the horned Antlar, the pearl-eating Gamakutira, the uranium-eating Gabora, the gold-eating Goldon, the murderous Gango, which is created from a space-stone that becomes anything one can imagine, the mutated astronaut Jamilar, Maglla (possibly a typo for Magilla), Chandlar, Redking, Suflan (a giant plant), Gomora, Telesdon, Jirass, Woo, Pester, Guigass, Gudis, Guigazaurus, Broads (pronounced Bro-adds), Bogun, Ragon, Degola, Barrangas, Zebokon, Majaba, Kodalar, Kilazee, and others.

Comment: Produced by Toho, home of Godzilla, and conceived by Godzilla's creator, special effects artist Eiji Tsuburaya, the original series ran for 39 half-hour episodes that were enormously successful in Japan, but moderately so when dubbed and syndicated in the United States in 1967. Successive seasons—including one done in animation—went by different titles. In the second series, *Ultra Seven* (1967–68), Agent 340 is sent from Nebula M78 to map the Milky Way. Intrigued by Earth, he decides to study it more closely by adopting the human identity Dan Moroboshi and joining the Ultra Garrison, an elite, six-person government team devoted to protecting the Earth from extraterrestrials (hence, the title of the series). Whenever monsters or aliens attack, Moroboshi puts on his Ultra Eye glasses to become Ultraman.

The 49 episodes of *Ultra Seven* were followed by *The Return of Ultraman* (1971–72), *Ultraman Ace* (1972–73), *Ultraman Taro* (1973–74), *Ultraman Leo* (1974–75), *Ultraman 80* (1980–81), and added a variety of Ultramen (the Ultrabrothers) who looked more or less like the original, including Zophy, the hero's superior; the improved New Ultraman (a.k.a. Ultraman Jack); the youthful Ultraman Taro; Ultraman Leo; and Ultraman Ace, who is formed when Seiji Hobuto and Yuko Minami press their Ultra-rings together. To date, there have been 395 episodes of the show.

A 1990 incarnation, *Ultraman: Towards the Future*, produced by Tsuburaya Productions and the South Australiian Film Corporation, returns to the original one-Ultraman concept. This time, Ultraman (who is referred to in press materials as Ultramangreat) has cornered the monster Gudis (pronounced Goo-dis) on Mars. They're spotted by UMA astronauts Jack Shindo and Stanley Haggard; when Gudis kills Haggard, wrecks the spaceship, and flees to Earth, Ultraman merges with Shindo and follows. Unlike Hyata, Shindo does not rejoin his group but operates as a loner.

The animated series, *Ultraman II*, tells a slightly different origin tale. In it, the near-future Earth Defense Force is organized to protect our world from "aggressive planets." After serving a year in space, Lt. Harris—along with other crewmembers, including the chicken-like robot PDQ—are heading back to Earth when Harris is drawn into a misty limbo. There, Ultraman II explains that he and the other Ultramen look after humankind but cannot function in our dimension unless they inhabit a human body. Since the Ultramen know that ice-breathing dinosaurs are about to ravage the planet, Ultraman II enters Harris's body. Thereafter, whenever his powers are needed, all Harris need do is remove a blue star from his belt, hold it to his forehead, and voila! He's Ultraman II. However, he can remain in this form only for a few minutes. If he tries to stay longer, both the hero and Harris will perish. Harris's conveyance is the laserfiring rocket-sub *Superstar*.

The character's most recent TV appearance has been in the Hollywood-made *Ultraman: The Ultimate Hero*. In this retelling of the legend, the hero works in tandem with the Worldwide Investigative Network Response team, whose specialty is battling monsters from space. The half-hour series debuted in the United States in syndication in the fall of 1994. Scott Rogers stars in the Ultraman suit.

In 1979, two *Ultraman* feature films were edited together from episodes of the first TV series: *Urutoraman* was pieced together from four episodes: his origin, adventures on the monster-infested Tadara Island, and the spectacular battle with Gomora. This was followed by *Urutoraman—Kaiji Daikessen* (*Ultraman—Big Monster Battle*). A feature film, *The Six Ultra Brothers vs. the Monster Army*, was made in 1974 and released in the United States as *Space Warriors 2000*. Set on the Planet Ultra, it combines some new footage with monster battle scenes from various TV episodes.

Another feature, *Urutoraman Sutori* (*The Ultraman Story*) was made in 1984. This one centers around the growth and training of Ultraman Taro. Before Taro is quite ready, Earth is attacked by the wicked space tyrant Judah and Enmahgo, the King of Hell. While the Ultrabrothers have their hands full with Enmahgo's towering robotic monster Grandking, Taro is forced to tackle Enmahgo himself. Victorious, Taro flies into space to help his Ultrabrothers fight the monster on a deserted world. Finally merging into one all-powerful Ultraman, the heroes defeat the monster.

A videogame was produced for the Super NES Nintendo system in 1991, and a comic book from Ultracomics, a division of Harvey Comics, began publication in 1993, based on the characters seen in *Ultraman: Towards the Future*. That same year, Nemesis—also a Harvey division—was formed to take over both *Ultraman* and a new title, *Ultraman Negative One*. In 1994, Viz Comics began publishing English translations of the Japanese Ultraman comic books that have been published since the character's inception.

THE UNIGEN (L)

First Appearance: "Winner Lose All" by Jack Vance, December 1951, *Galaxy*.

Physical Description: An intelligent life form, the unigen is made of "mobile nodes of a luminous-substance which was neither matter nor . . . energy." These millions of nodes are connected to one another by tendrils forming "a great brain." The unigen feeds on energy and, when there's enough of it, it splits into more nodes. When hungry, it roams through space "glowing only feebly," stalking "planets, satellites, meteors, and dark stars" for nourishment. The unigen can concentrate heat in just a few nodes, generating extreme temperatures. The emotionless nodes can see and sense changes in electrostatic fields.

Biography: Unknown to one another, both the unigen and a spaceship from Earth arrive at a new, uninhabited Earthlike world at the same time, one to feed on uranium, the other to explore. The reconnaissance party encounters the unigen—which regards the humans as "land-worms"—and captures a node, unaware that it is an integral part of an intelligent being. The unigen attacks, melting holes in several explorers' spacesuits, and the humans respond with electrical blasts. The two life forms decide the struggle isn't worth it and abandon the world—unaware that a third life form, native spores apparently roused by the to-do, use the uranium to launch themselves into space, "toward different stars."

Comment: Other worlds referred to in the story include Alexander with its yellow water, Coralasan with waters of red, and Antaeus with vines 30 miles long.

THE U.S.S. ENTERPRISE (TV, L, C, MP)

First Appearance: *Star Trek*, September 1966, NBC.

Physical Description: In its original incarnation, the *Enterprise* was a Declaration-class liner, one of 900 such ships that traveled between Earth and Alpha Centauri from 2123 to 2165. Little is known about it.

The second *Enterprise*—NCC-1701—is one of 13 Constitution-class starships. It measures 300 meters and consists of a saucer-section 127 meters in diameter, 11 decks deep and with a bridge on top. A slanted "neck" connects the saucer-section to the conical engineering section, which has a slanted stanchion on either side, each supporting a 153.6-meter-long matter/anti-matter nacelle. The

The U.S.S. *Enterprise* from the original *Star Trek* series.
© Paramount Television.

hangar in the rear of the engineering section contains a minimum of two seven-passenger, box-like Class F shuttlecraft, including the Columbus, Copernicus, and Galileo. Vertical and horizontal turbolifts connect the bridges and respond to voice commands. The ship weighs 172 million kilograms and is armed with 400 photon torpedoes, three phaser (ray) banks, and defensive shields. The ship travels at sublight (impulse) and faster-than-light (warp) speeds. Warp speeds increase geometrically, the speed being the cube of the warp factor: warp 2 is eight times light speed ($2 \times 2 \times 2$), warp three is 27 times light speed, etc. Though warp 6 is the maximum safe speed, the *Enterprise* has reached speeds of warp 14.1. The warp drive is powered by dilithium crystals, mined on alien worlds like Troyius and the hardest mineral known to science.

The crew of 430 is two-thirds male and comprised of 387 enlisted personnel, the rest officers. (Prior to Captain Kirk taking command, the crew capacity was only 203.)

The third *Enterprise* is a refitted version of the second, and the fourth is the same as the third, rebuilt. The fifth and sixth *Enterprises* are Excelsior-class and Ambassador-class vessels about which little is known.

The seventh *Enterprise* is a 42-deck Galaxy-class starship with a crew of 1,014 and a detachable saucer-section (solo, it can travel only via impulse power). The "neck" is narrow from side to side but long front to back, and the engineering section is flatter than the original. The nacelles are also flat, rising from the side of the ship on J-shaped stanchions. In addition to shuttlecraft, the new *Enterprise* carries smaller shuttlepods, life boats for escape and rescue, a captain's yacht, and other vessels. Notable additions include family compounds, schools, and a holodeck that can create realistic, relaxing environments, complete with the appropriate weather.

The second through the seventh *Enterprise*s all have transporters, which can instantly transport people or goods through space; their range is 16,000 miles.

Biography: Commissioned circa 2245, and launched from the San Francisco Yards in Earth orbit, the starship undertakes its first five-year mission under the command of Captain Robert April. After a minor refitting, the *Enterprise* sets out on its second five-year mission in 2251 under Captain Christopher Pike. Pike commands two five-year missions, served both times by Science Officer Mr. Spock. Captain James Kirk takes command in 2264, Spock again serving; after this five-year mission the *Enterprise* undergoes an 18-month refitting, which increases engine performance, enlarges the sick bay, and modernizes the vessel in other ways. Commander Willard Decker is in charge of the ship during the renovations, which are completed in 2271.

After Kirk, MR. SPOCK, and the *Enterprise* defeat the menace of V'ger, Kirk undertakes a new five-year mission. When this is completed, Kirk returns to the ship one last time to battle his old enemy Khan. Kirk destroys the *Enterprise* in 2285 to keep it from falling into Klingon hands. After Kirk is tried and demoted for insubordination, he is given command of the new U.S.S. *Enterprise,* NCC-1701-A in 2286. Kirk continues to serve as its captain at least through 2293.

Little is known about the NCC-1701-B or C, save that the latter was commanded by Captain Rachel Garrett and destroyed.

The last *Enterprise* (to date), NCC-1701-D, was launched from the Utopia Planitia Fleet Yards circling Mars in 2383 under the command of Captain Jean-Luc Picard. It remains in service as of this writing.

Other "U.S.S." ships seen in the *Star Trek* chronicles include the *Bozeman* (NCC-1941), *Constellation* (NCC-1017), *Constitution* (NCC-1700), *Excalibur* (NCC-26517), *Excelsior* (NCC-2000), *Exeter* (NCC-1672), *Hathaway* (NCC-2593), *Hood* (NCC-42296), *Intrepid* (NCC-1631), *Phoenix* (NCC-65420), *Potemkin* (NCC-1702), *Republic* (NCC-1373), *Stargazer* (NCC2893), *Tsiolkovsky* (NCC-59311), *Victory* (NCC-9754), *Antares, Carolina, Defiant, Drake, Farragut, Grissom, Horizon, Lexington, Trieste, Tripoli, Valiant,* and *Yorktown.* Smaller "S.S." ships include the *Beagle, Botany Bay, Colombia, Dierdre,* and *Huron.*

The classes of starships are the obsolete Declaration and Constitution classes, replaced by the Enterprise Class, Excelsior Class, Reliant Class, Federation Class, Dreadnought Class, and Decatur Class. These, in turn, are supplanted by the 24th-century Galaxy Class and new Excelsior Class.

The "NCC" designation, never explained, appears to have been derived from Earth's amphibious Navy Curtis Craft.

Comment: The refitting of the *Enterprise* under Decker (Stephen Collins) is recounted in *Star Trek: The Motion Picture.* The destruction of the ship occurs in *Star Trek III: The Search for Spock,* the return of the *Enterprise* is seen in *Star Trek IV: The Voyage Home,* and the completely redesigned ship is seen in the TV series *Star Trek: The Next Generation.* The new version of the ship was introduced in events portrayed in the motion picture *Star Trek Generations* (1994).

See also *Data*; Appendixes C and D.

USSF STATION (MP)

First Appearance: *Project Moonbase,* 1953, Galaxy Productions/Lippert.

Physical Description: The space station is a big, white disc with a docking port located at every 90 degrees around the side. It orbits the Earth 10 times daily. Rockets in the film are standard V-2-type missiles. The vehicle used to visit the moon is a Lunar Excursion Module-style ship with a round top, cylindrical body, and spidery legs.

Biography: By 1970, the United States Space Force has established a space station to be used as a staging area for the first mapping mission to our natural satellite. Onboard the three-person lunar craft are Colonel Breiteis (a woman), Major Moore, and Dr. Wernher—who, it turns out, is a communist spy. He and Moore fight, causing the ship to spin out of control and waste fuel. The trio is forced to land on the moon and await a rescue ship. Wernher falls and dies while on an EVA; a chaplain weds Breiteis and Moore over the TV, since the government and the U.S. public are uneasy about having a healthy, single young man and woman stranded on the moon.

The U.S. president is also a woman.

Comment: The film is comprised of two episodes of the unsold TV series *Ring Around the Moon.* Donna Martell is Breiteis ("Bright Eyes"), Ross Ford is Moore, and Larry Johns is Wernher. Richard Talmadge directed from a script by the great science fiction author Robert Heinlein and Jack Seaman.

V

VALCOM-17485 AND AQUACOM-89045 (MP)

First Appearance: *Heartbeeps*, 1982, Universal Pictures.

Physical Description: The talking humanoids have gold faces. ValCom-17485 has plastered gold hair and wears a gold, pinstriped suit and gold bow tie; AquaCom-89045 has golden steel-wool hair and dresses in a gold and pink dress with long sleeves and a ruff-style collar tilted so it's higher on the left than on the right.

Phil is a squat, silver, square-headed, green-eyed robot with dish-like ears, two arms, and a pair of caterpillar-treads. Catskill is a silver-skinned, balding, cigar-smoking robot in a black suit. The Crimebuster robot is a rolling, black gumdrop with a rotating head. It's equipped with a flamethrower, a pair of TR-16 machine guns, and a cannon.

Biography: In 1995, ValCom-17485 has been programmed to be a valet, and AquaCom-89045 is designed to be a hostess. The two robots meet at their San Francisco GM factory, where they've been brought for repairs. They fall in love and decide there has to be more to life than serving humans. They run away with the robot, Catskill—a standup comic who usually sits down—and hole up in a junkyard owned by Calvin and Susan Gort. The Gorts sympathize with the robots' plight and help them elude Charlie and Max—humans hired by the factory to recover the renegade duo—and the fierce Crimebuster robot. The Gorts also help the lovers start a family, providing spare parts so they can build a child, Phil.

Comment: Andy Kaufman stars as ValCom-17485 and Bernadette Peters is AquaCom-89045, with Randy Quaid as Charlie, Kenneth McMillan as Max, Melanie Mayron as Susan, and Christopher Guest as Calvin. Jack Carter provided the voice of Catskill; Phil is a real robot. Allan Arkush directed from a script by John Hill.

See also GNUT.

VALENTINE MICHAEL SMITH (L)

First Appearance: *Stranger in a Strange Land* by Robert A. Heinlein, 1961, G.P. Putnam's Sons.

Physical Description: Smith is "a slender young man with underdeveloped muscles and overdeveloped chest" from having spent his entire life on Mars, where the atmosphere is relatively thin and the gravity less than Earth. He possesses a "bland, babyish face" but with eyes that "would have seemed at home in a man of ninety." Smith is able to speed up or slow down his heart or respiration, increase his tactile sensitivity, and cause people to disappear.

The Martians are "not human." They look quite different in "nymph" and adult stage: As the former they are "fat, furry spheres," and as the latter they look like "ice boats under sail." All nymphs are females who metamorphose into male adults. The Martians live in "faerie, graceful cities," revere Old Ones for their knowledge (this is especially true of the nestlings or "eggs," the young ones born of nymphs); they strive to "grok" to fullness objects, people, and events—that is, to achieve complete understanding—before acting on them; they bond as fully trusting "brothers" to those with whom they've shared water; and they "discorporate" upon death, though the discorporate Martians still communicate with their fellows.

The *Envoy* is not described, though the crew is comprised of Captain Michael Brant, the pilot and captain; Dr. Winifred Coburn Brant, a nurse and historian; Francis X. Seeney, astrogator and second pilot; Dr. Olga Kovalic Seeney, biochemist; Sergei Rimsky, engineer and chemist; Eleanora Alvarez Rimsky, geologist; Dr. Ward Smith, surgeon and biologist; and Dr. Mary Jane Lyle Smith, engineer.

Biography: The first ship to Mars, the *Envoy*, isn't heard from after landing. Twenty-five years later, the ship *Champion* finds just one survivor: Smith, the son of a union between Mary Jane and Captain Brant—the mother having died in childbirth, her unhinged husband having cut Brant's throat and then his own. (It isn't known what happened to the others.) The Martians raised Smith as one of their own; even now, not yet having grokked humans, they do nothing to harm him (unlike the beings of the fifth planet, whose world they reduced to the rubble that is the asteroid belt).

Much more alien than human, Smith is taken to Earth with the blessings of the Martians, who hope to better grok humans through the young man. Nurse Gillian (Jill) Boardman watches over him at his Washington, D.C. hospital as her lover, journalist Ben Caxton, tries to find out why the government is holding him, whether or not he is the legal heir to the Lyle Drive (space engine) invented by his mother, and whether he "owns" Mars in the eyes of Earth law. Fearful of what the government may do to Smith, Jill sneaks him to her apartment. When men come to arrest her, Smith causes them to vanish.

With no one else to turn to, Jill brings Smith to the paternal, influential attorney, philosopher, and author Dr. Jubal E. Harshaw, who lives with his devoted secretaries Miriam, Anne, and Dorcas on his estate in the Poconos. While the humans learn about Smith, he studies books and learns about humans. He becomes the object of veneration and founds the Church of All Worlds, Inc., teaching others the ways of the Martians, though he's viewed as an outlaw and a blasphemer to those who don't understand him or the naked, sexually liberated members of his Innermost Temple. Ultimately, Smith goes before his enemies and is stoned and shot to death. His discorporate self prevents Jubal from committing suicide, his new religion goes on—comanaged by Ben—and the Martians, finally grokking humankind, figure we're not worth their concern and don't waste another "split eon" on us. As for Michael—now, Archangel Michael—he isn't quite so ambivalent as he settles into eternity filled with ideas for "changes" he wants to make.

Comment: *Stranger in a Strange Land* is one of the great science fiction novels and became something of a "bible" to many young people in the late 1960s. This was a longer, meatier novel than Heinlein's earlier works, and his output thereafter tended toward more expansive works like *I Will Fear No Evil* (1970), in which an old man has his mind placed in the body of his young secretary; *Time Enough For Love: The Lives of Lazarus Long* (1973), in part a time travel tale of a man who beds his mother; *The Number of the Beast* (1980), set on various worlds and boasting the return of Jubal Harshaw; and *Friday* (1982), in which an Artificial Person secret courier is hunted in the rebellion-plagued future.

An unabridged edition of *Stranger in a Strange Land* was published in 1991. This was Heinlein's original 220,000-word draft, and it followed the same general narrative structure as the 160,000-word edition, which had been cut at an editor's request.

VALLEY FORGE (MP)

First Appearance: *Silent Running*, 1972, Universal Pictures.

Physical Description: The ship is approximately 2,000 feet long and comprised of a straight and narrow metal skeleton with six geodesic-dome greenhouses clustered in groups of three around one end. The living quarters are located in two flat "wings" midway along the ship.

The drones are each approximately a yard high, with flat, squarish bodies. They have an arm in the front and waddle about on two legs, one on either side.

Biography: It's 2008, and botanist Freeman Lowell has spent eight years onboard the American Airlines space freighter *Valley Forge,* one of three ships carrying the surviving specimens of flora and some fauna from nuclear holocaust-ravaged Earth (the other ships are *Geosylva* and *Telopor*). The hope is that one day Earth can be refoliated. The younger astronauts—Wolf, Barker, and Keenan—

Freeman Lowell and a pair of drones onboard the *Valley Forge.*
© Universal Pictures.

Amazing companions on an incredible adventure...that journeys beyond imagination!

"silent running" starring **Bruce Dern**

with Cliff Potts • Ron Rifkin • Jesse Vint • and The Drones

Original Songs Sung by JOAN BAEZ • Original Music Composed and Conducted by PETER SCHICKELE

Written by DERIC WASHBURN & MIKE CIMINO and STEVE BOCHCO

Directed by DOUGLAS TRUMBULL • Produced by MICHAEL GRUSKOFF

A MICHAEL GRUSKOFF / DOUGLAS TRUMBULL PRODUCTION

A UNIVERSAL RELEASE • TECHNICOLOR* | G | GENERAL AUDIENCES ALL AGES ADMITTED

ORIGINAL SOUNDTRACK ALBUM NOW AVAILABLE EXCLUSIVELY ON DECCA RECORDS

Advertising art showing the dome of the *Valley Forge* (left) and the entire ship (to the right), along with Freeman Lowell and a drone. © Universal Pictures.

couldn't care less about their precious cargo, and when the crews receive orders from Earth to destroy the pods all are delighted except Lowell. Murdering his three shipmates as they attempt to set nuclear devices to destroy the domes, he makes it appear as though the *Valley Forge* is out of control, then heads away from Earth, aided by the "drones" (robots) Huey, Dewey, and Louie, which he's reprogrammed to be his friends. Unfortunately, while the ship survives a rocky, off-course encounter with the rings of Saturn, Lowell is injured and the plants begin to perish. Though he himself is dying, the botanist sets up lamps to provide the flora with artificial sunlight and, in the

end, jettisons the pod with a robot caretaker, blowing up *Valley Forge* to cover his tracks and hoping that the plants may even outlive the human race.

Comment: Bruce Dern stars as Lowell, Cliff Potts as Wolf, Ron Rivkin as Barker, and Jesse Vint as Keenan; the film was directed by Douglas Trumbull from a script by Deric Washburn, Michael Cimino (of *The Deer Hunter* fame), and future TV producer Steven Bochco. John Dykstra (*Star Wars*) worked on the special effects with first-time director Trumbull, who had cocreated the effects for *2001: A Space Odyssey*.

Many of the scenes on the *Valley Forge* were filmed on the decommissioned aircraft carrier of the same name.

VAMPIRELLA (C, L)

First Appearance: *Vampirella* #1, 1969, Warren Publishing Co.

Physical Description: In every way, Vampirella resembles a very attractive young Earthwoman with long, brunette (later, raven-black) hair. However, she has a long, slender fang on either side of her two upper front teeth and drinks blood to survive.

Though she occasionally wears terrestrial clothing, her preferred attire is a skimpy red bikini bottom with a gold bat design on the front, and a thin red strap running from either hip to a high white collar. She also wears spike-heeled black boots, a gold armband on her right arm, and a pair of large, gold, crescent earrings.

Vampirella has the ability to transform herself into a bat (in early stories, she could also sprout bat wings and retain her human form). In human form, her reflexes are much faster than those of an Earth person.

Biography: On the planet Draculon (later spelled Drakulon), "a world of cooling breezes and soaring, towering burnished spires," a humanoid race known as the Vampyr (which means "Gentle people, kind of heart") survive by drinking the "flowing waters" of the planet, the "equivalent . . . [of] mammalian blood." But volcanoes cause the planet to spin off its axis, inverting the poles; the life-preserving "creatone layer" deteriorates, and the planet's twin suns bake the world. As the "waters" dry up and the race dies, Vampirella breaks the most sacred law of the Vampyr: not to kill. She encourages Tristan to drink the blood of the boar-like Gronos she's slain, and he is disgusted.

Vampirella in the midst of bloodlust, drawn by Jose Gonzalez. © Harris Publications.

Shortly after, the Arthur Clarke Geosurvey Expedition No. 3 lands on Draculon. The explorers shoot at Vampirella and Tristan attacks them; he is so revolted by having broken the law himself that he goes mad. Reluctantly, Vampirella leaves him, taking the spaceship back to Earth. Initially, she poses as "Bambi Aurora" and preys on humans, then runs afoul of the sorceress Evily, the Princess of Vaalgania, who is Vampirella's cousin (the relationship is unexplained). In time, she meets scientist Tyler Westron, who amputates her wings and creates a serum that serves as a blood substitute. Leaving his estate, she is pursued by Conrad Van Helsing and his son Adam, descendants of Dracula's nemesis, supernatural researchers who are looking for the vampire that killed Conrad's brother Kurt (he was already dead when she drank his blood). Ducking into a carnival, Vampirella makes a lifelong friend in Pendragon, "the world's greatest third rate magician." Later, while battling the demon Skaar, the "Drakulonne" explains all to Adam, and she becomes the pair's "ally in the struggle against the forces of chaos."

Vampirella's twin sister, the blonde Draculina, appeared in the second adventure, but her existence was never explained.

Comment: The character was created by science fiction historian and literary agent Forrest J. Ackerman and by publisher James Warren. The story recounted above also includes elements of the expanded original tales written by J.R. Cochran (*1972 Annual*) and Budd Lewis (#46).

Warren published 112 issues of the large-size, black-and-white comic book through 1983, as well as a yearbook (1972) and a full-color *Vampirella Special* (1977). Harris Publications brought the title back as a color comic book, starting with #113 in 1988. After an irregular publishing schedule, the comic book was cancelled and relaunched in April 1994 as *The Vengeance of Vampirella*, starting with #1.

In 1974–75, Warner Books published six Vampirella novels by Ron Goulart: *Bloodstalk, On Alien Wings, Deadwalk, Blood Wedding, Deathgame,* and *Snakegod.*

Hammer Films began preproduction on a Vampirella motion picture in 1975. However, the company shut down before the film could be made. Test shots of actress Barbara Leigh in the Vampirella suit appeared on the cover of several issues, beginning with #67.

THE VINDICTIVE (L)

First Appearance: "The Bureaucrat" by Malcolm Jameson, April 1944, *Astounding Science Fiction.*

Physical Description: The *Vindictive* is a "stumpy old sky monster" of the cruiser class, powered by Ekstrom repulsors and equipped with Mark XX katatrons (cannons). The conn contains a "black visiplate" for viewing what lies ahead. The *Pollux* is a cigar-shaped vessel, and the *Vindictive* apparently is the same.

Biography: The former "queen of the fleet," now a "clumsy old monitor," the *Vindictive* was scrapped years ago only to be recommissioned and stationed in space, in an orbit that keeps it over New York—despite the fact that Earth's at war, the planet is in no danger of being attacked. Turret Gunner Roy Benton wants a transfer to where the action is, and goes to see Grand Admiral Bullard, his father's old and beloved skipper. Bullard looks into matters and discovers that the ship was reactivated to provide a safe haven for sons of the rich. Bullard orders it readied for action; during target practice, however, its hastily rewired, upgraded engines accidentally kick it into an enemy sector. It arrives just in time to battle two prowling enemy "maulers," after which it returns to the moon in triumph. The new "bronco" drive is renamed the Benton effect, and Lt. Commander Benton is put in charge of the ship "for the duration of the war."

Other ships mentioned in the story include the *Pegasus,* the *Altair,* the *Pollux,* the *Relentless,* the *Implacable,* the sky-cutter *Gnat,* and the target control ship *Alferatz.*

Comment: Jameson, a former navy man, sold his first story to *Astounding Science Fiction,* "Eviction by Isotherm," in 1938. "The Bureaucrat" was part of his Bullard series, which began in 1940. The stories were collected as *Bullard of the Space Patrol* in 1951. "The Bureaucrat" was not included in the 1955 edition; his story "Devil's Powder" (1941) appeared in neither. Jameson died in 1945.

THE VISION See THE HUMAN TORCH.

VOL See GOR.

VOLCAN ROCK (T, C)

First Appearance: *Power Lords,* 1982, Revell.

Physical Description: Disguised to resemble a volcanic planetoid, the synthetic Volcan Rock was created by ancient Power Lords as an arsenal for the most powerful space-warfare weaponry extant, most notably an Ion Cannon able to vaporize a planet with one blast. "Capable of traversing the universe at faster-than-light speeds," Volcan Rock has sensors that "track incoming enemy starcraft with pinpoint accuracy." The armaments here can be activated only by a burst of "cosmic energy . . . [from] the power jewel" worn by each and every Power Lord.

Biography: Toran is a "mighty planet" thriving in a three-sun system. Respected throughout the galaxy, the high-tech world and its human inhabitants are governed by the Power Lords, "an eons-old caste of philosopher-rulers" who safeguard the peaceful worlds of the galaxy. But they haven't

done quite as good a job as they should have: Toran is attacked by aliens of the Extraterrestrial Alliance, forces from the worlds of Krondar, Morda, and Zomar, ruled, respectively, by Arkus "the Evil Dictator," Raygoth "the Goon of Doom," and Ggripptogg "the Four Fisted Brute." As the palace falls, Izah, King of the Power Lords, and his Queen Moira are slain, though not before their devoted herald Shaya uses a molecular-disassembler to send their son Adam to "an environmentally hospitable planet" in space sector QE-24—Earth.

Adam goes to work at an observatory with no memory of his past until Shaya arrives in a Power Ship Attack Cruiser, pursued by a four-legged green alien Trigore. She restores Adam's memory and takes him to Volcan Rock, where he leads the counterattack against the Extraterrestrial Alliance.

Comment: In addition to the popular toy line, created for Revell by Strongin/Mayem International and designed by Wayne Barlowe, the characters appeared in a DC comic book that ran for three issues in 1983.

THE VOLES (L)

First Appearance: *Planet of the Voles* by Charles Platt, 1971, G.P. Putnam's Sons.

Physical Description: The Voles, "frighteningly serene" humanoids, are commanded entirely by females, who stand roughly a head taller than the males. The Voles are able to project their thoughts across great distances and move objects; using other minds as amplifiers, Vole telekinesis can actually reach through space.

The world they've captured is covered by a prehistoric jungle. The atmosphere is nearly like that of Earth, and the gravity is .9 that of our world. There are no edible animals below, and only a few edible plants.

The Vole spaceship is pink, "thin and wide . . . like a ray, swimming." Shaped like an equilateral triangle, it is covered with "bubble-cells arrayed in rows around one larger cell, at the geometric center."

The Earth ship is 500 meters long and 50 meters in diameter, built to hold 1,000 passengers. It carries an escape pod designed for limited flight.

Biography: Sent to reclaim worlds conquered by the hitherto unknown and still-mysterious Voles, a troop carrier is gassed by Voles and goes down on a world only 500 square miles of which had been colonized by humans. The nameless planet was used as a resort for big game hunting and safaris and later to train warriors before being conquered by the Voles. Janitor Jon and artist Tomas are the only two who remain awake, and the two men are captured. But Tomas gets away in the escape pod, and when Jon is spirited away by a giant bird, Tomas is able to rescue him. Picking their way through the jungle, the men meet a man named Snipe, who's a one-man resistance movement. Everyone else has been turned into a zombie from drugged foodstuffs provided by the Voles.

The three men use birds to carry them into the massive Vole fortress, where they steal a carrier and blast off. Though the Voles are able to gas them, Tomas remains awake thanks to rock dust he'd inadvertently breathed. They are able to elude the Vole fleet that's waiting for them and return to the planet. There, they discover that the fortress is a decoy "designed to appeal to warrior-psychology," and that the real Vole stronghold is elsewhere. Rousing the soldiers in their old transport by using the newly discovered antidote, Jon and Tomas provide Captain Shallup with the location of the real fortress, based on a photograph they've taken. The attack is successful and, confronting the leader Gavina, Tomas learns that he was allowed to survive the initial gassing of the carrier because his own birth is actually a product of Vole telekinesis. Because he is a half-breed, a human being with Vole mental prowess, his genes have been manipulated so he could work as an infiltrator for them. But Tomas chooses to work with the humans, and Gavina departs in a huff.

Comment: Platt, an English author, also wrote *Garbage World* (1967), about the dumping-ground asteroid Kopra, as well as other science fiction titles.

VOLTRON (T, TV)

First Appearance: *Voltron: Defender of the Universe*, 1984, syndicated.

Physical Description: Comprised of five robot lions, each of which can function separately or in teams of two, three, or four, the fully-assembled Voltron is a towering humanoid with: two lion-head feet, one yellow, one blue, like his legs; lion-head hands, one red, one green, like the arms; a yellow-horned silver, red, and blue robotic head; and a pair of rigid red "wings" jutting from his shoulders. The fifth lion, the black lion, forms his torso. He carries a huge sword.

Biography: In the 25th century, a group of space explorers set out to find the fabled lion-robots that unite to form Voltron. When this is done, the robot from the planet Arus becomes the protector of its own galaxy and those around it, fighting the likes of the Alien Mice, the evil Alliance, Merla the Queen of Darkness, and others. It is joined, in its crusade, by other robots.

Comment: World Events produced a whopping 125 half-hour episodes. Matchbox Toys produced an enormously successful action figure line, which, the following year, expanded from one robot to the Voltron Warrior Force, featuring different robots.

Voltron is the same figure as Golion of the GODAIKIN ROBOTS.

THE VREMEATRON (L)

First Appearance: "The Technicolor Time Machine" by Harry Harrison, 1967, *Analog*.

Physical Description: The original model is a "hulking mass of machinery . . . a metal platform set on thick insulators." It's run by a nearby control board. The second model, used by Climactic Studios, is "larger . . . far more festooned with wires and glittering coils . . . and a heavy-duty diesel motor-generator." Two dozen large truck tires on the bottom absorb the shock of landing, and pipes are set up "to delimit the edges of the time field" (anything outside them, from a truck tail pipe to a human arm, will be left behind).

Vremeatron is from the Serbo-Croatian *vreme*, or "time."

Biography: Climactic Studios is on the verge of bankruptcy when producer Barney Hendrickson learns of Professor Hewett's time machine. Studio head L.M. Greenspan agrees to an experimental trip. He sends Barney, stuntmen Tex Antonelli and Dallas Levy, UCLA philologist Dr. Jens Lyn, studio technician Amory Blestead, and a truck back to the 11th-century Orkney Islands to see if it would be feasible to shoot a movie there. They return with a Viking named Ottar, whom they select to costar in the epic *Viking Columbus*. This time, the Climactic team returns to the past with cameras, lights, generators, trucks, boats, crew, a script by Charley Chang (whom they sent back in time to write it, then brought him back an hour after he left), and stars Slithey Tove and Ruf Hawk. By making their film, not only does the team return with an epic adventure that saves Climactic, but they enable Ottar to sail to Vinland and found a Viking settlement there—causing the ruins that, when discovered in the future, convince archaeologists that Vikings came to the New World before Columbus and inspire the movie in the first place!

After the film is completed, Tex and Dallas use the machine to offer safaris to prehistoric Earth.

Comment: The serialized novel—a hilarious send-up of moviemaking—was published in book form that same year. Popular author Harrison sold his first story, "Rock Diver," to *Worlds Beyond* in 1951.

VULCAN (TV, L, C, MP)

First Appearance: *Star Trek*, September 1966, NBC.

Physical Description: Vulcan is a Class M planet, a world on which humans can live without life-support systems of any kind. Vulcan has no moon, an extremely bright sun, and seems a deep red when viewed in natural light; this is due to the great yellow and umber deserts that cover the world. The seas have little salt, and the thin air doesn't appear to support clouds. The average daytime temperature is a dry 140 degrees F.

Biography: Civilization on Vulcan was originally governed by the families of powerful warriors. During a period of devastating warfare, the philosopher/historian/telepath Surak persuaded the major warring family heads to lay down their arms and embrace logic, rather than combat. This lifestyle swept across Vulcan and brought both peace and achievement to its people. The achievement of ultimate logic, kolinahr, became a goal of every Vulcan. Surak is memorialized with a towering statue near the capital city of Shikhar, where he performed the first kolinahr ceremony and where all others are now performed.

Vulcan children enter school at three, the first year consisting largely of meditation. The Vulcan Science Academy is considered the finest such institution in the known universe. At the Vulcan Hall of Ancient Thought, the katras (mind and soul) of departed Vulcans are available for consultation.

At some point in the past, a race of beings known as the Preservers came to Vulcan and, fearing that its harsh climate would cause its people to become extinct, spirited away a portion of the population to another world. These transplanted Vulcans became Romulans, a race of courageous if deceitful warriors. The Romulans spread outward from their two-world system, though Ch'rihan and Ch'hauran remain the center of their empire.

Vulcan words include:

Kah-if-farr: Begin the ritual act
Kal-if-fee: Act of challenge
Klee-fah: No
Koon-ut kal-if-fee: Marriage
Kroykah: Stop
Plak tow: Frenzy
Plomeek: Soup
Pon far: Mating time
Tal-shaya: Merciful execution
Tasmeen: The name of a Vulcan month

The Vulcan greeting is a hand gesture in which the fingers are separated in two pairs. (This was inspired by the shape of the Hebrew letter shin; the hand symbol is used by rabbis to bless the congregation on the high holy day Yom Kippur.) In Vulcan, the greeting is usually accompanied by the phrase "Live long and prosper."

See also MR. SPOCK; U.S.S. ENTERPRISE; Appendixes C and D.

THE VULTURE (TV)

First Appearance: *Salvage 1*, January 1979, ABC.

Physical Description: Nineteen feet of the 33-foot, six-inch-tall ship consists of a cargo cylinder (made from a gasoline truck tank) with three booster rockets along the side, each of them as long as the cylinder. An octagon-shaped two-passenger capsule (made from a cement truck mixer) is perched atop the cylinder with six small retro-rockets facing up and a "bubble window" on top. The entire ship sits capsule-up on a tripod with automobile tires on the bottom to absorb the shock of touchdown.

Biography: Based in Southern California, Harry Broderick and his Jettison Scrap and Salvage Company thrive on the exotic: capturing rare spider monkeys from Bantu Larova for a zoo; heading to Burma to find the B-25 Harry flew during World War II; saving a girl from a sealed fallout shelter in an earthquake zone; removing a ghost from a haunted house (a spirit who turns out to be an alien); and surviving an attack by a Universal Soldier android with an impaired program. However, the most exotic missions of all don't take place on Earth. With the help of demolition and rocket fuel expert Melanie Slozar, former astronaut Skip Carmichael, and aerospace engineer Mack, Harry constructs a spaceship to retrieve valuable satellites from space and expensive equipment from the moon. In one two-part adventure, they also salvage Skip, who returns briefly to active duty and is stranded onboard NASA's *Skylab* space station.

The "flight patch" of *Salvage 1* shows a vulture with a wrench. Harry's nemesis is FBI agent Klinger.

Comment: The hour-long series blasted off with a two-hour pilot; the show ended in November 1979 after 12 more episodes. Andy Griffith is Broderick, Joel Higgins is Skip, Trish Stewart is Melanie, J. Jay Saunders is Mack, and Richard Jaeckel is Klinger. The show was created by Mike Lloyd Ross.

W

WALTER THE WOBOT (C)

First Appearance: "Judge Dredd," 1977, *2000 A.D. #2*, IPC Magazines, Ltd. (England).

Physical Description: Standing approximately five feet tall, Walter has a TV-shaped head, thick, coil-like arms that end in three sharp fingers, a stocky oval body, and a pair of three-toed feet. The robot is quite intelligent, though he pronounces his "r"s as "w"s.

Biography: After World War III in 2070, a new civilization arises governed by the Declaration of Judgment. The edict decrees that an army of judges be given unrestricted power to hunt down criminals. (To become a judge, children of unusual intelligence and physical ability are trained for 15 years, from the age of five, at the Academy of Law.)

Judge Dredd entered the academy in 2071. Now 35, he is a judge in Mega-City One, a huge metropolis that sprawls from the Atlantic Coast to where Pittsburgh used to be, and from old Toronto to what was once South Carolina. He is ably assisted in his work by Walter, a Servo-Robot, who also does the housekeeping and shopping.

Walter has also had solo adventures, most notably his run-in with Doc Frankenheim, who tries to transfer his servant Ygor's mind into Walter's metal body.

Comment: The characters were created by writers John Wagner and artist Brian Bolland. They also appeared in the seven-issue *Judge Dredd* comic published by Eagle Comics in England but widely distributed in the United States.

THE WATCHERS (C)

First Appearance: *Fantastic Four* #13, 1963, Marvel Comics.

Physical Description: The Watchers are hairless humanoids—some, macrocephalic—who stand approximately 10 feet tall and wear white robes beneath high-collared blue togas, blue boots, and golden gloves. Some wear blue robes with white togas.

Thanks to exposure to "Delta rays," the Watchers are apparently immortal. They are also telepathic, can create illusions, and thanks to "cosmic anti-matter isotopes," which they absorb, they can transform themselves into "living energy" for rapid transit through space.

Biography: The Watchers are an ancient people who originated on an unnamed planet in a solar system outside our galaxy. At some point in the past, they decided to bring "the gifts of health, and wealth to other races!" and went to the planet Prosilicus, a world of pointy-eared green humanoids. The Watchers give the Prosilicans atomic energy to "advance your civilization by a thousand years." But the Prosilicans use it to make war on one another and attack a neighboring planet. The unnamed world retaliates, and both planets are destroyed. Thereafter, the Watchers agree that they must only observe and learn, not interfere and educate.

Among the few Watchers who have been named are the bearded Ikor (the blood of the gods in Greek mythology), his son Uatu, Emnu (Leader of the High Tribunal), young Aron, and Ecce. Ecce witnessed the birth of the villainous GALACTUS (see entry) in our universe. Failing to prevent it, he knew that "for ages yet uncounted, I may regret the decision I have made this day." Uato is assigned to our solar system and, though he does not help us per se, he gives advice to heroes like the Fantastic Four and they act on his suggestions.

In addition to watching our own dimension, the Watchers have begun peering into other realms, including alternate realities.

Comment: The origin of the characters was revealed in *Tales of Suspense* #53, 1964. The Watchers also host the ongoing title *What if . . .*, which began publication in 1977 and wonders what would have happened if Conan walked the Earth today, if Spider-Man had never become a crimefighter, if Iron Man were trapped in the time of King Arthur, etc.

WATT 4 (C)

First Appearance: "The Rejects," 1968, *Witzend* #4, Wallace Wood.

Physical Description: The conical ship has two slender wings toward the rear, with three rocket engines in the middle on the underside, a larger engine on the wingtip, and two engines where the wings meet the fuselage. The tail fin has two rockets and there's a cluster of rockets in the rear; the hatch is located in the side, and the bridge has a bubble-window.

The ship travels "at near-sonic speed" and its equipment includes a hyperspace warp rationalizer, a null psionics justifier, a thousand-foot-drop scanner, and a cybernetically programmed chronofram.

Wally Wood's wonderful *Watt 4*. © Wallace Wood.

Walter the Wobot, drawn by Brian Bolland. © IPC Magazines Ltd.

Biography: In their one adventure, the crew of the *Watt 4* lands on a planet of Liquefactionist Deviates, religious nuts who try to sacrifice them to their god. The crew of the ship is comprised of the giant Glomb from Jupiter, the diminutive Wee Witt, the furry Hairy James, the superheroic Blue Banana, Venus (a Martian), the microscopic mutant Miniman, the odd Dimentius, the brilliant I.Q. and his companion Kenneth Banghead, a Hammerbird whose nose is a rock-hard weapon. After surviving a near-sacrifice, the crew heads off to battle their nemesis L. Sprague De Freeb.

Comment: The characters were created by the brilliant artist Wood. Their only adventure was reprinted in *Woodwork* in 1980.

THE WERSGORIX (L, MP)

First Appearance: "The High Crusade" by Poul Anderson, July–September 1960, *Astounding Science Fiction* (name changed to *Analog* with September issue).

Physical Description: The aliens stand "about five feet tall" and are very broad. The skin is "hairless and deep blue," and they have a "short thick tail." The round head has "long and pointed" ears on either side, though they are "less acute" than human ears; the "blunt-snouted face" has amber eyes and a high brow.

The Jairs are "a little taller" than a human with "soft gray fur" all over the body and a "cat-whiskered" face with "enormous purple eyes." The hive-dwelling Pr?*tans (the ? is a whistle, the * a grunt) have a "tentacled shape," while the Ashenkoghlis are described as centaurs.

The Wersgorix ship is a smooth "gleaming pillar" and is equipped with an "automaton-pilot" and "blinding hell-beams" for weapons.

Biography: In 1345, a Wersgorix ship arrives in England intent on conquest. However, accustomed to high-tech combat, the aliens are unable to fend off a close-combat attack by arrows and battleaxes. The ship is taken by the forces of the baron Sir Roger de Tourneville, while Brother Parvus works with a captured alien named Branithar to understand how it works. The craft is dubbed *Crusader,* and a crew of Englishmen sets out to conquer the Holy Land. But Branithar betrays them and they head into space. Making the best of a bad situation, the crew decides to conquer the planet Wersgorix and its hundred-world empire.

The first world of the empire they reach is Thraxian, whose fortresses fall to the plucky Earthlings, after which a "super-light drive" voyage brings them to the planetary system Bodavant. There, they bluff the native Jairs as well as aliens from Ashenk and Pr?*t into joining their anti-Wersgorix campaign. Despite the misdeeds of the traitorous Sir Owain, they triumph over the Wersgorix and establish the benevolent Christian kingdom of New Avalon in space. Centuries later, a ship arrives from Earth and the New Avalonians ask the spacefarers if the Holy Land was ever liberated from the infidels. "Yes," says Captain Yeshu haLevy of the Israeli Empire.

Comment: One of the most imaginative and enduring science fiction authors, Anderson sold his first story, "Tomorrow's Children," coauthored with F.N. Waldrop, to *Astounding Science Fiction* in March 1947.

The High Crusade was published in book form the same year as its serialization. It was made into a motion picture in 1995, directed by Holger Neuhauser and Klaus Knoesel and starring John Rhys-Davies.

See also THE HOKAS.

THE WHEEL (MP)

First Appearance: *The Conquest of Space*, 1955, Paramount Pictures.

Physical Description: The smooth, gleaming *Wheel* orbits 1,075 miles above the Earth and consists of a core with a bulb at the top, middle, and bottom. The rim of the *Wheel* is connected to the core by three long, narrow cylinders that radiate from the central bulb. The hub is roughly 130 feet long, and the wheel is approximately 250 feet in diameter.

The Mars ship is a delta-wing craft with rocket engines. The ship, which is approximately 500 feet from wingtip to wingtip, lands on its belly and carries a passenger rocket on its back. When it's time for the astronauts to depart, the V2-like rocket is raised to the vertical and lifts off. The rocket is approximately 125 feet tall.

The film also features a space taxi, a roughly 10-foot long, X-shaped sled with an engine on either end.

Biography: In the near future, a rocket from Earth brings Dr. George Fenton to the *Wheel*, which was built by Colonel Samuel Merritt whose estranged son, Captain Barney Merritt, is also aboard. Fenton is there to oversee the departure of the Merritts, along with Sergeant Imoto, Sergeant Fodor, and Jackie Siegle, on the first flight to Mars; eager Sergeant Mahoney stows away. En route, the ship has an uncomfortably close encounter with an asteroid; Fodor—during a spacewalk to repair an antenna—is killed when a micrometeoroid penetrates his suit; and, shocked by Fodor's death, Colonel Merritt becomes a religious nut. Feeling that they've offended God, Merritt tries to crash the ship as he glides it in for a landing on Mars; his son takes over and manages to set them down safely. Later, the colonel sabotages the water supply and pulls a gun on his son when Barney tries to stop him; the elder Merritt is accidentally shot to death during the ensuing struggle. Fortunately, Martian snow provides water for the crew during the months that they must sit tight waiting for Earth and Mars to be realigned for the return trip. The soil supports transplanted terrestrial plant life, and after surviving a Marsquake that nearly wrecks the rocket, the crew heads for home.

Comment: William Hopper stars as Fenton, with Walter Brooke as the elder Merritt, Eric Fleming as his son, Mickey Shaughnessy as Mahoney, Benson Fong as Imoto, Phil Foster as Siegle, and Ross Martin as Fodor. The film was produced by veteran science fiction filmmaker George Pal and directed by Byron Haskin from a screenplay by James O'Hanlon, based on earlier scripts by Philip Yordan, Barre Lyndon, and George Worthing Yates. All were loosely based on concepts put forward in the nonfiction book *The Conquest of Space* (1949) by scientist Willy Ley and artist Chesley Bonestell.

THE WIDE-PURPOSE WARDEN (L)

First Appearance: "In Man's Image" by Terry Carr, 1971, *Amazing Stories*, Vol. 45, #4.

Physical Description: The humanoid robot has "logic processes" housed in its torso and is in constant contact with the public computer—pubcomp—which has a faster brain. The robots are humorless and, for the most part, emotionless.

Mike Kaluta's interpretation of the *Wide-Purpose Warden.*
© Ultimate Publishing Co.

Biography: "Over three hundred years" in the future, the air is unbreathable—and has been for about a half-century, despite the domes that cover Earth's cities—and humans may be extinct. But the Wide-Purpose Warden believes that one may survive and enters a long-sealed apartment tower to check it out. He finds an embittered drunk with a broken ankle and sends for "medical crewmen" robots to help; the two talk while they wait, and when the crew arrives and takes the man away, the Warden is wiser and more human from the exchange.

In the tale, early robots were built "as street sweepers and industrial workers"; later models are more sophisticated, such as the Wide-Purpose Warden, and they refer to the previous models as "classics."

Comment: Not a prolific author, Carr is best-known for his work as an anthologist.

WIDGET (C)

First Appearance: *Excalibur* #2, 1988, Marvel Comics.

Physical Description: In his natural, ovoid form, Widget is approximately 18 inches in diameter. The robot consists of a toothless mouth, two small "nose slits" above it, and a pair of large white eyes with red pupils. By consuming anything made of metal, Widget can use the digested metal to construct things. Widget can speak, fly—though its means of levitation and propulsion are unknown—and also has the ability to generate magical energies that open doorways into other dimensions. However, only beings who possess magical powers can use the portals.

Biography: Widget was created by the blue, ape-like Tweedledope of the Crazy Gang, a band of other-dimensional criminals. The British-based superheroes known as Excalibur tangle with the Crazy Gang and Widget, though the latter is not malevoient by nature.

Comment: In common usage, a widget, of course, is any small, simple mechanical device, especially one whose name is unfamiliar or cannot be recalled. The word appears to have come about as a contraction of "which gadget."

WINGNUT AND SCREWLOOSE (C)

First Appearance: *Teenage Mutant Ninja Turtles Adventures* #8, 1989, Archie Comics.

Physical Description: Wingnut is a blue-skinned, six-foot-tall humanoid bat with black hair, yellow eyes, purple gloves, and an orange belt. He has four fingers on each hand and two toes on each foot. Because of a birth defect, he has underdeveloped wings and must wear metal wings to fly. Screwloose is a three-foot, two-inch purple-skinned mosquito who wears green gloves.

Biography: For millions of years, the bat- and mosquito-like creatures of the planet Huanu have lived in symbiotic harmony on this world of perpetual red-light night, the latter drinking the blood of the former and serving as companions of sorts. When the evil Krang destroys Huanu, Wingnut and Screwloose take off and have many adventures throughout the galaxy.

Comment: The characters appeared in several issues of *Teenage Mutant Ninja Turtles Adventures* before moving over to *The Mighty Mutanimals* with #1 in 1991.

See also STUMP ASTEROID.

THE WONDERTWINS (TV, C)

First Appearance: *The All-New Superfriends Hour*, September 1977, ABC.

Physical Description: More or less human save for their pointed ears and upswept eyebrows (like all Exorians), the teenagers are shape-shifters, a capability they activate whenever they touch one another, knuckle-to-knuckle, and chant, "Wondertwins' powers, activate!" The can become anything within certain boundaries: Zan is restricted to water (including mist and ice), Jayna to animals ranging from houseflies to mythical monsters. (In the comic book, they have no such restrictions.) The two wear purple bodysuits, Zan with a "Z" on his chest, Jayna with a "J."

Biography: Teenagers from the planet Exor, the twins hop into a spaceship and run away from their unpleasant guardian Dentwil, owner of a carnival. Eluding the Tracer Department, they reach Earth and study under the galaxy's greatest heroes, the Super Friends (Superman, Batman, Robin, the Flash, Wonder Woman, and Aquaman). They are accompanied by their blue monkey-like pet Gleek, who can stretch its tail great distances and once belonged to Illik the Laughmaker at the carnival. The Twins spend a great deal of time in the superheroes's satellite headquarters.

In one of their most daunting missions, the Twins battle fellow Exorians Yeltu and Fegla, evil shape-shifters from the carnival who impersonate Superman and Wonder Woman, among other superheroes.

Comment: The series ran through September 1978. There were 60 episodes, four airing on each hour-long show. The first of these would be a four-minute adventure featuring the Wondertwins in a non-science fiction adventure among ordinary teenagers in trouble. This would be followed by a half-hour adventure featuring the twins and the Super Friends, after which two six-minute adventures (featuring one or two Super Friends only) would air. Michael Bell provided the voices for Zan and Gleek, Louise "Liberty" Williams for Jayna. The series was narrated by actor Ted Knight. The Wondertwins also appeared in *Challenge of the Super Friends* on ABC from September 1978 to September 1979. They were not featured on other Super Friends TV incarnations (see SUPERMAN).

In print, the characters starred in the DC comic book *Super Friends*, which lasted 47 issues from 1976 to 1981.

WOOKIEE See CHEWBACCA.

WORF See DATA; KLINGONS; U.S.S. ENTERPRISE.

X

XANDAR (C)

First Appearance: *Nova* #1, 1976, Marvel Comics.

Physical Description: The planet, apparently larger than Earth and able to support terrestrial-style life, is destroyed early in the chronicles; it is "rebuilt" when four great, inhabited chunks of the planet are connected by great bridges.

Biography: When their world is consumed by the planet-eating GALACTUS, the Luphoms under the warlord Zorr attack Xandar. The war causes the destruction of the planet itself, though with the aid of THE WATCHERS, groups of Xandarians survive on four large segments of the world. Using their advanced technology, the aliens build bridges between the fragments. But peace is short-lived as the new Xandar is attacked by THE SKRULLS, who want the world to become part of their empire. The aliens are defeated with the help of Nova; Earth's superheroes, the Fantastic Four; and a newly-created band of defenders known as the Champions of Zandar, comprised of both Xandarians and Earthmen. Alas, the Champions and all of Xandar are destroyed in one last invasion, this one launched by the super villain Nebula.

The war with Zorr also involved an Earthman, Richard Rider, when he was struck by a beam from space. Taken to a hospital, he is contacted by the Centurion Nova-Prime Rhomann Dey of Xandar, who has suffered a mortal wound fighting Zorr, who is the last surviving Luphomian. Dey transfers his powers of superstrength, superspeed, and flight to Rider, who distracts Zorr while Dey locks onto the warlord and teleports him to his ship in Earth orbit, where they both perish. Assuming the name Nova, Rider battles criminals on Earth and also helps the Xandarians fight the Skrulls. After that war, he remains on the planet to help rebuild the world and then hangs up his blue-and-yellow costume.

Dey's onboard supercomputer is known as Computer Prime. Among Nova's terrestrial foes are the huge Earth-Shaker, a walking iron mole with a drill-head and arms and a rocket-firing chest (#5).

Comment: The world was created by writer Marv Wolfman and artist John Buscema. Nova and the Xandarians starred in 25 issues of Nova's own title, through 1979. The planet was also featured in *Rom*, *The Fantastic Four* and other Marvel titles.

THE XENOMORPHS (MP)

First Appearance: *It Came from Outer Space*, 1953, Universal-International.

Physical Description: In their natural form, the aliens are approximately eight feet tall. They are bulbous and smooth-skinned with a single, large eye in the center and a tangle of stringy, gelatinous limbs. When an alien wants to impersonate a human, it releases a mist that surrounds the person and turns the alien into a copy. In human form, the aliens are pale, have stilted speech, and can look directly into the sun without going blind. They do not eat terrestrial food and leave a silvery trail where they walk.

The alien spaceship is a huge sphere with hexagonal designs all over its surface. The creatures carry wands that can slice through most objects, and there is a large disintegrator beam on their ship.

Nothing is known about the planet from which the aliens hail.

Biography: En route from their world to another, the alien ship crashlands in the desert outside of Sand Rock, Arizona. Setting up a repair shop in the abandoned Excelsior Mines, the creatures abduct seven Earth people and take their places, in order to get the material they need to fix the ship. The townspeople suspect that "Martians" are among them, and amateur astronomer John Putnam knows they're right: He saw their ship crash and took his fiancee Ellen Fields to check it out. To avert disaster, the aliens take Putnam into their confidence; they not only tell him what they happen to be doing here, but also promise that if they're hurt, they will kill their hostages and the rest of the Earth will suffer "things so terrible you have yet to dream of them." When the angry villagers finally head for the mine, Putnam uses dynamite to seal it. The aliens are able to finish their repairs and, true to their word, release their prisoners and leave.

Comment: The film stars Richard Carlson as Putnam and Barbara Rush as Ellen. Jack Arnold directed from a script by noted science fiction author Ray Bradbury and Harry Essex (who received sole credit), based on a screen treatment called "The Meteor" written by Bradbury. In the treatment, the creatures are reptilian and don't shape-change but use mind-control to take charge of humans.

The creatures are never called "Xenomorphs" in the film, although that is what author Bradbury and others call them. It is Greek for "Alien form."

X'LOR (C)

First Appearance: "Strange in a Stranger Land," *1982, Creepy* #135, Warren Publishing Co.

Physical Description: Made of green, "star-forged metal," the circa-15-feet-tall, bipedal robot fires a blistering heat wave from his eyes and has powerful flashlights for hands. It possesses "prodigious strength."

Its master is a giant, spider-like robot quadruped approximately eight feet tall.

Biography: The small fishing village of Terrance Point, Maine, is alarmed one day as a tall robot emerges from the sea, tearing up the town until it finds a boy and his dog. The robot takes them to its spaceship under the bay: Inside, a giant, wounded dog-like (four-legged) robot explains that while mapping Earth, the ship malfunctioned and caused the quadruped serious injury. It sent its "pet" X'Lor out for help, the giant robot naturally assuming that only a four-legged creature would have the intelligence necessary to aid its injured master. The dog cannot help, of course, nor can the boy—and the alien "dog" perishes.

Comment: The story was written by Rich Margopoulos and drawn by Peter Hsu.

A pair of the *XRO robots,* drawn by Royston Evans. © Star Rider Productions.

THE XRO ROBOTS (C)

First Appearance: *Star Rider and the Peace Machine* #1, 1982, Star Rider Productions (Canada).

Physical Description: The vaguely humanoid robots (at least seven in number) stand approximately eight feet tall. They have cylindrical bodies, slightly tapered toward the waist; gumdrop-shaped heads with a T-shaped visor in front; and powerful-looking arms and legs made of metal, pipes, and wires.

Biography: When an armed missile goes off course, the heroic Steel Chameleon—pilot Edward Holman, who wears a metal plate on his scarred face—chases it with his supersonic fighter and literally leaps on the missile, disarming it, before parachuting to safety. Six hundred kilometers away, a nameless megalomaniac with a robotic right hand—a hand he lost in a battle with the Steel Chameleon—complains to a scientist flunky that while this plan has failed, he will lure the Chameleon out some other way and send his XRO "beauties . . . [to] tear him limb from limb!"

Comment: The confrontation never occurred: The characters appeared in the one and only issue of writer/artist Richard Comely's black-and-white comic book.

Y

THE YARNANS (L)

First Appearance: "The Ice World" by Ross Rocklynne, Summer 1946, *Thrilling Wonder Stories*.

Physical Description: The telepathic, bipedal, "reptilian-eyed" amphibious creatures hail from a world "fathomless light-years distant." They have "leaf-green" scales, gills, "powerful arms" with seven-fingered clawed hands, and "crocodile mouths."

The alien ship carries approximately a hundred crewmembers.

Biography: In the future, the sun is dying and only one city, with a thousand inhabitants, remains on glacier-covered Earth. Though the Elders accept the coming extinction of humankind, young Starnik refuses to do so—especially when an alien ship arrives from Yarnan, crash-landing in front of his tractor. The occupants tell the youth that their goal in life is to re-ignite dying suns, to "renovate the universe so that dying races" can be revived. Unfortunately, he says, they have run out of "sorbal, an isotope of uranium," which they need

A *Yarnan*. © Standard Magazines.

to save the sun. Starnik obtains some for them, only to learn that the real reason they're saving Earth is so its ice will melt and they can migrate here from arid, dying Yarnan. Starnik pretends to become an ally of the aliens; once the process of restoring the sun has begun, he slips deadly, radioactive U235 into the pools in which they sleep, killing them.

Comment: Rocklynne (real name, Ross Rocklin) sold his first story, "Man of Iron," to *Astounding Science Fiction* in 1935. He created many unusual civilizations in dozens of space stories. His stories about huge, living space-clouds that move among the stars during their multimillion-year life spans, written from 1940 to 1951, were collected in *The Sun Destroyers* (1973).

THE YARS (VG, C)

First Appearance: *Yars' Revenge*, 1982, Atari.

Physical Description: The Yars are blue-skinned humanoid flies. They have four arms with two fingers on each hand and stand erect on two hind legs. Each has two sets of wings, and they fly through space, unprotected. The Yars "can devour any substance," which, in turn, they can convert "into energy missiles powerful enough to vaporize solid rock."

Biography: Flies are accidentally allowed onto Earth's first interstellar vehicle, loaded along with food. When the ship reaches the Razak solar system, it collides with a radioactive object; the vehicle crashes on one of the worlds and the flies mutate into Yars. Over time, they populate the third, fourth, and fifth planets of the solar system, where they establish orderly and productive civilizations. Although they develop the invincible Zorlon Cannon to defend their worlds, Planet IV is destroyed without warning by the evil beings the Qotile, who are based on a moon circling Planet Epp, farther out in the solar system. Donning silvery armor, the Yars go to war against the Qotile.

Comment: The characters were featured in the videogame for the Atari home videogame system, and in a comic book adventure that was packaged with the game.

THE Y ROBOTS (L)

First Appearance: "The Machine Brain" by David V. Reed, July 1940, *Thrilling Wonder Stories*.

Physical Description: The original Y robots are 15 feet high, weigh half a ton, and have "an eye in each of its three tentacles and in each of its four steel legs." The robots speak, are smarter than humans, and are run by "a broadcast of radio waves which are converted into current." They can be "ripped . . . apart" by magnetic rays or stopped by a blue light that shuts down their "control photo-electric cell."

The Super Y model is "a violet-glowing metal monster" that stands 20 feet high, is five feet across at its broadest point, and has eight tentacles on its trunk. Each tentacle is "thickly studded with large photo-electric cell eyes," which have a "pinkish glare." There's a "colorless glass

Jack Binder's interpretation of a *Y Robot*. © Ziff-Davis Publications.

mound" beneath the tentacles—a ray beam that burns anything it touches—and a "short, hollow nozzle" below that. The robot stands on three "stumpy, massive legs."

The Master Y is violet, "taller and broader" than the rest, with more eyes, has five legs with small wheels, which can be retracted, and has two glass mounds. The K model robot is "tall" and "tread-mounted" with three arms.

The *Southern Star* is a "sleek white" ship that possesses artificial gravity and carries 1,200 passengers.

Biography: The first Y robots are built by the Lenox Physiology Laboratories "to perform simple dissections." But they turn on humans, killing several to examine them—not from hate, but curiosity. The police destroy the rebels and the model Ys all recalled.

As the Interplanetary Luxury Lines flagship *Southern Star* returns to Earth from Exota, word reaches passengers Geoffrey North and George Raleigh of the Department of Science that the model Y robots have escaped the Manufactory in New York and headed into space on stolen ships. But the warning comes too late: The robots snare the ship in a magnetic ray and tug it to a planetoid, where the new model Y robots—Super Ys built by the old models—plan to use the passengers as guinea pigs. North overcomes a menial K model sent to feed them, and programs it to help. The robot, K-71, takes North and Raleigh to the Y warehouse, where they find the Master Y being educated by others. Using an ES Generator to fill himself with static electricity, North touches and shorts one of the robots attending the powerful Master. As the robot aide dies, North is able to program the Master Y to destroy the command center. That done, and all the robots shut down, the ship is able to leave.

Comment: Reed is a pseudonym for David Vern, who sold his first story, "Where Is Roger Davis?," to *Amazing Stories* in May 1939.

Z

THE ZANTIS (TV)

First Appearance: "The Zanti Misfits," December 1963, *The Outer Limits*, ABC-TV.

Physical Description: The six-legged, antlike creatures are approximately six inches long, have two anteannae, and fuzzy dark/light-striped abdomens like flower flies or bumble bees. They have outsized, vaguely human heads with large eyes (humanlike, not compound), mouths with lips and teeth, and somewhat pointed chins. All of the dozens of Zantis appear to have tufts of hair on their heads; some have white muttonchops, others goatees. The Zantis speak in a high, largely expressionless voice; they do not speak English. Their bite is apparently poisonous to humans.

Their silver Penal Ship One is shaped like a pointed gumdrop, approximately five feet tall with a dark tip. It rests on a flat base slightly larger than the base of the gumdrop.

Biography: Because the denizens of Zanti are a "discipline-oriented society" incapable of killing their own kind, the Commander of the Planet persuades Earth to become a "place of exile" for their criminals and misfits—threatening us with destruction if we refuse. Accompanied by guardians of the "same spoiled persuasion," the Zanti misfits land in the California desert, where a quarantined area has been set aside for them. In the nearby ghost town of Morgue, a military unit under General Maximilian R. Hart, along with historian Stephen Grave, monitors the Zantis' arrival from an outpost in a hotel. Meanwhile, robber Ben Garth and his girlfriend Lisa Lawrence crash through a barricade and drive onto the desert. There, Garth spots the landed Zanti ship and goes to investigate. The Zanti First Regent emerges, kills him, and chases Lisa; hopping in a jeep, Grave races to the desert to try and assure the Zantis that the intrusion was unauthorized. Instead, he ends up rescuing Lisa and crushing the alien with a rock.

Grave returns to Morgue and the Zanti ship arrives in town shortly thereafter. The alien hordes attack the soldiers—which, it appears, had always been their plan—and the shooting, stomping, blasting G.I.s are victorious. As Hart frets that the Zanti home world will retaliate, the Commander radios that they never intended to attack the Earth. They knew that we "could not live with such aliens" in our midst and would kill them, since we are "practiced executioners." The remains of the Zantis are burned in a bonfire, the menace ended.

Comment: The episode was written by Joseph Stefano and directed by Leonard Horn. Michael Tolan stars as Grave, Olive Deering is Lisa, Bruce Dern is Garth, and Robert F. Simon is Hart. Robert Johnson and Vic Perrin provided the voices of the Zantis.

ZARZ (C)

First Appearance: *Magnus, Robot Fighter* #1, 1963, Gold Key Comics.

Physical Description: Like his fellow aliens, the light blue-skinned Zarz stands approximately 10 feet tall. The aliens have ribbon-like legs and arms that can be perfectly straight or curl (compensating for the fact that they lack knees and elbows) and a long, rectangular body and football-shaped head, with the "football's" ends on the sides. The aliens have two big black eyes, two fingers on each hand, and wear purple bodysuits with flared shoulders and hems and a purple helmet. As long as the helmet is on, Zarz is able to survive in outer space.

Some of the aliens wear "disinto-jets" on their helmets.

Zarz's spaceship looks like a big red lawn dart.

Biography: Hundreds of years in the future, two years and 3,000 light-years from Earth, Captain Johner and the crew of his silver, blimp-shaped ship met the first alien spaceship ever encountered by humans. Fearful of one another, the crews go to war until Johner bravely shuttles to the alien ship with a "tele-translator." The aliens and the humans make peace, with Zarz and several aliens agreeing to join the Earthship for the voyage to Earth, and four of Johner's crewmembers joining

321

the alien trip to their (unnamed) home world. The humans survive anti-human intrigue on the alien home world and face other dangers, and Zarz does likewise on Johner's ship and on Earth.

The alien planet has a variety of exotic life forms including Dream Makers, creatures that can look like whatever they choose. The illusion is broken only when someone touches them. The Dream Makers "are the secret service agents" of the alien world and are "always camouflaged."

Other aliens include Zarz's second-in-command, Bul, and Ora, who is suspicious of alien races.

Comment: The characters appeared in *Magnus, Robot Fighter* through #28. Two issues of *The Aliens* appeared, one in 1967, another in 1982, reprinting adventures from the earlier comic book. The late, great Russ Manning handled the art on the series.

ZAZZALA (C)

First Appearance: *Justice League of America* #23, 1963, DC Comics.

Physical Description: The humanoid woman wears a leotard with horizontal black and orange stripes and flared shoulders; orange boots (later red) and gloves (later black); and an orange headband (later discarded). She has a pair of diaphanous wings that grow from her body and enable her to fly.

Zazzala possesses a "magno-nuclear rod" that controls bees, stores and releases magnetism, and both compels others to do her bidding or turns them into small, insect-like creatures. She also has bombs capable of destroying entire worlds; the explosives explode or are deactivated solely at her "personal mental command."

Zazzala flies through space in her hive-shaped Hive Ship, which is protected by "anti-discovery devices."

Biography: Born on the planet Korll, Zazzala is queen of a race of humanoids who evolved from insects. Centuries before, Korllian scientist Per Kazz discovered an elixir of immortality. To determine who was the "wisest, healthiest, and strongest person on all Korll," and thus the one most worthy of possessing the elixir, he hid it in three vials on the cloud-covered planet Somalar, with monsters protecting each. Per Kazz perished on the world, as have the Korllian queens who have gone looking for his potion.

But Zazzala—also known as the Queen Bee—has a plan. She comes to Earth and threatens to destroy our world unless the superheroes of the Justice League get the elixir for her. For the heroes, it's a no-win situation: If she gets it, Zazzala plans to conquer the universe. Complying, they deliver the formula to Zazzala, who finds that it has one small drawback; once she takes it, she is paralyzed. Using her magno-nuclear rod, she enslaves the superheroes and sends them to find an antidote. They do, but the diminutive Atom is able to use the rod to paralyze her anew. In time, Zazzala discovers a way to become immortal by using her rod to draw magnetic energy from people, and she remains a formidable force for evil in the universe.

Comment: Over at Harvey Comics, the antennaed, humanoid Queen Bea, would-be conqueror from the Martian moon Deimos, battled the superhero B-Man in *Double-Dare Adventures* in 1967.

ZELDA (TV)

First Appearance: *Terrahawks*, October 1983, syndication.

Physical Description: The android looks like a classical witch, with a long face, pointed chin and pointed nose, and warts on both. She has dark circles around her deepset eyes, and a wild spray of silvery hair on her head.

The silvery Zeroids have cylindrical bodies, no limbs, and spherical heads with white eyes and a horizontal slot for a mouth.

Biography: In 2020, Zelda, the Imperial Queen of the planet Guk, attacks NASA's base on Mars and replaces it with her own headquarters. Her goal: the extermination of the human race. Three years before, having feared such an attack, NASA had turned to Dr. Tiger Ninestein—the ninth clone of Professor Stein—to organize a small, crack international force to defend our world. Called the Terrahawks, the team sets up shop at the Hawknest base in South America and now turns its resources against Zelda, her "younster" Yungstar, her android "sister" Cystar, and Cystar's son Itstar.

The other Terrahawks are the brilliant Lt. Hiro, who creates their Computer Command Center and flies the Spacehawk; Captain Mary Falconer, pilot of their spaceship Battlehawk; Captain Kate Kestrel and Lt. Hawkeye—a pilot with microcomputer-assisted eyes—who fly the Hawkwing fighter; and Zeroids Sergeant Major Zero and Space Sergeant 101, a pair of alien robots.

Among the aliens encountered by both sides during their long struggle are Moid (the Master of Infinite Disguise), the evil Lord Sram, Yuri the Space Bear, Tamura the Space Samurai, Sporilla the giant gorilla, the Space Cyclops, and others.

Comment: Zelda's voice was provided by Denise Bryer. Bryer was also the voice of Mary, Windsor Davies was Zero, Ben Stevens was Hudson, 101, and Yungstar, Jeremy Hitcher was Ninestein, Johnson, and Hiro, and Anne Ridler was Cystar and Kestrel. The pilot was written by creator/producer Gerry Anderson; all but one other show were written by Tony Barwick using a variety of "Stein"-clone pseudonyms, including Frank Instein and Sue Donymstein.

The series replaced producer Gerry Anderson's Supermarionation (see SUPERCAR) with Supermacromation, a form of puppetry in which the figures were operated from below with hands and rods, like more realistic Muppets. There were 39 half-hour episodes; the series ran through July 1986 in England. It debuted in syndication in the United States concurrently, but lasted only 13 weeks.

ZEN (C)

First Appearance: Zen Intergalactic Ninja #1, 1987, Entity Comics.
Physical Description: Standing approximately five feet tall, the blue-skinned, bare-chested humanoid Zen wears black tights and orange sandals, laced nearly to the knee. He has a silver Z belt-buckle. Zen has four fingers on each hand, two black eyes, and no nose, mouth, ears, or hair. The alien communicates telepathically and carries on his back a wooden staff for fighting.

In his original, black-and-white comic books, Zen is extremely muscular. In the Archie Comics, he is a more slender figure.
Biography: On the planet Baltoon, in the Rigel System, the blue-skinned natives perform genetic experiments "designed to produce a superior being." The resultant creatures are considered failures, but the compassionate female Teslah simply cannot destroy another living being. Instead, she launches the latest failure into space in a T-pod (transport pod). After traversing "numberless galaxies," the space sphere lands in a marsh on the planet Om, near a community of "ancient masters." The mysterious humanoids teach Zen meditation and martial arts; grown to young adulthood, he sets out in a spaceship to roam the worlds, hiring himself out as a mercenary. He is eventually employed by the tall, green-skinned, humanoid Gordons to go to Earth and protect a human teenager, Jeremy Baker, who has been appointed the wielder of an ancient, alien geocrystal that enables him to harness the planet's "eco-power" and protect the environment from the evil Lord Contaminous and his minions.

By using the "recyclotron" on Zen's spaceship, Zen and Jeremy transform shovelfuls of recyclables into five superheroic aides: the robotic Can-It, the grassy Lawnranger, the stealthy flying Lights Out, the massive Pulp, and the diamondlike Bandit.
Comment: The character was created by Steve Stern and Dan Cote. In addition to the ongoing comic book, Entity also published the one-issue *Zen Intergalactic Ninja Christmas Special* in 1992 and two miniseries in 1993–94: *Zen Intergalactic Ninja: The Hunted* and *Young Zen.*

In 1992, Archie Comics published a three-issue "children's" version of the title, *Defend the Earth,* with new stories, followed by a regularly published comic book also called *Zen Intergalactic Ninja.*

THE ZENGS (L)

First Appearance: "Top Secret" by Eric Frank Russell, August 1956, *Astounding Science Fiction.*
Physical Description: Apparently humanoid, the Zengs are described only as having "long, skinny arms." They are able to speak just as humans do.
Biography: When the Earth empire places 20,000 settlers on the planet Motan, the peaceful Zengs settle two worlds in the same system, Korima and Koroma. The blustery, inept human military worries about the potential for hostilities, and makes plans to destroy Zeng beam (communications) stations in the event of war. A top-secret message is radioed to Centauri, an Earth staging post: "In event of hostile action in your sector the war must be fought to outstretch and rive all enemy's chief lines of communications."

The message they receive is: "An event of hospitality your section the foremost when forty-two ostriches arrive on any cheap line of communication." Plans are put into motion to get ostriches to Motan, and the Motanese radio to ask why. The answer they receive: "Will amuse you." In fact, however, the message that had been sent was, "Will emus do?"

As it happens, the worrying was for naught. The Zeng emissary Tormin arrives on Motan and explains that prisoners on Koroma included a number of convicts, who have rebelled. A message is sent from Motan to the Earth military: "Civil war is taking place among local Zengs. They are asking for assistance." But the message the military receives is, "Sibyl Ward is making faces among local Zengs. They are asking for her sister." Alas, no help is sent, and the military decides that the settlers of Motan have gone mad.

Comment: Russell, a British author, sold his first story to *Astounding* in 1937. Among his works is a series of stories written from 1941 to 1943 about the humanlike robot Jay Score; these were collected in the book *Men, Martians and Machines* (1956).

THE Z-15 (L)

First Appearance: "Coffin of Life and Death" by Robert Wade, April 1948, *Fantastic Adventures*.

Physical Description: The rocket is not described, though it has a genie-screen for video communication and special instruments for navigating the asteroid belt.

Biography: Trumble, Inc. of Earth, robot manufacturers, sponsors a contest to create a robot that will obey every command and never fail. Scientist Peter Shad of Mars intends to win first prize, $15 million, and hires pilot Blake Wallace to bring him to Earth. Shad also entrusts Blake with the Martian words that operate the robot—which Blake presumes is in a coffin they're carrying—since Shad is dying. As it happens, Shad dies in the office of James Drake Trumble moments after ordering the confused Blake to recite the words. Incredibly, Shad's corpse responds to the commands. Gruesome as the display is, Trumble has to admit it fits the criteria, even though Shad isn't a robot, and he pays up. Trumble is glad to do so, however, as Shad's will stipulates that the money be used to further his research into finding a cure for a Martian form of catalepsy. Inside the coffin is his granddaughter Gloria Williams, who is the first one to be cured.

The Martian words provided in the story are:
rela: forward
steepa: stand up
twan: stop

Comment: This was the first story of little-known author Wade. That same issue featured Lee Francis's story "Flight Into Fog," an adventure set on Monoon, the "forgotten" moon of Mars; and G.H. Irwin's "Lair of the Grimalkin," pitting Earthmen against Venusians on the second planet in the year 2020.

ZODY (C)

First Appearance: *Zody the Mod Rob*, 1970, Gold Key Comics.

Physical Description: Zody is about six feet tall and made of green metal. It has round grids for eyes, no nose, and a big lower jaw. Its chest is a cylinder, its neck is a thin pipe, and its legs jut from a sphere attached to the chest by a tube as thin as the neck. Its arms are jointed at the elbows, its legs at the knees, and it has five fingers on each hand. Its feet are toeless plates. An inverted gray bowl with two antennae sits on its head and gives the "tin head . . . an eight-hundred I.Q."

Biography: Young Randy of the Tinker High *Times* goes to interview Professor Ipsof Acto. Acto has proved "the existence of astrological energy waves," and anyone who wears his specially-designed helmet will receive them—and become a super-scientific genius also able to see into the near future. Randy dons the helmet, builds Zody at his high school, and leaves the helmet on the robot overnight. Zody comes to life as a hippie because it's a "tuned-in . . . Aquarian"; to help him blend in, Randy outfits the automaton with a red poncho, beads, and a mop-head for hair. Zody becomes a reporter, teaches dance, and finds a bomb in the school.

Comment: There was only one *Zody the Mod Rob* comic book; its contrived and belated hipness has made it something of a cult favorite.

ZOGG   See OGG.

ZUNAR 5J/90 DORIC 4-7   (MP, C)

First Appearance: *The Cat From Outer Space*, 1978, Walt Disney Productions.

Physical Description: The telepathic cat looks exactly like a terrestrial cat; thanks to his high-tech collar, he has the ability to levitate objects and stop time.

The cat's ship is a gumdrop-shaped vessel that vaguely resembles a cat's head. It has four stubble landing struts and is approximately 10 feet tall.

Biography: When his spaceship breaks down, Zunar 5J/90 Doric 4-7 lands on Earth. In order to make his rendezvous with the mothership, the cat must replenish his ship's power source with six cubits of Org-12—$120,000 worth of gold—within 36 hours or be stranded here forever. The ship is found by NASA and taken to the Energy Research Lab, and while kindly Earth physicist Dr. Frank Wilson, his girlfriend Dr. Liz Bartlett, and their friend Link try to help the cat, whom they nickname Jake. General Stilton tries to find the invader. Meanwhile, the evil millionaire Olympus and his henchman Stallwood also search for the cat

Zunar 5J/90 Doric 4–7, better known as "Jake," in *The Cat From Outer Space.* © Walt Disney Productions.

to try and obtain its collar. Ultimately, the bad guys kidnap Liz and her cat Lucy Belle, with whom Jake has fallen in love. In order to save them, Jake must choose between making his rendezvous and remaining on Earth. He opts for the latter, saving the ladies and being made a U.S. citizen.

Comment: Jake was played by the Abyssinians Rumpler and his sister Amber, and Spot played Lucy Belle. Ken Berry stars as Frank, Sandy Duncan is Liz, MacLean Stevenson is Link, Harry Morgan is Stilton, William Prince is Olympus, and

Roddy McDowall is Stallwood. The film was directed by Norman Tokar from a script by cartoonist Ted Key (*Hazel*).

The film was adapted in comic book form in *Walt Disney Showcase* #46, 1978.

ZUR (L)

First Appearance: "A Gift from Earth" by Manly Banister, August 1955, *Galaxy Science Fiction*.

Physical Description: Located "sixty-odd light years" from Earth, Zur is a world extremely poor in metals but wealthy in clay. The Earthlike planet is inhabited by humanoids who are capable of breeding with humans.

Biography: Travelers from Earth come to medieval Zur, upsetting the rich pottery merchants by introducing cheap, metal pots and pans, then setting up telephone lines, constructing oil pipelines, introducing automobiles, and making other changes to which most Zurians quickly become very accustomed. Desperate, the members of the family-run Pottery of Masur business complain to the Earth-run Merchandising Council, set up to help native companies hurt by Earth's activities. The Council gives the Masurs a loan, with interest, which the aliens can't repay—just as the government and military can't repay *their* loans. The Zurians realize too late that they have been conquered by a means that is "better—and more sure—than war and invasion by force."

Comment: Banister, who wrote sporadically for the science fiction pulp magazines, published only one novel, *Conquest of Earth* (1957), in which humankind battles the extraterrestrial Trisz.

APPENDIX A: COMIC BOOK ALIENS

The following is a selection of unusual extraterrestrials from Marvel, DC Comics, and EC Comics. Issue number denotes first appearance.

Aakon Yellow humanoids from the planet Oorga, second world from Mira in the Milky Way, in Marvel Comics' *Captain Marvel* #8, 1968.

A'askvarii Green humanoids, with six squid-like arms, from O'erlanii, third world from the star Deneb in Marvel's *Black Goliath* #5, 1976.

Acanti Two-mile-long fishlike beings in Marvel's *X-Men* #156, 1982.

Achernonians Purple humanoids from Achernon, fourth world from Alpha Unakalhai, in Marvel's *Thor Annual* #6, 1977.

A-Chiltarians Furry purple humanoids from A-Chiltar III in Marvel's *Tales to Astonish* #46, 1963.

Alexander K. Gator The alien alligator-like parasite who poses as a hand puppet and takes over humans in EC's *Weird Science* #16, 1952.

Alpha Centaurians Purple, scaly humanoids from Arima, third planet from Alpha Centauri A in the Milky Way in Marvel's *Sub-Mariner* #17, 1969.

Amphibions Amphibious beings from Xantares in Marvel's *Tales to Astonish* #73, 1965.

Arcturans Humans from Arcturus IV in Marvel's *Fear* #23, 1974.

Astrans Golden humanoids from Astra, second world of Mu Cephi in the Milky Way, in Marvel's *The Incredible Hulk* #6, 1963.

Autocrons Iron-based, blue-skinned humanoids from Cron, sixth planet of Betelgeuse, in Marvel's *Machine Man* #3, 1978.

Axi-Tuns Humanoids from the planet Tun, orbiting S'vihn-Hoont in the Ring Nebula M-57 in Marvel's *Invaders* #1, 1975.

Ba-Bani Yellow-skinned humanoids from the planet Ba-Banis in the Milky Way, in Marvel's *The Avengers* #219, 1983.

Bamunoans Roughly three-foot-tall scientifically advanced humans on Earth's twin world, orbiting the sun on the opposite side, in EC's *Weird Fantasy* #7, 1951.

Betans Purple-skinned, bat-winged humanoids from Beta, orbiting the star Mirpet in the Milky Way in Marvel's *Godzilla* #12, 1979.

Bfan See GLUN.

Brah See HVAH.

Brx See LTH.

Bwhalli See INTALLA.

Captain Krydd A humanoid space villain with red skin and three-clawed hands in DC's *Adventure Comics* #471, 1980.

Centurii Yellow-skinned humanoids from Centuri-Six, orbiting Proxima Centauri in the Milky Way in Marvel's *Thor* #258, 1977.

Chznonz and Tmnop Giant roach-like aliens who find Earthlings in their salad in EC's *Weird Fantasy* #15, 1952.

Ciegrimites Tortoise-like bipeds from Ciegrim-7 ("The Distiller's Planet") circling Omacron in Andromeda in Marvel's *Hercules*, Vol. 1, #4, 1982.

Clavians Humanoids from Clavius, orbiting Clyph in the Milky Way in Marvel's *Rom* #71, 1976.

Contraxians Humanoids who are half pink-skinned, half brown-skinned (left and right), hailing from Contraxia, which circles Elidra in the Milky Way in Marvel's *Jack of Hearts* #1, 1984.

Courga Light brown-skinned humanoid canines of Courg, circling Bledsoe in the Milky Way in Marvel's *Marvel Presents* #5, 1976.

Craniac and Zarno White-skinned humanoid space criminals from Saturn's moon Rhea in DC's *Mystery in Space* #106, 1966.

Cxargx and Zlafg Fishlike bipeds from a water world in EC's *Weird Science-Fantasy* #23, 1954.

Czuk and Trark Doglike bipeds on an unnamed planetoid in EC's *Weird Fantasy* #16, 1952.

Dakkamites Humanoids from Dakkam, circling Beta Rigel in the Milky Way in Marvel's *Silver Surfer* #6, 1969.

Darbians Hulking, pink-skinned humanoids from Darbia in Marvel's *Fantastic Four* #298, 1987.

Deonists White-skinned humanoids from Deo, orbiting Denebola in the Milky Way in Marvel's *Thor* #261, 1977.

Dr. Xol Debbio A blue-white-skinned, bald humanoid scientist in DC's *Mystery in Space* #108, 1966.

Druffs Small, puffy-pink humanoids, natives of Ryas, circling Psori in Andromeda in Marvel's *Fantastic Four* #37, 1965.

The Duplorians An aggressive humanoid race ruled by Torr the Terrible; all denizens of Duplor look identical due to "an accident of evolution" in DC's *Superman* #178, 1965.

Elan Green, 10-foot-tall, frog-like humanoids with slender limbs; they dwell on Elanis, orbiting the Milky Way's Beta Scorpi in *Fantastic Four* #21, 1963.

Entemen Entem, circling Donatut in the Milky Way, is home to leopard-like bipeds with tentacles for arms and legs in Marvel's *Marvel Presents* #5, 1976.

Ergons Powerful, red-skinned humanoids who dwell on Ergonar, orbiting M. Canum Venaticorum in the Milky Way in *Thor* #259, 1977.

Flb'Dbi These brown-furred quadrupeds have two tentacle-arms, a dark brown tail, and a round head ringed with dark brown fur, red eyes, and two tendrils on either side of the mouth. They are natives of Jhb'Btt, orbiting Beta Lyrae in the Milky Way in *Fantastic Four* #221, 1979.

Fomalhauti The denizens of Pumor, circling Fomalhaut in the Milky Way, resemble sunnyside-up eggs, with a single eye in the center, in Marvel's *Thor* #258, 1977.

Fonabi Obese, round-bodied, 16-plus-foot-tall humanoids with extremely slender legs and arms and a big head, in Marvel's *Fantastic Four* #269, 1984.

Froma The denizens of Chize, circling Delee in the Milky Way, are tall, green-skin humanoids who can levitate in Marvel's *Tales of Suspense* #68, 1965.

The Galactosaur A giant orange-skinned snake with tiny arms, the "mineral-eating space beast" lives in deep space in DC's *Superboy* #213, 1975.

Gegku Brown-green, reptilian humanoids from Wilamean, circling Gabansaa in Andromeda in Marvel's *Hercules*, Vol. 1, #2, 1982.

The Girafon An alien with an elephantine body, giraffe-like skin, a beaked mouth, and a horn on its head; it attacks a cargo ship and releases the captive, bull-sized, sheepdog-like Sheepies in DC's *Tales of the Unexpected* #53, 1960.

Glun and Bfan Praying mantis–like aliens who spearhead an invasion of Chdnar (Earth) in EC's *Weird Science* #13, 1952.

Glx Tall, yellow humanoids with extremely flat heads, natives of Glxx orbiting Zpist in the Milky Way in *The Incredible Hulk* #182, 1975.

Gramosians Blue-black humanoids from the planet Gramos in the Milky Way in Marvel's *Thor* #208, 1973.

The Green Glowers A race of hairless, noseless, three-fingered humanoids at war with the similar Red Glowers in DC's *Tales of the Unexpected* #99, 1967.

Groster and Klobe Circa 15-foot-tall, blue-skinned, three-fingered, humanoid Jovians with a long, thin head and antennae instead of ears, in DC's *Strange Adventures* #108, 1959.

Grunds Tiny, yellow-skinned, cherubic, antennaed humanoids from Grundar, circling Quat in the Milky Way in Marvel's *Giant-Size Defenders* #3, 1975.

Guna Frog-like humanoids with three clawed toes, natives of Gunava, circling Janoth in Andromeda in Marvel's *Tales of Suspense* #55, 1964.

Herms Light-orange humanoids with brown spots, two-clawed feet, fishlike heads and bodies, four-fingered hands, and wisps of fins on their arms, back, and head; the Andromeda natives appeared in Marvel's *The Incredible Hulk* #136, 1971.

Hibers Humanoids from Hiberlack, orbiting Hunyock in the Milky Way in Marvel's *Rom* #67, 1985.

Horusians Brown- or yellow-skinned humanoids from Horus IV in the Milky Way in Marvel's *The Incredible Hulk* #145, 1973.

Hujah Serpent-like denizens of Hug, orbiting Zuccone in the Milky Way in Marvel's *Avengers Annual* #7, 1977.

Hvah, Brah and Zkoh Spacefaring aliens with a ratlike body, face like a blowfish, mohawk stretch of hair from head to tail, and two large antennae, in EC's *Weird Fantasy* #17, 1951.

Hydra-File A one-horned dinosaur-like quadruped on the planet Rullah in EC's *Weird Fantasy* #8, 1951.

Intalla and Bwhalli Frog-faced, orange-skinned, circa 20-foot-tall aliens in DC's *Tales of the Unexpected* #20, 1957.

Interdites Blue-skinned humanoids with pointed ears, denizens of Interdis circling Tartaru in the Milky Way in Marvel's *Warlock* #15, 1976.

Jovian Water Blaster A purple-feathered, yellow-beaked bird with a yellow sack under its bill, the bird releases high-pressure streams of water in DC's *Mystery in Space* #103, 1965.

Judans Brown, four-armed heads with legs who stand 12 feet tall and live on Dyofor, orbiting Palyn in the Milky Way in Marvel's *Strange Tales* #180, 1975.

Kallusians Pointy-eared humanoids from Kallu, in orbit around Andromeda's Kallu-Kan in Marvel's *Avengers* #14, 1965.

Kamado These hulking humanoids dwell on Mikkaz, circling Dopner in the Milky Way in Marvel's *Defenders* #125, 1983.

Kawa Ten-foot-tall, ant-like bipeds with two arms, the Kawa dwell on an eponymous planet circling Bawa Kawa in Andromeda in Marvel's *Hercules*, Vol. 1, #3, 1982.

Klklk The blue, cockroach/iguana hybrids are eight feet long and dwell in La'kil, circling Ti'bik in the Milky Way in Marvel's *The Incredible Hulk* #259, 1981.

Klobe See GROSTER.

Knogs Humanoids with two large arms, six smaller ones, four legs, a tail, and a slug-like head, the Knogs keep humans as pets in EC's *Weird Science* #12, 1952.

Kodabaks The porcine, bug-eyed humanoids dwell on Kodaba, circling Grosgumbique in the Milky Way in Marvel's *Marvel Two-in-One Annual* #2, 1980.

Korbinites Golden-skin, noseless humanoids, the Korbinites dwell on Korbin in the Burning Galaxy in Marvel's *Thor* #337, 1985.

Kosmosians Reptilian, with a vaguely human face, the 50-foot-long denizens of Kosmos, orbiting Zokka in the Milky Way, appeared in Marvel's *Tales to Astonish* #44, 1963.

Kronans The stony, silicon-based, orange-skinned humanoids dwell on Ria, orbiting Krona in the Milky Way in Marvel's *Journey into Mystery* #83, 1962.

Kronons Warlike beings who invade the planet Rur in *Bill Black's Fun Comics* #4, from Americomics in 1983.

Krylorians Slender humanoids with three fingers on each hand and two toes on each foot, the Krylorians dwell on Krylor, orbiting Andromeda's Aceta in Marvel's *Rampaging Hulk* #1, 1977.

Kt'kn The tiny, spiderlike golden globes dwell on Kn'kn, which circles Tk'kn in the Milky Way in Marvel's *Astonishing Tales* #2, 1970.

Kymellians Slender, horse-headed, peaceful bipeds with highly advanced technology, in Marvel's *Power Pack* #16, 1986.

Landlaks These humanoids are covered with white spots and live on Birj, a moon of Marman in the Milky Way in Marvel's *Fantastic Four* #211, 1979.

Laxidazians The denizens of Laxidazia, orbiting Dolenz, are short, elfin humanoids, in Marvel's *Strange Tales* #179, 1975.

Lem Red-skinned, the Lem have human torsos, serpentine bodies, and long heads—with just eyes and large, fanlike ears. These denizes of Lemista, circling Atianti in the Milky Way, appear in Marvel's *Shogun Warriors* #19, 1980.

Levians The blue-skinned humanoids dwell on Levia, circling Nelweni in the Milky Way in Marvel's *Thor* #256, 1988.

L'on A roughly 10-foot-tall, blue-skinned alien with yellow cat-eyes, pointed ears, and three fingers, searching for his friend Vaar—a circa four-foot-tall, orange, two-tentacled alien, in DC's *Tales of the Unexpected* #84, 1964.

Lth and Brx Each alien is a human-sized "protoplasmic mass" with four pseudopods and a single eye above a gaping mouth, in EC's *Incredible Science Fiction* #30, 1955.

Lumina The humanoids dwell on Lumin, orbiting Sh'Mengi (a tribute to SCTV) in the Milky Way in Marvel's *Shogun Warriors* #1, 1979.

Makluans The huge dragons dwell on Maklu-IV in the Milky Way in Marvel's *Tales of Suspense* #6, 1959.

Mandos The nine-foot-tall green humanoids, with monstrous teeth, dwell on Mand, orbiting Tumbla in Andromeda in Marvel's *Warlock* #15.

Marvanites Green-skinned, 40-foot-tall, dome-headed humanoids on Marvan, orbiting Manwolf in Marvel's *Marvel Two-in-One Annual* #3.

Megans Red-skinned, big-handed, big-eared cyclopeans from Mega, which orbits Mirpet in the Milky Way in Marvel's *Godzilla* #12.

Mekkans Blue-skinned humanoid robots of Mekka (renamed from Maarin, its name under humanoids killed by a virus), circling Kirthom in the Milky Way in Marvel's *Fantastic Four* #91, 1969.

The Meteor Monster A small, crab-like alien with a skull-like human face and hypnotic powers, in EC's *Weird Science* #13, 1950.

M'Ndavians Yellow-skinned humanoids with diamond-shaped heads, inhabitants of the planet M'Ndavi, orbiting B'Ibwo in the Shi'ar Galaxy in Marvel's *Fantastic Four* #262, 1984.

Mn'torr A green-skinned, red-eyed space prophet in DC's *Adventure Comics* #470, 1980.

Mobians Orange-skinned humanoids of Mobius, orbiting Lemivell in Andromeda in Marvel's *The Incredible Hulk* #136, 1971.

Moko A diminutive, hairless, monkey-like, antennaed, bug-eyed denizen of Rullah, in EC's *Weird Fantasy* #8, 1951.

Morani Brutish, green-skinned humanoids of Moran, orbiting Andromeda's Jark in Marvel's *Tales of Suspense* #58, 1964.

Mun Zeerohs A humanoid Martian, approximately seven feet tall, with an oversized head, slender body, two spindly arms, and two tentacles behind them, in EC's *Weird Science-Fantasy* #24, 1954.

Myndai Humanoids of Mynda in the Milky Way in Marvel's *Shogun Warriors* #1.

Nanda Green-skinned humanoids with wide, oval heads. They dwell on Nanda, orbiting Particulus in the Milky Way in Marvel's *Shogun Warriors* #19.

Nymenians Wolf-headed, purple-skinned humanoids with three fingers on each hand and two toes on each foot. They inhabit Eomuma, circling Myunimo in Andromeda in Marvel's *Hercules*, Vol. 1, #1, 1982.

The Ollans Huge green-skinned humanoids at war with the (unseen) Lankmars, in DC's *Strange Adventures* #134, 1961.

Ovoids Yellow-skinned, eight-foot-tall humanoids with large egg-shaped heads. They live on Birkeel, circling the Milky Way's Janstak in Marvel's *Fantastic Four* #10, 1963.

Pegasusians The denizens of Lar, circling Stinlar in the Milky Way, are green-skinned humanoids with reptilian heads, bug eyes, and pointed ears, in Marvel's *Strange Tales* #178, 1975.

Phantoms Humanoids who inhabit Phantus, circling Phalbo in the Milky Way in Marvel's *Avengers* #2, 1963.

Pheragots Brutish blue-skinned humanoids with a wide ridge of bone over the eyes. They dwell on Arago-7 in Andromeda in Marvel's *Hercules*, Vol. 1, #1, 1982.

Plodex Blob-like yellow creatures in Marvel's *Alpha Flight* #1.

The Probers Four-eyed alien quadrupeds with two arms, hairy, bloblike bodies, and a mass of tendrils on their heads and chests, in EC's *Weird Science* #8, 1951.

Procyonites Human-sized, stegosaur-like bipeds of Perratin, circling Procyon in the Milky Way in Marvel's *Thor Annual* #6, 1977.

Queega Green-skinned, reptilian bipeds who can generate defensive electrical charges; natives of Queeg, circling Quolan in Andromeda in Marvel's *Daredevil* #28.

Quists Humanoids of Quistalium, circling Uistraa in the Milky Way in Marvel's *X-Men* #20.

Quons Brown-skinned amphibious humanoids from Quon, orbiting Byjak in the Milky Way in Marvel's *Fantastic Four* #97, 1970.

Rajaks Burly, blue-green-skinned humanoids of Rajak, in Marvel's *Tales of Suspense* #57, 1964.

Reptoids (1) Bipedal reptiles of the playet Tayp, circling Kormuk in the Milky Way in Marvel's *Thor Annual* #6, 1977.

Reptoids (2) Bipedal, human-sized, tyrannosaur-like aliens who defend their planet Renak against a horde of skeletal, white-skinned humanoid aliens, in DC's *Mystery in Space* #112, 1980.

Rhunians Three-hundred-foot-tall, pointy-eared humanoids with arched brows who dwell in Rhun, a planet of Vulliger, in Marvel's *Thor* #219, 1974.

Rigellians Yellow-skinned humanoids from Rigel-3, founders of a sprawling intergalactic empire, in Marvel's *Thor* #129, 1966.

R'malk'i Asparagus-like creatures with arms and a half-dozen short, rootlike legs. The human-sized denizens of R'malk'i, orbiting C'lehr'ee in the Milky Way, appear in Marvel's *Warlock* #15, 1976.

Roclites Reddish-brown humanoids with white eyes and ferocious teeth. They dwell on Rocklon, circling the Milky Way's Tarl in Marvel's *Iron Man* #55, 1973.

R'zahnians These inhabitants of R'zahn, orbiting Lahj'kk in the Milky Way, have red skin, no hair, and pug-like faces, in Marvel's *Weird Wonder Tales* #20, 1977.

Sagittarians Gray-skinned humanoids, these natives of Berhert orbiting Rempit in the Milky Way debuted in Marvel's *The Incredible Hulk* #111, 1968.

Sarks Blue-skinned humanoids of Sarka, circling Tilnast in the Milky Way in Marvel's *Strange Tales* #179, 1975.

Saurids Green-skinned, nine-foot-tall amphibious humanoids with three claws on each foot, one of which is in back. The reptile-faced natives of Timor, circling Varanus in the Shi'ar galaxy, debuted in Marvel's *X-Men* #107, 1976.

Shi'ar Highly advanced humanoids who originated on a planet called the Aerie and have created a galactic empire, in Marvel's *X-Men* #97, 1976.

Sidri The creatures possess six slender limbs and a single eye in the center of their flat, triangular-shaped bodies. They evolved in deep space and first appeared in Marvel's *X-Men* #154, 1982.

Sirians Humanoids from Sirius III and IV in the Milky Way, they debuted in Marvel's *Avengers* #36, 1967.

Siris These green octopi (albeit, with nine tentacles) have five-fingered hands on two of their arms. They originated on Yomot, circling Sirius in the Milky Way in Marvel's *X-Men* #37, 1967.

Sirusites The humanoid natives of Sirus X, circling Al'Ma'an in the Milky Way, debuted in Marvel's *Strange Tales* #179, 1975.

The Skrann The blue-skinned, three-fingered humanoids with big eyes, saucer-shaped ears, and balloon-like heads—with the balloon neck for a mouth—appear in DC's *Mystery in Space* #67, 1961.

Sligs The six-foot-long, spider-like creatures have eight thick, tentacular limbs, the front two of which can be used for grasping; two antennae; and a carapace. The denizens of Ryneb's planet—Ankara—in the Milky Way debuted in Marvel's *Fantastic Four* #209, 1978.

Smellies Green, blobby aliens surrounded by long tentacles and topped by two eyestalks with orange eyes; each is "like a sponge coated with slime," in DC's *Time Warp* #1, 1979.

Sm'ggani Humanoid, with orange skin, a brown shell on the chest and pelvis, three toes on each foot, and a frog-like face with eyes on stalks, these natives of M'ggani, circling T'letio in the Milky

Way, debuted in Marvel's *The Incredible Hulk* #230, 1978.

Sneepers Green-skinned, macrocephalic humanoids, the Sneepers dwell on Sneep, orbiting the Milky Way's Snuup in Marvel's *Tales of Suspense* #49, 1964.

The Solarites Beings who live inside the sun, in Coresun, beneath a thick wall of lead. Young Davos and his android aide Arman fight crime on Earth in the short-lived 1979 comic book *Solarman,* from Pendulum Press.

Solons Blue-skinned humanoids with pointed ears and a diamond-shaped orange patch around each eye, the Solons live on an eponymous world circling Nardea in the Milky Way in Marvel's *Fantastic Four* #237, 1981.

Sssth The eight-foot-tall, green-skinned reptilian humanoids have three clawed toes on each foot, a long tail, and a shock of red hair on their heads. They live on Sslirteep's second world, Sszardil, in the Milky Way in Marvel's *Thor* #212, 1973.

Stenth Yellow-skinned, hairless, pointy-eared humanoids from Stent, orbiting Duggil in the Milky Way in Marvel's *The Inhumans* #7, 1976.

Stonians Inhabitants of Stonus I through V, the hairless, horned, goatlike humanoids debuted in Marvel's *Astonishing Tales* #21, 1973.

Technarchy The metallic, robotic, gangly armed humanoids feed on energy. They hail from an unknown world, in Marvel's *New Mutants* #18, 1984.

Tektons Purple-furred humanoids, the savage Tektons hail from Tekton, orbiting Tacuspar in Andromeda in Marvel's *Fantastic Four* #91, 1969.

Thantos A circa-eight-foot-tall humanoid with red skin, three eyes, and a cone-shaped head; able to split into three identical beings, in DC's *House of Mystery* #168, 1967.

Thurans Tiny, green-skinned scientists of the planet Thura, in DC's *Superman* #102, 1956.

Thuvrians The big-headed, hairless humanoids dwell on Lomyra's planet—Thuvria—in the Milky Way, in Marvel's *Rom* #19, 1981.

Tmnop See CHZNONZ.

Trark See CZUK.

Tribbitites Troll-like, orange-skinned humanoids, the Tribbitites have goatlike legs with two toes on each foot. They evolved on Kroke, orbiting Ouin in the Milky Way, then moved to Tribbit, a.k.a. Toadworld. From Marvel's *Rampaging Hulk* #2, 1977.

Tribunals Ghostly energy beings from an unknown world, the Tribunals can take any form, manipulate energy, and move through time. They debuted in Marvel's *Defenders* #124, 1983.

Tsiln A lumpy, oranged-skinned race, the humanoid Tsiln have large, three-toed feet, long tails, pointy ears, and sharp teeth. They dwell on Broi, circling Wyllys in the Milky Way in Marvel's *The Amazing Spider-Man* #103, 1971.

Tsyrani Humanoids with great physical strength, they hail from the planet Tsorcherhi, orbiting Elia in the Shi'ar Galaxy in Marvel's *Spider-Woman* #36, 1982.

The Ullan When an Ullan, a Larooite, a Tragoite, and a Raaganian inadvertently attack the human space pilot Ace Arn at the same time, they give him their combined powers in the "Ultra the Multi-Alien" strip, which ran in DC's *Mystery in Space* beginning with #103.

Ul'lulans Six-tentacled, eellike giants of the planet Ul'lula, circling Ul in the Milky Way in Marvel's *Defenders* #13, 1974.

Vaggo Xat The wrinkled, red-skinned Martian exiled to Earth (and receiving mail from Mars via the U.S. Postal Service) in DC's *Strange Adventures* #42, 1954.

Vch-Nazzarites Purple-scaled humanoids with three-fingered hands and fishlike faces, in DC's *Mystery in Space* #117, 1981.

Vegans The horned humanoids stand approximately 30 feet tall and dwell on Vega Superior, orbiting Vega in the Milky Way. They debuted in Marvel's *Tales to Astonish* #58, 1964.

Vipswarzznee The circa-15-foot-tall god of an alien world has a body like a rotted tomato, with seven green tentacles on its head, a mouth filled with wormlike tendrils, two long arms, and two stumpy feet, in DC's *Time Warp* #2, 1980.

Vorms Red, dragon-like creatures over 16 feet long, these inhabitants of Vormir, orbiting Helgentar in the Greater Magellanic Cloud, debuted in Marvel's *Avengers* #123, 1974.

Vradv and Xnortk Circa-eight-foot-tall cricket-like bipeds who plan to lead an invasion of Earth, in EC's *Weird Science* #14, 1952.

Vrellnexians Purple-furred, six-limbed, ant-like creatures, these aliens live on Vrelinex, circling Cetsin in the Milky Way in Marvel's *Thor* #212, 1973.

Wilameanis These Earthlike humanoids dwell on Wilamean, orbiting Andromeda's Yalnot in Marvel's *Hercules,* Vol. 1, #2, 1982.

Wobbs Purple-skinned telepathic bipeds, the Wobbs have pug-like faces circled with blue hair, two-toed feet, and two antennae. They dwell on Wobb-Lar, circling the star Filipima in Andromeda in Marvel's *The Incredible Hulk* #137, 1971.

Xantareans Red-skinned hulking humanoids who stand over seven feet tall, the Xantareans dwell on Xantar, circling Xantares in the Milky Way in Marvel's *Tales to Astonish* #73, 1965.

Xantha Diminutive, pale-yellow-skinned macrocephalic humanoids, the Xantha dwelt on Xanth, circling Jatskan; they presently live on New Xanth, orbiting New Jatskan. They first appeared in Marvel's *Fantastic Four* #7, 1962.

Xartans Golden-skinned humanoids with pointy ears, these natives of Xarta, circling Zugano in the Fornax Galaxy, first appeared in Marvel's *Journey into Mystery* #90, 1963.

Xeronians Nearly seven-foot-tall humanoids with two-toed feet and three-fingered hands, the orange-skinned Xeronians are hairless and possess beetled brows. They dwell on Xeron in the tri-star system of Aerim, Honj, and Verserin in the Milky Way. They debuted in Marvel's *The Incredible Hulk* #103, 1968.

Xixix These natives of Xix, orbiting Xaravaran in the Milky Way, are red-skinned, spindly-limbed humanoids, hairless with apelike faces. They debuted in Marvel's *Fantastic Four* #261, 1983.

Xnortk See VRADV.

Yirbek Natives of Yirb, orbiting Bek in Andromeda, the Yirbek are green-skinned humanoids with oversized torsos and an even more oversized, bulldog-like head. They first appeared in Marvel's *Avengers* #14, 1965.

Yrds Green-skinned bipeds with a fishlike face and single horn in the center of their head, these denizens of Yrest, orbiting Corinum in the Draco Galaxy, debuted in *Tales of Suspense* #54, 1964.

Zarno See CRANIAC.

The Zato An eight-eyed, octopus-like, "slime-covered," tentacled Martian, from EC's *Weird Science* #9, 1951.

Zkoh See HVAH.

Zlafg See CXARGX.

Z'nox The brown-skinned humanoids have virtually no forehead, with an oversized mouth full of oversized fangs. They dwell on Z'nox in Andromeda's Huz'deyr system, and debuted in Marvel's *X-Men* #65, 1970.

Zundamites Yellow-skinned humanoids with extremely spindly limbs, the Zundamites have a flat, oversized head with giant red eyes, two slits for a nose, and a horselike mouth. They stand nearly 12 feet tall and hail from Zundam, circling the Milky Way's Fakowi in Marvel's *Fantastic Four* #207, 1978.

Zyrkx A robot with a cone-shaped head, humanoid torso, and bullet-shaped pelvis with a single wheel for mobility; an explorer from a machine world, in EC's *Weird Science* #18, 1953.

APPENDIX B: OUTER LIMITS ALIENS

Below are listed aliens that appeared on *The Outer Limits* television show. See also ADAM LINK; ANNEX ONE; THE EMPYRIAN; THE GALAXY BEING; THE OUTSIDER; TRENT; THE ZANTIS.

Aabel A wasp-faced humanoid from the planet Eros who wants to mate with human women and produce male children, in "The Children of Spider County."

Alien Brain A pulsing brain that lives in an ancient house, studying humans, in "The Guests."

The Antheonite Before Weblor One is launched to the planet Antheon, a light-being from that world inhabits a plant, turning it into a giant, vine-like being warning us away, in "Counterweight."

The Bellero Alien A shimmering humanoid alien from a world "just above the ceiling of your universe," brought here by a Bellero Corporation laser machine, in "The Bellero Shield."

The Chromoite An alien "exchange student," a blob-like mass with slender arms from the front of its chest, ending in pincers; two legs, and a nub of a featureless head, in "The Mice."

Diemos See PHOBOS.

The Ebonites Slender, winged, devil-faced humanoids who accidentally attack the Earth, in "Nightmare."

Eck An electrified, four-armed, four-eyed creature who escapes a two-dimensional plane by accident and can't return to its world, in "Behold, Eck!"

The Grippians Anemone-like aliens who flee a tyrant and land their soccer ball-sized spaceship on the moon, near a U.S. base, in "Moonstone."

Ikar A dome-headed humanoid alien with three horizontal slits beneath its eyes and four fingers on each hand, who swaps a scientist scientific information for the scientist's emotions, in "Keeper of the Purple Twilight."

The Invisibles Twelve-legged, crab-sized, cyclopean creatures that resemble prehistoric trilobites and take over humans, in "The Invisibles."

Luminoids Denizens of a super-hot world, close to its sun, these humanoids have melted-clay-like skin, in "A Feasibility Study."

The Martian "Sand Sharks" Seven dinosaur-like creatures that menace the crew of the M-2 Mars probe, in "The Invisible Enemy."

The Megasoid A fierce, shaggy, apelike alien on the loose on Earth in 2025, in "The Duplicate Man."

The Microbe A lumpy (Venusian?) spore, the size of a refrigerator, that crawls along the floor and menaces the human captives of an alien space probe, in "The Probe." (The spore is not the life form that sent the probe.)

Mr. Zeno A denizen of the planet Xenon who tutors Earth youths in climate control, dematerializing, undiscovered elements, and more as a prelude to invasion, in "The Special One."

The O.B.I.T. Monster A cyclopean, silvery humanoid with four fingers on each hand, trying to take over the Earth via surveillance devices known as Outer Band Individuated Teletracers, in "O.B.I.T."

Phobos and Diemos A Martian Senior Solar System Inspector, Phobos comes to Earth and contacts Accredited Earth Caretaker Diemos (sic) to study our "custom" of murder, in "Controlled Experiment." Both are humanoids (Barry Morse and Carroll O'Connor, respectively).

The "RNA Meteors" Incapable of reproduction, aliens send their genetic matter out in meteors. When the ore is used in bullets that strike several Earthmen, it turns them into geniuses who build a spaceship to bring handicapped children to a new world, where they aren't crippled, in "The Inheritors."

The Rocks Protoplasmic aliens who communicate telepathically and can turn to ooze or solid rock, in "Corpus Earthling."

The Spores Latching onto a Project Adonis space station, alien plant spores return to Earth and take root, the towering poinsettia-like plants spitting lethal powder, in "Specimen: Unknown."

Thetan A nitrogen-breathing, chicken-legged, bug-eyed alien with a huge V-shaped head, dreamed up by scientists trying to convince Earth it's being invaded, in "Architects of Fear."

The "Tumbleweed" Aliens On a hard-luck expedition, aliens (unseen) take over what they presume to be an intelligent Earth life form, tumbleweeds, and then take over a corpse, in "Cry of Silence."

The *Venusian* from ''Cold Hands, Warm Heart.''

Venusian Scaly, slender, floating stalk with two arms, glowing eyes, and long, stringy hair, in ''Cold Hands, Warm Heart.''

The Wolf 359 Alien A malevolent white, ghostlike bat that evolves when Dundee's Planet, a simulation of a planet orbiting Wolf 359, is created in a lab, in ''Wolf 359.'' (A draft of the script called the creature a Plag.)

The "Yellow Planet" Aliens Crash-landing on Earth, a pair of peaceful, cat-eyed, humanoid aliens contend with a human infiltrator, genetically mutated to appear as one of them as they repair their saucer, in ''The Chameleon.''

APPENDIX C: STAR TREK ALIENS

This appendix contains brief entries on extraterrestrials from the original *Star Trek* series, animated series, motion pictures, and comic books. See also MR. SPOCK; U.S.S. ENTERPRISE; VULCAN.

Andorians Blue-skinned humanoids with white hair and two antennae.

Aquans Humanoid merpeople of the planet Argo, with green hair, webbed extremities, and dorsal fins.

Argelians Pleasure-loving humanoids of the planet Argelius II.

Aurelians Birdlike natives of the planet Aurelia.

Berengarians Dragons who dwell on the planet Berengaria VII.

Caitians A race of catlike humanoids; bipeds, they have human hands, cats' feet, and lionlike tails.

Capellan Power-Cat One of the fiercest creatures in the galaxy, a bear-sized, bobcat-like animal with red fur, brown spikes along its back, and the ability to generate a deadly electrical charge.

Cheronites A race of humanoids, some of whom are black-skinned on the right side and white-skinned on the left, and vice versa.

Deltans Natives of Delta V, the bald humanoids are extremely intelligent, possess ESP, and are a highly sexual race. They take oaths of celibacy before serving on Federation starships.

Denebian Slime Devil Nothing is known about these creatures, though their name seems to say it all.

Dimorusians Ratlike creatures who attack intruders with poisoned darts.

Dramians Circa seven-foot-tall, golden-skinned humanoids with big eyes and large, bald heads.

Edoans The natives of the planet Edos are red-skinned humanoids with long necks, three arms ending in three-fingered hands (the odd arm is located in the center of the chest), and three legs, which are human on the top and doglike on the bottom (the odd leg is in the back).

Elasians and Troyians Elas and Troyus are the two inhabited worlds of the Tellun star system; the warring inhabitants are all humanoids. The Troyian men are violent, while the women have a chemical in their tears that, upon touching a man's skin, forces him to fall in love with her.

Excalbians Rock-like humanoids with two bear-like claws on each hand, they live on a planet whose surface is made of lava.

Eymorgs Humanoid females who live on Sigma Draconis VI. Though they are simpleminded, they are more advanced than the males of their species, the Morgs, whom they capture and use for mating and protection.

Fabrini Humanoids who live in the Fabrina star system.

Flying Parasites The size and shape of rolled, uncooked pizza dough, these red-and-ivory-colored denizens of Beta Portalan, Lavinius V, Theta Cygni XII, Ingraham B, and Deneva are able to fly short distances and "bite" other beings, surviving as parasites. Each creature is a cell of a single consciousness. They have two small eyes toward the front and tiny teeth underneath.

Gamma Triangulians Primitive, immortal, red-skinned, white-haired humanoids of Gamma Trianguli VI who are ruled by the computer Vaal. The planet also has poisonous plants that fire deadly thorns.

Giant Eel-Birds Denizens of Regulus V who, every 11 years, return to the caves where they were born in order to mate.

Gideonites Intellectually, physically, and spiritually highly advanced humanoids.

Gorgan The sole survivor of the planet Triacus, Gorgan is a portly humanoid with ulcerated flesh—though, dressed in a shimmering silver cloak and enveloped in a green glow, he projects an image of white-haired, kindly-faced benevolence.

Gossamer Mice Nearly transparent mice-like creatures used as experimental animals onboard the U.S.S. *Enterprise*.

Halo Fish Small fish surrounded by a rainbow-like circle; the colors fade when something non-native is introduced in the waters.

Hortas Silicon-based life forms on Janus VI, the circa five-foot-long, dark-orange Hortas are slug-like "rocks" that have a series of small, crab-like legs on their underside. They bore through rock (and kill) by exuding a powerful corrosive. Every 50,000 years or so, the entire race dies save for one member, who cares for the eggs and then for the newborns.

Iotians "Extremely . . . imitative people," these humans form a society based on the book *Chicago Mobs of the Twenties*, left behind by the starship *Horizon*.

Kanutu Dark-haired humanoids who live on the planet Neural and possess rudimentary ESP.

Kelvans Huge creatures with hundreds of tentacles and the ability to assume other forms, they hail from Kelva in the Andromeda Galaxy.

Kohms See YANGS.

Kzinti Natives of Kzin, the creatures are catlike beings who stand roughly eight feet tall. Barrel-chested, with four fingers on each hand, the warlike beings have individual markings on their fur.

Lactrans The inhabitants of Lactra VII are approximately 20-foot-long slug-like creatures with a long, elephant-like trunk that ends in three fingerlike tendrils.

Le-matya A large leopard-like creature with leather-like skin, colorful markings, and poisonous fangs and claws. A native of the planet Vulcan.

Medusans Reportedly so vile-looking that their appearance can drive an observer mad, they appear—through special visors—to be a miasma of bright lights infused with a green glow.

Megan A tall, extremely slender female with cat-like eyes and a crescent-like arm of hair sweeping out from each side of her head. The mind reader hails from the Omega Cygni system.

Melkots Possessing giant, yellow, catlike eyes and tiny nostrils, the floating creature appears to Captain Kirk to be "all head and neck and very colorful." The head is cubelike.

Mellitus A vaporous alien of Alpha Majoris I who, at rest, becomes a solid, sponge-like mass.

Metrons Tall, slender, silver-haired humanoids. See *Comment* section of entry for THE OUTSIDER.

M113 Creature A vampire that sucks the salt from humans. The creature is humanoid, with long, thick hair, pasty skin, a circular mouth, small deepset eyes, and no nose. It is the last survivor of its once-civilized race.

Mugato A white, human-sized ape with a pink face and a huge horn on the top of its head. The Neuralese native has poisonous fangs.

Organians The Organians exist in a pure energy state and possess extraordinary powers, can create bodies for themselves if they wish, can generate intense heat (for example, to make weapons too hot

to handle), and apparently live for thousands of years.

Orions Humanoids comprised of a variety of types: green-skinned with tails, claws, and black hair; golden-skinned; and white-skinned.

Phylosians Plant beings with a mass of tendrils for arms, three stalk-like legs, a mushroom-shaped head, and a pair of eyestalks. Also living on Phylos are the Retlaw plants, which are roughly a half-foot tall and have a fuzzy purple top and dark roots, which the plant uses to become ambulatory.

Platonians Humans who live for thousands of years and possess psychokinetic powers.

Sandbats Creatures who dwell on Manark IV and appear to be mineral—until they launch themselves at trespassers.

Sarpeids The humanoid inhabitants of Sarpeidon, the only planet circling Beta Niobe.

Scalosians Humanoids who move at a highly accelerated rate, making them invisible to the human eye.

Sehlats Giant, bear-like creatures with large fangs. They are native to the planet Vulcan.

Skorrians Winged, taloned humanoids with a feathery covering and eagle-like faces.

Sord A bipedal, intelligent, human-sized, humanoid-dinosaur hybrid.

Sur-snake A giant native of the planet Argo, the snake spits deadly venom.

Talosians Bald-headed telepathic humanoids with extremely large braincases. Their mental abilities are such that they can create illusions that other beings believe are real.

Tellarites Because Tellar is an extremely cold world, the humanoid denizens are covered with fur. The chunky, pink creatures have cloven hooves, three-fingered hands, pointed ears, and piggish noses.

Thasians Bodiless beings from the planet Thasus.

Tholians Reddish-gold, crystal-like beings with white, triangular eyes.

Tribbles Small balls of purring fur, Tribbles come in an assortment of earth colors; they have mouths but no teeth, eat anything they are fed, and have an unknown means of locomotion. Their home world is not known.

A genetically engineered creature known as a Glommer does nothing but eat the fast-multiplying Tribbles.

Triskelions Also known as the Providers, the aliens once "had humanoid form, but we evolved beyond it." Now, they are simply disembodied brains dwelling on Triskelion in the trinary star system M24 Alpha.

Troglytes   Brutish humanoids who work in the mines of Ardana.

Troyians   See ELASIANS.

Ursinoid   A bipedal, intelligent, bear-like creature on Motherlode, an Arcadian mining world.

Vendorians   Possessing roughly the same mass as a human, each Vendorian can rearrange itself into any shape that has the same mass.

Vians   Large-headed, bald humanoids of the planet Minara II.

Yangs and Kohms   Respectively, the warlike and peaceful humanoids who inhabit Omega IV, descended from American (Yangs) and Oriental Earth-people.

Zetarians   Energy-beings able to travel through space and take over the bodies of other beings.

APPENDIX D: STAR TREK: THE NEXT GENERATION AND STAR TREK: DEEP SPACE NINE ALIENS

This appendix lists aliens that appeared on the TV series *Star Trek: The Next Generation* and *Deep Space Nine* (indicated by "9" after the title). See also DATA; DEEP SPACE NINE; KLINGONS; U.S.S. ENTERPRISE.

Acamarians   Humanoids of Acamar III, copper-skinned with clefts in their foreheads.

Aldebaran serpent   Three-headed lizard.

Allasomorphs   Intelligent shape-shifters of Daled IV. Their natural shapes are unknown.

Angosians   Pacifistic humanoids of Angosia III; many were chemically converted into supersoldiers to fight the Tarsian War.

Antideans   Fishlike beings from Antide III.

Arkarians   Waterbirds that live on Arkaria.

Bajorans   Spiritual humanoids with an ancient civilization (and a scalloped ridge of bone on the nose), the Bajorans hail from the planet Bajor.

Bandi   Humanoids from Deneb IV.

Baneriam (9)   A hawklike creature.

Barzans   Somewhat catlike humanoids of the planet Barzan.

Benzites   Blue-skinned humanoids of Benzar.

Beta Renna Cloud   A vaporous creature that can take over the bodies of other life forms.

Betazoids   Telepathic humanoids from the planet Betazed who can read the minds of all but a few alien races, such as the Ferengi.

Bolians   Humanoids with a ridge down the middle of their face; natives of Bolarus IX.

Brekkians   Humanoids from Brekka, fourth world of the Delos system.

Bynars   Large-headed, bald humanoids from Bynaus who are electrotelepathically linked in order to exchange information.

Cardassians   Swarthy humanoids with deep-set eyes and bony ridges on their forehead and chin.

Crystalline Entity   A large, intelligent snowflake-like being.

Crystilia   Flowering plants of Telemarius III.

Devidians   Living outside of normal human time, the featureless, vaguely humanoid beings feed on neural energy.

Diomedian Scarlet Moss   Red plant with feathery appearance.

Douwd   Intelligent energy creatures who can assume the likeness of other beings.

Garanian Bolites (9)   Bacteria-like creatures that irritate human flesh.

Gilvos (9)   Creatures that live on Corvan II and look like tree branches.

Gomtuu   A living, teardrop-shaped spaceship, Gomtuu is the last of its kind.

J'naii   Androgynous humanoids.

Joranian Ostrich (9)   Alien bird that hides its head in water when frightened—and drowns. Unrelated to the ostrichlike Gunji Jackdaw.

Kataanese   Humanoids of the planet Kataan who lived in a somewhat medieval society; now extinct.

Ktarians   Humanoids with large foreheads and cat-like eyes.

Lynar   Bat-like native of Celtris III.

Mintakans   Vulcan-like humanoids.

Promellians   Lizard-like humanoids, now extinct.

Takarans   Another group of reptile-like humanoids.

Talarian Hook Spider   A spider that stands a half-meter tall.

Tamarians   Humanoids with batlike nostrils and heads that are lizard-like from the forehead back.

Targ   Furry pig of Qo'nos.

Ullians   Telepathic humanoids.

Wadi (9)   Extremely tall humanoids from the Gamma Quadrant.

Wanoni Tracehound (9)   Fleet, canine-like hunter.

Zakdorns   Humanoids with folds of flesh on their cheeks.

Zaldans   Web-fingered humanoids.

Zalkonians   Humanoids with extremely deep, horizontal "creases" in their faces and the blossoming ability to become noncorporeal.

APPENDIX E: STAR WARS WORLDS

Below are listed worlds in the Star Wars films, novels, and TV shows. See also CHEWBACCA; EWOKS; MILLENNIUM FALCON; R2D2 AND C-3PO.

Abregado-rae   A planet in the Abregado system.
Af'El   A mining planet of underground cities.
Akrit'tar   A penal world.
Alderaan   A key world in the Old Republic and in the Rebellion against the Empire.
Altor 14   Home world of the birdlike Avogwi and the lizard-like Nuiwit.
Ammuud   A feudal world.
Annoo   An agricultural world inhabited by the reptilian Annoodat.
Aquaris   A water world.
Aridus   A desert world.
Arzid   Home planet of the giant Arachnor spider.
Barab 1   Home of the black-scaled reptilian humanoids the Barabels.
Barhu   A dead, extremely hot world in the Churba system.
Baros   Home of a race of two-legged reptiles.
Berchest   A beautiful world on the border between the New Republic and the Empire.
Bespin   A gaseous world circled by the moons H'gaard and Drudonna, among others.
Biitu   A farming world.
Bimmisaari   Pleasant home of the peaceful, furry Bimms.
Bnach   A parched prison world.
Bogden   A swampy moon circling an unnamed world.
Bonadan   A yellow-colored factory world.
Boonta   A planet renowned for its racetracks.
Brigia   An underdeveloped world.
Byss   A fertile world in the binary star system of Byss and Abyss.
Calamari   A water world.
Chad   A lush, civilized world.
Chandrilla   A world of humanoids.
Churba   The fourth world in a system that also includes Barhu (number one), Hurcha (number eight), and New Cov (number three).
Circarpous XIV   The last world of the Circarpous Major star system. Circarpous V is also known as Mimban.
Clak'dor VII   A planet in the Colu system, home of the bipedal, large-headed Bith.
Columus   Home of the tiny-bodied, large-headed humanoid Columi.
Commenor   A trading world.
Cona   A hot planet in the Teke Ro system.
Corulag   A planet of humanoids.
Coruscant   A world of enormous beauty, wealth, and culture.
Dagobah   A swamp world and home of Yoda, the Jedi Master; the planet Bpfassh is located nearby.
Dantooine   A remote world, and a key base for the Rebel Alliance.
Da Soocha   A water planet in the Cyax system; it has at least five moons.
Dellalt   A watery world with two moons.
Deneba   A desert planet.
Derra IV   A world in the Derra star system.
Devaron   A world of humanoids.
Duro   A planet used for the storage of toxic wastes.
Elom   A cold, harsh world famed for the ore lommite.
Endor   A planet whose forest moon is the home of the Ewoks. Another moon is named Eloggi. (Some accounts say that the forest moon itself is named Endor, and that it is one of two moons orbiting the planet Tana.)
Etti IV   A pleasant world circling the star Etti.
Fornax   A planet circled by five rings of fire.
Galand   Home of the religious leader H'kig.
Gamorr   Home of the warlike, humanoid boars the Gamorreans.
Gargon   A planet once raided by Han Solo.
Giju   Home of the large, bipedal race of Herglics.
Honoghr   Fourth world of the Honoghr system. Companion planets include Kuthul—the most distant—but only Honoghr is capable of supporting life.
Hoth   An ice world, the sixth planet in an eponymous star system.
Ingo   A harsh, cratered world.
Ithor   Fourth world in the Ottega system, the verdant, tropical home of the Hammerheads.

Jomark The second of six worlds in its star system, and the only one that can support life.

Kabal Locale of the Conference of Uncommitted Worlds, following the events in *Star Wars*.

Kalla A planet famed for its universities.

Kamar A desert planet infamous for its murderous Badlands and deadly digworms.

Kashyyyk Home of Chewbacca.

Kessel A world of labor camps and the lucrative spice trade.

Kir A planet of crystal mines.

Kirdo A desert world.

Kowak Home planet of the monkey-lizards.

Kyryll's World Home of the tiny, barbell-shaped Pui-ui.

Lafra Home of gray-skinned humanoids.

Lianna An industrial planet.

Lorrd Home of a humanoid race.

Lur A world of unending storms.

Manda Home world of the Babob Merchant Fleet.

Mima II A tropical planet in the Lar system.

Miser A small, iron-rich world in the Bespin system.

Moltok Home of the nature-loving Ho'Din.

Myrkr A world on the border between the New Republic and the remnants of the Empire.

Mytus VII A desolate, airless world with two moons.

Nar Shaddaa A smugglers' moon that orbits the planet Nal Hutta.

Nkllon A mining world in the Athega system.

Norvall II A planet in the Norval system.

Obroa-skai An Earthlike world that houses a massive computer database.

Ord Mantell A world on which Han Solo spent some time.

Ord Pardron A key world in the defense of the planets Ando, Filve, Crondre, and various worlds menaced by the Empire in its war with the Republic.

Orin A hostile planet in the Bespin system.

Orron III A planet in the Orron system.

Orto A cold world in the Orto system.

Oslumpex V A world of the Oslumpex system.

Ossus A planet on which the Jedi Knights may have originated.

Ottega A star system with 75 planets and 622 moons.

R'alla A planet famed for its mineral waters, much in demand on the planet Rampa.

Ralltiir One of the first rebel worlds.

Rampa A heavily industrialized world.

Rishi A hot, damp world circling Rish.

Rodia A planet in the Tyrius star system.

Roon A planet that hosts the famed Colonial Games, Roon is surrounded by small moons and planetoids; one side exists in endless night.

Rudrig A planet of universities.

Ruuria A planet of insect-like creatures.

Ryloth A world in the system of the same name, home of humanoids with tentacled heads.

Saheelindeel Home world of intelligent apelike beings.

Sedri Home of seal-like humanoids.

Sisk World of the spider-like Sic-six.

Sljee Home of tentacled, flat beings with a highly developed sense of smell.

Sluissi Planet of humanoids who are snakelike from the waist down.

Stenness A star system of seven mining planets.

Sullust A planet in the star system of that name. The Sullustans are humanoids with large jowls, huge ears, and big eyes.

Tammuz-an A world of humanoids.

Tatooine A desert world circling the binary stars Tatoo I and Tatoo II.

ThonBoka A water world.

Tibrin Home of the Ishi Tib, big-eyed, beak-mouthed beings who build their cities on Tibrin's coral reefs.

Togoria A planet of humanoid felines.

Toola A freezing world in the Kaelta system.

Toprawa A rebel world.

Trian Another world of humanoid felines.

Tund A world of magic.

Tynna A cold forest world.

Ukio A farming world in the system of the same name.

Urdur Base world of an outlaw band.

Verdanth A jungle world.

Wayland A planet inhabited by the Myneyrsh, tall, thin, four-armed humanoids with crystalline skin.

Yag'Dhul Home of the skeletal Givin.

Yavin A huge, gaseous world in the Yavin star system, Yavin has at least 13 moons. Other worlds in the system include Fiddanl and Stroiketcy.

Z'trop A tropical planet with volcanic islands and exotic beaches.

FURTHER READINGS

Barbour, Alan J. *Cliffhanger.* Secaucus, N.J.: Citadel Press, 1977.

Battle, Kemp B. *Great American Folklore.* Garden City, N.Y.: Doubleday, 1986.

Bell, John. *Canuck Comics.* Montreal: Matrix, 1986.

Benet, William Rose. *The Reader's Encyclopedia,* 2nd ed. New York: Harper & Row, 1965.

Benson, Raymond. *The James Bond Bedside Companion.* New York: Dodd, Mead, 1984.

Botto, Louis. *At This Theatre.* New York: Dodd, Mead, 1984.

Brombert, Victor. *The Hero in Literature.* New York: Fawcett, 1969.

Brooks, Tim and Earle Marsh. *The Complete Directory to Prime Time Network TV Shows, 1946–Present,* 5th ed. New York: Ballantine, 1992.

Brosnan, John. *James Bond in the Cinema,* 2nd ed. South Brunswick, N.J.: A.S. Barnes, 1981.

Bulfinch, Thomas. *Myths of Greece and Rome.* New York: Penguin, 1981.

Buston, Frank and Bill Owen. *The Big Broadcast, 1920-1950.* New York: Avon, 1973.

Carpenter, Humphrey and Mari Prichard. *The Oxford Companion to Children's Literature.* Oxford: Oxford University Press, 1984.

Del Rey, Lester. *The World of Science Fiction, 1926-1976.* New York: Ballantine, 1979.

Dille, Robert C., ed. *The Collected Works of Buck Rogers in the 25th Century.* New York: Chelsea House, 1969.

Drabble, Margaret, ed. *The Oxford Companion to English Literature.* Oxford: Oxford University Press, 1985.

Estren, Mark James. *A History of Underground Comics.* Berkeley, Calif.: Ronin, 1987.

Foster, Harold. *Prince Valiant in the Days of King Arthur.* New York: Nostalgia Press/Franklin Square, 1974.

Gerani, Gary. *Fantastic Television.* New York: Harmony, 1977.

Gerber, Ernst and Mary. *The Photo Journal Guide to Comic Books,* vols. 1 and 2. Minden, Nev.: Gerber, 1989.

Gifford, Denis. *The International Book of Comics.* London: Hamlyn, 1984.

_____ . *Space Aces!* London: Green Wood, 1992.

_____ . *Super Duper Supermen!* London: Green Wood, 1992.

Gould, Chester. *The Celebrated Cases of Dick Tracy, 1931–1951,* ed. Herb Galewitz. New York: Chelsea House, 1970.

Grossman, Gary. *Saturday Morning TV.* New York: Delacorte Press, 1981.

Hancer, Kevin. *The Paperback Price Guide.* New York: Harmony, 1980.

Harmon, Jim. *The Great Radio Heroes.* New York: Ace, 1967.

Horn, Maurice. *Comics of the American West.* South Hackensack, N.J.: Stroeger, 1977.

_____ . *Women in the Comics.* New York: Chelsea House, 1977.

_____ . *The World Encyclopedia of Comics.* New York: Avon, 1976.

Kyle, David. *The Illustrated Book of Science Fiction Ideas and Dreams.* London: Hamlyn, 1977.

Lang, Andrew, ed. *The Arabian Nights Entertainments.* New York: Schocken, 1967.

Lee, Walt. *The Reference Guide to Fantastic Films,* 3 vols. Los Angeles: Chelsea-Lee, 1972.

Lord, Glenn. *The Last Celt, A Bio-Bibliography of Robert E. Howard.* New York: Berkley Windhover, 1977.

Lupoff, Richard A. *Edgar Rice Burroughs: Master of Adventure.* New York: Ace, 1968.

Marill, Alvin H. *Movies Made for Television.* New York: Da Capo Press, 1980.

McNeil, Alex. *Total Television.* New York: Penguin, 1980.

Miller, Don. *The Hollywood Corral.* New York: Popular Library, 1976.

Nicholls, Peter, ed. *The Science Fiction Encyclopedia.* New York: Dolphin, 1979.

Okuda, Michael and Denise. *Star Trek Chronology.* New York: Pocket Books, 1973.

Overstreet, Robert M. *The Overstreet Comic Book Price Guide.* New York: Avon, 1993.

Peary, Danny. *Cult Movie Stars.* New York: Fireside, 1991.

Pickard, Roy. *Who Played Who in the Movies.* New York: Schocken, 1981.

Ransome, Arthur. *Old Peter's Russian Tales.* Middlesex, England: Puffin, 1974.

Raymond, Alex. *Flash Gordon in the Planet Mongo.* New York: Nostalgia Press/Franklin Square, 1974.

Resnick, Michael. *Official Guide to the Fantastics.* Florence, Ala.: House of Collectibles, 1976.

Robinson, Herbert Spencer and Knox Wilson. *Myths and Legends of All Nations.* Totowa, N.J.: Littlefield, Adams, 1976.

Robinson, Jerry. *The Comics.* New York: Berkley Windhover, 1974.

Roseman, Mill. *Detectionary.* Woodstock, N.Y.: Overlook Press, 1977.

Russell, Alan K., ed. *The Rivals of Sherlock Holmes.* Secaucus, N.J.: Castle, 1978.

Sampson, Robert. *Yesterday's Faces,* Vol. 1: Glory Figures. Bowling Green, Ohio: Bowling Green University Popular Press, 1983.

Seymour-Smith, Martin. *Dictionary of Fictional Characters.* Boston: Plays, Inc. 1992.

Standring, Lesley. *The Doctor Who Illustrated A–Z.* London: W.H. Allen, 1985.

Steinbrunner, Chris and Otto Penzler. *Encyclopedia of Mystery and Detection.* New York: McGraw-Hill, 1976.

Thomas, James Stuart. *The Big Little Book Price Guide.* Des Moines, Iowa: Wallace-Homestead, 1983.

Van Hise, James. *Pulp Heroes of the Thirties.* Yucca Valley, Calif., Midnight Graffiti, 1994.

Weiss, Ken and Ed Goodgold. *To Be Continued . . .* New York: Crown, 1972.

Wells, Stewart W., III. *The Science Fiction and Heroic Fantasy Author Index.* Duluth, Minn.: Purple Unicorn, 1978.

Woolery, George W. *Children's Television: The First Thirty-Five Years,* 1946–1981; Part 1: Animated Cartoon Series. Metuchen, N.J.: Scarecrow Press, 1983.

Entries are filed letter-by-letter. **Boldface** headings indicate extensive treatment of a topic. *Italic* locators indicate illustrations and captions.